The
Two Worlds
of American Art

THE PRIVATE AND THE POPULAR

Barry Ulanov

THE MACMILLAN COMPANY, NEW YORK
COLLIER-MACMILLAN LIMITED, LONDON

*This book is affectionately dedicated
to the memory of Norman Bel Geddes,
distinguished contributor to both
worlds of American art.*

❀

*By the kind permission of the publishers, excerpts are quoted in this book
from the following works:*

From *Here Come the Clowns* by Philip Barry. Copyright 1939 by Philip
Barry. Reprinted by permission of Coward-McCann, Inc.

From "The Cow," copyright 1950 by Theodore Roethke; from "The Sloth,"
copyright 1950 by Theodore Roethke; from "The Open House," copyright
1941 by Theodore Roethke. All from the book *Words for the Wind* by Theodore
Roethke. Reprinted by permission of Doubleday & Company, Inc.

From *America and Alfred Stieglitz.* Copyright 1924 by Doubleday & Company,
Inc. Reprinted by permission of Doubleday & Company, Inc.

CONTENTS

PREFACE

THE PROTOCOL of prefaces requires an author to make acknowledgments to those who have given him special aid in the making of his book, and that I propose, very briefly, to do here. The major acknowledgment, however, cannot be to a person or even to a group of persons. It must be to the two worlds I have attempted to explore in this book, to the arts themselves, the arts of this century in America, the private and the popular arts. Their presence in my life has been extraordinarily commanding and almost equally rewarding, and from an age so young that it barely qualifies as one of consciousness or reason. The delight I received from the first concerts I attended, from the first films I saw, the first vaudeville acts, the first plays, the first paintings, was such that almost every element of the experiences remained with me—and they remain with me still.

To some extent, then, this book is a testimony to the presence of the arts in America in a time which, for all the glaring pretensions and sickening inadequacies and galling betrayals of various performers on various occasions, has been one of triumph for art in America. As is so often true of any real achievement in America, America has been the last to recognize this triumph. I am not particularly anxious to call attention to the triumph now. It is enough, I think, to remind ourselves of the presence, the inalienable presence, of the arts in our midst, and to see with what equanimity our artists have continued to function in panic and prosperity, in war and peace, to recognize with what dignity they endow us all when against the problems of the race they assert the primacy of each individual's life and death and when they answer the terror of the bomb with their wonder over almost every sound, every color, every texture they have encountered.

It is important to say that not all the artists of quality and significance in this country in this time are represented by name or by work in this book. The achievement is too great to cover in its entirety. I will certainly not be unhappy if the large number of men and works I have tried to examine in some detail call attention, for any reason at all, to others of distinction.

Many of the artists who are discussed in this book have been my tutors in their arts, again too many to acknowledge by name. The greatly gifted man to whom this book is dedicated will have to stand as their representative, for the generosity with which he shared the knowledge of his several crafts in lengthy discussions over many, many years, and for the dedication to those crafts he continued to display in spite of all sorts of disillusioning and even demeaning experiences. It is worth adding, I think, that musicians in all the spheres of music, actors, playwrights, directors, designers, novelists, poets, painters, sculptors, vaudeville and radio and film and television people, photographers, dancers, and architects—all kinds of artists, at every level of skill and of eminence—have been similarly generous with their time, with their skills, with themselves. Equally, distinguished critics and scholars of the arts, some of whom were my classroom teachers, have been, over the years, marvelously accessible and constantly stimulating, not the least of them that splendid group with whom I have been associated since 1951, my colleagues at Barnard College.

One particularly valuable set of experiences involved in the writing of this book was gathered from traveling to the countries of Europe and Asia, to match my state-by-state experience of the arts in this country. A very long stay in England and visits to most of the countries of Europe, including Russia and Poland, to the Middle East and all around India, were made possible by grants from the John Simon Guggenheim Memorial Foundation and the American Council of Learned Societies. Those grants were directed toward research in another project, but they were of great assistance in the last stages of writing of this volume.

All my books have benefited from the wisdom and patience and hard labor of my wife, contributions too great, perhaps, to be adequately acknowledged according to the protocol of prefaces, but not, as I hope these words make clear, ever forgotten. I should like also to indicate my gratitude to the several editors who gave my large manuscript good care in its several stages: Emile Capouya, Dan Hayes, June Herman, and Robert Markel.

BARRY ULANOV

INTRODUCTION

TO EUROPEANS, the word American or the United States conjures up an image of a huge monolithic structure. To some of them it is terrifying, to some beneficent, but to all it seems to be massive, relentless, overpowering, in its march across the twentieth century. As much as the vast Russian and Chinese political empires, we have assumed the force of a single-minded entity to others, and not only Europeans, but Asians and Africans and South Americans as well. With varying degrees of cautiousness and conviction, they all make generalizations about American culture. Some of the generalizations are friendly. At least as many are not. But almost all are spacious generalizations, joining together all the regions and all the people and all the arts of the United States in a single block.

Americans when they appraise their culture are inclined to be a little less roomy in their summary statements. They have been cautioned by the complex machinery of the social scientists' statistics and chagrined by the constant reminder during the last war that we were not fighting for the foods of America or the games of America— hot dogs and baseball were simply not in it. Were we fighting, then, for the books of Herman Melville or the paintings of Albert Ryder or the poetry of Walt Whitman? Or for a later art, the music of jazz, the drama of the motion pictures, the photographic realism of the hard-boiled detective story? Or was there somewhere underneath all of this a reality, difficult to define but genuine enough, which some Americans at least had in mind when they went to defend their country?

It is not absolutely essential to define what is American about America,[1] any more than it is of any urgency to make similar pronouncements about the French, the British, the Germans, the Russians, the Irish, the Italians, the Spaniards, or any of the others about whom such proclamations will continue to be made as long as there are nations. We all recognize by now how inflammatory any such definition must be to someone somewhere, how far from complete, how inattentive to detail. Can we not, then, pay attention to the detail, go well beyond the well-rounded emptiness of the simple

9

summation of a people and its culture? Is it not possible to forget the simple figure of the European—or Asian or African or South American—editorial evaluation of American culture and the statistics, American or European, and the futile contentions about the last war, and to find out something in some detail about the culture of Americans? It is, I think, if we are willing to explore not the single culture of Americans but the several cultures, the cultures and the arts of native and naturalized Americans, of Americans from all parts of America, of VIP's and very small people, of businessmen and ballet dancers, of jazz musicians and gas-station attendants, of politicians and painters, of gangsters and college professors, of drugstore cowboys and bona fide cattlemen, of FBI men and Communists, of movie stars and bobby-soxers, of professional military men and government-issue soldiers, of psychiatrists and farmers and poets.

Many countries and many cultures can claim almost as many kinds of people and professions as the United States. In no other country, however, is the range of art and culture at once so wide and so full. The British certainly have a top as widely separated from the bottom as we do, if by top and bottom we understand degrees of learning and competence to deal with the complexities of art and culture. But in between the two extremes, the British do not begin to touch as many bases as we do, moving up and down and across from our upper-uppers through our middle-middles and lower-middles to the lowest orders, as class and caste are ranked in this sort of classification. The French have a marvelously stratified set of middle-class tastes, with so many layers of likes and dislikes that one begins to wonder after a while in France if agreement is ever possible among them. But the French do not have a bottom cultural land like ours, in spite of their every effort to follow after us, or even to lead us, in jazz, and in spite, too, of the terrifying success of their own version of the rock 'n' roll wheezers, whiners, and blasters. And in the same way, the Russians, with their ardor for a top-directed culture of the mass, have produced an unequaled lower-middle-class culture, unequaled, that is, in its constant reiteration of lower-middle-class tastes and values, but the vulgar, in the most honorific sense of the word, is absent from the arts in Russia, and anything very different in quality from lower-middle-class art is the province of an elite so far removed from the rest of the Russians that they live their lives as they find their art, in secret.[2]

American culture has much in common with these and other cultures in the West. It has its elites, too, with arcane tastes that are only occasionally discussed in the magazines or newspapers or over the air or before television cameras. But they *are* discussed, and more and more discussed as the rage develops to use all our mass media for educational purposes. American culture has a fair variety of middle-class likes and dislikes, even as the French, and, as noted above, a separation between its extremes of taste as broad as the British. But American culture is the largest of the democratic cultures of the West. It exhibits its characteristics, those it shares with other democratic cultures and those which are fairly much its own, with an intensity and a consciousness of size that no other country can quite match, even such a huge country as Russia, which in the narrowest sense of the word has made every attempt to build a democratic culture, a culture of the masses. But Russia has severely limited its culture wherever possible to one or two levels of communication, preferring for all sorts of doctrinal political reasons to let regions make for diversity rather than finding its variety in differences of education or temperament or skill.

In a democracy, there are always—speaking very broadly—two kinds of culture. In the modern world, anyway, a world of masses and mass media and a world of more specialized and individual tastes, there is always a popular culture and a private culture. Each has its own set of arts, popular arts and private arts, each dedicated to different purposes, each making use of different skills.

The private artist is a man who communicates to one man at a time, seeking, like Socrates' image of a noble dialectician at the end of the *Phaedrus,* a listener particularly congenial to him and to what he has to say. Every endowment, every interest, every special gift of the private artist is directed to the individual, the individual who understands and, he hopes, also speaks his special language. The particular concern of the private artist is to distinguish himself from the mob. Everything about him is directed to special concerns, special languages, special textures, a special audience.

The popular artist is differently motivated, differently organized, differently directed. Everything about him—his interests, his skills, his special gifts—leads him to box-office returns, to the largest possible audience for his work. He must become a best seller; his programs must achieve a high rating; he must find a response from the millions, or at least the hundreds of thousands, or fail to survive. Everything about him is orientated in this direction, not only by concern for money or prestige or power, but often because of a set of talents specifically directed to mass responses.

We must recognize that neither set of endowments, adaptations, skills, or temperamental qualities is necessarily good or bad. This is neutral ground, morally and aesthetically. A book is neither good nor bad if it sells well in hard covers and phenomenally in paperback. A song is not to be despised simply because everybody is humming or whistling or singing it. Neither, on the other hand, is a painting good or bad because it is obscure, or a piece of music worthless because it is seldom played and rarely to any large show of enthusiasm. These are simply the conditions of being of the arts, the private and the popular arts, and of the artists who work in them. Neither success nor failure, neither easy understanding by masses of people nor a recherché communication that only a very few are equipped to get—none of these things is to be canonized. This really is neutral ground. It simply defines status, not stature.

If one looks, however casually, at the world of the private artist and of private culture, one discovers quickly enough that in this world are located the sounds, the textures, the words, the gestures, the movements, the colors of the arts traditionally denominated as major, the arts we usually call arts. But in them for many years the obstacles to understanding for the ordinary man have been very great indeed. There has been nothing like a universal vocabulary for almost a century now, with a growing obfuscation since the general acceptance by private artists of the symbolic apparatus that we associate with the poetry of Baudelaire and Rimbaud and Mallarmé or of the highly personal painting idioms of the Impressionists and Post-impressionists and Cubists or of the even more oblique structures of the composers who followed the expansions of Wagner and Mahler and César Franck and Debussy with the near destruction of fixed tonality.

Unless one is very specially prepared for it, recent music in the private domain presents to the listener a very strange world of sound. But it is an enterprising world, a serious one, in spite of its divorce from the symmetries of diatonic music—or perhaps even because of it. Happily for the unprepared ear, it is a music that generally (in the West, anyway) stays within the octave, not often dividing its vibrations into smaller segments than the half-tone in its ventures into realms inaccurately called "atonal," since its materials are still quite unmistakably tones. This is a music, too, that is accessible in its narratives, its dramatic recitals or operas or settings of poems, or in its halfway-house life as background for film and radio and television drama, for mystery stories, or for any other line of dramatic development in which something like a chilling or a startling or a less-than-familiar sound is required. The world of modern music remains a small one, however, the smallest, the most private of the worlds of private art, its citizens those with advanced education or long experience in its several strange languages.

What about modern painting? Here the language, once very private indeed, has become almost well known, if not altogether acceptable, to masses of people. The two-dimensional picture plane to which the modern painter reduced his pictures, insisting, as he did so, upon following the nature of his materials, no longer terrifies anyone: it has been used so often in advertising in magazines and on television and even on billboards. Some people are still bothered by the retreat from representation that followed the loss of perspective in painting, but it is clear today, as the worlds of private and popular painting begin to coalesce and large numbers of people find increasing satisfaction in the violence of action painting and the fun and games of pop art, that this is a less than anguishing kind of privacy, that, in fact, privacy is only barely respected in it any longer, so eager has the rush been to reach and join the public that has come flocking to the museums and the galleries.

Modern poetry uses words. That gives it at least the appearance of universality. Modern American poetry uses conventional forms. That makes possible something like the openness about his experiences without which a lyric poet could not write and a dramatic poet would feel severely constrained. But modern poetry, even at its most open, still has its private areas, where the elusive symbolism and complex syntax of the French seem to be echoed or where the references insist upon an education that goes well beyond a grounding in poetry. But this, of course, is an ancient problem with the poets and their audiences. It was not T. S. Eliot who first translated theology into poetry; Dante did it a long time before him and with far more recondite materials that all the music of his verse could not make limpid.[3]

The modern novel which follows Joyce in its fragmentary presentation of the bits and pieces that turn up in the subconscious minds of its central characters provides some difficulties, but not the formidable obstacles of *Ulysses,* and no one has attempted again a multilingual puzzle on such a scale as Joyce did in *Finnegans Wake.* Private literature in our time is restricted to the theater of the absurd, the novel of the grotesque, and the short story of character and situation that lacks conventional narrative structure. None of these presents any harrowing difficulties for anybody. They simply cater to tastes different from those nurtured and sustained by the mass arts. Like the modern dance, like even the most accessible of modern poets and composers, these specialized genres require concentration and a certain amount of reflection. They provide some of the few meditative exercises of our culture, and, quite properly, they do so in privacy for those with a strong taste for the private.

What about popular culture? Certainly it requires no great effort. "Concentration" is a television quiz game, not an attitude of mind one must often adopt in dealing with the medium. Most people in America relax happily when they can turn the little dial and settle back to their nightly anodyne at home. There is a little more effort involved in going to the local movie house, a little less comfort, perhaps, in the torn leather and worn springs of the once luxurious seats. In both surroundings, people are alternately harangued and caressed by the technological arts and, in spite of a great deal of evidence to the contrary, addressed by technological artists as well and moved by artists whose performances are only incidentally concerned with technology. It may be hard to believe, as one looks at the sagas of the psychotic and the depraved or times one's laughs to the canned giggles and cackles that accompany the comedy shows, that anything in the way of technique or schooling or special skill goes into the organization of the long weary treks across the plains or the larruping of Lucy and her brethren. But the fact is that it does take skill, even upon occasion a skill with words, certainly some knowledge of cameras, often a real talent for direction and production, for scene and costume and lighting design, just to put on the horsy horrors and the human ones. Television has not yet matched the performance of the American film at its best, but it is not for lack of pretension or of technical resourcefulness.

There are large skills buried in the technological jungle of the popular arts, skills which have emerged just often enough to justify a serious examination of the growth and development and regression —where there has been regression—of these arts. When people became literate in quantity, it became necessary that books in quantity be provided them. When the technology of the film, of radio, of television, and of the phonograph record was developed, it became inevitable that some degree of art would have to follow that development, however stumblingly.

These, then, are the two kinds of art in America, the two kinds of democratic culture. But generalizations about them are not enough. They are not much more satisfactory, really, than generalizations about the American people, or the British, or the French, or the Russian. One must come very much closer to the arts, peer into their faces as closely as the television camera does in its interviews, get close enough to see the face of each of these arts in precise detail, even if in that close look one is for a moment affronted by creases and wrinkles and pockmarks. When we come that close to any of the arts, popular or private, we come that much closer to the people in the arts. For even if we do not leave that encounter with more confident insights into the general nature of American culture, we are bound to discover a good deal more about a certain number of Americans. That may be all we can accomplish, but that may be enough. For what we will be doing is what the arts do, each in its separate way, offering the facts of humanity for humanity to contemplate.

MUSIC

OF AMERICA'S private artists none work in greater privacy than its composers. They remain almost completely undisturbed by conductors, performers, and audiences. Their names are little known and one even barely knows what to call the art they practice. Classical music? Serious music? Or just music? To the mass of Americans "music" means Rodgers and Hammerstein, Gershwin, or the great names of the classical concert-hall repertory, Bach, Mozart, Beethoven, Brahms, Tchaikovsky, Wagner. Almost all of our native composers, from the late Charles Ives to the young and middle-aged twelve-tone writers, are dubious "modernists" who write in an idiom so remote from the possibility of an enjoyable musical experience that it need never really be taken seriously.

If one includes on one's list of American composers the major figures of European music deposited on American shores as gifts of the Russian Revolution and Hitler—Rachmaninoff, Schönberg, Bloch, Bartok, Stravinsky, and Hindemith—then perhaps it can be said that some contemporary names outside the sticky circle of operetta and musical comedy have made their way into the American consciousness. Certainly among record collectors, at least, these distinguished Europeans are well known. Rachmaninoff, with the aid of Hollywood and some pop-tune transformations, has taken his place beside Tchaikovsky as one of the composers who define the Russian national sound, and Stravinsky, having had the longest birthday celebration on public record to celebrate his coming of the age of wisdom, at least as television marks eightieth birthdays, including a festive occasion in Washington, finds himself set beside Robert Frost as one of those few who have received the good White-Housekeeping seal of approval.

In spite of a fair number of festival performances of their works, a respectable place in the record catalogs, and even occasional inclusion in the programs of the major symphony orchestras, most of the native-born composers of "serious" music remain hopelessly obscure. Even those who break through for a while, like Aaron Copland, who had a popular work in his *El Salon Mexico,* whose name has appeared in large type in film credits, and who has written several successful books explaining music in general and modern music in particular in popular terms, even such composers are something less than household names. Leonard Bernstein, who wears a shining dress shirt and a tousled hairdo with an aplomb that a younger Leopold Stokowski might have envied, and who springs upon a podium with an élan that is barely matched by our most accomplished trampoline artists, is everything that a classical musician should be. He looks good. In spite of an occasional orotundity that dangles too long on the palate, he sounds cultured. He explains obscure music, from Bach to jazz, so it stays explained. And, besides, he has the good taste to write scores like *West Side Story,* which can be whistled.

If taxed, a radio listener or television viewer could come up with another name—Gian-Carlo Menotti. He may not be sure whether Menotti is Italian or American, especially in view of some vague association with some fights at an Italian music festival that his newspaper reading has left him with, but he knows he's a pleasant sort of fellow, full of hummable, slightly acrid, Puccini-ish tunes, and nice opera plots that move with nimble oscillation back and forth between the macabre and the sentimental. He has seen most of Menotti's operas on television at least once, and one, *Amahl and the Night Vistors,* a TV commission, he has suffered through happily every Christmas since 1951. That leaves only the sizable accomplishment of modern American music unaccounted for.

American composers are not unendowed, either with native gifts or with substantial donations from the foundations. They have had in this century an organization, the League of Composers, generally devoted to the cause of modern music, American and European, but most particularly concerned to find audiences and advance the reputation of the American product. They themselves have been effecttively involved in an American Composers Alliance and in an American branch of the International Society for Contemporary Music, which in its time presented a large number of excellently performed concerts of modern American music. Several educational radio stations and a great many FM channels have regularly played recordings of American composers, and even have paid out of meager budgets for live performances of American works. One of them, WNYC in New York, has for years sponsored an annual month-long celebration of the breadth and depth of contemporary American composition in recorded performance and live, in round-table discussion and lecture. And on campuses of all sizes and budgets, native composers are welcomed with almost as much enthusiasm as native poets, as artists in residence, instructors, or whatever form their temperaments and talents will permit their employment to take. But still the audiences are less than large, the interest dim. The breakthrough which occurred in American painting a few years after the Second World War has not yet happened in music. A snobbism or a very particular judgment seems constantly to elect the European over the American in music. If a dazzling percussion is called for, or an electronic sound, an adventure in *musique concrete* or "totally organized" music, the private artist sought out will be the European rather than the American, even when the American has been well recorded, intelligently explained, or at least well quoted on the dust jacket, and, insofar as these things can be measured, is quite obviously a composer or arranger or laboratory technician of equal merit with his German or French competitor or clearly his superior. [1]

There has been enough special pleading for American music which has failed to make clear that special pleading is not the answer to American composers' problems. Regular performance, outside festivals and special radio celebrations and campus culture weeks, may be one good answer. A serious examination of the music by all who intend to spend any amount of time in serious consideration of the arts in America may be another good answer. But clearly the best will be more than regular performance, more than examination of the music now and then as part of a conspectus of American culture; it will have to be concentration for years on the work of American composers, all sorts of performances by all sorts of conductors and orchestras, chamber groups and singers, to the extent that Americans come to know Ives's *The Housatonic at Stockbridge, Paracelsus,* and *Concord Sonata,* Wallingford Riegger's *Dichotomy, Study in Sonority,* and *Third Symphony,* and the chamber music of Roger Sessions at least as well as they know the orchestral works and chamber music of Rachmaninoff, Bartok, Stravinsky, Schönberg, and Hindemith.

This is not to insist that Ives, Riegger, Sessions, or any other native-born American composer is necessarily of the stature of that remarkable quintet of naturalized Americans, though I suspect that Ives will stand up to the comparison and there may be others of like quality. But the fact is that until we have had a chance to know the works of our composers, to hear them differently interpreted and performed, by heavy-handed conductors or those who are light with their hands, by Germanic, by French, and by Slavic conductors, by Midwestern, Eastern, Southwestern, and Northwestern musicians, we shall not be in any position to judge them. It is foolish to imagine that one recording, even an excellent one that is certified as thoroughly satisfactory by the composer, can bring a composition fully alive to audiences, no matter how often repeated. Music, notoriously the most difficult of the arts to explain, to find words for, must be lived with. That means close acquaintance, not simply the token introduction which we get from George Szell's performances of the works of Easley Blackwood with the Cleveland Orchestra or the light sprinkling of contemporary American works that Leonard Bernstein offers listeners of the New York Philharmonic or the multiple summonings up of emotion, all at once patriotic and musical, with which every few years on February 12th Roy Harris's *Lincoln Symphony* is trotted out by one orchestra or another. It means not only a few names, variously well known, variously attractive, either because of newspaper reputation or conventional melodiousness. It means far more, then, than Barber, Menotti, and Copland, Harris and Virgil Thomson, Walter Piston and William Schuman, Norman Dello Joio and David Diamond. It means a full and constant representation of American composers of unmistakable professional ability and even of some whose eccentricities of style or aberrations of form (as these things are usually looked at) make classification of any kind impossible. Until such a time, all judgments of American music must, it seems to me, be tentative and far from complete, except perhaps in the cases of the most trivial works or the most commanding, and even then, until we have had a chance to hear them again and again, as for example we have heard the Gershwins' *Porgy and Bess* and Copland's *El Salon Mexico,* we should recognize that we don't really know what we are talking about when we make our noises of acceptance or rejection.[2]

It is not altogether clear why the music of Charles Ives has not found a larger number of eager sponsors and listeners. If any composer ever came out of the American earth, it is he. His early influences were a Connecticut village fiddler and the bands and church choirs of his father. The figures deliberately evoked by his music are

Emerson, Hawthorne, the Alcotts, and Thoreau, after whom the four movements of his 1909–15 *Concord Sonata* are named, as well as Lincoln and the Americans who celebrate or are celebrated by the country's major holidays. He writes about Central Park in New York and the Housatonic River in Connecticut, the hills, the waters, the birds, the people of New England. He wrote four symphonies of a Whitmanesque girth and motion and intensity and a group of thirty-four songs that touch all the stops of the American emotional organ, choral music with a fine, if somewhat acrid edge of hymn sounds. He has music for the violin and piano which is reflective, somber, harsh, ebullient, peaceful, and chaotic by turns, with all the quick shifts of emphasis—emphasis only barely placed, emphasis sometimes apparently misplaced—which the American temperament, so happily attuned to volatility, should find deeply moving. And for those who like to make discoveries, there is the startling one to make in Ives's music, when one learns the dates of composition, that suggests he happened upon almost every variation and methodization of tonality which was later to be systematized and made persuasive to the more conventionally educable composers by Arnold Schönberg.

Ives was a lover of sound, as no one who has listened to his music for any length of time can miss observing. He loved sound, one might think, without discrimination, and gathered it up in masses of notes, throwing them into measures of any size, shuttling them back and forth in rhythms of any shape, hardly worrying about where they fell or how they fell upon the instrument or the ear. Attitudes do not come easily out of such a music. One rarely knows with any certainty whether what one is hearing in, say, the great, nervous, and showy *Third Symphony* (1901–1904) or the marvelously unstable setting of Robert Browning's poem *Paracelsus* is meant at any given time to be "noble"—an adjective often associated with the symphony—or reverent or impious or even sour. *Paracelsus* is an early dramatic poem of Browning's; in it the poet is highly rhetorical, but not insensitive to the complex figure he celebrates. Near the end of the last scene, which Ives set with particular vitality, are some lines given to Paracelsus that seem to reflect Ives's wandering speculations through his music.

> man, once descried, imprints for ever
> His presence on all lifeless things: the winds
> Are henceforth voices, wailing or a shout,

A querulous mutter or a quick gay laugh,
Never a senseless gust now man is born.

The morn has enterprise, deep quiet droops
With evening, triumph takes the sunset hour,
Voluptuous transport ripens with the corn
Beneath a warm moon like a happy face:
—And this to fill us with regard for man.
With apprehension of his passing worth,
Desire to work his proper nature out,
And ascertain his rank and final place,
For these things tend still upward, progress is
The law of life, man is not Man as yet.[3]

Ives's music moves as quickly as Browning's words from the enterprise of morning to the drooping quiet of evening, with a voluptuous sunrise and a triumphant sunset. He is a composer clearly
unafraid of the images of calendar art and yet altogether open to
abstractions of an abstruseness and indirection few other composers
were daring or gifted enough to feel in the first quarter of this century,
when he wrote most of his music. It is this enormous openness to the
experience of man in his most natural setting that makes Ives so
beguiling to listen to, even without any clear guidelines of program or
setting, or even with pointers that seem to restrict one's responses to
the stock figures in the stock landscapes of New England. Neither
guidelines missed nor pointers followed can confuse or confine the
meditative listener to his rows of tones, to his ragtime, his polyrhythms, his constantly shifting accents. Like an enormously learned
and gifted but drunken Fourth of July orator, he has something he
knows he wants very much to say, something he knows is very much
worth saying, but he seems not quite sure what it is. Is it his country
he wants to praise? Is it his people he wants to castigate? Is it an apprehension—in both senses of that splendid Victorian word—of man's
passing worth he wants to communicate?

There are all sorts of ways to go through Ives's music—looking
for techniques, praising techniques, spurning techniques. He has all
the gracelessness of William Faulkner at his worst, without anything
like the rules of grammar or syntax to find him out. He has all the
sentimentality and folksiness of Robert Frost at his most contrived,
without any of the countless repetitions in textbooks and other anthologies to find him out. He has, too, an eloquence that no writer in

America seems quite to have matched, and no other composer seems quite to have attempted, about all the voices that seem to rise—wailing, shouting, muttering, laughing—out of the soil of America. For he has the requisite volatility to match the most sudden appearance or evaporation of feeling in Americans. And he long had the intuition of grandeur in the American land and the American people, had it long before it was obvious either to the people themselves or to their friends or to their enemies. When he came to set a psalm it was the 67th he chose, the simplest, briefest burst of praise.[4]

Ives never himself attempted to find an audience for his music, and in spite of the earnest support of a few other composers, such as Henry Cowell, and a few performers, such as the pianist John Fitzpatrick, and late but warm critical approval, he has never been given any large attention by the record companies, the radio and television networks, the symphony orchestras and chamber groups and recitalists. Now, however, that American art has begun to interest Americans almost as much as it interests Europeans, Ives may be played, played by different people in different ways, played often, played well. Once played, he may find for his music something like the support he found for the insurance policies he sold day after day in Wall Street to make the living that permitted him to go home to Connecticut to write his music and, when he retired in 1930, to leave the wealthiest firm of its kind in the insurance business.

There is no other American composer outside of jazz with quite the gusto or depth of feeling of Ives, but there are several of great originality, with musical personalities, once one comes to know them, that are absorbing, entertaining, provocative—all the things that the human person can be in music, perhaps to a more intense and disturbing degree than in any other art. Wallingford Riegger is a master of the tone-row of such a skill and such a range of enterprise as to keep any instructor in tone-row techniques keyboard deep in examples—eleven-tone, twelve-tone, thirteen-tone rows and almost any and all multiples thereof. His is a philosophical mind in music, displayed with that mixture of innocent gravity and sophisticated intricacy that makes the writings of Ludwig Wittgenstein so engaging to read. In any rational musical world his 1927 *Study in Sonority*— a word used with masterful precision here—for ten violins, his *Dichotomy* (1931–1932), for chamber orchestra, his various sets of *Variations*—for one piano, for two pianos, and for violin and orchestra—would be standard repertory items. And so, too, would his marvelously compact *Third Symphony* (1946–47), which though it won the New York Music Critics Circle award in 1948 has been more appreciated in Europe than the United States. And finally, now that audiences have begun to open their ears to the terse precisions of Webern and the late Stravinsky, perhaps there will be time for Riegger's songs—fine, angular, unsentimental settings of Emily Dickinson, Dylan Thomas, Whitman, Burns, and Shakespeare—and piano and organ pieces. Not much time will be needed. Most of them are two, three, four, or five minutes long.

The technical problems taken up by Carl Ruggles are so engaging to other composers and to those few writers about music capable of translating them into words that, insofar as any impression at all has been conveyed to the musical public about him, he has been described as the most private of private artists, a colleague of Ives, Riegger, Edgar Varèse, and Henry Cowell in the Pan-American Association of Composers and if possible more recherché than any of them. He is rarely performed; his transformation of Gerhart Hauptmann's moving antimaterialist allegory, *The Sunken Bell,* is unpublished, unrecorded, and of course never done; his arcane studies of men and angels for odd groupings of instruments—six trumpets, four trumpets, and three trombones (or as many violins and cellos)—seem as remote to the makers and players of the present repertory as angels themselves. But he is not, for all the neglect, an inaccessible composer. His polyphonic experiments, while they are not filled with convenient little echoes of Bach and Handel, are of a sufficiently open construction to compel the attention of anyone who is delighted by the motion of lines against each other—and who is not? His brief *Evocations,* for piano (1937–1945), is lean, lofty, a work close in style to the row composers, in spirit to the Elizabethans, a fitting set of evocations for a native of Massachusetts who ended up in Vermont, looking and acting a Vermonter, writing his music on brown paper with colored pencils.

It seems incredible that Edgar Varèse had to wait until the sixties for any large recognition in his adopted country, of which he became a citizen in 1926, at the age of forty-one. He had by that time been a restless entrepreneur of new music for almost a decade, most successfully with the International Composers Guild, which he founded in 1921, the first society devoted entirely to the presentation of modern music, and probably, in the range of its programs over a six-year life, in the number of new composers introduced, and its openness to experimentation in sound, the most daring and the most vital organization of its kind. In everything he did, Varèse was passionately dedicated, as he believes a composer must be, to reflecting his own time, its ideas, its sounds, its rhythms, no matter how strident or straining as judged by conventional musical standards. And so he moved from the comparatively docile sounds of the traditional symphony orchestra to percussion instruments alone, and finally to all the soundmakers of our world which can be caught on a tape recorder—airplane propellers, vacuum-cleaner motors, pneumatic drills, factory machines, etc. The unlikely intervals and pulsating polyrhythms of the 1923 *Hyperprism,* or *Amériques* or *Arcana* of the same period, fade before the thirty-five percussion (played by thirteen men) of the 1931 *Ionisation,* and all dim before the concretization of the world of the late fifties in his *Poème Electronique* and *Deserts.* The fading is literal. The early works sound dated. But that is probably exactly what they should do.

Varèse's concern to reflect his own time makes inevitable that his music of the twenties will, more than most of the music of that period, reflect the twenties, in quite the same way as *Le Sacre du Printemps* reflects the years just before the First World War and has a dated sound. As a pioneer in electronic sounds in this last phase of his career, Varèse will undoubtedly always have about his music an innovator's associations, but with how much more fullness of idea and richness of investigation than most of the others who have been working with the same materials! He has not as yet produced anything that is likely to win a large audience, even of record buyers, as the much younger German composer Karlheinz Stockhausen has with his *Kontakte,* in which electronic sounds are so ingeniously combined. But Varèse has managed a handsome harsh support for sung words in his *Nocturnal,* a setting of words by Anais Nin; and the separations of sounds in *Deserts,* which began this extraordinarily fertile late period of Varèse's, are almost literally hair-raising as they insinuate their clattering, splattering, crackling, grating, grinding ways into the skull and make sense of a sort and even a kind of meditative experience of the noises with which we have no choice but to live at this end of the twentieth century. The sense comes from an artist's organization of these sounds. The meditation comes from what follows, as ineluctably we are drawn to think and to feel our way around the characteristic tones of our time, around the character of our time. No one has been more thoughtful about his own music or the music of his own time than that most articulate of American composers, Roger Sessions. He has written with particular sensitivity of the musical experience of the composer, the performer, and the listener, finding words of unusual simplicity and directness to express himself and something at least of the nature of his art. His remarkable response to words is reflected in the texts he has chosen to set—the murky but highly provocative symbolist drama of Leonid Andreyev, *The Black Maskers,* for which he composed incidental music when he was twenty-seven, in 1923; Brecht's coolly ironic play, *The Trial of Lucullus,* which Sessions made into an opera in 1946 and for which he might conceivably find a receptive audience in 1976, by which time Brechtian detachment, in music as in words, should not too much offend a generation gradually being weaned from the theater and the concert hall and the opera house of the vicarious; the *Idyll of Theocritus,* in a felicitous English translation by Robert Trevelyan, composed in 1954 for soprano and orchestra, a work of more emotional intensity than most of Sessions' music, with suggestions of the atmosphere and method of Schönberg's *Erwartung,* but not its actual texture, and some of the *Angst*—call it Kierkegaardian, dodecaphonistic, Auden-Episcopalian—of Berg's *Wozzeck.* The *Theocritus,* with its thick orchestral writing and unusually exposed emotional qualities, is a handsome reminder that Sessions began his career as a disciple of Ernest Bloch, an influence probably less active technically in his mature writing than Schönberg's, but possibly closer to his life of feeling and to the interior life of his recent music. In a more reasonable world than that of American music, Sessions would not be a remote composer, his musical speculations would be at least as widely available as his verbal, and it would be possible to hear his settings of Brecht and Theocritus, his two string quartets (1936 and 1951), his concertos for violin (1935) and piano (1956), and his four symphonies (1927, 1946, 1957, and 1958) with something like the regularity their musical strengths and philosophical depth deserve. But instead we shall have to make do with the more favored Americans, Copland and Thomson, Foss and Schuman, Dello Joio and Diamond, Piston and Hanson, Barber and Menotti.

One has no difficulty understanding the preeminent position of

Aaron Copland in American music. He has written in almost every musical form. He has written for the private audience, speaking to one listener at a time, and he has composed in every possible popular medium, for film and theater and radio, for the dance, for the phonograph record. And in almost every medium he has touched his audiences, small or large. He touched them with bubbling satire in the 1925 *Music for the Theater,* and with the dry acerbities of the 1930 *Piano Variations* and the 1929 trio on Jewish themes, *Vitebsk,* and the short orchestral pieces of the early thirties, and once again he reached them with the populist themes of *El Salon Mexico* (1936), *Billy the Kid* (1938), *Rodeo* (1942), *A Lincoln Portrait* (1942), *Appalachian Spring* (1943), and his film scores. So effectively, in fact, did he shift from solemn thoughts at home to gay thoughts abroad, and so thoroughly did he bring himself out of his native Brooklyn environment to the folksy atmosphere of nineteenth-century ballet America, that anything he wrote after the forays into springtime Pennsylvania and dance-hall Mexico and the prairie of the badman was bound to be listened to for its evocations of the measured wilds of Agnes De Mille, John Steinbeck, and Metro-Goldwyn-Mayer. Somehow the staccato rhythms which he early learned from close listening to Stravinsky and the impressionist textures he analyzed with his teacher Nadia Boulanger and his years of sober musical reflection combined in his populist pieces to make a definitive sound of folk culture.

Stravinsky—French impressionism—and a lean and hungry music—hardly, one would think, the background for the dance pieces or the films, *Of Mice and Men, The Red Pony, Our Town,* and James's *The Heiress* (née *Washington Square*). But the staccato rhythms had a beat and the impressionism offered a simple kind of tune and the years of reflection about the nature of his craft had turned Copland into an eager writer for mass media. He performed with distinction the duties set for him by his new colleagues, the ballet choreographers, the film directors, the broadcasting company producers. He did his work almost too well. There is a homeliness in *Appalachian Spring,* for example, which borders on the cloying. The composer's own descriptions of the several sections of his setting for Martha Graham's ballet read like a caricature of a scenario of a film about life down on the old farm: The characters are introduced, "one by one, in a suffused light." A duo "for the bride and her intended—scene of tenderness and passion." When a revivalist enters, the feeling is "Folksy . . . suggestions of square dances and country fiddlers." With the bride's solo dance a "presentiment of motherhood. Extremes of joy and fear and wonder." Finally, after the couple have made their way among their neighbors, they are left alone, "quiet and strong in their new house." Perhaps the most significant words are those in which Copland describes a section for muted strings just before the close of the work, "like a prayer." This sort of writing of his is never prayerful but like a prayer, and never really of the folk but folksy. It is the equivalent in music of the prose of James Agee and the poetry of Carl Sandburg, with all the surface manner of the peepul, but very little of their matter, for all the echoes of hymns and cowboy songs and dances.

It was fitting that Richard Rodgers and Oscar Hammerstein should have commissioned Copland to write an opera for the thirtieth anniversary of the League of Composers in 1954 and that the attempt should have had the title of *The Tender Land,* a fair indication of its flaccid content. But it is not fitting that a composer of Copland's gifts should be known almost entirely for his folksy effusions or that his influence should lead others to do much more writing of this same kind. In his brief excerpts "From a Composer's Journal" in a recent volume of his, he concludes with a terse comment on "Genius in a Small World": "It takes a long time for a small country to get over a great man—witness Finland and Sibelius. Norway has taken fifty years to get over Grieg, and it looks as if Denmark would need as long a time to get beyond Carl Neilsen. If I were any of these men, it would not make me happy to know that my own work engendered sterility in my progeny." [5] Did those words come from reflection on his own progeny? Has Copland begun to regret the proliferation of his kind of prairie Americana? Certainly his recent music seems to mark a return through the discipline of twelve-tone techniques, adapted rather than adopted, to the dry wit of *Music for the Theater* and the reserve of the *Piano Variations.*[6]

Even if Copland does sell his home on the range, the populists will go marching on. Those badly bitten by prairie dogs seem to have recovered from the worst effects of the bites. At least they have not perpetrated any recent hymns for irrigation canal and orchestra. Virgil Thomson, since the scores for Pare Lorentz's documentary films, *The Plough that Broke the Plains* (1936) and *The River*

(1937), for Robert Flaherty's *Louisiana Story* (1948) and his own reflection, *Wheatfield at Noon* (1948), seems to have been quiescent. Perhaps his years of enforced critical detachment on the music desk at the *New York Herald Tribune* produced a distaste for jus' folks sentimentality, which in spite of his Missouri origins seems very far removed from the witty personality of the Paris-trained, New York-developed composer of the operas *Four Saints in Three Acts* (1928) and *The Mother of Us All* (1947), both on librettos by Gertrude Stein.

Lukas Foss seems altogether to have abandoned the role of paean-ist for the people which he took up in 1944 under the inspiration of Carl Sandburg's poem *The Prairie.* He was only twenty-one when he made the Sandburg ode into a cantata and only six years a resident of the United States. Thereafter he went to the Bible for his cantatas, to Isaiah (1945), and to the Song of Songs (1946), and to a variety of sources which showed him remarkably attuned both to popular and sophisticated tastes—O. Henry, Mark Twain, Rilke, Auden, A. E. Housman, Kafka, Nietzsche. He has written a tribute to Albert Schweitzer—a *Symphony of Chorales* (1958)—and has for several years now toured at home and abroad with an improvising chamber group, which for some listeners has the vitality and resourcefulness of a first-rate jazz group. There is no question of Foss's large talents, as composer, conductor, and pianist, nor of his literary sensibility. But in spite of his affecting setting of some of Rilke's *Stories of the Dear Lord,* for narrator and symphony orchestra (as *A Parable of Death* in 1953), and the skillful writing in *Time Cycle* (1960), the sequence for soprano and orchestra in which he makes use of texts by Auden, Housman, Kafka, and Nietzsche, he has not yet found a channel for his gifts which is either recognizably or compellingly his own.

The search for a recognizable identity has plagued American composers of the last few generations and left them with little to offer audiences in search of clear personality vigorously asserted but the bloody marks of the search. For a while William Schuman seemed an unmistakable Americanist, with an *American Festival Overture* (1939), a setting for chorus of Whitman's *Pioneers* (1937), transla-tions into music of poems by Genevieve Taggard, a *William Billings Overture* (1943), a *Prayer in Time of War* (1943), music for the theater and for the dance (including the very successful collaboration with Antony Tudor, *Undertow,* in 1945) of the professional kind our Americanists can turn out. As late as 1956 he produced a *New England Triptych* based on tunes by Billings. And earlier, in 1953, he made an attempt to turn "Casey at the Bat" into an opera, *The Mighty Casey.* But the enduring Schuman seems rather to be in the works sans program, the symphonies, especially the *Sixth* (1948) and *Seventh* (1960), the chamber music, especially the *Third String Quartet* (1939) and the *Fourth* (1952), in spite of the predilection of Pulitzer Prize committees and the public for the works of a more open populism. Schuman is, in any case, accessible enough to popular tastes in his works without program. His wide-ranging dynamics, assertive writing for brasses, and neatly modernized adaptations of baroque counterpoint are bound to please. It is only the embarrassing Americanism that stands in the way of easy acceptance by those for whom the best ballads for Americans never wave a flag or even name their patriotic purposes.[7]

Enough people recognized personal voices in the music of Norman Dello Joio and David Diamond to pull them out of the mass of highly competent but not easily recognizable American composers. Both have their plaintive moments, a kind of dramatic melancholia to which the public always responds happily. Dello Joio has done his bit for the pioneer trade, too, settings of texts by Whitman and Whitman redivivus, Stephen Vincent Benét. He has also tuned his orchestra to the medieval modes and Renaissance forms, perhaps under the influence of his teacher, Paul Hindemith, most impressively in the *Three Ricercare for Piano and Orchestra* (1946) and the orchestral *Variations, Chaconne and Finale* (1947). Diamond is another skilled worker in the neoclassical tradition, with a taste for Shakespearean suites (*Music for Romeo and Juliet,* 1947, and a sketch for orchestra illustrating *Timon of Athens,* 1949) and a considerable ease in symphonic forms, demonstrated by over six symphonies and three concertos, as well as his popular *Rounds for String Orchestra* (1944), before he was forty. Audiences may not always find themselves at ease in Diamond's increasingly thick orchestration, but like Dello Joio and such quite different older men as Walter Piston and Howard Hanson, he seems to have won an open place in symphonic repertories.

With Piston, four notably lucid music textbooks and a sprightly ballet score, *The Incredible Flutist* (1938), reworked as a suite for orchestra, have opened the way at least to polite hearings for his highly competent, better than textbookish writing for orchestra. With Hanson, a lifetime of conducting, teaching, and publicizing American music, and a generous romanticism in the best sentimental tradition have combined to make listeners of a similar disposition happy with his echoes of late-nineteenth-century orchestral writing. But none of these composers has caught and held the public fancy so firmly as Samuel Barber and Gian-Carlo Menotti, each a decade younger than Aaron Copland, each at least two decades older in taste and texture.

Barber's stylish lyricism early attracted the attention of Arturo Toscanini, who performed the economical *Essay for Orchestra,* written in 1938, and the compactly meditative *Adagio for Strings,* written two years earlier. In spite of several changes of manner and an increasing openness to complicated rhythms and fluctuating tonality, Barber's music remains at an emotional level that vast numbers of people can follow agreeably, and more, vicariously. The significant touchpoints after the early demonstrations of professional skill are probably the incisive setting of Stephen Spender's poem about a soldier dead in the Spanish Civil War, *A Stopwatch and an Ordnance Map* (1940), for men's voices, tympani, and brass; an entertaining adventure in *concerto grosso* structures, the *Capricorn Concerto* (1944); a 1948 setting of the first chapter of James Agee's *A Death in the Family* for soprano and orchestra, as *Knoxville: Summer of 1915,* somewhat less agglutinated than the original text; his ballet for Martha Graham, *Medea* (1955); and his opera *Vanessa* (1958). Some of the dramatic power of the Spender setting can be found in the far more complex music for *Medea* while Barber's lyricism, conventional but moving, carries the inanities of Gian-Carlo Menotti's libretto for *Vanessa* to a point where it is possible to be interested even if not deeply affected by characters out of the dreariest reaches of the Teatro del grottesco and the drawing-room drama of the twenties and thirties.

What Menotti does limpingly for Barber, he does with far greater élan for himself. His own librettos are juicily melodramatic, made to order for his slightly sour versions of Puccini. You have your choice with this Italian-American melodramatist—a variety of inconsequential comedies, *Amelia Goes to the Ball* (1934), *The Old Maid and the Thief* (1938), *The Telephone* (1946), *The Last Savage* (1963),[8] or a variety of inconsequential dramas, *The Medium* (1946),

The Consul (1950), *Amahl and the Night Visitors* (1951), *The Saint of Bleecker Street* (1954), *Maria Golovin* (1958). Only the most shameless sentimentalism could translate the terrors of displaced persons into the treacle of *The Consul.* As for *Amahl* and *The Saint,* one can only wonder at the sort of spirituality that can confuse the stickiness of the first and the hysteria of the second with genuine religious experience; a parodist could hardly do better. By comparison, the unpretentious craftsmanship amid conventional musical structures of Douglas Moore, in his one-act *The Devil and Daniel Webster* (1938) and two-act *The Ballad of Baby Doe* (1956), is a joy to hear, and Marc Blitzstein's operas of social conscience, *The Cradle Will Rock* (1936) and *Regina* (1949), seem almost restrained, and certainly closer to a world of genuine emotion, however much simplified to fit Marxist dogma.

The best of American operas remains Virgil Thomson's *Four Saints in Three Acts.* The sheer joy of Gertrude Stein's versions of Teresa of Avila and Ignatius of Loyola and the confidantes she has invented for them, Saints Settlement and Chavez, is caught in abundance by the music, which rolls round the words and settles them with unmistakable unction in the mouths of any singers unselfconscious enough to sing them as if they make sense—because they do. The Negro cast gathered together by the composer provided such singers for the Stein text and Thomson's music. They understood Gertrude's characters and the two characters Virgil added, a *Compère* and a *Commère,* twin surrogates for the layman and for the audience, that is, for those who are not saints or at least are not canonized. They were not embarrassed by the bubbling vernacular they were given to sing nor made uneasy by Florine Stettheimer's cellophane scenery and velvet costumes. Everything went together. Nothing was excessive in that first wonderful production of *Four Saints* in 1934. No set of words and music in our music is so satisfactorily, so delightfully, so wittily, or so wisely joined together. One wonders, then, what it will take to give *Four Saints* its proper place in the opera houses or to convince producers to try out the less interesting but still absorbing opera Virgil Thomson made out of Gertrude Stein's *The Mother of Us All* (1947), a softly solemn tale of Susan B. Anthony and the fight for votes and other rights for women in the United States. As long as the melodramatic absurdities and saccharine pomposities of Gian-Carlo Menotti are equated with grand opera, then Stein and Thomson must remain a part of the past, and the best instruction American musicians and audiences are ever likely to have in the mysteries of music drama will be denied them.

It may be that the denial will be brief, for it is quite clear that a new period is beginning in which the eager hopes of all the organizations for the defense and illustration of American music of the twenties and thirties have at last some likelihood of being realized, in which experimentation is in itself an honorable badge for the composer, and the private artist has some chance of communicating to enough people to avoid the dangers of an empty solipsism in his music, and the public composer need not be so blatantly public, and may even, in fact, retire his chewing gum, his lasso, and his worn 48-star flag without contemplating a replacement for any of them.

Of the private composers, perhaps the most striking are Elliott Carter and Milton Babbitt. Both offer a music of an obscurity suitable to their position, Carter with conventional instruments, Babbitt with traditional instruments as the agents of his complex logic of sound and rhythm and with electronic voices. In neither case is the aim or the effect one of obscurity for obscurity's sake. We are in a realm now of advanced speculation, in which no time-marking or choice of register or pitch or dynamic is ever in any way accidental. But neither are we dealing with a kind of control which precludes feeling. Indeed, if my own response is in any way typical, this is rather a kind of control of musical resources in the service of feeling. The amount of feeling possible in Carter's idiom is probably most openly exposed in the string quartets of 1951 and 1960, in which each part is marked by an individuality which is as clearly dramatic as roles in a play, and no easier nor more difficult to follow than the ambiguous exchanges of the characters of Samuel Beckett or of Jean Genet. Carter's affinity for the serial composers in the Schönberg tradition may strike some listeners to his 1955 *Variations for Orchestra,* but it is not that connection, which is really quite remote here, but the interdependence of the ten variations which absorbs the attentive ear and the undeniable fact that this is a work complete in itself, which requires no comparison with other works in the modern repertory for understanding. It can be followed as any significant work of art must be, as for the moment self-generating, not as a part of history, but as a presence in and for and by itself.

No American composer has worked longer with what has been called "totally organized" music, or sometimes *musique concrète,* than Milton Babbitt, and none has as a result more effectively removed himself from the interest or understanding of mass audiences. But Babbitt's compositions, whatever their mathematical precisions, do not require the learning or musicianship of their composer to be listened to, nor should they be shunned because, as with the poetry of William Empson or the painting of Alfred Manessier, one must bring something more than a boiling subconscious to them. They sit squarely in the twelve-tone idiom, whether liberated from the uncertainties and inaccuracies of human performers by the controls on amplifiers, preamps, speakers, and tape decks or left to the vagaries of temperament and temperature and audience atmosphere to which live musicians are subject. If one comes, then, with some education in the serial method, by the book, by the phonograph record, or the concert hall, one has more than a passing chance of hearing what is going on, even when the method is extended beyond the choice and ordering of tones to cover all the other values connected with the sounding and the duration of notes. With at least that much background, one may find in Babbitt's 1947 *Composition for Four Instruments* (flute, clarinet, violin, and cello) or his *Composition for Twelve Instruments* (1948), his *Composition for Viola and Piano* (1950), his song cycle *Du* (1950), or his writing for jazz musicians, *All Set* (1957), an idiom of great refinement, cool, as the jazzman inflects that adjective, and worth many hearings.

Because all of these works of Babbitt's are on records, they are bound to reach a fairly large audience, but that will not give them or other works of similar merit by the composer the constant hearing they deserve in concert halls. A work designed for recorded rather than live performance, Babbitt's *Composition for Synthesizer* (1964), is likely to hold more interest for the ordinary ear. For untrained that ear may be, but unconditioned it is not. The electronic sounds that make up this composition have been dinned into every man's hearing many times, but never have they been arranged so elegantly, with such intellectual rigor and responsibility. Listeners of all sorts, trained and untrained, may much of the time find themselves shut out of Babbitt's fragments, but they are almost certain some of the time to be caught up in the steely music, whether because of its novelty or its intrinsic worth. They will recognize, if they listen long enough and hard enough, a fine, independent mind, a composer in the twelve-tone tradition who has gone well beyond musical tradition in his open acceptance of the technology of the twentieth century. In doing so, he may be giving us an insight into the art of the future, art that is fully alive to modern technology and not forever bound to eighteenth- and nineteenth-century sentimentalities.

One cannot help connecting music like Milton Babbitt's with that of other composers who have experimented with electronic devices or percussion instruments only, with various ways of augmenting or attacking the piano or deploying one's instruments and performers around a hall. Otto Luening and Vladimir Ussachevsky, Babbitt's colleagues in the Electronic Music Center, have used a tape recorder with imagination in constructing works which extend the range of traditional instruments, change textures, multiply rhythms, and move the parts of an orchestra around with a calculated but not reckless abandon. John Cage has moved a long way from the "tone clusters" Henry Cowell used to draw from the piano with his arms on the keyboard right up to their elbows: by "preparing" his piano with an apparatus of hardware and software, ranging from nuts and bolts to pieces of rubber and felt, Cage was able to simulate most familiar percussion sounds, Eastern as well as Western, and a great many not so familiar. To this kind of experimentation, he added some playing around with radio receivers, improvised batteries of bowls and bells and bars and jars, and some writing for electrically amplified instruments. His music, apparently disorganized and devoid of any recognizable continuity, makes an appeal to the public not unlike the two- and four-bar phrases of the arrangers in the Fletcher Henderson jazz tradition.[9] It is an appeal matched in a way by Henry Brant's movement across and around a hall of small groups of musicians, each playing a work apparently disconnected from the others in time and tonality and almost everything else. There are connections in both cases, of course, whether intended or accidental, whether planned by the composer or placed there by the listener.

What the public will have to decide is whether it wants to continue making the connections or prefers, say, the elegances of Gunther Schuller, out of jazz, the twelve-tone tradition and a long personal playing experience, or the wit of Teo Macero, from a similarly cross-grained background, including that most contemporary and most exacting of musical experiences, splicing the many takes of a recording-

studio performance, a duty that falls to Macero in his capacity as a
recording director for Columbia Records. It is fairly clear that the
public will elect some such music, either along jazz lines or electronic
or both, and that it will do so with a degree of conscious responsibility
for what it is doing. The chief appeal may be that of novelty: it is
titivating to find oneself listening to jazz instruments in a setting recognizably solemn, if not quite what one used to mean by the word "classical." When, as in *Fusion,* Macero's ingenious joining of five improvising jazzmen and a symphony orchestra carefully scored for, the two
worlds come boldly together, audiences may go beyond mere sensations to a deeper experience of the potentialities of the different kinds
of music of their time and their place. Or again, in the Luening and
Ussachevsky tape recorder pieces the mass audience may discover the
opening to musical development that modern technology offers, or in
the work of Cage, or perhaps even more of Edgar Varèse and Milton
Babbitt, the remarkable connection between the commonplace noises
of their epoch and the far from commonplace organization of those
noises which a graced ear can effect. And then, perhaps, though the
appeal has been one of novelty rather than any more significant
effect of serious listening, the preoccupation with sound that could
result might send listeners back to Charles Ives, who was after all
a great lover of sound, and to some if not to all of those who followed
and continue to follow in his distinguished direction. And if listeners,
why not performers, conductors, orchestras, singers, even record
companies and television networks?

POPULAR MUSIC

THE NAME tells the story. The concern of the composers and lyric-writers of popular music has always been box office at any price. The condition of their being is fifty million whistlers of their tunes and twenty or thirty million singers of their words (words are always harder to remember than melodies). They have had to list with the passing wind. They have had to stand up tall with the constant taste—if there is any such thing in American popular music. If the public fancy goes to waltzes, then so do the songwriters; if to fox-trots, tangos, rumbas, mambos, bossa novas, then so do they. If novelties are in the wind, then these riders of public transport must cup their ears to hear exactly what kind of novelty is called for by the people who do the calling—nonsense lyrics with a lilting tune, nursery rhymes with a jazz twist, or just an inane tune surrounding a vacant set of words, an idiot's delight, a twist.

With such limitations of expression, it is remarkable that so many talented men have been attracted to the field and have stayed in it, producing work year after year of charm, of wit, of a robust and enduring character, and sometimes even of beauty. It is even more remarkable that such work has been produced under the surveillance of just exactly the kind of men one would expect to have the power of yea and nay in a field as restricted to the universally acceptable product, the inoffensive, the commercial, as popular music.

Something like constant achievement, if not constant taste, has been the record of the best of the popular-song composers, those who write musicals, or, if one prefers the more elegant term, those who write for the American musical theater. A catalog of the best of their work since the turn of the century is one of very high distinction. It shows, if one approaches it chronologically, a spiraling movement away from the sentimental bonbons of Victor Herbert and Reginald de Koven, first in the direction of every kind of humor—blowzy, caustic, genial—then onward and upward toward "significance"—musical, dramatic, sociological. It shows, if one looks at it in terms of form, a flexibility to fit all the demands of the musical theater, which are almost all the demands of the theater; in the long

36

list are torch songs and whispering serenades to innocent young love, topical commentaries, dances for almost every kind of dancer, and as one comes closer and closer to the present, ballets of a considerable breadth and arias that go well beyond the pastries of the Viennese operetta in their ambition to present slices of life in three-quarter, four-quarter, and six-eighth time. If, finally, one turns over the catalog to assay the particular performance of individual composers and lyric-writers, one finds at least a half-dozen masters of the pop tune whose work transcends the contributions of their word-writing associates, no matter which ones, in no matter what style, and then about as many teams of songwriters, handsomely matched, who have produced songs that can be compared, without apology, with the words and music of Gilbert and Sullivan.

The earliest of the enduring names of popular music in the twentieth century is Victor Herbert. But his tunes, for all their undeniable mechanical perfection, are directed almost exclusively toward the exaggerated sweetness of the second-rate Irish tenor and the third-rate American soprano. It takes a strong stomach and a weak ear to listen often to "Ah, Sweet Mystery of Life," or "Kiss Me Again" or "I'm Falling in Love with Someone" or "Sweethearts" as they almost demand to be sung—with hand on heart and voice pitched for the second balcony. That there is a larger melodic strength in Herbert's work has been suggested now and then by jazz or dance-band arrangements, such as the one Glenn Miller did of "Indian Summer." But as long as inferior tenors and sopranos insist on making Herbert the center of their affections, doubt must remain about his work.

Jerome Kern was certainly not an acidulous composer. There is a substantial amount of schmaltz in his melodies, from "They Didn't Believe Me," in 1914 (from *The Girl from Utah*) to "The Last Time I Saw Paris," written in 1941 with Oscar Hammerstein as a kind of lament for the city, then occupied by the Nazis. But the tunes of that extraordinarily gifted melodist go well beyond the service they have seen. They remain, to hold jazz musicians, amateur and professional sentimentalists, good singers and bad singers, in thrall. The list is very long, but a few are classics of a sort; they define the possibilities for melodic talent working in a commercial mold. They suggest that the mold is not impossibly confining.

From the Princess Theatre shows of the First World War, written by Kern in collaboration with Guy Bolton and P. G. Wodehouse, one song remains captivating, "Till the Clouds Roll By" (from *Oh, Boy!*): It was used as the title tune for the 1949 film based on Kern's life that was written by Bolton. For Marilyn Miller, Kern wrote the durable "Look for the Silver Lining" (from *Sally,* 1920) and "Who Stole My Heart Away?", the last from his first collaboration with Oscar Hammerstein, *Sunny,* in 1925. Two years later the two men turned out *Show Boat.* Hammerstein's adaptation of Edna Ferber's novel was full of *dese-dem-dose* Negro diction, and the Mississippi showboat rocked with melodramatic exaggerations, but it was an attempt to force-feed some life into the musical-comedy libretto, and for it Kern wrote the fine music of "Ol' Man River," "Can't Help Lovin' Dat Man," and "Bill," as well as the more conventional "Only Make Believe" and "Why Do I Love You?" It took a diseuse like Helen Morgan, rather than a straightforward singer, to make convincing some of the curious mixing of talking and singing in "Bill," not unlike the *Sprechstimme* technique of Arnold Schönberg. A little more of the same mixture gives an edge to "Why Was I Born?" also written for Helen Morgan (*Sweet Adeline,* 1929). In *The Cat and the Fiddle* (1931), Kern offered his orchestrator, Robert Russell Bennett, the material for a fuguetta in "She Didn't Say 'Yes' (She Didn't Say 'No.')" In *Music in the Air* (1932), some handsome echoes of southern Germany were filtered through a faintly mocking set of melodies—that is, if one cared to do songs like "I've Told Every Little Star" and "The Song Is You" that way. *Roberta* (1933), perhaps the best Kern score of all, followed. The famous tunes, "Smoke Gets In Your Eyes" and "Yesterday," and the less famous ones, "The Touch of Your Hand" and "You're Devastating," all show the kind of firm control of the medium and constant flow of fresh tunes that were to distinguish Kern's work as long as he lived. For Fred Astaire's *Swing Time* (1936), he did the gently sweetened "The Way You Look Tonight" and the gently soured "A Fine Romance"; for other films, he composed "Dearly Beloved" (1942) and "Long Ago and Far Away" (1944), two tunes of impeccable construction. And in between, he wrote that model song, beloved of arrangers and improvising pianists, "All the Things You Are," for the ill-fated musical *Very Warm for May* (1939).

No composer of popular songs can match Kern's record for freshness of line and brightness of construction, year after year, in every sort of vehicle, writing for the stage or for films. There are longer lists of hits than his, such as Irving Berlin's and Cole Porter's. There are other musicians who manage, as Kern did, to be interesting no matter how drab or inept their collaborators, such as Harold Arlen, Vernon Duke, and Vincent Youmans. And apart from the incomparable teams—the Gershwins and Rodgers and Hart—there is at least one other composer with an identity just as securely his own as Kern's and perhaps more gifted as a musical commentator on his own times—that is Kurt Weill. But for sheer melodic quality, of the distinction and durability of the work of the Johann Strausses and Franz Lehar, and yet with some of the intensity of feeling and drive we generally associate with jazz, no one can quite touch Jerome Kern.

Irving Berlin is the consummate professional, as composer and as his own lyricist. When ragtime expressed the *Zeitgeist,* he produced "Alexander's Ragtime Band" and "Everybody's Doin' It," among many others of like craftsmanship. For the First World War, he rolled out "Oh, How I Hate to Get Up in the Morning"; for the Second, "This Is the Army, Mr. Jones." For Ziegfeld, he produced, to order, "A Pretty Girl Is Like a Melody"; for the Music Box Revues, "Say It with Music" and "What'll I Do?" For topical revues of the Depression years, he did "Let's Have Another Cup of Coffee" (*Face the Music,* 1932), and "Heat Wave" (*As Thousands Cheer,* 1933). For Ethel Merman, he tailored two glistening scores, *Annie Get Your Gun* (1946) and *Call Me Madam* (1950). *Annie* is filled with tunes that cannot be faulted, at least in context—"The Girl That I Marry," "Doin' What Comes Naturally," "They Say It's Wonderful," "Anything You Can Do," "There's No Business Like Show Business." And they are good enough on their own to explain the choice of Berlin to do this score after the death of Jerome Kern, who had expected to do it, and what is more, to do it without delay. He is the supreme professional. Patriotic song? "God Bless America." Christmas song? "White Christmas." Film tunes? "Cheek to Cheek," "I've Got My Love to Keep Me Warm." Single songs, outside of shows? "All Alone," "Always," "Remember," "Blue Skies," "How Deep Is the Ocean?" "Russian Lullaby." Need one say more?

Cole Porter's record is almost as impressive as Berlin's for consistency over a very long period and for the special ability to produce an unending series of scores reeking with urbanity, 86 proof. His songs fall into fixed grooves; they tend to be much alike, and almost all quickly likable. Some of the very best are among the earliest,

"Let's Do It" (*Paris*, 1928), "Love for Sale" (*The New Yorkers,* 1930), and "What Is This Thing Called Love?" (*Wake Up and Dream,* 1930). His taste for erotic melodrama is best represented by "Night and Day," written for Fred Astaire (*The Gay Divorcee,* 1932). Its mood is variously echoed in "I've Got You Under My Skin"(for the film, *Born to Dance,* 1936), "Get Out of Town" (*Leave It to Me,* 1938), "I Love You" (*Mexican Hayride,* 1944), and "So In Love" (*Kiss Me Kate,* 1948). His taste for jazzy tunes, equally useful to jazz musicians and to cocktail pianists, is well illustrated by almost all the tunes from the celebrated collaboration with Porter of Wodehouse and Bolton, Lindsay and Crouse, *Anything Goes* (1934)—the title song, "I Get a Kick Out of You," "You're the Top," and "Blow, Gabriel, Blow." It is even better demonstrated by "Just One of Those Things" from *Jubilee* (1935), an unjustly uncelebrated work for which he also did "Begin the Beguine" and "Why Shouldn't I?" Sooner or later, all the Porter songs recommend themselves to jazz singers and instrumentalists, as witness the gradual emergence of "It's All Right with Me," from the 1953 *Can-Can,* as a standard tune for improvisation. The short staccato phrases into which most Porter tunes sort themselves, with or without simple witty lyrics to guide the performer, make them natural material for elaboration. It is a considerable compliment to Cole Porter's style to point out that even when his melodic lines are changed beyond recognition and his chord progressions heavily altered, something of the texture of the original remains. A not-quite-bitter wit, a taste for satire bordering in late years on self-caricature—these elements have so infused his music that they cannot ever be altogether suppressed.

Vincent Youmans was a more tenderhearted composer than Porter, but like him given to melodrama and to terse phrases that allow performers every opportunity for those nuances which establish their own styles. The melodrama is at its worst in "Without a Song," from *Great Day* (1929); the terse phrases are at their most compelling in "More Than You Know," from the same show, in "Tea for Two" and "I Want to Be Happy" (*No, No, Nanette,* 1925), "Sometimes I'm Happy" (*Hit the Deck,* 1927), and "Time on My Hands" (written for Marilyn Miller's *Smiles,* 1930, but removed at the star's request). He also did a memorable score for Fred Astaire's first starring film, *Flying Down to Rio* (1933), including the title song, "Carioca," "Music Makes Me," and "Orchids in the Moonlight."

While working as rehearsal pianist for Vincent Youmans' *Great Day*, Harold Arlen produced a fetching countermelody of his own for one of the Youmans songs. He was immediately encouraged to develop it. With lyrics by Ted Koehler, it became the very successful "Get Happy," and Arlen and Koehler shortly afterward went to work producing songs for the revues at the Cotton Club in Harlem. After doing "Between the Devil and the Deep Blue Sea," "Stormy Weather," and its sequel, "Ill Wind," Arlen became an unusually adroit writer for nightclub performers of all kinds, no matter what the original intention of his songs. Thus the great success in clubs, on records, and television of his musical monodramas for films—"Blues in the Night," "That Old Black Magic," "Over the Rainbow," and "Happiness Is a Thing Called Joe"—and that elegantly elongated torch song, "Come Rain or Come Shine," which he wrote for the stage (*St. Louis Woman*, 1946). Quite unlike these, two other Arlen scores require performers with special accents and special skills. Both are West Indian tales, the first, *House of Flowers* (1954), with dialect-ridden lyrics by Truman Capote, who wrote the book for the show; the second, *Jamaica* (1957), with more workmanlike lyrics by E. Y. Harburg. Neither has the naturalness or the easy simplicity which made Vernon Duke's collaboration with John La Touche in *Cabin in the Sky* (1940) so satisfactory and continues to make songs from that particular tale of Negroes stand up about as well as any that have ever been written by white men—the title song, "Taking a Chance on Love," and "Honey in the Honeycomb." An unselfconscious straightforwardness is Duke's abiding virtue, whether he is writing a song for a revue, such as "April in Paris" (*Walk a Little Faster*, 1932), or "I Can't Get Started" (*Ziegfeld Follies*, 1936), or a full-length score, such as *Cabin in the Sky* or *Sadie Thompson* (1944). The last was a critical and a box-office failure but was much more interesting musically than the pretentious works that, following *Oklahoma!* (1943), were to become the great hits of the American musical theater.

The taste for the operatic which has hung over the musical theater since the late thirties, like a mist over Catfish Row, can be traced back to George Gershwin's *Porgy and Bess* (1935). For many, no other work comes close to being *the* American opera. For others, no doubt a minority, *Porgy and Bess* is a fine collection of tunes, not quite as shapeless as Gershwin's Piano Concerto or *Rhapsody in Blue* or *An American in Paris,* but like them more a series of tunes than a work of indissoluble unity. It also indulges in that version of Negro dialect, more fanciful than accurate, which makes Uncle Remus read like a fastidious grammarian. The technique of Ira Gershwin, formidable as it was, was not quite up to giving the Gullah Negroes of South Carolina an authentic voice. His craft, developed in musical comedy, from *Lady, Be Good* (1924) to *Let 'Em Eat Cake* (1933), was unashamedly built of Broadway elements. He was brittle, bumptious, tender, as required. He was rarely sentimental, frequently ironic, always matching sonic patterns in the words to the sound structure of his brother's music. His are singing syllables in these musical-comedy songs because everything in them—except good sense—is at the command of the tunes. It is a fair enough arrangement; the tunes, as a whole, are among the best ever written for the American musical stage, and on the basis of present performance nobody seems likely to challenge the Gershwins' accomplishment.

George Gershwin wrote some fair songs in his first years as a professional songwriter—"Swanee" for Al Jolson's *Sinbad* (1919), "Somebody Loves Me" for the last of the five scores he did for George White's *Scandals* (1924). But it was not until *Lady Be Good* that his collaboration with his brother was complete and his remarkable career fully under way. Fred Astaire, who figures in so many of the distinguished scores for stage and screen, was the star with his sister Adele. The title song, sung by a less than respectable lawyer to some ladies of equal integrity, makes a bid for companionship on the basis that he is alone in the city, much misunderstood, "just a lonesome babe in the wood," so . . . The show also had the effective "Fascinating Rhythm," "The Man I Love," which was withdrawn from the show because it didn't overwhelm the Philadelphia tryout audience, and "The Half of It, Dearie, Blues," a fair indication of the wit to come in songs by the brothers. The next year, for *Tip-Toes,* the Gershwins produced "That Certain Feeling," "Sweet and Low-Down," and "Looking for a Little Boy." In 1926, for Gertrude Lawrence in *Oh, Kay!* they wrote "Someone to Watch Over Me"; in 1927, for the Astaires again, in *Funny Face,* " 'S Wonderful"; in 1928, sharing the score for Marilyn Miller's *Rosalie* with Sigmund Romberg, their most lasting contribution was "How Long Has This Been Going On?" "Liza" was the best thing about *Show Girl* (1928).

"I've Got a Crush on You," "Soon," and the title song provided the brightest moments of *Strike Up the Band* (1929), the first of the collaborations with Morrie Ryskind and George S. Kaufman. The book—antiwar, antibusiness, antigovernment—was less than polished, but it was a spirited introduction to the kind of satire to come two years later in *Of Thee I Sing,* and the Gershwins showed themselves quite ready to translate ridicule and scorn into popular-song forms.

Before their major effort at political satire, the Gershwins took one last fling at conventional musical comedy in 1930. The title of the inconsequential book set the mood—*Girl Crazy*. The tunes followed the mood, half seriously, half satirically. "I Got Rhythm":

> I got music,
> I got my man—
> Who could ask for anything more?

"Boy, What Love Has Done to Me":

> You get to know life
> When married to a low-life—

"Sam and Delilah"—a set of variations on a familiar theme (*cf.* "Frankie and Johnny," *passim*):

> And she tracked him
> And hacked him
> And dug for Sam a grave.

"But Not for Me"—advice to the lovelorn by a lorn lover who has reached that time when she desperately needs a "friend":

> When ev'ry happy plot
> Ends with the marriage knot—
> And there's no knot for me.

And finally, among the handsomely turned tunes of the smoothest of shows, there was "Bidin' My Time" (" 'Cause that's the kinda guy I'm") and "Embraceable You," an equally irreverent song in spite of the sickly sweet performances to which it has for so long been condemned—

> In your arms I find love so delectable, dear,
> I'm afraid it isn't quite respectable, dear.

Of Thee I Sing (1931) is filled with similarly felicitous rhymes and rhythms. But with the exception of the title tune, "Love Is Sweeping the Country," and "Who Cares?" its songs are so much a part of its plot that they do not mean much when sung out of context. But how well they fit into Kaufman and Ryskind's wild tale of a candidate for President—John P. Wintergreen—who runs on a campaign of love and wins, with the exquisitely named Alexander Throttlebottom as his Vice President (exquisitely played by Victor Moore). *Let 'Em Eat Cake,* the sequel to *Of Thee I Sing* in plot and characters but not in tone, was too strong for 1933; it failed, not quite dismally, running less than three months. But its exercise in canonic songwriting, "Mine," is one of George Gershwin's brightest inventions, in both its prime melody and countermelody. The irascible humors of *Let 'Em Eat Cake,* involving a Communist revolution and dictatorship, are superbly translated into song lyrics by Ira Gershwin. The members of the Union League Club have never been better apostrophized than in the song named after them:

> When we wake, which is infrequent,
> We keep wondering where last week went. . . .

Depression-era agitation is accurately summed up in "Union Square":

> Down with one and one make two,
> Down with ev'rything in view!
> Down with all majorities;
> Likewise all minorities!
> Down with you, and you, and you!

Misanthropy was not in fashion in the thirties, in spite of excellent conditions for its growth and development. *Let 'Em Eat Cake* failed to run a full season. And so, curiously enough, did *Porgy and Bess* in its first appearance in 1935. The New York critics were not enthusiastic. But the tunes hung on, as tunes will when they have the quality of "Summertime," "I Love You, Porgy," "A Woman Is a Sometime Thing," "It Ain't Necessarily So," and "Bess, You Is My Woman, Now." And thus on revival in New York in 1942 and on tours throughout the world, *Porgy and Bess* has been an unqualified success with audiences (and even with most critics, now) who hang on to the tunes and through them get caught up in DuBose and Dorothy Heyward's melodrama. Whatever its limitations as a picture of Negro life, and however narrow its vision of its genre, *Porgy and Bess* satisfies that taste for the sensational and the violent that is normally catered to by *Pagliacci* and *Cavalleria Rusticana* and other operas of the same kind that have made the word "grand" stand for tawdry.[1]

The journey of Richard Rodgers from Hart to Hammerstein is like George Gershwin's peregrination from the *Scandals* to grand opera. With Larry Hart's collaboration, Rodgers wrote fine scores for the *Garrick Gaieties* of 1925 and 1926 (tunes like "Manhattan" and "Mountain Greenery"), for *The Girl Friend* of 1926 (the title song and that incomparable parody of popular songs, "The Blue Room"), for *A Connecticut Yankee* in 1927 ("Thou Swell," "My Heart Stood Still," "On a Desert Island with Thee"). The two men had found a precision of phrase, verbal and musical, that has only been matched by the Gershwins. Witness "You Took Advantage of Me" (from *Present Arms,* 1928), and the mellifluous measures of the songs from *Jumbo* (1935), "Little Girl Blue," "The Most Beautiful Girl in the World," and "My Romance." Or the song made to order for Ruth Etting's nasal poignancy, "Ten Cents a Dance" (1930). Or the gallic humor of "Mimi," written for Maurice Chevalier's film *Love Me Tonight* (1932). Or the tickling chromatics of "Lover" (1933), written as a waltz, but altogether successful too when swung into four-quarter time by a jazz band.

Starting with *On Your Toes* (1936), the ambitions of Rodgers and Hart lifted them to the level of ballet choreographed by George Balanchine, but the libretto for the ballet ("Slaughter on Tenth Avenue") was happily only a takeoff on gangster films, with a couple of infectious jazz tunes spliced together to fill it out and keep it at the scale of musical comedy. Balanchine remained the team's choreographer in the less than nobly plotted *Babes in Arms* (1937), which was loaded with good songs—"Where or When," "My Funny Valentine," "The Lady Is a Tramp," "I Wish I Were in Love Again."

I'd Rather Be Right (1940) was a political satire by Kaufman and Hart (Moss, not Larry), all built around the New Deal, with George M. Cohan playing President Roosevelt and the songs fitted firmly into place in the plot. Ballet and Balanchine again added tone to a Rodgers and Hart musical in *I Married an Angel* (1938), this time without a score of any particular distinction, except for "Spring Is Here." But two of the last four collaborations of the pair cannot be faulted. It is best to skip *Too Many Girls* (1939) and *By Jupiter* (1942), though each was a box-office success, and each had its moments that were at least adroit, if not exactly inspired. But *The Boys from Syracuse* (1938) and *Pal Joey* (1940) were astonishing translations into musical theater of Shakespeare's *Comedy of Errors* and of John O'Hara's tales of a professional stinker. Only the plot and characters of *The Boys,* really, were Shakespeare's; the lines were George Abbott's, all, except two of them held over from the original. The tunes were *echt* R & H—"This Can't Be Love (I feel so well),", "Falling in Love with Love," "The Shortest Day of the Year." *Pal Joey,* for which a better case can be made as a masterpiece of the American lyric theater than for *Porgy and Bess,* was not a great success at first, but it came back twelve years later to set a record for a revival. Like the *Porgy and Bess* songs, its tunes too had hung on— "I Could Write a Book," and "Bewitched, Bothered and Bewildered" in particular. And nobody now could fail to appreciate the brilliantly corrosive humor of Larry Hart's lyrics. None of the people involved has ever done more craftsmanlike work, not Rodgers, not O'Hara (who constructed the book out of his own stories), and certainly not Hart, who before he died did only one other musical, *By Jupiter,* and spurned the offer from the Theatre Guild to transform *Green Grow the Lilacs* into musical theater. Nor, by comparison, do the flatulent expansions of the musical theater of the postwar decades reduce its charms.

In his collaborations with Richard Rodgers, Oscar Hammerstein II offered the composer every kind of folksiness—Southwestern folksiness (*Oklahoma!* 1943), New England folksiness (*Carousel,* 1945), Polynesian folksiness (*South Pacific,* 1949), Siamese folksiness (*The King and I,* 1951), and Tyrolean folksiness (*The Sound of Music,* 1960)—all with *haute couture* tailoring. In every case, he took a work already successful in another form—the Lynn Riggs play that had earlier been refused by Larry Hart, Molnar's *Liliom,* Michener's

Tales of the South Pacific, Margaret Landon's *Anna and the King of Siam,* and the autobiography of Baroness von Trapp. The pattern is the surefire middlebrow one of broad humor and melodrama, especially surefire when gravely mixed with barrel-chested tenors and baritones, personalities like Mary Martin, Gertrude Lawrence, Yul Brynner, Ezio Pinza, and Theodore Bikel, and dances, where they fit, designed by Agnes De Mille and Jerome Robbins. To confess to being unmoved, or worse, slightly sickened, by songs like "Oh, What a Beautiful Morning" and "The Surrey with the Fringe on Top," "June Is Bustin' Out All Over" and "You'll Never Walk Alone," "Some Enchanted Evening" and "I'm Gonna Wash That Man Right Outa My Hair," "Hello, Young Lovers" and "Do Re Mi" is to declare oneself a candidate for investigation by the House Un-American Activities Committee. The fact is, however, that Rodgers and Hammerstein were masters of *kitsch,* and when they constructed their own material, as in *Allegro* (1947) and *Me and Juliet* (1953), they produced soap opera, the first about the inherent virtues of country doctoring as against the perils of big, black city practice, the second a backstage story of the depth of one of the early talkies with a similar setting. There is more of the same in Rodgers' solo work, *No Strings* (1962), where he joins a tantalizing love affair, mixing white and Negro (suitably light, as played by Diahann Carroll), to an ending that can offend no one except those who find the final separation of the lovers either an undignified concession to middlebrow tastes or just poor plotting. At least it has some good tunes, including one candidate for jazz honors, the title song.

Alan Jay Lerner and Frederick Loewe served a brief apprenticeship in conventional musical comedy before they turned so successfully to their version of *kitsch* with *Brigadoon* (1947) and *Paint Your Wagon* (1951). The first has a Scottish setting and one distinguished song, "Almost Like Being in Love." The second is a California Gold Rush story with songs with titles (and lyrics) like "Wandrin' Star," "There's a Coach Comin' In," and "I Talk to the Trees." Both were staged with dances by Agnes De Mille. Both owed much to the good golden pioneering of Rodgers and Hammerstein. *My Fair Lady* owes much to Bernard Shaw. Rodgers and Hammerstein had been approached with the idea of turning *Pygmalion* into a musical and could not see it. Lerner and Loewe saw it, heard it, made it. Theirs is certainly the most good-natured of the large-scale musicals of the postwar years. It lacks the bite of the Shaw play, in spite of the generous portions of the original it retains, but it does have a constant sweetness that does not often fall over into coyness or sentimentality, either in Lerner's words or Loewe's music. Not as much can be said for the team's collaboration in the film *Gigi* (1959), which simply adds yards of lace to the carefully revealed petticoats of Colette's whores and paramours, or the less-than-lilting score they drew from T. H. White's delightful *Once and Future King,* which in their hands simply became a craggy and crenellated *Camelot* (1960).

One doesn't know, for a moment, quite where to fit Leonard Bernstein's, Arthur Laurents', and Jerome Robbins' *West Side Story* (1957). That is its securest virtue; it has no clear category—at first, anyway. But on second thought, one realizes that its transmutation of *Romeo and Juliet* into a battle between adolescent gangs in New York, one Puerto Rican and one not, hits the *kitsch*-lover where he lives, right in the middle of his brow. Jerome Robbins' dances turn teen-agers into epicene caricatures of themselves. Bernstein's music falls, like so much of this kind of writing, into that wide stream of innocuousness, just this side of Muzak, in which the musical theater has been swimming so ingloriously in recent years. His score for *Candide* (1956), setting a fine book by Lillian Hellman and fresh lyrics by the poet Richard Wilbur, John La Touche, and Dorothy Parker, was much more alive, much more original, and more impressively varied in form and mode. But whatever the limitations of *West Side Story,* nothing is quite so distasteful to those who dislike it as the attempt to make the ugly racial tensions that burst into rumble warfare into a frothy entertainment, complete with a pious expression of high hopes at the end, even as in *Romeo and Juliet.* But Shakespeare, at least, intended his ending to be ironic.

Can seamy tales be turned into musicals? Is slice-of-life naturalism at its most fetid a proper mode for this kind of theater and its composers and performers? Kurt Weill's attempt to turn Elmer Rice's *Street Scene* into a musical (1947) argues well for the mode. He produced no great arias, no bright pop tunes, but he did synthesize a strong, lean supporting music, with occasional flowerings, like an embellishment of plainchant. He had done much the same sort of thing for Paul Green's antiwar play, *Johnny Johnson* (1936), shortly after coming to this country from Germany. And once more, he did as much for *Lost in the Stars* (1949), Maxwell Anderson's adaptation of Alan Paton's novel *Cry, the Beloved Country,* with a fine boogie-woogie accompaniment for a ballet based on the refining of gold, and some brilliant writing for a chorus, given a more adventurous role here than ever before or since in the American musical. Weill's characteristic minor-key laments were excellently suited to such assignments. They also were useful for erotic purposes, as they proved in *Knickerbocker Holiday* (1938), giving a very persuasive voice in "September Song" to an old Peter Stuyvesant seeking the love of a young girl; in *Lady in the Dark* (1941), translating the fantasy life of the editor of a leading fashion magazine into a happy dream motif, "My Ship"; and in *One Touch of Venus* (1943), finding just the right insinuating sound for the exchange of desires between a barber and a statue of Venus, in the show's most enduring tune, "Speak Low." In each of these cases, Weill had superior collaborators—Maxwell Anderson at his most compressed in *Knickerbocker Holiday,* Ira Gershwin in *Lady in the Dark,* and Ogden Nash in *One Touch of Venus.* But Weill was never uninteresting. The bits and pieces he used to hold together *The Eternal Road* (1937), Franz Werfel's pageant of Jewish history, were constantly provocative, adding alternately soft and pointed musical commentaries to Max Reinhardt's sumptuous staging. The similar function he performed for Alan Jay Lerner's *Love Life* (1948), a kaleidoscopic view of American history from 1791 to the middle of the twentieth century, blossomed into several fine songs—"Green-Up Time," "I'm Your Man," and "Woman's Club Blues," the last perhaps the best among them.

In his fifteen years in the United States (he died in 1950), Kurt Weill never again achieved the sardonic brilliance of his collaborations with Bert Brecht, *The Three-Penny Opera* (1928) and *The Rise and Fall of the City of Mahagonny* (1930), nor did he produce anything for an English text as biting as his setting of the German of Brecht again in the song cycle *The Seven Deadly Sins* (1933). But he did demonstrate that it was possible for a composer of original gifts and of great seriousness to work with some frequency in the musical theater, to write songs within the commercial forms, and to do so without any significant compromise. And he showed that this could be done without the airy musical gestures of the new American grand opera.[2] How good that is. For the swollen musical rhetoric which now dominates the American stage may in time turn out to be the worst of the concessions made by popular culture to *le bourgeois gentilhomme,* as it invades our days and our nights, our radio and our television sets, our elevators and our jets, and its kitschy-kitschy-koos, scored for a hundred strings, pursue us down the street and into our homes like the most terrible of the inventions of science fiction. The Thing may turn out to be a Rodgers and Hammerstein score played by The People.

One of the real catastrophes of American music has been the inflation that gradually overwhelmed popular songs in the thirties, forties and fifties. First it was the souped-up scores of the movies, musicals and straight pictures both, blowing up inoffensive little songs into symphonic blasterpieces, with the aid of patches of Richard Strauss, Ravel, early Stravinsky, and any other composer whose work could be used for the aid and comfort of lovers of bombast. Then it was the orchestras in the radio and recording studios, like those of André Kostelanetz and David Rose, following the same loud lead. Finally, it became the whole industry, providing cues for television in the sticky movie manner, turning out hordes of LP's for the home and tapes for the elevator, the jet, the restaurant, the doctor's waiting room, all thick with sound, with high-fidelity flatulences.[3]

In all this great wind it is entirely possible to miss the contribution of the journeyman songwriters. It is their pieces, after all, that are being inflated, their very good pieces, the ones that have lasted well beyond the first industrious plugging, long after the years in which they were born. One thinks, in this enormous category, of the ebullient creations of Buddy De Sylva, Lew Brown, and Ray Henderson, "The Birth of the Blues," "Black Bottom," "The Best Things in Life Are Free," "You're the Cream in My Coffee," and "Button Up Your Overcoat"; and of songs like Fats Waller's "Honeysuckle Rose," "Ain't Misbehavin'," "Keeping Out of Mischief Now," and "I've Got a Feeling I'm Falling." One remembers the delightful songs from the *Little Shows*—Ralph Rainger's "Moanin' Low," Kay Swift's "Can't We Be Friends?" and Herman Hupfeld's "Sing Something Simple" and "When Yuba Plays the Rhumba on the Tuba"—and their successors, *Three's a Crowd* (1930), in which Libby Holman sang Johnny Green's "Body and Soul," and *The Band Wagon* (1931), the last of the appearances of Fred and Adele Astaire together, in which Arthur Schwartz's "Dancing in the Dark" and "I Love Louisa" appeared. Of the same period, there is the fine score Gus Kahn and

Walter Donaldson wrote for Eddie Cantor's *Whoopee* (1928), including "Making Whoopee," "Love Me or Leave Me," and "My Baby Just Cares for Me."

There are literally dozens of able songwriters who have made their substantial contribution, moved on to triple A rating in ASCAP (the American Society of Composers, Authors and Publishers)—and oblivion. The average listener who enjoys their work, in reasonably contained performance or inflated, rarely knows their names. Some deserve to be rescued from that obscurity. Isham Jones, who led a better-than-average dance band, wrote better than average tunes, too: "I'll See You in My Dreams," "It Had to Be You," and "Swingin' Down the Lane" are three of them. Johnny Burke's most famous song before he began to collaborate with Jimmy Van Heusen was "Pennies from Heaven," written for a Bing Crosby film.[4] Three of the most enduring of the Burke and Van Heusen songs, all written for Crosby films, are "Sunday, Monday, or Always," "Swinging on a Star," and "But Beautiful." Van Heusen, who in effect moved from the Crosby camp to the Sinatra clan, continued to write handsome tunes, with Sammy Cahn doing the lyrics, the best of them the Oscar-winning "All the Way" and the Sinatra song that did double duty as John F. Kennedy's campaign song, "High Hopes." An older writer of the same dependability as Van Heusen is Jimmy McHugh, who with Dorothy Fields doing the lyrics wrote "On the Sunny Side of the Street," "Exactly Like You," "I Can't Give You Anything But Love, Baby," "Diga Diga Doo," "I'm in the Mood for Love," and "Singin' the Blues."

Of the trusty professionals, perhaps the best known is Hoagy Carmichael, not only for his great successes—"Star Dust," "Rockin' Chair," "Lazybones," "Georgia on My Mind," "I Get Along without You Very Well"—but for his twangy voice and dry humor as a film actor and singer. Frank Loesser, who collaborated with Carmichael, doing the lyrics for "Small Fry" and "Two Sleepy People," turned composer with "Praise the Lord and Pass the Ammunition" during the war (1942), and then afterward continued in both capacities, offering Ray Bolger an entertaining song for *Where's Charley* (1948) —"Once in Love with Amy"—and making Sidney Howard's play *They Knew What They Wanted* into a serious musical, *The Most Happy Fella* (1956), operatic but not too grand for the musical-comedy stage. But Loesser's masterpiece is *Guys and Dolls* (1950), in spite of the fact that no one song stands out in the score. It is that masterly blend of imaginations—Jo Swerling's and Abe Burrows' for the book, Loesser's for the songs—that suggests what vitality and wit there may still be in musical-comedy song forms. A similar box-office success, crowned with Pulitzer Prize approval, Burrows' and Loesser's *How to Succeed in Business Without Really Trying* (1961), does not show the same ingenuity in using those forms, but it is evident, once again, that craftsmen are at work.

Whatever remains of the craftsmanship of the popular song in popular singing after the trying inanities of the rock 'n' roll years must be found in the performances of Frank Sinatra most of the time, of Perry Como every once in a while, of Margaret Whiting and Lena Horne and Ella Fitzgerald almost always. Not exactly a young crowd. But the youngsters have not been available. They have been plucked, almost as soon as they were out of diapers, for screeching duty down at the record studio, or, if they have stumbled on into college, and have learned to sing three-part harmony while fumbling over a fret and wearing a blazer, they have had a banjo thrust at them and have been told to make like folks.

One should never despair about popular singing, however. It has never been very good. At the same time that Mildred Bailey and Bing Crosby were performing their labors for Paul Whiteman, and making so much of anything of quality in a pop song—a good line, a swinging phrase, anything—Rudy Vallee was everybody's leader, and an audible sinus condition often passed for a song style as all over the country singers imitated Vallee's constricted sound. When Bing Crosby was battling it out with Russ Columbo, a few years later, for gulping and scooping honors, movie musicals and the musical-comedy stage were full of tenors and baritones whose lifeless voices sounded as if their owners had been altered. And during the swing years, all the big orchestras, including the jazz bands, featured male singers, as they were lightly called, of a zombielike stillness of phrase, of body movement, of voice. So used to this stillness by the bandstand did audiences become that when Kay Kyser's boy sang "He Wears a Pair of Silver Wings" during the war, nobody even cracked a smile. And people for years applauded Carmen Lombardo.

It is astonishing how humorless American pubescents and adolescents can be. How else account for the hypnotic effect upon them of Johnnie Ray, Elvis Presley, Conway Twitty, Fabian, Paul Anka, the Beatles, and all the rest of the toneless wonders of the purple note? And how much more sensitive to sound can their elders be— if by "elder" be understood only a difference in physical age—when they can put up year after year with the sixty-cycle hum that passes for folk singing and with folk songs that no self-respecting illiterate would ever sing, much less listen to?

The loathsome level to which popular music, rather than popular singers, sank during the late fifties and early sixties can be measured by the fact that it is unimaginable that any singer of quality could or would do even the best of the rock 'n' roll or pseudo-folk songs. Some of the rock 'n' roll writers use the sounds of labor rooms, pig-sticking contests, and those made by drowning men for their material. Some of them write songs that are deliberately meant to be funny, such as "The Witch Doctor" and "The Purple People Eater," "The Little Blue Man," "I'm a Mummy," and that fine adventure in the subway tunnel, "Ambrose." Who can forget the immortal lyrics of "The Witch Doctor"?

> Ooh, eeh, ooh, ah, ah,
> Ting, tang, walla, walla, bing, bang.

And who can imagine Ella Fitzgerald bothering with them? Or Sinatra? Not even Bing Crosby at the top of his career, when he would sing *anything*—hillbilly songs, Hawaiian strangulation cries, hiccups in Latin tempo—not even Bing would have done such songs.

While the songs that the little boys in blazers sing are not quite so primitive as rock 'n' roll, they are hardly fit for civilized company, and be it said for the rationality of the few singers of popular distinction still around, none of them has tried to tame and use this material either. The songs that interest singers—as distinguished from hummers and screechers—are the songs of Kern and Berlin and Porter, of the Gershwins and Rodgers and Hart, of De Sylva, Brown, and Henderson, of Burke and Van Heusen, of Kurt Weill, of Hoagy Carmichael, of Frank Loesser. If, for the moment, no young composer or lyric-writer of quite such skill and professional integrity seems to be developing, there are some signs that all has not gone to the dogs, to grand opera, or to grand ol' opry. There were the felicitous collaborations of Richard Adler and the late Jerry Ross, *The Pajama Game* (1954) and *Damn Yankees* (1955), each with a song or two of quality—"Hernando's Hideaway" and "Hey There" in the first, "Whatever Lola Wants (Lola gets)" in the second. And *Bye, Bye, Birdie* (1960) made superlative fun of the worst of rock 'n' roll and still managed to offer some good songs of its own—"Put on a Happy Face" and "Kids." [5] And hundreds of old songs of quality continue to be sung and played, sometimes by just a singer and a rhythm section, sometimes by just a pianist, often with taste, occasionally with musicianship, almost always with affection.

JAZZ

JAZZ IS an art of feeling. Its performers nurture their feelings with the tenderness of a parent, the tension of a frustrated adolescent, and the violence of a dispossessed adult. To find feelings and to hold them, jazz musicians use every means known to art and some new ones that they themselves have invented. Their procedures are alternately controlled and disorderly, anarchical and academic. They have developed virtuoso playing techniques to fit them. They have established a whole new series of traditions. All are in the service of feeling.

Feeling for the jazz musician is either physical or conceptual, or both. It may be evoked by a person, a place, an atmosphere, an object. It may spring, as the sounds which express it so often suggest, right from the blood. It may be the result of a surface speculation, or of a more deeply seated meditation. It may come floating tortuously to the lips or the fingers as the consummation of some union of emotion and intellect. Whatever its source, however it comes, wherever it ends, it is feeling, feeling all the way. This is the subject of the jazz musician's discourse, the substance of his art, the object of his life.

Few will dispute the preeminence of feeling in a jazzman's life. It is obvious in the special language he speaks, in the adjectives he relies on to indicate the temperature of his feelings (*hot* or *cool*) or the intensity of his translation of his feelings into music (*jumping, leaping, wailing*). It is clear in the anguish or jubilation or tightly withdrawn attitudes of jazzmen, all immediately visible as one watches them playing on a nightclub stand, on a stage, or even in a recording studio. It is unmistakable in the music itself, which either elicits or reflects these moods, the music which gives final form to the feeling.

Few will, few can, argue about the high place of feeling in jazz. More can—more will—debate the extent to which what the jazz musician makes of his feelings can be called art.

Perhaps it does not matter whether or not we call it art. The first-rate jazz musician will go on playing first-rate jazz with or without the encomium and probably less self-consciously and more forthrightly without it than with. But he can remain indifferent only so long. In search of approval, of status as an artist, he is likely to do what he or his predecessors have so often done in the past: turn out large-scale works of a high literary and musical tone and very little else and perform these works at concerts which only come alive in the brief intervals allotted to improvisation between the weighty compositions with which he is making his ambitious thrust at art.

On the other hand, if he is a jazz primitive, either a bona fide ancient of one of the first generations of jazz or one whose performances are consecrated by association with the ancients, he will settle back into his small repertory convinced that any attempt to make jazz into art will inevitably destroy its and his original rude power. As a result, he will play the few pieces he plays the same way each time, and the improvisation and the attempt to make something fresh of each performance will disappear and with them the original rude power.

Jazz musicians achieve their place as artists only by the most devious means. They must cultivate a balance of primitive and sophisticated approaches, one which permits them to play with all the gusto of the early- and middle-period jazzmen and still gives license to do anything they may want with the inherited tunes, established forms, sacred playing procedures.

They cannot go too far from the blues. When they lose contact altogether with the harmonic symmetries and melodic asperities of the blues, they seem to lose some of their identity as jazz musicians, too. But they cannot wallow in the blues either, not any more, not this many years after the founding mothers, Ma (Gertrude) Rainey and Bessie Smith, and their inspired accompanists. When they wallow, they come out muddy; their playing is coarse, but not vigorous; their thinking, monotonous; their feeling, synthetic, or at least it appears to be.

Mere imitation of the past usually produces a music of little consequence and with it an embarrassing apparatus of gestures, grimaces, laughter, language, and clothing—the stereotypes of the race-conscious America in which jazz was first played and jazzmen first accepted, if acceptance is the right word for the patronage bestowed on men viewed as clowns and panders.

The best jazz musicians have always been both adventurers and craftsmen, capable of producing endless variations on the blues, as for example the young Louis Armstrong did on the trumpet, or Jimmie Noone did on the clarinet, or Earl Hines did (and still does) on the piano, by constructing engaging little two- and four-bar figures (Armstrong), or fresh countermelodies (Noone), or a brilliant hammering obbligato in trills (Hines).

They have been gifted with a melodic fertility that has made moving new tunes out of hackneyed old ones, as the late Charlie Parker did almost every time he took up his alto saxophone and under almost all circumstances, in the company of genuine jazzmen, or with the curious race of musicians that makes its living in radio, television, and recording studios, or with symphonic performers. Really talented jazzmen have consistently resisted the double appeal of the familiar—those tunes that they know best and therefore need examine least and that the public enjoys most and therefore will come to hear most frequently—as Duke Ellington resisted that appeal with his constant building of a new repertory of all sizes and shapes and degrees of experimentation.

After more than forty years of leading jazz bands and writing for them, Ellington was still capable of finding on-the-spot wit and joy in the mere gathering together of nine percussionists in a studio to sit in with his orchestra, or of drawing elegant jazz tunes out of a reading of a number of Shakespeare plays, or of wresting from the best-known and most often played blues a whole new set of insights into the individual tunes in particular and the blues form in general.

Because jazz musicians are improvisers they are also experimenters. No matter what feeling inspired a particular performance, there is almost always in their work a kind of academic exercise in experimental procedures.

They constantly probe their experience as musicians, as, for example, when the Woody Herman band, collectively, made over the Rodgers and Hart waltz "Lover" into a tumultuous jazz piece in four-quarter time, or when pianist Mary Lou Williams translated eight-to-the-bar boogie-woogie motifs into a waltz. They test themselves and their idiom every time they make the startling rhythmic changes which more than anything else set off one jazz era from another, as the musicians of bebop did when they broke with the syncopated patterns of all earlier jazz in the mid-forties and created a kind of one-one-one-one beat so even in texture it barely required the intervention of bar lines to mark off the measures by which musicians hold themselves and their performances together.

It is in the area of rhythm that jazz has its most striking contributions to make. As it has become free of the restrictions of syncopation, it has become aware, or at least some jazzmen have, of the enormous possibilities of a kind of counterpoint of rhythms, setting lines in different times against each other to produce balance and imbalance, tension and relaxation. Rhythms in jazz, more than any other element, have proved the fitting counters for jazz musicians' feelings, physical or conceptual. But in the past they have been confined to one beat at a time and thus to one line of development in any one performance.

Now, as the pianist Lennie Tristano has demonstrated, a boldly imaginative music can be constructed out of lines in seven-eight, seven-four, five-eight, and five-four, just to name a few possible times, played against each other as well as against a conventional four-quarter time. With this sort of improvisation in rhythm as well as in melody, some of the complex feeling that has in the past often eluded jazz can be expressed.

Thus one has the matching and clashing of times in two piano *Requiems,* one conceived by Tristano to memorialize Charlie Parker, the other by pianist Bernard Peiffer to record his grief at the death of Art Tatum, a major figure in the history of jazz piano. Both Tristano and Peiffer make ample use of the blues. Both shift time frequently. Both make the listener well aware of the experimental nature of their thought. Both communicate a considerable flow of emotion: tenderness, tension, even violence. Jazz remains an art of feeling.

Jazz has not been a consistent art. It has moved in and out of popularity. In the years after the Second World War, it split into two quite different expressions, one designed to entertain, the other to communicate feelings more or less as any private art does, to one person at a time, in language suitably oblique. For an understanding of the private expression, only a long exposure to the music of jazz in all its most significant evolutionary stages could prepare one. For a response to the other jazz, all that is ever necessary is a normal amount of blood.

Early jazz was an audacious music. Its conversion of hundreds of strains of folk melodies and dance patterns, of hymn tunes, work songs, marches, and the rhythms of Southern speech into an orderly playing procedure and a music of a recognizable structure would have been an astonishing achievement even if the procedure and the structure had not endured. Simply to wrest order from such a motley collection of materials, to make the amalgam something that doesn't fall apart at the first tampering with it, is arresting. But to have provided for a continual flow of improvisation within these forms, without destroying the forms, is a work of such daring imagination as to deserve the kind of superlatives with which writing about jazz has been filled for so long and to make acceptable comparison with the felicitous undertakings of a similar nature of sixteenth- and seventeenth-century organ improvisers, and even with the most considerable figure in that tradition, Bach.

Nobody in New Orleans jazz or any of its tributary expressions bulks as large as Bach, and it is unlikely that anybody would make any such claim now that the first wonder at the achievement of the early generations of jazz musicians has begun to die down. But the melodic ingenuity of these performers is worth exclaiming over. It produced a whole repertory of jazz tunes within a few years, blues and rags, chiefly, on which jazz has been feeding well ever since. It is unlikely that any one of the performers was ever as good as his own or other people's colorful recollections suggest, but there is no doubt that pianists like Jelly Roll Morton and Richard M. Jones, clarinetists like Alphonse Picou, Johnny Dodds, and George Lewis, cornetists like Bunk Johnson and Joe (King) Oliver, trombonists like Kid Ory and Honoré Dutrey, and rhythm-section men like Johnny St. Cyr (banjo) and Baby Dodds (drums) were gifted musicians. They fall somewhere between the pioneers and the perfecters, in chronology, in equipment, and in style. There could not have been a Bach among them because there was not an old enough or firm enough tradition upon which any musician could build so individual, so precise, and so carefully worked out an identity. People had been playing this sort of music for decades by the turn of the century, but it was only then that all its sources and all its personalities were beginning to coalesce into something recognizable as itself and not simply a half-dozen or more elements tossed together to make a compound, loose or tight.

Jazz may not have been a big-city music to begin with. It reached clearly enough into the hollers and shouts of revival meetings at country crossroads and workers in the cotton field for its fast-moving tunes and free ways with them; and collections of singing and playing made in the backwoods of Alabama and Louisiana and Mississippi show a music that was obviously of great influence upon the early jazzmen, although by the time the collections were made the influence must for some years have been working in the other direction.

For all the country music in jazz, however, it needed the city, needed it for growth and sustenance, needed it for the development of playing personalities and for the organization of audiences of some openness to the new sounds, of some awareness of its styles and stylists, of the general responsiveness without which personality in an improvised art cannot develop. For all the association of jazz with the bordellos in Storyville, the sporting-house area of New Orleans, and in other red-light districts in the cities of the South, it did discover and develop its own followers.[1] The aficionados of the new music either prefaced or followed or accompanied their pursuit of other pleasures with some enthusiastic recognition of the pianist, the clarinetist, the cornetist, or the singer in the house. It was enough, anyhow, to become an advertising point for the houses. Jazz was by the time of the First World War an acknowledged part of big-city life. It played a variously significant part in an ancient commerce, the hold-door trade, as Shakespeare called it. It had a large and supple repertory of tunes, gathered from the mournful exercises of the marching bands (marching to the cemeteries) and the mirthful (marching back again), from the organized bands, such as King Oliver's and Jack Laine's, and from the players in the back rooms at the brothels and the barrelhouses. And as the tunes became respectable—a startlingly quick metamorphosis, no matter what the original intention of the words or association of the music—so did those who sang and played them. By the time jazz was evicted from its red-light shelters, under the official auspices of the Secretary of the Navy, who closed up all such quarters shortly after the United States entered the war in 1917, it was a highly acceptable product to all sorts of people to whom a dirty word was a dirty word and for whom a sporting house was no place at all for fun and games. When the bands hit the cities of the North, they found a warm reception and good jobs waiting for them—the Original Dixieland Jazz Band at Schiller's and the Del'Abe Cafe and Casino Gardens in Chicago and Reisenweber's in New York and Rector's in London, King Oliver at the Lincoln Gardens Cafe in Chicago—the same sort of delight in their music that marked the response of the riverboat customers to jazz.

The jazz diaspora was not an unhappy one, in spite of the great changes of climate, cultural as well as geographical, and the lifetime of scuffling in the cold cities of the North that some of the musicians let themselves in for. Wherever they came from, most of the jazz musicians, white and Negro, were at ease playing a big-city music in the big city, recording its delights and its laments and reporting them in dark smoky rooms, from late at night until early in the morning, to those who found their culture comfortable to take in those places at those times, especially when communicated with a beat. Wherever they went, they made converts. In Chicago, the visiting bands from the South laid the foundation for the development of jazz for years to come.

Out of the performances of the New Orleans Rhythm Kings, something less than a first-rate jazz band, came the impetus for the music of the Chicago gang, of that swinging crowd that went to Austin High School and of those who went along with the Austin kids. All the young musicians associated with the legendary clarinetist Frank Teschemacher in the middle and late twenties were formed by the New Orleans jazz that they had listened to so avidly and imitated so well in the early twenties. Thus there came into their own Muggsy Spanier and Jimmy McPartland on cornet, Bud Freeman on tenor sax (a striking departure from Southern instrumentation), Joe Sullivan on piano, Eddie Condon on banjo, Jim Lannigan on string or wind bass, and Gene Krupa on drums. These musicians, just a few years younger than the men they admired and imitated, picked up from their sources the classical repertory of Dixieland jazz—"Tiger Rag," "Panama," "Eccentric," "Clarinet Marmalade," "I Wish I Could Shimmy Like My Sister Kate," "Maple Leaf Rag," "That's a Plenty"—and added their own tunes to the books, the ones more or less contemporary with them, at least in popularity—"Nobody's Sweetheart," "Sugar," "China Boy," "Shim-Me-Sha-Wabble," "I've Found a New Baby," and "There'll Be Some Changes Made," just to name some of the most lasting sets of notes and chords.

Lots of musicians of quality worked with the Chicagoans at one time or another in the twenties and thirties: men from the Paul Whiteman and Jean Goldkette orchestras, those great federations of all the sounds of popular music and jazz of the period; men from the Ben Pollack band, which was a kind of Chicago gang all by itself; almost all the white musicians of quality that the hard-hustling organizers of that jazz—Red McKenzie and Eddie Condon, Miff Mole, Red Nichols, Phil Napoleon—could bring together. An occasional Negro musician would make a date with them. Don Redman, that broadly gifted saxophonist and arranger, was one of the few. But on the whole racial ranks were kept. The result was that the most considerable of the musicians to be associated with Chicago jazz, the cornetist Bix Beiderbecke, never really recorded with his equals, except, perhaps, for the trombonist Jack Teagarden and the clarinetist Benny Goodman, neither of whom was yet at his peak.

Considering the quality of Bix's associates, it is remarkable that so much of enduring beauty emerges from his recordings. In spite of rhythm sections that do not swing and a succession of dull solos by the cliché experts who surround him, Bix never falters. He swings. He produces long, soft, impeccably molded melodic lines, in as sweet and evenly inflected a tone as the cornet or trumpet has ever boasted. His predilection for the whole-tone scale and related appurtenances of French impressionism is not as clear on cornet as it is in his few piano pieces—"In a Mist," "In the Dark," "Flashes," "By Candlelight"—but it is always obvious that one is listening to an experimental mind, incapable of contentment with commonplace ideas, and equally incapable of ever making a sloppy statement. It is hard not to speculate about the contribution he might have made to jazz if, like Teschemacher and so many other gifted jazzmen, he had not died so young.[2]

The career that parallels Bix's and then, if only by longevity, eclipses it, is Louis Armstrong's. Louis, born in New Orleans on July 4, 1900, just three years before Bix, was as fortunate in his collaborators as Bix was not. He was, in effect, brought up as a musician by Joe (King) Oliver, himself a broadly talented trumpeter and leader of one of the best of the early bands of jazz. In Chicago, Louis gathered some of the Oliver musicians around him, including Johnny Dodds, Johnny St. Cyr, Baby Dodds, and Kid Ory, to make the brilliant Hot Five and Hot Seven records. Then he combined with Earl Hines on piano in a series of performances which demonstrate the special power of this music when men of equal strength are brought together. Each toughened the other. Hines's so-called "trumpet style," a muscular jazz piano of extraordinary resourcefulness, grew out of Louis's forceful blowing. Each man was capable—as Earl remained right into the 1960's—of adding endlessly engaging countermelodies to the tunes at hand, to the blues, to show tunes, to whatever came along.[3] And they had with each other that rapport upon which really distinguished collective improvisation depends, the same kind of feeling for tunes, tones, modes, moods, beats, that Hines had for the clarinetist Jimmie Noone, another New Orleans musician of large gifts, with whose great flowing sound he merged his vigor for several years at the Apex Club, in duets and ensemble performances that are, as they should be, legendary.

Louis was never at a loss for the music to express his feelings, and, after his records began to achieve wide circulation, other jazz-men were never at a loss for fetching little phrases with which to fill out their performances when they could not dredge up the material from their own inner supply. From Louis they took a succession of riffs, swinging two- and four-bar phrases into which both the blues and thirty-two-bar tunes break up accommodatingly, that is, if one has as fertile a source of supply as Louis. The whole pattern of making tunes, of whatever distinction, into middle- and up-tempo swing-pieces, after a chorus or so of fairly straightforward performance, is essentially Louis's. No other musician in the twenties fixed it so firmly in the jazz consciousness, as no other so forcibly made singers aware of what could be done to turn popular-song treacle into solid jazz. All that was needed were some grunts here and there to make a phrase stand up and move, and gravel-throated inflections, either to remove the cloying effect of words and music of little or no dis-tinction or to heighten the impact of lyrics and tunes of quality. All that was needed was Louis Armstrong. Louis sang with experience. What he couldn't pull out of his own imagination, he could draw from the magnificent singers he had accompanied at one time or an-other—Ma Rainey, Clara Smith, Trixie Smith, and the incomparable Bessie Smith, whose majestic way with a blues nobody has ever matched, not even Louis.

Bessie Smith had a built-in bellows; her voice cut through a theater or a ballroom with the resonance and intensity of a power-house turbine. But she also had taste, such taste that no matter how crude the lyrics assigned her, she made them over into a kind of jazz aria, not pretentious exactly, but full-throated and with an overwhelming suggestion of complete control that made one glad she had been given this or anything else to work out on. Listening to the moving plaints she made out of the obscenities to which she and other Negro performers were reduced in their efforts to challenge the injustices of the white man's world, one recognized the commanding stature a blues singer could assume. Watching her walk across a stage was to be presented with the same feeling of authority, total, undismayed by clinkers in the band, hecklers in the audience, or embarrassments of any kind.[4]

That is the mark of jazz, to take any tune, no matter how drab, and almost any combination of instruments, and to make it all fall into place, with a propelling force that lifts everything before it, that often makes second-rate musicians eloquent and almost as frequently gives lasting life to songs that really deserve nothing but obloquy and extinction. That constant resourcefulness of jazz, one that goes far beyond mere expediency, was not widely recognized until, after some years in limbo, jazz leaped into public consciousness again with the success of the Benny Goodman band in 1936. Suddenly, through records, through magazine articles, through radio programs, and through avid listening in theaters and ballrooms and nightclubs, Americans became aware of the size of the jazz achievement. Only those who read the special magazines that dealt with jazz and followed the music very closely, however, really recognized the contribution of Fletcher Henderson, who was writing some of Goodman's best pieces and who for more than a decade before that had established the systematic translation of a free-swinging jazz solo into a big-band arrangement upon which the swing era and its orchestras ultimately depended. And even his substance as arranger and leader had to wait until much later for adequate recognition. That came in 1961, nine years after his death, with the release of a collection of four LP's, encompassing sixty-four performances by Henderson bands. Here could be heard Henderson's revitalizing way with a tune and the kind of setting thus provided for some of the finest musicians in jazz—Jimmy Harrison (trombone), Coleman Hawkins and Chu Berry (tenor sax), Roy Eldridge (trumpet), Benny Carter (alto sax), and many, many others. The only comparable list in jazz is the personnel of the Duke Ellington bands from the early twenties to the early sixties, with many fewer changes over the late years.[5]

Duke Ellington has never lacked for somebody's attention. He is himself a personality of such commanding size that even those who

have just passed through a club or a theater where he has played
have been made permanently aware of him. His music is not always
so clamorous for attention. His is, on the whole, a music of subtleties
that one must search out. In spite of several periods in the forties
and fifties when he was writing large-scale works and presenting them
in concert performance, Ellington's usual procedure is, as it has been
most of the time, to offer his extraordinary meditations on jazz materials in the form of recordings. Those recordings, for years confined
to the three-minute form of the 78 rpm shellac record, have generally
required the kind of close attention that not many people like to
give popular art. Even when liberated in time by the long-playing
record, Ellington's compositions have continued to make their points
by hint and suggestion, by the innuendo of his most distinctive voices—
Johnny Hodges' alto or Harry Carney's baritone sax, Lawrence
Brown's trombone or one of the growling trumpeters, Bubber Miley
to begin with, then Cootie Williams, or Tricky Sam's growling trombone—rather than by the great brawling asseverations of which all
his bands have also been capable. His music always has a beat, no
matter how gently inflected. No band, not even the Stan Kenton and
Lionel Hampton orchestras of the forties augmented with strings, has
ever matched the range of color which Duke Ellington has been able
to command, either because of his own or Billy Strayhorn's multifaceted scoring or the shades and tints of his solo horns. It is hard to
think of an effect in big-band writing or playing that was not anticipated or brought to perfection by Ellington. The freedom with which
reeds are now combined follows his example in doubling the conventional alto lead with baritone saxophone. The imitations by jazzmen of the sounds of human happiness or misery, down to the least
sniffle, up to the last guffaw, were certainly given their greatest impetus by the trumpeters and trombonists of the Ellington band, who
with felt hat and brass hat, with plumber's plunger and all the known
mutes, made their instruments over into voices for expressing feelings
to which no mere larynx could do justice. And as one would expect
of a musician of such stature, Ellington has unceasingly produced
work worthy of close inspection, ever since the time of the First
World War when he began his career, giving his remarkably articulate soloists not only good tunes and chord progressions on which to
improvise, but carefully worked backgrounds against which to display themselves.

Every Ellington period had its rewarding moments. In the late twenties and early thirties in the New York clubs, there were inconsequential jump tunes of a raggy bumptiousness and the first fleshing out of the repertory with more ambitious compositions like "Black and Tan Fantasy," "East St. Louis Toodle-oo," "Black Beauty," "The Mooche," "Mood Indigo," "Creole Rhapsody," and "Creole Love Call." In the mid-thirties, there were the so-called concertos, featuring Cootie Williams, "Cootie's Concerto," Rex Stewart, "Trumpet in Spades," and Barney Bigard, "Clarinet Lament," and a wistful, but vertebrate set of variations on a theme, quite accurately called "Reminiscing in Tempo." Then after a long series of handsomely worked little pieces in the late thirties came the incomparable Ellington period, from late 1939 to 1946, from the advent of Jimmy Blanton on bass and Ben Webster on tenor and Billy Strayhorn as general assistant to Ellington. The writing and the playing and even the singing (by Ivie Anderson and Herb Jeffries, by Joya Sherrill and Marie Ellington and Kay Davis and Albert Hibbler) of this period are almost uniformly first-rate. The ensemble has the swinging quality of the best of the Jimmie Lunceford band. The soloists have only themselves to compete with, moving through a whole tapestry of colors and textures with what might be called hauteur in small masterpieces like "Ko-Ko," "Jack the Bear," "Sepia Panorama," "Chelsea Bridge" and "The Perfume Suite." So accomplished is the band at this point, that even the loosely organized scraps and pieces of the forty-five-minute *Black, Brown, and Beige* seem to hold together, with a coherence drawn from the matching of individual reminiscences with Ellington's own narrative, made up of events half from his own life and half from the life of the Negro people. Nothing that comes afterward can match the effortless perfection of this era, not the few large works such as *A Drum Is a Woman* and *Such Sweet Thunder,* not the many small ones. The band is never less than interesting, Duke Ellington's own mind never less than alert. But that perfect wedding of composer and performers which the band of the forties was—a wedding not without its own voluptuousness and intensity of spirit—will probably never be equaled again in jazz.

One large organization that came close to the spirit and power and freshness of the Ellington orchestra of the early and middle forties was the Woody Herman band of the middle and late forties. Once again, a single composer-arranger, in this case Ralph Burns,

JAZZ 67

had much to do with the quality. Once again, there were many soloists, to give Burns and the other talented men who occasionally wrote
for the band almost any voice they wanted: Flip Phillips, a conventional leaping tenor; Stan Getz, an unconventional cool tenor; Bill
Harris, a garrulous barrelhouse trombone; and trumpeters of every
description, for tones and textures of every description. The band
moved into the restrained elegances of early cool with the same confidence it had displayed in late hot. Only the suddenly abrogated
staying power of Woody Herman could end the band's triumphs.
Woody, an able clarinetist and even better singer of the loose vibrato
school founded by Red McKenzie, came back with new bands more
than once, but never again with such a group of musicians. It was
too late for that in the fifties and sixties.[6]

There is an achievement more precisely like Ellington's in the
various editions of the Count Basie band led by the pianist since
bringing his raucous group out of Kansas City in 1936, following
close on the heels of Benny Goodman's success in the spring of that
year. Basie has never lacked for soloists, from the most memorable
of them, Lester Young, to all the other able men who have played
for him, Harry Edison and Buck Clayton and Joe Newman and Thad
Jones on trumpet, Dickie Wells and Henry Coker on trombone,
Hershal Evans and Buddy Tate on tenor, and all the driving rhythm-
section men who have joined their talents to his tinkling, tingling,
always swinging piano, most notably and most durably the guitarist
Freddy Greene. He has had two incomparable blues singers—Jimmy
Rushing, who contributed his round roars in the early years of the
band, and Joe Williams, who added his lean hollers for a while in
the later years. There has never been any shortage of good manuscript, though no particular arranger has had any more to do with
the quality of the band's sound than the plentiful supply of infectious
jazz figures supplied by Basie or one of the soloists or that great and
steady source of material, tradition, which for all its largesse is almost
never credited with a tune on a record label or a piece of sheet music
or a stock arrangement.

Tradition is, as a matter of fact, Basie's strongest ally. He goes
far back into jazz tradition himself, having worked with the most representative Kansas City band of the twenties and early thirties, Bennie
Moten's, and with that wittiest of pianists and full-time antisentimen-
talists, Fats Waller. In his band he has always stayed very close to the

line of least resistance in jazz, the short figuration that swings. Like the frisky bands of Chick Webb and Teddy Hill in the thirties and forties, like Don Redman's memorable outfit of a slightly earlier day and Jimmie Lunceford's and Lionel Hampton's powerhouses a little later, Basie's groups have always made rhythm the major vehicle of feeling. No matter what the period or what the edition of the Basie band, it was always just a little ahead of everybody else in catching the spirit of the time—literally, the time, the tricky time, the identifying beat of jazz that nobody has ever quite been able to catch on paper, either in words or in numbers or in dots or anything else. Time changes in jazz, sometimes subtly, sometimes boldly. Now it is syncopated. Now it is, as in the bop and cool years, an even beat, without any marked change of accent. And now, as in the time of hard bop, it returns to a crunchy syncopation all over again. Basie's band is always with it or ahead of it. If you want to know the spirit of the time—or rather the time appropriate to any spirit in jazz—listen to Basie.

For a more limited period in jazz, the same is true of Billie Holiday, or of her records, anyway. In her couple of decades she did not change her style very much. She did adjust her sense of time, the truest and the most delicate and the most languorous in the history of the music, to meet the varying demands of a swing band, of a bop group, of six men or sixteen, of an arranger or of a head arrangement put together in a few frantic minutes in a recording studio. Her behind-the-beat drawl did slow almost to a crawl in her last years, when she was herself so slowed with drink and drugs and less and less certain of what she was doing at any given moment or why. But the great wounded sound she produced out of her misery—early misery, late misery, misery in-between—remained incomparably magnetic to jazzmen. And they all came to play with her, to make records with her, to sit in on that rare occasion when she would permit somebody other than her accredited accompanist to back her on a club floor. As good a record as we have of the sound of the late thirties and the forties is to be found in Billie's records with Teddy Wilson and then in her own many dates. And again, as jazz arrangers and jazz audiences found themselves more and more bemused by the possibilities of strings, one finds in Billie Holiday's backgrounds the concern and the conception of a music striving to get somewhere outside itself, nowhere very good, but managing with the majestic tortured voice at the center to transcend all the difficulties and the pretensions and the emptiness in the music as they had been transcended by Billie Holiday in the life.

There is no such sound of misery or torture in the singing of the few who deserve with Billie Holiday, in the modern era of jazz, to be called jazz singers. Mildred Bailey was almost as much a lure as Billie for jazzmen of quality, even with a sweet and clear voice, a voice with no touch of raucousness or rasp, because she was so appreciative of jazzmen of quality and because she could mix her sweet sound with theirs, like another instrument. The torture in her life emerged in her singing in the ironic furbelows that she cut around a tune and in understatement, never in blasts or booms of any kind, never in rough sounds of any sort. She was a *Lieder* singer in a music that didn't know it possessed such songs or people to sing them. She was a musician, and with her husband of the time, Red Norvo, she led a band, a very good one, the quietest, the coolest, in some ways the most musicianly of the swing era. For it Eddie Sauter did his best arranging. And Mildred Bailey her best singing.

The singing of Ella Fitzgerald and Frank Sinatra was formed in bands, by bands, for bands, Ella's with Chick Webb, Frank's with Tommy Dorsey. Ella was a virtuoso. She was capable of mixing it up with a studio orchestra of fifty or sixty musicians or of singing with Ellis Larkins at the piano, alone, sans bass or guitar or drums or rhythm accompaniment of any kind except those few percussive sounds Ellis was willing or able to strike. Her scatting around a tune was always a little mechanical. She never made all she could of her instrumental qualities. But she moved with enormous confidence and matching control to encompass in her singing every form with which jazz or popular music could challenge a singer, as in a very different way Bing Crosby had when he moved out of the band world into the movies and radio and records. She never lost her feeling for jazz, never lost her beat, as Bing did; but something went, not to disappear altogether, but to turn up only in an occasional performance, in one LP collection out of three or four. It was a more painful loss than it would have been if Sinatra had drifted out to the edges of his profession, as he moved from band to solo voice to the films and finally to his own small kingdom within the Hollywood imperium. But Sinatra had elected nothing quite as demanding as Ella had, nothing quite so debilitating to a jazz sound. He simply preferred tunes that swung to

those that did not and backings that supported a beat to those that
did not. And with that preference clearly elected, he made his voice
felt as others, not much less gifted, did not. He became more pro-
ficiently rhythmic as his voice deepened, more skillful at introducing
his charm into a performance in lieu of any feeling for true improvisation. In a time of epicene sounds, his unmistakably virile voice stood
out. Supported by a beat, it found a place for itself in jazz.

Other singers, truer to the jazz feeling than Ella Fitzgerald or
Frank Sinatra, never found so secure a place for themselves in the
music, for all sorts of reasons but most notably, most painfully, for
the reason that the very life that gave such persuasive tone to their
singing made impossible much of a career as a singer. For example—
take away from Anita O'Day or Mary Ann McCall their instabilities
of temperament and what would happen to their voices? Their assaults on pitch and broken-phrase running obviously represent their
experience as hard-living human beings with great intensities of feeling. They are not the stuff of which commercial success is made,
though Anita O'Day has certainly had a large audience for her singing
and Mary Ann McCall, at least in her days with Woody Herman and
just after, has had more than the support of a coterie. Similarly, it was
impossible for Joe Turner, a brilliantly equipped blues singer, ever to
find an atmosphere on the road or even in New York that fitted him
so well as Kansas City in the years when Basie was hanging out there.
Dozens of others, with powerful voices and a good beat and a fully-
fleshed repertoire of blues, made a couple of appearances on the
Negro theater circuit that extended in the Northeast from New York
City to Washington, showed up at a couple of breakfast dances or
with bands at the ballrooms where jazz was either featured or at least
tolerated, and then disappeared when big bands began to disappear
just after the war, in the late forties. A few more jazz singers of some
style, of some identity, of some swinging quality turned up in
the years of swing's decline and bop's rise and fall—the rhythmic
whisper of Jeri Sothern, the good taste of Terri King, the entertaining scat-talking of Babs Gonzales are part of that era as of the next.
But the large contributions were over until, in a period of decline and
desuetude for jazz, vitality was returned to jazz singing by the translation of instrumental music into vocal lines by Dave Lambert, Jon
Hendrix, and Annie Ross, and by the sheer exuberance of Ray
Charles.

The change that occurred in jazz at the end of the Second World War was a very great one. It was, in fact, a revolution, the revolution of bop. Bebop and cool jazz, its successor, combined with economic exigencies to make the big band as much a novelty in their period as the small band had been in the swing era—more, really, because at least in the classical structure of the swing epoch, every large city had its street or neighborhood where small bands flourished, such as *the* Street, 52nd in New York, or the Loop in Chicago. Now, only fresh musicians, able to play a fresh music in tight little bands, were wanted.

The bop revolution did not occur because there were not enough swing musicians of quality around. There were, if anything, too many to keep up with, an encyclopedia full of pianists and tenormen and trumpeters, almost as many trombonists and altomen, and certainly enough drummers, bass players, guitarists, and players of the more exotic instruments of jazz (vibraphone, mellophone, bass sax) to fill all the clubs and theaters and ballrooms all the time. But playing procedures had become hackneyed. Improvisation was a word to describe fewer and fewer performances. For the famous performances had to be adhered to note for note: an extraordinarily large number of people knew by heart things like Coleman Hawkins' "Body and Soul," Mildred Bailey's "Rockin' Chair," Billie Holiday's "Fine and Mellow," Ella Fitzgerald's "A-Tisket, A-Tasket," Art Tatum's "The Man I Love," Lester Young's "Lester Leaps In," and Roy Eldridge's "Rockin' Chair," and would suffer no changes in them. And the others, less famous or utterly unknown, had become uncomfortably mechanical, certain chords inevitably calling forth certain phrases, and phrases calling to phrases with a deadly sameness that made jazz, for all the talent of its best performers, some of the time seem a dying music or at least an inert one.[7]

The bop musicians did valiant combat against the inertia that had set in during the swing era. With varying degrees of consciousness and conviction, they set about retiring the clichés and constructing a playing procedure which would not only allow but actually demand originality. They had the impressive examples of Lester Young and Roy Eldridge, Charlie Christian and Jimmy Blanton to build upon. Young had made a resolute attack on the cloying melodic line, even, when absolutely necessary or just rhythmically effective, reducing a statement to one note, repeated again and again, measure after measure, with slight but unmistakable differences of inflection. He had, at least for those who understood and appreciated his kind of stinging ideas, wiped out the vibrato as a clumsy pomposity for his own instrument, the tenor sax, and for other horns as well, thus preparing the way for cool jazz. Roy Eldridge, though a traditionalist in the way he formulated melodic figures, pushed his lines to longer and longer utterances in the early forties, with something like the even beat that bop was soon to install. Christian and Blanton demolished forever in jazz the foolish notion that their instruments, the guitar and bass, were limited to rhythm-section duties, requiring them to nag away at the syncopations, weak beat by strong, weak beat by strong, far far into the night. They made their own long fresh lines, even while keeping the beat steady and the tone large and round, and added enormously to the delights of big- and small-band performance, Christian with Benny Goodman, Blanton with Duke Ellington. Both, sadly enough, died of tuberculosis the same year, 1942, both having been born the same year, 1919.

Lester Young's inconsistent performances in his last years have diminished his place in the memories of many jazz listeners, if not altogether wiped it out. Jazz musicians have not been so forgetful. They turn to no other performer so regularly for guidance in sound, in sense, in ways of constructing a solo line and in modes of playing it. For no other performer could make so much of a single note or a sequence, played once or over and over; none surrendered so completely to the characteristic textures of his own horn. That none of this was simply an accident was demonstrated in Young's brief experiment with the clarinet when he was still with Count Basie. In a few weeks, and on one record, "Texas Shuffle," he showed a possible direction for the instrument along which, years afterward, musicians like Jimmy Giuffre, for all their squeaky ingenuity, have not advanced very much. After his time with Basie, Lester Young subsided too often into sloppy whispering and whistling sounds, rather like a hissing speech defect that makes all the sibilants s-s-s-s-sound too long and too loud and too harsh. But there were often echoes of his great days with Basie, when he could construct an almost endless melodic line out of almost any material and make it leap all the way, so sure was his invention and his beat, so sure and so economical, never letting a note go until he had squeezed all the possible swing out of it, never missing a likely interval if it could give shape and substance to a tune. He did for long lines in jazz what Lewis Carroll and Guillaume Apollinaire did for them in poetry—gave them a witty contour, an attractive content, and brilliant continuity.

The long line was bop's first substantial resource. Its founding musicians, Charlie Parker and Dizzy Gillespie, did not simply tie two- and four-bar phrases together; they burst forth in large cadenza flourishes, filling in as many notes between band statements as seemed apposite, and sometimes that was a great many indeed. The designation for their cadenzas on paper was one hundred to the bar, the conventional way of indicating "Blow as many as you would like, man." Everything about their new conception was linear. They moved ahead horizontally; they thought less and less in vertical, or harmonic, terms. They broke down the iron bars of the measured line, which clicked the common time of jazz, 4/4, so monotonously into place, with an even 1-1-1-1-1-1-1-1 that for all practical purposes made the listener, at least, forget the bar lines. They encouraged any eccentricity of melodic thought or performance which would break down the familiar shapes and contours of jazz solos. They encouraged young musicians, some of them far from mature, but with an unmistakable flair for the bop line, especially for the acid comments that led, often so entertainingly, to the concluding flatted fifth, which was in itself a delicate gesture of scorn for the time-dulled resolutions of Western music on the tonic or dominant—distinctly not flatted.

Among the best of the young musicians who clustered around bop was Fats Navarro, a trumpeter of extraordinary elegance and fluency. Clifford Brown, dead, like Navarro, in his middle twenties, was another trumpeter of exhilarating agility, almost rococo in his spendthrift showers of notes, but with something less than Navarro's depth. One could hear the melancholy echoes of Fats Navarro's drug-shattered life in his playing. Brownie was more like Dizzy Gillespie, a wit, a wonder-worker on his horn, ripping through everything in great horizontal tiers of notes, like his model. It was a lip-breaking pace that Dizzy had set. Remarkably enough, there were trumpeters to follow him, rarely with his humor, but often enough with parallel technical virtuosity.[8]

By the late forties, the special concern of all boppers, of whatever age, on whatever instrument, was to get Bird's alto-saxophone sound, to imitate Charlie Parker. It was obvious, soon enough, that this was a musician of incomparable dimension in jazz, one who could, in the best tradition of the music, make any piece worth listening to, and often with only the slightest alteration of melody or rhythm. He literally played the rests, made every pause significant in the lines he cut into place with such precision, with such marks of permanence, like a sculptor in granite. Good tunes, bad tunes, blues—Parker made them all worth hearing, for one heard him, not the tunes, really, even when he went to some lengths to preserve the original melody. He himself could "hear" anything, could find something worth examining and expressing in almost any set of sounds, because for him there was always room for some fresh variation, some manipulation of materials, for which he always seemed to have the inspiration, even when his energies were clearly reduced or weakened, apparently beyond rebuilding, by the disorderly life he led in his little more than ten years as a major figure in jazz, which ended with his death in 1955.

At about the same time as Charlie Parker was beginning to formulate his style and to develop his influence, another musician of the same stature was playing, teaching, talking, writing, first in Chicago and then in New York. Lennie Tristano, like so many other pianists of his time, emerged with touches of Art Tatum in his playing, but also with marks of the ideas of Paul Hindemith, at first, anyway, and then with an independence which since the late forties has set him apart from all other musicians in jazz. Of all those who have given much thought to the purposes and possibilities of jazz, he has been most consistent in his concern to express his feelings, meaning by that something far more than the negligible emotional outburst which in the attrition of words "feeling" has come to denote. It is a totality of experience that Tristano looks to articulate in piano solos and in small-band performances with some of the gifted musicians who have studied with him, such as the alto saxophonist Lee Konitz and the tenorman Warne Marsh. He has the intellectual and the pianistic equipment to work out for himself fascinatingly intricate polyrhythms. But perhaps more important, he has such ease and relaxation as an improviser that he can forget the underlying intellectual formulations and the hours of practice when he is playing at a club, in a concert hall, or for recording purposes, and let himself go, allowing the feelings to come through, permitting the fullness of his personality to speak. It does not speak, many may think, in general enough terms. It is too demanding a personality, some say, for jazz. All they are saying, really, is that Lennie is not an entertainer but a serious musician, a private rather than a popular artist. He has not made the concessions which in his case would be necessary to set him comfortably in jazz audiences' ears alongside the musicians who found wide acceptance as members of the cool school in the early fifties or leaders of hard bop in the late fifties and early sixties or as amiable eccentrics and originals in the same period.[9]

Cool jazz added a useful restraint to the general equipment of all modern jazzmen. Out of the vibrato-less playing of Lester Young and Charlie Parker, it developed a strong taste for restraint and understatement. Though it sometimes approached an unhealthy frigidity, the cool school did open the way for some delicate arabesques by the trumpeter Miles Davis, the sometime associate of Parker, whose gentle assaults on pitch are pleasant enough unless they deliquesce in a sentimental sea, as they often do. In something of the same way, the pianist Dave Brubeck, his altoman Paul Desmond, and their bassist and drummer have delighted many listeners—more perhaps than any other bona fide modern jazz group—with a tender mixture of jazz and nineteenth-century romanticism, and terse acerbities which keep the touches of Schumann and Liszt and Chopin from dissolving into a convulsive saccharinity. Gerry Mulligan, with a pianoless quartet and a big band, with new tunes and old ones sedulously recaptured from the jazz archives, has also made restraint into a resourceful style, if one of limited range and depth.

The hard boppers moved against the formulations of cool jazz with all the model precision of a Hegelian antithesis lining up for duty against a thesis. They boomed and they stomped, they pummeled and they sweated—Sonny Rollins and John Coltrane on tenor, Cannonball Adderley on alto and his brother Nat on trumpet, Horace Silver on piano, Art Blakey on drums—with authority, with a beat, with a blast. The beat too often returned to chunky syncopations, the blast too frequently overwhelmed their lines, but the authority was unmistakable, perhaps not so much their own authority as that of the earlier jazz they were recalling, by intention or not, the music of Charlie Parker and the early Dizzy Gillespie, of Fats Navarro and Clifford Brown.

Against such limited conceptions, the deliberately odd perambulations across jazz of saxophonist Ornette Coleman and the musicians he has led may seem fresh. Certainly what he has done leaves a way open to experiment and permits such a gifted associate as trumpeter Don Cherry to express himself with imagination. But there seems to be more chaos than invention in Coleman's involuted music. He does not strike one as having the bold wit of a Charlie Mingus, who, as bass player and composer, has been able to make wildness and amusement on the surface stand for a greater turmoil and more twisted humor inside. Mingus demands and gets serious attention. He has his pompous and pretentious moments, but they do not obliterate the beat or remove all traces of improvisation as in the work of some of his more learned contemporaries, writing in that curious compound of jazz and music of other genres and traditions which goes by the name of "Third Stream" (as distinguished from Mainstream jazz and the Modern variations which remain inside jazz). One can make use of jazz forms in a symphonic setting, as Teo Macero showed in *Fusion,* his work for small band and symphony orchestra, and as Gunther Schuller showed in his ballet score built around the Modern Jazz Quartet. But as in those engaging works, one must always leave room for feeling to show through. There must, constantly, be an opening so that every aspect of a musician's personality may be expressed, either on the spot, without any immediate preparation, or after long weeks of careful rehearsal, but always, always, may be expressed with a large measure of spontaneity. That is, after all, what gives jazz as an art its identifying character.

Few jazzmen have been more concerned to express every aspect of their persons than Thelonious Sphere Monk. His middle name excellently describes the rounded rear view of him his audiences get when he conducts a pick-up band at a concert or when he shuffles and wiggles and bumbles his way around stage in what is no dance, but is not a walk either, or a run, or anything else of any easily describable nature. He makes much of his hats and his goatee. He makes less of his piano. He is no virtuoso. He is a small, contained melodist, whose tunes swing and lend themselves to easy improvisation—especially when others play them. Whether because of temperamental or technical limitations, he makes his dynamics obvious, sometimes ploddingly obvious. He catches public interest, as he does journalistic copy, because of his beard, his hats, his shuffles and wiggles. He holds the interest of musicians because his tunes are good and his own slow-moving variations on them seem to hold some inexplicable depth, humor maybe, a meditative reach perhaps. Whatever it is, it has some of the marks of a genuine spontaneity, and this remains, in jazz, the

most beguiling and the most significant of identifying marks, if also
the most mysterious.

The urge to be spontaneous in jazz has sometimes produced mere
novelty. The tinklings of the pianist Bill Evans, so close to cocktail-
piano vacuities, do not seem to me to rise much above novelty. Neither,
for all the unmistakable jazz skills of Cecil Taylor, do his experimenta-
tions at the piano. Mary Lou Williams' simple swinging precisions even
when she is merely repeating a familiar piano piece of her own, almost
note for note with the original recording, seem to me to remain fresh,
illuminating, and, if only because of the rhythmic pulse in them, altogether spontaneous.

Spontaneity is not simply a matter of playing ad lib, without a
score. As the monotonous music of the late swing years proved, it is
possible to improvise without adding anything new to a tune or set
of chords. Bop was conceived as a revolt against that monotony and
lack of spontaneity, but in time, when bop had calcified into hard
bop, it was producing its own terrible brand of tedium. Equally, the
resourcefulness of the Modern Jazz Quartet in turning to the music
of Bach and Mozart for some of its forms and dynamics soon seemed
to run out, and what began as a fresh exploration ended as an enervating preciosity. Some jazzmen seem, fortunately, to be so generously
endowed with vigor that nothing, not even their own bad taste, can
altogether dam their creative spirits. Dizzy Gillespie is such a musician. His own humor, good or bad, invariably delights him and he
sometimes gets carried away with it, but the beat remains, just as the
fine rasping tone of his trumpet remained even after he twisted the
horn into a right-angled caricature of the instrument. Ray Charles is
another such jazzman. No matter how crude his attempts at commercial exploitation of his own voice and the band and the singers
with which he supports it, he remains a jazz singer, an uncommonly
convincing one in a time of famine for the art of jazz singing. Charles
has that intuitive grasp of when to let go of pitch or time and when
to take both up which marks the real thing. He is good enough,
really, to use as a kind of measuring sound. Against what he does,
the success or failure not only of other singers but of other performers on any of the jazz instruments can be accounted for. It isn't
a matter of a tear in the voice, like Charles's, or a pounding, locked-
hands beat like his at the piano, but rather the unbroken flow of feel-

ing, orderly, disorderly, by the book, by the heart, by the head, by the viscera. That, ultimately, is what unites all the greatly skilled performers of jazz—Hines, Armstrong, Beiderbecke, Parker, Tristano, Young, Ellington, Bessie Smith, Billie Holiday—and makes their art such a compelling one.

PAINTING

THE CHARACTER of American painting in the twentieth century has been determined by two disciplines: the arithmetic of illustration and the calculus of contemplation. For forty years most American painters struggled to see the world around them accurately and to get others to see what they saw. For a little more than twenty years, as the result of several influences and the natural evolution of art in this country, a large number of American painters have been concerned with the design of a canvas and the extent to which a painter's emotions can be expressed in it, by design or otherwise. The result of the two impulses is a severely bifurcated art, two arts really. They came together briefly in the WPA art project. But then the illustrators were middle-aged if not older, well placed in the art world, and complacent. They tolerated the strange youngsters and even worked side by side with them. Now, however, the split is complete; there are no government agencies to bring them together again; and nothing else, not even the materials they use, seems likely to draw them close again. They look for different things; they look for different ends; they look in different ways.

It may seem ungenerous to give the name of illustrators to the men who established American painting as a serious art. But that, in fact, is what most of them were. The four men who gathered around Robert Henri at the end of the nineteenth century, George Luks, William Glackens, John Sloan, and Everett Shinn, were all employed as illustrators at the *Philadelphia Press,* and many of those who exhibited with them in New York afterward were illustrators by profession or by inclination.

Robert Henri had a gift for people, for words; for teaching, for talking. As a painter, he lacked much. He did not mediate between his models and his canvases. He offered the viewer what he saw, and what he saw seemed to be the surfaces of people, painted quickly but not exactly vigorously. There is more vitality in Luks; his people are friendly, warm, in the manner of those of Frans Hals, who was much admired by all of Henri's circle. It is hard not to find engaging his dancing young ladies, with the shining hair and eyes and teeth, *The*

Spielers (1905), who are so pleased with themselves. Everett Shinn was content to play with theatrical lights and shadows, to scoop little bits of Paris earth onto his canvases, but never enough to dirty them.

The men whose adventures in the soiled earned for the whole group the name of the Ashcan School were Glackens and Sloan. As a newspaper illustrator, William Glackens had to feel and to communicate the immediacy of an event. His paintings, especially those which follow the example of Manet, are newspaper stories, not very important ones but pleasant enough. Some of Turner's mist, but none of his brooding, is in his *Park on the River* (1905), and several of the French Impressionists seem to be mirrored in the glass behind the Jamesian figures of *Chez Mouquin* (1905). The events in the paintings of John Sloan are not arresting, but the places are. The New York tenement houses, in front of which the ash cans stood guard, are preserved for the record. The taxicabs and the people of the city of New York, the streets and the lights, some of the waters around it, and many of the different lights in which one could see it—all this Sloan recorded, although not often with the spareness of tone and color which makes *The Wake of the Ferry* (1907) more than merely evocative.

A series of exhibitions brought people out in increasingly large numbers to look at the ash cans, the ferries, the tenements, the diners, and the dancers. Henri's group was joined by three artists of more delicate stomach, Ernest Lawson, Maurice Prendergast, and Arthur B. Davies, to make up the first of the shows at a midtown New York gallery in 1908. Viewers were startled, diverted, and instructed by the pictures of The Eight. The impression was reinforced by the noisy illustrations of George Bellows—who in his paintings of prizefighters seemed to be mixing punches with his subjects—and others not quite so violent who joined with him in the show of independence in a loft on 42nd Street across from the Public Library. But the circus was still to come.

The Armory Show of 1913 had eighteen rings, wrapped in burlap by Bellows, who had become adept at mounting exhibitions. It was superb theater, especially on the opening night, when there were speeches and all sorts of crowd noises, hooting, howling, applause. It was also a dramatic introduction to the painting of the School of Paris, the honorable dead—Cézanne, Van Gogh, Gauguin—and the honored living—Matisse and the other Fauves and Cubists, Rouault,

Vlaminck, Picasso, Braque, Léger, Bonnard, Picabia, Dufy. There were a few paintings from other schools, notably some by Kandinsky. There was Marcel Duchamp's *Nude Descending a Staircase,* a figure all right, but not one that was recognizably naked, going somewhere, but not clearly downstairs; everybody talked about it, and newspaper cartoonists drew it.[1]

There were Americans at the Sixty-Ninth Regiment Armory, too —Bellows and his Independents, The Eight, and many, many more: there were fifteen or sixteen hundred paintings altogether. What the show, staged so effectively, really did was to make America safe for French art. The new American painters, the antiacademic ones, went on painting and being shown. But the most earnest looking was at Europeans. When, in 1916, the Society of Independent Artists was organized and allowed anyone to show, hundreds of Americans sent in their paintings. But the works that caught everybody's attention were by Braque, Gris, Matisse, Picasso, and the sculptor Brancusi, not to forget the *Fountain by R. Mutt,* the urinal contributed by Marcel Duchamp, one of the first of his "ready-made" works of art. Duchamp's joke embarrassed the Independents, who promptly hid it, arousing the indignation of all those who admired either Dadaist gestures or urinals or both.

The note of defiance in American painting has not always been as amusing, as ironic, or as sanitary as Duchamp's. But it has been there, at least from the moment that painters decided that the strictures of the Academy were confining and brought their easels or their sketchbooks out of the studio and into the world. It was a defiance shaped by a sense of mission and conditioned by a series of rejections. The mission was shared with the European artists, especially the French, with whom they also shared exhibition space; the rejections were shared with Americans in other arts who also had to take a certain number of gratuitous insults before they could get critics or reviewers to see or hear or read what they were actually doing.

Most American artists, watching the struggles and successes of the French, picked up from them the fervor to which they were able to join a native evangelical tone, but the direct influence of French painting was not significant, except for those who studied in Paris, and even they never seemed quite able to get the point of the Cubist design or the purpose of Fauvist color. The Armory Show opened hundreds of walls to French painting in American museums and collectors' houses. It bit deep into the consciousness of American painters; it frightened some of them, made others nervous, left many with a feeling of inferiority to the Europeans, a feeling which continues to afflict a large number of American painters who must have approval for their work from Paris before they can rest secure in it.

Rejection did not last very long. There were hooting and catcalls when the Armory Show toured, and even the burning of Matisse in effigy in Chicago by students at the Art Institute. But quickly enough the Europeans were accepted, and within a half-dozen years the Americans made the rounds of the galleries and the large-scale annual competitions without any danger of bonfire, cartoon, or editorial. The Academicians never quite conceded; many of the reviewers on the major newspapers were at worst hostile and at least uncomfortable with the new painters. But how long could hostility and discomfort remain in the face of paintings that in essence took up no greater challenge than the technical one of replacing the lithographers and engravers of the nineteenth century?

An art of illustration is a public art, and that is what American painting became for twenty years between the wars. Even when painters took unpopular political positions, they took them in terms anybody could understand. The distance of most American painters from their paintings was not very great: In a manner very different from the French, they invited their viewers to witness a scene, to admire a building, to become part of the nature or the lives they painted, or to reject either violently. Without quite descending to the level of an Aesopian morality, many painters did invite conclusions of a startling fatuity. These are the rewards of a superficial realism that invokes no sensation more significant than that of a "lived" reality: Somebody has been here before; this is an actual place; people do look like this. In this kind of painting there is no room for allegory, symbol has the force of a slogan or a trademark, and design contributes no more than a pleasing composition. Even those sensitive to the tensions of the art and its power to transform objects were caught up in the objects themselves. Even the painterly painters found it hard to escape painting endless homages to the "thing."

Those who went to Paris after the turn of the century managed to avoid the worst excesses of what Ortega y Gasset calls "feeling intervention." [2] Alfred Maurer started with objects and ended with colors; even before breaking up his pictures into Cubist planes he recognized the power and honesty of a non-, not antinaturalistic palette. Arthur Dove, with a somewhat greater independence, departed from precise renderings of form and color. He painted chattering abstractions—which he called by that name—as early as 1910 and translated what he saw on a farm and viewed from a houseboat anchored off downtown Manhattan into lively paintings that reminded those who would look at them of how much could be seen by a painter with an eye to form and color.

The experience of Paris left in the work of Abraham Walkowitz and Max Weber, Marsden Hartley and Charles Sheeler and Joseph Stella, unmistakable elements of form, color, composition; but their choices of subject remained American, and in their works subject dominates. A strict logic balances *The Bridge* (1922) of Joseph Stella, dividing the picture into two Gothic arches illuminated like stained-glass windows. But the painting stops there; it confirms our notions of symmetry. Similar limitations narrow the view provided by Weber and Walkowitz of workers, figures of Jewish life, the city; sometimes their work verges on caricature or cartoon; almost always it has a kind of body warmth. Abstraction is an approach, not a conclusion, in this sort of painting. It is what makes so unsatisfying any merely formal approach to a landscape or a still life.

Marsden Hartley had sharp intuitions of form, which he followed with great deliberateness at the beginning and end of his career. He learned much about the bold application of color in his time in Europe before the First World War and used what he learned in an attack on the German military caste he had come to know in his three-year sojourn in Berlin. His *Portrait of a German Officer* (1914) is a portrait in terms of symbol—*Hackenkreuz,* flag, medal; its color is strong, its iconography simpleminded. After years of vacillating between dedication to the imagination and distrust of it, Hartley came in his last pictures to his most significant understanding of form. Personal emotion enters into these pictures; like Dove and Maurer, Hartley drapes nature in his own colors, but there is a serenity in these paintings that the other men never quite achieved. Maine trees, flowers, waters, woods, are segmented and then tied together in a way that recalls the works of a great French painter of the same period, the late thirties. Hartley here seems a blunter Braque.

All these painters exhibited at one time or another at the galleries of Alfred Stieglitz, the photographer. Maurer and Hartley and Dove were introduced at the Photo-Secession Gallery, better known as "291," after its Fifth Avenue address. Weber and Walkowitz received their first large-scale exhibits there. There, Rodin's drawings were introduced to the United States, and there Matisse made his American debut in 1908, when the gallery opened. There, Henri Rousseau was introduced to America, and Picasso and Braque paid early homage in 1911 and 1914. Hartley called the little gallery "an enormous room . . . because it let a few personalities develop in the way they were believed in, and find the way to develop of themselves." They developed there and at the succeeding showrooms, the Intimate Gallery, and An American Place, they, the "few personalities." How much Stieglitz and his galleries meant to the people who exhibited there, they demonstrated in their contributions to *America and Alfred Stieglitz, A Collective Portrait* (1934). Arthur Dove wrote about the man:

When asked what Stieglitz means to me as an artist, I answer: everything.

Because I value his opinion as one who has always known.

I do not think I could have existed as a painter without that super-encouragement and the battle he has fought day by day for twenty-five years.

He is without a doubt the one who has done the most for art in America.

John Marin wrote about the place:

A place that is never locked for those who can produce a key.
A place that is never locked to anyone—
anyone can enter and walk about—
but if one got nothing then the *Inner* remained closed—
they hadn't the key.

To realize such a place—
a very tangible intangible place was and is this man's dream.

How much realized.—Well—this man being human—
working and being associated with working humans—

Those round about and many there are—
have sensed that things had happened—that things were happening—
that work had been done and was being done—

that the way had been lighted up—
that cheer had been given to many to carry on—
that the place has carried on with the conviction that
the place does exist.[3]

The man and the place were vital for John Marin. There he showed every year between 1909 and 1917, and in the new galleries, once they were opened, again annually. Those shows almost defined American art between the wars. Marin's triangular and diamond-shaped visions, his slashing lines and shimmering colors, brought the Maine seascape into New York. His yards of small watercolors and then, later, tightly contained oils, demonstrated quickly, rudely, brightly, what could be drawn from the ancient elements, earth, air, fire, water. The older he got, the more abstract he became. With or without intending to do so, he helped impress upon the American artist's consciousness the power of the two-dimensional picture plane.

The French understood very well the nature of their materials. The Cubists took apart and put together again the flat planes into which they reduced all objects to fit the two-dimensional nature of canvas, paper, whatever they drew or painted upon. American painters, reluctant to depart from illustration or narrative, held strongly to the third dimension. Perspective was parted with very slowly, and even where it is merely vestigial, as in the later Marin, it is unmistakably there in a horizon line, a depth of sail, a clear array of objects placed one behind each other and separated by definable if not defined distances. Georgia O'Keeffe, closest of all the artists to Stieglitz—she became his wife—scooped from the photography with which she was surrounded great panels of icy flatness and translated them into buildings in New York or pelvises and skulls in the Southwest, or calla lilies or windows or doors. The third dimension remains in O'Keeffe, however, the perspective that neither the photographer nor the illustrator can ever quite lose; even when she folds shutters tightly against a house, as in her incisive *Lake George Window* (1929), she lines up each of the layers of space behind the others: shutters, clapboards, window frame, window, and the door seen through the window.

The photographer's view is also that of Charles Sheeler, whose paintings often resemble the pictures he took with his camera, except for a range of color that is distinctly a painter's. Perspective sits high in Sheeler's paintings; the eye rises to the third dimension in them, up to the top of bridges, across railroad tracks, to the chimneys of the Ford River Rouge plant, from the bottom to the top of Shaker buildings in Pennsylvania or skyscrapers in New York. It is all very clean space, perfectly arranged, every inch of it clear to the eye, and but for the intrusion of the spectator at the time of viewing, out of time.

Time dominates the work of the painter who protests an indignity done to a class or a color of people, a painter whose only abstractions are political or social principles. One is so much aware of time in a painting that screams about social injustice that one can only wait for the death of the scream and the painting, too. Such a painting dies very quickly, like a newspaper story or comment in a weekly journal of opinion. It is not because the painting is topical that it dies, but because we are asked to live it, not to look at it, to become one with it or to make its cause ours. This sort of response may be pleasing to the painter; Ben Shahn says as much when he describes the pleasure given him by his paintings dramatizing the Sacco and Vanzetti case:

> The ensuing series of pictures was highly rewarding to me. First, I felt that my own work was now becoming identified with my person. Then there was the kind of response which met the pictures; not only did the customary art public receive the work kindly, but there was also an entirely new kind of public, a great influx of people who do not ordinarily visit galleries—journalists and Italian immigrants and many other sorts of sympathizers.[4]

William Gropper and Philip Evergood made violent comments that must have given them a similar pleasure; certainly the same public that responded to Shahn responded to their castigations of police brutality and the stupidity of legislators. Calumny, detraction, anger—they were all contagious in the Depression years, and the painters who gathered in congress and in union, around political figures and political magazines, went after their enemies like vigilantes—but not like painters. Some of the men changed—those with a respect for the design of a painting, for form and space; those who recognized that no matter how topical or turbulent a subject for a painting it could have in it elements that were universal, it could be looked at in tranquillity. Thus Shahn "crossed the terrain of the 'social view,' and . . . would not return." His explanation for the change is simple and eloquent:

I was impelled to question the social view of man to which I had adhered for a number of years without actually doubting that it might be either a right view or a natural one to me. Now it dawned upon me that I had always been at war with this idea. Generalities and abstractions and vital statistics had always bored me. Whether in people or in art it was the individual peculiarities that were interesting. One has sympathy with a hurt person, not because he is a generality, but precisely because he is not. Only the individual can imagine, invent, or create. The whole audience of art is an audience of individuals. Each of them comes to the painting or sculpture because there he can be told that he, the individual, transcends all classes and flouts all predictions. In the work of art he finds his uniqueness affirmed.

Shahn's later work does emphasize the individual; it also beckons to him to join the individual that is Shahn in some expression of general sympathy or special grief. But Shahn is not content merely to observe; he must comment. And so the viewer is forced to comment, too, and to become involved in what is at best a skillfully worked pathos, of young lovers, of musical instruments engraved with figures, of hands, even of landscapes.

There is no room for the tragic vision when a painter stays so full of protest. There is not even room for irony, but only for a simplifying kind of sarcasm that makes some of the paintings of Jack Levine offensive to many who have no objection to satire directed at politicians or generals. There is more to elicit lasting speculative examination in such a painting as Levine's *King Saul* (1952), a foreshortened icon viewed from above, part modern playing card, part Oriental potentate, part businessman, part Scriptural figure. The trouble with this sort of painting, as with the sometimes sharp, sometimes bludgeoning canvases of Levine's friend Hyman Bloom, is its explicit statement. Such painting seems to demand algebraic substitutions of meaning on the part of the viewer, or identifications even more obvious, as Peter Blume did in *South of Scranton* (1931), which once explained loses its poetry and becomes a travelogue, a Surrealist postcard of a trip from a Pennsylvania coal mining town into a Southern city by the sea, with the mines, German sailors exercising on a warship, and clay-roofed and flat-topped houses making obvious points of emphasis.

Others besides Blume have tried to anthologize or synthesize their impressions of America, rarely with any success when they have insisted upon precisely identified detail. They have come too close to advertising art in their illustrations. Bring up one of the signs into bolder light, focus the spectator's attention on a particular building or store, and you have a Coca-Cola ad. Put a leaf of tobacco in the hands of one of the figures, and you sell Lucky Strikes. There is no doubt that the public likes this sort of art, just as it does the soft drinks and cigarettes sometimes sold by it. It also enjoys the polished portraits and simple vistas and not-too-rankling acerbities of Grant Wood. After the first hurt and suspicion died down, nobody in the Midwest could be much offended by *Daughters of the Revolution* or *American Gothic* (1930), and could even chuckle a little over the dry portraits. The Gauguin Kansas figures of Thomas Hart Benton and the fondly handled Wisconsin soil of John Steuart Curry do not even arouse a momentary hostility.

There is more thoughtful reproduction of people and places in the painting of Charles Birchfield and Edward Hopper. Ohio has been seduously examined by Birchfield, its landscape, houses, skies, light and darkness, days, weeks, seasons. His painting has grown from fair copies of industrial and domestic scenes to canvases flatulent with light and color, but not indigestible, touched all at once by fairy-tale-like imagery, an explosive energy like Marin's, and by Ohio, which seen this way reveals far more than any turnpike tourist ever sees. Edward Hopper sees New York with the ash cans removed—and with most of the people missing, too. When in his paintings there are figures on a stoop, peering out of a window, or sitting at a lunch counter, they are figures only; they have no clear identity; they might just as well be plants or lamps or coffee urns. Hopper is the painter of cities without people, of buildings without tenants, of kiosks leading to subways that do not run. His is an anthropologist's eye view of modern civilization, a film director's, an architect's, a scholar's. He represents, without any comment except that of selectivity, the softness, the calm, the majestic impassivity of large buildings. Such painting demands at least a mildly meditative response, at least the briefest of pauses.

Hopper's painting is, on the surface at least, a public art. To those who know big cities, the New York scenes are likely to be appealing. To almost anybody, his pictures of houses on and near the New England coast are likely to be attractive, if not compelling. But this is only to look at surfaces and to miss the musing that has gone into these paintings, the long period of gestation which describes both the years in which Hopper was emerging as a painter and his approach to any one painting. He offers viewers a sophisticated and contemporary vision of the Peaceable Kingdom: a peaceable democracy of brick and iron. The urge in Hopper is still to illustrate, but in depth and with a sense of design.

Design comes only with detachment. Because of the distance from his subjects that Charles Demuth was able to keep, his paintings, even those that are merely washes over pencil drawings, have structure. There is form in his vaudeville vignettes, in his pictures of the city which are so much like Marin's, and in his portraits in oil. His mixture of architectural detail and tenderly applied textures will hold anybody who has ever attempted a watercolor. His ideas of order are much like those of Wallace Stevens; but his aestheticism is never so fragile as the poet's, nor, unfortunately, so deeply pondered and probed.

The respect for the concrete object of those artists who led the way to abstract painting in the United States is a wonder to behold. Like Demuth, Stuart Davis fills his paintings with objects, palpable, visible objects, and in some cases all but audible ones. Influenced by the paintings of the Cubists he saw at the Armory Show, Davis spent hours, months, a good part of a lifetime, examining objects closely. He painted an electric fan, gloves, and an eggbeater over and over again and drew from them patterns of design that became for him a personal vocabulary, a calligraphy, a poetry. His paintings have an unmistakable identity, their own and his. Letters, symbols, objects tell you where you are in the city: in a nightclub, in a street, listening to jazz musicians, looking at a newspaper. Davis abstracts from the concrete in a series of steps as precise as those of a man climbing a flight of stairs; over each of the steps he draws a transparent veil of color which makes almost all his work tuneful, as simply melodious as the airs of the Dixieland musicians whose playing has so influenced his painting.

Design is the crucial element in the significant American painting of the last twenty-five years. Even in the highly representational portraits of Franklin C. Watkins, there is a prevailing structure of color or line or texture, carefully arranged, that leads the viewer into the recesses of the human person. The putrefying particulars of Ivan Le Lorraine Albright, whether of a door painted over a period of ten years (*That Which I Should Have Done I Did Not Do*, 1941) or of people placed on canvas a little more rapidly (*Room 203*, 1930-1), arrange themselves in an iconography of the maggot, in which every minute detail has been conscientiously designed.

With increasing speed and grace and understanding, the object was filtered out of American canvases in the late thirties, the forties, and the fifties. The scenes of sea or land painted by Milton Avery show a recognizable tree, or waterline, or sail, but it is design and color that hold the eye in flat areas that recall the work of Hartley and Dove. There are streets, buildings, birds, flowers, even human figures in the work of the recent painters of the Northwest. But their paintings add up to a romanticism abstracted—abstracted in both senses of the word, reduced to the essentials of design, and preoccupied, withdrawn. Mark Tobey went to Seattle in 1939 by way of his native Wisconsin and Chicago; his painting moved far beyond his locus into the Orient. Over almost all his work done in the Northwest, Tobey spun a web of white runic brushstrokes, lines or dots more or less fine or stubby, linked together in mazes which his titles proclaim to be contemplative: *Written Over the Plains* (1950), *Meditative Series Number Seven* (1954), *Space Ritual Number Six* (1957). Morris Graves has made his paintings into a series of discursive prayers in a private language, but one that is not too difficult to follow. The language is chiefly of birds, whose flights or stationary poses make contemplative exercises for those who will pause over them. Some of the birds start their flights in the world of nature: *Preening Sparrow* (1952), *Wounded Scoter* (an Arctic seabird, 1944), *South American Bush Bird* (1944). By color or attitude, cast of wing or look of eye, by the wild waves or black sun surrounding them, they quickly move out of nature and into the world inhabited by Graves's other birds, his birds of the Inner Eye, painted in the early forties, his *Bird Maddened by the Sound of Machinery in the Air* (1944), his *Spirit Bird* (1956). Graves, like Tobey, feels an affinity with the Far East, to which he made several trips as a youngster and where he would have gone again right after the war, if permitted to do so by the American Military Government in Japan.

In New York, the exercises of contemplation were more mathematical, constructed after seasoned disciplines in painting; their sources were the Dutch painters of *de Stijl,* particularly Theo van Doesburg and Piet Mondrian. In 1935 Harry Holtzman organized the American Abstract Artists group, and the works of these men, variously warm and cold, personal and detached, vibrating and still, became an important part of American painting. They led the way in the destruction of the three-dimensional image and toward the construction of the two-dimensional picture plane. They influenced the design of textiles, of page layouts, of books, of advertisements, of homes and even of office buildings. When Mondrian was brought to the United States by the American Abstract group in 1940 to spend the last four years of his life in New York, this influence was made decisive in all the realms of public art which rest so heavily upon the procedures of the private. So widespread has the influence in applied art been, that many have forgotten that it is an influence and that it started with the work of particular private artists who have names of their own. Fortunately, the AAA continues to exhibit, and members of the group or those on its periphery continue to develop, although not always along geometrical lines.

There is no definitive AAA orthodoxy, and even the lines of derivation, which at the beginning could be traced like a genealogy, are no longer—happily—so clear. There is still much of Mondrian in their work, some of Hans Arp, a little of Klee, and much of the other Bauhaus painters. One of the Bauhaus faculty, Josef Albers, has contributed to this school a searching analysis of color, split surgically into squares superimposed upon each other. His paintings have taught us much about the tensions that exist in basic forms and flat colors.

In almost all the work of the American geometricians, even the most chaste and reserved, there is a volatility which should hereafter be recorded either as a mark of the American temperament or of the materials of painting used by these Americans. Even in the large symmetrical black balances of the recent paintings of Ad Reinhardt, there is some restlessness, some motion, some tension, if it is only the faintest tipping of a balance on one side or the other, or the shade of an imperfect equation of spaces.[5]

Geometric tension creates contention. In the middle forties and afterward there was debate, uncertainty, disagreement among AAA members about the place of geometric form in their work. Some thought the geometry had begun to harden into a new academic convention. Others found themselves increasingly attached to a symbolic palette. There were expulsions from the AAA, retirements, all sorts of collisions over practice and vocabulary. Art critics, always anxious to classify, always busy applying new and old terms to artists, called some of the old members "classic" geometricians, some of the dissident ones "romantic," a few of each "Neo-Plastic." Out of the turmoil, as so often happens after imbroglios among painters or musicians, individuals arose; artists of a notable independence emerged.

A late emergence was that of Barnett Newman, who after eight years without an exhibit placed enormous canvases on show in the winter of 1958 and contributed a bristling statement to the catalog of the *Exhibition of the New American Painting* which was sent to Europe in the same year. Newman's statement begins in the middle of things, as the great stripes of his paintings do. His words have the pugnaciousness of one of Sören Kierkegaard's tracts against the Established Church. Newman wages war to end war, or at least to confine the fighting to the canvas:

It is precisely this death image, the grip of geometry that has to be confronted.

In a world of geometry, geometry itself has become our moral crisis. And it will not be resolved by jazzed-up kicks but only by the answer of no geometry of any kind. Unless we face up to it and discover a new image based on new principles, there is no hope for freedom.

Can anyone, therefore, take seriously the mock aesthetic war that the art journalists and their artist friends have been waging against the new Pyramid—while they sit in it under a canopy of triangulation—with their feeble frenzy-weapons of the hootchy-cootchy dancer?

I realize that my paintings have no link with, nor basis in, the art of World War I with its principles of geometry—that tie it into the nineteenth century. To reject Cubism or Purism, whether it is Picasso's or Mondrian's, only to end up with the collage scheme of free associated forms, whether it is Miró's or Malevich's, is to be caught in the same geometric trap. Only an art free from any kind of the geometry principles of World War I, only an art of no-geometry can be a new beginning.

Nor can I find it by building a wall of lights; nor in the dead infinity of silence; nor in the painting performance, as if it were an instrument of pure energy full of a hollow biologic rhetoric.

Painting, like passion, is a living voice, which, when I hear it, I must let speak, unfettered.[6]

The drive to let paintings "speak unfettered" did not start in one place at one time. But the antecedents of the New American Painting are clear enough. The gallery the architect Frederick Kiesler designed for Peggy Guggenheim in 1942 in New York offered some of the painters space to hang in a Surrealist arcade. Among those who exhibited were William Baziotes, Robert Motherwell, Mark Rothko, Clyfford Still, and several times, Jackson Pollock. The atmosphere of the gallery had its liberating influence; so did the association, however tenuous, with the Surrealist painters who had retreated to New York from the Second World War, among them Marcel Duchamp, André Masson, Max Ernst, and Yves Tanguy.

The European painters thrown up on American shores by the Nazis and the war had a profound effect on American painting. Their works were like the Armory Show all over again in their introduction to new ideas, new forms and personalities. But theirs was no exhibition of a month in New York with brief repeats in Chicago and Boston; they offered tutelage by continuing example and direct instruction.

As many of the geometricians had picked up both process and conviction from Mondrian, so did other artists, less mathematical in their approach to painting, learn from Hans Hofmann, who arrived in New York from Germany in 1932. Hofmann in his teaching and in his own painting placed particular emphasis on the painting process, indeed equated process with reality. In the paintings of Cézanne each individual brushstroke has a clear and definable value; the whole is the sum of all the parts, but the parts have an individuality which can be discovered by anyone who looks closely enough. In the paintings of Hofmann, no one stroke signifies very much; it is the whole that counts and the whole is simply the sum of the whole. No matter where one starts in the tumult of color and texture which is any one of Hofmann's canvases, one must go on. The lines and colors lead one round and round, like the swirls of tragacanth in a Victorian endpaper. It is hard to stop, once one has begun this process of inspection, and equally difficult to find one's starting place. No one thing shines forth; the whole *thing* does. That is how it achieves its being, by becoming. It becomes what it is each time one looks at it—so much of the process of painting has the artist put in the painting itself.

In the painting of Hofmann and of those who have learned either directly from him or from experiences like his, all the central procedures of painting in the twentieth century can be seen. Here is the breaking down of the object into planes of color and texture; here, the recovery of the object, painfully, piece by piece. But what is recovered at the end is not the original object, but its colors and textures and lines. What is perceived is its form. The painter has had something like an apprehension of an inner form in painting of this kind. He has painted what Gerard Manley Hopkins calls the *inscape* of a thing. He has painted not the *whatness* of an object, not the fact that it is a horse, a telephone, a guitar, a book, an apple, but its *thisness,* the fact that it is a particular horse of a particular color and size and texture and form, a particular telephone, a particular guitar, etc.[7]

The painter of inscape has come far past the surfaces of landscapes and seascapes and individual objects. He has not come that long distance as Hopkins did, through the study of Thomas Aquinas and Duns Scotus or any philosopher. He has made his journey as a painter, helped by other painters. He has benefited hugely from the analytical discoveries of the Cubists and the synthesizing operations that followed. He has learned from Matisse about the physics of color, its mass and its extension, its power in repose and in motion, its reserves of energy. From the Surrealists he has learned about the concealed meanings in objects, the overtones that the most trivial thing contains; he has learned about the erotic significations of objects and other significations more remote; he has learned that pictorial imagery accompanies all processes of thinking and from Bonnard he has learned how much the process of painting can be the subject of a painting, even one that sets out to reproduce an object faithfully. He has gathered from Van Gogh what very few have of the thousands who have bought books about him and reproductions of his paintings: that his art has a contemplative center and that upon it his superb sense of design fastens; that upon it his jubilant color sits; that upon it rests his penetrating examination of a chair, a billiard table, a cornfield, a homely woman of Arles.

Design is the end product of these discoveries. It is nothing less than a triumph. "Look," these painters can say, "look, we have come through!" The development of American painting has reached a climax and probably an irrevocable separation of ways. The illustrators can contribute very little more; they can keep a certain number of painting exercises alive. The painters of design have transformed painting in America, as they have transformed themselves.

The transformation was a fairly slow process and very much a process. It did not start the night Jackson Pollock threw his easel out the window and began to squeeze and drip paint across the canvas stretched on the floor before him. It did not begin at a party at which Arshile Gorky danced or when Gorky died or when Willem de Kooning suddenly discovered release in violent attacks on an oversized canvas. The transformation is not the result of any number of nights in a barroom or a club for painters. Each of the painters of design has a personal history, a painting history. Each came to his present position because he looked so hard at painting, thought so hard about it, felt it so deeply, and made it all—the looking, the thinking, and feeling—a part of his own painting. Those who come to look at the paintings of these men now will have to look hard, too, will have to think about the art of painting and feel it deeply. Without having shared some of the experiences of these men, they will not find it easy to respond to their work or even to look at their paintings. Without having understood the evolution of painting in America, or lived through it, in however compressed or synthetic a way, they will probably not feel much at all, except maybe disquiet or a more stormy emotion. They will miss, then, the design and the form; and the triumph. They will not understand how much it means for painting and for painters—for art in America—to have come through.

What in fact has it meant to "come through"? For the painters themselves, a series of remarkable personal discoveries; how remarkable and how personal, every statement of theirs in words or paint makes clear. Robert Motherwell, for whom words come easily, says that the process starts with separations of value of a moral kind: "I believe that painters' judgements of painting are first ethical, then aesthetic, the aesthetic judgements flowing from an ethical context . . ." One of the principal ethical values "respected by modern painters" is "venturesomeness" as Kierkegaard understands it: "the ethical . . . teaches us to venture everything for nothing, to risk everything, and also therefore to renounce the flattery of the world-historical . . ." Other values that Motherwell lists are other aspects of the ethical venture: "integrity, sensuality, sensitivity, knowingness, passion, dedication, sincerity, and so on . . ." As a group, these values "represent the ethical background of judgement in relation to any given work of modern art." It is all, in sum, "a question of consciousness . . . ethical consciousness." Without ethical consciousness, Motherwell concludes, "a painter is only a decorator . . . the audience is only sensual, one of aesthetes."

There are elements of crusade in this sort of thinking, but this is not a group movement issuing manifestos, in spite of the fact that, for the time being at least, the painters of action and abstract expressionism always hang together, rise together, and fall together. Separations of value are, for example, quite personal in Motherwell's own painting, and have been for almost two decades, in medium-size brown-paper collages, in synagogue mural, and in mural-size canvases. The forms of a work of his called simply *Wall Painting IV* (1954) either advance or retreat, depending upon the way one reads it, from left to right or right to left; whichever they do, they strike out, they seem to mark an emotional crisis of some kind, like the monstrously inflated Rorschach inkblot with which such painting is sometimes jeeringly compared. The comparison is not inapt and, equally, not necessarily invidious. For emotion is clearly involved, emotion of some "integrity, sensuality, sensitivity, knowingness, passion, dedication, sincerity, and so on . . . ." How can one miss it in the great boulderlike forms of Motherwell's *Elegy for the Spanish Republic XXXV* (1954-8)? Whatever way one reads the forms, however much or little of oneself one puts into the events behind the canvas, the painting itself is an event: something happens in it and something will happen to the viewer because of it, if his ethical consciousness is aroused, as Motherwell intends it should be, as his apologetics of painting tells us, as his title tells us, as his painting tells us.

In 1943, Adolph Gottlieb and Mark Rothko insisted in a letter to *The New York Times* that "There is no such thing as good painting about nothing. We assert that the subject is crucial and only that subject-matter is valid which is tragic and timeless. That is why we profess kinship with primitive and archaic art." The kinship was professed by both men in a series of paintings of small figures— microscopic in terms of the dimensions of their present work. Adolph Gottlieb was for a long time known chiefly for his pictographs, explorations of the unconscious in a series of signs enclosed in graphlike boxes. The signs were adapted but not directly copied from the symbol systems of primitive societies. The boxes which enclosed the signs were carefully but not sharply indicated; there was never the precision of the geometricians in any of the lines or blocks of color, and even when the painting seemed to be a monochrome exercise, closer acquaintance would show a touch of color or texture that would dispose of that impression. The discipline that Gottlieb rigorously applies to his work now is directed to free his feelings. He does not seek to find images for his emotions, but to get onto canvas the "intangible and elusive images" that for him "have meaning in terms of feeling." To ask precisely what the images mean is to ask "the wrong question. Visual images do not have to conform to either verbal thinking or optical facts. A better question would be, 'Do these images convey any emotional truth?' " [8]

As Gottlieb's paintings have increased in size, so have they in clarity. The picture writing has become more intelligible, although not easily susceptible of translation into verbal formulas: the paintings are paintings, not "the restatement of restatements." His ways are still labyrinthine, but now one can walk through them with the ease and with the pleasure with which one goes through the maze at Hampton Court Palace, pulled to one side or the other, impelled to go forward, compelled to go backward, but always moving, always alert. In his most recent work, the writing is more compressed than ever before, bolder, richer. The double image of *Burst* (1957) may in time come to be for American painting what the winebottles, newspapers, guitars, African masks, and the young ladies of Picasso's Avignon were for art in France. The three-foot red sun poised over the three-by-four black Chinese character explodes into stillness. Here, after a small effort, one can rest.[9]

There is more tension, perhaps, in the great rectangles of color of Mark Rothko, their brush-filled edges bringing them fuzzily together and keeping them fuzzily apart. Rothko was once a painter of the underbrush of the unconscious, too, but his paintings grew bigger and so did his signs. Fussy detail disappeared. A shining cottony color took its place. Rothko has as a result a clearer identity, and so has color.

Identities are not elusive in this kind of painting. The signatures of Jackson Pollock and Willem de Kooning are all over their canvases;

one need not look for their names at the bottom to identify the drippings of one or the slashes of the other. In the same way, one comes to recognize, after a few viewings, the continents of color, broken up by small inlets and seas and lakes and rivers, of Clyfford Still and the coagulations of color toward some undefined center in the recent paintings of Philip Guston; the shattered blocks of color of James Brooks and the colored protozoans that cluster across the walls of canvas of the expatriate Sam Francis; the huge black and white calligraphy of Franz Kline that was beginning to change shape and color when he died suddenly in 1962; the colored rain of Jack Tworkov. The flora and fauna, buildings and landscapes of the imagination of William Baziotes are close enough to the natural history and geography of the Surrealists to make his work seem familiar, although it is by no means merely derivative. The explicit evocations of places of Grace Hartigan, chiefly New York City places, stop short of description or illustration, not because she abstracts fruit in a market, a sign on Broadway, a billboard, an awning, or a marquee, but because the places that her large paintings are "about" are dwelling places for form and color.

Jackson Pollock's work evokes what? According to one man, "An ocean's tides and a personal nightmare, the bursting of a bubble, and the communal clamour for a victim are as inextricably meshed in the coruscation and darkness of his work as they are in actuality." [10] That there is feeling of such an intensity in Pollock's walks across a canvas is clear enough; that it need be expressed in such terms is not at all clear. There are elements in his paintings that might stimulate images of nightmare and "the communal clamour for a victim"— whatever that means. But they are not really suitable as illustrations for Raymond Chandler or Mickey Spillane, Franz Kafka or an anthropologist's notebook. The colors Pollock mixed in such disturbing clots and channels have a commanding interest in themselves. His unwillingness or inability to give any one color dominance in any one of his paintings reduces their drama; it also gives them a certain reticence, large and tumultuous as they are. In some there is even a touch of elegance.

There is more of burlesque than elegance in De Kooning's paintings—not that any of them is likely to stimulate much laughter. His is the burlesque of Joyce's *Walpurgisnacht* in Dublin; his woman, painted over and over in the last decade, is an incubus or succubus. Her image will haunt painting for a long time. Blowziness has not often been blown up to such proportions, and that is not to speak merely of the dimensions of the canvases. "Art never seems to make me peaceful or pure," De Kooning says. "I always seem to be wrapped up in the melodrama of vulgarity." [11] The Grand Guignol of his painting has as yet no Punch to go with its Judy; it certainly has all the requisite action and something like a proscenium arch to frame it. Color turns and twists, drips and trickles on a De Kooning canvas; it is pierced and punctuated by charcoal; and somehow, finally, it coalesces and fills the flat space with a performance that almost never extends outside the painting, that moves in no direction except forward, toward the viewer, in an inversion of perspective.

The motion forward disturbs the Miró-like figures of Arshile Gorky's late paintings. His space is decorated, scented almost, with color. His figures arouse tactile responses; they seem to be soft, unfinished, incomplete. The lines which sever the figures, or indicate the directions in which they might perhaps grow, break his compositions into parts. After one has seen these paintings frequently, one learns to hold the parts together visually, and thus to build a kind of point and counterpoint out of them. All the senses, except perhaps that of taste, may be engaged by Gorky's works, though they need not be. But speculation or experimentation, development of some sort, must be aroused by paintings of this kind, at least among painters.

There is an abundance of suggestion, too, in the heavily worked surfaces of the paintings of the late Bradley Walker Tomlin. In his last years Tomlin produced a series of canvases which from a distance seem little more than ornamental. On close inspection, however, it becomes clear that the designs are made up of many shapes, of letters and numbers, of geometrical forms, of the figures on branding irons and arrows, the trailing impressions of drying brushes, all united by cursive white lines, the serifs of Tomlin's calligraphy.

Many painters have been influenced by the closely worked space of Pollock or the broad open spaces of Clyfford Still. Both approaches appeal to an artist of baroque sensibilities. Both satisfy the urge to bring larger and larger areas under control and to make heroic statements, even if the control is less than masterful and the statement assumes only the postures of the heroic. Both have the necessary concern with the processes of art though imitators of these painters often do nothing but manipulate paint—a hardware store's as well as an art supplier's—and maneuver canvases.

The number of those who have been directly influenced by the work of Gorky is small, although certainly he is today much admired by painters. The possibilities for development that his paintings hold forth—and to a lesser degree, Tomlin's—will probably be explored by painters when sheer size and boldness are no longer quite so fresh, when filling canvases with buckets of paint is no longer quite so compelling, when manipulating paint and maneuvering canvas are no longer quite so satisfying.[12]

Sheer size and boldness are not new traps for American artists, although painters have not so often been snared by them in this country as those in the other arts have. The young painter climbing up ladders to unleash his buckets at the canvas may just as easily turn into the Gericault of abstract expressionism as the Rubens. Unconsidered leaps into the processes of painting may produce a romanticism that is feeble in spite of all its violent gestures, or worse, a Whitmanesque rhetoric without any content except self-admiration.

Self-admiration has become the necessary foundation of a great deal of American painting today. As an art that is essentially private has become public, trademarks have had to be established. Without recognizable identities, painters' market prices decline and their markets soon disappear. The price tag is in the open style. Immediate recognition is called for; not a shock of recognition, however, but a tender response, rather like seeing a familiar movie face. There is an abundance of simple sexuality in abstract painting, none of it simpler than in the area of recognizable identities.

The extent to which painters pander consciously to the public's desire to fix identities permanently is not important. What is, is the reduction of a painting consciousness to a machinery of reproduction, in which one or two devices become inflated far beyond their intrinsic value and the best one can achieve is a kind of billboard-sized graphic art. Nicolas de Staël, the most arresting of postwar French painters, is a good case in point, making patchwork quilt after patchwork quilt of his marvelously inventive squares of color until, if one sees a large enough number of them at once, the joy in them seems only euphoria and the insights become banalities. In the generation that followed Gottlieb, Rothko, and Pollock, Motherwell and De Kooning and Kline, the same rapid transit from a fresh style to a trademark can be seen. Ellsworth Kelly's meticulously painted giant forms, as bold in color as in shape, become after a while little more than decorative backgrounds. The entertaining simplicity of his *N.Y., N.Y.* for exam-

ple, dwindles into a chamber-of-commerce sign; the architectural precisions of his paintings tire one; they do not stand up to a long day's
viewing. Robert Rauschenberg, who is an able draftsman and has a
shrewd sense of composition, has become an ironic vaudevillian, not
only a painter of objects but an impresario of them. Coca-Cola
bottles, clocks, all manner of working objects, enter into his "combine" paintings, as well as the traditional materials of the Cubist
montage. They are plausible entertainments. They hold one a few
times. But how often can one go on making the same kind of assault
upon the painting of one's time? How long this way can one hold the
private viewer, who has not come to see a star turn on the stage but
an exhibition of paintings?

Kelly and Rauschenberg are among the best of this second wave of
abstract identities, and by no means the most insistent upon their
identities. Jasper Johns's encaustic (paintings in melted wax) reproductions of targets, numbers, names, the American flag are more
open entertainments still. Their ironies may not be the ones the
painter intended, for they fall limply, for some of us at least, into the
lower circles of interior decoration. That same descent yawns before
Landès Lewitin's procession of calligraphic forms, Western brand
marks, and related shapes. Enough of them and everybody will know
who he is, a splendid achievement for the painter intent upon markets, but not necessarily a way toward an art of any significant
quality.

One recognizes a large set of skills in these artists and many
others who have not been quite so facile in their plotting of identities.
But one sees also a destruction of the meditative purpose of art that
must inevitably end in the abolition of the viewer's consciousness.
What, finally, can one do after the first sense impression of paintings
that are only faint variations on other paintings by the same artist, an
artist who has reduced himself to a handful of emblems, and very
simple emblems at that? The next step for the painter and the painter's public, after such a reduction in meditative power and purpose,
has to be pop art.

Others more impressed by the glib precisions and self-castigating
gestures of the pop artists may want to trace in detail the development of the painting of a Campbell Soup can, a comic strip, a couple
of automobile doors running into each other, a comic-strip frame, a
necktie and all the other commonplace objects of pop art, from their

first appearances in the combines of Rauschenberg and the encaustics of Johns, or to go back farther to the objects recorded or simply exhibited by Marcel Duchamp and Max Ernst and the other European votaries of the object who are really the Grandadas of pop art. It is enough, I think, to note the obvious connections and recognize the response to abstract expressionism which is involved in pop art and to speculate upon its great destructive energies.

There is no difficulty in seeing the graphic power of the pop artists' massive reconstruction of the detritus of the big-city landscape. Their objects are the objects of our world, at least as significant in the twentieth-century city as the furniture and the bibelots were in the London and Paris and Venice and Amsterdam interiors of the eighteenth century. The modern exterior is a lot more arresting to the eye than the eighteenth-century interior. There is more shock appeal in billboard art, highway art, advertising art, especially when blown up to the size of the billboard, than there is in the conventional accouterments of the naturalistic portrait or landscape or genre subject. The trash of our lives—and what a superfluity of waste materials an affluent society can produce!—provides materials for a great many violent paintings, especially with the additional assault value of smears of bold color all around it. But why stop at inoffensive trash? Why not the waste materials of the bathroom? Just think what a fine smeary painting can be made of human excrement! In our homage to the object, why not the baby's diaper? the sanitary napkin? And then the overflow from operating rooms—what splendid objects there are for pop artists in the flesh and blood and bone droppings that accumulate after a day's hard sawing and cutting in surgery! Why stop at pop art? Why not slop art?

The truths of pop art are very small truths, for all the inflated size of the canvases and boards. They are the truths of naturalism. They are Zola's truths, writ even smaller than in Zola. They are the truths of surfaces repeated over and over again, as Andy Warhol's paintings repeat the images of Marilyn Monroe or Elizabeth Taylor over and over again. At its best, pop art is cute, coy, archly contrived like a perfume- or bra-ad designer's adaptations of Klee or Mondrian. At its worst, pop art is altogether sterile, a retreat from the object, which is presented without visible reflection or meditation. All that the pop artist adds to his commonplace objects is a faint curl of the lip, the most obvious sort of irony. He ends by ridiculing himself and his art.

For his inflation of commonplaces has not exposed them in any new way, has not made them either more ugly or more attractive, but only demonstrated the susceptibility of a large number of painters of several generations to the machinery of the obvious, just so long as it is bright and loud and large enough.

Brightness, loudness, and largeness can be virtues in art. The art student who is not entranced by them is not quite alive, either to himself or his art. But they require some serious examination and development if they are to fill an artist's canvases over and over again. Perhaps it is enough to work one's way through one kind of emptiness of content after another, until, sated with the emptiness, one can extract everything possible from the techniques exposed by contentless painting. That seems to have been part at least of Larry Rivers' experience as he worked his way through figure painting, *George Washington Crossing the Delaware,* and all the ordinary world around him, until he was left with what he calls "A smorgasbord of the recognizable, and if being the chef is no particular thrill, it was as much as I could cook up." That is, of course, a calculated understatement of the quality of his variations on familiar themes, in which he plays the happy humorist to the well-known visual object, just as in England Francis Bacon plays the disconsolate and demonic attendant upon the object. Rivers disclaims edification, "Gorgeousness," virility, and moral uplift in his painting and tells his own zoo story to explain such purpose as his works may contain:

Well, when I was very young and went to the zoo a lot, I once went with my father, who is quite strong. He was feeding a deer through the wire fence and then began playing with the deer's antlers. Suddenly the deer backed away and a part of its antlers broke off and there was my father holding them in his hand, and the deer charging off in the distance. Aside from expectations of glory, all I can hope for from my work is that it arrests your attention with no more or less insistence than the breaking of a deer's antlers. That something in my work obliges you to forget for a few minutes the absurdity of your life.[13]

There are enough color and wit in the large bits and pieces of people and places that drift across Rivers' works to absorb any viewer's attention for a while. Rivers is a superior entertainer. The wit which is in his writing is even more substantial in his painting. But one would like to see his facility and humor reach beyond virtuoso twirls and twists to more demanding material, though it is something in a time when the surfaces of pop art and the emblems of easy identification absorb so many painters to find even entertainment that requires a little thought, a brief pause.

Rivers' facility extends to figure painting, may even be most intelligently, as well as intelligibly, employed on the human figure. Certainly his *O'Hara,* a variation on a famous Gericault standing male nude, is one of his most felicitous canvases and an attractive indication of the continuing interest of painters in the human figure. That interest blossomed in the early sixties into a renewed interest in figure painting. The interest was not, one quickly gathered, a rejection of the abstract. Many of the most agile and widely exhibited of the figurativists—Lester Johnson and Elaine de Kooning, for example—have the closest personal and stylistic ties with the New York abstractionists and actionists.[14] Their work is still deeply centered on the painting process. Many of the figure painters are students of Hans Hofmann, with that same earnest concentration on texture and stroke and color, as ends in themselves, which frees their work from the illustrative and journalistic dullness of the social-conscience and society-portrait figure painters of earlier decades. It is true that some of the figure painting of the sixties flattens out into the vacuous cereal and canned-soup likenesses of pop art. But there is enough of it that comes, like all the best of modern American painting, out of long hard examination of what painting is about, that one can believe that this branch of the art is growing up too.

There are some painters still concentrating so hard on their paintings that the viewer is forced to concentrate, too. It does not mean that a precise sort of communication has been achieved, but it is impossible, for example, in the great turmoil of Helen Frankenthaler's paintings or the conflagrations of color and texture Richard Lytle makes out of literary and mythological themes not to respond with some matching intensity of feeling, even if one ends ultimately by rejecting both the feeling and the painting that elicited it. There is, I think, a still larger range of feeling and a greater opening to rejection in the paintings of Gandy Brodie. Brodie, who has always responded with feeling to feeling, is unusually adept at translating a jazz musician's tones from sound to color and form, to the line of a small drawing or the thickness of a heavily painted canvas. Feeling is almost always his subject, feeling which, though broken down into a saxophonist's parabolic lines or a trumpeter's circles or a bird's burrowing pinches at the soil, never can be categorized in very simple terms. When his points of references are particularly clear, his meditation is at its most extended. Then one must look and look—"must" is not the word; one *will* look and look, as, for example, at the bold white figure of an Italian boy, of a fine stubborn centrality, who stands in front of a familiar slogan, one that is scrawled on many Italian walls, "NO ALLA GUERRA ATOMICA." Some of the letters are hidden by the figure, but the slogan, like the texture of the walls on which it is written and the atmosphere in which the boy lives and the hard reflection in which all were painted—all of this is clear enough. What one does with these several clarities is dependent upon the extent to which one can still contemplate subject matter in painting —a boy, a bird, a musician, an idea—and work from surfaces to something beneath them, which they conceal or reveal, reveal immediately or very slowly, depending upon the procedure of the artist.

Op art, or if one prefers, the art of perceptual abstraction, is concerned almost entirely with concealing and revealing. The game of optical effect and optical illusion is an entertaining one, as such of its ancient players as Josef Albers and Ad Reinhardt have long demonstrated, and as such of its newer performers as Frank Stella and Ellsworth Kelly have shown again. The great limitation of this sort of elaborate geometry is that, for all its engaging color and agile invention, it does not often rise above the level of sleek advertising art to the plane of meditation.

The point about the kind of painting that emerges from meditation and leads back to meditation, whether it is a series of drippings or smears or emblematic forms, whether it uses recognizable objects or simply concentrates on the technique of painting, is that what the painting evokes in the viewer is not very different from era to era, from style to style, from content to content, or from contentlessness to contentlessness. Color, texture, line, form—these always force themselves upon the senses, in the marvelous balances and imbalances of a Mondrian painting or the excruciating clumsiness of a piece of kitchen linoleum, in the pressed tin of the Moscow subway or the glass skin of Lever House, in Ad Reinhardt's black on black paintings or in all the colors of a Philip Guston medley of strokes and hues. One comes to look, and one stays to reflect, and perhaps to feel, in large part because of these obvious and essential elements. They are not the only elements, however, even at this point in the history of painting. It is possible now as it always has been to deal in any way, in every way, with the world around one. A mere representation, a simple illustration, may be more quickly exposed in its banality than in earlier years. So, soon enough, will the attenuated abstractions of those who have run quickly after the successful style, the marketable imitation of an imitation of a De Kooning or a Pollock or a Gottlieb or a Rauschenberg. The large concerns of serious artists can be turned with freshness and strength into recognizable persons or places just as easily as they can into designs.

There is in American painting, perhaps more than any other art in America, a terrible tyranny of school or movement or style. It has increased its power with the enormous expansion of the audience for painting, as the art has moved from private precincts to public exposure. Now that a successful painter, no matter how odd or obscure his style, is almost by definition a popular (though not necessarily a pop) artist, most painters ambitious of such success follow the leaders. We have had a decade or more of abstract expressionism, in which the styles of the New York School of painters dominated painting all around the country. We stand a chance of almost as many years of pop art, op art, and their various combinations and permutations. If one looks at the prices quoted in *Art News,* one can get a fair idea of the going school. If one goes to the New York galleries, one can get the same idea, at a slower and more depressing pace. The major museums, too, tend to follow rather than to lead. Incredibly enough, it was not until 1963 that Hans Hofmann was given a full-sized exhibition at the Museum of Modern Art.

In spite of the tyrannies and timidities of the art world, however, a substantial independence is still open to the artist. He cannot turn away from the new painting in America. He must be aware of the effect of the great change from illustration to design, from a second- or third-rate kind of nativism to international leadership in painting. But he need not choose the going school or the one that seems on its way to taking over in the popular marts. He need not be an imitator. He can do much more than scar the surfaces of his paintings with other men's experiences. There are no petitions for him to sign, no buttons to wear, no membership cards. There are, it is true, certain saloons, certain salons, but he need not fret if he either cannot be admitted or does not want to attend. He can follow his own pace, if he wants to, come to maturity slowly, as the New York painters did in the Depression years and those right after. He has the same right to every sort of self-questioning uncertainty as they did. But because of them he can now find space more easily in the galleries. If he has great integrity, he can resist the transformation from private to popular artist a little longer. He can spend some time scrutinizing paintings for himself, to find inner forms and the outer designs that signify them. He can develop his own consciousness. That should be enough. American painting has reached the point in its matching of mind and eye where one can hope for it what at its best it has suggested it can attain—the dizzying heights of the possible.

SCULPTURE

SCULPTURE WAS the last of the private arts in the United States to approach maturity. Not until after World War II did it wholly emerge from its Memorial Fountain and Alma Mater stage, a stage which had lasted for more than a century and had produced the greatest collection of monumental junk with which a country has ever been afflicted. Finally, in the years of the television era, sculpture became a significant art in America, partly as a corollary of the great accomplishments in painting in this country, partly as the result of the dedicated efforts of a handful of distinguished men, émigrés mostly, who had labored assiduously between the wars to rescue American sculpture from the hacks of the FM and AM crowd.

Even amidst their gilded hackery, the makers of meaningless monuments knew something of what sculpture was about, or at least once had been. Charles Caffin, a great admirer of the attenuations and travesties of Phidias, Praxiteles, Michelangelo, Donatello, etc., practised by the American drudges, concluded a book on *American Masters of Sculpture* in 1903 by saying, ". . . the end of art is not to teach, but to make us feel; to refine and elevate the operation of the senses, helping us through visible, tangible and audible beauty to catch at something of the mysterious infinitude of beauty." [1] Unfortunately, in spite of the enormous difference between their world and the worlds of the Greeks, the Romans, and the Italians of the Renaissance, men like Augustus Saint-Gaudens and George Grey Barnard, Daniel Chester French and Frederick Macmonnies felt that nobility and beauty—"the mysterious infinitude of beauty"—could be achieved only in endless imitations of the past, which had apparently frozen forever the essence of the mystery in its reliefs and rounds.

One could quarrel at length about the limited view of the "past" that these sculptors and their supporters and admirers held, a view which kept even so discriminating a collector of medieval sculpture as Barnard from discovering the large opening to feeling that lay in some of the procedures and devices of medieval sculptors. One could bemoan the high walls against feeling they erected in their large cold figures of presidents and generals, American horses and Greek gods.

But one should save one's anger for the tight guard they mounted against others discovering what they had failed to discover, against others feeling what they had not felt, in the courses they themselves taught or allowed or did not allow others to teach in the American schools and academies where sculpture was taught.

The anger, one might think, is unnecessary now. The struggle is over. The day of the wistful maiden, the drooping pony, and the public figure whose head is too heavy with affairs of state to hold upright is over. Newspapers and congressmen are still affronted from time to time by abstractions too bold for their imaginations, as they were, for example, when judges awarded the prize in the competition for a Franklin D. Roosevelt memorial to an ingenious construction of steps and slabs, emblazoned with the words of Roosevelt. But the danger now, for all the lack of imagination in America, is not that we will be overrun with ponies and maidens and heavy-headed public figures again. There is much more likelihood of a new academicism of wire and welding and the inane inflations of pop art, against which a sculptor of the tender classicism of an Aristide Maillol, if he should turn up in the United States, would have little or no chance. That would be a very high price indeed to pay for the freedom which has made metal the dominant medium in American sculpture and made it possible for the welders and brazers, the breakers and twisters to construct anything at all, out of anything at all, that might in any way translate their feelings or satisfy their sense of design. It would, in fact, be the end of that freedom.

The freedom of the American sculptor is no small thing. It came very fast and it was used very quickly. Within a few years after World War II, American sculpture had raced through the multiple developments, extending over more than a century, of modern painting, with particular emphasis upon the analytical and synthetic stages of Cubism. Sculptors in this country, as they became more and more aware of their freedom to do anything they pleased, anatomized the world around them, took it apart and put it together again. They did not do this simply by sign and symbol and reconstruction. They took the things up themselves, and especially those *things* with which our life is so filled, iron things, wooden things, things of steel and things of string, whatever could be found around us and particularly whatever could be found in that great historical record of our era, the junk-yard. They investigated things and they liked what they saw and then they presented us with those things, they did not *re*present them. And then, as artists inevitably must do, they performed their own vital ontological function: they made their own things, a whole new imagery of the world, often with familiar names, but rarely with familiar likenesses, except to those who have extraordinary accessibility to their subconscious minds.

Though the new sculptors owed much to the earlier work of the illustrious émigrés, Gaston Lachaise and Elie Nadelman and Jacques Lipchitz, they did not often show how much they owed in the form of obvious influence or open homage. They had much more in common with the mobiles of Alexander Calder, in some ways the most significant of their American precursors, and with the great master of abstractions in iron, the Spaniard Julio Gonzalez, who it is hard to believe died as long ago as 1942. But their debt to Lachaise, Nadelman, Lipchitz, and others of that generation, for exposing audiences to vital nonacademic sculpture and giving them pleasure in it, is very large.

Just how much pleasure Gaston Lachaise has to offer we can now see with the freeing of his last works for general exhibition. Many of these pieces—11, 18, 24, 25, 37 inches high—are very small alongside the monumental bronzes with which we usually associate Lachaise. But they possess—or better, are possessed by—an intense sexuality that nothing done by him or anybody else in the late twenties or early thirties can match. Here the tight waist and great rounded buttocks and breasts of his heroic woman are celebrated once again, but now with a tumult of feeling that is given a new eloquence in his studies of pendulous bosoms and upthrust swollen nipples and a new force in his sculptured couplings of men and women, couplings which, small or large, have some of the ecstatic beauty of the temple sculpture of Khajuraho and Konarak in India. It is hard to understand the timidity that dictated the withdrawal of these handsome figures from circulation for more than thirty years. For in them, what is given such articulate expression and unmistakable dignity is no conventional figure of woman, nor simply an unconventionally large and well-developed woman, but rather woman herself, woman as an instrument of feeling, woman made more beautiful and attractive by the distortions wrought in her body by feeling. To be offended by these bronzes is to be offended by the very existence of woman, by heterosexuality, by sexuality itself.[2]

Though he was born in Poland, Elie Nadelman was, like Lachaise, trained in Paris; like him too, he developed his style in this
country. The content of Nadelman's sculpture, quite unlike Lachaise's, cannot easily be described. On the surface, it seems to be all
surfaces, a decorative history of the frivolities and flippancies of the
first half of the twentieth century, made in marble and bronze. On
closer examination, Nadelman's sculpture reveals itself as a series of
speculations about the dimensions of sculpture. Each piece is as
abstract a handling of the problems of mass and extension in sculpture as one can get without altogether departing from recognizable
forms. That his works also possess a cheerful and never quite clear
fantasy of their own is all to the good. He was, in the best sense of
the word, an original.

Jacques Lipchitz is a Cubist, a philosophical Cubist. We have his
own word for it. In Cubism, he finds a view of nature, a vocabulary
and a grammar indispensable to his way of shaping objects. He takes
things apart—and in this one sees the germ, at least, of recent American sculpture—almost visibly, before the viewer's eye. But at the
same time, in a remarkable duality of movement, he puts them together again to make a shape agreeable to him, each part that he
retains quite differently hinged to its neighboring part from the way it
was originally hung together. Like the Cubist paintings of Picasso and
Braque and Juan Gris, his sculpture is a sculpture of parts, with the
totality not always easy to see as such and not always agreeable
either. But Lipchitz is not fixed as to style, for all the apparent
permanence of his Cubist attitudes. There is an enormous leap from
the early pieces made in Paris—the 1917 *Man with Guitar,* the 1918
Guitarist, the even earlier heads—with their sharp angles and surface-
centered compositions, to the work done after his move to America in
1941. What emotional power the later pieces have—the intertwined
Mother and Child (1941-45), which sits beside a pool at Frank
Lloyd Wright's famous Kaufmann house in Bear Run, Pennsylvania;
the great pear-shaped *Our Lady of Rejoicing* of 1948, bringing dove
and womb, Lord and Lady, together in as fine a piece of religious
sculpture as we have had in our time; the echo of that masterpiece in
the 1958 *Between Heaven and Earth,* in which the dove and womb
crown gnarled shrubbery like the New Testament rising from the Old
in a brilliant, burning perpetual movement. The early works have
everything in common with the other sculptors of Cubism, Ossip

Zadkine, Alexander Archipenko, Henri Laurens, Raymond Duchamp-Villon. The later ones, from the transitional period of the thirties on, have their own softness, roundness, airiness, agitation, their own insistence upon inner states of being, their own considerable humanity, for all the continued presence of abstract forms.[3]

Sculpture in the United States before the Second World War did not often achieve the strength or the eloquence of the originality of Lachaise, Nadelman, and Lipchitz. There was some fine stone-cutting by William Zorach and John Flannagan, though with something less than a Rodin-like originality of idea or boldness of form.[4] There was the inevitable social conscience, expressed in photographic likenesses of misery and depression, most of them a great deal less effective in their naturalistic outlines than photographs of the same depths of despondency and defeat, and almost all of them afflicted with a simple indignation too unmediated to rise above petulance or plaintiveness. By comparison to these little laments, so close to despair and so far from expressing it, the abstractions of Alexander Calder, Isamu Noguchi, and David Smith take on something approaching splendor.

Calder's *Mobiles* are a translation of the impish humor of Joan Miró into three dimensions, a reflection of Russian constructivism and of Dutch linear painting, a conversion into spatial sculpture of animated film cartoons and a fine piece of modern engineering. As soon as they were freed from the motors which drove them at first, they jumped into a poltergeist existence of their own, infusing many museum rooms with wit and confusing many gallery goers who, in spite of all the temptations to do so, had never found much to laugh at in modern painting and sculpture, except in philistine derision. Calder's is the sort of investigation of things that has proved epidemic in postwar American sculpture. Most of his things move, but not all of them. And whether a huge *stabile* or a small *mobile,* each has the same lacy and fragile sweetness which his line drawings possess. But no matter how delicate his works become, or how romantic, they also have a stubborn strength, perhaps because the materials involved are so often those of an engineer, perhaps because there is obviously such good engineering involved.

Noguchi has come closer than anyone else to domesticating Constantin Brancusi's forms and insights in this country. He himself studied with Brancusi. He had the skill as well as the taste to make Brancusi's kind of reduction to fundamentals his own. No birds in flight for him, but rather a shape, cut into a piece of wood or a chunk of stone, that links modern life on Manhattan Island with ancient life on Easter Island in a continuous primitivism. A certain complexity has entered Noguchi's work with the division of his years between the United States and Japan, a highly agreeable complexity of image and form and material. He has not rejected the primitivism, as his wittily worked set of three columns, *The Family,* will show anyone who passes by the Connecticut General Life Insurance Company building in Bloomfield, Connecticut, before which the stolid and amusing pictographic figures stand. He has made his humor more open and considerably broadened the arena of his meditations, as his entertaining little set of terra cotta figurines, *Even the Centipede* (1952), will show, or equally his large stone garden, a garden for philosophical growth, constructed in 1958 for the UNESCO building in Paris.

The growth and development of David Smith since he first started welding iron in 1933 has been philosophical, technological, literary, coloristic, semaphoric. Smith acknowledges the influence of Julio Gonzalez, but there is much more of European art in his sculpture than that. The whole range of abstract art, from Kandinsky and Klee and Mondrian to the American abstractionists, is represented in his iron and steel, represented and absorbed, brought freshly alive in the form of birds, totemesque figures, dialogues and pictographic letters in forged iron, and bright signals on a sculptor's highway—sentinels and ziggurats, Smith calls them—cut and folded out of steel and painted in striking colors. The influences may or may not be conscious; but the forms look as if they were popped right out of canvas and cast or bent into iron and steel—the coagulated drippings of Mathieu, the cattle brands of Bradley Walker Tomlin, the arcs and circles of Kandinsky, just to name a few that come quickly to mind. Does this make Smith any less a sculptor? I think not. For whether he wriggles in wire and pipe, bends sheets of metal, or welds and brazes, he produces forms that loudly proclaim their third dimension. But the forms themselves have an unmistakable association with painting, if not a precise source in it.

The painting of our time casts a long shadow over the sculpture of our time, and especially over the abstract sculptors who have worked so quickly and so industriously at their art since World War

II. The surrealism of David Hare, the spikes and spindles and arrows of Herbert Ferber, the iron flora and fauna of Seymour Lipton, the bronze and copper and nickel and chromium networks of Ibram Lassaw, the wire geometry of Richard Lippold and Harry Bertoia— all have unmistakable points of contact with individual painters or schools or movements in painting.[5] Indeed, when photographed against a flat shadowless background, their sculpture often looks more like a two-dimensional painting than a three-dimensional piece of sculpture. The point is to avoid such indirect experience of sculpture, any sculpture, but this sort of abstract work above all. One must see it, touch it (if its guardians will permit), know it as a work of art in its own medium, a work possessed of its own dimensions and of its own individuality.

Categories no longer matter much in sculpture, as is shown by the rapid expansion of materials once the breakthrough from stone and wood to metal, and from carving and casting to welding and brazing had become general. Painting has led the way in the visual arts in our time and so sculpture, like type design and architecture and billboard layout and the packaging of everything from depilatories to detergents, shows its dominating influence. But as a younger generation of welders has begun roaming the junkyards, a quite different sort of sculpture, related to painting only in the way that the urinal and all other objects admired by the dadaists are related to painting, has begun to show itself.[6] Thus we get the portrait of a political *Candidate* by Richard Stankiewicz, with a head made of a hollow television tube and a body consisting mostly of yards of exposed pipe, like so much intestine open to the winds from above. Thus we have the huge collection of canvas and rods and a plexiglass bomber turret brought together by Lee Bontecou as an image of *1964,* flying (more or less) against the wall of the New York State Theater in Lincoln Center in New York City.[7] Thus we have a world inspected with a thoroughness that is really quite new, even after a hundred years of outdoor painting and a half a century of examining objects bit by bit in the hallowed Cubist manner. At its worst, this sort of inspection turns into a specious act of homage to the commonplace and the tawdry, in which Marcel Duchamp's "ready-mades" are constantly re-made, with all the beauty and the charm and the wisdom of a television commercial played over and over again. At its best, this restless probing of our environment turns up the real beauty that can often be found in the ordinary world around us, if we look hard enough and with enough wit. It shows us, as again and again we must be shown, that the machine-made objects of this century, whether fresh and shining and new, or old and bruised and broken, have as much in them "to make us feel; to refine and elevate the operation of the senses" as any material ever presented to an artist to work on. It is just a matter of finding the right man to tease or to tear the feeling out of the object.

It will be a long time before anybody really knows how right these men really are for the objects they have been working upon. It will be enough for a long time to look at the objects and to discover in them something of what the persons who present them to us have found in them or something else entirely, to discover a little, perhaps, of the persons themselves. One thing is abundantly clear: sculpture is not dying, as for so long it seemed to be. It is once more very much alive in the studios, in the galleries, in the museums. Architects are once again making use of sculpture, not as an ornament to be grafted onto the finished product, but as an integral part of their conceptions, as they themselves have more and more been influenced by the shapes and forms and procedures of sculpture. But best of all, perhaps, sculpture in America is now well within its own time. It is no longer lost in an empty, irrelevant reconstruction of the past. It may still be producing junk, but now it is junk openly, even proudly, acknowledged.

PHOTOGRAPHY

IN FEBRUARY, 1921, Alfred Stieglitz wrote a prefatory statement for the catalog that accompanied a retrospective exhibition of his work, starting in 1886. "This exhibition is the sharp focussing of an idea," he began.

The Exhibition is photographic throughout. My teachers have been life—work—continuous experiment. Incidentally a great deal of hard thinking. Any one can build on this experience with means available to all.

Many of my prints exist in one example only. Negatives of the early work have nearly all been lost or destroyed. There are but few of my early prints still in existence. Every print I make, even from one negative, is a new experience, a new problem. For, unless I am able to vary—add—I am not interested. There is no mechanicalisation, but always photography.

My ideal is to achieve the ability to produce numberless prints from each negative, prints all significantly alive, yet indistinguishably alike, and to be able to circulate them at a price not higher than that of a popular magazine, or even a daily paper. To gain that ability there has been no choice but to follow the road I have chosen.

I was born in Hoboken. I am an American. Photography is my passion. The search for Truth my obsession.

ALFRED STIEGLITZ

In 1934, in the volume called *America and Alfred Stieglitz: A Collective Portrait,* in which twenty-five writers celebrated Stieglitz's many contributions to many arts, the photographer Paul Strand summed up:

Stieglitz does not label his work "art," he does maintain that it is photography. The question is an academic one and can be left to those who are greatly worried about whether this or that is or is not art. One needs but to go to the Boston and Metropolitan museums, see their few but fine examples of Stieglitz's work, to feel grateful that life has again been enriched by a new beauty, another heritage being preserved for future generations. And beyond what these photographs give in themselves they may also be seen as symbols of the machine used not to exploit and degrade human beings, but as an instrument for giving back to life something that ripens the mind and refreshes the spirit. They give hope of, and perhaps prophesy, a new world, humanly speaking, which is not an absurd Erewhon; but one in which people have learned to use machines with a different attitude towards them and towards each other. In such a world the machine would take its place, not alone as an invaluable tool of economic liberation, but also as a new means of intellectual and spiritual enrichment.[1]

In the same volume, Harold Clurman, one of the founding directors of the Group Theatre, hailed Stieglitz as "the great pioneer of American group work in the arts" and his photographs as "the greatest individual achievements in American art." The volume itself was a Literary Guild selection, an indication that the directors of the book club, whether or not they agreed with Clurman's high evaluation of Stieglitz's work, felt that an examination of it would interest a mass audience.

Photography does have a mass audience today, perhaps the largest of all the audiences for mass media in the readers of magazines and newspapers and the viewers of television, in which each year still photographs play a more and more significant role.[2] Photography is the special art of the amateur in America, who is no longer simply the collector of "memoranda of . . . every-day life, objects, places or people" for whom George Eastman produced the first Kodak camera in 1888, but a dedicated artist, both in taking films and in developing them. It may even be that photography has become the means for some of the intellectual and spiritual liberation that Paul Strand looked to it to effect. Certainly it regularly brings millions out into the sunlight to examine each other and the world around them with something like contemplative calm if not detachment. Certainly through photography more people have learned at firsthand something about composition and texture and tone in the visual arts than through any other means, have been forced to develop their imaginations along with their photographs, and have had to construct something like a philosophy of art with which to guide themselves in choosing size, electing a composition of symmetry or asymmetry, and in deciding what portions of their original negatives to keep and what to crop. In spite of all this, the critical examination of photography is still very much a private art, the work of a few dedicated people writing for a few dedicated people. The very magazines that have

accomplished Stieglitz's "ideal"—mass production of first-rate prints
at a cheap price—rarely analyze or even call attention to the work of
the men and women on whom they subsist.

   To some extent photographers themselves are responsible for the
lack of interest in or understanding of photography as an art. Paul
Strand's dismissal of "art" as a word to describe Stieglitz's work has
been followed by a corresponding reticence on the part of photographers to discuss their own work in print. Their chief argument seems
to be that the photograph would somehow cease to say anything if
anything were said about it, or that the words would act as a damag-
ing apologia for the picture, confessing the picture inadequate to
achieve its end. In two successive sections of the 1957 American
Society of Magazine Photographers' *Picture Annual,* this point is
made. Richard Avedon explains of a group of fashion photographs
that because he feels "strongly that photography is its own medium,
and speaks for itself," he will limit himself to the time and place in
which the photographs were taken, the name of the magazine in
which they appeared, and the kind of camera with which they were
taken. Elliott Erwitt, commenting on two pictures of his wife, one
pregnant and one with the newborn child, complains:

Little is more irritating to me than photographers pontificating about
photography or talking about their pictures in public, unless these photographers have just come back from China or the moon, or have something
very particular to say, or a great new technique and approach to talk
about, or are interesting and intelligent personalities. They should stick to
talking through their pictures. Not particularly falling into any of the
first categories, I will only say about my two pictures herewith produced
that I like them. . . .[3]

And so one learns almost nothing about photographs of considerable
intrinsic interest, and the anti-intellectual atmosphere in which photography always seems to be wrapped is thickened.

   Stieglitz's attitude was anything but anti-intellectual. He was determined to increase the numbers of skillful American photographers
and to win the widest possible viewing for their work when he began
his half-century struggle in behalf of photography in this country in
the 1890's. He not only exhibited widely himself, he was a tireless
arranger of exhibits for others. He edited the *American Amateur
Photographer* for a year, then founded and edited the publication of

the Camera Club of New York, *Camera Notes*. In 1902, he organized, edited, and published *Camera Work*. In its fifty issues, produced over a period of fifteen years, the gradual emergence of a hard, precise, unsentimental photography out of a cocoon of furry elegance is documented. One sees the work of the Photo-Secession, the group of photographers in New York (with a corresponding group in London called the Linked Ring) who were brought together when New York Camera Club members protested Stieglitz's publication of photographers outside the club in *Camera Notes*. Among them are Edward Steichen, a close associate of the editor, Clarence H. White, whose study of women, "In the Orchard" (1902), and Gertrude Käsebier, whose picture of mother and child. "Blessed Art Thou Among Women" (1900), are tender examples of turn-of-the-century photography. Steichen was working in the same soft idiom as White and Käsebier, but with the insight of genius into painterly textures and lighting. His "Rodin—the Thinker" (1902) brought sculptor and sculpture together in a pair of profiles which are saved from collapse in a dreamy haze by the presence in the brightly lighted background of the sculptor's great head of Victor Hugo. His portrait of J. Pierpont Morgan (1903) focuses on black eyes, a little more frightened than frightening in their piercing stare, and a left-hand grip on a chair arm which, with the twisting of the light, becomes a small dagger. Steichen's Paris photographs of these years—such pictures as "Yvette Guilbert" and "Steeplechase Day, Paris: After the Races" (both 1905) and "Balzac by Rodin" (1908)—are impressionistic, romantic, lighted for the stage. They record the postures and hopes and wistful pretensions of a period rather than the period itself, or its places or its people, as do Stieglitz's horsecar and steaming horses ("The Terminal," 1902), immigrants ("The Steerage," 1907), and studies of a wet Paris boulevard (1894) and wetter New York square (1897).

By the time of the First World War, the attention of American photographers had moved out of doors. Like the Impressionist painters, like Stieglitz, they had discovered the sterility of the studio and the corresponding vitality of the city, of the country, of land and clouds, of people and machines and buildings, discovered it, now, with great force, in their own streets, their own yards, their own countrymen. Paul Strand photographed sewer pipes, driftwood, fences, his own film-making equipment; he caught people unawares, close up, angrily alive. Charles Sheeler photographed the sides of Pennsylvania barns, the well of a staircase, concentrating with Mondrian's kind of linear fixation, a painter's concentration, on sharply defined rectangles. After the war he moved on to industrial subjects (such as the Ford River Rouge plant in 1927), in which an occasional circle or cone or cylinder varies the pattern, and to photographing medieval architecture and ancient sculpture.

American photography in the twenties remained the work of recognizable individuals. This is so in spite of the development of tabloid newspapers and the popularity of sepia-colored rotogravure supplements to the other papers, in which was caught, in a kind of large, ill-defined clutter, on Saturday and Sunday, some of the violence, some of the smell and the noise which the New York *Daily News* and *Daily Mirror* and *Evening Graphic* were evoking in more memorable single, full-page photographs. News photography was live enough, colorful enough, startling enough even in the more polite papers; it was not yet the inviting field for the self-conscious performer it was to become with the advent of the picture magazines. The artist in photography, like the painter, was still a man apart. He worked, like Edward Weston, not for a market or for an audience, but to solve problems of texture and definition, of subject matter and ways of looking at it. Not only did he work to solve problems, he worked to create them, to find the essential problems of his craft, to find his craft.

Weston followed the pattern of American photography in his development of a style. He moved in the twenties from soft to hard definition with a triumphant clarity. No photographer did more to fix the power of sharp focusing on the American consciousness than he did. None presented more vividly the paradoxical attainment of abstract composition out of a realist's fervor for exciting detail. None made more of light and shadow where light and shadow count most —out of doors. His nudes, the most determinedly photographic of all nudes, huddle or stretch out on the sand, in sunlight, marking their presence by formal elements that are as abstract as recognizable buttocks, breasts, shoulders, arms, legs, feet, and hair can be. They have the geometric coolness of the forms of Ben Nicholson or Hans Arp or Nahum Gabo, but they are not paintings or sculptures and they are not cadavers; they are photographs of women or parts of women; there is a recognizable human element always—a wrinkle of the skin at the neck, a motion of the spine over the melon halves of the rump, a drawing together of the thighs, an unmistakable gathering of flesh around the nipple. Weston does not present us with abstractions in the way a painter does. He does not offer a complicated symbol system. "If there is symbolism in my work," he explains, "it can only be the seeing of parts—fragments—as universal symbols. All basic forms are so closely related as to be visually equivalent." Thus, like Baudelaire's, his is a system—if system it is—of universal analogy. Thus, reasonably enough, he has had "a back (before close inspection) taken for a pear, knees for shell forms, a squash for a flower, and rocks for everything imaginable." [4]

Weston's preoccupation is with form as a photographer may observe and record it. He is a ground-glass photographer. What he sees on his glass is what he photographs. He sees it whole, in an 8 x 10 camera which makes a picture the precise size he wants it, without enlarging or reduction (he does not even own an enlarger). He sees it in all its detail, with a kind of simultaneity of vision which is the camera's special contribution to modern seeing, offering us all at once what we normally see in sequence, offering us detail, depth, range, which we cannot get by ourselves, which require the mediation of the photographer and his instruments.

Most photographers have been content to restrain their mediation to the choice and grouping of subjects, the control of light, the selection of parts or wholes in the developing process. A small number in Europe in the twenties insisted upon roles more exactly like a painter's, with light as subject and object and the camera put aside in favor of direct manipulation of sensitized photographic paper. Even negatives could be varied in this way by exposure to white light in the development process. The result was a kind of Surrealist photography, at least at first, in which the bizarre and the eccentric seemed to be the central values and to outweigh more serious considerations of design or composition. But out of this school there came some work that was more than merely precious, in which useful experiments were performed with over- and underexposure and temperature changes in the emulsifying process, and a whole set of degrees was added between the two poles of the developing process, the negative and the positive. Among the most eccentric of the experimenters—as many thought in the twenties—was the American expatriate Man Ray. His "rayographs" are a record of this kind of interest, the photographic equivalent of the verbal and typographic games his friends and associates were playing in *transition* and the various organs of Dadaism. Whatever the limitations of his own work, it was, along with Ladislaus Moholy-Nagy's and Christian Schad's, the foundation for work of high excellence in graphic design—in book jackets and magazine illustration and the organization of the type page—three and four decades later.[5] Furthermore, Man Ray was at the same time a portrait photographer of uncommon perception when those who sat for him were in some way related to him, in taste or skill or interest. His 1926 portrait of Arnold Schönberg, like a death's-head, all black and white, the flesh seemingly bloodless, the eyes fixed in a kind of hypnotic stare, has the power to hypnotize: it leaps from a wall or the pages of a book with the violence characteristic of the composer who is its subject. His 1933 portrait of Picasso is almost the opposite: the eyes once again stare at one, but gently, the whole face somewhat tired as it rests on the painter's left arm, which is in turn supported at the elbow by his right hand. Dressed in a trench coat, Picasso looks like a weary victim of the rain, sitting for a photographer for whom one cannot manifest any emotions but true ones.

One senses that every emotion is a true one in the extraordinary series of portraits Edward Steichen made in the twenties and thirties for *Vanity Fair*. More than any other contributor, he gave that magazine distinction, and still does, years after its demise. His is a record of personalities constructed to fit the headlines, to suit the fashions or to reflect them. But the structure has unusual depth. It preserves more than names and reputations; it holds safe against time the human person and makes thoroughly understandable the cult of personality of the era.

Steichen joined Condé Nast in 1923 and photographed for *Vanity Fair* until it was discontinued in 1936. He photographed actors and actresses, prizefighters, opera singers, pop singers, torch singers, writers, aviators. For each he found just the right light, just the right pose or repose. His shadows are rarely dramatic, never melodramatic; his light, never harsh, not often sentimentally soft, only occasionally severe. Profiles and full-face pictures dominate the series. Props are important but do not slap one in the face; they say what they must. Like the knifelike thrust of J. P. Morgan's armchair, the walking stick and hat of H. G. Wells speak for his urbanity, real or imagined. The arch of a chair back and the pattern of a Chinese chair insist upon Harold Nicolson's manner, almost as much as the cut of his hair and the slice of his smile. More often a Steichen background is gray or black or striped with shadow, vertical or horizontal or diagonal, to act as furniture of the atmosphere, upon which Rudolph Valentino may lean precariously, John Gilbert may sit more confidently, Leslie Howard may rest one arm speculatively, Leopold Stokowski another arm less tentatively. Couples—Charles MacArthur and Helen Hayes, Norma Shearer and Irving Thalberg, Edna Best and Herbert Marshall—and casts—*Green Pastures* and *Journey's End* and *Anything Goes*—remain alive in the stained glass with which the time was illuminated, the glossy pages of a magazine. It is a tribute to Steichen's photography to say that these figures do not seem glamorous, as their press agents might have called them, but substantial; the whole period, in such a record, seems to have substance.

Steichen's eye was always open to the enduring. His Paris was Rodin's and Matisse's and Cézanne's and Picasso's, before World War I, before the years of the expatriates; he supplied Stieglitz with some of his best exhibits for "291," as his gallery in a Fifth Avenue brownstone will always be known. He recorded two world wars, fliers in Europe in the first, the Navy in the Pacific in the second. The first war brought his painting career to an end and led him to study photography all over again, light and shadow, animate and inanimate subjects. The second war turned him into the impresario of photography, the organizer and director of *The Road to Victory* and *Power in the Pacific* at the Museum of Modern Art, and then, later, in his position as Curator of Photography at the Museum, as producer of *The Family of Man*. What Steichen crammed into that incomparable show was birth and death and everything in between, everything that anybody in the middle fifties thought could be photographed and many things that nobody realized had been. All of it was held together by Steichen's judgment, judgment of size and sequence and the right words to go with the pictures. The words were few enough, but they contributed something, too: Molly Bloom's warm assent to sexual love at the end of *Ulysses* (" . . . and then I asked him with my eyes . . . and yes I said yes I will Yes."), some wise words by Pueblo and Sioux and Kwakiutl and Navajo Indians, by the composer Scriabin, by Euripides, the Biblical writers, the *Bhagavad-gita,* William Blake, St. John Perse, Plato and Lao-Tse and Montaigne and Homer and Virgil and Shakespeare and one or two others. What the exhibit had at the museum and still has in a book, even in pocket-book size, is in two lines Steichen used from the medieval Indian poet Kabir, "The hills and the sea and the earth dance. The world of man dances in laughter and tears." Without a dull picture, without a stereotype, without a banality, the world of man dances through these pictures. Photography defines its place and finds its dignity here.

Steichen used much from magazines, from newspapers, from wire services, "Photographs concerned with man in relation to his environment, to the beauty and richness of the earth he has inherited and what he has done with this inheritance, the good and great things, the stupid and destructive things." He looked for states of being, for moments infused with the fullness of life and the emptiness of death, "Photographs concerned with the religious rather than religions. With basic human consciousness rather than social consciousness. Photographs concerned with man's dreams and aspirations and photographs of the flaming creative forces of love and truth and the corrosive evil inherent in the lie." [6] From over two million pictures, he chose 503, some by famous photographers—Henri Cartier-Bresson, Margaret Bourke-White, Werner Bischof, Andreas Feininger, Gjon Mili, Barbara Morgan, Edward Weston—some by unknown photographers, amateur and professional. He used a few famous pictures, properly famous pictures, taken for the Farm Security Administration in the Depression by Dorothea Lange and Ben Shahn, pictures aching with poverty and hunger and bewilderment and depression. He used a great many from the archives of *Life,* a fair indication of the many photographers of quality who have done work worth preserving for the magazine since its founding in 1936, and an indication too of the extent to which photojournalism has dominated photography in *Life*'s third of a century.

There have been two kinds of American documentary photography, both more or less "straight," as the photographer uses that term, that is direct picture-taking, without retouching or otherwise distorting the print. One is a permanent record, unconcerned with editorial requirements, or any other, except holding onto the moment, the place, the people. The other is made for a particular day's or week's or month's audience in a particular journal. The first was practiced by the sociologist Lewis W. Hine in the early years of this century at Ellis Island and in the slums of New York City, as he traced the lives of immigrants from arrival to settlement and decay. He did as much again with Red Cross workers in Europe after the First World War and with American labor in the collection called *Americans at Work* (1932). The Farm Security Administration photographers picked up every possible particle of dust as they filmed the eroded lands and people of the Southwest in the mid-thirties. Many years, many boom years, later the pictures still make their points eloquently. Perhaps the most affecting sequence is Dorothea Lange's—she concentrated on faces; she listened to voices. Some of her vision and her hearing are preserved in *An American Exodus* (1939), which she did with Paul Taylor, printing in it snatches of her subjects' conversation to go along with the pictures.

The photojournalists, the second group of documenters, work within tighter restrictions. They not only have a deadline, they must produce illustrations to fit a carefully planned story, or must arrange their recording of an event, a manner, a fashion, a splice of nature, or serving of geography so that it falls easily into a narrative. With all these limitations, however, they have at least one compensating advantage: they may shoot hundreds, perhaps thousands, of pictures, 35 mm. or Rolleiflex or Speedgraphic or any combination of them or other cameras. They leave little to chance. What will not happen according to plan they do their best to make happen according to plan. The picture of a Chinese baby sitting in the debris of a bombed-out railway station in Shanghai, abandoned, crying, became an emblem of horror of the Japanese invasion of China; but the baby, though unhappy enough, was not actually deserted; it was placed there by the photographer, N. Wong of International News, with the parents' consent.

Magnificent photographs have come from photojournalism, but so have yards of dull or glib or merely workmanlike performances. Photojournalists can perhaps point to Mathew Brady, the Civil War photographer, as their progenitor in this country. But only a very few have been able to concentrate as stoically on the material to be photographed as Brady did, capturing a general in front of a tent, a hospital ward full of soldiers, the ruins of houses in the city, of a bridge in the country, without seeking heroes or villains, without sentimentalizing the scene, without in some way reducing the eloquence of what is observed to make room for the eloquence of the observer. The destructive element in the photojournalist's work is the need to comment, often at top voice. Sometimes it is a political comment, often a sociological one, too frequently a sentimental one. The sentimentality is most often not for the subject, though it may be the occasion for burning tears or reverent laughter; usually it is a shiver of self-appreciation that goes rippling through the photographer and slobbers over onto the finished photograph: See, the picture says, see how sensitive a photographer took this picture: See the warmth: See the wit: See the wisdom.

Perhaps the most reserved of documentary photographers is Walker Evans, one of the FSA group, but before that and afterward a remarkable historian of places and recorder of manners. Ossining, New York, and Havana, Cuba, a worker in Wallabout Market, the destitute sitting or sprawling on South Street, the Sixth Avenue El and cars and a Negro woman heavy in furs—the early thirties are singularly alive in such pictures, each moment, each place stopped down to as much light and expression and movement as the emotionless machine will permit. Evans's is never a crude naturalism: there is no apparatus of interpretation pressing an implacable determinism upon the viewer of his pictures. He photographs a tattered movie poster on the side of a building, an ornate water pump in Maine, a stolid sharecropper's family in 1936, of whose six members only one half-naked little girl shows some vitality. More than thirty-two photographs gathered together in the front of the book he did with the writer James Agee in 1941, *Let Us Now Praise Famous Men,* more than twice that number in the revised edition of the book, make their austere points without title or gloss. This sort of photography does speak for itself, though the lengthy text that follows is not a useless appendage, for all its verbosity. Nor does one resent the commentary Lincoln Kirstein supplies for the two groups of pictures called *American Photographs,* published in connection with an exhibition of Evans's work at the Museum of Modern Art in 1938.

One is grateful, too, for the laconic titles and dates that go with the pictures in Berenice Abbott's collection of pictures of New York in the thirties, *Changing New York* (1939). Parts of the city that have changed very much since then, ways of life that will never be the same, buildings that have been torn down or much redecorated—these are looked at with some feeling but no great intrusion of personality. The photographer had returned to New York from Paris at the end of the twenties. She had obviously learned to look with the special kind of respect for a stone, a building, a street, a square that a long sojourn in Paris or any European capital confers. You do not take anything for granted, not rubble, not store-window displays, not signs, no category of ugliness, no sort of beauty. You find your picture or it finds you, as in Berenice Abbott's "Union Square: 1932": the arena to which Depression-era workers always took their riots is full of broken stones, dirt; there are suggestions of the litter of workmen making repairs in the background; in the foreground a statue of Lincoln lies, fallen or shoved or carefully removed from its pedestal. Is this a riot? Is it a landscape changing peacefully, by plan? No, it is simply Union Square: 1932. "Every other artist begins from scratch," Steichen says, "a blank canvas, a piece of paper, and gradually builds up the conception he has. The photographer begins with the finished product. When that shutter clicks, anything else that can be done afterward is not worth consideration. At that point the difference between photography and any other medium stops, because the photographer has brought to that instant anything any artist in any medium has to bring into action for the creative act." [7]

Photography today is an art and an industry. It is crowded with brilliant technicians. There is almost no event, trivial or significant, that is not photographed from every angle. Perhaps the best of the photojournalists, the most thoughtful as well as the most experienced, are gathered together in an international organization called "Magnum," twenty-eight all told, nineteen full members, three associates, six contributors, with Henri Cartier-Bresson and Elliott Erwitt (the first executive officers), and Dorothea Lange, Cornell Capa, Wayne Miller, and Ansel Adams among the American members. In every country there are abstractionists, photographing whatever they can find that resembles an abstract canvas or arranging things—paints, wood, metal, anything at all—to get the abstraction. Color is the abstractionist's best medium; his work seems less synthetic in color than in black and white. And equally, when abstractions come out of nature or the city, with little interference from the photographer, they give to color some of the conviction that black-and-white photographs by Stieglitz, Weston, Steichen, Evans, and Abbott have, freeing it of that look of an advertisement which sometimes spoils even the work of so accomplished a photographer as Anton Bruehl.

The best of the color, whether intended as an advertisement or simply suggestive of one, is still part of the industrial or journalistic side of photography. But some of the abstractions surely do call for critical examination as private art. If the abstractionists work long enough and with enough meditative direction, they may come within reach of the photographs Stieglitz made in the twenties and thirties, before ill health forced him to stop, a full ten years before he died.[8] In what he called "Equivalents" (for a particular mood or attitude or experience), he shot hundreds of views of the sky, of clouds, of the sun, making unpretentious contact prints of the pictures he took with a 4 x 5 Graflex. In what might be called equivalents of the "Equivalents," he photographed New York City from the windows of his apartment in the Hotel Shelton and from his gallery, An American Place, and the upstate New York country around Lake George, and his wife, the painter Georgia O'Keeffe, her face and her hands.

If the abstractionists are simple enough, they may find somewhere near them a subject as various and as satisfying as the shadblow, a tree by a pond, that Steichen spent more than four or five years photographing. "Here was something in nature which repeated everything that happened in life, even to human relationships." He photographed it at different hours of the day, in all seasons, in every kind of weather. Every kind of emotion, every sort of conviction became bound up with that tree until the need for a kind of musical continuity made color slides inadequate and decreed the use of a motion-picture camera. With one tree he has said again what *The Family of Man* says, what photography must say: "The hills and the sea and the earth dance. The world of man dances in laughter and tears."

ARCHITECTURE

CHICAGO WAS as much the birthplace of modern American architecture as New Orleans was of jazz. Other architects in other cities made lasting contributions to the new architecture, but it was the Chicago school that most clearly enunciated the principles of the new way of designing buildings and defined them in the buildings themselves. In Chicago adventitious ornament was first chased off the faces of buildings openly enough so that any passerby could recognize the naked splendor of the structure for what it was. In Chicago the structure was admired for what it was and allowed to show right through the finished work. In Chicago the materials of buildings—stone, steel, glass—were looked at by architects and they saw that they were good.

Henry Hobson Richardson was a lover of French Romanesque buildings, of their simple forms and great granitic construction. He translated that love into his designs in America, most notably perhaps in the solid stone structure of the 1887 Marshall Field Store in Chicago, a building in which all depends upon the expressive power of large blocks of stone and simple bands of windows articulated in two- and three-story vertical panels. It is an easy dependence. Stone and glass can carry almost anything if they are designed well enough, which is to say, really, if they are entrusted to do enough.

The full strength of this sort of trust was most convincingly demonstrated by Louis Henri Sullivan in buildings in Chicago, Buffalo, St. Louis, Salt Lake City, Owatonna, Minnesota, and Grinnell, Iowa, buildings which are of the importance to modern American architecture that those of Inigo Jones, Christopher Wren, Nicholas Hawksmoor, and John Vanbrugh are to English architecture, and before them those of Brunelleschi, Alberti, Bramante, and Palladio to Italian architecture. In Sullivan's major works, and some of his minor as well, the force of an immensely gifted architect's feelings is thrust behind a limited set of functions to produce the enduring forms of the modern high-rise building at its best. Sullivan himself defines that force in a paragraph in his *Autobiography of an Idea*, famous among architects the world over for its italicized slogan, *form follows func-*

tion. He is discussing the liberating effect upon his designing of achieving partnership with the very well organized Dankmar Adler in 1881. As always in the *Autobiography,* he speaks of himself in the third person:

Now Louis felt he had arrived at a point where he had a foothold, where he could make a *beginning* in the open world. Having come into its responsibilities, he would face it boldly. He could now, undisturbed, start on the course of practical experimentation he long had in mind, which was to make an architecture that fitted its functions—a realistic architecture based on well defined utilitarian needs—that all practical demands of utility should be paramount as basis of planning and design; that no architectural dictum, or tradition, or superstition, or habit, should stand in the way. He would brush them all aside, regardless of commentators. For his view, his conviction was this: That the architectural art to be of contemporary immediate value must be *plastic;* all senseless conventional rigidity must be taken out of it; it must intelligently serve—it must not suppress. In this wise the forms under his hand would grow naturally out of the needs and express them frankly, and freshly. This meant in his courageous mind that he would put to the test a formula he had evolved, through long contemplation of living things, namely that *form follows function,* which would mean, in practice, that architecture might again become a living art, if this formula were but adhered to.[1]

It was some years before this formula was adhered to by large numbers of architects, but there is no doubt about its defining function in the growth and development of American architecture. Until very recently the creed of all avant-garde architects in the United States could be summed up as *form follows function.* Every really modern adaptation of American, European, and Eastern styles to business buildings, college campuses, churches, and private houses has insisted upon the pivotal importance of function in establishing form. And equally, from Frank Lloyd Wright's convulsive reiteration of Sullivan's ideas to the more restrained prose of Louis Kahn, almost every American architect of quality has insisted too upon the central place of "living things," of nature, in a word, in the evolution of an architect's style. What many have missed, I think, is the full force of Sullivan's statement: "This meant in his courageous mind that he would put to the test a formula he had evolved, through long contemplation of living things. . . ." It is the contemplative element that draws one again and again to the wide arches which spin and turn the Chicago Auditorium of 1889 through its stately arabesques, from the three that welcome one at the main entrance to the proscenium arch, to those that curve round one at both sides of the hall inside, and finally, outside again, in the side entries and above each vertical course of the main bands of windows and the lesser tiers near the top and near the bottom of the building. I can speak from experience too of the beguiling effect of these arches and all the rest of the well-barbered decoration of the auditorium upon speakers and performers on its stage. The hall fits its functions well; its live acoustics are in splendid contrast to the stillborn auditoriums of recent creation.[2] But functional achievement is not the Chicago Auditorium's only excellence. It is also a work of art, born of contemplation, that induces contemplation.

A similar contemplative quality infuses the Carson Pirie Scott Building of 1899 (originally the Schlesinger and Mayer store) with continuing interest today. Its open display of its structural frame is impressive; the intricately interwoven cast-iron decoration which surrounds the windows of the bottom two floors, set against the cool undecorated large windows of the building's upper stories, is even more engaging. A similar decorative power is not really to be found again in Sullivan's work until the 1908 Security Bank (originally the National Farmer's Bank) of Owatonna, Minnesota, and the 1914 Merchants' National Bank in Grinnell, respectively Assyrian and Persian in motif, and very close in spirit to the best of Wright's *art nouveau* performances. What the famous large buildings of Sullivan lose in decorative detail, however, they gain in sheer massiveness. The 1889 Walker Warehouse in Chicago, the 1891 Wainwright Building in St. Louis, the Dooly Block of the same year in Salt Lake City, and the Guaranty Building of 1895 in Buffalo are all handsome examples of the expressed skeleton of the large structure, with in every case but the Wainwright the eloquent arches Sullivan favored somewhere in evidence to lighten the mass and point up the entrance or the window detailing. In the St. Louis building, one of Sullivan's most graceful performances, there is just enough decoration to frame the recessed windows and crown the structure, a tender horizontal element set against the severe vertical lines of the window treatment.

In the Guaranty Building, a top course of circular windows acts as a series of charming periods to the vertical lines of the recessed windows.

Each of Sullivan's buildings can be described as he described everything in nature. They all "have a shape, that is to say, a form, an outward semblance, that tells us what they are, that distinguishes them from ourselves and from each other." And that goes not only for the brilliant office buildings but for the flamboyant Transportation Building at the Columbian Exposition of 1893 in Chicago, for the restrained little Russian Orthodox Church, St. Trinity, he built in Chicago in 1903 around a motif of incised roof and window and porch arches, and for the bold Josephine Crane Bradley house he built in Madison, Wisconsin, in 1909, with its fine thrusting porch sailing in the air like the bow of an ancient Norse ship. Other members of the Chicago school made significant contributions—William Le Baron Jenney (entertainingly and accurately described by Sullivan as an engineer, as "a free-and-easy cultured gentleman, but not an architect except by courtesy of terms") for his inauguration of steel frame construction; Daniel H. Burnham and John Root, for the undulating wit of the bays they fixed round their Reliance Building in 1890, their firm exposure of the skeleton of their building, and their expressive use of the wide "Chicago window," [3] and for their Monadnock Building of 1891, once again with a splendor of bays and an openness of construction, in undecorated but marvelously decorous walls which literally had to bear the weight of the building. But for all the undeniable skill and innovating courage of these men, it was Sullivan's contemplative exercises, with Adler and alone, that gave American architecture its identifying breadth and vigor, its forward motion, its experimental texture, its resemblance at its commanding best to living things. It would be years, decades, before American architecture would go as far forward as Sullivan's beginnings invited it to go, but at least there would be in the intervening era brilliantly gifted eccentrics like Bernard Maybeck and a follower of enormous gusto and irresistible mass appeal such as Frank Lloyd Wright.

Bernard Maybeck was America's Gaudi, a fantasist in architecture who worked in California, where fantasy should have gone down without a protest. But he was out of step with his time or any time, like Gaudi, a speculative architect into whose meditations in wood and plaster almost every style of the past entered for the duration of a beam, a carving, a column, a dome, but who was also quite aware of the advantages of modern steel and concrete construction. His pink stucco Palace of the Fine Arts, designed for the Panama-Pacific Exposition in 1915, is possibly San Francisco's most notable building, in spite of all the decay and lack of interest which it has suffered. Its animate arches and perfectly scaled dome could serve the pleasure of Kubla Khan. His First Church of Christ Scientist in Berkeley, built in 1910, is a marvel of carved wood inside—organ loft and organ screen, trusses and piers and capitals—and of trellis and glass outside. It is a temple for Ibsen's Peer Gynt or Strindberg's Stranger on the Road to Damascus. Elegance, caprice, romanticism—the words inevitably associated with Maybeck do not quite do justice to an architecture which is at once openly out of the French Beaux Arts tradition, in which the architect was trained, classical in its balances, and nativist in its off-center pirouettes in wood. His output was too small, his personality too retiring, to compete with the great continuing exhibition put on over most of the years of his career by his near-contemporary Frank Lloyd Wright, but when more time and study are given to his work and a more precise photographic record made of it than we have now, he may, like Gaudi, find a position in the history of our architecture at least as honored as Wright's, if not so public.

When Frank Lloyd Wright died in 1959, the obituaries accepted his own generous estimate of himself as America's greatest architect, as for long years most of the books and magazines devoted to architecture in the United States had been doing. Certainly he was the most skillful architectural publicist of the modern era. In his generation only Bernard Shaw could be said to have written better advertisements for himself. The question of his actual accomplishment remains, his accomplishment in stone and concrete, wood and glass as well as in words.

He was an original in the eighteenth-century sense of the word, and like most eccentrics very much of his own time and place. His buildings in the Chicago suburb of Oak Park, in Wisconsin, Arizona, California, in Tokyo and in New York, look their age, speak their periods unmistakably. Sometimes, as in the 1956-1959 Guggenheim Museum in New York, the periods Wright's buildings suggest are many years before those in which they were built. For the principles he defined in his 1894 architectural creed remained central to his working method: as few rooms as possible; openings "as integral features of the structure," forming, "if possible, its natural ornamentation"; everything assimilated into "the design of the structure," all fixtures, and all pictures, which should be "incorporated in the general scheme as decoration." He insisted upon the closest relationship between building and site: "A building should appear to grow easily from its site and be shaped to harmonize with its surroundings if Nature is manifest there, and if not try to make it as quiet, substantial and organic as She would have been were the opportunity Hers." [4]

The executive word is "organic." It is Wright's chosen name for his own architecture. To the extent that the "gently sloping roofs, low proportions, quiet sky lines, suppressed heavy-set chimneys and sheltering overhangs, low terraces and out-reaching walls sequestering private gardens" that he prescribed for buildings in the Midwest can be found in his own early works, they can be said to be organic. The Oak Park houses and Unity Temple are handsome exercises in horizontal line and plane, very much a part of their flat sites. But sometimes one wonders, looking at the struts and planes of Taliesin West in Arizona, or the heavy brick detailing of Taliesin East in Wisconsin, or the cantilevered slabs of the Kaufmann house in Bear Run, Pennsylvania, "Fallingwater," whether his buildings grow out of their sites or whether Wright has simply surrounded them with nature. And when one sees the open principle carried to its logical conclusion, as in the famous 1936-1939 administration building of the Johnson Wax Company, in Racine, Wisconsin, one is reminded only of the design of Victorian office floors, hundreds of desks lined up beside each other in a deadly monotony which reproduces all the worst features of the factory and is hardly relieved by the great palm-tree columns with which Wright intersects the space and, so many are there, reiterates its wearisome changelessness.

As late as 1949, in the large glassless façade of the V. C. Morris Gift Shop in San Francisco—ironically enough a store with a large stock of glassware—Wright was still working in the angles and curves of *art nouveau* and other turn-of-the-century design patterns and methodologies. The same is true of the finely pointed gable of the First Unitarian Meeting House in Madison, Wisconsin (1947), and its stone and glass interior, very much like the 1911 Taliesin East. And in spite of his often expressed contempt for the architecture of the Bauhaus, for Gropius, Mies van der Rohe, Le Corbusier and other creators of that modern architecture he described as "Organic-architecture deprived of a soul," his own 1938 designs for Florida Southern College in Lakeland look in parts uncomfortably like early Mies van der Rohe or Le Corbusier, or worse, like a poor perform-ance in the box school of international style by one of "the white-paint-men" for whom Wright reserved his deepest contempt.

Wright never did get very far from the shapes and forms of his youth and middle age. To the extent that those structures, following the occult inclination of his own limited taste, also reflect the taste of millions of other Americans who grew up in a world of horizontal lines and planes, of "gently sloping roofs, low proportions, quiet sky lines," etc., Wright was a major American architect. And equally, to the degree that he made Americans conscious of architecture as a significant art in which their own tastes could be expressed, in the design not only of their homes but of their towns and cities, he was a major contributor to the development of his discipline in this country. But his achievement as an architect is conceivably not much greater than, say, Maybeck's. At his best, he is a maker of decorative houses and churches, most of them finished before the First World War, heavy but not unpleasing arabesques drawn from his rococo imagina-tion. At his worst, he is a maker of factorylike open enclosures, whatever their purpose or function, the arch-example of which is the antimuseum designed for the Guggenheim trustees. On the outside it is a bad piece of 1925 geometrical sculpture, bearing no visible con-nection with its upper Manhattan site except its bilious beigeish color. On the inside it is a kind of side show version of Dante's Inferno, a spiral ramp which pushes the viewer up or down and gives the paint-ings on exhibit almost every possible disadvantage except absolute darkness. The architect is in charge as Wright clearly intended that he should be. Hadn't he written as early as 1894, "Pictures deface walls oftener than they decorate them"?

Wright's high rank in American architecture is not entirely the result of his own eager pamphleteering. After the pioneering of Sullivan and Richardson, there were few in America besides Wright with the necessary toughness of skin and courage of conviction to fight for an architecture of some breadth and depth and at least a modicum of individuality and contemporaneity. Maybeck apparently lacked Wright's self-confidence and ability to dramatize himself.

Wright's own students were large in number, well spread out across the country and many of them were in places of influence, but they produced among them few works that served either to identify themselves or their teacher—which may be a compliment to Wright, who emphasized with all the words in his power the place of the individual in architecture. There were, between the wars, some heavy centers of building activity, but they were more notable for the identity with which they provided geographical areas than for their picking out of the persons of architects.

In California, the Austrian Richard Neutra established a level for international style in housing which has withstood intense attacks both of elephantiasis of the imagination and of the conspicuous consumption which has been endemic in the southern half of that state for most of this century. Neutra came to Los Angeles in 1925, after serving time with distinguished architects in Vienna (Adolf Loos) and Berlin (Erich Mendelsohn) and with a large well-established firm in Chicago. Within a few years he had established his level—preferably the side of a small mountain—and his style— sharply accented glass, concrete, and steel lines, with a geometry of balconies and windowpanes in which the sun announces its axiomatic presence with the precise economy of a Euclid. Two of Neutra's best performances are the 1948 Tremaine house at Santa Barbara and the 1947 Kaufmann Desert House at Palm Springs. In both, rock and earth and tree play significant roles. The Kaufmann house has a particularly attractive openness about its architecture: even nature seems to be arranged to fit the structure, rather like a chaste version of a Wright building, with no pretentiousness about the large areas of glass or the chimney, and no rhetoric about the cactus being placed there by a beneficent and unusually self-conscious nature. The consciousness is all the architect's and he is not ashamed to admit it. But neither is he blatant about it.

The social usefulness of Neutra's open-faced architecture could be seen ten years after he settled on the West Coast in his 1935 Corona Avenue School in Los Angeles. There, what has since become commonplace in American school design, was demonstrated with charm and conviction: great areas of glass set the tone for classrooms which quite literally open to the sun wherever possible, on sliding panels. Trees and grass are also absorbed into the architectural scheme, quietly and rather formally, with no visible attempt to make a city landscape into a country one. The same principles obtain in Neutra's most dramatic performance, the Channel Heights Housing Project of 1942-44. In six hundred unpromising acres atop Los Angeles Harbor, Neutra proved it was possible not only to make dullness into beauty, but to turn the necessarily standardized forms of public housing into a collective work of art, unified but far from monotonous. "The duality of a separate beauty and utility," Neutra has written, "surely does not exist in outer nature around us, which, after all, is our precedent. When does a parrot or a blooming tree stop being beautiful and start to be utilitarian?" And in the same passage in his book *Life and Human Habitat*, he asks, "Can we stand a painfully chopped-up setting or is our very nature frustrated by it? The human organic system is an entity, a oneness." [5] And so, motivated by a conviction of the unity of the life process, Neutra eschews simplified systems of architecture and life which, as Le Corbusier sometimes seems to do, make everything rest on a unit of measurement like the golden section of the Renaissance architect. "If man, woman and child are our subject of love and study, we must recognize that they are not governed by some over-simplified, static, geometrical, or mystic 'modulor.' " [6] And yet what gives Channel Heights much of its special eloquence is its candid display of certain repeated forms— corners of timber paneling, horizontal balcony rails, outside stairways without vertical risers, windows which rise to the roof line, to be cut there like the photographs which "bleed" at the edges of a modern book or magazine layout. Perhaps what takes the sting out of it, what keeps it from becoming a blatant exhibit of modular architecture, is the fact that the repeated forms are living forms and forms for living —windows, balconies, stairs—rather than merely decorative embellishments. The decoration is in the function. Rarely has Sullivan's dictum been so successfully demonstrated.

Other California architects have not always been so successful in avoiding senseless display. In spite of the impressive early examples of Maybeck and the brothers Greene, whose 1909 Gamble house is a monument of taste and skill and resourcefulness in the ornamental manipulation of roofs and balconies, hundreds of architects all through the Southwest have for most of this century laid their designs on a foundation of adventitious ornament. Missing the bounding romanticism of Maybeck or the lightness of the Greenes and untouched by the feeling for form displayed as early as 1917 by Irving Gill in his stucco box patterns for Ellen Scripps (in La Jolla) and Warren Dodge (Los Angeles), and once again by the Austrian Richard M. Schindler a decade later in his ingenious exercises on a vertical motif in the Catalina Island house of C. H. Wolfe, they have succeeded only in demonstrating how much money their clients have given them to spend. The result is a series of caricatures of international style to be added to all the others in that lunatic architectural anthology which has been springing up all over southern California ever since the Hollywood colony discovered that it was just as possible to reproduce Hadrian's Villa and the Palace at Cnossos as houses to live in as to make cardboard copies of them for films. But these parodies cannot quite conceal the work of quality which has been allowed to grow up in between the fakes and the follies in the Hollywood hills and valleys and on the Santa Monica beaches. There is a record of the pursuit of the sun here which is classical for the modern house, and a conversion of bare mountain, grubby hill, and scrubby desert into garden, swimming pool, and playing field which may, if the world faces its population problems rationally, turn the least promising wasteland into oases.

Would that as much could be said about the solution of limited urban space made by the designers of high-rise buildings after the first generation. The skyscrapers of this century, until the time after the Second World War when American architecture came alive again, offer little more to the admirer of form or function than a series of broken records for height and the number of stories following aimlessly after each other, like the pages of an almanac devoted to the narrative of pole-vault and high-jump exploits in the same period. In New York, engineers moved from Daniel Burnham's Fuller Building of 1902 (better known as the Flatiron Building, because of its wedge shape) to the Metropolitan Life Tower of 1909 to the Woolworth Building of 1913 to the Empire State Building of 1931, finally stopping there with 1,250 feet, 102 stories, and miles of dreary space. One can still be amused by the way the Flatiron megalith fills its three-cornered space at the confluence of three major traffic arteries. One can still be entertained by the scale of the Gothic ornament of the Woolworth design of Cass Gilbert, a worshipful monument to the religion of big business that should have made passersby shudder when the building was still white and its crowning buttresses and tower still the shining crown of the New York skyline. Nobody with a sense of architectural form, tutored or not, could help but be appalled by the pile of ornaments that made up the Metropolitan Tower, a junk heap consisting of almost every known architectural excrescence, from cornice and pavilion to spire.[7] As for the Empire State, it failed as a mooring mast for dirigibles; it made a traffic hazard for low-flying planes, one of which did in fact crash into it; it made an excellent foil for King Kong, the mountain-sized gorilla in the film of the same name, and it has turned out to be a fine height for the antennae of the chief television stations of New York. As a work of architectural art it lies somewhere between the Eiffel Tower and a Bronx apartment house, lacking the airiness and circusy splendor of the first but missing none of the fatuity or featurelessness of the second. In its symmetrical balances—conceivably a concession to style on the part of its designer, Richmond Shreve—it lumbers into setbacks at the twentieth, thirtieth, and sixtieth floors to form the world's largest foundation for the world's largest phallic symbol, which only absolute innocence or humorlessness could have permitted Shreve to move from his drawing board to the top of New York. Some may argue, however, that it is a not illogical symbol for the city it surmounts.[8]

A much stronger case can be made for the building with which Chicago found its skyscraper identity, the 1925 Tribune Building of Raymond Hood and John Mead Howells. As a last gasp of irrelevancy in midair, it has a certain grandeur. Not even the Woolworth buttresses can compete with the Tribune's for meaninglessness. It is a formidable Gothic lump that says nothing, means nothing, and adds nothing except so much filled space to its handsome location by the Chicago River. In every way it was an admirable building to house its titular tenant, Colonel McCormick's newspaper, the *Chicago Tribune*.

Raymond Hood was not committed to Gothic. He was capable of topping a massive black building of some small distinction with golden ornament which all at once resembled the decoration of a Louis XIV bedchamber and the undulating forms of the product of the client for whom he built his tower on New York's Bryant Park in 1925, the American Radiator Company. He also managed wedding-cake modern for McGraw-Hill in 1931, a green symmetrical structure, beribboned with multipaned windows that stretch around every floor, and with setbacks so placed as to remove whatever elements of tension and drama the successive bands of glass and of green and blue terra-cotta surfaces might have yielded if allowed to proceed in an uninterrupted ascent or in less conventionally balanced symmetries. A year earlier, in the New York Daily News building, he and John Howells produced a moderately effective imitation of unrolled newsprint in an alternation of recessed windows and high-rising thin slabs, all of which emphasized the building's vertical axis. These pleasing lines were in strong contrast to the irregular setbacks, which occurred just often enough and extended just far enough back each time to reaccent and reassert the essential vertical strength of the structure. But once again, the points chosen for setback seem almost frivolous, like the adaptations of Cubist painting and sculpture for novelty furniture and decorative art in the twenties and thirties. If there is a conscious style involved in the choice of balances and imbalances, of essential points of vertical and horizontal emphasis, it is one of no great depth.

One feels a similar absence of any great organizing principle in the original buildings of Rockefeller Center (1931-1937), in which Hood was one of eight participating designers. The ground plan is impressive; it establishes a principle for the organization of space in a city that is self-evidently intelligent and practical, indeed a most expeditious way of combining goods and services and office facilities in the world of the white-collar worker. This principle was revolutionary for its time. It may still be—the self-evidently intelligent and practical does not often recommend itself to real-estate developers and corporation executives. But the rest of Rockefeller Center required no great intellectual or spiritual strain on anybody's part. Once again office workers could be herded together in great central spaces, or bands of offices could be wound round each other until they reached inner cubicles built on the enduring architectual principle of the Black Hole of Calcutta. The recessed windows and rising slabs of the News Building were repeated, offering the eye a conventional set of façades, a tone not in the least harshened by the precise center balance of the building arrangement, of Radio City, all of it set off in equidistant straight lines from the hub of the Center, the tall, lean, and almost-fresh-looking 30 Rockefeller Plaza. The sunken restaurant-terrace cum skating rink in front of that building and the gardens which eventually topped the small Fifth Avenue buildings and were built into some of the side terraces of the other structures suggested what could have been done with so large a plot of land if landscaping had ever been a serious part of its design.

Design seemed to come in fits and starts in the twenties and thirties. Never a whole section of a city, apart from Rockefeller Center, and rarely a whole building. The closest to an exception to this dismal rule is the 1932 Philadelphia Saving Fund Society Building of George Howe and William Lescaze. Its continuous windows and spandrels achieve a unity which the similar bands of the McGraw-Hill Building do not. The alternation of light gray brick and glass gives the thirty-three-story building, a colossus in the Philadelphia of its time, a remarkable lightness and delicacy, an impression supported by the handsome contrast between its two sides, one broad, the other narrow. The cantilevering of the walls beyond their supporting columns makes possible a wealth of light inside the building like the great shafts of sun Albert Kahn was bringing into the truck and automobile plants he was designing for the Detroit manufacturers about the same time. Whatever the limitations of the PSFS Building—and one can quarrel about its imposing but not quite integrated bottom stories—it is surely the most successful skyscraper of the period between the wars, one of the few buildings that suggests the character of the architecture to come, its boldness and freedom and adaptability to human needs, its sheer delight in being architecture.

The great vitality and versatility of present-day American architecture can be seen in hundreds of projects across the United States in which the simplifications of the international style have been altogether scrapped or amended or combined with other styles, original or imitative, to make the restless, constantly changing, provocative building design of the sixties. Shopping centers such as Roosevelt Field on Long Island and rebuilt city centers such as that in Knoxville, Tennessee, sprout malls in which fountains and benches and courts play the part in contemporary streets and architecture that they once did in Renaissance Italy. Apartment houses that boast little distinction in other ways beckon to the prospective purchaser or lessee (perhaps all too successfully) with ingeniously cantilevered canopies or umbrella marquees, and whatever their other failures at least decorate their streets with incisively angled bays, great glass-curtain walls, and gracious balcony patterns. On a Long Island sand dune four two-story wheels, called appropriately enough Round

Dune, draw the sun from every angle, open as they are in the center as well as faced with glass all around. Airports begin to look like what they are: anterooms to the most far-flung and entertaining of Luna Parks, especially New York's Kennedy, in which the large, round, brightly lit Pan-American Terminal (Tippets, Abbott, McCarthy and Stratton) greets customers like an amiable drive-in hamburger stand and the TWA bird in flight (Saarinen) looms before one like the entrance to the wildest roller-coaster ride of them all.

Some of the new banks look like supermarkets, a few like grade schools, one or two have the harem look, a great many are large and spacious and so lighted that by day or night they look like nothing so much as a museum of modern art. None of them looks like a bank, that is like the Pantheon, the Parthenon, St. Peter's, St. Paul's, or the old Columbia University Library, which were for so many years the molds from which banks were stamped. With the museum or school design, conspicuous culture remains the shining face of the banking institution, but there are even some banks, and ones not so badly made at that, which proclaim their function with outdoor deposit windows to which cars may roll up. And almost all the new banks are well landscaped. A tree may soon come to be as much a symbol of banking as a Doric column or a Corinthian capital, and people, especially those who spend their lives in cars, may come to enjoy going to the bank almost as much as going to the supermarket. The only trouble is that banks cannot offer their customers samples of their merchandise as supermarkets can. They will have to settle for greenery. That of course is quite fitting. It may in fact explain the willingness of so many bank directors to go along with grass and trees and bushes.

Next to savings banks, the dullest buildings in America used to be its churches. No more conventional architectural patrons could be found than pastors and their building committees. There were some noble exceptions at the turn of the century—Wright's Oak Park Temple and a variety of wooden churches with great descending gables and bold interior arches that gathered from *art nouveau* inventiveness and from much older American design an impressive freedom of movement and continuity of form. But the prevailing modes were heavy-stone Gothic and heavy-wood meeting hall, with a few motions backward and aside in favor of Romanesque simplicity or baroque extravagance. Much of that has changed now. The "contemporary" is the acceptable style, whatever that means to the pastor and his committee. Fortunately it frequently means allowing an architect to proffer architectural solutions to problems of site, budget, size of congregation, and, to the extent that church rubrics permit, even the ritual of worship. The results at best have been superb community churches and churches for religious communities, such as Pietro Belluschi's mixture of brightly colored glass, fieldstone, and redwood for the Baltimore Church of the Redeemer, with its unmistakable *art nouveau* associations, and the leaping roof and prow design for the First Unitarian Church of Westport, Connecticut, by Victor Lundy, which has all the stateliness and ingenuity of curve and line of a clipper ship.

All over the country church windows have taken on a new splendor with the polychrome abstractions of modern designers, whose ministrations have not been limited to new churches, but like the superb new glass in the windows of the Cologne Cathedral have been set beside older forms and styles to provide a leaven of color and texture and shape. Creamy white baroque and dull gray Gothic have both benefited by the contrast, even in some cases by a blunt conflict of styles. As much again can be said for the appearance of Marcel Breuer's Abbey Church for the Benedictine Monastery at Collegeville, Minnesota, and its college, St. John's. Set next to the drab colors and dreary forms of mid-nineteenth-century Minnesota church architecture, its large concrete theatricality lifts everything around it into significance, even at the very least in a supporting role to its bold center-stage histrionics. Outside, the 112-foot-high bell banner grips the eye. Inside, the lighting canopy, held over the altar by rods and wire, and the subtle hierarchical structuring of pews, choirs, sanctuary, and abbot's chair arrest the mind. Its drama is further enhanced by the simple rectangular geometry of the monastery wing also designed by Breuer.

Frank Lloyd Wright's churches are fussy, broken up into bits and pieces, like his furniture designs, that often require distance or architect's drawings to sort out. But his last church, the Greek Orthodox Church of Annunciation, in Wauwatosa, a suburb of Milwaukee, is a titillating exercise in light and air and circular form. Inside it seems almost an anthology of church styles, its receding balcony moving blithely into lunette windows much like the upper galleries of Wren or Hawksmoor, its fretwork and filigree iconostasis offering just the barest suggestion of a traditional chancel screen, its wide-open pew and pulpit arrangement evocative of the simplest sort of Congregational meetinghouse, its church-in-the-round structure curiously reminiscent of Father Coughlin's Shrine of the Little Flower in Royal Oak, Michigan. Outside, its undulating lines rise to a large blue saucer turned upside down to make the flattest of domes, its sprightly lines picked up again in the parabolic roofing of the main entrance. The church has its inevitable clumsinesses of detailing, its fidgety decoration, but they are less distracting than usual in Wright's work. It is at once a reminder of the strength of his first designs and the force of recent church design in the States.

Schools trigger tempers as almost nothing else in contemporary architecture. Everybody feels he has a role to play in their design, in their location, in their budgeting. Everybody pays taxes for schools. And into schools goes more than a monetary investment: our children live a third of their young lives there, grow up there, find their tastes there. But the central concern, as voters in New York City proved a few years ago, is money. Almost no one was disturbed by the ugliness of old schools, middle-aged schools, and modern schools in New York. Almost no one brought up the issue of the education of the eye involved in every other kind of education that takes place in our schools, that is shaped by the kind of materials used in them and developed by the way they are used, the eye that becomes an altogether urban eye or a city-and-country eye to a large extent as a result of its school surroundings.

Stock plans are the usual solution to the monetary problem, a solution not much better than the mechanical one of the second half of the nineteenth century which proliferated the dark red-brick and white-cornice monstrosities of American towns and cities, with their separate entrances for boys and girls, their scarcity of greenery, and ornamentation reduced to the wire netting over the lower-floor windows, which though designed only to protect the buildings from marauders at least were designed. The best of stock plans has a prefabricated look, with little or no personality of its own. But a mixture of stock elements and individual variations, designed for only one school, one site, one set of problems, can offer a school board a handsome freedom from assembly-line vacuities, especially if it makes good use of the surrounding land, as Mario Ciampi has in his recent school designs for Daly City, just below San Francisco. The best of them, Oceana High School, is cut, in sweeping radial arcs of concrete, into a hill over the Pacific Ocean. But Ciampi, at least after his first few designs for Daly City, did no stock-room work on his schools.

Too many school designers today surrender quickly to the exigencies of budget and the rhetoric of educationists and produce the low-lying string of huts and cabanas, capped with bubble-gum skylights and orientated to the sun, which any traveler across America soon comes to recognize as the second surest harbinger of an approaching town. The first, of course, is the string of gas stations, uglier in every way than the schoolhouse continuum, but an equally poor solution to a problem, with every easy concession made to utility and almost none to beauty. The school designer can boast of having given lots of light and space to the children who must use his buildings. The gas-station designer—if, in fact, any such man exists—can boast of having given just the right amount of light and space to the automobiles that will use his buildings. Neither has given anything much to the eye of the mere beholder. The children can correct this with their drawings and paintings. The automobile, unlike the chimpanzee and the child, has not yet produced its own form of abstract expressionism.

Skidmore, Owings & Merrill is a corporation name with all the impersonal coldness and lack of public identity of such a name. But its architectural performance for more than twenty-five years deserves a warmer response. In New York alone, it has produced a battalion of distinguished buildings—Lever House, Union Carbide, Pepsi-Cola, the 43rd Street Manufacturers Hanover Trust Company branch, Chase Manhattan—which rise literally and figuratively well over the fatuities and mediocrities with which they are surrounded. Skidmore, Owings & Merrill buildings have something in common: they tend to be geometrical, cool, precise, and to proclaim their measurements in exposed modules that can be counted off in segments of glass like soldiers in an infantry review. Where the firm designs—O'Hare Field in Chicago, the Yale Rare Book and Manuscript Library, a new wing for the Buffalo Art Gallery—it designs firmly, with few concessions to conventional taste and always with professional skill. It has designed so well for so long now that soon it will have to face a problem of its own making: its standards are very close to becoming the new conventions.

The depredations of Skidmore, Owings & Merrill imitators have all but ruined Lever House, the 1952 masterpiece of the firm's chief designer in New York, Gordon Bunshaft. All around it, glass-curtain walls have sprung up in profusion, a profusion worse propounded by glass tinted almost exactly the same green as that in Lever House and set in a geometry of precisely the same scale as the great soap company building. But the hack designers of the other green glass structures, following the line of least resistance in making their adjustments to New York's upper-story setback laws (now happily defunct), have swept their walls onto shelves as ill-conceived as the laws with which they were conforming. Where Lever House rises from stainless-steel columns and a garden arcade into a band of offices before plunging into its majestic glass rectangle, the imitators simply rise story by implacable story before achieving their dusty shelves.

The power of the simple elements of Lever House can be seen most clearly if one contrasts them with two clumsy imitations in London, the Castrol Building, which rests its large glass vertical substance on a horizontal strip of the same materials, almost exactly as in the original Bunshaft design, and New Zealand House, an imitation in glass and concrete of the right-angle, reverse-L structure. The Castrol Building is the clumsiest of mimicries, its proportions lacking any sharpness of contrast, its detailing cluttered and everywhere exposed to the eye in all its clutter. New Zealand House is not quite such a disaster; its proportions are closer to the severely articulated contrast of Bunshaft, with a stubbier foundation strip and a fatter, squarer vertical element. But by the time the building was dedicated by Queen Elizabeth in 1963, its concrete was already soiled by rain and soot and its curious flattop roof resembled nothing so much as one of the less inspired head coverings of the Queen's grandmother. The glistening glass wall, which reflects everything around it—sky and buildings and people—so handsomely, is a necessary part of this sort of incisive design. It is the mark of coolness and control which Bunshaft clients must toe if they want their buildings to retain their distinction. No papers should be out of place in these models of glass sobriety, the Manufacturers Hanover Trust Building at 43rd Street in New York (1954) and the Pepsi-Cola Building at 59th and Park Avenue (1960). And while no one can peek in the windows of the Connecticut General Life Insurance Company headquarters in Bloomfield, Connecticut (1957), or just up and over the hill into the great glass slab of the Emhart Manufacturing Company (1963), that sits quite beyond eye level on rows of concrete stilts, the impulse of all who work in these buildings must surely always be to keep their desks impeccably clean.

The emotional range of Skidmore, Owings & Merrill buildings is something less than wide, but it is very satisfying in the way that precision tools are satisfying, and new automobiles, and jet planes, and a hard, deep fall of snow on a well-made ski slope. And unlike tools and cars and planes and snowfalls, these buildings retain their look and feel of newness and seem likely to do so for a long time to come. One may tire of the precision and the unvarying newness. One may come to feel uneasy at the constant sense of exposure, real or imagined. One must be grateful for the clarity and cleanliness—real or imagined—which the Bunshaft and related Skidmore, Owings & Merrill structures contribute to their streets and hills and surrounding neighborhoods and countryside. This way lies a city with some continuity of style and coherence of street and avenue. And this way, too, older buildings, even those of no great distinction, such as the pseudo-Renaissance Racquet Club across the street from Lever House, take on a certain contrasting warmth and vitality, and the great tumbling variety which a city like New York necessarily pours onto its streets suddenly seems to make sense.

The place of the old buildings in American cities has never been so dramatically presented to the eye as in recent years. With the constant destruction of buildings of all styles and shapes and sizes and ages to make way for better-paying new ones and the shocking contrast provided by the glass-curtain walls and steel and concrete precisions of such buildings as Bunshaft and Mies van der Rohe's, all sorts of people who have never before bothered to think about the streets and buildings around them have begun to take their surroundings seriously. The disappearance of a landmark is moderately disturbing. The removal of all that gave a city, or a part of it, its identifying tonality is highly upsetting. And the objections are not necessarily trivial. More than mere sentimentality or a tenuous argument based on grounds of familiarity may be involved, as Jane Jacobs has shown so well in her book *The Death and Life of Great American Cities*. A thorough plundering of ancient blocks, even of slums and even for the most noble motives, shows up most of the time as senseless. For what it removes from the city is a great deal more than streets and buildings. It sucks character from its neighborhoods and reduces living to the barest fulfillment of mechanical functions—or at least tries to. It empties a city of its past and withdraws elegance from the lives of all but the wealthiest of its citizens, who can buy their kind of elegance by the square foot from interior decorators and install it in their hermetically sealed drawing rooms and foyers, far from the madding crowds.

The humanists of the Italian Renaissance gave elegance a street address. Theory was not enough. The ideal could not be allowed to remain a mere speculation on paper. Paper had to be translated into stone, the ideal into the real. The result was a *palazzo* around every corner, a *piazza* in every quarter—and not just palaces and squares, but museums and monuments of every size. The modern city is not so carefully put together. It is not even a modern city, but a series of cities of different epochs, arranged as well as time and attrition and the helter-skelter repairs of variously conscientious governments would permit. But even the most debauched of present-day cities has an honorable past. Even the most unlovable may have a future.[9]

The Renaissance city did not harden into a museum; it was designed to be one. Sculptors and painters, architects and town planners worked together to reproduce ancient Rome in modern dress, with a halo hovering just overhead, the perfections of this world and the next indissolubly cemented and glued together by masons and joiners. Fifteenth-century Florence was the New Jerusalem for the Florentines, sixteenth-century Venice the heavenly city for the Venetians.

When Francisco Zurbaran came in 1629 to paint a saint's vision of the holy city of the Apocalypse, he was quite content to settle for a segment of the Spanish town of Avila, walls and buildings and people and all.

Zurbaran's New Jerusalem rolled out of the clouds of his canvas, but it was very much on earth. It was Avila. It could have been Seville or Toledo or Madrid, Venice or Rome or Florence. It could have been any one of hundreds of small towns planned with art and ruled by artists. The state may or may not have been a work of art in the Renaissance, but the city surely was, all of it, the streets and alleys, the inner squares and outer promenades, the palaces, villas, churches, loggias.

The city of the Italian Renaissance was as much the work of the moral philosopher, poet, and painter as of the architect. But that was usually because the architect was at least two or three of those things. Leone Battista Alberti was all four and more—athlete, musician, botanist, mathematician, and physicist, sociologist of the family, political satirist, raiser of sunken ships. All his skills, all his interests enter into the work by which he is best known, the *De Re Aedificatoria Libri Decem,* ten books on the art of building, written in the middle of his life and of his century, the fifteenth. This book is, directly or indirectly, the source of most of our notions of what a city is—or should be—or could be.[10]

As an architectural theorist, Alberti remains a mathematician, musician, and moral philosopher. He sees an order in the arts based upon a universal harmony which he believes can be reduced to formula and design. It is entirely a harmony: Alberti draws his proportions from the intervals of the musical scale. In fourths and fifths and octaves, he finds delight, majesty, dignity, and beauty, which can be produced in space, if the same proportions are maintained.

We should find it hard today to accept Alberti's precise principles of proportion, but not the central importance of a theory of proportion. For from such theory has come the emphasis on the module, a basic unit of measurement which assures the modern architect or city planner of that harmony of parts which would be made, if not ugly, at least disagreeable, by the removal, addition, or alteration of any single part.

The Renaissance city was not only satisfying on its own grounds; it was complete. There was no clumsy mixing of town and country. Cities were cities, surrounded by country, but quite content not to reproduce it or even to make fumbling gestures in its direction. There was art enough, life enough, function enough in a palace, a group of houses around a square, a carefully planned district radiating around a monumental circle. All were well equipped, or could be. There was space for parades, formal and informal, space to hang flags and to stretch banners. There was space for flowers and gardens, flowers arranged in boxes, gardens ordered formally, to suit a city's needs. There was space to linger over a walk, to meet neighbors and to talk. There was space conceived as space, served as space, admired as space. There was space.

The same balance can be found in Lisbon, a city of many eras, medieval and Renaissance and modern, but one which achieved its harmony in the eighteenth century. "Achieved" is not quite the word. The harmony was imposed by the Marquis de Pombal following the earthquake, fire, and tidal wave of 1755. But what an extraordinary city was thus created: a city on hills, a city clearly of three dimensions, not only of squares but of cubes.

The suburbs of Lisbon, at least in two directions, are the sea. But even so, it is threatened with the same proliferation of garden cities and housing developments that promises to make the land from Washington to Boston into the Metropolitan Area of the future. There are good reasons for what William L. Whyte in *The Exploding Metropolis* calls "urban sprawl." [11] We all know them. There are also bad reasons, the worst of them a double disaffection, both for the city and the country. Americans have turned, many of them anyway, to their compromises-by-the-turnpike because they really enjoy shuttling between shopping center and housing colony. They have relegated the country to farmers and vacationing academics. They have relinquished the city to commuting businessmen by day and carousing delinquents by night.

New York will not lose its big corporations or the big buildings in which they conduct their business—more and more openly, through plain glass. It may lose its little companies, guilds almost, of flower merchants and booksellers, and its vendors of odd goods and exotic talents, such as taxidermists and horologists. One can still be overwhelmed by the fragrance of ten thousand gardenias in the town of flowers on Sixth Avenue in the upper twenties, or overcome by the fumes of fertilizer that protects the outdoor nurseries on the Lower West Side just above the financial district. But the booksellers are beginning to leave Fourth Avenue, forced out by parking lots and apartment houses, and it is getting harder and harder to get a moose stuffed or to find a face for an ancient calendar clock.

When the elevated tracks were removed and Third Avenue was exposed to the light again, some of the handsomest wrought iron north of Worth Street was uncovered with it. But this too shall pass, along with the moose and the calendar clock and all the other monuments of Middle Monstrous and Late Hideous that give our cities so much of their distinctive character.

Some architects are fighting to preserve the city *qua* city, if not in New York, at least on its distant outskirts, in Washington and Montreal. I. M. Pei and his associates have connived with the past in

Montreal, filling in the great open pit in the middle of town, where the railroad trains used to steam in, with a cruciform building that is not only a marvel of cantilever construction in itself, but also a fine foil for the cathedral with which it shares the Place Ville Marie. In Washington, just southwest of the Mall and along the river, in the acres that stretch from A to P Streets and from First to Twelfth Avenues, the same architects have put up small buildings next to large, surrounding four apartment houses with six to seven hundred town houses, gathered around commons. Like Renaissance architects, these men work with concepts of space, to which buildings, streets, squares, and whole cities are subject. Their principles are those of most of the architects of today whose thinking extends beyond the charm of a spiral or a latticework. The return to planned space, ornamental as well as functional, gives one hope that elegance will once again be given a street address in the city of the future.

Historical reconstruction makes sense more often, I think, than city officials and architects will admit. There are many periods of architectural achievement still visible in the slummy remnants of the past that clutter American cities, from which many sizable areas of distinction can be carved by careful restoration, street by street, house by house, and by thoughtful town planning, region by region, function by function. But even if all possible reconstruction is entered into, there still remain miles of mess in our cities, a litter of buildings in which human beings are condemned to live in dirt and ugliness on such a scale that no quaintness or genuine historical importance as architecture could recompense them for the indignity of their lives. These are the streets and buildings that must be begun again, best of all as part of a large plan for each city as a whole, but at the very least as part of a reorganized segment which will accomplish more than to replace dirty little rooms with clean little rooms soon to be dirtied again and to substitute for streets filled with children and garbage tall buildings filled with adults and garbage. More often than not in the last twenty years the replacements have been architectureless boxes, clothed in pockmarked red or orange or yellow or beige brick, and set in rows on a just barely planted landscape, like the miles of drab masonry with which Russian cities are achieving their post-Stalin-era identity. Against such buildings, in which mere dullness unaccompanied by anything really hideous is a mark of achievement, the worst of the old slums stand up very well.

There is, of course, the alternative of good architecture. But good architecture generally costs more money than housing developments should cost, at least as private investors and government agencies compute these things. The result, on the rare occasion that a development of quality actually does go up, is that the old slum dwellers are priced out of the new houses or that money has had to be saved at the cost of detailing and clean finishing or both. In New York, I. M. Pei's bold Kips Bay Plaza apartments retain their vigorous outlines. From a distance the great rectangles of glass and concrete look very much like the simplified Italian Renaissance shadow boxes of Giorgio di Chirico's early paintings, with handsome shadows forming across the setback windows and under the ground-floor supporting columns. But close up one sees all sorts of sloppiness of detail, like the rough finish and uneven seaming which one notices all around the edges of so many recent buildings, most glaringly, perhaps, in Frank Lloyd Wright's Guggenheim Museum. And the cost of the apartments is not even remotely within the budgets of the people who used to live in this area. Still, the buildings add much to the neighborhood of Bellevue Hospital, as in his project in Washington, where Pei's mixture of tall multistory dwellings and small houses has added variety and rhythmic tension to the warehouse and savings-bank architecture of the center of the District of Columbia.

The new monuments in American cities are buildings. They make better memorials than the pseudoclassical statuary and other Greek and Roman echoes of all our cities, from Washington, D.C., to Seattle, Washington, though perhaps they do not so often recall the events or persons they are meant to memorialize as the soldiers and sailors mounted in heroic pose around the edges of parks and in the center of great city squares. In this way, however, not only do the living salute the dead, but the dead salute the living. In Milwaukee, the first unit of the County War Memorial Center (built in 1957) is a museum and assembly hall in the shape of a tight, cleanly designed tetragon in the parkland on the lake in downtown Milwaukee. Its symmetrical lines are all one notices at first, but then, on the site, one sees its lower stories, cut into the ground in such a way that monotonous balances are overthrown, and within the building, just visible through the openings between the piers that support the tetragon, there is a glass-walled stair, free-floating, which brings the eye down to rest on a reflecting pool and the roll of war dead around it. In this way, Eero Saarinen, the center's architect, has made the center's point. Portland's Memorial Coliseum is not so impressive by day, when its small site is all too visible. But at night its oval arena encased in a square of glass walls is a spectacle of light on the Willamette River, with some of the arresting quality of a mobile abstraction as people move around in it. This should be one of the constant pleasures to reflective passersby in the Oregon city, as it is watching people change the shapes and textures of the Deutsche Oper in West Berlin, through similar curtains of glass, or noting the lines of motion of cars arriving and departing at Cobo Hall in Detroit. It need only be a corollary concern of an architect to add to the drama of his building and its site a suitable background for the colors and shapes of cars and people, but it can never be altogether disregarded without a great loss of pleasure and perhaps even more, of ordinary ease, on the part of those who use his building or any of the land around it.

The Royal Festival Hall in London, the city's chief concert hall and its only modern one, is not only remote from the central sections of the city, but poorly situated on the south bank of the Thames, with no cafés or restaurants or related buildings of any kind around it and only its own rather inadequate eating establishments to make up for this emptiness of facility and atmosphere. New York's new Lincoln Center for the Performing Arts, which gradually shuffled off the drawing board and out of hoardings into life in 1963 and 1964, shares this disability. It has around it several housing developments of a featureless architecture, a few churches, some derelict hotels, and some automobile salesrooms. Into these surroundings half a dozen buildings, designed by Saarinen, Max Abramovitz, Wallace K. Harrison, Philip Johnson, and Pietro Belluschi are being introduced, with only a certain relationship to tropical architecture in common and nothing to link them with their neighborhood. This is as serious an objection to the enterprise as the poor acoustics of the first of the buildings to be finished, Philharmonic Hall, or the World's Fair appearance of the composite model of the center.[12] Milwaukee backs its art center with a park. Portland and Detroit and London front their civic and cultural assembly halls with their rivers. New York, always remarkably shy about using its rivers, and never altogether conscious of the significance of its neighborhoods or of their traditions, can offer only apartment houses and automobile salesrooms, and does not have even the small comfort of handsome traffic movement with which to lull and beguile the discontented eye.

The eye that settles on Chicago from the air is bound to be charmed. Seen from above, the city's gridiron plan has all the neatness and precision of a prosperous farm, the blocks falling into position as inexorably as well-plowed fields. Close up, on the ground, Chicago is not always enchanting. The grid remains, but the way it is filled in is almost always haphazard. One has to know details of Daniel Burnham's 1909 plan for Chicago to recognize the way some of the streets and bridges follow a conscious design of variation on the symmetrical theme. Michigan Avenue openly proclaims its self-conscious elegances. Grant Park frames the lakefront broadly and brightly enough. But the double-deck construction of Wacker Drive must be sought for, and the zigzag motion of the bridges across the Chicago River can only be fully appreciated from certain promontories along the narrow riverbanks, preferably from up high in one of the city's central skyscrapers. And even where there are new buildings of great force or fantasy, such as Bertrand Goldberg's Marina City, twin cylinders, lipped for sixty-five stories with scalloped balconies, there are also ugly little buildings, one- and two-story taxpayers, crouching in the shadows, like hoodlums about to pounce, preventing the city from achieving its full measure of grandeur.

Almost as arresting a sight as Marina City in the new Chicago architecture is Perkins & Will's United States Gypsum building. Set at a forty-five-degree angle to the streets around it, the seventeen-story building dominates its corner site and all the structures close by, both the moderately interesting and the downright ugly, by its shrewd positioning and the fine long white sculptured lines that fix it firmly in place. The sculpture is unmistakably architectural, just barely ornamented with spikes at the top. But it is enough to give the building the fresh crisp appearance of a priest robing for mass, shining white marble surplice over opaque black slate soutane. Like Harrison & Abramovitz's small masterpiece for the Phoenix Mutual Life Insurance Company in Hartford, Connecticut—fourteen glass stories sitting in elliptical splendor on a three-story foundation, and occupying all its own block—the Gypsum building fights free of everything around it. It will not, like all too much of the fine design of our time, be wrapped in the winding sheets of dead architecture.

Chicago's achievements in architecture have always been shrouded by the shadows of other buildings, little buildings, big buildings, ugly buildings. The great granite arcs of Louis Sullivan's and Dankmar Adler's Chicago Auditorium of 1889 have never been fully appreciated by Chicagoans, although the city's musicians have long celebrated the vibrant acoustics of the handsome wooden hall within —not enough, however, to keep it in good repair, although present activities promise to make amends for this fact. Sullivan's 1900 revelation of the wonders of the steel frame openly exposed, naked and unashamed, the Carson Pirie Scott Department Store, has had to live with shabby neighbors, and has had something less than the tender care its glass and steel splendors deserve. One hopes for something better now that the city has moved from the era of Sullivan and Wright to that of Mies van der Rohe, now that architecture has been conceded a central role in the future development of the city. Mies's four high-rise Lake Shore Drive apartment houses of 1951 and 1956 make a brilliant black aluminum and glass curtain for the new city. From their incisive accents and those of the same architect's buildings for the Illinois Institute of Technology, the precisions of the Skidmore, Owings & Merrill projects—the completed Inland Steel and Harris Trust buildings, the Equitable Tower, the Brunswick Building—take their cue and find their balance. And Mies himself is represented in more of the same sort of steel, concrete, and glass geometry in the new Federal Center downtown and at 2400 Lakeview, an uptown apartment house of twenty-nine stories.

Chicago's shadows will be less mottled in future. The lines of growth and development will extend the grid upward in clean, clear, straight lines, most of which have already begun to form. Will this require an immediate contrary movement in circle and oval and arc? Will the new brutalism in architecture have to settle here to correct the flat precisions of Mies and his followers with its corrugated savagery?

These are questions that architects in many more places than Chicago have begun to ask themselves. For with the work of Mies and Philip Johnson and the Skidmore, Owings & Merrill designers and Saarinen's General Motors Technical Center and CBS building and I. M. Pei's Mile High Center in Denver and his cruciform office building in Montreal and the great inheritance from the years of international style which is deposited in city after city in the United

States, clean, clear, straight lines have begun to be banal and boring straight lines. For in spite of all the unmistakable qualities of Mies's marvelously well proportioned Illinois Institute of Technology buildings and apartment houses and private houses and the bronze precisions of the Seagram monolith that he and Philip Johnson designed and that has become along with the green glass and reverse-L of Lever House one of the classical architectural statements of New York's Park Avenue, the rising grid has become a threatening convention. A massive monotony has begun to set in along the business streets of New York and Chicago, and people of very particular tastes in modern design who never thought they would come to such a point have begun to be grateful for the neo-Byzantine and neo-Gothic and not-so-neo-Romanesque with which the *kitschy* structures of the first forty years of this century were faced and topped. In Chicago, the scallops of Marina City are being welcomed as a round of relief for the short-term but acute sufferers from the straight and narrow as in London the new Post Office Tower seems a blessing to those who find even the inept boxes of that city's postwar architecture too straitlaced to be endured.

What is needed here, obviously, is the sort of revitalization that Le Corbusier gave to architecture in Europe with his sculptured Chapel of Notre Dame du Haut in Ronchamp, finished in 1955, and his Dominican Convent of Ste. Marie de la Tourette, near Lyons, finished in 1961. "Finished" is perhaps not the appropriate word for these astonishing performances. For both make much use of reinforced concrete deliberately left unfinished, or sprayed on to capture the virile texture of the material, and all shaped into forms that affront the eye used to the restful squares and rectangles and polished surfaces of Mies van der Rohe and Gropius and indeed of earlier Corbu. Architectural students, usually a few years ahead of their masters, have for a decade now been moving toward the new brutalism, hoping to translate into building designs some of the opening to the subconscious, some of the sweeping spontaneity, of abstract expressionism and similar eruptions in postwar painting as Le Corbusier drew from Cubism and its succeeding movements in French painting the emotional freedom and force of his architecture. Some movement in that direction can perhaps be traced in the warm response of many viewers to the buildings of Edward D. Stone and

Minoru Yamasaki, and more, much more, in the spectacular fantasies of Eero Saarinen.

It is perhaps unfair to the architecture of Edward Durell Stone to inspect much of it at once. For if one sees picture after picture of his buildings, one comes to think of him as the great harem architect of our time, adding to the workaday functions of embassies, schools, art galleries, hotels, and office buildings, a heavy suggestion of the erotic. Working much of the time in the round, building up from podiums, he almost invariably drops a curtain of lacelike stone around his buildings or supports his umbrella roofs with thin columns that move round the large central edifice like silent Indian sentinels. The grill-work is a splendid invitation to the occupants of the building to climb up the walls—an invitation, I was told in New Delhi, that the first family to occupy the American Embassy in that city did not hesitate to accept. Wherever Stone's designs go, some of Islam goes along, even to the projected Trappist abbey in South Carolina, Our Lady of Mepkin, which, at least in the first published models, looks more like a mosque than a Christian cloister. But that is quite in keeping with the ecumenical temper of the recent popes, and certainly, considering its purposes, far better a mosque for the architectural motifs of a Cistercian monastery than a harem.

If Edward Stone's architecture frequently evokes the harem, Minoru Yamasaki's almost as often suggests the elaborate tombs built for the too-early-dead wives of Oriental potentates. His buildings at Wayne State University in Detroit seem to spring from the Agra and the Delhi of the Moghuls, especially when Yamasaki's works are seen in photographs. Exposed to the naked eye, they seem too small in scale for their bold conception. The screens against the sun which Yamasaki drops in delicate concrete cutouts around his buildings seem a clumsy kind of mocking irony in the light—very dim—of Detroit weather. Neither in size nor form do they solve the housing problems of a large metropolitan university. There is more of the same in his 1959 Reynolds Aluminum Building in Detroit, which translates Eastern ornament and portico structures into the materials of the sponsoring company and looks a little like the overgrown product of a "boy's own" construction set. By contrast, the St. Louis Airport building that Yamasaki designed, together with George Hellmuth and Joseph Leinweber, is an unquestioned success. Its barrel shells emphasize the hangar motif which has been so effectively used by European architects ever since Eugène Freyssinet designed his hangar on a parabolic arch for Paris's Orly Field in 1916. Once again, however, the scale is not quite up to the conception, though the hall is large. Walking through the halls, I at least have the feeling that still larger spaces are called for, that what is required is something closer to the *Grand Palais* rather than the *Petit* in Paris, which the airport design so much resembles. But there is charm in the design, a suggestion at least of the kind of playful wit that animated the great Crystal Palace of the last century, and for this we must be grateful.[13]

Eero Saarinen played games with his buildings. He was never entirely frivolous in his design, but he did, obviously, mean to delight the viewer and the user of his architecture and most of the time he succeeded. If he did other things, too, so much the better. But in a time when so many buildings achieve a somber monumentality as well as a certain utility, it is good to be allowed to find pleasure in a work of concrete and steel and glass as well as a certain utility. His most openly good-humored works have much in common: the TWA terminal at Kennedy Airport, Saarinen's bird in flight (1956–62), is not far in spirit or symbolic value from his Dulles Airport Terminal in Washington, D.C. (1962–63), a triumphant hammock of a building held together by massive leaning pylons; both recall the zestful undulation of the great roof of the Yale hockey rink (1956–58) and the sauntering concrete arc over glass walls of the Massachusetts Institute of Technology auditorium. By comparison, the neatly spaced cubes of the General Motors Technical Center (1951–57) seem staid and conventional, so orderly as to be uninteresting, and his American embassies, in Oslo (1955–59) and in London (1956), clumsy and dull, no matter what their excellences of detail and openness to the multiple demands of the Foreign Service. These buildings do not signify. At no point do they proclaim that joy with an assignment which gives the airport designs such lilting delight, and makes, at least for portions of their expanse, Saarinen's college buildings so pleasant to work or to live in, as for example in any portion of the central court or its hacienda-like balconies in the women's dormitory he designed for the University of Pennsylvania (1957–60), or just walking alongside the variously pointed roofs and spires of Concordia College in Indiana (1953–58), which develop such engaging silhouettes against the sun or moon.

The achievement measured even in sheer tonnage or footage is enormous. A walk around the 1,000-foot curve of the 1956 IBM Research Center in Westchester, New York, demonstrates some of the weight of Saarinen's architecture. In the sunken garden that separates the curving building from its attendant parking lot, he has caught some of the delicacy and tension of scientific research. The four bridges that span the garden moat seem to be the building's only connection with the outside world. Symbolically, at least, these corridors are free from the world's pressures.

The new CBS Building in New York offers another example of this urge to isolate his buildings from everything around them. It is that rarity in a big city, a free-standing building, all vertical lines when the shadows fall correctly, barely touched by the clop and clutter of the Avenue of the Americas and its side streets because it is literally untouched by other buildings and sunk below the surface of the street. Its isolation may not have any symbolic significance, but it does at least suggest the power a sensitive and tasteful building patron may exert upon a city, like Seagram's and Lever Brothers before it.

The thin shell and soaring lines of Saarinen's TWA bird and the leaping parabola of the central ribbing of his ice rink at Yale are fair samples of the daring and the delight of recent architecture in the United States. They have the additional virtue as popular art goes of making immediate contact with their users and viewers. There is no mistaking the powerful thrust of the ice rink and its dramatic concentration of architectural and thus of crowd interest upon the arena. Similarly the symbolism of the airport design could not be more obvious, though it loses some of its power if in a mood of algebraic substitution of forms one tries to find a precise birdlike meaning for the accordion-pleated gangways that open up to meet the airplanes.

The rhythms of Paul Rudolph's designs for schools, and especially his 1959 Art Center at Wellesley, are not likely to have a broad popular appeal, though surely they fit the curious assortment of college styles at Wellesley at least as well as, say, Gropius's Graduate Center fits into its milieu at Harvard, and with rather more liveliness and suggestion of emotional depth. The work of Louis Kahn will probably rest at an even greater distance from mass understanding and may even for some time elude other architects, for it fits into no clear categories, follows no particular school or leader, though in various ways and at various points it seems to have affinities with the designs of Frank Lloyd Wright, of Le Corbusier, with late medieval and early Renaissance architecture in Italy, and even with the most conventional patterns of international style geometry. But if one man can be said to show the strength of the present period in American architecture and to assure it of a substantial growth in future if it follows his kind of meditative freedom, it is Kahn.

With the work of Louis Kahn, American architecture returns to the contemplative spirit of Louis Sullivan. Everything about his architecture breathes the contemplative. "A great building," he says, "must begin with the unmeasurable, go through measurable means when it is being deisgned, and in the end must be unmeasurable. The design, the making of things, is a measurable act. . . . But what is unmeasurable is the psychic spirit. The psyche is expressed by feeling and also thought and I believe will always be unmeasurable. . . . You must follow the laws, but in the end, when the building becomes part of living, it evokes unmeasurable qualities." [14]

One rarely feels the urge to measure Kahn's buildings. Even during its construction in Philadelphia, the Richards Medical Research Building (1960–64), his masterpiece and perhaps the most striking performance in American architecture since the Philadelphia Saving Fund Society Building, so obviously subsisted in the realm of feeling that measurements were as irrelevant as they would be in the realm of feeling. Architects were interested, as they should have been, in the system of trusses, in the way the beams were cantilevered, in the handsome adaptations of precast concrete. Scientists were interested, as they should have been, in the system of interior spaces, adaptable to many different kinds of partitioning to accommodate many different sizes of research groups. But the mere viewer could see much more. He could see the towers, tossed about the small site with the occult abandon of the medieval towers at San Gimignano, in Tuscany, now close to each other, now far apart, spaced according to some inner spirit that measures distances in terms of spirit, a function at least as important as a laboratory procedure. He could see the detailing of air-intake holes and the openings at the top of stair towers, in which unfilled space becomes a sculptural element as moving as great areas of white or black or unpainted canvas in the painting of our time or as an unfigured sky over a multifaceted landscape. He must see the open laboratory rooms, which terrace over each other in their towers like the balconies of a maharaja's palace, a modern maharaja whose empire is all glass and concrete and brick and whose lions and tigers are visible only under a microscope. He must, finally, be moved, if this sort of thing can move him at all, by the skyline the cluster of towers makes by itself on the University of Pennsylvania campus, a small city of beauty in a dreary urban landscape. Certainly he is invited to be moved, for in Kahn's architecture of unmeasurable quantities, the mere viewer becomes sovereign patron. Wherever his eye goes with pleasure and rests with ease is where it is meant to go.

Another excellent example of the kind of invitation Louis Kahn's architecture constantly offers to the viewer is in his 1951–53 addition to the Yale University Art Gallery. A glass wall, set at right angles to two brick walls, draws the passerby into the entrance doors beneath as in a 1936 New Jersey housing project for the Resettlement Administration, on which Kahn was assistant architect, a glass wall set at a right angle to the entrance wall drew visitors onto a small patio and into a warm view of the dining area of the house. In the Yale Gallery a pause is almost inevitable. One must contemplate the linear exercise in planes of half a dozen sizes, in lines of almost as many thicknesses, perhaps the most successful of all the recent adaptations in this country of Mondrian's painting for architectural purposes. On the inside, once again one must stop to examine the shapes and textures of the reinforced concrete, which is unretouched, the construction exposed to the eye to see all its richness of form and style. The ceilings in particular, with their tetrahedrons winking at the viewer like so many star-shaped beams, offer all the visual arts, but especially sculpture, the most accommodating of modern settings.

On the basis of Louis Kahn's architecture, no prediction can be made about American architecture except that today it is unpredictable. This is its strength. This is its honesty. For when it proceeds without dogmatic assumptions and even without stylistic presumptions, it proceeds with the openness of a mature art which recognizes each new problem as unique and each new solution as equally without any precise analogy in the past. This is neither to reject the past nor to glorify the present, but to work as Louis Sullivan did, "through long contemplation of living things . . . that architecture might again become a living art. . . ."

POETRY

IT IS very difficult for a poet to strike a private pose. He is always making a public show of himself, however obliquely. If he does not want us to share his joys or miseries, he has a philosophy, a sociology, a politics, an anthropology, a religion for which he seeks converts. At his most open he is a preacher, a revivalist, a street-corner medicine man, a houri before a tent. More guarded, he constructs pulpits for others, makes their tents, bottles their medicine, or sets fire to their temples, opens a hole in their canvas, poisons their medicine. At his most covert, he reveals little or nothing of himself, sews his metaphors in tight sacks of impenetrable verbiage, and runs away from any confrontation with his puzzled readers. But even then, he is there, somewhere in the jungle of words, taunting, teasing, usually quite anxious to be found, no matter what his pose. For even when he finds himself looking only at himself, believing only in himself—

> I could believe that I am here alone,
> And all the world my dream;
> The passion of the scene is all my own,
> And things that seem but seem.[1]

—even then he must share the experience. Like Vermeer's girl looking at herself in the mirror, he is only too happy to be seen at that curiously satisfying moment, in the self-regarding stance.

At the turn of the century American poetry seemed lost in poses hardly worth making. Sentimentality and what passed for gentility were the ruling tones. Only a few scholars and scholar translators, such as Charles Eliot Norton, had any notion of what gentility was all about, or how rare it was even to aspire to that distillation of the virtues which Renaissance poets so much admired. True feeling was glanced at in a poem or two by Stephen Crane. William Vaughn Moody, not without a certain rhetorical gift, was incapable of either the harshness or the indirection his cries of outrage at mischance and baseness and greed required; his poems, after a few fair pictures, fell off into editorial gestures and grimaces that now seem tainted with selfrighteousness. Trumbull Stickney, a better poet than most of his contemporaries, wrote in his brief years a poetry appropriate to brief years—

> These are my murmur-laden shells that keep
> A fresh voice tho' the years lie very gray.

His counsels are melancholy, his predictions desolate—

> Live blindly and upon the hour. The Lord,
> Who was the Future, died full long ago.

> Awake! Give thyself to the lovely hours.

> Thou art divine, thou livest. . . .[2]

In his handsomely turned country memoir, "Mnemosyne," the landscape he rescues from the past has its warmth, but also, and more insistently, its cold, its emptiness, its loneliness, its darkness.

In this mood of landscape painting and self-regard, the poets who were to return American verse to its mid-nineteenth-century peak found little instruction. They were assailed with doubts about life; their tone was melancholy often enough. But they preferred the plangent notes of incisive character portraiture to the poignant ones of sad complaint. Their landscape was filled with figures, out of the Midwest, out of New England, out of small-scale histories, out of large-scale history, and out of cities that sometimes seemed larger than the country of which they were a part. The graveyard that comes to life in Edgar Lee Masters' *Spoon River Anthology* (1915) is a fair sample of the new characterization at its simplest, clearest, and most openly dramatic. The people who speak from beneath the earth and under the stones are all the people of a town—judge, newspaper editor, housewife, priest, Civil War soldier, poet—presented in moderate depth, in lines of a deliberate flatness. The ancient conflict between appearance and reality, brought briefly and superficially alive, acts as leaven for a cemetery of dead souls. As a record of small-town life, it has the same sort of interest that Thornton Wilder's *Our Town* has; its philosophy is no richer; its prosaic lines are perhaps more compelling on the stage than they are on the page (or at least they were to those who made the 1963 stage adaptation of

Spoon River into a deeply felt personal cause). It has some of the
smell of life if not much more, even as Carl Sandburg's clumsy
cadences devoted to Chicagoans—to the ice handler, the fish crier,
the milkman, the policeman—to "the people—the mob—the crowd
—the mass." But there is nothing in Masters as toneless, as trite, or
as unselectively plastered together as Sandburg's love songs to the
people, the people "who will live on," the people for whom he offered
his exultant affirmation, *The People, Yes.*

The best that Sandburg could offer was an essay spaced in free-
verse cadences like an editorial by William Randolph Hearst, and
about as rich in content. Vachel Lindsay did not have much more to
say, but he had an ear and an eye that could follow after his hobo
journeys through America with a jubilant poetry of the senses. He
could space the sounds and the images with a constant beat—the
sounds and the images of politics and of evangelistic religion, of
traffic in the Southwest and of life among the Negroes. His rhetoric
far outreached his observation. The China of his poems is of the
dimension of the vaudeville and film and circus figures he also celebrated so gladsomely. Negroes like his in "The Congo: A Study of
the Negro Race" were clichés out of the pulp magazines, out of the
slicks, out of jungles of Hollywood fantasy. His Altgeld, his Bryan,
his General Booth, his Abraham Lincoln, his John L. Sullivan, his
Barnum, are highly simplified figures, but they are sung well, sung
with conviction, by a man with an ear and an eye and a good songwriter's gift of phrase. At their very best, radio and television and
musical comedy might perhaps match this sort of singing line:

> Election night at midnight:
> Boy Bryan's defeat.
> Defeat of western silver.
> Defeat of the wheat.
> Victory of letterfiles
> And plutocrats in miles
> With dollar signs upon their coats,
> Diamond watchchains on their vests
> And spats on their feet.
> Victory of custodians,
> Plymouth Rock,
> And all that inbred landlord stock.
> Victory of the neat.

Defeat of the aspen groves of Colorado valleys,
The blue bells of the Rockies,
And blue bonnets of old Texas,
By the Pittsburgh alleys.
Defeat of alfalfa and the Mariposa lily.
Defeat of the Pacific and the long Mississippi.
Defeat of the young by the old and silly.
Defeat of tornadoes by the poison vats supreme.
Defeat of my boyhood, defeat of my dream.[3]

Lindsay had a beat, Sandburg and Masters some of the tang of life; Edwin Arlington Robinson had all the attributes of a major poet. Robinson's senses were open wide. Robinson's mind was restless and roofless, open, too, to the tempests and the winds and the bits of balmy air and sunlight that sometimes strayed his way. He wrote his portrait-poems, as Masters did, but with what a world of difference! How much more thoroughly he considered and how much more fully he drew the Maine people who inhabited his "Tilbury Town": Luke Havergal, who mourns a dead love; Richard Cory, who seemed to have every rich reason to live, but could find none, and "one summer night went home and put a bullet through his head"; Cliff Klingenhagen, who made a ritual of bitterness. Robinson could turn a lilting line if he wanted to, but he rarely did so without an ironic kick as an afterbeat. Of that, there is no better example than "Miniver Cheevy," the romantic drunkard with utterly unrealizable dreams of the past.

With these poems, endlessly anthologized, and the blank verse monologue which so engagingly apostrophizes Shakespeare, "Ben Jonson Entertains a Man from Stratford," Robinson has regularly been thrown at high-school students. With his Arthurian trilogy, *Merlin* (1917), *Lancelot* (1920), and *Tristram* (1927), he won a substantial audience—and the Pulitzer Prize. Later narratives, right up to *King Jasper,* published in the year of his death, 1935, present at a length that is sometimes tedious and always tortuous the struggles of a brooding mind to rise above the plentiful darkness to the light, the thin, the distant, the only barely perceivable light. He mocks a too easy pessimism, which diminishes into the grim farewell of Job's wife:

Whatever suns may rise or set
There may be nothing kinder for him here

Than shafts and agonies;
And under these
He may cry out and stay on horribly;
Or, seeing in death too small a thing to fear,
He may go forward like a stoic Roman
Where pangs and terrors in his pathway lie,—
Or, seizing the swift logic of a woman,
Curse God and die.

But he offers no easy hope with which to allay the fears and futilities. His emblematic "Man Against the Sky" is a troubling surrogate for us all:

> Whatever drove or lured or guided him,—
> A vision answering a faith unshaken,
> An easy trust assumed of easy trials,
> A sick negation born of weak denials,
> A crazed abhorrence of an old condition,
> A blind attendance on a brief ambition,—
> Whatever stayed him or derided him,
> His way was even as ours;
> And we, with all our wounds and all our powers,
> Must each await alone at his own height
> Another darkness or another light, . . .[4]

This Robinson, of the sour-sweet metaphysical meditations, this Robinson, of "The Man Against the Sky" and "Eros Turannos" and "Dionysus in Doubt," this is a poet to mark the size of American poetry by. His language is never self-consciously colloquial; his is an educated man's vernacular. His thoughts do not spring into modish styles; he set no fashions, he followed few. But in lines of passion and images of every kind, he presents a land, "a land where all days are not fair," a poet's land, a philosopher's land, like his New England, a place where irony is a guiding virtue and a drunkard's honesty provides a kind of comfort against the empty, the foolish, the falsely intoxicated:

> Here where the wind is always north-north-east
> And children learn to walk on frozen toes,
> Wonder begets an envy of all those
> Who boil elsewhere with such a lyric yeast

Of love that you will hear them at a feast
Where demons would appeal for some repose,
Still clamoring where the chalice overflows
And crying wildest who have drunk the least.

Passion is here a soilure of the wits,
We're told, and Love a cross for them to bear;
Joy shivers in the corner where she knits
And Conscience always has the rocking-chair,
Cheerful as when she tortured into fits
The first cat that was ever killed by Care.

For a while Robinson shared the post of laureate with Robert
Frost, a sharing dictated by their age, their New England origins, and
their often dissimilar, sometimes complementary approach to the
American landscape. But Frost spoke more directly to the mass of
readers, spoke more clearly, with an easier reach into the soil, onto
the tree, across the mowings, and over the fences. His very name
became an icon of his poetry, a hissing, purring, soft, and friendly
symbol of life lived close to a nature at once destructive and benevolent. Frost had his unmistakable intuitions of gloom, but rather than
Robinson's "blind atomic pilgrimage Whereon by crass chance
billeted we go," Frost suggests a sudden end, as he looks out on the
Pacific—

It looked as if a night of dark intent
Was coming, and not only a night, an age.
Someone had better be prepared for rage.
There would be more than ocean-water broken
Before God's last *Put out the Light* was spoken.[5]

He speculates about two possible doomsdays, one of fire, one of ice,
in a handsomely chiseled nine-line poem, which offers fire if destruction comes in one blow, ice if twice, like a double helping of the
bowels of Dante's hell. But even when his images are frightening and
his intuitions are of doom, the sweet clean lines hold no terror but
only a tune, and that one a folk melody familiar and quick to take
shape on the tongue. Talk of death is an almost certain harbinger of
death, as in the perfectly planted, hoed, and furrowed "The Death of
the Hired Man." Differences between men are not often solved by

men; no point in choosing sides or building fences which wall a man in as well as out. And besides, out of the darkness and the uncertainty, there is not much can come—except darkness and uncertainty:

> at an unearthly height,
> One luminary clock against the sky
>
> Proclaimed the time was neither wrong nor right.
> I have been one acquainted with the night.

Frost was never without his sense of tragedy, the function of an inflexible will in nature. But tragedy, his poems used to say, was no more worth weeping over than the cold which accompanies the snow; tragedy was no more worthy of complaint than the distance a man must go in a day, in a night, in a lifetime, before he can sleep. Nature's will looked at this way is not ill will; nature's will is simply its will. But Frost was not content with the dignity of the world he found when he took unfamiliar paths, when he stopped to contemplate the snow; he was not as much at ease as his pictures of a finely, firmly designed world suggested. He had glosses of unhappiness to write on the text of a world moving too far, too fast, into its future. It was as if the loneliness really did catch him "unawares," as he says in his "Desert Places" (1936)—

> And lonely as it is that loneliness
> Will be more lonely ere it will be less—
> A blanker whiteness of benighted snow
> With no expression, nothing to express.

And so he wrote in his late years poetry of an obliqueness remarkable for one once so public in his tunes and his rhythms, in his tales and his people and his philosophy. And in 1947 he published a "Directive" just mischievous enough, just mocking enough, just mysterious enough. He would take his readers

> Back out of all this now too much for us,
> Back in a time made simple by the loss
> Of detail, burned, dissolved, and broken off
> Like graveyard marble sculpture in the weather, . . .

There they would find an old house, and near the old house the brook
that fed it its water, and hidden in an old tree beside the brook,

> A broken drinking goblet like the Grail
> Under a spell so the wrong ones can't find it,
> So can't get saved, as Saint Mark says they mustn't.
> (I stole the goblet from the children's playhouse.)
> Here are your waters and your watering place.
> Drink and be whole again beyond confusion.

The mystery is in the broken goblet, of course. Frost's Grail, the
point of his parable, will never be understood by those (following St.
Mark) who seeing do not perceive, and hearing do not understand.
They must not be converted; *they* are outside the kingdom; *they* shall
not be converted. What kingdom? Ah, there is the mischief and the
mockery. God's kingdom or nature's? Or are the two kingdoms the
same? The poem ends much as does the fifth book of Rabelais's
Gargantua and Pantagruel, with a firm command to drink of nature's
plenty. Take up your goblet and drink, says Frost the Evangelist.

A similar mischief-making continues in some of the poems
gathered into Frost's last volume, *In the Clearing* (1963). He is most
engaging in the title poem, or rather the poem which fills out the title,
"A Cabin in the Clearing." In a fanciful dialogue between Mist and
Smoke that reads like some of the aery-faery talk between beggars
and fools in the poems and plays of Yeats, the inhabitants of the
cabin are gently mocked. "I don't believe," says Mist, "the sleepers in
this house Know where they are." Smoke doesn't understand why
they have not asked the natives of their world, and most particularly
the Indian, where they are and what they are; they have asked philosophers, they have asked preachers; they go on far into the night
muttering their questions to themselves. But "who they are"—or
rather, "who *we* are," to make the obvious interpretation—

>   is too much to believe—
> Either for them or the onlooking world.
> They are too sudden to be credible.

Thus speaks an old man on the brevity of life and the folly of those
who live it and cannot see it for what it is: a moment's habitation, a
cabin in the clearing:

Here are your waters and your watering place.
Drink and be whole again beyond confusion.

Frost never had the philosophical depth of Robinson, but his themes were not so far removed from those of the poet of Tilbury Town as they first seemed to be. Most of the poets of that commanding first generation of American moderns were concerned with the same subjects, with the conflicts between skepticism and faith, the tensions between appearance and reality, the too familiar, great brooding darkness that seems to settle over all so much of the time, the rare moments of light. Whether they did their meditating at home, like Frost and Robinson and William Carlos Williams, or abroad, like Ezra Pound and T. S. Eliot, or settled their minds with abroad thoughts at home, like Wallace Stevens, their themes were the true themes, the grand themes, the everlasting ones. They asked the fundamental questions about innocence and guilt, about transience and permanence. And wherever they finally settled themselves and their philosophy, upon eternity or the most transient mortality, they settled with a firmness of image and a brightness of sound and a contagion of rhythm that set a dozen other poetries going, as just a little earlier the French had with their distillations of the symbol and sensitizing of the human ear to anything that could be spelled out.

In a lecture on "The Relations Between Poetry and Painting," delivered at the Museum of Modern Art four years before he died, Wallace Stevens said, "Modern reality is a reality of decreation, in which our revelations are not the revelations of belief, but the precious portents of our own powers. The greatest truth we could hope to discover, in whatever field we discovered it, is that man's truth is the final resolution of everything." [6] The poetry of this successful businessman, vice-president of a major insurance company, is a constant meditation on human powers and the truths accessible to man. It is a meditation in color and texture and sound. The mind has tones in Stevens' poetry; every idea has a hue and a surface palpable to the touch. And far from decreation, his restless aestheticism is always building worlds, synthesizing from all the specters of the dead that haunt his poems an awareness of the endurance of essences that in time amounts to an irresistible conviction of the permanence of beauty. Like a piano-playing Plato with a penchant for the loud pedal, he hears the overtones of infinity in each note he strikes. But

unlike Plato or any other philosophical idealist, he finds an abiding
satisfaction in the shadows. The flesh does not mock him; it is all he
has—all we have—of immortality.

> It may be that the ignorant man, alone,
> Has any chance to mate his life with life
> That is the sensual, pearly spouse, the life
> That is fluent in even the wintriest bronze.[7]

Being is frozen in being. It cannot disappear as long as we and our
artifacts are here. This, Stevens said in handsome ways in his first
book of poems, *Harmonium,* in 1923, and in handsomer, even better-
sounding ways in the last volumes of his poetry. It may be a while
before the delights of "Credences of Summer" and "Esthétique du
Mal" and "To an Old Philosopher in Rome" and "The World as
Meditation" become as familiar as the delights of "Le Monocle de
Mon Oncle" and "The Emperor of Ice-Cream" and "Sunday Morning" and "Peter Quince at the Clavier," but they will, in time, fall
into place, blue, green, yellow, black ideas invoking a hope for order,
as they find their place in our imagination. And if our prayers, like
Stevens', are prayers for man, as the supreme being, prayers to man,
as the supreme being, it will be enough to feel with Stevens a
"Blessed rage for order":

> The maker's rage to order words of the sea,
> Words of the fragrant portals, dimly-starred,
> And of ourselves and of our origins,
> In ghostlier demarcations, keener sounds.[8]

Nothing seems more tangible than the world of William Carlos
Williams, a New Jersey obstetrician's world. But it is a world, too, of
ghostly demarcations, of chinoiserie in New Jersey. Little things, little
people, dripped, dropped into little lines in which the vital mark of
punctuation is the lowercase letter with which almost every line begins. Like one of the marvelously economical brushstrokes of a Chinese calligrapher, Williams writes a word and composes a person:

"The Widow's Lament in Springtime"—

> Sorrow is my own yard

"Rain"—

> As the rain falls
> so does
>   your love
>
> bathe every
>   open object
> of the world—

And "Rain" again—

> The rain
> falls upon the earth
> and grass and flowers
>
> come
>
>   perfectly
>
> into form from its
>   liquid
>
> clearness
>
>   But love is
> unworldly
>
>   and nothing
> comes of it but love [9]

The world has been more receptive to the typographical experiments of E. E. Cummings than to those of Williams and his opposite number in Brooklyn, Marianne Moore. But none did better than these two with the art of the typesetter, the special amanuensis of the poet, if the poet will give him the necessary dictation. What Miss Moore says about her art in her famous poem about "Poetry"—

> I, too, dislike it: there are things that are important beyond
>   all this fiddle.
>   Reading it, however, with a perfect contempt for it, one
>   discovers in
>   it after all, a place for the genuine.

—can also be applied to all the things of this industrial world, to all animals, to all people, to our minds. Like Williams, Miss Moore finds

enchantment just by looking about her. Like Stevens, she finds beauty
permanent, even in the midst of war and hate—

> Beauty is everlasting
> and dust is for a time.

And best of all, she finds no weapon so strong as a poet's imagination:

> What is more precise than precision? Illusion.[10]

Ezra Pound thought constantly about poetry, worried about how to
take advantage of Harriet Monroe's new magazine, *Poetry: A Magazine of Verse,* in 1912, to drive home to Americans the virtues of the
hard, clear image, and the vitality of the traditions inherited from the
Provence of the troubadours and the Florence of the *stilnovists,* from
the music and the logic and the meaning of Dante and Guido
Cavalcanti and Arnault Daniel and Bertran de Born. He wrote
poems. He wrote critical pieces. He argued in restaurants in London
and Paris and Venice. He translated from the Provençal and the
Italian for those who could not read those consecrated languages and
he adapted and paraphrased and translated from the Chinese and
the Japanese for those even greater numbers of people to whom the
wisdom of the East would have to come through the efforts of the
great missionaries of art—such as Ezra Pound. He offered instruction
in reading and writing and for a while had some takers—those who
ate and argued with him in restaurants and invited him to join their
movements, the Imagists, Hilda Doolittle and Richard Aldington and
John Gould Fletcher and their friends, and T. S. Eliot, who sent him
his manuscripts to be corrected. But the Imagists, for whom Pound
wrote some splendid manifestos, changed direction a few times and
then changed leaders, and when that happened, when they became
the Amygists, as Pound called them, with Amy Lowell setting the not-
so-hard, not-so-clear ground rules, Pound left them, as he eventually
left almost every group or magazine of which he was a part. But he
left them, as he left his friends, his enemies, his readers, his world,
touched with his enormous appetite for the past. Nobody else ever
could wolf down a culture as Pound could, but anybody, as he liked
to point out in his manuals of self-instruction for the "culchur"-

hungry, could read the necessary few volumes in the accredited translations, if not in the original, and become wise as Pound was wise and
as, soon enough, Eliot was to be, too.

All sorts of arguments are possible about Pound's wisdom, a
wisdom that led him to become an ardent supporter of the dubious
Social Credit economics of Major Douglas and of the Fascist politics
of Benito Mussolini, which in turn led to propaganda broadcasts for
Italy, his adopted country, during the Second World War, to his
imprisonment by the American Army and a lengthy stay at St. Elizabeth's Hospital in Washington as the most distinguished of the country's asylum guests. But very little argument can be sustained about
the quality of Pound's verse technique or the debt of modern poetry
to his assorted activities, a debt that the United States officially acknowledged in freeing him a few years ago. His most considerable
work, his *Cantos,* has gone well beyond the projected mark of one
hundred and well over the heads of most of its readers, no matter
how learned. Its Chinese letters, patches of quotation from ancient,
medieval, and Renaissance writings, and fragmentary syntax make
any kind of long sustained reading impossible. There are, however,
magnificent trumpetings in the *Cantos,* like the great blasts from hell,
especially the comparatively well-known indictment of usury,
"Contra naturam," of Canto XLV; a superb dip into ancient Argive
seas in the opening cantos; and through the contempt and misery and
ugly temper of the Pisan cantos, written behind the barbed wire of an
army prison camp, there are lovely cadences and lingering insights
into what he gathered so well "from the air"—"a live tradition"—as
one might gather "from a fine old eye the unconquered flame." [11]

The *Cantos* are a mottled work, an immense cryptogram for
scholars and pseudo-scholars. But one must be grateful for the echoes
in them of the Pound of the early translations and paraphrases, of the
snotty and the impish and the charming poems about his friends, his
enemies, his loves, and his hates. And if they send readers back to
those little works and the first large ones, the *Homage to Sextus
Propertius* of 1917 and the *Hugh Selwyn Mauberley* sequence of
1920, that will be enough. For upon these works Pound's enduring
reputation as a poet can comfortably depend, in them his personality
can comfortably be found. It does not ultimately matter how much
one makes of the complicated exchanges of mask which make
Mauberley into a kind of unsympathetic criticism of Pound ironically

presented by Pound in the persona of the critic. One need not find the exact substitutions for the other personages of this poem any more than one need be a classical scholar to appreciate the elegances of the *Homage*. It is enough to have such a compendium of ancient and modern custom, of mythology and the tabloid, as this:

> Who, who will be the next man to entrust his girl to a friend?
> Love interferes with fidelities;
> The gods have brought shame on their relatives;
> Each man wants the pomegranate for himself;
> Amiable and harmonious people are pushed incontinent into duels;
> A Trojan and adulterous person came to Menelaus under the rites
>   of hospitium,
> And there was a case in Colchis, Jason and that woman in Colchis;

Or such a portrait of the artist as a young man as this:

> His true Penelope was Flaubert,
> He fished by obstinate isles;
> Observed the elegance of Circe's hair
> Rather than the mottoes on sun-dials.
>
> Unaffected by "the march of events,"
> He passed from men's memory in *l'an trentiesme*
> *De son eage;* the case presents
> No adjunct to the Muses' diadem. [12]

The conspicuous consumption of the princely poets of the past that Pound practiced was even more openly affected by T. S. Eliot. He called Pound "il miglior fabbro," the better craftsman, in his dedication of *The Waste Land* (1922) to him, but he worked harder than Pound at displaying everything he knew about his craft, from fairly familiar tags from Wagner and Dante and Shakespeare and Baudelaire, to splendidly obscure bits of Tarot lore and Sanskrit. Pound was content to quote Villon in French and Homer in Greek and pun on Pindar in Greek and English. Eliot required signs and pointers: he appended a scholar's tail of notes to *The Waste Land,* most of which helped very little, and none of which explained the magic of his own lines. Perhaps it was a ritual magic, drawn from Jessie Weston's literary anthropology. Perhaps it was a colloquial magic, the rhythm of common speech as Wordsworth had never heard it or reproduced it, drawn from barroom talk and pop songs and the excellent examples of Jules Laforgue and Tristan Corbière. Whatever it was, it transcended its own pretentious and nearly useless notes; it went far beyond wide reading and Pound's tutelage. To some extent, perhaps, it was the open exposure of a soul, not as open as the exposures to come, but clear enough to make it all an engrossing spectacle, for the soul was a superior one and sensitive as few had been for decades to the language of religious experience. The shore that Eliot sat upon in the last lines of *The Waste Land* (that Pound had pruned so well) was the shore of the sea of faith, and now it was not retreating; the roar that one heard was of the sea coming in.

The roar, if the well modulated Anglican accents of the Reverend Mr. Eliot (as Pound called him) could be so described, increased. The world would end with a whimper, he predicted, as he made a melancholy attack on the vacuity of a life lived without hope, but the big bang of the world that did not end but kept recreating itself was a sound Eliot really heard clearly and he had hope as he heard it, in spite of all the causes for despair all around him. It was a world that constantly erred. It did not understand its rich Christian past. It did not heed the advice of Eliot or the wise men gathered round him in the pages of *The Criterion*. Only a very small part of it was, like Eliot, Royalist in politics and Anglican in religion and classicist in literature, and even that part did not take its politics or its religion very seriously, and besides it made noises much more like a romantic than a classicist. And because Eliot shared so well, in the manner of the discredited romantics, his prayers and his passions, his doubts and his aridities, he could always be sure of an audience for his struggles up to the top of Arnault Daniel's (and Dante's and Augustine's and Plotinus's) stairs, tier by tier, to where he found "strength beyond hope and despair," as he told us in *Ash-Wednesday* (1930), where he heard himself intoning over and over the *Domine non sum dignus,* the most noble of all confessions,

> Lord, I am not worthy
> Lord, I am not worthy
>
> but speak the word only.[13]

The sea of doubt of the early poems, of the Sweeney poems and "The Hippopotamus" and "Gerontion," had quite retreated by those extraordinary years in the middle and late thirties when Eliot was bringing poetic drama alive again in English with *Murder in the Cathedral,* his Canterbury Festival tale of the temptation of the worldly Archbishop who became St. Thomas à Becket, and *The Family Reunion,* a baptism by Fury of the Oresteia. But nothing in these plays quite warmed the heart so well as the *Four Quartets,* which had come out chapbook by chapbook until they were finally complete in 1943: earth, air, fire, water; "Burnt Norton," "East Coker," "The Dry Salvages," "Little Gidding." The last great long poem in the language, it still strikes many of us as an incomparable statement of faith. It will not satisfy an inquisitor; it is too honest in its doubts, too irregular in its passions, too ambitious in its spirituality. It cannot please a doctrinaire secularist; it is too closed in its certainties, too regular in its rejections, too neurotic in its dejections. But it must satisfy a lover of language, an admirer of meditation, a student of versification. For here, in the exquisite golden chain Eliot has made of the matter of St. John of the Cross and the manners of Dante and Donne, of the Angelus and the *Bhagavad-gita,* of Heraclitus and Henri Bergson, is a soul exposed in brilliant light, and the brilliance, one comes to see, is its own. The pretensions of *The Waste Land* are at most protections now. The affinities and affiliations no longer matter. Royalist—Anglican—classicist—these or any other categories are not really in it. It is the figure of Eliot, a figure of sufficient dimension, presented in verse of sufficient beauty, to hold us all enthralled and to turn us from his self-regarding stance to our own, not unlike John of the Cross and Dante and Donne, the *Gita* and Heraclitus and Bergson. And so we follow on through the drawing-room comedy cum mystery play, *The Cocktail Party* (1950), and the drawing-room comedy cum morality, *The Confidential Clerk* (1954), and even sit quietly and with close attention through the elegant inanities of *The Elder Statesman* (1960), for whatever may be revealed in this scene or that of the further adventures of this most happily public of private poets, whose privacy was never anything but a pose, whose public position was never anything but deserved.

The exaltation in the best of Eliot was never matched by any of his contemporaries or near-contemporaries. But it was a generously endowed generation that deserves the most lasting and significant of tributes, constant reading, rather than the strained attempts of literary historians to file its members in schools or movements, and then, almost inevitably, to forget them. Even a more considered appraisal by ideology or affinity tends to lose the individual poet in the group, to lose the thinker in the thought, or just as frequently to drop altogether the unfortunate fellow who fits into no slot at all. Thus we tend nowadays to leave undisturbed the septic shriekers who people Robinson Jeffers' narratives, all except his version of the "case in Colchis, Jason and that woman in Colchis," [14] whose name Judith Anderson's portrayal will bring to many lips, though not necessarily with pleasure. Edna St. Vincent Millay and Elinor Wylie are distant voices, a little more throaty than we like to hear now, with a tendency to gush which young girls at college and their college-haunted mothers perhaps do not mind. The Southerners, the Agrarians, those who were going to bring their debilitated countryside alive again and with it the nobility of their countrymen, can hardly help but seem superannuated now, after Little Rock and Birmingham and Selma, Alabama, battles of greater significance, it may be, than those of Chancellorsville and Chickamauga and Gettysburg, and fought to achieve a greater nobility than is dreamed of in Allen Tate's "Ode to the Confederate Dead." Conrad Aiken and Archibald MacLeish, much honored names, public names, have other associations. Aiken is an autobiographer, his short stories have at last been collected and so too his criticism; the fullness of his achievement now obscures his achievement. MacLeish has held a Harvard chair and is certainly better known for his play *J.B.* and perhaps better remembered for his sudden and violent outburst of patriotism in 1940, *The Irresponsibles,* than for all but one or two of his poems, though in 1952, twenty years after winning the Pulitzer Prize for *Conquistador,* he won it again for his *Collected Poems.* Hart Crane and E. E. Cummings, the long dead and the recently dead, are still widely read and even believed; they have the gift of sentimentality, which can be a gift when crossed with enough irony or satire or humility, though a bitter one. Only the oldest of the generation, John Crowe Ransom, who still writes, seems altogether to have grown with the years, to have grown as a poet while, for some of us, he has shrunk as a critic. His great grace is to speak his mind. He speaks it best according to the logic of verse, an Aristotelian logic—as he understands Aristotle—

In all the good Greek of Plato
I lack my roastbeef and potato.

A better man was Aristotle,
Pulling steady on the bottle. [15]

Jeffers' long unclean probings of the proud flesh of the hill dwellers and horse riders of northern California will perhaps be long forgotten, perhaps deservedly, but one hopes that not all the unchained lines of this bilious Whitman of the West will fall into disrepute. He asked a fair question:

> This coast crying out for tragedy like all beautiful places,
> (The quiet ones ask for quieter suffering: but here the granite
>   cliff the gaunt cypresses crown
> Demands what victim? . . . .) [16]

He answered it badly. But those who ask the fair questions are our best citizens, our necessary Socrates'; if we forget them, we must at least remember their questions.

Allen Tate wrote a better poem in prose about the Civil War, *The Fathers* (1938), than ever he wrote in verse, a better book than any other we have about the Civil War, sick with the conflict, macabre with it, mournful and compassionate, and written in a style fit for love. The novel is moving as none of the poems are, nicely done as they are, neatly done as they are. His short-lived confrere, John Peale Bishop, left behind a poetry of more urgent life, doleful with the death of F. Scott Fitzgerald ("The Hours"), mirthful with the tragedy of Othello and Desdemona ("Speaking of Poetry"), simple again and again with the simplicity of adolescent, of Freudian dreams, like his novel about a race-crossing, race-battering sexuality in a not very distant South, *Act of Darkness* (1935).[17]

The poetry of Archibald MacLeish is professional, assured, well versed in the different manners that at different times win different prizes. But in spite of many attempts, much energy, a great flapping of wings, like Leonardo or Lindbergh about to take off, it is not a poetry with any special power to rouse either the many or the few to any of MacLeish's militancies. I myself would rather face the morning, noon, or night with Aiken's Senlin, standing before a mirror tying his tie, make my overtures and recapitulations in his simple and always singable keys, and stand with him at seventy as at forty, letting his self-regard stand surrogate for all others, remembering that

                              we who divine
          divine ourselves, divine our own divinity
                              it is the examination
      of godhead by godhead
                              the imagination
      of that which it is to be divine. [18]

Hart Crane's cleft pallet never caught a dream intact. He was joggled too much in his sleep, broken too much when he awoke. He wrote of "The Harbor Dawn,"

      Insistently through sleep—a tide of voices—
      They meet you listening midway in your dream,
      The long, tired sounds, fog-insulated noises:
      Gongs in white surplices, beshrouded wails,
      Far strum of fog horn . . . signals dispersed in veils. [19]

But it was not only the dawn that brought its tide of voices. Every hour for Crane was an hour of long, tired sounds, which he rationalized, now with the open sentimentality of a patriot, now with the closed sentimentality of a frustrated lover. His patriotism was not only for his country, but for his country in his time, when it was building bridges and playing jazz and riding the subways and staying awake all night, as uncomfortable in the automobile, the nightclub, the subway car, as Crane on his shapeless bed underneath the bridge, beside the river, in Brooklyn. His love was bound to be frustrated; it was bound to a homosexuality that never brought fulfillment, though occasionally it seemed very close to it, and once or twice was accompanied by a genuine if brief friendship. But perhaps the broken condition of such a life, snapped shut with a sudden leap from a ship, was the only one that could snap open so rewardingly for others the time of Crane's life, the twenties and the first of the thirties, to see so quickly, so harshly, so well, the legend latent in things, in American things, in Brooklyn things, in a bridge, in a river, in the

Damp tonnage and alluvial march of days—
Nights turbid, vascular with silted shale
And roots surrendered down of moraine clays. . . .

That vision will remain, remain in spite of jagged lines, jerky rhythms, clumsy rhetoric, fractured dreams. The fragments, sentimentalized but convincing, are enough.

E. E. Cummings goes down more easily than Crane. His verse is better oiled, funnier, nastier, wittier, wiser, more entertaining by far. The trouble with the wit, the trouble with the fun, the trouble with the nastiness is the familiar trouble with this sort of game: it stales the third time round; it embarrasses; the contrivances hit one in the eye, in the mouth, in the mind, until one doesn't want to see them or say them or even think them. And the trouble with the sentimentality is that one grows older than it and gets over it. But neither trouble should dim the eye or close the mouth or the mind to the wisdom. The wisdom is there, inside the maneuverings of syntax, the contortions of punctuation, the adoration of the blatantly lowercase word. It is a wisdom of warnings—diagnosis,

> Progress is a comfortable disease:

leading to prognosis,

> We doctors know
>
> a hopeless case if—listen: there's a hell
> of a good universe next door; let's go

It is a wisdom of a timeless unconcern; take the world as it is or you will be taken:

> Blow soon to never and never to twice
> (blow life to isn't: blow death to was)
> —all nothing's only our hugest home;
> the most who die, the more we live

It isn't the most sturdy of metaphysics he offers, but it is an affirmation of life as large as the furtive mechanics of a satirical sentimentalist can allow it to be. At its most open it turns tender, turns joyous, turns loving, and a technique so often in the service of affectation,

serves affection instead. The handsomest examples of the openness
reach back in time through the poet's life, none more movingly than
the poem that begins "my father moved through dooms of love" and
ends

> though dull were all we taste as bright,
> bitter all utterly things sweet,
> maggoty minus and dumb death
> all we inherit, all bequeath
>
> and nothing quite so least as truth
> —i say though hate were why men breathe—
> because my father lived his soul
> love is the whole and more than all [20]

How much of the time Theodore Roethke was reviewed with
reservations, how often cast in the too familiar role of the poet who
has not quite fulfilled his great promise, as if he had given an under-
taking to produce volumes of greatness, signed a note at a bank—so
many volumes of greatness a decade, so many in a life. Now his life is
over and we will have to take him as he was, unfulfilled, undelivered,
just a poet sweet in words, marvelously easy to read; uncomfortably
imitative, especially in the meters and matters he cribbed (with open
acknowledgement, like a thief at confession) from Yeats; slightest,
like so many others, when most determined to be substantial; most
delightful, like very few others, when he simply allowed the words to
come, when they were simply *Words for the Wind,* as he called his
most careful culling of his poems for collective publication.

He hears "the flowers drinking in their light." When reincarnation
enters his random meditations in a field, he thinks he will come
back

> As a snake or a raucous bird,
> Or, with luck, as a lion. [21]

He pipes the songs of childhood:

> There Once was a Cow with a Double Udder.
> When I think of it now, I just have to Shudder!
> She was too much for One, you can bet your Life:
> She had to be Milked by a Man and His Wife.

Of the sloth, he reports:

> should you call his manner Smug,
> He'll sigh and give his Branch a Hug;
>
> Then off again to Sleep he goes,
> Still swaying gently by his toes,
> And you just know he knows he knows.

He is painful, pleasing, full of personal hurt and the strained happiness of love at the edge of the grave, in his poems of mourning, "The Lost Son" and "Elegy for Jane." Let us by all means reject Roethke's awkward imitations, have none of such poor assemblies of other men's metaphysics as the quartet of poems called "Four for Sir John Davies" by this least metaphysical of poets. But let us not, while we are rejecting, reject too much, nor be taken in too quickly by the bright square openness of the title poem of his first volume, *The Open House:*

> My truths are all foreknown,
> This anguish self-revealed.
> I'm naked to the bone,
> With nakedness my shield.
> Myself is what I wear:
> I keep the spirit spare.

The spirit may have been spare; the flesh was not, nor is the verse it bodified, through health and illness, through jubilation and despair. It was enough that he wore himself; himself was enough to wear. It is cause for weeping that he wore himself out. For no one who comes after, no one writing in America today, is quite as much fun to read, none so natural a poet as he.

There is a plenitude of good poets, of good poems, in America today. That only a few have broken through to the public consciousness, even among those who have been publishing for two decades or more, is no reason to mourn the state of our poetry or find us low in poets. The first shock of self-awareness is over. We know now that poets do grow up in America, that they come one after the other, that they come in remarkable number, though not all are to be numbered

among the remarkable. The most startling thing about them is how
easily they write, how often, with what absence of ceremony. Like
Karl Shapiro, in his "Elegy Written on a Frontporch," the occasion is
very frequently ordinary; it may even, in fact, be ordinariness:

> The sun burns on its sultry wick;
> Stratus and cumulus unite.
> I who am neither well nor sick
> Sit in a wicker chair and write. [22]

The view is not like El Greco's Toledo or Tintoretto's Venice. In
spite of the Reverend Mr. Eliot and the rather differently reverent
Yeats, the vision is a truncated one, lacking any outer distances
except those that can be measured. Shapiro's measurements and
views are of some years ago, but the sentiments are up-to-date:

> I face a heaven half-destroyed,
> A skyscape alabaster, dead.
> One living shadow on the void,
> A Flying Fortress drones ahead.

The modern landscape in which the castles are all in the air
(Flying Fortresses), and the most dazzling stratus or cumulus may be
the stream of a supersonic jet, has not yet produced an enduring
poetry, but it has provided a background for poets, one which they
have literally put at their back, as they have moved away from it. In
many cases, the motion, like its motivation, is academic; the vocabulary, the references, the whole tone are drawn from other men's
verses; the poetry becomes, then, a poetry of poetry, in which all that
is unmistakably genuine is the reading experience of the poet; no
other experience is really presented to view. But there are other cases,
other kinds of poetry, in which all the experiences mix, as in the
poems of John Berryman or Delmore Schwartz or Richard Wilbur,
where the reading and the living are one, and enough feeling rises to
the surface to make an experience for the reader. But this is a mixture
that becomes increasingly hard to prepare. Even our most gifted
poets find it ever harder to bring all that they are and do and believe
into the texture, into the tone, into the life of their poems. They turn
then, some of them, too many of them, to case histories, confessions

from the couch or brought hot from the group-therapy oven where numbers are cured together. Inevitably the cases whose histories they know best are their own and those of their family, and it is those they regale us with and to which we must pay the kind of embarrassed attention that comes from trying to fill in all the interstices—how long was it that Robert Lowell was put away for? Was he really in jail as a CO? What sort of breakdown did he suffer? What's that really mean, about the Miltown and Mother's bed and getting drunk with the Rahvs? Anything like the drinks he drank with Delmore Schwartz? And what *really* happened between W. D. Snodgrass and his wife? Who made whom gray, who brought on the dullness? Some people enjoy this sort of revelation. I would rather follow Eliot's footnotes wherever they lead, even when they only lead from ritual to romance, and track down Pound's Chinese ideograms stroke by stroke, even when they bring me no closer to the *tao* than the name of an obscure emperor.

The real failure of these *Life Studies,* as Lowell calls them, is a failure of matter. With nothing more significant to write about, or nothing in these experiences that signifies any more than the experiences themselves, the poets who offer us this sort of anatomizing are reduced to the thinnest sort of naturalism. It is the Henry Miller of the *Tropics* without even the slightest gloss of fiction; letters from bed, from the bathroom, from a desolate day in the attic, made a little more tolerable to the squirming spectator by the finished manner of the poets. And the manner is good, impressive, metrically sure, sonically sound. As we read Lowell now, we still remember the elegant craftsmanship displayed in "The Quaker Graveyard in Nantucket" (1946)—

> Atlantic, you are fouled with the blue sailors,
> Sea-monsters, upward angel, downward fish:
> Unmarried and corroding, spare of flesh,
> Mart once of supercilious, wing'd clippers,
> Atlantic, where your bell-trap guts its spoil
> You could cut the brackish winds with a knife
> Here in Nantucket, and cast up the time
> When the Lord God formed man from the sea's slime

—still remember the skill brought to such a shine in "Falling Asleep over the Aeneid" (1950), where an old man's dream is given a young

man's urgency, and the classicism of Rome and of Boston meet trem-
blingly through eighty-six well-made lines; near the beginning—

> I hold
> The sword that Dido used. It tries to speak,
> A bird with Dido's sworded breast. Its beak
> Clangs and ejaculates the Punic word
> I hear the bird-priest chirping like a bird.

—and at the end—

> I hold
> His sword to keep from falling, for the dust
> On the stuffed birds is breathless, for the bust
> Of young Augustus weighs on Vergil's shelf:
> It scowls into my glasses at itself.

The skill still permeates the agonizing confessions of *Life Studies,* but
how much better, in the same volume, the more detached wit and the
bemused tone of "Skunk Hour" or the compassionate monologue
written as "Words for Hart Crane." [23]

Snodgrass's careful inventories of his emotions are not quite so
self-revealing, not quite so agonizing, as the recent Lowell, in spite of
his insistence "that our only hope as artists is to continually ask
ourselves, 'Am I writing what I *really* think? Not what is acceptable;
not what my favorite intellectual would think in this situation; not
what I wish I felt. Only what I cannot help thinking.' " But his
energies as a poet of the tortured and the threatened, the sick and the
sickened, are enormous, and his skill as a spinner of assonances and
drummer of beats is very large. His colloquies with himself are variously painful, affecting, cautionary. His fight with a bird, "A Cardi-
nal," is a fine tussle with religion, philosophy, the academic mind,
and the academic vocation. But nowhere is he more effective than in
that splendid long poem of love and fission in the family and in the
world, "Heart's Needle," the best of Snodgrass's plaints. This is
Snodgrass offering us what he *really* thinks and feels, in the most
universalized of his plaints. Family separation and a sense of sterility
produce a sense of oneness with Onan and all the incomplete, the
truncated, the unborn:

        I stand by the unborn,
    by putty-colored children curled
        in jars of alcohol,
    that waken to no other world,
    unchanging, where no eye shall mourn.
        I see the caul
        that wrapped a kitten, dead.
    I see the branching, doubled throat
        of a two-headed foal;
    I see the hydrocephalic goat;
    here is the curled and swollen head,
        there, the burst skull. . . .[24]

A similar anguish snakes its way through the jungle of the Beats, but it never finds a comparable eloquence. The universality of Beat emotion is the language of the tabloid and the jazz joint and the saloon. The depths are rarely touched in the poetry of the Beats, not in Allen Ginsberg's "Howl," where the number of letters in the title is too often the cipher of the poem's philosophy, not in the more skillful lines of Lawrence Ferlinghetti or Gregory Corso. The Beats work too often with plasticene, with mud, with manure. But, as Denise Levertov, a poet with a full share of ordinary man's language and emotions, says in her variations on a well-known theme by Théophile Gautier,

            The best work is made
            from hard, strong materials,
                obstinately precise—
            the line of the poem, onyx, steel.

            It's not a question of
            false constraints—but
                to move well and get somewhere
            wear shoes that fit.

            To hell with easy rhythms—
            sloppy mules that anyone can
                kick off or
            step into.[25]

This is not the time of the poets of the hard file; Horace's age in America is long past and will not come again for this world or these woes. Woe-sayers speak now a less polite language, crumple hearts like playing cards, come happily tousled, dirty, and sticky from their beds of misery. But no matter how pleased the public becomes with displeasure, no matter how large the profits of confession and contrition expressed in autobiographical works, there will always be some to attend the austere ceremonies of the other kinds of poetry, the rituals of restraint.

Critics will admire the poetry of Richard Wilbur and reject it at the same time for its facility, its admirable precisions that too quickly solicit admiration, its unmistakable, its unshakable professionalness. But if one examines in detail and at length all the poetry of Wilbur, as on two occasions now I have done—the four volumes of 1947, 1950, 1954, 1961; his translation of Molière's *The Misanthrope*; his lyrics for the Lillian Hellman–Leonard Bernstein musical version of *Candide* —one ceases soon enough to cavil about perfections that roll too easily on and off the page. It is enough that such ease, Wordsworthian almost, comes into our speech, realizes a twentieth-century American childhood, draws together laundry and St. Augustine, makes familiar objects classical, and turns anguish into a stately literary language:

> What can I do but move
> From folly to defeat,
> And call that sorrow sweet
> That teaches us to see
> The final face of love
> In what we cannot be? [26]

This is the precision of some of the best poetry of our time, of Delmore Schwartz's masterpiece of meditation on the indissolubility of body and soul, "The Heavy Bear," which provides the careful reader with a gloss of a line by Whitehead, and an addendum to Augustine; of John Berryman's *Hymn to Anne Bradstreet,* of the sea poems of Philip Booth, and the largeness of his condensed writing, say in "Marin," which brings all his excellences together; of the verbal sleight of hand of George Starbuck; of the university poems of Louis Simpson, Robert Pack, and John Hollander, the works of a constant consciousness, of a rigorous critical apparatus, of a regnant intellect, which may not know what it really thinks, but knows at least that it really thinks. And that, though often a private affair, expressed in a language reserved and remote from the slogans of despair and the formulas of failure, should be enough to keep the art alive. And surely it will be enough as long as these poets, like Vermeer's girl, are happy to be seen at their private devoirs, in those curiously satisfying moments when they look at themselves and find, of all people, us, even if only one of us at a time.

THE SHORT STORY

THE MODERN American short story is an acquired taste, not like olives but like the art song, with which it has a great deal in common. It is, at its best anyway, a matter of feeling, conveyed by all manner of means, but almost always quickly: a few notes of characterization or even fewer of setting; all character sketch, or all place; a symbol, stretched and pulled so that its outlines can only be barely recognized through the elastic distortion, or a sign algebraic in its exactness, insisting on immediate substitution on the part of the reader—one person for all persons of a certain type or one incident for every other of the same category; and over and through everything a personality, the author asserting himself with a demand for attention not unlike a young child neglected too long by adults.

The generalization may seem too precise, inapt as a description, for example, of the naturalists who make in their short stories as in their novels so large a pretense of objectivity, presenting not Theodore Dreiser's world or Stephen Crane's, not Ring Lardner's or Sherwood Anderson's, but the World. But even in their pieces, the plea of the person is heard, the tone of an identity rings through again and again, the same identity, the same person, the author, demanding attention as he does not in his novels, pulling sentences this way and that, organizing character and situation, whether he means to or not, finally to reveal himself.

Obviously much of this is the result of the exposed technique of the short story. It always shows. There is no missing it, even in the long story posing as a short novel or novella. There must be a fineness in the handling of detail, a precision in the shaping of people and places and events, which will give quick value but not so quick that all the reader is aware of is the speed. The selection that the writer makes is often, then, apparent, written on the surfaces of his sentences, written in the words that one sees and in those that have been cut away. Here, he says, this is the way I give you a neglected child in a rotting family, finding moments of dry life under the dampness and decay of those around him, in his own nature. Here, she says, this is how I will discover for you the thousand tortured emptinesses of old ladies in the South, tortured but somehow amusing, full of laugh wrinkles, if only you can forget for a moment, under the spell of my prose, that the wrinkles are the wrinkles of old age.

The triumph of the short story in America in the years after Henry James is its openness to inspection, its confident asseveration of itself, of its own modes and manners. Very much like the art song, it proclaims itself, forces us to follow its form, hangs its meaning on the hooks and buttons of form. And like the art song, too, the more it thrusts its form at us, the more it mystifies us, mystifies and enchants us, holds itself only so close, close enough to make us lunge for meaning, but not so close that we can catch it. We have heard some handsome sounds, have been drawn through a fragment of a person's life, caught up warmly in the carefully shaped sentences and paragraphs, twisted easily or uneasily through the whole structure of the work, only to be pushed aside at the end, unfulfilled, without any clear control of the characters, quite uncertain about whether they live happily or unhappily thereafter, or whether they live at all.

The effect of this sort of experience may be frustration, or a less pronounced dissatisfaction, or a fixed taste for the preciosities and fragments of the American short story. It is distinctly a private taste, in spite of the sporadic attempts of the great supporters of the short story to make a cause of it, to find supporters for it as one might for a political cause, and in spite of the more consistent efforts of the editors of textbook collections of stories, whose introductions and afterwords and sets of questions surrounding the chosen examples of the craft all seem to say that this is a public art—solve the puzzles, find the ciphers, and you will be in possession, you and a million other high-school students, you and every other college freshman in the land.

But the short story cannot be reduced to such questions, not at least the short story that deserves to be memorialized in a collection that illustrates the best qualities of the genre. Who can answer with certitude of a story of any subtlety of tone or richness of revelation of the human person, "Why does the writer shift from a first person narrator to a third person? What is the meaning of the last sentence?" Who, asked to examine the structure of a particular sentence or paragraph can then describe its "intent" as the editors of short-story collections for students demand? Who can say why a character is bitter or sweet or anything else with the precision that the questions ask for? Analysis of any one of the stories is surely worth making, but any analysis that attempts so firmly to fix the writer's intention and the character's motivation must end by destroying the individual story and, perhaps more, the whole apparatus of the short-story form by which the psychology of human character is so handsomely preserved, not only the character in the story, but the one behind it, the writer's.

We have learned enough by now in our analysis of American literature not to reduce even the totally exposed structures of Poe's and Hawthorne's stories to the bones and cartilage that we see. We have come to recognize depths where shallows seem to confront the eye. Even in spite, for example, of Poe's insistence on the planning of effect from the first sentence, "with deliberate care," every facet to reveal a "tendency, direct or indirect, . . . to the one pre-established design," we continue to look for more in his stories than effects.[1] The preconceived scheme may call for revelations that are only just touched off by the symbolic cask. The tale the telltale heart tells may be far more oblique than the simple scaring entertainment that it first appeared to be. In our own time, we must be more attentive still to resonances, much less willing to trust quick impressions, still more open to long ripples of meditation.

How does one know when to listen attentively? How does one prepare for the meditative ripples? If the writer is James or Jamesian, the response is inevitable. The signs point all the way, as in that incomparable tour de force, "The Beast in the Jungle" (1903), which quickly announces its mode in the first paragraph. We are, as so often in James, at a house party.

There had been after luncheon much dispersal, all in the interest of the original motive, a view of Weatherend itself and the fine things, intrinsic features, pictures, heirlooms, treasures of all the arts that made the place famous; and the great rooms were so numerous that guests could wander at their will, hang back from the principal group and in cases where they took such matters with the last seriousness give themselves up to mysterious appreciations and measurements. There were persons to be observed, singly or in couples, bending toward objects in out-of-the-way corners with their hands on their knees and their heads nodding quite as with the emphasis of an excited sense of smell. [2]

"There were persons to be observed. . . ." It is far more than a hint; it is a positive shove in the direction essential to late James and to every short story that follows anything like the same modality. And so we nod, "quite as with the emphasis of an excited sense of smell."

The sense of smell is aroused, too, by a much simpler technique, say Sherwood Anderson's. No delicate sniffing is necessary here. The smell comes quickly to the surface. Titles, as in the twenty-three stories of *Winesburg, Ohio* (1919), say much: "Hands," "Queer," "The Philosopher," "The Teacher," "Godliness," "Loneliness," "The Strength of God." A title may be expressionistic, to reveal a type rather than a single person, ironic, wistful, but it counts for much in this sort of storytelling. The reader is started on a road in which there will be all the guidance he can ask for. The writer will take him along the ways of a small town in Ohio in the second decade of this century, underscoring the truths not always exposed to the eye, and emphasizing the "grotesque," Anderson's own word for those odd things and people that most appealed to his imagination. There is in the constant proclamation of his own working procedure by Anderson a grotesqueness that he could not have intended. It is rather like the signpost, the cue, by which a popular magazine writer or the composer of musical backgrounds for movies or television prepares the emotions of his audience for quick delivery. Of Anderson's teacher, we learn, for example:

Although no one in Winesburg would have suspected it, her life had been very adventurous. It was still adventurous. Day by day as she worked in the schoolroom or walked in the streets, grief, hope, and desire fought within her. Behind a cold exterior the most extraordinary events transpired in her mind.

Of each of the characters in *Winesburg,* some such line of inquiry is developed—and delivered. When the young reporter, through whom all the other people in the book are seen, leaves the small town for the big city, he is carried off—and the book with him—with placards of predication:

The young man's mind was carried away by his growing passion for dreams. One looking at him would not have thought him particularly sharp. With the recollection of little things occupying his mind he closed his eyes and leaned back in the car seat. He stayed that way for a long time and when he aroused himself and again looked out of the car window the town of Winesburg had disappeared and his life there had become but a background on which to paint the dreams of his manhood. [3]

Predication is a cut above prediction. We could have been left with a Dickensian look into the future, predicting all that is to come for our young man with the passion for dreams. Instead we have an anticipation of the writing career to come, the one, we realize now, with something less, perhaps, than the nervous thrill the writer had intended, that *Winesburg, Ohio* itself represents. We have, it is true, once again the familiar note, Anderson's dominant note, without which he could not conclude a story: Appearances are deceiving: "One looking at him would not have thought him particularly sharp." Ah, but we know better; we have read his book.

In spite of such clumsiness, Anderson is not without his resonances. The sensitive reader can move over the too carefully prepared ground into the depths that lie just beyond. If he moves through the other books of stories—*The Triumph of the Egg, Horses and Men,* and *Death in the Woods*—he will find a growing ease with a few facts, the simplest narrative structure, and a prose lean enough to hold everything in place, which makes that much reworked story, "Death in the Woods," so satisfying. "The whole thing," the narrator says shortly before the end of the story, "the story of the old woman's death, was to me as I grew older like music heard from far off. The notes had to be picked up slowly one at a time. Something had to be understood."

It was a music Ernest Hemingway heard, too, and perhaps understood. He made his short stories even more simple than Anderson's, more mannered in their simplicity, mannered in style, mannered in character, mannered even in incident. The style, out of Sherwood Anderson by Gertrude Stein, is all over, into everything. The blocks of ordinary man's speech, whether ordinary men are speaking or not, whether, in fact, anybody is speaking or not, break up a fishing tale, a story of gangsters or bullfighters or sexual impotence, into nervous staccato rhythms. One either finds these captivating or tedious, a way of staying with all the events in Hemingway's stories, significant or inconsequential, or a dead weight on the imagination and a frequent obstacle to one's interest. But like it or not, the consciousness of style remains with one, as it has remained with other American writers since. Whatever James or Anderson did not supply to the short-story writer in self-consciousness and the courage to build a story style around it, Hemingway did.

Some of the tricks stand out like the gold on a matador's clothes.

Perhaps today they are more like the tarnished gold of a beaten-down bullfighter playing the provinces. The reiteration of "bright boy" in "The Killers," for example, has all the subtlety of a Wagnerian leit-motif. The scene directions with which many of Hemingway's stories open are less than inspired prose and not quite revealing enough in their briefness to move one as, in a different way, James's first para-graphs do. The constant attention to virility, not only in the stories' content, but in the two-fisted prose, is also less than deeply affecting. But there is a larger impression, emerging from the totality of Hem-ingway stories, linking all his people—in the Midwest, in Paris, in Africa, in Spain; young boys growing up, bullfighters growing old, prizefighters winning and losing, women mostly losing—linking them and giving them a collective eloquence. It is that group identity that gives the little Spanish boy Paco of "The Capitol of the World" (1929) his force.

Madrid is full of boys named Paco, which is the diminutive of the name Francisco, and there is a Madrid joke about a father who came to Madrid and inserted an advertisement in the personal columns of *El Liberal* which said: PACO MEET ME AT HOTEL MONTANA NOON TUESDAY ALL IS FORGIVEN PAPA and how a squadron of Guardia Civil had to be called out to disperse the eight hundred young men who answered the advertisement.

Paco

was a well built boy with very black, rather curly hair, good teeth and a skin that his sisters envied, and he had a ready and unpuzzled smile. He was fast on his feet and did his work well and he loved his sisters, who seemed beautiful and sophisticated; he loved Madrid, which was still an unbelievable place, and he loved his work which, done under bright lights, with clean linen, the wearing of evening clothes, and abundant food in the kitchen, seemed romantically beautiful.[4]

Paco, who waits on table at the Pension Luarca, has bullfighting ambitions. In a mock fight, performed with a chair, to which knives have been tied with napkins to simulate a bull, Paco is gored to death. Within the terms of the story itself, his death is painful in the way that sentimental tales breed pain, but in the larger context of all of Hemingway it is perhaps more touching than that, as Paco takes his place beside the other figures of foolish bravery who work so hard at being men. Hemingway, in effect, denied that there was anything of mystery in his bare-bones tales, but the mystery of the human person supervenes, in spite of him, maybe, or more likely because he put it there, or struggled to put it there, and then did not quite have the courage to admit the struggle.

Faulkner, in his stories as in his novels, was less shy about putting in and acknowledging the mystery. Like the darkness in "Old Man" (1939), which has the paradoxical advantage of obscuring the rain and lighting up everything else for the convict escaping in the flood waters of the Mississippi, the atmosphere of black tragic mystery in Faulkner's stories is in spite of its obscurities a constantly revealing one.

It was full dark now. That is, night had completely come, the gray dissolving sky had vanished, yet as though in perverse ratio surface visibility had sharpened, as though the light which the rain of the afternoon had washed out of the air had gathered upon the water as the rain itself had done, so that the yellow flood spread on before him now with a quality almost phosphorescent, right up to the instant where vision ceased.[5]

Wandering in and out of Faulkner's stories is that great consciousness of the South which gives all his work, of any length or design, an unmistakable unity and clarity. Even more than Hemingway's stories, Faulkner's hold together, not only with each other, but with the novels. Whether or not they fit into the Yoknapatawpha pattern, they come from the same soil, are washed with the same rivers. Their people are initiated in the same rites of manhood and womanhood, in the same freedoms or restrictions of whites and blacks, in the same great consciousness of the South. Only one clear distinction, apart from size, seems to attach to the stories: they expose more clearly the refusal to admit something fundamental, one way or another, the refusal to yield to death, which is what the unwillingness to acknowledge defeat in the Civil War comes to. The mind takes in quickly the long stubborn fight of Miss Emily Grierson against death in "A Rose for Emily" (1931)—yes, and taxes, too. It is only her death that reveals her lover's. But her death does not compromise her struggle or the South's or Faulkner's, each in a different way, to hold, to hold hard, to hold to the end, for life against death, for man against everything around him, time included, and to celebrate those who hold hardest, even when their holding is insane. The celebration has a particular vitality in the briefer narrations that the large-scale works do not offer, unless we read them in excerpt, as so often we do, pulling out "Spotted Horses" from *The Hamlet,* "Old Man" from *The Wild Palms,* and setting loose "The Bear" from its imprisonment in the *Go Down, Moses* collection, to take only the most conspicuous examples. Then we see Faulkner in a dimension that makes the seeing altogether tolerable. We are not engulfed by a tumultuous prose which, for all its monumental force in the larger works, is often sunk in the muddy mists of run-on chapters. We are held, as Faulkner's heroes hold. We can stand still even through the slogging transitions of "The Bear," because the movements in that remarkable multiple tale—of an animal hunt, a hunt for manhood, and a hunt for the legacy of the Southern land—are such captivating movements, such whole ones, such exposed ones, open to the sight in the best traditions of the American short story, to be seen, to be contemplated, to be understood, although surely never to be understood in terms of formulas or slogans.

The mixture of conscience and consciousness in Faulkner is a troubled and troubling one. Darting back and forth like glints of shining trout in the stories, just for seconds, the symbols of a sick South touch us, worry us, but do not quite sicken us. At least we are never quite sure how much we are meant to be sickened. How much, for a fair sample of this sort of disorder, are we to be caught up in the fears of the Negro washerwoman Nancy in "That Evening Sun" (1931)? She is victim, she is victimizer; she is haunted, she haunts. She will do as a symbol of the South if we do not press her too firmly into doing duty for all the sins the South itself has committed and all those committed against the South. Perhaps she will do best of all if we remind ourselves as we stand aside—like the children of the story, a little frightened, but convinced that we are not involved because we are not in Nancy's case—remind ourselves that we are altogether wrong to stand aside. We cannot, like the children in the story, go down into the ditch and come right up out of it again. We cannot leave Nancy as easily as they do—as so often all of us do—escaping from the sight, hearing only a few distant sounds, concerned more about the inconveniences to us than the woman's terror. Faulkner's parabolic style has never been more to the point. It points the largest of fingers at the spectator from the North without for a moment excusing the South for creating the spectacle:

> We went up out of the ditch. We could still see Nancy's house and the open door, but we couldn't see Nancy now, sitting before the fire with the door open, because she was tired. "I just done got tired," she said. "I just a nigger. It ain't no fault of mine."
>
> But we could hear her, because she began just after we came up out of the ditch, the sound that was not singing and not unsinging. "Who will do our washing now, Father?" I said.[6]

The other Southern writers of stories who follow after Faulkner are as conscious of their locale as he is and of the color of their characters, but their consciences are not so sorely troubled. Katherine Anne Porter, Eudora Welty, Peter Taylor, Flannery O'Connor, Carson McCullers, Truman Capote—to mention a particularly impressive half-dozen—have their parables, too, their grievances, their many tales of sickness and despair. But the appeal in their work is not so often to conscience as it is to one's sense of the quaint, the curious, the strange, the rather sadly and sweetly strange. If the bizarre types one meets in their stories also strike us as aliens in our world, hangovers from a mammoth drunk involving all the people of their world, it is not because they hurt or worry us or in any serious way involve us in their troubles, but because they are so strange, so far removed from us, so completely driven into their own customs, their own speech, their present permanently suspended to make room for their past.

Nothing, perhaps, so insistently clamors for technical virtuosity in the short story as the strange. And conversely, a concern to display that virtuosity invariably leads to the choice of odd people who do odd things in odd places. What an opportunity to fool with the role of the narrator, to work out all sorts of schemes of concealment or revealment, to give the teller of the tale omniscience or to bring up from the slumbering depths of the unconscious a trail of accidents and incidents that in effect explain themselves, like so many chattering nerve ends. The special charm of the Southern writers, the ladies especially, is that while they are anything but shy about their performances, they do not so impose style upon us that we lose people. Furthermore, their style, almost to a woman, has the edge of an enchanting conversation, the limitations of which are only apparent at some distance. And if we get sufficiently involved with the conversation, in large enough gulps, we never again quite achieve the distance. Thus, in the stories of Eudora Welty, we may fail after a while to see the elegant struttings and preenings with which she fills her prose and be content with the tales that emerge, at various tilts and slants, through the carefully measured rhythms and oh, so balanced compositions. For something does emerge, especially in the earlier stories, stories of fragmentary people told in fragments, so much a series of shards, in fact, that even when death occurs it is not conclusive, as in "Death of a Traveling Salesman." It is a handsomely modeled story of a man running for his life, only to die after a night spent with an impossible pair of people, a husband too young and a wife too old, not in age but in appearance and in attitude. In another of the early stories, "Lily Daw and the Three Ladies," a feeble-minded woman either is successfully dispatched to an asylum or finds asylum with a xylophone player. We are never altogether sure. We never altogether care.

When Eudora Welty does make us care in some of the later stories, it seems to be because she has worked harder at plotting, found herself more concerned with her people, found herself people more like other people, less strange, if not less estranged. The odd people in their lives are "other people," like the outsized Spanish guitarist in "Music from Spain," who in a long, tortuous adventure assuages the grief of a man who has married his landlady, unhappily, and, through death, lost the daughter who might have made the marriage tolerable. And other people do not often help, like the poor girl in "The Whole World Knows," who is made to act as a betrayed husband's unhappy accomplice in an unsuccessful attempt to forget his wife's unfaithfulness with a parallel act on his own part.

Style is as much as ever a part of these stories. We are acutely aware of the plaintive calls of the numbed husband in "The Whole World Knows," calling out to his father, who a long time earlier had deserted his family, an aching parallel to his deserting wife: "What you went and found, was it better than this?" And then in a paragraph by itself, the last three words of the story, almost unspoken words, "And where's Jinny?" But in these stories, as in the long ones that purport to be novels, *The Robber Bridegroom* and *Delta Wedding* and *The Ponder Heart,* style is often an intrusion. It stands too boldly beside the facts of the stories. The art song has been violated by enlargement, to do double duty as an operatic aria and a Schubert *Lied,* and it doesn't come off as well as the brilliantly polished fragments that preceded it. There is too much of the art song still to allow the disorder of tortured lives to push through convincingly. And there is too much tortured life to make all the exquisite contours of the art song quite acceptable as a way of telling us about it.

Katherine Anne Porter's stories manage plot and style better by never allowing either to overwhelm the other, and by keeping firmly to a literary mode of such complexity that reality, as she sees it, must always be examined at a distance, with some detachment. Even passion itself must be experienced dispassionately—as in "Flowering Judas" and "Maria Concepcion"—if "experienced" is the word for what the reader has undergone. Her people sit for portraits, like Henry James's, and the psychological insights that we are privileged to make must be grabbed at, turned over quickly in the mind, as we do a hastily whispered story about somebody who is within hearing distance; and we can never be sure if we have heard correctly, the word "hear" may have been "leer" or even "rear," so muffled were the whispers; and we cannot ask again, or in any way settle ambiguities, for all sorts of reasons, of tact, of taste, of our own insecurity.

As in Faulkner, death hovers over Miss Porter's South. Sometimes it waits almost forever, as with the old white Grandmother and equally old Negro Nannie of some of her stories. Sometimes it performs its work with terrible dispatch, as in the 1939 "Pale Horse, Pale Rider," where the influenza epidemic at the end of the First World War makes a young girl named Miranda, perhaps the most constant character in her stories, into a configuration of Eve. She gives her fiancé, a soldier significantly named Adam, the virus which kills him. She herself recovers from her long illness, in which her feverish hallucinations and those of wartime have been cruelly mixed, everybody and everything made evil, as by a sudden squall of evil, as by the terrible visitation after the Fall.

In "Pale Horse, Pale Rider," Miss Porter allows herself some leisure in which to mix good and evil, delirium and clarity. The symbolic figure of the title, the figure of death on his horse, saunters rather than gallops into our consciousness. In the 1930 "Flowering Judas," an incomparable demonstration of technical power, she moves through a conflict between types and attitudes, upbringings and downfalls, with all haste, the impression of dazzling speed and matching virtuosity considerably heightened by the tense in which the story is told, the present. The central character is a cool, almost frigid American girl, a schoolteacher in Mexico, who becomes involved with revolutionists. The revolutionary leader tries to seduce her; she is at once pulled toward him and repelled, and made full of the disturbances left in her by the conflict between her attraction to him and her Catholic faith. She has taken pity on one of the young revolutionists, now in jail, and frightened because his leader apparently will not help him to escape; she has brought him drugs, with which the boy promptly kills himself. In the last paragraph of the story, all its events are mixed together; its title gives it its final shape as, in a dream, the boy calls her "Murderer" and offers at the same time to lead her to a new country. In the rhythm of dream, and following its logic, she climbs to the top of "the Judas tree that bent down slowly and set her upon the earth." She is offered the "warm bleeding flowers" of the tree to eat; she holds them to her lips and sees that the boy's hand is without flesh and his eyes without sight. And finally, in the concluding moments of the story, the only ones altogether in the past tense, she eats "the flowers greedily for they satisfied both hunger and thirst. Murderer; said Eugenio, and Cannibal! This is my body and my blood. Laura cried No! and at the sound of her own voice, she awoke trembling and was afraid to sleep again."

The ironies are clear and blurred by turns in "Flowering Judas." It is clear enough that the girl's faith has contrived her repression and her guilt. It is equally clear that her compassionate feeling for the people she has tried to help, as teacher and as an ally of the revolutionists, has betrayed her, leading her into a tormented sexuality and leaving her with the tortured knowledge that she was an accessory in the suicide of young Eugenio. But the transfiguration of Eugenio into the Christ of the Last Supper is a confusing image, in part a function of the story's rhetoric, in part, of its psychology. All one can say for certain of the girl's faith at the end is that it has left behind trails of guilt, blossoming in her subconscious like the blood-colored flowers of the Judas tree. Salvation has been torn from her, like the flesh from Eugenio's hand and the light from his eyes. Every redeeming motion of hers has brought betrayal. The final irony, blurred though it may be, makes her into a kind of Judas, and, by uneasy but inescapable inference, associates attempts to bring surcease to suffering with more suffering, efforts to end tyranny with more tyranny, and love and redemption with an ugly parody of both. We open our mouths for the flesh of Jesus and find we have swallowed Judas. The bitter estimate of human affairs of *Ship of Fools* seems well anticipated here.

Few other short-story virtuosi allow such bitterness to rust their ironies. But simply because their virtuosity rests to a large extent on the oblique, a cynical edge is always open to view in any story of theirs that presents a calculated ambiguity to the eye or the mind. Nobody ever prospers in their accounts, except to somebody's else's disadvantage, or, sooner or later, to their own. Almost everybody worth writing about is a grotesque, and far more strange these grotesques than Sherwood Anderson's. What does not meet the eye or regale the mind when one confronts a Southern town like the "dreary" one of Carson McCullers' "The Ballad of the Sad Cafe" (1951) is far more frightening than anything hidden behind the façades of Winesburg, Ohio. The dreariness of the town, dark and dingy and with nothing in it to do, conceals a frightening history, the history that is the substance of Mrs. McCullers' ballad. It is a tale of "a dark, tall woman with bones and muscles like a man," of a hunchback who is "a great mischief-maker," and a man just returned from the penitentiary and due to return there, who brings bad luck with him wherever he goes. It is a tale told in a high style, like most of Carson McCullers' stories, but more important, perhaps, told with some passing comments on the nature of love and lovers that serve fairly well for all this species of ironic private art.

The most outlandish people can be the stimulus for love. A man may be a doddering great-grandfather and still love only a strange girl he saw in the streets of Cheehaw one afternoon two decades past. The preacher may love a fallen woman. The beloved may be treacherous, greasy-headed and given to evil habits. Yes, and the lover may see this as clearly as anyone else—but that does not affect the evolution of his love one whit. A most mediocre person can be the object of a love which is wild, extravagant, and beautiful as the poison lilies of the swamp. A good man may be the stimulus for a love both violent and debased, or a jabbering madman may bring about in the soul of someone a tender and simple idyll. Therefore, the value and quality of any love is determined solely by the lover himself.

It is for this reason that most of us would rather love than be loved. Almost everyone wants to be the lover. And the curt truth is that, in a deep secret way, the state of being beloved is intolerable to many. The beloved fears and hates the lover, and with the best of reasons. For the lover is forever trying to strip bare his beloved. The lover craves any possible relation with the beloved, even if this experience can cause him only pain.[7]

The relationship of lover to beloved here outlined might well describe the connection between these writers and their characters. For apart from the joys that must accompany virtuoso display, there can be only pain in the chronicles of the treacherous and the greasy-headed, the jabbering madmen, the poison lilies of the swamp to which they have for so long dedicated themselves. Marriages are polluted by drunkenness, such as the wife's tippling which produces Mrs. McCullers' "Domestic Dilemma," or pulled apart, at least for a moment, by an aimless lechery, such as the husband's in John Cheever's "The Country Husband." A woman is doomed to learn, as so many of the people who inhabit these stories are, that joylessness is her fate (as it is almost everybody's) in "Beatrice Trueblood's Story" as Jean Stafford tells it: "She was certain that sweetness could put an end to strife; she believed that her tolerance was limitless, and she vowed that when she married there would be no quarrels." "But," we are told, "there were. The dew in her eyes as a bride gave way nearly at once to a glaze when she was a wife." [8] It is a glaze that remains, in spite of all her sweetness and limitless tolerance, remains through one marriage after another. For hers is the typical marriage of the virtuoso short story, mostly torture and pain, the kind the married couple hears about in John Cheever's "The Enormous Radio," as it reports, by means of its monstrously endowed, utterly graceless circuit, the quarrels and infidelities, the thousand empti-nesses, of life in all the apartments of a large New York apartment house, and finally reduces the couple who own the terrible instrument to the same kind of misery. It is not a misery that will disappear, either. When the radio is restored to conventional performance, the news it reports is essentially of the same kind:

The voice on the radio was suave and non-committal. "An early-morning railroad disaster in Tokyo," the loud-speaker said, "killed twenty-nine people. A fire in a Catholic hospital near Buffalo for the care of blind children was extinguished early this morning by nuns. The temperature is forty-seven. The humidity is eighty-nine." [9]

The only thing that is normal in this world is abnormality.

By comparison to the bitterness and misery of the virtuosi and their victims, the anger or toughness or wistful yearning for a better life of some of the other writers seems like downright good humor. There are anxieties in their stories, and even anguish, but there is either hope of resuscitation or revolution, or a warm sentimental affection for the friendless and the oppressed, or a burst of comedy, like a shot from a vaudeville cannon, to light up the atmosphere, to soften or palliate or actually remove the anguish. F. Scott Fitzgerald's poor little rich boys watch life blow up in their faces; but they themselves have lit the fuses, and we have watched them as they have done so, and so we cannot mourn too long; we can only mumble an act of contrition with them or an act of love for them and praise the Lord that we are not in their condition and would not be caught dead in it—for the only way, after all, anyone is ever caught in their condition is dead. Even the repentant figure in this social drama, who is perhaps the most touching of Fitzgerald's characters, Charlie Wales in "Babylon Revisited" (1931), leaves us in peace. The logic of his misery is all too clear: having locked his pregnant wife out in the snow, in one of his festive brawls, and killed his wife as a result, he is permanently suspect as a father; no penance, no repentance can earn him the right to take his daughter to live with him. We pity him, perhaps, but a burning compassion we do not feel.

Similarly, Kay Boyle's victims seem classified rather than compassionated, especially the victims of the Nazis she has placed so precisely in their settings—in Austria in "The White Horses of Vienna," written at the time of Anschluss, 1936; in the United States in "Winter Night," written ten years later. One reacts to the poignancies in which her people are involved—like the little orphan boy in "His Idea of a Mother," whose emotions must be prepared by him to meet situations in the way that he has heard children with living parents are likely to behave—with accustomed responses, but not with a matching involvement. That sort of reaction is saved for the Depression victims of Tess Slesinger and George Milburn. They have been dealt blows too hard to turn aside but deeded nothing like adequate defenses with which to meet them. And they draw one in, like Lawyer Parnell in "The Nigger-Lover," the first story in Milburn's *Oklahoma Town* collection, or Charlie Wingate, the title character in the same writer's "A Student in Economics" (1933), who works all night at a diner and sleeps through his classes all day. It is not a vicarious experience to which one is drawn, but rather to under-standing, to sympathy, or to that spluttering distaste for any attack on human dignity which motivated so much writing in the thirties. The grim fixation on money which comes at the lowest and the highest times of our economy is one of the surest causes for alarm in such writers, and almost equally certain to evoke an answering unhappi-ness in their readers. When the father of a two-weeks' dead girl in Milburn's "Sugar Be Sweet!" uses the coupons gathered as a dividend from her expensive funeral to bid down a tough old farmer in a "Lucky Moon Auction Sale" for a hundred-pound sack of sugar, he reduces his wife to a terrible stillness, "her eyes hard with loathing." The reader may share the wife's emotion, but surely it will be directed to a different end and for a different purpose. This sort of writing is more than classifying. Its poignancies demand more than an accus-tomed tear. With whatever chances of success, against such indignity one must stretch the weapons of amelioration.

After a gap of some decades, a new group of short-story writers not ashamed to make special pleas has turned up. Their pleas are variously open or covert, made with utter seriousness or great good humor. Irony, the prevailing tone of what might be called the well-made short-story, is invariably present, but its inflections are as many as those given the tones of the diatonic scale in the music of our time. No one can miss the angles of love from which the writers of pro-nounced Jewishness view their people. Bernard Malamud's collection is properly called *The Magic Barrel,* after one of its celebrated stories, but also, one hopes, as a fair description of its happy-unhappy protagonists and antagonists, so closely related in simple, not quite sober resignation to the people of Sholem Aleichim. It is hard to know how much meaning Philip Roth attaches to "Goodbye Columbus," but one would have no trouble accepting "Hello Broad-way" as the completion of the phrase, for he has given a kind of wry musical-comedy twist to the events in which his New York-New Jersey Jewish adolescents figure, with all the turns in which they come onstage just close enough to the solos and duets of the ingenues to be recognizable and just parodied enough to make their attempts to live like other people, grown-up people, non-Jewish people, rather pathetic.[10]

J. D. Salinger's family of Glasses achieves its brittleness through a mixture of Jewish and Irish blood, but the inflections of Franny and

Zooey, Seymour and Buddy, and all the others, Mrs. Glass, the mother, not least among them, are very much New York modulations, and, let us say, more in texture like those of Central Europe than Great Britain. In fact, when Salinger writes dialogue for a thirteen-year-old English girl in "For Esme—With Love and Squalor," he has her emphasize syllables in the same way as Franny Glass, and he fixes the reader's ear with the same insistent use of italics he makes for the Irish-Jewish-American college girl, though with a little more restraint. Esme is not trying to fix the Jesus prayer in her life as a kind of mystical counterpoint to her actions, but she has all the marks of a Salinger character, earnestness, eager affection, and a determination to find the same intense metabolism in those around her. As in the living examples of the species, it is an engaging set of characteristics in small doses; it is only when one is forced to live with it through many hours or many pages that one realizes how superficial it is as an approach to Yale boys, God, the way of the Pilgrim, quiz programs, or any other god*damn* subject.

Salinger's books are all about growing up, at whatever age, with whatever success, confident, like the television-actor Glass, Zooey, or confident and despairing by turns, like Seymour, who commits suicide. So are the books of James Baldwin, the novels, the essays, the stories; about growing up into blackness in a white world, a color appropriate to a Calvinist consciousness but hardly acceptable to an insensate society, which has little enough time for a Negro and almost none at all for a Negro apologist for homosexuality, except one, perhaps, who is willing to plead openly for his complicated cause, in many ways, and with a full specification of the agencies and instrumentalities involved. For all the frankness of detail, in the American novels and the French, and in the stories and the debates with himself which go by the name of essays, there is a certain preciousness in Baldwin's work which one cannot help comparing to a similar tonality in the stories of Truman Capote. But what Capote's mannered arabesques never touch—what perhaps no other American writer about people who are all feeling has ever touched—is the violence with which the feelers search out feeling. A long time ago, as this genre of short story goes, Willa Cather tried to hold some of it on paper with "Paul's Case" (1920), a story of a Pittsburgh slum-dwelling adolescent with a preternatural feeling for music. But, in spite of all sorts of surface details that ring true, Paul's case is too much a case of things, not enough one of self. When he commits suicide, it is more to fill out a literary design than the inescapable downward spiral of loss of feeling.

Baldwin's Sonny, in "Sonny's Blues," is more convincingly a man in search of himself, and determined to find himself with and through things, and to be more a human being as a result of his adventure with things, not less. In his case, the things are those that make up the piano—"so much wood and wires and little hammers and big ones, and ivory." Sonny is a jazz musician whose self-seeking search has led him through heroin to jail, and then back onto the piano and into God knows what else. He is, unlike almost every other attempt to fix a jazzman in words, in novel or short story or film, a real person, as well as a jazz musician, and recognizable as both. He is caught up in his music and in his search. He is lost at times in the means he uses—"I needed a fix, I needed to find a place to lean, I needed a clear space to *listen*—and I couldn't find it, and I—went crazy, I did terrible things to *me,* I was terrible *for* me." But he is never lost to the reader. He never becomes one of those papier-mâché figures, speaking an aery argot, that readers of jazz stories know too well but that jazz musicians do not know at all. By comparison, Eudora Welty's "Powerhouse" is a trifling fantasy about jazz.

When, at the end of Baldwin's story, Sonny and a small band play the blues, his brother, who tells Sonny's story, reports:

. . . the music tightened and deepened, apprehension began to beat the air. Creole [the bass player] began to tell us what the blues were all about. They were not about anything very new. He and his boys up there were keeping it new, at the risk of ruin, destruction, madness, and death, in order to find new ways to make us listen. For, while the tale of how we suffer, and how we are delighted, and how we may triumph is never new, it always must be heard. There isn't any other tale to tell, it's the only light we've got in all this darkness.

The description will do for Sonny's blues and it will do for Baldwin's story and all the others with which the short-story writer in America has moved into such commanding control of his medium. It is true of all those described in the paragraphs above and of others, differently gifted, not so consistent in their skills, less certainly directed to this kind of story, but still of the same breed: Erskine Caldwell when he was writing, early in his career, about the charming, fumbling sexual maneuvers of adolescence in "Indian Summer," or the indignities of life in the beauty parlor, in "We Are Looking at You, Agnes"; or John Updike, in the early stages of his career, some decades later, chronicling life in the automobile age, with a sweetness in the face of futilities and fatuities that recalls, if in a more ordered way, the early Caldwell; George P. Elliott, writing setting-up exercises for the imagination, satires on anthropology, sociology, and pseudoscientific method, such as "Among the Dangs" and "Sandra," that make their own contributions to the anthropology and sociology of modern America. The list could lengthen, perhaps should lengthen. But what is important is not the number of names, but that they represent something. What? Baldwin has said it: ". . . while the tale of how we suffer, and how we are delighted, and how we may triumph is never new, it always must be heard. There isn't any other tale to tell, it's the only light we've got in all this darkness." [11] Or at any rate, it is the only light these writers, talking each one to one other person at a time, can see. What makes it all worthwhile is that they describe that light, and the darkness which surrounds it, so well.

THE NOVEL

AMERICAN WRITERS have lived for a long time in an atmosphere of judgment. They have written with critics' judgments large against their pages, those already made or those about to be. They have written with publishers' judgments moving before them, slowly, pitifully, arousing contempt in them, perhaps, but also arousing their share of worry. They have written with more or less awareness of public judgments, ashamed to be concerned, conditioned to be concerned, determined to be concerned, arousing contempt in the public or hoping they would or hoping they would not. They have written to make their own apodictic judgments, no mere decalogue but a hundred or more dismissals and affirmations in which American society has been picked up and put down with all the tenderness and all the ruthlessness with which a three-year-old handles a doll that is older than she is.

There is no escape from judgment. Against judgment a book is published, read or not read. Against judgment a writer is judged. In a culture sitting uncomfortably on a cushion of value judgments, writers are expected to make more of them, more, more all the time, to keep stuffing the cushion, so that as one judgment flattens out another may be quickly puffed to take its place. In such a culture critics and reviewers, even anonymous carpenters of one- and two-inch notices, have a special place, a magisterial one. They can tell us what the novelists tell us or what the novelists do not. They can tell us whether what the novelists tell us is worth telling us.

What the critic can never do is to give a writer the sense of fulfillment. The public may be assured that it has just been handed the third great American novel or the thirtieth; it may, month after month, rest content with high accomplishment delivered in neat packages by the book clubs. The writer never finds that assurance. His are all the short-term achievements: position, prestige, skills of a sort and perhaps the freedom to use them, even money, if the book clubs use his work to fill their packages. But endurance—what of it? What capacity for life does he have—do his works have? Will his judgments hold? Will the judgments on his judgments hold?

The American writer has for long been in the position of Milly Theale in *The Wings of the Dove* (1902): a wealthy young girl, "conscious of a great capacity for life," but sick with a fatal illness and destined to die young and thus unfulfilled. James outlines her position—and the writer's—in the Preface he later wrote for the novel:

One would see her then as possessed of all things, all but the single most precious assurance; freedom and money and a mobile mind and personal charm, the power to interest and attract; attributes, each one, enhancing the value of a future. From the moment his imagination began to deal with her at close quarters, in fact, nothing could more engage her designer than to work out the detail of her perfect rightness for her part; nothing above all more solicit him than to recognise fifty reasons for her national and social status. She could be the last fine flower—blooming alone, for the fullest attestation of her freedom—of an "old" New York stem . . . There goes with it, for the heroine of "The Wings of the Dove," a strong and special implication of liberty, liberty of action, of choice, of appreciation, of contact—proceeding from sources that provide better for large independence, I think, than any other conditions in the world—and this would be in particular what we should feel ourselves deeply concerned with. I had from far back mentally projected a certain sort of young American as more the "heir of all the ages" than any other young person whatever (and precisely on those grounds I have just glanced at but to pass them by for the moment); so that here was a chance to confer on some such figure a supremely touching value. To be the heir of all the ages only to know yourself, as that consciousness should deepen, balked of your inheritance, would be to play the part, it struck me, or at least to arrive at the type, in the light on the whole the most becoming.[1]

James felt called upon "to assist" at the ordeal of consciousness —as he called it—of Milly Theale. To the ordeals of consciousness of their writers, Americans have been summoned, as to levees. They have watched with varying degrees of awareness writers with varying intensities of consciousness awakening to their own sensations, their own feelings, their thoughts, their intentions, their obligations. The display for forty years or so was public in the most vexed sense of the word: an exhibition for all who would come and ogle; a demonstration for all who would pay close enough attention. The reward for attendance and attention was a sharing of consciousness: they would

—or at least they could—awake together, writer and reader. What was achieved, not for the writer alone, but for Americans generally, was consciousness as Paul Valéry describes it, an awareness of strange events in a totally darkened theater, an awareness that was part of the events, which consists, as we come to realize upon close inspection, not only of a spectacle but of the spectators who view it.[2] It was an awareness in James that was in part a matter of spirit, in part a matter of geography. The distance Americans had to travel added to the perspective of each new discovery; their spirit, to the freshness; their psychology, to the intensity. Charlotte Stant's view of London in *The Golden Bowl* (1904) is an instance: she has just come back from a trip to America; she is accompanied on her tour of inspection by Prince Amerigo:

It had rained heavily in the night, and though the pavements were now dry, thanks to a cleansing breeze, the August morning, with its hovering, thick-drifting clouds and freshened air, was cool and grey. The multitudinous green of the Park had been deepened, and a wholesome smell of irrigation, purging the place of dust and of odours less accepta- ble, rose from the earth. Charlotte had looked about her, with expres- sion, from the first of their coming in, quite as if for a deep greeting, for general recognition: the day was, even in the heart of London, of a rich, low-browed, weather-washed English type. It was as if it had been waiting for her, as if she knew it, placed it, loved it, as if it were in fact a part of what she had come back for. So far as this was the case the impression of course could only be lost on a mere vague Italian; it was one of those for which you had to be, blessedly, an American—as indeed you had to be, blessedly, an American for all sorts of things: so long as you hadn't, blessedly or not, to remain in America.[3]

That is in a sense the public view. It is also the hedonist view, an inspection eager and alert, but the eagerness chiefly for pleasure and the alertness compromised by personal interest. That is the view that another such American—Sophy Viner—herself offers to the eye of an observer in *The Reef* (1912) of Edith Wharton; the observer is an official at the American Embassy in London:

He had immediately classed her as a compatriot; her small nose, her clear tints, a kind of sketchy delicacy in her face, as though she had been brightly but lightly washed in with water-colour, all confirmed the evidence of her high sweet voice and of her quick incessant gestures. She was clearly an American, but with the loose native quality strained through a closer woof of manners: the composite product of an enquiring and adaptable race.

Mutability is her element; it defines her look—

Sitting opposite, in the compartment from which he had contrived to have other travellers excluded, Darrow looked at her curiously. He had never seen a face that changed so quickly. A moment since it had danced like a field of daisies in a summer breeze; now, under the pallid oscillating light of the lamp overhead, it wore the hard stamp of experience, as of a soft thing chilled into shape before its curves had rounded: and it moved him to see that care already stole upon her when she slept.[4]

—it defines her life: when the book ends, Sophy is off to India, having given up all chance for a life of quality ("But," it is explained, "Sophy's restless—always was—and she's taken it into her head she'd rather travel . . .").

The private view is not very different on the surface. Once again in Edith Wharton's *The Fruit of the Tree* (1907), a figure, a face, a character offer contrasts:

John Amherst's step was singularly noiseless. The nurse, sensitive by nature and training to all physical characteristics, was struck at once by the contrast between his alert face and figure and the silent way in which he moved. She noticed, too, that the same contrast was repeated in the face itself, its spare energetic outline, with the high nose and compressed lips of the mover of men, being curiously modified by the veiled inward gaze of the grey eyes he turned on her. It was one of the interests of Justine Brent's crowded yet lonely life to attempt a rapid mental classification of the persons she met; but the contradictions in Amherst's face baffled her, and she murmured inwardly "I don't know" as she drew aside to let him approach the bed.[5]

It takes 610 pages before the veil is lifted from the inward gaze. Amherst has married the nurse, fallen in love with another woman, compromised both with his business affairs, separated from his wife and returned to her. The return is accompanied by "an unwonted intensity of perception"; he knows his wife now as he has not before —he sees her, he feels her:

He noticed how her full upper lids, of the tint of yellowish ivory, had a slight bluish discolouration, and how little thread-like blue veins ran across her temples to the roots of her hair. The emaciation of her face, and the hollow shades beneath her cheek-bones, made her mouth seem redder and fuller, though a little line on each side, where it joined the cheek, gave it a tragic droop. And her hands! When her fingers met his he recalled having once picked up, in the winter woods, the little feather-light skeleton of a frozen bird—and that was what her touch was like.

Amherst's is not a small perception; its reach from inward gaze to outward touch is rare enough, even in the novel of subjective sensibility. But it is not of the depth or the intensity of Maggie Verver's in *The Golden Bowl*, of her perception of others, of her perception of herself, or of her perception of the art of perceiving. She is the American dove again; but her wings are not clipped, though they certainly come close enough to being cut off. The act of contemplation saves her. She has facts to learn: James's Greek chorus in the book, Colonel and Mrs. Assingham, explain it to us. To Maggie, somehow, the nature of wrong must be shown, though she is "the person in the world to whom a wrong thing could least be communicated." She must open "her sense" to the wrong, to the very, *very* wrong, "To what's called Evil—with a very big E: for the first time in her life. To the discovery of it, to the knowledge of it, to the crude experience of it. To the harsh, bewildering brush, the daily chilling breath of it." [6]

The record of Maggie's growing consciousness of the world around her, of herself, and of consciousness itself, in two chapters of the book (25 and 26), is an exhausting experience for the attentive reader of James. It offers something closer to a vicarious experience, perhaps, than any other passage in the late period of the writer. In her expansions of consciousness, Maggie makes, for the first time, her own acquaintance: she is aware now of having refused and resisted reflection about the central situation in her life, though it had pressed in upon her and occupied "the garden of her life . . . like some strange, tall tower of ivory, or perhaps rather some wonderful, beautiful, but outlandish pagoda, a structure plated with hard, bright porcelain, coloured and figured and adorned, at the overhanging eaves, with silver bells that tinkled, ever so charmingly, when stirred by chance airs." She had known she could enter; she had repressed the knowledge, escaped the situation—to a point:

She had not, certainly, arrived at the conception of paying with her life for anything she might do; but it was nevertheless quite as if she had sounded with a tap or two one of the rare porcelain plates. She had knocked, in short—though she could scarce have said whether for admission or for what; she had applied her hand to a cool, smooth spot, and had waited to see what would happen. Something *had* happened; it was as if a sound, at her touch, after a little, had come back to her from within; a sound sufficiently suggesting that her approach had been noted.[7]

The change in her has the character of a "semi-smothered agitation." She becomes aware of the relationship between her husband, Prince Amerigo, and Charlotte Stant, her closest friend and now her stepmother. The images her consciousness notes need no comment: "There passed across her vision ten times a day the gleam of a bare blade. . . ." Before the fire, "She might have been watching the family coach pass and noting that, somehow, Amerigo and Charlotte were pulling it while she and her father were not so much as pushing. They were seated inside together, dandling the Principino and holding him up to the windows, to see and be seen, like an infant positively royal; so that the exertion was all with the others. . . ." Finally, "the first shock of complete perception" ends with Maggie feeling "very much alone" and helpless:

she sat there, in the solid chamber of her helplessness, as in a bath of benevolence artfully prepared for her, over the brim of which she could but just manage to see by stretching her neck. Baths of benevolence were very well, but, at least, unless one were a patient of some sort, a nervous eccentric or a lost child, one was usually not so immersed save by one's request. It wasn't in the least what *she* had requested. She had flapped her little wings as a symbol of desired flight, not merely as a plea for a more gilded cage and an extra allowance of lumps of sugar.

The desired flight comes. Maggie's sense has been opened to evil; but the experience has not been crude only, not harsh or bewildering alone. For what is most important is not what her sense has been opened to, but that it has been opened, and that in the process conduct has been joined to sensibility. Knowing herself, she has come to know others and they to know her, and through her, goodness. The book ends in a series of sacrifices and separations and comings together, all as a result of her conduct, as her conduct has been an effect of her new sensibility. Her father takes away his wife—her friend and her husband's mistress. Her husband brings himself back —her friend and her lover—"his whole act enclosing her."

Maggie Verver's expanding consciousness draws in all around her, even, one gathers, the mute Principino, her baby. James describes the same process in detail in the case of Milly Theale in *The Wings of the Dove*. All those who are part of Milly's life, part of her action, are "drawn in as by some pool of a Lorelei"; one sees them "terrified and tempted and charmed; bribed away, it may even be, from more prescribed and natural orbits, inheriting from their connexion with her strange difficulties and still stranger opportunities, confronted with rare questions and called upon for new discriminations." Before he has brought Milly to "full-blown consciousness," the figure of the Rhine maiden has changed for James to "that whirlpool movement of the waters produced by the sinking of a big vessel or the failure of a great business . . . the strong narrowing eddies, the immense force of suction, the general engulfment that, for any neighbouring object, makes immersion inevitable." But all those in Milly's neighborhood do not go under. Her dying movements recall other motions of her soul to Merton Densher, whose pretended love for her, caught up in self-interest, has become at her death something like the real thing, liberated by selflessness. Her old generosity has provided him with a large inheritance; his new generosity does not permit him to take it or even to discover how large it is. He is still quite willing to marry the woman for whose sake he has pretended and plotted and looked toward the inheritance he now refuses, but his fiancée now refuses in her turn. "Her memory's your love," she says to Densher. "You *want* no other." He insists: "I'll marry you, mind you, in an hour." "As we were?" "As we were." She turns to the door with her closing words, the drama's closing words and James's: "We shall never be again as we were!"

One would like to see in this theatrical exit the drama of America brought, if not to a close, at least to one of several flattering climaxes; as one would also like to see in Milly Theale's abundant generosity of means and extravagance of spirit a fair symbol of Americans. One need not stretch the canvas too far to make it present this picture. James has identified Milly as that "certain sort of young American" who is "more the 'heir of all the ages' than any other. . . ." He sees her, as anyone with half a gift for the oracular must have seen

America sixty years ago, "devoted and exposed, a creature with her security hanging . . . by a hair. . . ." [8] But it remains a private view, in spite of the clear outline presented in James's Preface and the spaciousness of the finished painting, following in such extravagant detail the cartoon with which James in his generosity has, so to speak, after the work of art, provided us.

In *The Wings of the Dove* and *The Golden Bowl* and *The Ambassadors,* James was producing—in 1902 and 1903 and 1904—a "literature fully aware of the difficulties of the American situation and able, in some sense, to meet them," that Van Wyck Brooks demanded in 1918. James was, as Brooks required, one of the writers who "are the pathfinders of society; to [whom] belongs the vision without which the people perish." [9] But the vision is not always offered directly to the people. Sometimes it comes in terms devious and far removed from those of the mass of people, a vision presented slowly, tortuously, in mysterious colors, as true visions have a way of presenting themselves. The critic can find the path for himself and perhaps for others—so at least James, who knew something of the craft, taunts the critic in his Preface to *The Wings:*

Of course, as every novelist knows, it is difficulty that inspires; only, for that perfection of charm, it must have been difficulty inherent and congenital, and not difficulty "caught" by the wrong frequentations. The latter half, that is the false and deformed half, of "The Wings" would verily, I think, form a signal object-lesson for a literary critic bent on improving his occasion to the profit of the budding artist. This whole corner of the picture bristles with "dodges"—such as he should feel himself all committed to recognise and denounce—for disguising the reduced scale of the exhibition, for foreshortening at any cost, for imparting to patches the value of presences, for dressing objects in an *air* as of the dimensions they can't possibly have. Thus he would have his free hand for pointing out what a tangled web we weave when—well, when, through our mislaying or otherwise trifling with our blest pair of compasses, we have to produce the illusion of mass without the illusion of extent. *There* is a job quite to the measure of most of our monitors—and with the interest for them well enhanced by the preliminary cunning quest for the spot where deformity has begun.[10]

Having discovered "the spot," having identified beyond a shadow of a doubt all of James's dodges, the critic still will not be able to make

James's method in his parables of "the American situation" universally agreeable or even acceptable. The indirection he practices is a contemplative exercise that requires some matching meditative energy on the part of the reader. One works one's way through the later James in waves of expanding consciousness, like Maggie Verver's or Merton Densher's; aware that one must keep watch, like Maggie, "to distinguish places that must serve, from within, and especially far aloft, as apertures and outlooks," willing, like Densher, to shrug off personal advantage, even the advantage of an absorbing tale that lifts one from oneself into somebody else's person and life. For with only very infrequent exceptions, the detachments one practices in taking with James the private view brings one closer to oneself and farther from that imagined participation in the lives of others that we call vicarious.

Henry James was, as he described himself to Henry Adams, "that queer monster, the artist, an obstinate finality, an inexhaustible sensibility." He could see his aloofness as no detachment at all but rather the constant plumbing of the depths of his own consciousness, an "act of life" in itself, involving an endless making of notes, hachures marking the gradations of people's surfaces and marks even more birdlike indicating things below the surface; notes of opening and closing moves in a conversation and of all those in between, of overt responses and covert. His art, he explained, was the art of the brush and not of the slate pencil; he really could not write "on that two-and-two-make-four system on which all the awful truck that surrounds us is produced"; the gift of life to him was the gift of consciousness, "an illimitable power. . . ." The participation in the lives of others that his sensibility offered was not in any way vicarious; it left each man square in his own place, though never too far from the places of others. The private view guaranteed privacy, but insisted on sharing the privacy: He wrote to Henry Adams in 1914,

I still find my consciousness interesting—under *cultivation* of the interest. Cultivate it *with* me, dear Henry—that's what I hoped to make you do— to cultivate yours for all that it has in common with mine. *Why* mine yields an interest I don't know that I can tell you, but I don't challenge or quarrel with it—I encourage it with a ghastly grin. You see I still, in presence of life (or of what you deny to be such,) have reactions—as many as possible—and the book I sent you is a proof of them. It's, I suppose, because I am that queer monster, the artist, an obstinate finality, an inexhaustible sensibility. Hence the reactions—appearances, memories, many things, go on playing upon it with consequences that I note and "enjoy" (grim word!) noting. It all takes doing—and I *do*. I believe I shall do yet again—it is still an act of life.[11]

There were times when James made his private view too public —or at least seemed to himself to be doing so—when there were too many marks on paper; when every word, every sound, every gesture signified too much; when he became too anxious about those he observed and when he tried to make their lives conform to his observations. Then his detachment once again delivered him and he saw himself and his method as worthy of parody and produced his elegant caricature of himself as the figure of the meddling observer of events, the narrator of *The Sacred Fount* (1901).

Of the writers and readers of the 1860's, Henry Adams wrote, "Henry James had not yet taught the world to read a volume for the pleasure of seeing the lights of his burning-glass turned on alternate side of the same figure. Psychological study was still simple. . . ." Forty or fifty years later the remark needed no amendment. In America, psychological study was still simple; the figures created by the public writers of the 1900's did not have alternate sides. But the new literature of realism did have a side—one side, clear or muddy, turned up for all to see, with an accompanying moral or emotional tone of about the same depth. What the public saw was what the public writer saw—there was no more to see. What the public felt was what the public writer felt—there was no more to feel.

It is a commonplace of American cultural history that the writers of this country have most of the time lived apart, alienated by temperament and by choice, choosing to reject society and thus to be rejected by it. Those writers who raked through muck with joy, rebuilding in mud what others had built in steel and concrete, found joy again in the sympathy they aroused and in the hostility, too. Those who, like the painters of 1900, fought to change fashions in subject matter, won the fight because they so clearly enjoyed new subjects; because censuring or praising, accepting or rejecting, they really saw art in ash cans. But unfortunately their judgments were shallow, Aesopian: signboards of defeat track Frank Norris's McTeague through Death Valley; emptiness engulfs Theodore Dreiser's Sister Carrie after she has lost track of her man. Whores, in this literature, almost invariably have hearts of gold, gold that sounds disagreeably like tinkling brass. Coincidence and contrivance suck the life out of situations; melodramatic manipulation makes the characters jerk eccentrically on their strings. No matter how much offended anyone —publisher, reviewer, reader—may have been when asked to linger so long over refuse, no one was really irritated by the conclusion reached after the dirt had been sifted through. The homely virtues remained, served in the breach at the very least. Greed was condemned. Loyalty was saluted. The art of Frank Norris and Theodore Dreiser was as public as that of David Belasco.

Only a delicate shade of irony withheld Stephen Crane's *Maggie* from immediate public success and made it fitting that it should at first have been issued privately. The fury that lights up *The Red Badge of Courage* is cinematic, episode after episode catching the reader in an experience that is all climaxes; and even a public that was not a film-going one was caught. Crane became a public artist after all—all of him, even the chronicler of Maggie.

The public writer like the public painter was an illustrator and fortunate to be one in the new century. It was the time to see things. Photographers were searching out form in windows and doorways, compositions in city streets and harbors, character in people's faces. Painters were coming before the photographers or following after and staying longer in the streets or down at the docks or at their easels, confronting the strangeness of ordinary people who had never before been stared at that way. Newspapers were sending men around the world to bring back pictures of wars and alien races and odd people doing odd things. American sight was opening almost to full width. Only a small astigmatism remained: A sense of propriety, Puritan and Jansenistic, imposed a custody of the eyes on the average man that cut his view off at the top and at the bottom and in the corners, wherever the dirt might gather.

Oppressed by what seemed to them a false propriety and encouraged by what seemed to them the naturalness of the new naturalism in writing, American novelists and journalists and poets and playwrights began to turn up the corners of carpets to look for the dirt so that they might confront the average man with it. Their hearts palpitated with only barely concealed pleasure as they found the dirt they looked for, the low behavior in high places, the *condottieri* in railroads and banking and beef and newspapers and their mercenary troops in politics. The ordeal of consciousness was not long for such writers. They had found their villainy and if necessary could manufacture villains to account for it. Not for them the incessant sound, "the hoarse bass of *vanitas vanitatum, omnia vanitas*" which William James heard between the lines of "that strange contemporary Parisian literature, with which we of the less clever countries are so often driven to rinse out our minds after they have become clogged with the dulness and heaviness of our native pursuits." Not for them either "the hour of terror at the world's vast meaningless grinding," or any part of an "inward remedilessness" in which "the world appears to us potentially as what . . . Carlyle once called it, a vast, gloomy, solitary Golgotha and mill of death." They may have seemed at times, the most lumbering of them, slipping into slime, or the most nimble-footed, dancing in it, to have surrendered to what James calls "the attitude of gnostical romanticism," which "transforms life from a tragic reality into an insincere melodramatic exhibition, as foul or as tawdry as any one's diseased curiosity pleases to carry it out." [12] But their romanticism actually lay elsewhere, doing its own kind of transforming, manufacturing its own melodramatic exhibitions out of an aching sincerity. Theirs was the romanticism of the new enlightenment, of the new heroes of the combat against the *condottieri:* Upton Sinclair's Jurgis Rudkus in *The Jungle* (1906), who survives every contact with the stockyard jungle and the lions and leopards of politics to emerge a good Socialist; Jack London's more euphoniously, more melodramatically, more allegorically named Ernest Everhard, who organizes and leads a band of revolutionaries to snap and bite at *The Iron Heel* (1907) of American fascism. They were determinists almost as much as their French predecessors and progenitors, but the causes they found for the ugly effects of finance capitalism did not lie in any irremediable gloom inherent in the human state: there were no Golgothas in their bibles. The same sequence of causes that produced beef trusts and robber barons would in time yield Rudkuses and Everhards, serfs and vassals determined to overthrow their feudal lords.

A meliorism so down-to-earth, so determinedly practical, created leaflets rather than literature. Into the Socialist tracts went much of the noise of life, but little of life itself. Compared to the squeals and roars of Sinclair's and London's beasts, the figures of Frank Norris and Theodore Dreiser talk like men. Furthermore, no matter what the biases of the authors, they remain excellent observers of the world they have come to reform. In rooms described—especially by Dreiser—in scrupulous detail, the shoguns of finance make their monstrous moves, the moves of men, with some of the dignity of men, preserved for a few paragraphs at least, recorded right next to their depravities. What Dreiser could do, even with all the limitations of his lumbering prose, is demonstrated by the setting he gives one of the many unattractive meetings of Philadelphia's double-dealing financiers and politicians in *The Financier* (1912). We are at the house in Rittenhouse Square of Senator Simpson—a man with all the Philadelphia virtues: Quaker background, some taste in the arts, and a large skill in money matters, which has given him a central place in conservative circles in Washington. Dreiser furnishes his house in precise detail:

The house that he occupied, of Venetian design, and four stories in height, bore many architectural marks of distinction, such as the floriated window, the door with the semi-pointed arch, and medallions of colored marble set in the walls. The Senator was a great admirer of Venice. He had been there often, as he had to Athens and Rome, and had brought back many artistic objects representative of the civilizations and refinements of older days. He was fond, for one thing, of the stern, sculptured heads of the Roman emperors, and the fragments of gods and goddesses which are the best testimony of the artistic aspirations of Greece. In the entresol of this house was one of his finest treasures—a carved and floriated base bearing a tapering monolith some four feet high, crowned by the head of a peculiarly goatish Pan, by the side of which were the problematic remains of a lovely nude nymph—just the little feet broken off at the ankles. The base on which the feet of the nymph and the monolith stood was ornamented with carved ox-skulls intertwined with roses. In his reception hall were replicas of Caligula, Nero, and other Roman emperors; and on his stair-wells reliefs of dancing nymphs in procession, and priests bearing offerings of sheep and swine to the sacrificial altars. There was a clock in some corner of the house which chimed the quarter, the half, the three-quarters, and the hour in strange, euphonious, and pathetic notes. On the walls of the rooms were tapestries of Flemish origin, and in the reception-hall, the library, the living-room, and the drawing-room, richly carved furniture after the standards of the Italian Renaissance.[13]

Like a Victorian portrait painter pointing to the opulence of his sitter's life, or a painter of the Flemish Renaissance, filling in details half in joyous collusion with the financier, half in mockery, Dreiser goes along with the Senator—at least as far as his furniture. As strongly as Sinclair and London, Dreiser took sides against the malefactors of American society—not a hard thing to do, since for him the sides were so clearly drawn. Thus it is society that corrupts Sister Carrie and traps her into a hollow life in the theater, one which is only superficially successful, and it is society again, conspiring with a haunting, time-consuming sexuality, which forces quotation marks around the epithet with which Dreiser describes his painter of the Ashcan School, Eugene Witla, in The "Genius" (1915). And society must take the blame for An American Tragedy (1925), the dissolution of Clyde Griffiths, a victim of the American dream. His abandonment of whatever it is that is his own, and not simply the manipulation of a studiously simple superego, is traced out in a series of events that is obvious but anguishing. He has been moving in two directions: onward and upward in a collar factory in upstate New York, including the inevitable attachment to a girl of wealth and class; downward and under with one of the factory girls, who is growing big and oppressive with his child. He cannot face the test of pregnancy out of wedlock. He had earlier deserted his sister when she was faced with the same problem. He now makes the weakest of determinations to kill his factory girl by drowning. She dies in what is apparently an accidental upsetting of their boat, but Clyde is held guilty of her death.

The burden of Dreiser's accusations will never be too much for American society, at one class level or at many, to bear. But the strength of his observations, with or without the accompanying bill of attainder, is that they document with remarkable fullness of detail the world of finance in the Frank Cowperwood trilogy (of which The Financier is the first volume), the world of commerce women were just beginning to come into in large number in Sister Carrie (1900), the life of the American artist fifteen years later in The "Genius," and the squalid setting in which success was wooed in the middle twenties in An American Tragedy. There is no great ordeal of consciousness in any of Dreiser's people, though he is not unaware of some of the symptoms of that ordeal. They lie crushed by the shattering weight of society's one immutable force, its force for destruction. Or they join the destroyer-behemoth. Crude, clumsy, much of this, and dubious social history, and yet so admirably complete in its furnishings—houses, rooms, cities, towns, the exteriors of people and, where they were accessible to a very simple psychology, their interiors—that we must find in Dreiser a very satisfactory naturalistic performance. He was incapable of James's detachment or his perceptions, but his works complement James's just the same. They give us enough to draw some conclusions for ourselves, about his people, about their society. And they never leave us so utterly at the mercy of partial parables and skimpy satires as the books of Sinclair Lewis and John Steinbeck do.

Sinclair Lewis's sense of humor was never large enough to turn his indictments of life on *Main Street* (1920), of *Babbitt* (1922), of religious fakery like that of *Elmer Gantry* (1927), or of native American Fascism (in *It Can't Happen Here,* 1935), into the satirical masterpieces they keep promising to become. He sniggers at the gaucheries of Gopher Prairie, Minnesota, in *Main Street.* He giggles at the loudmouth idiocies of George Babbitt. Then the snigger turns into a snarl in *Elmer Gantry* and the giggle into a gasp of horror in *It Can't Happen Here,* as the allegorically named small-town Vermonter, Buzz Windrip, blasts his way to the Presidency and thereafter through every democratic institution. Lewis's causes are self-evidently "good" ones today. They were never altogether without supporters, though in the early twenties they did require some special pleading and one must remember that even as late as 1935 the terrors of a Huey Long were not clear to many people. But the very intensity of Lewis's special pleading, relieved only by snigger and snarl, reduces the power of his plea. It is, too much of the time, as if he himself has not full confidence in his argument, has not the necessary assurance with which to construct the sensitively balanced shafts of satire.

One sees at least one good reason why he could not raise impolite laughter into satirical guffaws when one turns to the positive people of Lewis, those he admires. They are wooden; they are figures of virtue, not virtuous persons. There is Martin Arrowsmith, in the novel named after him (1925), and there are his associates, for example, medical idealists. Arrowsmith's life makes a splendid tale for boys, a rollicking version of Ibsen's *An Enemy of the People;* today, it could be easily turned into a musical for the new musical theater; as a matter of fact, Rodgers and Hammerstein were not so

far from it in *Allegro*. The terms of the tale are ridiculously simple—
St. George in a lab coat does battle against the dragon of medical
corruption. They are not much more complex in *Dodsworth* (1929),
in which the long-suffering hero, car manufacturer Sam Dodsworth,
must somehow make his peace with a frigid wife, with European
snobbism, and American automobile monopolists. Lewis is a little
closer to people of dimension here, but still incapable of any great
depth of analysis or the sort of detachment that would allow him to
do more than snipe at Dodsworth's enemies and (as he clearly believed) America's. And far from gaining in depth or detachment after
Dodsworth, Lewis became something of a hack novelist, turning out
work after work of no distinction, except that familiar one of the
second-rater, manifest good intention. In performances like *Ann Vickers* (1933), which takes care of social work and workers, *Gideon
Planish* (1943), which settles philanthropy and philanthropists, and
Kingsblood Royal (1948), which disposes of the Negro problem, this
tends to give even good intention a bad name.

John Steinbeck's *exempla* are better constructed than Lewis's.
They serve a somewhat less narrow view of society. Society is still
sick, still must be cured, but there is more joy in the cure than Lewis
allowed because there is more worth in the patient. On the basis of
Tortilla Flat (1935), one could even conclude that illness is only a
trick of the eye, that in the formidable bedragglement of the Mexican
section of Monterey, California, there may be more peace than futility, more sanity than oppression. This book of tales, drawn together
by an amusing central figure, seems, finally, more an indictment of
materialism than of any particular form of materialist society. Not so
what follows, however. It is all class struggle through *In Dubious
Battle* (1936), as California fruit-pickers organize, strike, are pursued by vigilantes and lose. Their heroic organizer, Communist Jim
Nolan, is killed. All is not really lost, however, Mac, the old Red pro,
tells the crowd at the end of the book. But that is not the answer. It is
only the question in this book, as it is in *Of Mice and Men* (1937),
the fatalistic tale of the mentally retarded physical giant who is too
strong to be allowed to live with such mental weakness. Steinbeck
allows ironies to creep into the union battle; the professional agitators
are, if not corrupt, untrustworthy, if not stupid, clumsy. In the tale of
overlarge Lennie with the crushing hands, everything moves too
swiftly for ironies to appear openly. But they are implicit, however

simple. Man is tricked by an indomitable genetic force, the equivalent, as it works its ignoble wiles upon its unprotected victims, of the devastating mutations in the weather that produced the dust bowl in Oklahoma, and in conjunction with an unplanned economy, sent Okies like the Joads in *The Grapes of Wrath* (1939) careering down the road to disaster. There are signals of hope: Lennie has a friend to shoot him, like a horse with a broken leg, before a posse can come and get him. The wife of Connie Joad, symbolically named Rose of Sharon, can wet-nurse a dying man with her full breasts when all other food gives out. And once again, at the end of Steinbeck's ambitious *East of Eden* (1952), Adam Trask, the dying paterfamilias of a family apparently doomed to an eternity of hatred, leaves his son Caleb a one-word inheritance. The word is Hebrew: *Timshel;* its meaning, as explained by the book's Chinese sage, "Thou *mayest* rule over sin." In other words, freedom is all. Certainly, in this *mélange biblique* of Steinbeck's, it accounts for all—for good and evil, for two sets of Cains and Abels, or Jacobs and Esaus, depending on how one twists the tale, and for at least one Adam and one Eve. Scripture suffers some in the telling. There is no scene so vivid as Rose of Sharon's unbosoming at the end of *The Grapes of Wrath,* no character so neatly and precisely fashioned as Lennie, although for all the book's many scenes and many pages, no character is presented in any greater depth than Lennie, with any more motivation or meaning. But there is at least open hope, a becoming note in any writer, even when produced in this theatrical fashion, like the grunts of Indian Joe at a séance.

Unfortunately, Steinbeck did not go on from Eden to cross the Jordan. He went back to Monterey for *Sweet Thursday* (1954), a sequel to a sequel, *Cannery Row* (1944), which was a kind of appendage to *Tortilla Flat.* One could do a short piece, perhaps, on Steinbeck's fascination with brothels and brothelkeepers in *East of Eden* and *Sweet Thursday,* if the subject had enough intrinsic interest. One could lament the need to return to a genre at best of limited value—the linked set of tales, built around a group of people, with only one of any special importance, in this case a marine biologist of doggedly eccentric beneficences. The essential sadness is that compulsive return to old forms and figures which has plagued a number of American writers, all, curiously enough, with a predisposition to naturalistic determinism, politically orientated.

John Dos Passos has repeated himself so often since *U.S.A.* (1930–36) that the initial accomplishment has almost been forgotten. Dos Passos has, in fact, been much neglected by critics and literary historians, not entirely forgotten, but relegated to a place in the past, the honorable confrere of Hemingway in remodeling the American novel, but a much smaller figure, a more distant one, though he has lived on beyond Hemingway. The distance increases with each new book, too much like the old ones except for an embarrassing change of political conviction, from left to right. It is almost an article of literary faith that a novelist who is as violently disaffected with the New Deal as Dos Passos is in *District of Columbia* (1939–48), his second trilogy, should no longer be taken seriously, especially when he adds to his disloyalty a rejection of the sacred cause of the liberal, the anti-Franco position in the Spanish Civil War. Assuredly, the second trilogy is not the astonishing performance that the first is. There are no new devices of the freshness of the Newsreels and Camera Eyes of the books that make up the first group, *The 42nd Parallel* (1930), *1919* (1932), and *The Big Money* (1936), though there are biographies of leading figures of the period placed strategically through the second set of volumes, as in the first, biographies that are brief, and always apposite. In *U.S.A.,* Dos Passos was a historical determinist of the left, looking toward a convulsive change in the social system to make imbalances right and give people something better—just what, is never made clear. It is significant, perhaps, that the last line of the last volume, concluding a brief study of a vagrant, is "A hundred miles down the road." No character is too well defined, for all the shuttlings back and forth, like crosscuttings in a film, among half a dozen central figures. The collective figure is Dos Passos' achievement here, class by class, group by group, not the individual. In the second set of volumes, *Adventures of a Young Man* (1939), *Number One* (1943), and *The Grand Design* (1948), one man, Glenn Spotswood, is clear enough, to the mind as well as the eye. And since the second volume is clearly based on the life and times of Huey Long, its demagogic protagonist is concentrated upon in the utmost detail, producing a book no less absorbing than Robert Penn Warren's *All the King's Men* (1946), and with none of the concealed or unconscious admiration for its Fascist hero that Warren's novel reveals and none of its dubious metaphysics either.

Dos Passos is still a designer of novels, as he has been from the very beginning in *Three Soldiers* (1921), where he presented the AEF of World War I in microcosm, and *Manhattan Transfer* (1925), where he did as much for the city of New York, over nearly a quarter of a century, with a small group of characters pulling everything together, including news events, songs, and speeches by public figures. After *U.S.A.*, in spite of a lack of fresh design, he continued to cut his pieces with skill, exposing his structure much as certain recent architects have. In spite of his strong political convictions, he remains at some remove from his people, from his plots, and from his settings. There is no inward gaze in any of his characters; that is not his way. But there is in him always a remarkable capacity for life, the ultimate palm he awards his country. For even though the country is, as it has been for decades, grossly ill, according to his separate diagnoses, swollen with different kinds of bigness, first with big business, then with big government, there is still in the United States a marvelous cross-grained vitality, and it is his special joy to describe the markings. This he still does, with a technique less obviously indebted to James Joyce now, somewhat more confined, but still quick, nimble, and precise, as the lines fall into place, like a great geodesic dome of prose.

Design in the novels of James T. Farrell is not often apparent, for all the sensitivity the writer has shown as a critic of literature, even as a philosopher of literature. His books, even the best of them, read like a series of confessions, recorded at first- or secondhand, thrown up into the ears and eyes, tossed at the senses, of his readers. The twenty-nine years of Studs Lonigan are of an unparalleled brutality in our literature, as they are recorded in *Young Lonigan* (1932), *The Young Manhood of Studs Lonigan* (1934), and *Judgment Day* (1935). In the Danny O'Neill books, the brutality is sifted more thoroughly, studied over Talmudically, one would be inclined to say, if one did not know so well that Farrell's preparation was Catholic and his scholasticism learned on the South Side of Chicago, from Irish priests. It is not notably improved by the studiousness: hoodlumism does not requite a pedantry with art, it just spins itself out in painfully repetitious pages. All one can say after the third, the fourth, the fifth installment of the O'Neill saga, is that one has been there before, and before, and before, an impression not one bit lessened by the fact that this series is not in chronological sequence and that one really has met Danny before: he is a character in the second volume of the Lonigan trilogy.

Farrell needs the annealing effect of time on his books—not a few years but a lifetime. Though they are not constructed as social history, they have, like the best of Dreiser, the virtue of scrupulous observation, precisely recorded, and thus they will remain, no matter what the writer's intention, documents of a time and a place and a people, and of a necessary stage in the development of a literature. It was not enough to have the recordings of Dreiser; we also needed the lucubrations of Farrell, more studied than Dreiser's, more laborious, more firmly tied to a view of history. It is our good fortune that in Farrell we found a historicism sufficiently unorthodox to avoid the crudities of the proletarian novelists and a psychology sufficiently direct to understand the motivations of his *Lumpen*-proletarians and a compassion sufficiently large to care about them. In time, we—or those who come after—may want to take chunks out of the O'Neill series and hold on to them, or to bits and pieces of the Bernard Clare (or Carr) trilogy. We will certainly be able to take, intact, one of the most neatly turned of Farrell's novels, *Ellen Rogers* (1941), a Zola-esque tale of a Catholic girl's descent into despair and suicide, and the less well finished but not less affecting story of *Tommy Gallagher's Crusade* (1939), a deservedly harsh translation of the anti-Semitic hoodlums of the Christian Front from the newspapers into a novel. Because Farrell's books are demonstrably accurate and just, it may even be that many of those who have been most offended by Farrell's treatment of the progeny of "good Catholic families," that is, good Catholic families, will in time come to recognize the blunt honesty of his narratives, and even find in the constant repetition of the same episodes and the nagging reiteration of the same failings a reflection of their own inevitably tautological discourse. What priest in parishes like those of Lonigan and O'Neill, Ellen Rogers and Tommy Gallagher, has not found himself blasting the same sins in the same way with the same examples week after week? Sin does not change. Neither do its narratives. They both tend to be repetitious.

Nelson Algren is a more inventive writer than Farrell, but his is not necessarily a useful kind of invention. His Chicago is not without its resemblance to life, but it is a life hurried along, pushed into high gear with narcotics, surrendering people to sensation under the guise of a superrealism that must never skip anything. So we go down skid row and up the hypodermic needle's edge, bump by lump, visiting at length only with the derelict and the depraved, who, by that inverted system of judgment which Algren has helped to make acceptable, are the only members of our ignoble society worth knowing. The incidental intelligence about Chicago in *Never Come Morning* (1942) is not without its insights: Algren has looked earnestly and lovingly at his city. The picture of dope addiction in *The Man with the Golden Arm* (1949), however, is a romantic one. Algren's compassion is constantly mutilated by his fantasies about addicts and whores, never more sadly than in *A Walk on the Wild Side* (1956), which sentimentalizes an illiterate Southern boy who achieves a brief maturity of muscle and gland, mostly in New Orleans, in the early thirties. "Earthy lyricism," one reviewer called it; it is earth-colored all right, a drab and dreary mixture of clay and dung, and the lyricism is rock 'n' roll, some twenty-five years too soon.

Chicago's book is Saul Bellow's *The Adventures of Augie March* (1953), from the opening lines, Augie's lines:

I am an American, Chicago born—Chicago, that somber city—and go at things as I have taught myself, free-style, and will make the record in my own way: first to knock, first admitted; sometimes an innocent, sometimes a not so innocent. But a man's character is his fate, says Heraclitus, and in the end there isn't any way to disguise the nature of the knocks by acoustical work on the door or gloving the knuckles.[14]

Bellow does not wear gloves, kid or any other kind. But, in spite of the suggestion of nose-thumbing truculence in the opening paragraph, neither Augie nor his author is out to shock. Sensation comes as it should, by the senses, always more alert to the city than anything else:

Well, this is how it was in Chicago when I came back. I stayed on the South side. I got my case of books back from Arthur and I read in my room. The heat of June grew until the shady yards gave up the smell of the damp soil, of underground, and the city-Pluto kingdom of sewers and drains, and the mortar and roaring tar pots of roofers, the geraniums, lilies-of-the-valley, climbing roses, and sometimes the fiery devastation of the stockyards stink when the wind was strong.

There are failures of tone in the book: Augie is too many different people, least convincingly of all a schooled philosopher, when we know and see and feel how utterly unschooled his philosophy is, but since Heraclitus makes his motto for him at the beginning of the book, he can claim a constant fidelity to change and let it go at that. Augie's Grandma, too, is some of the time more a product of the literary imagination than of life, an accommodation that would be entirely acceptable if Augie, the most convincingly self-conscious of recent heroes, showed himself aware of how much he was refracting his articulate grandmother out of focus.

There are also triumphs of tone in *Augie March:* a tumultuous mating process, to the flapping of an eagle's wings in Mexico, to the mechanical noises of Chicago, a mating with a rich girl who is, for once, more than just a glandular exercise on the writer's part; and the roundest of characters, one Einhorn, a product of the literary imagination, not entirely Bellow's imagination, but that of the middle-European Jewish world that formed Einhorn—or malformed him, if we want to take the fact that he is a cripple allegorically. One of Augie's summations of Einhorn has some of the delight of the man:

Jesus, he could be winsome—the world's charm-boy. And that was distracting. You can grumble at it; you can say it's a ruse or feint of gifted people to sidetrack you from the viper's tangle and ugly knottedness of their desires, but if the art of it is deep enough and carried far enough into great play, it gets above its origin. Providing it's festive, which sometimes it was with Einhorn, when he was not merely after something but was gay. He could be simple-hearted. Nevertheless I was down on him occasionally, and I said to myself he was nothing—nothing. Selfish, jealous, autocratic, carp-mouth, and hypocritical. However, in the end, I every time had high regard for him. For one thing, there was always the fight he had made on his sickness to consider. No doubt smiting the sledded Polack on the ice was more, or being a Belisarius, and Grail-seeking was higher, but weighing it all up, the field he was put into and the weapons he was handed, he had made an imposing showing. . . . He knew what retributions your devils are liable to bring for the way you treat your wife and women or behave while your father is on his deathbed, what you ought to think of your pleasure, of acting like a cockroach; he had the intelligence for the comparison. He had the intelligence to be sublime. But sublimity can't exist only as a special gift of a few, due to an accident of origin, like being born an albino. If it were, what interest could we have in it? No, it has to survive the worst and find itself a dry corner of retreat from the mad, bloody wet, and mud-splashing of spike-brains, marshals, Marlboroughs, gold-watch-consulting Plugsons, child-ruiners, human barbecuers, as well as from the world-wide livery service of the horsemen of St. John. So why be down on Einhorn, afflicted with mummy legs and his cripple-irritated longings?

Augie is always right when Einhorn is in the book: when the literature is running deep, it is on the sly, like the covert reference to Hamlet ("No doubt smiting the sledded Polack on the ice . . .") and all the conspicuous knowledge of history, tossed in as that kind of autodidact would. Einhorn is more of a true picaro than Augie, or a true picaro's teacher; he brings out the rogue in Augie and gives it body room and provides the impetus for growth, for growth of all kinds, of spirit, of heart, of understanding, that makes this one of the few really distinguished growing-up books in the literature. For with Einhorn, and all that he brings, the book has character as well as Chicago.

Character as Bellow delineates it is etched in the acid of pain. Tommy Wilhelm, the small-scale *misérable* of *Seize the Day* (1956), is memorable because his torture is not only clamorous but real; he commands our pity in spite of his smallness as a human being. Moses Elkanah Herzog, the large-scale acher of *Herzog* (1964), has intelligence, has tenderness; he also has trouble, which, with his self-directed tenderness and misdirected intelligence, he enlarges into torment. In spite of the breadth of Herzog's imagination and the charm of his talk (chiefly to himself), his torment is not convincing; it seems out of proportion to its causes; a toothache has been inflated into an intellectual melodrama. But the talk, the undelivered letters to the living and the dead, the intermittent glosses on the history of ideas—these give the book and the character dimension and make Herzog a figure to set beside the judge-penitent of Camus' *The Fall,* who is almost as much the victim of his own heated self-pity as Herzog.

Bellow's other books are trimmer than these sagas of suffering, and more nearly neutral, in spite of occasional indications of a position. In *Dangling Man* (1944), the isolated figure seems an emaciated version of Dostoevski's Underground Man, incapable of the great thrusts into life of the little fellow from between the Russian floorboards which give him enough material for a judge-penitent's notebook and our sympathy. In *The Victim* (1947), there is an exchange of positions between the anti-Semitic persecutor and the persecuted Jew, not quite described or defined, which makes what seems for a while only a contrived tale for sophisticated tears a fine paradoxical exercise. The allegory in *Henderson the Rain King* (1959) is too trim for discomfort: the middle-aged American who lands his lion cub, finally playing his African role well after a couple of poor rehearsals, is too neatly wrapped in symbol (especially after all the funny things we know about him, that he himself has told us) before getting down to allegorical business. The Henderson who stands for America in the second half of the book is not really half as interesting or as large a figure (even though he still wears the same outsize clothes) as the Henderson who simply stands for Henderson. Bellow's gift is gusto, is character, is people. It is a larger gift than that of the symbol-minded.

A gift for character is not enough, but it carries a writer far, when he has an ear such as Herbert Gold's. Motivation is often obscure in Gold's books and his plots are scrappy, but the speech is good and the atmospheres and settings are carefully shaped around it so that one always has a sense of human presence. There is in his books, too, a comely variety—a moving portrait of love in middle age that does not quite fall over into sentimentality in *Birth of a Hero* (1951); some good carnival atmosphere and a compelling figure of loneliness that turns to desperation under the force of drugs in *The Man Who Was Not With It* (1956); a study of politicking at the local level in *The Optimist* (1959), and some entertaining sketches of adolescents growing up in Cleveland in *Therefore Be Bold* (1960). The disappointment is *The Man Who Was Not With It*. It is a much better novel than *The Man with the Golden Arm;* there are no fantasies about drugs or drug addicts in it; much about it has the unmistakable conviction of reality, closely and well observed. But Gold's poor old carny victim springs too quickly at us: we do not know where he came from or why he is not with it; when he is trapped on a bridge leading to Canada, he might just as well be a runaway animal, for all his kindness to the boy through whom the book's modicum of feeling is allowed to escape.

Bernard Malamud chooses feeling above all in *The Assistant* (1957), a brilliant exploitation of pathos, quivering and without shame, but brief enough to permit at least a semblance of restraint. It is all closer to the better writers for the Yiddish theater than to Chagall, with whom Malamud has several times been compared. There are no goats in the Brooklyn sky of The Assistant, who comes

to rob a poor, miserable parody of a Jewish grocer and ends by
becoming, as best a young man who is not Jewish can, his double.
The experiences briefly related in *The Assistant* may not have the
resonances of profundity or grandeur that the book's most ardent
enthusiasts find in it, but they are told with a striking economy and
without any great stirring of symbols. In *The Natural* (1952), baseball is forced onto the field of myth, where it sits, stands, runs, and
finally strikes out: the whole thing belies its title: it is far too artificial, with a theory about popular culture that is more appropriate to
a speculative essay than a novel. Mark Harris's *Wake Up, Stupid*
(1959) does the same thing with a much less fancy windup, more
naturally. Malamud's third novel, *A New Life* (1961), is written in a
curious amalgam of the two styles. Pathos there is, pathos for the sad
lot of the college instructor, especially if the college is secondrate and
he isn't any better. There is an additional poignancy, not quite
planned for: the material has been presented so often, indifferently,
by indifferent novelists, that it is hard to respond to a better writer
who has nothing much better to offer. When deeper meanings come,
they come in the usual mode of books with this setting: the long,
wobbly shadows of impotence play fitfully among some dancing
satyrs and nymphs of the English department. Why not the engineers
or the physicists, for a change? Don't their wives ever leave them? Is
the pay so much better? Or the sex? Kinsey doesn't say, and neither
does Malamud.

The alienated man pursues the reader of recent American novels
feverishly, furiously, down the chapters, brandishing misery like a
marriage certificate. The paths of justification are certainly greater in
number and more devious than Luther ever realized, the sounds of
complaint surely more various and more strident than the first American writers to wind up their characters for whining ever intended.
Oh, with what invention, with what love, with what longing, the case
for alienation has been made, by novelists pleading for children, by
novelists pleading for Negroes, by novelists pleading for Jews, by
novelists pleading for the South, by novelists pleading for college
instructors, by novelists pleading for themselves. Can you blame
them? What would you do if you were a college instructor, especially
an impotent one married to an importunate wife, with another fellow
hanging around down the hall, sneering at you at parties between
leers at your wife, a fellow whose problem is obviously quite the

opposite of yours? What would you do if you were a Southerner? A Negro? A Jew? A Child? Obviously, you would write a novel or find a novelist to write one for you. Obviously, you have.

Perhaps the reason that Ralph Ellison's *The Invisible Man* (1952) continues to bear close inspection more than a decade after publication is that it makes no overt pleas for the downtrodden Negro, bursts with no sense of outrage. There is anger in the book, but not the violent kind of Richard Wright's *Native Son* (1940) or Chester Himes's *If He Hollers Let Him Go* (1945); it is the pugnaciousness of a boy who goes through more rites of initiation than were ever dreamed of by an African tribe or an anthropologist, to learn that he must protect himself with belligerence or with irony. The wonder is that Ellison, having served an apprenticeship in the tents of the bellicose, Communist Party-line periodicals, should come down so hard on the side of a Dostoevskian irony. He inspects color like a painter or a dancer, making splendid little arabesques of his whirls around the color line. If there is a plaintive note in the book, it is in the multiplicity of ironies let loose by the fragments of the blues that he has dropped into his narrative—still another color, the only right one, as the white man sees the black, to light up the darkness: it brings such comfort to the white man.[15]

Ellison's book is almost a private statement. It will be read in future, as it has been in the past, by a mass of people, but its modality requires, if not extended meditation, at least a pause in the judicial process. The answer to *The Invisible Man* is not a Supreme Court decision or a lifetime membership in the NAACP, however worthy both may be. It is, rather, like the answer one must give Dostoevski's Underground Man, an act of love. The terrors of Wright's Bigger Thomas, made everybody's enemy by everybody, including himself, can be dissipated by more simple means. More important, perhaps, because Bigger fits so well into the popular image of the criminal Negro, *Native Son,* the book about him, can be easily forgotten, as it has been by so many of us. Not a tract, not simply a tale of blood, and yet not quite touching, not quite right—that is the futility of the angry book about alienation, as it also is of the book that mixes anger with an irony so bitter it turns to sarcasm, Himes's *If He Hollers.* Himes moved through some shrewd writing about politics and the Negro in *Lonely Crusade* (1947) to a long, sad tale, *The Third Generation* (1954), about a gentle Negro college teacher, doomed by his intellectual inadequacies and sweetness of disposition to shabby jobs in shoddy Negro colleges, and the family doomed with him. Too long, too sad, the novel makes some eloquent motions in the direction of significance in the conflict between the genteel professor, content with his low lot, and his shrill wife, ambitious, anxious for rank, scornful of her husband's dark color—a terrible symbol of her frustrations.

What can be done with a Negro family is demonstrated in James Baldwin's *Go Tell It on the Mountain* (1953). Several salvations are mixed in the book, religious, racial, human. Out of a running fight between Gabriel, the father of the family, who is a preacher, and John, his illegitimate stepson, come all the tensions of the book. Gabriel's is a kind of annunciation; though by a means far from direct he leads John to a stunning religious experience. Whether it really transforms the boy or not, it must do something to the reader, brought through John's ecstasy to see, to hear, and to feel the kind of exposure the Negro has for so long been required to make of himself, even without any degrading confrontations with white men. Those, too, play a part in the novel, but they are only on the second level of exposure. Before going out to the marketplace, the Negro has had to go to the mountain.

The martyrdom of the Negro has been eloquently attested by Baldwin and Ellison and Himes. The holy witness of the homosexual is something less than convincing, in novels by, among others, Gore Vidal, Dorothy Baker, and James Baldwin. One recognizes, and not unwillingly, one hopes, that the agonies of homosexual love, male or female, are not less agonizing than those of the heterosexual, but that does not make any more acceptable clichés of character or plot or setting. A triangle is a triangle is a triangle, is the mournful effect of Dorothy Baker's book about the tortures of Lesbian love, *Trio* (1943), which suffers from a dullness of plot, just as does *Young Man with a Horn* (1938), her more celebrated novel, based, more or less, on the life of Bix Beiderbecke.

Fineness of perception intervenes in Baldwin's *Giovanni's Room* (1956), *fioritura* passages of splendid, spiky writing, quite fitting in a book about an American and an Italian in Paris. But the plot is the old triangular one, and the odd angles do not make for any more depth of interest, as the murder into which Vidal's *The City and the Pillar* (1948) slides does not either. Baldwin is more successful in his effort to give dignity and depth to homosexual love in *Another Country* (1962). On the basis, at least, of the furious genitality of that novel, the application of the adjective "unnatural" to homosexual relations seems unconvincing and not even altogether relevant. Unfortunately the half-dozen central characters of the book live only in their sexual organs. In their dragon-fly couplings they have an unmistakable strength. We may be annoyed, exhilarated, horrified, inspired; some of the time we are bound to be absorbed by the meticulous descriptions of a connoisseur of the dance of death. But for the rest, we have almost no clue. There is no meaningful life to the jazz playing and singing of the book's Negroes, brother and sister, musician and singer. There is no opening into the motivations of the two writers among Baldwin's sextet, or those of the actor or the neglected wife, except the opening of the thighs and the motivation of the glands. And for all the candor of the talk between the races about the races, there is no insight offered here either, but only sensuality, hostility, accusations, conjugations, the sweetness and the bitterness of lives lived entirely in the flesh.

In these tales of torment, a technical perfection that extends to every facet of novel-making remains the only expediency of the writer with a special plea to make, even if the plea is patently a just one. It is ultimately the elegance of Proust that makes everything and everyone acceptable in his book—acceptable as characters, not as people. It is often much easier to take the tortured, or even the torturing, in the flesh than on the page. Inept writing—motivationless characterization, flat plotting, constant pleading—is certain damnation for a pervert in a novel, whether he is accomplished or unaccomplished, wishful or real. In the hands of an artist, we confront a fellow human being's agony; with a less than highly competent writer, we deal with sodomy.

That is as much true for the ordinary agonies as it is for the more spectacular ones. Just a touch of Oedipus, with a small complication of Southern tension, is enough for the fullest anguish, as William Styron shows in his almost impeccably ordered *Lie Down in Darkness* (1957). The interior monologue of a dying girl, which comes just before the end of the book, is as searing a soliloquy of pain and desertion and the terrible awareness of approaching death as we have in the recent American novel. "Diuturnity is a dream and folly of expectation," are the last words from the epigraph taken from Sir Thomas Browne's *Urn Burial*. The girl's last words are:

Perhaps I shall rise at another time, though I lie down in darkness and have my light in ashes. I turn in the room, see them come across the tiles, dimly prancing, fluffing up their wings, I think: my poor flightless birds, have you suffered without soaring on this earth? Come then and fly. And they move on past me through the darkening sands, awkward and gentle, rustling their feathers: come then and fly. And so it happens: treading past to touch my boiling skin—one whisper of feathers is all—and so I see them go—oh, my Christ!—one by one ascending my flightless birds through the suffocating night, toward paradise. I am dying, Bunny, dying. *But you must be proper.* I say, oh pooh. Oh pooh. Most be proper. Oh most proper. Powerful

Oh most Powerful
Oh must [16]

Diuturnity has been a dream for the girl; it has not been much more real for her father, the "Bunny" of the concluding prayer, though certainly his life has had its plentitude of tangled tangibilities— another daughter, early dead; a wife never fully alive; a mistress live enough, but not much else. The implausible days fill in the waiting moments at the station dock, as father and mother wait for the train bringing their daughter's body back to them, rescued from New York's potter's field, an island of faceless people, where bodies are dumped like fill in Jamaica Bay. It is Styron's accomplishment to have filled in some faces and to have made us hold still for a long chronicle of the enemies of expectation, not a friendly gesture to our own hopes. He does not do as well in his other large book, *Set This House on Fire* (1960), though freedom is its ultimate election and the text for his lengthy sermon is another lofty one from the seventeenth century, this time from a sermon by John Donne. But this tale and its writing seem to get beyond Styron, to send him round and round the literary devices and the literary places—in Italy and in the South—with a murder in it that is better suited to one of Patricia Highsmith's little horror tales.[17]

A relationship between father and daughter not unlike that in *Lie Down in Darkness* is the center of action and analysis in Harvey

Swados' *Out Went the Candle* (1955), with Jewishness as surrogate for the Southern cross. There is more to this father than the other, if less to the girl, with neither granted the felicity of such a constant making of phrases as Styron deals his characters. But there are scenes to stir pity, if not horror—the father almost piercing his dulled consciousness in London at the time of the great raids, the daughter submitting to the most graceless of sexual experiences, again and again and again, with a soldier who might just well be a dog tag with genitals, on a ride across America. Everything that occurs in darkness is tinged with death in both books, a darkness that begins at the center of corrosion and decay in the modern American novel, the family. Both are highly literary works, with endings of carefully worked craftsmanship that do not quite ring true, a difficulty almost impossible to surmount in a fictional mode that insists so much upon naturalistic detail that every less than precise speech or descriptive passage must inevitably sound precious and strained by whatever distance it departs from verisimilitude.[18]

It is by that measure that the war books that report in deepest dirtiest detail the sound of guns and the groans of soldiers, that work in plenty of anatomical and psychological details to go with the battle strategy, carry the deepest, dirtiest impression, the one everyone wants of war. So it is that the books of the Second World War were John Horne Burns's *The Gallery* (1947) and Norman Mailer's *The Naked and the Dead* (1948) and James Jones's *From Here to Eternity* (1951) and Herman Wouk's *The Caine Mutiny* (1951) and Irwin Shaw's *The Young Lions* (1948), slick books, all of them, thick books, with character so incisively, so colorfully rubbed into the protagonists of each of the books that it is very hard to see the people for the shiny cosmetics piled on them. It is all more like the "life-tone" makeup advertised in the funeral directors' magazines than anything living people wear. Shaw, Jones, and Wouk wrote superior movie scenarios this way; Mailer got himself under way as a writer, full of little touches of several other writers and big smears of Dos Passos; and Burns, not without the influence of Dos Passos, too, managed to sneak some dignity for a couple of soldiers and more for the people of Naples into a book which finally defeats its own contrivances, pseudoliterary and *echt* naturalistic, and presents a fair record of American soldiers in the Italian war which may even stand up as a document of the wandering American, in or out of war.

A better book than any of these about the war is *The Patriot*
(1960) of Evan S. Connell, Jr., a novel about the systematic disillusionment through the good offices of the Army Air Force of a Kansas
original—a sweetly, almost shrewdly, altogether rightly gullible boy.
The whole thing—from first high hopes to last low certainties, from
mishaps in a plane, to idiocies as an art student, to a miraculously
ordinary marriage—is a little as a chronicle of such events might be if
it were written by Smollett or Fielding. The ironies are good-hearted,
as they never are in the big war books (not that *The Patriot* is small,
exactly) or in the tightly turned short stories or novellas about the
hellish military, like William Styron's *The Long March* (1952), in
which the Marines, old specialists at this sort of villainy, plot the
nasty boot-blasting trials. There are deaths in Connell's book and
villains to account for them, if one insists, but the hell of war is not
combat in this book, not dirty words and lives to fit them, but sham
at the air base, pretense in the barracks, fatuity in the psychologist's
office, and the destruction of simple patriotism, which doesn't stand a
chance against such odds, except in an inverted form, wistful, Fran-
ciscan, and not quite in touch with the world.

As it is with the war books, so too with the books about adolescents. J. D. Salinger is the preferred voice; Holden Caulfield's, in *The
Catcher in the Rye* (1951), is accounted the authentic sound. There
are some few readers who get goddam sick of Holden's goddams,
who are not comforted by the unmitigated preciosity of the recital,
Holden playing cute and self-critical to make us see through him
seeing through himself and make us love him as he loves his sister as
nobody else loves him and as he loves nobody else. But most adult
readers are content and adolescents are very content to find in
Holden Caulfield's madness in Manhattan a hook upon which to hang
their own happy discontent, as if somehow having caught the ragged
edge of prep-school syntax were a sign of deep understanding. Adult
readers, anyway, ought to know better and to remember with longer
and more faithful memories that incomparable record of two boys in
Chicago and at the University of Illinois, William Maxwell's *The
Folded Leaf* (1945). The naturalism there is sustained, worked
through with little chatty sociological asides, half-ironic, one im-
agines, but surely not meant to be disregarded either, and in any case
not easy to put aside. Nothing in the accumulation of sensitivity with
shame on the part of Lymie Peters or of manhood and a girl on the

part of Spud Latham can be put aside. They are teased out of the carapace of adolescence, as the lines from Tennyson suggest, following their own nature, following nature:

> Lo! in the middle of the wood,
> The folded leaf is woo'd from out the bud. . . .

Maxwell has done younger children an unaccustomed justice in that sad book built around a young mother's death, *They Came Like Swallows* (1937), and he has been faithful, at perhaps too great length, to some slightly older children, not long married, in *The Chateau* (1961). But his special accomplishment is *The Folded Leaf,* for which Huckleberry Finn need not be invoked, about which no great fuss need be made: it is simply right.

In the same way, if one may be allowed a smallness of vision for a moment, one may celebrate Jean Stafford's *The Mountain Lion* (1947) without underlining all the symbols in an unusually skillful allegory of the pains of emerging adolescence, without sitting heavily on the significance of the shooting of the lion which, with a horror that has few equals in our literature, we learn has also involved the shooting of the strange and wonderful girl who is the marvel of this short novel concerning herself and her brother, who is almost as wonderful as she is, if not quite so strange. The girl's name is Molly, the boy's, Ralph, and at the end of the first of the nine chapters there is enough about both of them to indicate some of the uncommon sensibility of the book:

Once Grandpa had said that Molly was "a deep one" and Ralph almost thought this was true. He had said it because she insisted that she had learned Braille in kindergarten, and though people would explain to her that what she was thinking of was the beads on a frame which you moved about to learn to count, she replied, "I said I learned Braille and I mean it."

"Will you listen to my poem?" she said pleadingly.

"How long is it?" Ralph did not care for poetry.

"It's real little." And then, without waiting for him to say "All right" she went on. "It's called 'Gravel,'" she said, "and this is it:
             Gravel, gravel on the ground
             Lying there so safe and sound,

Why is it you look so dead?
Is it because you have no head?"

"Say it again," said Ralph, puzzled now. And when she had repeated it, he said, "It doesn't make any sense. Gravel doesn't have a head."

"That's what I said. 'Is it because you have no *head*?' "

"Well, I don't know what you're talking about."

"You're merely jealous because you can't write poems yourself," said Molly, close to tears. She took her handkerchief out of the pocket of her middy and snuffled into it and beginning to cry, she said, "Now you've gone and made me have another nosebleed."

He did not even open his eyes. He knew that she didn't have a nose-bleed and he was so tired of her poems that he was just not going to make any effort to understand this one or to praise it. But neither did he want her to have a mad on him because that would spoil Grandpa's arrival and so he said, "Why don't you go write it down on a piece of paper and then maybe I can get the drift of it?" It was true that he never could hear things as well as he could see them and until just this year he had always thought that the song was "O Beautiful for Spacious Guys."

"I will! I will!" cried Molly and she ran to the house, chanting her poem.[19]

One need not push very hard at the symbolic structure of *The Mountain Lion* to discover in it a great deal about a disappearing openness and honesty in American life, dead, like Grandpa, like Molly, like the lion. What makes the novel so satisfying is its own openness and honesty, so much like a medieval fiction, accessible at any level at which one might want to grasp at it. Nor, having grasped, need one fear that one will come away with a sententious homily about the rugged values of the old West that we have cashed in for a tinseled modernity. The loss of values seems to be lamented all right, but as something inexorable, like growing up, like death. It is, as Gerard Manley Hopkins says, "the blight man was born for."

A similar spirit informs George Santayana's *The Last Puritan* (1936). The book is bound in green, Santayana's latter-day color at Scribner's, chosen, apparently, to distinguish his single novel and his memoirs from the solemn maroon of his volumes of philosophy. It should have had at least a small black band put around it, to signify its mournful tone and to do so in the manner of Santayana's genera-tion, for the passing of which this beautiful long elegy was written.

When he was first considering the book, in 1921, Santayana wrote to an old friend that it was "to contain all I know about America, about women, and about young men. As this last is rather my strong point, I have *two* heroes, the Puritan and another not too much the other way." It has been remarked that the heroes are at opposite poles: Protestant and Catholic, Puritan and hedonist, mournful and joyful. While that is true, it rather simplifies the novel and makes more of the polarity than Santayana does. For Santayana's real concern—obsession, almost—is the Puritan, Oliver Alden, named with allegorical precision after Oliver Cromwell and John Alden. Oliver is, as Santayana explained in another letter, "very much too fine in texture and feeling to be happy in his world, or to succeed in the things (including love-making) which it expects him to attempt; and so he peters out—which is so terrible a quiet tragedy that I have actually cried over the writing of it!" One shares his tears, however one makes one's identifications in *The Last Puritan*. Oliver tells us, as he tells himself in his last soliloquy in the book, what we have really known all along, that he "was born old," that he needs "to be honest . . . to be true . . . to be just," and that as a result of this "dreadful inheritance" he is quite out of fashion: "The world is full of conscript minds, only they are in different armies, and nobody is fighting to be free, but each to make his own conscription universal. I can't catch the contagion." This is spoken at the time of the First World War, just before Oliver goes to his death in France, but the words have much more than special application to one time and one place and one person. They have surely been spoken, or thought, by every man of good will in the twentieth century, no matter what his actual or ultimate convictions.

Oliver Alden is certainly not the last Puritan. Much better candidates for the distinction are the watered-down aristocrats of John Cheever's Massachusetts suburbia in *The Wapshot Chronicle* (1957) and *The Wapshot Scandal* (1964) and the liquored-up plutocrats and rustics of Peter De Vries' Connecticut exurbia in *Comfort Me with Apples* (1955), *The Mackerel Plaza* (1957), *The Tunnel of Love* (1958), *The Tents of Wickedness* (1959), and *Reuben, Reuben* (1964). To say that the distinction is made dubious, or invidious, by the candidacy of Cheever's and De Vries' defaulters and defeatists is not necessarily to rate their chronicles low. Default and defeat were seeded in the New England soil long, long ago, and these chroniclers are only showing the results of the ancient planting, and what's more, in uncommonly cheerful ways—Cheever with a gentility of style that is particularly fitting when he is dealing with his most attractive characters, his Wapshot ancients, Leander and Honora; De Vries with the most redoubtable punning and parodying in recent literary history. Still, the sagas of patrician attrition and middle-class malingering do sag, for all the good cheer, or maybe because of it. Scurrility should not be so cheerfully narrated, at least not over and over again, and without any particular depth of insight into it, for all the considerable skills of the narrators. One begins, after a while, to think that the writers have mistaken heartiness for heart, and one turns, then, if not for comfort, at least for a much deeper experience of evil, to De Vries in his great anguished outcry at the scandal of leukemia, *The Blood of the Lamb* (1961), in which his central character execrates a God he doesn't really believe exists. This may be confused thinking, but it is not superficial. And as with so many of the anguished and violent and biting performances of recent American writing—by novelists like Norman Mailer and John Hawkes and Mary McCarthy—it makes us measure the state of our own anguish or violence, the sharpness or dullness of our own bite.

It is easy to dismiss Norman Mailer. The newspapers have sometimes made him seem a mixture of fool and madman. His own translations of partial failure and fragmentary success and wishful conquest of the literary world into a torture chamber of exhibits, *Advertisements for Myself* (1959), have sometimes made him seem a barbarian. The contretemps that surrounded the publication of *The Deer Park* (1955)—refusal of publication by the publisher who had contracted for it and then by ten others, reputedly because of its unacceptable obscenities—made him seem an oaf. The reviews of *Barbary Shore* (1951) made him seem a one-book writer, the triumphant narrator of his own war experiences in *The Naked and the Dead* (1948). His fitful career as a columnist in a Greenwich Village weekly he helped to found and as a contributor to odd little magazines like *Dissent* and odder ones like *One* made him seem, as in the newspaper stories, a mixture of fool and madman. But dismissal won't do. *Barbary Shore* and *The Deer Park* are much better than their reviews. They show, both of them, an insight into the psychology of rebellion much more subtle and less proprietary than one would expect of a writer who is so busy so much of the time proclaiming his rebelliousness. The characterization of failure in *Barbary Shore*—failure to stay sane, failure to stay rebellious, failure to stay whole—is round, thorough, compassionate, and happily unconniving. The retrogression of character in *The Deer Park* is equally well conceived and developed: in its tumultuous, unargumentative way, it says much more about the terror of Congressional inquisition than Arthur Miller's *The Crucible,* or all the high-minded, agonizing editorials. If one can forget the sexual determinism that gathers in marginal knots around the edges of both books, one may find two well-turned tales of the terrors that turn up in Brooklyn Heights rooming houses and any houses at all in Hollywood. They are more startling tales, really, than any that turn up in the chain of griping, grunting, fighting, fornicating, roaring and dying that is *The Naked and the Dead,* and with far more assertion of Mailer's own skill and no egregiously derivative notes like those out of Dos Passos in the war book. "Please do not understand me too quickly," Mailer quotes André Gide at the beginning of *The Deer Park;* it is a fair request.

Irony and cynicism mix so well that sometimes in reading some of our professional ironists, say, James Gould Cozzens, Mary McCarthy, or John Hawkes, to take three who would probably shudder at being linked together, it is hard to know whether we are meant to come away bitter, bemused, or merely entertained. None of these novelists can escape the problem of intention. It is written all over their books. Their detachment is firmly marked. They affect many voices, deal, without any significant comment, with many different places, and not just different places but different kinds of places. All we have to be is attentive and through the many places, the different voices, the firm detachment, we will find—what? In Cozzens, a doctor, a lawyer, an army officer, each implacably professional, like Cozzens. In Hawkes, a Gothic horror, German or English or American, that doesn't horrify, because it is all just enough out of focus, just loosely enough assembled, set at a permanent tangent from human experience. In McCarthy, a not quite nimble-witted intellectual, a not quite lovable nonintellectual, an embarrassing attempt at creating a utopian community, an embarrassing attempt at creating a utopian college—all making the reader feel at least a little ashamed and embarrassed for those who have not quite made themselves bright or lovable or created any successful utopias, for certainly Mary McCarthy is not going to bother being ashamed or embarrassed. The question is, after performances like *The Oasis* (1949), *The Groves of Academe* (1952) and *A Charmed Life* (1955), by Mary Mc-Carthy, and *By Love Possessed* (1957), by Cozzens, whether we are going to bother. Cozzens has to answer now for having muddled professional detachment with a rhetoric so strained for large-scale irony that it reads like nothing so much as a mockery of itself. And McCarthy has left us so ensnared in her net of scorn that we find her books worthy objects of the same treatment; what, finally, is not contemptible? If Hawkes is exempt from the same charges, it is partly because he has chosen the safest distance of all, that of calculated obscurity, but equally because he can, without losing his obliqueness, tell an engrossing tale of human ugliness, such as the Nazi one, *Cannibal* (1950), or that most accessible of the lot, *The Lime Twig* (1961), about an English racetrack gang and its ritual murders, with connections reaching, not quite implausibly, back to the bombing of London in 1940.

Mary McCarthy, in her Foreword to *The Company She Keeps,* (1942), explains something about reaching back on the part of a character and the character's creator. She compares that reaching back, that search for the roots of a lost identity, to a woman who has lost something out of her pocketbook, "something ordinary and indis-pensable." The questions are the familiar ones—"When did you have it last?" "Was it here? Did you still have it at this point?"

It is not only scenes and persons but points of view that are re-visited—the intimate "she," the affectionate, diminutive "you," the thin, abstract, autobiographical "I." If the reader is moved to ask: "Can all this be the same person?" why, that is the question that both the heroine and the author are up against. For the search is not conclusive: there is no deciding which of these personalities is the "real" one; the home ad-dress of the self, like that of the soul, is not to be found in the book.[20]

The search is still inconclusive in *The Group* (1963), the most ambi-tious of the McCarthy novels, but there are at least a few indications of female personality that ring true, like an address that checks out. The class of 1933 at Vassar, Mary McCarthy's class, provides the members of the Group. Bitchiness, bafflement, incompetence, preten-sion, self-evasion, self-delusion—the mixture is to some extent as before, but the briefs are longer and more detailed and even, here and there, balanced. Unfortunately, along with the balance comes a dullness that makes one wonder why the author bothered with the search for her group and why we must bother after her. The identities of Vassar '33 as revealed here, though perhaps accurately hunted down and described, do not seem worth the trouble. In spite of a few entertaining sketches of bumbling old and stumbling young motherhood and a last-minute revelation of one of the Group as a Lesbian, which gives the book's concluding pages some momentary intensity; in spite of a sexual candor that is more apposite than usual and more deeply searched, *The Group* is remarkably like any other narrative of bitchiness, bafflement, incompetence, pretension, etc., written by a woman for women to discuss in their clubs.

Something like a search for a lost identity may be the motivation for Katherine Anne Porter's monumental display of human unworthiness, *Ship of Fools* (1962). One can only marvel that over the several decades she worked on the book, the writer was able to keep her eye and her mind fixed so steadily on smallness of spirit, on German smallness, on American smallness, on Mexican smallness, on the pettiness and the selfishness and the stupidity of the old and the young and the middle-aged, all gathered on a German ship bound from Mexico to Germany in 1931. No act of valor, no display of value, no depth of characterization, no breadth of narrative relieves the terrible tone of the book, the atmosphere of a sodden, sullen mediocrity, too witless to suffer or draw any significant lessons from its clotted condition. After such a voyage, all that is left to do is to see when the next sailing of Noah's ark is scheduled to be.

Like Sebastian Brandt, the fifteenth-century writer from whose *Narrenschiff* she took her title, Katherine Anne Porter was writing an allegory of human destiny. "I took for my own," she told an interviewer just before the book was published, "this ageless, almost universal image of the ship of this world on its voyage to eternity. I am a passenger on that ship." Brandt's ship is as packed with folly as Miss Porter's, but the guises he finds for foolishness are more numerous and the moral judgments he makes more various than hers and he leaves us at the end with something more than befuddlement to take with us to eternity. Of course, it may be that befuddlement is the identifying mark of twentieth-century fools, but surely it is not so universal nor so stupefying as Miss Porter makes out. In any case, other novelists, most of them women, curiously enough, have done a better job of looking behind this badge of contemporary folly to see why so many wear it.

Befuddlement sooner or later attacks most of the people of that old Southerner, Ellen Glasgow. Most of them die of it, some slowly, achingly, others all of a sudden, when they discover how miserable they are in their bewilderment and decide that a life that is uncertain is no life at all. Most of the men in Miss Glasgow's Virginia are well-heeled, well-behaved fools. Most of the women are good women but dull women, courageous women but not adventurous women, not in fact women at all. Love taunts the men. Love eludes the women. But befuddlement reaches them all.

As a reporter of life among the gentlefolk, she tends neither to edify nor to shock, but she does entertain. Her sagas of sexual failure among the magnolias are insufficiently detailed to serve as case histories, too delicate to touch the reader's nerves, too ironic to stir any passions. One wonders at her success in the twenties with the ladies who patronize lending libraries and the others, the truly genteel consumers of books, who buy special editions of books like the Old Dominion set of Ellen Glasgow's novels, a series of volumes bubbling over at the edges with fragrant blossoms and other insignia of the F.F.V. With whom did these ladies sympathize in these tales of frustration and impotence? Or did they find comfort in the numbers of finely crafted females who were born, perhaps like themselves, into a life of well-bred servitude? One hopes that they did not miss the ironies, or were not content to skip the larger jests for the smaller plays on words. One trusts that they did not read only to sneer at the selfish men, to weep at the unselfish women, and to cheer the few heroines who come through, like Dorinda Oakley, the long-suffering but ultimately triumphant farm girl in *Barren Ground* (1925). Dorinda is the center of a daytime radio serial's load of lamentable events. She is seduced and left for dead by her own true love, a doctor, who wants position and money and peace with his father more. The man she marries, finally, a village storekeeper, dies in a railroad accident. But her farm prospers, and when the doctor's mad wife kills herself and he has no resources with which to take up life again or to keep his farm, she buys the second and supervises the first. She does not love him. She loves no one, really. She is a manager, of farms, of people. No more marriages. No child of her own, just her husband's by a previous marriage. No seed in that ground.

And where is there seed? "For thirty-six years Judge Gamaliel Bland Honeywell had endured the double-edged bliss of a perfect marriage," *The Romantic Comedians* (1926) begins; "but it seemed to him, on this sparkling Easter Sunday, that he had lived those years with a stranger." One year after his wife's death, he tries "with all the strength of his decorous will" to remember what she looked like, and fails.[21] He rejects an old girl friend, who has the sentence of years upon her—she is 58—in favor of a young cousin of his wife, who is only 23, an appealing age to the 65-year old judge. His splendidly named wife—Annabel Upchurch, now Honeywell as well—promptly leaves him for the sonorities of one Dabney Birdsong, and the judge, determined not to be enfolded in withered arms, is in the last moments of the book showing strong signs of recovery from an illness as his glands respond to the patent nubility of his young nurse. "There," he thinks, "is the woman I ought to have married." The words of reflection which conclude the book have all the jubilant melancholy of a poem by Li Po:

> The vagrant thought came and went. After all, life was over. Or was it never over until you had gone down into the grave? There were men who had begun their best work, who had won their supreme happiness, only when the prime of life was well past. Beyond the warm room and the flickering firelight, the vital sap had risen again; flowers were already putting forth from the green earth. "Spring is here," he thought dreamily. "Spring is here, and I am feeling almost as young as I felt last year."
>
> Suddenly, beneath the dark sunset, an apocalyptic light rained from the sky, and in this light all the tender little leaves of April were whispering together.

Have the terms of superannuated concupiscence ever been more attractively or destructively described?

Miss Glasgow is a master of melancholy endings. The last of the three parts of *They Stooped to Folly* (1929) is called "False Spring." One knows by this title, as by everything else leading up to the final pages, that the central characters of the tale will, in a turbulence of symbols, pick their "way over the broken flagstones . . . the advancing dusk . . . saturated with the taint of despair." Father, then, to daughter: "If it is any comfort to you, my child, you have every reason to feel that [your husband] will come back in the end."

Daughter to father: "Doesn't everything come back if you wait until you have stopped wanting it?" What saves all of this from the brittleness of secondrate Oscar Wilde is the one certainty to be found in this book, perhaps the one certainty to be found in any of the Glasgow books, that, as the father of the piece says sometime after his own disillusionment with life, ladies, and Virginia has set in, "you can't grasp a moral sense by both ends." Hence appeals to the moral sense of most people are worthless, for they want not only to appease the moral sense of society but themselves, even if, as is usually the case, to serve themselves means to defy society.

The terms of the conflict are rarely larger than drawing-room debacle, or pathos by the petunias. But it is the gift of the ironist to hold one even when her characters do not. One remains in attendance for such a brilliant tour de force as the conclusion of *The Sheltered Life* (1932), which domesticates Ibsen's *Wild Duck* in Richmond, Virginia (called Queenborough in the novel), and succeeds in exposing adolescent concupiscence to as corrosive a commentary as the pangs of passion in the ancient evoke in *The Romantic Comedians*. The symbols are as blatant as in the Ibsen drama; they are, in fact, ducks, too, mallards, which another of Ellen Glasgow's Birdsongs, George, has just killed. "They were superb in flight," George says. "But he did not mean it," the young girl of the piece muses. "He enjoyed killing. He was possessed, she could see, by that strange exultation which comes to the sportsman when he has shot something that was alive the minute before." She would like to be possessed. "If I knew he cared, I shouldn't mind anything." The sequence of events that follows is swift, perfectly described, right to the point of this sort of possession. The young girl falls into the middle-aged duck-hunter's arms. His wife sees them. Within minutes, Mr. Birdsong has killed first Mrs. Birdsong and then himself. "Oh, Grandfather," cries the young girl, "I didn't mean anything. . . . I didn't mean anything in the world!" [22]

Compared to these delicacies the people and events of *Vein of Iron* (1935) and *In This Our Life* (1941) seem, if not commonplace, at least rather too familiar. The ironies are few; the writer, more crotchety now in her indisposition in the modern world, has lost some of her interest in the double-dealings by which man seems bound to be frustrated or to frustrate himself; the iron that remains is hard metal, a more rare ore than it might be generally suspected, and thus to be admired and to be described in detail when found. The result, in *Vein of Iron,* at least, is a portrait of an indomitable woman in which the feminist perspective is somewhat graceless. The other novel, her last, won a Pulitzer Prize and was turned into a "Warner Bros. photoplay," with excellent parts for two pairs of stock performers, Bette Davis and Dennis Morgan, Olivia De Havilland and George Brent: stock parts.

The ironies in Willa Cather are few, but so are the stock parts, unless, following the conventions of the categorizing literary historian, one feels one must classify her as a regionalist and her characters as essentially people of a region. Certainly she does settle her Antonia in the soil of Nebraska (*My Antonia,* 1918), and her Mrs. Forrester (*A Lost Lady,* 1923) in Colorado, and her Bishop Latour (*Death Comes for the Archbishop,* 1927) just as firmly as possible in New Mexico. Certainly her girls who go to Chicago and New York to sing—Thea Kronborg (*The Song of the Lark,* 1915) and *Lucy Gayheart* (1935)—come from the earth of Colorado and Nebraska and, in different ways, return to the earth. But it is the soil, the earth, literally, that is in and under almost all her characters rather than a particular part of the country. Her feeling for the prairie and the desert, for the country in and around small towns and villages, is for something palpable. She feels by being aroused to the touch, and those of her readers who have similar experiences, similar responses, will find their senses quickened in the same way by her writing.

Bishop Latour's first view of his cathedral city is *echt* Cather: "a sweep of red carnelian-coloured hills lying at the foot of the mountains . . . they curved like two arms about a depression in the plain; and in that depression was Santa Fé, at last!" The great spirals into towns which mark the pattern of so many Indian settlements in the Southwest act in *Death Comes for the Archbishop* like spinning tops of prose, to gather up the slow narrative in the whirling turbulence of the first societies of man. There is, for example, the approach to Arroyo Hondo:

One approached over a sage-brush plain that appeared to run level and unbroken to the base of the distant mountains; then without warning, one suddenly found oneself upon the brink of a precipice, of a chasm in the earth over two hundred feet deep, the sides sheer cliffs, but cliffs of earth, not rock. Drawing rein at the edge, one looked down into a sunken world of green fields and gardens, with a pink adobe town, at the bottom of this great ditch. The men and mules walking about down there, or plowing the fields, looked like the figures of a child's Noah's ark.[23]

The familiar metaphor for the huge rock formations on the mesas— "Gothic in outline, resembling vast cathedrals"—takes on freshness when Miss Cather explains that the great plain might have been a huge metropolis once, but now, "the smaller quarters destroyed by time," only "the public buildings" remained. And to finish this off, as always, there is the soil, sandy, gently seasoned with junipers, and "splotched with masses of blooming rabbit brush,—that olive-coloured plant that grows in high waves like a tossing sea, at this season covered with a thatch of bloom, yellow as gorse, or orange like marigolds."

Of a Navajo house where Bishop Latour spends a few days, in which sand seeps in through cracks in the walls, to stand up in ridges on the earth floor, Miss Cather writes, "one seemed to be sitting in the heart of a world made of dusty earth and moving air." It can be said that the Bishop founds his diocese by triumphing over such obstinate forces of nature. Or that he settles his church in the midst of the dusty earth and moving air, giving it the stability of earth, even dusty earth, finding it, as he finds the Navajo house filled with earth and sand, "favourable for reflection, for recalling the past and planning the future."

To some extent, all of the Cather books and stories are houses favorable for reflection. In them she recalls the past, her own and her country's and in *Shadows on the Rock* (1931), Canada's. In them, she allows her people to plan the future, and with just the faintest touch of cynicism snaps off a particular future or all future or suggests that it cannot be or will not be. The Bishop has his Navajo house, Godfrey St. Peter has his old home, *The Professor's House* (1925). He holds onto the old house when his family moves to a new and better one; now that he has reached a higher place as an academic, he must, by definition, have a richer dwelling. But it is the old house that has the significant tenantry; in it the professor recollects his life, gathers from it an expedition into a cliff city in New Mexico by his favorite student, Tom Outland, now dead, and brings his own boyhood figure back to threaten him with the emptiness of his age. As a boy in Kansas he had not been a scholar, but "a primitive":

He was only interested in earth and woods and water. Wherever sun sunned and rain rained and snow snowed, wherever life sprouted and decayed, places were alike to him. He was not nearly so cultivated as Tom's old cliff-dwellers must have been—and yet he was terribly wise. He seemed to be at the root of the matter; Desire under all desires, Truth under all truths. He seemed to know, among other things, that he was solitary and must always be so; he had never married, never been a father. He was earth and would return to earth.[24]

But the professor has married, has been a father. In spite of a sense of futility, of the end of life approaching, in spite of an attempt to yield to the fumes of a broken gas stove, the fumes of futility, he must recognize, as the dwellers of Cather houses always must, that he must return. He, like the others, can be allowed only "temporary release from consciousness. . . ." That proves beneficial for him; it may for others. It is the Cather version of depth therapy, the inversion of the coming to consciousness of the women of Henry James. In the cliffs of New Mexico and the earth of a Kansas boyhood, St. Peter finds the pagodas of his evanescent consciousness. But his is not to claim them, but to let them go, things too precious, we are told, to be relinquished consciously.

The annealing virtue in St. Peter's life, the surge of blankness under the gas fumes, leaves him without delight, "without joy, without passionate griefs"; but he is reconciled to that life and really gifted with a virtue that bears the name of virtue, "fortitude." The men and women in Willa Cather's books who obtain, obtain with fortitude. Defeat usually comes in cities, and comes to men and women of earth separated from the earth. Even when they return to their native soil, like Lucy Gayheart, they are restless, make plans to leave, and defeated, cannot. They have no place to go, except back to earth, where Lucy goes, drowned when a sheet of ice on which she is skating breaks off and her skate is trapped in a submerged tree. But even in defeat, even in death, even death by drowning, if one is of earth, one has a majesty in one's going. In her last moments, "Lucy was more stimulated than frightened. . . ." She was, we learn in the summing-up, the reminiscences of Lucy that conclude the book, a figure of "fire and blindness," who, on whatever occasion, one of love, or of pain, or of anger, had a "way of flashing with her whole self into one impulse, without foresight or sight at all. . . . When

she caught fire, she went like an arrow, toward whatever end." [25]
And as she is "wonderful" to the man reminiscing, she is wonderful
to us. She has lost her lover in the city; her lover in the country has
lost her—defeated, incomplete, brought suddenly, like a bird, to
earth. The book is as flawed, perhaps, as the girl, but it too has
majesty. This is the parable of reconciliation that Willa Cather offers.
The days of the founders are long past; the days of the pioneers are
gone too; success, when it comes, leaves a blotting out of the past as
the only set of terms on which we can live in the present and prepare
for the future. But for a few there is a merciful brevity, a suddenness
to life, that preserves the earth in them, the naturalness, and gives a
sacramental vitality even to their misfortunes. Their names are their
badges—Lucy Gayheart, Tom Outland; they live in another world,
the outland, where hearts can be gay. But they come alive into our
world; they offer us the wonder of their lives, which may perhaps
suggest how wonder can come into ours; they offer us the sun, the
rain, the snow, and the earth upon which all fall.

The American earth is in other characters, other books, other
writers. But only in one other in this century is it planted so deep and
is its hold so hard and its meaning so large. After Willa Cather, only
in the writing of that rare woman of Kentucky, Elizabeth Madox
Roberts, is the earth so rich or the love of earth so full, that one
would not leap startled from the pages to find a character so en-
raptured of the earth that he would kiss it in a moment of ecstasy as
Alyosha Karamazov does after what seems to him to be the return of
Father Zossima, and accompanying the resurrection of the priest a
vision of eternity, in *The Brothers Karamazov*. Nothing in the writing
of Miss Roberts is as passionate or in any way as intense as the
writing of Dostoevski. Her ways are those of indirection. Her style is
quiet, modestly discursive but marvelously witty in its rambles across
the gnarls and cuts and great warm smiles on the outside and the
darks and the lights on the inside of her mountain people. She has a
mountain wit; one would like to say an earthy humor, if the adjective
were not so beaten out of earth and into manure. It is the wit that
goes with wonder and grows in the soil like that of her young girl,
Ellen Chesser, in *The Time of Man* (1926). Ellen is pained by
adolescent growth and pleased by adolescent growth and entertained
by it. She looks at herself in a window just dirty enough with paint to
act as a mirror. She has just awakened and put off her nightgown.

With the bright light of morning to guide her, she bends "her neck to look at herself, stepping about to search out the ways of her movements":

"I'm ugly," she said, "and I might as well know it and remember. My hands are big and coarse and my skin is browned and redded in the wind. My eyes are slow and big, always a-looken at everything in the world and always expecten to see something more. My face looks like the ground and my back looks like ground with my old cloak pulled over it. I'm ugly. My hands, they're ugly and my feet have got on big old shoes. My feet are like roots of trees. I look like a board and I look like a rough old pond in a pig pasture. I'll remember. I'm ugly. Ugly. I'm ugly in the way I walk; sometimes a-goen fast and sometimes slow, scared-like. I might as well remember. No need for you to think about something pink to wear or something blue or yellow. No use to think about soft colors. You might as well wear one kind as another. Drab. Brown. Faded dark old shrunk-up anything is good enough. Why don't you just give up and be ugly? That's what you are. Ugly. That's all." [26]

The decision is a good one, a freeing one, like Godfrey St. Peter's release. She can go out now and cut dandelions and mustard greens, lettuce and lamb's-quarters and narrow dock: "A great load was gone from her body." She moves lightly: "No matter about her hands or her searching eyes or her heavy-shod feet. They did not have to be any other way. . . . The sun and the ground and the herbs to eat . . . to spring from one tuft to another on light-going arms and feet—that was a good way to be."

Ellen Chesser is a larger figure than any of Willa Cather's pioneer women or Chicago-trained singers; a firmer figure than any of Ellen Glasgow's iron-veined matrons, with depths of humor and wisdom to fill her out with a proportion like the greens she cuts for her dinner. She marries a sharecropper who has once, by accident, burned a barn. They have troubles in love, troubles in living together, but none is enough to separate Ellen from her husband, not even being forced to leave a farm they had hoped to buy and had seemed to be able to buy when a barn burned down and her husband was immediately suspect and a crowd moved against them, remembering that her man had once before burned a barn; none is enough to separate Ellen from her husband: "I'd go where you go and live where you live, all my enduren life. If you need to go afore sunup, why then I need to go

afore sunup too." And so they leave a little after midnight, when the
moonlight has begun "to pale the air. . . ." Ellen takes up her children, beginning to grow bright in her stoical ways: "Pap's not much
to talk, but he studies out a heap in his head." "If all the people in a
country turned against you why that would be a thing to study
over." She gathers them and her man and herself, and all go off, "a
long way while the moon was still high above the trees. . . . They
asked no questions of the way but took their own turnings."

Elizabeth Madox Roberts' people, especially her women, are people of the book, of a Scriptural flavor, hardened to life, made gaunt
by it, but still honied within. They speak the ancient tongue fashioned
by the Bible and the wondrous words current in the seventeenth and
eighteenth centuries when the first of their generations settled into the
southern Appalachians. They have the calm in the face of uncertainty
of the peasants of John Synge's Western World, and the charm and
the fatalism mixed with hope that always, short of despair, cures
depression and sometimes lifts unhappiness into joy, as when, upon
the death of Ellen's fifth child, she and her husband come together
again, forgetting their jealousy and suspicion of each other in a joyous grief that they alone can share.

Marriage is a trial for the mountain folk of the Roberts books,
one that takes a lot of "enduren." But it can be endured and its
goodnesses are such that others should be encouraged to bear its
pricking, fragrant thorns, as Philadelphia Blair does in *A Buried
Treasure* (1931). The book is just a long anecdote pieced out with
some of Miss Roberts' most entertaining people, especially the youngsters who are called indoors by Mrs. Blair to witness the pot of gold
her husband has found. Events contrive against the revelation of the
treasure, but the treasure is shared by Philly. She keeps her promise
to herself to "stop for a little spell themselves from talken love-talk
and kissen in dark corners under lilac bushes, and out on the road,
pretenden they're a-goen somewheres. . . . They'll all come, as
hearty as life itself, as if they're fitten to last forever, and as if love-
talk is a new kind they only discovered this year." Philly brings two
of them together in marriage and gets her henhouse a new roof with
money from the buried treasure and two thieves in the community are
as much fooled as they had hoped to fool the Blairs and the reader is
regaled with as funny an unfinished tale as ever wandered through
any old story, in which Philly, wise but not quite wise enough, is

certain a seventeen-year-old son of a family once big in these parts is
not himself but a ghost from a graveyard, especially since he admits
to having lived in the cemetery (as he had for a night) and gives it
out that he was driven indoors by the ants (as in fact he was): "You'd
be surprised to see how many. . . . They're under every foot of the
earth around in these parts." [27]

New world, old world, the world of the early settlers who walked
Daniel Boone's Wilderness Road (*The Great Meadow,* 1930), the
world of white men who fasten their flesh to Negroes for entertainment and of a white woman who feels some responsibility for the
offspring of the entertainments (*My Heart and My Flesh,* 1927), and
the world of the sacramental soil, to which farmers are attached by
lines more secure than any of rope or wire or any other material
known to man (*He Sent Forth a Raven,* 1935)—all this is Elizabeth
Madox Roberts' province. There is a little of fantasy in her tales, the
short ones as well as the long ones, and only a thin shadow of tragedy
to sharpen the edge of the misery in which her people generally find
their ease. She does not offer palliatives; she does not attenuate the
fullness of misfortune of her mountaineers or the depth of poverty of
her farmers. But neither does she lose sight of the consolations of this
people of the great crunchy speech and the toes naked to the earth.
The deep-seeing words of Thomas Hall, father of the wonder-walker
of *The Great Meadow,* Diony Hall, are her blazon, her emblem, her
creed: "Men, he said, were the mouths of the earth, and through
them the earth spoke in the general; but a man, in the particular
instance, might understand and interpret and might see the signs put
forth by the Author and the Designer to reveal what lay under the
outer show of properties and kinds." In a terrible moment in Diony's
life in the wilderness, when her mother-in-law is axed to death by
Indians, right before her eyes, and she is stunned, by the murder as
much as the force of a hatchet on her own head, she remembers the
creed.

A voice deeply within her forgetting part began to say, speaking with
swift syllables, "Since you can not deny that the great Mover and Author
of Nature continually explaineth Himself to the eyes of men by arbitrary
signs. . . . all those bodies that compose the mighty frame of the world
have not any substance without a mind. They take being through being
perceived or known . . . When not perceived by me they subsist in the

mind of some Eternal Spirit. . . ." She heard a horn blowing, great swift cries calling alarm to all scattered people, and she tried once again to close her will about the necessity to live, to arise and close the door, but she was enveloped in greater darkness and her pain turned back upon some inner and mightier frame, which had been as yet untouched and untested, and asked it again for some kindlier sign, some final explanation.[28]

Final explanations are few in Elizabeth Madox Roberts' books, but kindly signs are many, kindly as the Psalms speak of kindness, loving-kindness, not sentimental kindness, not contrived, except in the sense that to anyone who makes of any part of life a sacrament, there is something to reach for and to find deep within the "forgetting part" of all men, of any man. To find it, that meaning lost in "greater darkness," any contrivance will do. The difficulty in a novel or a drama or a short story or a poem is that what in all fairness can be a contrivance on the part of a character must not seem one on the part of the writer. Whether the texture of the work is naturalistic or antinaturalistic, the writer must live apart, or at least seem to live apart, from the surging ambitions of his people to reach for light and peace and warmth and understanding. It is Miss Roberts' special gift to have been able to stand aside, or at least to seem to, so that her people could speak for themselves and to themselves, could fall down into their ditches, dig down under their hearths, pull themselves up their mountains, grind their corn, carry their water, tan their skins by themselves. She is no mere folklorist, appreciating the handsome colors of a primitive rural people. She is no simple collector of mountain legend or mountain music. And she is no fashioner of homely moralities. She is a listener and a recorder, with an impeccable ear and a fine clear transcribing hand that makes dialect easier to read than anywhere else in the English-speaking world except Ireland. She is a mouth for the Kentucky earth.

At various times, earlier times, the writing of Elizabeth Madox Roberts, Willa Cather, and Ellen Glasgow has been highly celebrated in America, by the prize committees, by the book clubs, by the Saturday and Sunday literary supplements. Measured by the thermometer of torture and violence and sexual irregularity, their books do not produce much heat. But their inquiries into those things which support human dignity, as well as those which assault it, themselves have

dignity and deserve once again to be celebrated, as long as the celebration is not offered or taken as an indictment of the equally viable
literature of violence and irregularity.

The best things ever said about Gertrude Stein, apart from those
she said herself, were the simple clear things, the blunt appreciations,
usually by writers, of her writing. They were always a saying, not a
writing, even if they were intended for the pages of *The New Republic* or as an introduction to one of her books, as Sherwood Anderson's
were. They were infected by that drive of hers to make everything
over into talk that as much as anything else accounts for the charm
and the perverseness, the wit and the preciosity of the most famous
style based upon hers, Ernest Hemingway's. "She is laying word against
word, relating sound to sound, feeling for the taste, the smell, the
rhythm of the individual word," Anderson wrote in the magazine, in
1919, and he added, "she is not in a hurry." For him she was doing
her work in "her word kitchen in Paris," having "forgone the privilege of writing the great American novel," he explained in his introduction to *Geography and Plays* (1922), and of "uplifting our English
speaking stage, and wearing the bays of the great poets, to go live
among the little housekeeping words, the swaggering bullying street-
corner words, the honest working, money-saving words, and all the
other forgotten and neglected citizens of the sacred and half forgotten
city." [29]

She surely did forgo the great American novel, but she did not
miss much that a worker in words could do. From her own great
influence in the lives of writers, Hemingway especially, she directed
the remaking of American prose, if not the making of Americans.
And with more effect than small sales and a smaller coterie of ap-
preciators would seem to indicate, her books have gone out, to say
something about painting and painters (not just Picasso) and Paris,
France, and cooking and her lifelong friend and companion Alice B.
Toklas and writing, writing mostly by example. The most read of her
books is *Three Lives* (1909), as it must be, for the narratives are
entirely accessible, and the characters are, too: two Germans in
America, Anna, the housekeeper and Lena, the servant girl who becomes a serving mother, and a sweet uncomprehending Negro girl,
Melanctha, who is doomed to depression and decay by the life and
men she simply cannot understand.

In time, *The Making of Americans* (finished 1911, published

1925) may be read by more Americans, for it is not much harder to follow than *Three Lives,* just longer. The Americans whose making she reports are Steins for at least three generations (translated as Herslands, one man in each generation bearing the name of David). Her special concern is wholeness, for her a function beyond everything else of the verb: her style is all participles and gerunds. Where it leads is to a metaphysics that cannot easily be defined outside the whole book: "I know a good deal of it now though I am always puzzling, beginning again and again and again, feeling it all is fabrication and always I am knowing that really I see a very certain thing in my way of seeing kinds in men and women, that I am really understanding the meaning of the being in them." Some may dispute the understanding and many will mock the style, especially when they come across it in fragments like those in *Tender Buttons* (1914) which jump from bon mot to maxim to poetic reflection without discernible reason or structure. But others will listen as Hemingway did, listening with the eye as well as the ear, for the sounds of people, the ones they let other people hear, and the ones they don't. If they pay attention with all their senses to such a book as *Ida* (1940), the last of her novels, they will hear lots of the sounds they don't usually hear, from Ida, who had "decided that she was just going to talk to herself. Anybody could stand around and listen but as for her she was just going to talk to herself." They will meet Ida's dog Love and Ida's twin Ida-Ida and other people no odder and no evener. And though they may find some *longueurs,* they will also discover, along with some enlightenment about the way American talking can be made into American writing, a very lively sense of humor.

Laughter in Sherwood Anderson is, to use his own word for it, dark. He was a naturally unfunny writer, over whose works a long face is drawn, like a frozen Gothic shadow, settling everybody into gloomy place, with only an occasional touch of burlesque, as in a story like "The Triumph of the Egg," and a sweet run of cadences to enliven things. The cadences are sometimes almost enough, in spite of those long awkward Whitmanesque pauses when the writing turns sour with affectation, coy with deliberate solecisms, pretentiously unpretentious, like the worst of Hemingway, who probably caught the disease from Anderson. *Poor White* (1920), of all of Anderson's novels, suffers least from the writer's affectations. Some of its straightforwardness is put gently enough to rhythm and cadence to

make commonplace experiences take on some luster and to give to
the documentation of the coming of the Machine Age to a small Ohio
town a poetic force. Much of this force comes in paragraphs like this
one, giving stage directions for the final action of the story, out of
which will come regret for the stifling that industrialization brings and
hope where hope must reside, in simple human relations, but none of
it with a view to retiring from the age of machines, which, like the
automobile described here, is clearly here to stay:

> And now after the three years as a married woman Clara sat in the
> motor with her father and husband and with them was sent whirling
> swiftly through the summer night. The car ran down the hill road from
> the Butterworth farm, through a dozen residence streets in the town and
> then out upon the long, straight roads in the rich, flat country to the
> north. It had skirted the town as a hungry wolf might have encircled
> silently and swiftly the fire-lit camp of a hunter. To Clara the machine
> seemed like a wolf, bold and cunning and yet afraid. Its great nose
> pushed through the troubled air of the quiet roads, frightening horses,
> breaking the silence with its persistent purring, drowning the song of
> insects. The headlights also disturbed the slumbers of the night. They
> flashed into barnyards where fowls slept on the lower branches of trees,
> played on the sides of barns, sent the cattle in fields galloping away into
> darkness, and frightened horribly the wild things, the red squirrels and
> chipmunks that lived in wayside fences in the Ohio country. Clara hated
> the machine and began to hate all machines. Thinking of machinery and
> the making of machines had, she decided, been at the bottom of her
> husband's inability to talk with her. Revolt against the whole mechanical
> impulse of her generation began to take possession of her.[30]

The ending doesn't quite resolve the problem or end the revolt,
but we know with Clara's husband, the inventor who is the center of
the novel, as he hears the shrill night whistle of the factory mixed
with the sound of animals moving in his barns, that city and country
are irretrievably mixed now. That does not mean, however, that
farmhouse doors are forever shut to those who work with machines.
It is not a large wisdom or a significant morality that is contained in
such a judgment, but neither is it too little to deserve its books and to
merit our respectful attention.

Ernest Hemingway, who was sensitive to Anderson's music as he
was to Gertrude Stein's, was also from time to time possessed by a
revulsion for "the whole mechanical impulse" of his time, his place,

and his people. Though he used a Machine Age prose, coined in the factories and the subways and the ball parks, he gave it mostly to primitives and provincials to speak, or sent his city spawn into the veldt and onto the plains of Africa, across Spain and Italy and the back streets of Key West and Havana and the sea off Cuba, to watch the primitives and provincials and discover who was really provincial (if they did not already know) and be ashamed. He made fun of Anderson in *The Torrents of Spring* (1926), an inconsequential enough little satire which discovers its consequence in the parody of later Hemingway secreted away in the grunty dialogue and in descriptive sentences as short as those in the famous primer about Dick and Sally and Spot their dog. The first of its four parts is called "Red and Black Laughter," with a loud noise directed at Anderson; but underneath the title, there appears a line from Henry Fielding which hooks Hemingway as firmly as Santiago, the old man in *The Old Man and the Sea* (1952), snags his marlin: "The only source of the true Ridiculous (as it appears to me) is affectation."

On affectation, Hemingway lived from *The Sun Also Rises* (1926) on. He took his title from Ecclesiastes and his epigraph— "You are all a lost generation"—from Gertrude Stein and his people from Harry's bar and the English *Lumpen*-aristocracy and the Princeton Jewish aristocracy and the Spanish bullring and the hospitals of the late war. When he had them well mixed, or mixed up, according to the chapter and the liquor and the lay of the land, they did not come out so much lost as late. The book ends as it might have begun or could at any point have been slowed down to say:

"Oh, Jake," Brett said, "we could have had such a damned good time together."

Ahead was a mounted policeman in khaki directing traffic. He raised his baton. The car slowed suddenly pressing Brett against me.

"Yes," I said. "Isn't it pretty to think so?"

THE END

And so they go off singing "The We Could Have Made Beautiful Music Together If Only I Had an Instrument and You Knew How to Play It Blues."

Love is like that in Hemingway. You have or you have not. It's all in the having. In hospital beds (*A Farewell to Arms,* 1929) or in a shack in the Florida keys (*To Have and Have Not,* 1937), in sleeping bags (*For Whom the Bell Tolls,* 1940) or Venetian hotels (*Across the River and into the Trees,* 1950), it's in the having. I mean, you got it and then it's fine; you got it. Or not; and then it's not. "I know," says Catherine Barkley, the English nurse, to Lieutenant Frederick Henry, in *A Farewell to Arms:* "You haven't anything to do. All you have is me and I go away." Frederick Henry confirms her impression. "I'm sorry, darling," she says. "I know it must be a dreadful feeling to have nothing at all suddenly." Just how dreadful, Marie Morgan tells us in *To Have and Have Not* after her husband Harry gets himself killed running some rummy Cubans into their country—revolutionaries, they say they are.

I don't know, Marie Morgan was thinking, sitting at the dining-room table. I can take it just a day at a time and a night at a time, and maybe it gets different. It's the goddamned nights.[31]

It's a terrible thought. And it isn't as if she cared about the kids. Just Harry. She was wild about him.

Him, like he was, snotty and strong and quick, and like some kind of expensive animal. It would always get me just to watch him move. I was so lucky all that time to have him. His luck went bad first in Cuba. Then it kept right worse and worse until a Cuban killed him.

So what do you do now?

How do you get through nights if you can't sleep? I guess you find out like you find out how it feels to lose your husband. I guess you find everything in this goddamned life.

Except, "Jesus Christ, what do you do at nights"?

It's always the wrong ones get killed, too. Harry Morgan, he has to get himself killed, him, snotty and strong and quick, and the other guys, like that no-good writer Richard Gordon, does he get himself killed? No, not him. And what's he like? Slop, slop is the word for his kind of love, his wife tells him.

Slop. Love is just another dirty lie. Love is ergoapiol pills to make me come around because you were afraid to have a baby. Love is quinine and quinine and quinine until I'm deaf with it. Love is that dirty aborting horror that you took me to. Love is my insides all messed up. It's half catheters and half whirling douches. I know about love. Love always hangs up behind the bathroom door. It smells like lysol. To hell with love. Love is you making me happy and then going off to sleep with your mouth open while I lie awake all night afraid to say my prayers even because I know I have no right to any more. Love is all the dirty little tricks you taught me that you probably got out of some book. All right. I'm through with you and I'm through with love. Your kind of picknose love. You writer.

Like Anderson, Hemingway has little use for the whole mechanical impulse of his generation, and in fine brave stirring prose he tells us so.

What grows larger and larger in Hemingway's books, beyond the affectations of a muscular prose which is made for short stories and unmade in long ones, is a need for people. Not just one at a time, in bed, but groups, like the mixed bag that fight together for peace and democracy and the Spanish Republic in *For Whom the Bell Tolls*. One of the group, Pablo, gets another of the group, Robert Jordan, killed, and he the true one and the good one, but not before Robert Jordan has had a chance to feel the earth move in a sleeping bag with Maria, who provides the axillary motion, even though her hair has been cropped by some dirty Fascist dogs. The need for people is expressed with some fullness of plotting, the most involved Hemingway has ever gotten, interesting enough, almost, to make one forget for paragraphs at a time the inept devices Hemingway uses to translate the verb patterns and folk speech and strong invective of Spain, the most inept Hemingway has ever gotten.

And then, having made his plea for people in the mass, Hemingway points to the battle where it must finally be fought, with one enemy at a time. In *Across the River*, etc., it is the old man and the countess, he an American colonel with a distinguished past and a weak present, and she a child countess, Italian, and the conversation much funnier than intended but not funny enough to keep you going. But the refighting of some of the battles of the First World War has a certain interest and the love of Venice is real even if the other love is not and when you're just about to give Hemingway back his book and the check as well, the colonel has some lines that are good, if only as guidebook stuff. Like the dream of living in Venice forever, not in the fancy hotels, but just a little place, "and the tides and the boats going by. I could read in the mornings and walk around town before lunch and go every day to see the Tintorettos at the Accademia and to the Scuola San Rocco and eat in good cheap joints behind the market, or, maybe, the woman that ran the house would cook in the evenings." The colonel gets his wish: he doesn't have to leave; he dies with his boots on, quick, of a heart attack.

The big battle is *The Old Man and the Sea,* not a bad allegory as recent allegories go, though not to be held too firmly to account for all its details or for a large central meaning beyond the old one of the primitives and the provincials and who is really primitive and who is not. The style is cleaner than usual, as if to face the big fight with the marlin with a dignity appropriate to the old Cuban and to the fish. There is not much of that lifeless simplicity here that cripples some part of all the novels, but rather a respect for words like that in the best of the short stories, but without the playful manglings of syntax, the arch transformations of colloquial speech of the other books, where everybody comes out sounding like the dumb gangsters who provide the laughs in the films, whether Spanish Loyalists, Italian bar nobility, British Ladies, American lieutenants, or newspapermen.

Maybe a clue to the quality of *The Old Man* is that, novel though it is, it fits comfortably beside the best of Hemingway's full-length books, *Death in the Afternoon* (1932) and *Green Hills of Africa* (1935). Deep-sea fishing goes with bullfighting and big-game hunting in the Hemingway canon. It leads, like the other tests of virility, to some substantial reflection, open and covert, on the relationship between heroes and enemies, giving the devil his due with requisite splendor, for without such an adversary, the fight would be pitifully small, and not worth the inevitable loss. The loss must come, the way the marlin, beaten by the old man, is gobbled up by sharks that accompany him back to land after he has tied the great fish to his boat. The question is how it comes, with futility or clownishness or with grace. At his best, with Manolete in the bullfighters' book and with Santiago in the book about the sea, Hemingway has written about grace with grace.

Among the many who have affected the simple manner, few have managed to avoid a greater awkwardness than Hemingway at his most self-consciously prosaic or Anderson at his most strenuously poetic. The most ingratiating exception is Wright Morris. In twenty

years of novel writing he has become a crafty professional, but has
not cooled in the process, like Cozzens, or turned contemptuous of
his people, even the nastiest of them. His love for American places
has not grown less as his reach has lengthened; he has simply come to
use sounds as once, when he was a photographer, he used images,
working in a good music to go with the good gray Midwestern Goths
of his stories. It is a strong music of "little housekeeping words
. . . swaggering bullying street-corner words . . . honest working,
money saving words," like those Anderson praised Gertrude Stein for
using. It is a music which, most of the time, he uses where he should,
with people his Nebraska eye sees in something like exact outline and
even with some depth. Once, at least, in *Love Among the Cannibals*
(1957), writing about songwriters in Florida, he is hopelessly in-
exact, working against himself with characters that he will have to know
better than he knows these to produce the icy ironies he seems to
be looking for. But in *Man and Boy* (1951), *The Deep Sleep,*
(1953), *The Huge Season* (1954), and *The Field of Vision* (1956),
he has a gallery he does as well by as any living American, shabby
people, shaggy people, cut-up people, cut-down people, and none of
them ever too far from the unshaven hangdog folk who used to sit for
the photographers of the Rural Resettlement Administration in the
first years of the New Deal, people well ensconced in their misery, but
not ashamed of where they live and how and perhaps just a little bit
proud, as they have some right to be, of having held on so long
through so little.

Wright Morris's is an elusive achievement, one that more than
most requires examination and experience as a whole. Fortunately, it
also rewards that sort of serial reading. For besides the individual
narratives and their characters, so many of whom are alike, there is
also Morris's curious vision of America. It is a choppy vision, rough
and incomplete, but larger than any one of the books can indicate by
itself, and not quite meaningful until one has set alongside the shaggy
people of the first of Morris's gallery the much smoother ones of his
other group. Morris's second gallery is made up of Easterners, expatriates, writers. These people—the people of *The Deep Sleep*
(1953), *The Huge Season* (1954), *What a Way to Go* (1962), and
Cause for Wonder (1963)—provide an elaborate gloss and commentary on the people of the other novels. By means of parable and parody,
Morris makes fairly large philosophical pronouncements about the hu-

man condition, using his own fictions and those of other, better-known modern writers as the terms of his philosophy. What sort of philosophy? It is a philosophy very close to the processes of creation and the things and persons that are turned up in the processes. It is a philosophy that needs its own things and persons to be understood. It is a philosophy of acceptance of the world, resolute acceptance and, if one reads enough, an acceptance one comes to share, I think. But one must read a great deal, for the documents in the case are the books themselves, and without the documents there is no case.

It is easy to read the works of F. Scott Fitzgerald as a series of documents. He was himself superconscious of his time and of himself as its chronicler as well as chief victim. Who would know better, then, the right summary epithets? "It was an age of miracles, it was an age of art, it was an age of excess, and it was an age of satire," he said eleven years after he began to write about the Jazz Age. At thirty-five, looking back, listening to its "Echoes," he was sick and tired of "the most expensive orgy in history," and five years later he had a full philosophy of breakdown with which to explain the era—well, maybe not full, but compendious, anyway. He reported on it in that highly readable style of his, in the best, perhaps, of his *Esquire* pieces, "The Crack-Up":

> Of course all life is a process of breaking down, but the blows that do the dramatic side of the work—the big sudden blows that come, or seem to come, from outside—the ones you remember and blame things on and, in moments of weakness, tell your friends about, don't show their effect all at once. There is another sort of blow that comes from within—that you don't feel until it's too late to do anything about it, until you realize with finality that in some regard you will never be as good a man again. The first sort of breakage seems to happen quick—the second kind happens almost without your knowing it but is realized suddenly indeed.[32]

Fitzgerald's novels haven't much more to say than that, but still they are more than just bits of passing social history caught by an eager participant. They are shrewdly observed reports, for Fitzgerald's time, for our time, for any in which greed is a central motivation of human conduct. First they are not much fuller than vignettes of his own contemporaries—in *This Side of Paradise* (1920) and *The Beautiful and Damned* (1922)—though for a moment, at the end of his second novel, he reaches beyond fun and games at Princeton and the Plaza and on Wall Street for a nimble plot reversal and a fine last scene that shows his well-named major character, Anthony Patch, suddenly wealthy and all wound down, ready to lead a life of expensive emptiness. After these sketches comes the most celebrated of Fitzgerald's books, *The Great Gatsby* (1925), that fast drive by touring car over Long Island, to the Eggs, West and East. We drive to a tumultuous mixing of successful men, Wall Streeters and gangsters, and their women, in a brittle melodrama complete with symbol, the eyes of Dr. T. J. Eckleburg, "blue and gigantic—their retinas . . . one yard high," on a signboard, eyes "dimmed a little by many paint-less days under sun and rain," looking (brooding, according to Fitz-gerald) over a "solemn dumping ground." In spite of Fitzgerald's predilection for chapter endings lush with film-title prose (see my chapter on the movies), his book seems closemouthed, understated, a narrative with just about all the comment that the narrator, like Fitzgerald a participant in the events of which he writes, would be likely to make. Unlike most narrations of this kind, it actually sounds like a confidence, a long talk over a body only very recently dead, which is just about what it is. The insights into success in the mid-twenties, into bootlegging and parties and high and low finance, are not half as important as the sense of participation, so well managed that we have come over the years to take it for granted, as an ancillary virtue of the book instead of one of its most considerable accomplishments.

Tender Is the Night (1934), on the other hand, no matter what we may know about the resemblance of the schizzy wife of the central figure, Dick Diver, to Zelda Fitzgerald, Scott's wife, has a much more artificial air, as the point of view shifts from person to person in the story. The novel of manners, and this is one, requires a constant point of view, and preferably a single one, a participating one, austere but not outside events, like James's, or well inside, like Fitzgerald's in *Gatsby*. The brilliant device that is hinted at here is a shifting of viewpoints as, one by one, the forces that weaken and finally cripple Diver take up the story. But it is only suggested, not accomplished, and the demolishment of Diver at the end has to be passed off in a three-paragraph chapter, mixing fact and suggestion without much purpose and with still less power.

John O'Hara knows better than to wind up his stories in three paragraphs. He has become one of the most prolix writers in the business, and he is very much in business. He has a town of his own, Gibbsville, Pa., and a story not quite his own, about the failure of success or of blue blood or of both. A representative telling, which is not without its absorbing moments in passing, is *Ten North Frederick* (1955). When it comes to life it is reminiscent of that well-played overture to a suicide, *Appointment in Samarra* (1934), or the *Pal Joey* letters, or some of the bright, quick, witty stories O'Hara still turns out for *The New Yorker*. But these are short.

Nathanael West had in his four novels a marvelous economy. There are deficiencies of continuity, certainly, in the last of them, *The Day of the Locust* (1939), and something less than constant clarity in *The Dream Life of Balso Snell* (1931) and *A Cool Million* (1934), but there are no adventitious events or characters, no effect for its own sake. There are, instead, a series of miseries, deeply etched, with the acid still on them. The world is nobody's oyster; it is a worm that feeds on itself. If you get caught up in love, it is a hallucination, variously crippling and deforming, from which, if you are lucky, you may be quickly dispatched, as in *Miss Lonelyhearts* (1933). You are a worm, designing sets in Hollywood (*Locust*), writing an advice-to-the-lovelorn column (*Lonelyhearts*), dreaming dreams of art and life (*Balso Snell*), living dreams of Americanism (*A Cool Million*).

It is possible to overestimate West's accomplishment in a short life—he was killed in an automobile accident at the age of thirty-six—in just four books. Still, one must be impressed by the nearly perfect construction of *Miss Lonelyhearts,* with all the anguish in the overtones and none in the writing, and by the calm narration of Hollywood life, ending in a riot, right on schedule, in *The Day of the Locust*. The mockery of the other two books is easier to dismiss, leading one to look for a round moderation with which to view all four. But moderation will not do where immoderation is all. For if West has succeeded in two of his books, it is because he has sustained his tone all the way through, as, in fact, he has done in the others also, but with tones that require enharmonics at the very least, some slight variation in texture, to keep from deafening us with their bitter intensity. No other bitter humorist since has done so well, for almost all of them, like Vladimir Nabokov in *Lolita* (1958) or Henry Miller in his *Tropics* (*of Cancer,* 1931; *of Capricorn,* 1939), do not know where or when to stop. They cannot resist that proliferation of detail, which in *Lolita,* for example, after the hilarious introduction to Humbert Humbert and his relationship with his nymphet and her mother, soon makes the book fairly dull, in spite of some fine satire on sexuality in America and the way that American writers record it. Or, that endless narrative of encounters and encounterers in Miller's erotic zones, in which comic moments, dramatic moments, all the moments, finally fade into a set of utterly unmemorable events, like the blurred red lines of a bloodshot eye.[33]

Nabokov's wit is a comparatively private one, and an intensely academic one. Like so many American writers of the university establishment, he writes for his colleagues, or to be more precise, his ex-colleagues. The result in such a book as *Pale Fire* (1962) is a satire on scholars and scholarship, on poets and poetasters, and the devious means by which human beings convince themselves of their own worth, a satire which in just those details which give it its richest meaning is most carefully directed to the academic reader. It is actually no more elusive than *Gulliver's Travels.* Nabokov's invented language of Zembla is, like the land of Zembla and its king and its history, a fine piece of Slavofoolery, and probably a lot easier for most readers to understand than the shaded references of Swift to the Royal Society savants and the history and economics of his time. One is tempted to compare *Pale Fire* to *Gulliver* because Nabokov is a master of multiple satirical purpose, with somewhere beneath his verbal tricks and elaborate plotting a sympathy for his self-victimizing narrator like Swift's for all the human beings he made so large and so small in his voyage around eighteenth-century society. But there the re-Zemblance ceases. For while Nabokov's tour has great force, it is not a work of great heart or universal analogy as *Gulliver* is, but rather another demonstration, more beguiling than most, that poets, and professors, like kings, are desperate men.

The case for despair made out by John Updike's novels is one that does not convince his own characters, who achieve their virtue that way, just as the novels themselves do. For while the basketballer turned kitchen-appliance salesman in *Rabbit, Run* (1960) has every reason to run scared, he holds on, somehow, to that modicum of self-possession which is necessary to carry him through an insane aphrodisiac world in which everything—a spate of wife desertion, a casual and drunken and thoughtless shacking-up with a large lady whom he promptly makes pregnant, his wife's almost equally casual and drunken and thoughtless killing of their new baby, and his return to his wife—seems to be a servant of his appetites. In the same way, the high-school science teacher Updike has cast in the role of Chiron, the title character in *The Centaur* (1962), has every reason to turn tail and run far from the dreary life that threatens to trample his self-esteem and his myth together. But he is larger than life, as Updike's strange strained people always seem to be. His death perpetuates his myth as his life of fatuity and failure in the classroom somehow has as well. He will hold on, like his itchy son, a literally scabrous adolescent version of Prometheus, hold on long enough to work out his destiny and fix a place in our imagination for himself and all other creatures of the same stubborn dignity.

John P. Marquand also dealt with failure, the failure of success, the failure of blood, the failure of American society. It was moderately exhilarating in *The Late George Apley* (1937), as much because of the transformation of Marquand from a *Saturday Evening Post* potboilermaker to a serious novelist as for the comfortable satire on an outmoded Boston aristocracy, almost entirely without equipment to deal with the terrible twentieth century. It was less and less engaging with each novel, though in each one there are a couple of lively moments, usually of self-confrontation on the part of a stiff-necked, thick-bellied businessman. How good it would have been to see him try, after, say, the third retelling of the tale, an entirely new one; or, that failing, an entirely different approach to the old one.

The material in Louis Auchincloss's novels of American society is not quite the same as Marquand's, nor is the approach. There is more matching of form to content with each book, little elegances of diction and syntax, which almost make one think that the people and their problems are worth the effort. Certainly from *Sybil* (1952) to *The Great World and Timothy Colt* (1956), there is an unmistakable growth of confidence, which is not lost in *Venus in Sparta* (1958) or *Portrait in Brownstone* (1961), though neither of these books has quite as much story as the second, nor a character who makes himself so quickly engaging as Timothy Colt, whose upsetting of the establishment, however slight, provides a cheering spectacle. In the last books of Auchincloss, too, there is, along with the more flowing style, an unfortunate thickening of words, a noticeable loss of economy. That loss of economy may, of course, be illusory; it may simply be the impression of repetition within an individual novel that comes from the similarity of all the novels, tales of rising young lawyers or business executives, of querulous clients, of sexual conquests as well ordered as lawyers' briefs, of brownstone people in a brownstone world. That Auchincloss is capable of going beyond the single pattern is well demonstrated in *The Rector of Justin* (1964). Once again he tells a success story, this time of the founder and longtime headmaster of Justin Martyr, an Episcopal preparatory school in New England. The school prepares its boys for the same old brownstone world, but the preparation, as Auchincloss details it, is not without its attendant ironies. Not the least of them is the name of the school—that earnest second-century defender of the faith was martyred, after all, for his pains— or the relationship between the good gray headmaster and his daughter Cordelia, a relationship more leery than Learlike.

It is more obvious in *The Rector of Justin* than in any of his other books that Louis Auchincloss is making an attempt at a portrait of a good man, and especially trying to see whether or not goodness can withstand the perils of success. It is a speculation that has not escaped other writers. In the books of Edwin O'Connor, for example, it is a haunting preoccupation that may stay with the reader long after the surface foolery has disappeared from the memory. It is a genuine goodness, which possesses men, that preoccupies O'Connor, a goodness that is not stifled by city politics (*The Last Hurrah,* 1956) or church politics (*The Edge of Sadness,* 1961), nor entirely set aside by a vaudevillian's consuming egotism (*I Was Dancing,* 1964). One must read through a great deal to get at the goodness in these books —through long narratives insufficiently rich to justify their length and Irish Catholic stereotypes in the first two, through the inflation of a bright vignette into a rambling and unsubtle novella in the second. But goodness is, as somebody seems to have noticed, its own reward, and Boston politics is, as the whole world has probably begun to notice, not uninteresting. The priest-narrator of *The Edge of Sadness* says of a pastorate he takes up: ". . . in spite of all the obvious drawbacks, in spite of every sad expectation having been met, I was not unhappy at Saint Paul's—not even in those first hours of glum exploration." That, by slightly extended application, is a fair description of my own experience of O'Connor's books. That, while it does not specify the speculations about goodness which is at the center of O'Connor's books, at least echoes them, and may suggest why they are worth reading through.

In time, it may be possible to read one's way through Faulkner as one does through Proust, character by character, city by city, plain by plain, seeing it all with a wholeness which is not yet apparent, even with the aid of the surveying and mapping Faulkner himself did of Jefferson, Mississippi, and its surrounding county, Yoknapatawpha, in 1945, and the arrangement of excerpts from his works in chronological order that Malcolm Cowley performed for *The Portable Faulkner,* and any other bibliographical devices that somebody may think up. Till then, we must read him as he wrote, in pieces. We can read those pieces for simple pleasure or complex, for symbolism variously open and clotted, for intelligence about the old South or the new, for a full bag of myths and fables as good as anything along this line recorded by an American, and for the most striking use of Christian signs and symbols in recent American literature. "Use" is the executive word. Faulkner is a brilliant user of other men's themes and traditions, inherited signs and syntax, but use does not necessarily constitute endorsement. Faulkner is a committed writer, but not in any conventional sense a writer with a view, at least not one any more specific than the famous words of the speech of acceptance of the Nobel Prize, "I decline to accept the end of man. . . . I believe that man will not merely endure: he will prevail. He is immortal, not because he alone among creatures has an inexhaustible voice, but because he has a soul, a spirit capable of compassion and sacrifice and endurance. The poet's, the writer's, duty is to write about these things. It is his privilege to help man endure by lifting his heart, by reminding him of the courage and honor and hope and pride and compassion and pity and sacrifice which have been the glory of his past. The poet's voice need not merely be the record of man, it can be one of the props, the pillars to help him endure and prevail." [34]

To help man endure and prevail Faulkner has performed a hundred little services in his chronicles of madness and folly, of simple noonday terror and not so simple anguish in the middle of the night. He has created again and again the atmosphere of tragedy, if not the full drama, making man seem worthy of anguish, even idiot man, gelded man, incestuous man, even slaveholding and slave-hating man, even slave man. He has made the soul palpable in his books, even where he has seemed most beholden to psychology, for the obliqueness of his rhetoric is such that he is always protected from the simple reductions of a facile Freudianism. So much, in fact, are his novels alive with the disturbances of the soul, that one is constantly tempted to see, over and beneath and around all the myths and legends and symbols of the dying South, the central events of the passion and death and resurrection of Christ. Benjy the idiot in *The Sound and the Fury* (1929) and Addie Bundren, the old woman referred to in the title of *As I Lay Dying* (1930), and Joe Christmas, falsely accused of murder, who is himself murdered, in *Light in August* (1932)—all have the marks of the wounds; all seem to be Christ figures, though none so certainly as Christmas, who by his name and the circumstances of his birth and of his death must be so identified. Only in *A Fable* (1954) is Faulkner explicitly and openly Christian, telling what is literally the most fabulous of stories in terms of the First World War and making Christ into a corporal in the French Army and surrounding him with a Marthe and a Marya and a full set of characters parallel to those in the Gospels. The Fable gets lost in a spiral of paradoxical analogies, but it asserts, as all of Faulkner's books do, really, the essential point of his writing. In the midst of the colloquy between the old general who commands the Allied forces and the corporal, the famous words are spoken again: the general says, "I don't fear man. I do better: I respect and admire him. And pride: I am ten times prouder of that immortality which he does possess than ever of that heavenly one of his delusion. Because man and his folly—" The corporal finishes the sentence— "Will endure." And the old general says—"proudly," we are told—"They will do more. They will prevail." [35]

But the general argues for power against freedom, offering the corporal the world and the flesh and the glory with which the devil tempted Christ. He fails, as all the great tempters and temptations fail in Faulkner, not because they have not been successful, but because they cannot triumph. Something indomitable in the human spirit holds on through the saddest and drabbest and most monstrous of human couplings, through the imaginary horrors of miscegenation and the real difficulties, through sadism and voyeurism, through lynching, through murder of people of every age, not excluding an infant, through the fall of families of some nobility and the rise of families of none. We should not be surprised at the suggestion of calm at the end of the long day's dying of *Light in August,* nor be amazed at the view to the future when Addie Bundren finally is buried. We cannot be unduly disturbed by events in *The Sound and the Fury* if we see it only as a record of a sadly maundering region of the United States, fully capable in its aimless idiocy of gelding a feebleminded boy and selling off a girl after she has been seduced and watching her brother drown himself with the shame, which is in part, at least, however little he realizes it, the result of his own incestuous love for his sister. And perhaps if we see the book in all its analogies to the figures of Christ and his betrayers and those who loved him, then it may disturb us still less, though affect us more. What should startle us, however, no matter how we view the events, is the transformation of the Snopeses from furtive little hillbillies into full-sized figures worthy of their own trilogy, *The Hamlet* (1940), *The Town* (1957), and *The Mansion* (1959). Not only that, but they are capable of an avenging hero, Mink Snopes, who comes out of thirty-eight years of imprisonment to dispose of Flem Snopes, the leader and thus, as things must be in this family, the lowest of the clan. Mink is never much better than a ferret, but he is an amusing one, one of the really live people in a set of volumes of good fragments and bad that will surely of all of Faulkner's volumes most deservedly be read piecemeal.

For all its overpolished precisions of scarred and fouled sexuality, *Sanctuary* (1931) will continue to be read, for it is a better book than the conventional hard-boiled novel that it has too long been reputed to be. The early novels, especially *Mosquitoes* (1927) and *Sartoris* (1929), are also much more interesting than the quick dismissals as early tries or hack performances have made them out. *Requiem for a Nun* (1951) will pull *Sanctuary* back, because it brings back Temple Drake, that much-put-upon girl, now to be ravished by the murder of her infant by the drug-crazed Negro whore who is Temple's servant. The girl hopes to redeem herself through hanging for the crime, and at the same time to free Temple from the evil to which she has given herself. No clearing of issues is accomplished, though the girl dies with the certainty of Temple's forgiveness. But clear or muddy, because of its own intrinsic interest or for some other reason, every book of Faulkner's will be read. Certainly *Requiem for a Nun* will be examined for its use of dramatic form across the middle of the book and at the end, and *Sartoris* will be taken up for its introduction of the Yoknapatawpha legend, and the first two books, *Soldier's Pay* (1926) and *Mosquitoes,* because they are the first two, and *The Reivers* (1962) because it is the last, as well as a funny novel about a crazy automobile ride across country in 1905. The Joycean streams of *The Sound and the Fury* and *As I Lay Dying* will be crossed often, and the great symbolic structure of *Light in August* will be torn apart and put together again many times.

Perhaps the most read of Faulkner's books, in time, will be *Absalom, Absalom!* (1946), the great book about the South, the most ingeniously organized and the most fateful and compelling. It is the book that awards the South to the Negroes, first seeing to it that they come, by slavery and by freedom both, from all the good lines, white and black, Mississippian and Haitian. It is the book that commands, *"Tell about the South, What's it like there. What do they do there. Why do they live there. Why do they live at all."* And it's the book that in a long warm conversation in cold chambers at Harvard, always growing colder, more chillingly Northern, answers the command, with hate and love, as befits its Scriptural title, and a marvel of interior and exterior tales and a majesty of structure that is as much in the content as in the form. If ever a book showed the sins of the fathers visited upon the sons, this one does. And if ever a book freed all of them, in every generation, of a fullness of guilt while at the same time it insisted upon their complicity, it is this one. Like the other masterpieces of the literature with which it must be compared, it comes down, finally, to family. But the family doesn't have to bear the responsibility in *Absalom, Absalom!*, it is human mortality that does. And even that can be defeated. Death can be defeated. That is the ultimate reform, the one which the social reformers and the psychological reformers and all the others are really after. In his Introduction to *The Faulkner Reader,* in 1953, Faulkner wrote:

in its last analysis, this hope and desire to uplift man's heart is completely selfish, completely personal. He would lift up man's heart for his own benefit because in that way he can say No to death. He is saying No to death for himself by means of the hearts which he has hoped to uplift, or even by means of the mere base glands which he has disturbed to that extent where they can say No to death on their own account by knowing, realizing, having been told and believing it: *At least we are not vegetables because the hearts and glands capable of partaking in this excitement are not those of vegetables, and will, must, endure.*[36]

On the title page of his second novel, *Of Time and the River* (1935), Thomas Wolfe quoted from Ecclesiastes 3:21, "Who knoweth the spirit of man that goeth upward, and the spirit of the beast that goeth downward to the earth?" He subtitled the book, "A Legend of Man's Hunger in His Youth," and delivered his weighty tale to readers in eight books, each with a title drawn to give the impression of a work of epic importance (as well as proportions): Orestes: Flight Before Fury, Young Faustus, Telemachus, Proteus: The City, Jason's Voyage, etc. The mixture of figures of Greek myth and Faust, an unlikely Hellene, is moderately disturbing, perhaps. The jumble of impressions and expressions, tossed up in great tumbling unseparated lumps of prose, like a great cake too rich to hold down and too firmly baked to fall apart, may be more agitating. For no matter how thoroughly one may be warned about Wolfe, one must be unprepared for his books. His appetite for all the words that could somehow convey all the wisdom and all the wounds and all the animality of man—"the spirit . . . that goeth upward and the spirit . . . that goeth downward. . . ."—was boundless and so are his books, especially the most appetite-filled of them, *Of Time and the River*.

"Man's youth is a wonderful thing: It is so full of anguish and of magic and he never comes to know it as it is, until it has gone from him forever," Wolfe says in a pause in the Proteus section of *Time*. "A young man," he tells us, "is so strong, so mad, so certain, and so lost. He has everything and he is able to use nothing. . . . he is a wave whose power explodes in lost mid-oceans under timeless skies, he reaches out to grip a fume of painted smoke; he wants all, feels the thirst and power for everything, and finally gets nothing." It is not a bad description of Wolfe's great wasted strength, well tried in *Look Homeward, Angel* (1929), and then too well tried in his other books until there is nothing left to try but the reader. Who—especially one close to Eugene Gant's age—can fail to be moved by his gathering strengths and tensions, affections and determinations and disaffections, in the tensions, affections and determinations and disaffections, in the first book? Asheville, North Carolina (renamed Altamont for the book), is alive with the adolescent boy, in the book, and the boy alive with his town and his age, and not less but more living after the death of his cynical brother, because more himself, and permanently on his own, not separated, but severed from his family.

Who—apart from one close to Eugene Gant's age—can be moved by all the strengths and all the tensions gathered in such abundance in *Of Time and the River,* the multiple affections and determinations and disaffections, repeated and repeated, over and over again, with new names but old tales, in *The Web and the Rock* (1939) and *You Can't Go Home Again* (1940)? In a note to the reader at the beginning of his first book, Wolfe insisted, "we are the sum of all the moments of our lives—all that is ours is in them: we cannot escape or conceal it." His—and our—continuing difficulty is the need to arrange that sum in every possible combination of figures. The figures are good, bold, bright the first time; they still have some allure the second. The third and fourth times, even though the detachment is greater, the passion viewed with some continence and not simply recharged and relived, we can't go home again, not to Thomas Wolfe's home: the conversation doesn't change enough, the incidents are too familiar. And yet, for a master of the middle-of-the-page or zigzag method, who can dash down the chapters and across the books, at least the first two are an experience worth having, Harvard playwrights, Southern drunks, sensual Jewish students, European *Wanderjahre,* rambling prose poems and all. "In the end," Wolfe says of his strong young man, says of himself, really, "he is destroyed by his own strength, devoured by his own hunger, impoverished by his own wealth."

After Thomas Wolfe's books, Flannery O'Connor's *The Violent Bear It Away* (1960) and Carson McCullers's *Clock Without Hands* (1961) seem like very little books indeed. Each is just a page or two more than 240; the O'Connor is set loose and in large type. Neither is portentous with any other size to make up for the smallness of tale and conciseness of phrase—if they need any making up for. Both are about Georgia. Both deal with death almost in an offhand manner. Both do so with humor, the humor that comes from a sense of proportion, the humor that sits just the other side of gravity, keeping company with a corpse that must wait a little while to get buried and with a dying man who must wait just a little longer to get to be a corpse. Nobody is very anxious about these inevitabilities, not Francis Marion Tarwater, who must bury his uncle in Miss O'Connor's book, and certainly not J. T. Malone, who must die on the very last page of Mrs. McCullers'.

Most people who read the O'Connor book will be amused by a joyfully made young boy. Just before going to the city for the first time, Tarwater "had read facts in the almanac and he knew that there

were 75,000 people here who were seeing him for the first time. He
wanted to stop and shake hands with each of them and say his name
was F. M. Tarwater and that he was here only for the day to accompany his uncle on business at a lawyers." One must be entertained by
such a boy, but not so much, one hopes, that the sweet and terrible
tale will not have its effect. It needs no retelling. It has its own pain
and its own wisdom which the title, out of the Gospel of St. Matthew,
fairly and precisely sums up.

The McCullers book has not amused many people. Reviewers
were disappointed. It's hard to know what they expected. Maybe a
measure of grief more familiar and outspoken and inviting to others
to join in, the fitting emotions and gestures in the face of accumulat-
ing misery and certain death. Instead, they were offered fatuities and
jests and a funny old judge and ex-Congressman, impossibly reac-
tionary but not at all frightening, and a subplot full of race hatred and
race humor and another death, an ugly one but a funny one, too, a
death that is avenged, sweetly and not at all violently and with, of all
things, an abiding dignity.

These two books have dignity and scorn and wit, wit especially,
wit as in the Elizabethans, wit as in the middle of the seventeenth
century in England or the sixteenth in Spain, wit turning on indignity
and foolishness and the mortality of man. Death is the measure in both
books, not itself to be measured. From it and through it, life finds
its charm here in communications perhaps quite private, not at all for
widespread enjoyment, not to be cheered by reviewers, not to be
discussed in women's clubs, not to be crowned with prizes or selection
as anything of the month. But for the living, what a lot to be prized:
death, nothing less, for with it comes life, nothing less.

A new kind of wit has grown up among recent American writers.
An entertaining compound of naturalistic description and sheer
fantasy, it achieves its strength in its choice of people to examine in
this mixture of styles of attitudes. Most of them are preternaturally
odd, befuddled, but not unhappy, maladapted to their world, but
almost proud of it. What saves these characters and the treatment to
which they are submitted from dissolving into mere whimsy is the
intelligence that shines through their speech, and even, on occasion,
wisdom. They are clowns. They could be called "antiheroes," one of
the fashionable tags of literary criticism, if they were not so obviously
secure as protagonists of their books. For very literally, they play the

leading parts in their little dramas. And each drama is an "agon," a contest, in which the central figure, the protagonist, or better still, the agonist, fights a battle against one or more antagonists—people, things, the world. Often the battle is a silly one, as the world rates battles, but it is serious enough to the battler.

The battler is usually an innocent. He does not understand; he is not understood. He does not belong; he is not allowed to belong. Circumstances make it impossible for him to escape; he does not really want to leave; with a certain courage he would like to stay and understand, finally, even if he himself cannot be understood. The long vigil that Private Ellgee Williams conducts night after night beside the sleeping figure of Mrs. Penderton in Carson McCullers' *Reflections in a Golden Eye* (1941) is a fair sample of the struggle for understanding of these innocents. Private Williams is a dogsbody of a soldier; he has no Christian name, just the initials "L. G.," which the army converts for him into a name with an orthodox orthography. He understands horses some, people hardly at all. Somewhere there should have been somebody he could serve, maybe even Mrs. Penderton, if she were not as uncomprehending as he. But his dimness is no greater than that of those who are masters over him. He is simply the victim, as others of much greater perception are too at the Southern fort where all are held captives in this book. Others can paint watercolors and find language with which to express the things they see, such as the "tiny" and the "grotesque" reflections that the tiny and grotesque Filipino servant, Anacleto, sees in a fire, reflections in the "immense golden eye" of a peacock "of a sort of ghastly green." Private Williams can only watch and be watched, can only be disturbed and disturb, and finally, discovered where he should not be, be killed.

Carson McCullers' soldier is a difficult figure to meet, an unrevealing one, a curious clouded reflection. By comparison the plight of twelve-year-old Frankie Addams in *The Member of the Wedding* (1946) is a warming one, easy enough to follow, full of sweet talk and sorrowful events, leading from a beginning "when for a long time she had not been a member . . . belonged to no club and was a member of nothing in the world" to an ending when her little cousin John Henry West dies of meningitis in "a golden morning of the most butterflies, the clearest sky," and she is thirteen and at peace, even when she feels most strange, the strain of her loneliness broken now, largely through the mediation of the Negro cook Berenice. The drama

in Frankie and John Henry and Berenice defines itself; it is made to
order for a vicarious experience; it fitted happily into the theater,
drawing its laughs and tears on schedule night after night. Private
Williams' drama is private, not quite to be shared, his book as little to
be understood as he, a portrait hopelessly oblique for masses of
readers, directed to one viewer at a time.

The mannerisms of James Purdy, in his short stories and in his
novels, are private mockeries, most of them, of the artificialities of
the nineteenth-century novel and of the pretensions and harassments
of twentieth-century life. In a style round with small pomps, he
tells to those who will listen his strange tales of strange people, children of all ages, open to anything, unblinking in the face of anything,
determined somehow to make the odd even. "No one's too young to
hear anything about people!" says one of the characters in *Malcolm*
(1959). "I've seen from the beginning," says Boyd Mason to his sister
Alma, "you were determined to write a biography or a memorandum, or whatever term you wish to use, on the subject of Cliff,"
their nephew, missing in action in Korea (*The Nephew*, 1960).
The reader sees from the beginning of *Cabot Wright Begins* (1964)
that the novelist's view of events and character is predetermined, so
pointed by irrelevant conditions and considerations as to be pointless.
And so we get, in Purdy's books, "a biography or a memorandum, or
whatever term you wish to use," and we hear anything and everything
about people. Cliff may have run away with other people's money,
but he loved them, too; more important, Cliff's loss is the means of
finding him, of bringing him alive through colloquy and investigation,
of finding out how much more other people knew him than his aunt
and uncle did. In the pursuit of the nephew, the aunt and uncle
discover themselves and their town. Cabot Wright may or may not
have been the great rape-artist of our time. He is certainly the means,
beyond everything else, for filling other people's imaginations, other
people's appetites, even more than his own.

The people of Cliff's and Cabot's worlds are unmistakably off-
center. Those who live with Malcolm, and see him through the marriage that proves fatal to him, have never recognized any center or
lines that might lead from it in any particular direction. They do go
somewhere, however; their book gets somewhere. Round and round
the affectations and pretenses of our time they go, touching all the
self-conscious eccentrics and calculated eccentricities that the popular

novels and motion pictures of our time have made familiar. Urbane people, naïve ones, gangsters, whores, people of no income, people of great income, people on drugs, a midget, an undertaker—the list is long, the book is short, the experience is startling. The brittle, crazy glass, as George Herbert described man, is shaken once, twice, maybe a couple of times more, in a kaleidoscope, and the groupings described. Purdy's special accomplishment is not the description, however; it is the conviction with which he leaves the reader that, like it or not, amused or bewildered, he has been with people, not illusions.

An even greater conviction of reality assails the reader of Terry Southern's *Flash and Filigree* (1958) and *The Magic Christian* (1960), great bursting jokes of novels, which make fun of other books, of Hollywood, of high finance and low finance, of ordinary people, of people not at all ordinary. Guy Grand, the billionaire Magic Christian, spends millions "making it hot" for people. For example, he makes strange interpolations into a few highly successful films. He turns Mr. Miniver, Walter Pidgeon, in *Mrs. Miniver,* for just a second or two into a man meditating on the murder of his wife, by a close-up of a small penknife with which he is sharpening a pencil. He makes the part of the young amputee, who has hooks instead of hands, in *The Best Years of Our Lives* into Guy Grand Guignol: He is smiling at his girl, as if sweetly apologetic about his hooks, and she is equally sweet in her understanding. Then comes the insertion: "a cut to below the girl's waist where the hooks were seen to hover for an instant and then disappear, grappling urgently beneath her skirt." It all takes less than half a second; not many can believe what they have seen. That is Grand's kind of gesture and Southern's kind of incident, a fine roughing-up of literature, of incidents and of characters that are too familiar, too fatuous. The same can be said of the gestures and incidents which begin Southern's collaboration with Mason Hoffenburg, *Candy* (1964 in America, 1958 in Paris). The roughing-up given aimless sensuality is finely aimed and funny —for a few pages. But the joke soon ceases to be funny, after many repetitions, and the book becomes itself what it sets out to satirize.[37]

Warren Miller expressed what may be his temptation in the epigraph of *The Way We Live Now* (1958), a book about senseless divorce following perhaps even more senseless marriage. The source is William Congreve's *Love for Love.* "Therefore," Miller quotes Valentine in the play, "I would rail in my Writings, and be reveng'd."

Scandal answers, "Rail? At whom? the whole World? Impotent and vain! Who would die a Martyr to Sense in a Country where the Religion is Folly?" Miller does not rail at the whole world; he has not the temperament, apparently, of a Timon of Athens; he likes man too much, and woman even more. He does not quite rail; he rakes; he revels; he stabs; he laughs; and then, just on the point of weeping, he laughs again. His ear is, like all the others in this listening gallery of writers, very good. The girl the divorced agonist of this novel would like to marry explains how she keeps going back to her earnest, unsatisfying Boston husband: "I tried to leave him once. It was after about a year. I got only as far as the door. In the hall—we still lived in an apartment then—there was our laundry bundle; it had just been delivered. And I thought of all the things I had to do—" The agonist comments: "You always did like to make lists." The raillery is there, inside the unhappy man's constant dismissal of his work, his friends, his family, his love, and eventually himself. The not quite toneless narrator says of two other divorced men living in the monstrous Greenwich Village apartment house that seems to cater only to this category of shapeless living: "Eli and Oscar, for all that they smoked cigars, were the two most frightened men in the building." That is the color of tragedy in *The Way We Live Now*.

The colors of tragedy in *The Cool World* (1959) and *The Siege of Harlem* (1964) are black and white. With a remarkable ear for Negro diction, Miller has placed the terror of life behind the Harlem barricades on its own streets. He dramatizes that terror with a set of fables that depart far enough from photographic realism to make the people —and especially the children—of these books into first cousins, at least, of the figures of folk tale and legend. He turns the manner of Joel Chandler Harris's Uncle Remus into a cutting satirical genre in *The Siege of Harlem* and turns a literary mode, as a result, into a weapon, which he uses splendidly, entertainingly, and wisely in the fight for human dignity.

And so we have come, in the late fifties and early sixties, to the antiliterature of America. It is a kind of private art, but not half so firmly withheld from general circulation as its more somber French equivalent. Wit is its measure, and no matter how grotesque its characters or how Gothic its setting, its events do not terrify, do not freeze the reader, do not put him off at all. One can even imagine these books wandering into the view of a larger public, the public for popular art. For while they do not encourage vicarious experience, the experience to which the popular novel is dedicated and its readers devoted, these books offer no significant obstruction to involvement of some kind on the part of the reader, if only the involvement of his own self-awareness. Whether or not the present American reader is, like Henry James's "young American" in the preface to *The Wings of the Dove,* the heir of all the ages, he is almost inevitably concerned, as at the beginning of the century James hoped he would be, to know himself, to deepen his consciousness of himself and his world. Like the best of James's characters, he is always capable of being "most becoming" as a person. To that capability, it can be said, I think, that the American novel has made a major contribution.

THE MYSTERY STORY

THERE is no great mystery about the appeal of the mystery story. It is not a story of mystery at all, but of a problem, usually presented with exemplary precision, and then solved, neatly or messily. Mystification rather than mystery is its concern, best of all the kind of mystification that can be quickly dispatched. "The whole point of a sensational story," says G. K. Chesterton, explaining the art of the detective novel, "is that the secret should be simple. The whole story exists for the moment of surprise; and it should be a moment. It should not be something that it takes twenty minutes to explain, and twenty-four hours to learn by heart, for fear of forgetting it."

Simplicity and brevity are of the essence of the detective story or mystery, as Chesterton insists. In spite of a few remarkable exceptions, a very few, its model is surely, as Chesterton proclaims, the short story and not the novel. For the tale of mystification defines the basic pattern of popular art, to carry something through to its conclusion, with no missing pieces, no stray ends, all the suspense terminated, all the disorder cleaned up. Popular art, quite unlike private, feeds the richest of all fantasies, the dream of the golden age to come, in which perfection will have found its polity and all ailments, physical or mental, will be unknown. It is a dollhouse setting against which its dramas are played out. It is a mathematics textbook with all the answers to the problems worked out in back. No form of popular art, not even the motion picture, can offer such a spotless example of this antiseptic fantasy as the mystery story. For it leaves open to the imagination the fixing of the details that mean perfection, each individual imagination specifying its own details, each one spelling out for itself, in its own terms, its own vision of perfection. What the fairy tale is to the child, the detective story is to the adult.

The fact that the detective story is of such recent derivation may suggest something about the nature of our civilization. Reality has indeed become harder and harder for most people to face, and all our art, like the many branches of modern psychology, goes far to demonstrate that difficulty. The demonstrations are not always what might be expected, unless one recognizes with what complexity and elusiveness the mind structures its evasions of reality. Graustark is for a happier time. Simple romance is the product of a smoothly running society (or at least one that appears to be smooth) that is altogether prepared to label its escape mechanisms by their proper names. A society in trouble is usually a pretentious one. It has practiced so many evasions that it recognizes them all too easily. It has sought escape so often, and found most of the channels of release unsatisfactory so often, that it tends to look with quick disfavor on any mere entertainment, especially one that wears its function like an identification tag around its neck.

The all too breakable china figures of Victorian romance are out. Nor need the prince valiant apply who makes a career of rescuing beautiful princesses from the toils of those villains, once in such plentiful supply, who used to usurp kingdoms for a living. Now, as in the harem tales of late eighteenth-century French romance, we look to our nobles for sexual valor, as they rescue from frustration and impotent husbands that astonishingly large number of nubile women with which our literature has recently blossomed forth. No more happy clanking of beer steins in the Rathskellers of Old Heidelberg. *Gemütlichkeit* as we understand it now is the word for what happens after the drinking is over.

There is always a savior in this sort of tale, however, as there always has been and always will be in the reduction of religion to the rituals of simple fantasy which is the special function and general appeal of popular art. But the form the new savior takes, the clothes he wears, the duties he performs are much more commonplace than those of the old ones. Or rather, unlike the old ones, he makes no pretenses. He comes right to the point. He calls a spade a spade—no, not a spade; it has one letter too many. The only disguises he wears are those of shabbiness. He is so much like ordinary men that it takes several glances to make him out. Often his only conspicuous quality is his virility. That is why women with matching endowments are so quick to sniff his presence.

The handsomest description of the redemptive activity of the hero of the *roman policier* is Chesterton's. It was written at the turn of the century, quite a while before the emergence of the private detective; thus all the eyes of which he speaks are public. But the terms apply to others than police officers—to Sam Spade and to Philip Marlowe, the most celebrated of the shamuses, to James Bond and all the other secret-service agents so generously gifted in brain and gonad, and of course with absolute exactness to the American precinct officers and all the inspectors and superintendents of Scotland Yard, of the Sûreté, and of Interpol who have been making the world safe for detective-story writers and their dreaming readers.

While it is the constant tendency of the Old Adam to rebel against so universal and automatic a thing as civilization, to preach departure and rebellion, the romance of police activity keeps in some sense before the mind the fact that civilization itself is the most sensational of departures and the most romantic of rebellions. By dealing with the unsleeping sentinels who guard the outposts of society, it tends to remind us that we live in an armed camp, making war with a chaotic world, and that the criminals, the children of chaos, are nothing but the traitors within our gates. When the detective in a police romance stands alone, and somewhat fatuously fearless amid the knives and fists of a thieves' kitchen, it does certainly serve to make us remember that it is the agent of social justice who is the original and poetic figure, while the burglars and footpads are merely placid old cosmic conservatives, happy in the immemorial respectability of apes and wolves. The romance of the police force is thus the whole romance of man. It is based on the fact that morality is the most dark and daring of conspiracies. It reminds us that the whole noiseless and unnoticeable police management by which we are ruled and protected is only a successful knight-errantry.

Knights-errant, the heroes of the modern tales of detection surely are, whether they ride to the rescue of young ladies or old gentlemen, whether it is because of the lure of the lady or the old man's purse, whether they ride in Bentleys like gentlemen or parade their profession vulgarly in police cars with the red light on top swinging round its arc like an ebullient Christmas ornament. But still these knights conceal their true nature. Habitually laconic, they turn positively mute when confronted with the splendor of their achievements. One requires no special commendation, they seem to be saying, for attacking apes and wolves. Nor need one be motivated by a more consuming thirst for justice than is normal because one does everything possible to stamp out a brush fire or to combat a plague. One thing only will they admit to—the best of them, anyway—and that is to a love of puzzles. And with the love, they will also concede a certain skill, as lovers so often will, even the most bashful of them—in this case, a skill of a mathematical kind in solving puzzles. And because so much of our interest in them is in this area, we allow them to become more than a little overbearing as they go about their untangling and deciphering. We are even pleased to hear Sherlock Holmes and Nero Wolfe boast about their prowess; we are entertained by their impatience, delighted at the range and robustness of their vanities. Let them boast, let them strut, we say; their gifts are prodigious; they will do just what they promise to do. It is startling when a man does something in defiance of physical law and human finitude; it is more than that, it is charming as well, when, like Houdini and all other first-rate magicians and escape artists, he predicts just what he is going to do and then does it.

Robert Louis Stevenson reports as a complaint about the police novel, at the end of *The Wrecker,* that "the mind of the reader, always bent to pick up clues, receives no impression of reality or life, rather of an airless, elaborate mechanism and the book remains enthralling but insignificant, like a game of chess, not a work of human art." His remedy for this misfortune (as he regards it) is to construct around the machinery or within it a thoroughgoing novel, complete as to characterization, social manners, and class conflicts. It has been the remedy of others, too, and the result has been, in almost every case, a greater misfortune. It is not the peculiar beauty of the detective story to have charted social or political or economic or cultural history. It is not its lasting contribution to have left us characterization in depth for us to mull over when we have run through the supply previously left us by Stendhal, Balzac, Dostoevski, Joyce, and the others who are our usual purveyors. It is just that elaborate airless mechanism with which Stevenson is discontented that enthralls us; that alone, without anything else of a more striking importance. The game of chess is enough. When it starts exuding social or psychological significance and demanding that we learn from it, as we do from volumes of higher wisdom, it has ceased to be a detective story. Far from having dissipated mystery, it has left us with it, the same one or another, it doesn't matter. We are hopelessly entangled in sign and symbol and all the egregious apparatus of the detective story which is determined to be recognized as a modern novel, forever waving its techniques at us and drawing all our attention to its profundities, and letting the puzzle which first drew us to it go hang.

The fact is that the true detective-story writer spurns the devices of Dostoevski and Joyce. His unveilings are not of character. His history is not a serious addendum to the epoch. None of this is to say that he deliberately affronts all the literary canons or goes out of his way to distort history. There have been some excellent makers of character among the detective-story writers—Conan Doyle, of course, Dorothy Sayers, Francis Iles, Helen Eustis. Several others, in no precise attempt to chronicle their time, have in fact provided useful supplementary reading for social historians—Frances Noyes Hart in *The Bellamy Trial,* based on the Hall-Mills murder case, Dashiell Hammett in his first gangster stories, *Red Harvest* and *The Dain Curse,* and those two masters of secret-service extravagances, Eric Ambler, for pre-World War II adventures, and Ian Fleming for postwar exploits. But whatever use Ambler's greasy Balkan villains may be as an introduction to behind-the-arras diplomacy between the wars or Fleming's rather better manicured Soviet mastodons as an image of the struggle between the East and the West ever since, they are not the reasons for our continuing interest in their volumes. Reason is the reason. We read them because their puzzles are beguiling, because they can be solved, and because when solved they come to a clean, an orderly, and a satisfying conclusion, like the final clink of the tonic note or clank of the dominant in the coda of the last movement of a classical sonata.

Thus those who insist upon listing Dickens' *Bleak House* or Dostoevski's *Crime and Punishment,* Dreiser's *An American Tragedy* or Cozzens' *The Just and the Unjust,* as detective stories or mysteries of the same genre are making a criminal mistake. The puzzle is not uppermost in those novels; character, or manners, in the largest sense of the term, or a speculative social psychology, which involves both character and manners, is central to them. They have elements of detection in them; so do the speculations of archaeologists and cultural historians. An element of detection does not make a detective story, nor does a prevailing atmosphere make a mystery story. In fact, if the atmosphere prevails long enough, it is clearly something else entirely, played according to very different rules, if rules are in it at all. The true work of detection is quite theatrical. Its fogs are made of gauze and they are lifted promptly at the last curtain so everybody can take a bow in full light. Its thunderclaps are made by machine, its lightning cut by hand. Those who look for profound insight into human nature from the behavior of its people are as far from reality as those who judge the weather outside a theater by the events onstage.

Reality does come into the detective story, but as is fitting in a tale of crime and criminals, it sneaks in. We come in time to know a great deal about the hero-detectives, about their most obvious mannerisms, usually very carefully cultivated, and their tastes, usually hardly cultivated at all. But we never know so much that we can reduce them to the dimensions of ordinary people who would be baffled by the complex puzzles with which they are confronted. In fact, it is unlikely that their creators know very much more about them than we do, as for example Raymond Chandler made abundantly clear when he was asked all sorts of detailed questions about Philip Marlowe and, after doing his best to supply answers where answers seemed reasonable, suggested that his questioners probably had a better idea about the tastes and habits and convictions of Marlowe than he did. Furthermore, even as much as the reticent Chandler does say about Marlowe, that is, outside his novels about him, is too much. It is disturbing to be told by his creator that he is a failure as a man; that sort of judgment seems altogether outside the precincts of Chandler's kind of characterization. It is enough to watch Marlowe at work fighting corruption and venality and holding juvenile nymphomania at a bemused distance; taking just enough time to pick a few older flowers while he goes about the somewhat more bloody business of unraveling mysteries and exposing murderers. If we worry about an ambition unfulfilled or a talent left undeveloped, we lose sight of the only really significant fact about the private eye—that he is a superb private eye.[1]

In their determination to fix our attention on other things, detective-story writers often allow the central problems of detection and their solution to sneak by them. They become perfunctory in their development of puzzle plots, while they concentrate on moderately interesting details of character which with each book become less absorbing. Nero Wolfe's beer-guzzling and orchid-fancying and the abashed admiration of his ostensibly scornful amanuensis, Archie Goodwin, are just so interesting. After a couple of dozen times around, even the patent literacy of Wolfe's writer, Rex Stout, will not do; it has not been put to demanding enough use in all the years since 1934, when Wolfe made his first appearance in *Fer-de-Lance*. The same is true of that most perspicacious of amateurs, Ellery Queen, who has been written about since 1929 by two cousins, Frederic Dannay and Manfred B. Lee, who for no discernible reason write under the pseudonym of their detective—but in the third person! The plotting is always a little better than pedestrian in the Queen books; their authors are excellent detective-story magazine editors and anthologists and can always examine their work against the performances of the world's best, from Voltaire, Poe, Vidocq, Wilkie Collins, and Emile Gaboriau to the present. Nonetheless, the confident son of Inspector Queen has become a bore, as S. S. Van Dine's Philo Vance did before him and Erle Stanley Gardner's Perry Mason after him. Many of us can take just so much of these detectives and. the rigorously established and rigidly applied patterns in which they work before they turn into adult versions of the Bobbsey Twins, Nancy Drew, Tom Swift, and the Rover Boys.

The staying power of these series is not in any way helped by the addition of other media to their fields of operation. For not only have we had reams of paper devoted to Queen and Mason, to Frances and Richard Lockridge's Mr. and Mrs. North, to Dashiell Hammett's Nick and Nora Charles (the Thin Man and his similarly proportioned wife), and to Earl Derr Biggers' Charlie Chan, but we have had to suffer as well radio and motion-picture and television reiterations of their heavily stressed eccentricities, their encapsulated wisdom, the pubescent attachment of the secretaries of those who have had secretaries, the senescent uxoriousness of those who have had wives. In the light of these amplifications of personalities already too familiar, the conspicuous intellectual consumption of Philo Vance now seems a less offensive showing off on the part of his creator, the art critic and general cultural fancier, Willard Huntington Wright (S. S. Van Dine), than it used to seem. And equally, the beldam mannerisms of Stuart Palmer's Hildegarde Withers and the Cape Cod inflections of Phoebe Atwood Taylor's Asey Mayo and the determined whimsy of Carter Dickson's secret-service senex, Sir Henry Merrivale, and the parallel orotundities of John Dickson Carr's Dr. Fell (in girth and in rhetoric modeled on G. K. Chesterton) have become less irritating as their books have fallen further into the past. The eccentricities of these detectives have become less nagging because no longer omnipresent.

It is hard to find an ideal detective-story writer or an impeccable work of detection. The work that more or less begins the species, in 1841, Poe's *Murders in the Rue Morgue,* contemporary with the development of the police force in the modern metropolis, is, for all its excellences, a somewhat creaky exhibit. Sherlock Holmes's exploits, which continue to enchant us as almost no other set of detective adventures, also have their awkwardnesses: their all too obvious mechanics; their rather too insistent dwelling on the willful eccentricities of the rogue hero, which range all the way from violin playing to drugs; and the rather too forgiving indulgence of the great man in all his habits by the always fond but sometimes fatuous Dr. Watson. And submitted to scrupulous analysis, how much can one say for the intuitions on which Chesterton's Father Brown draws his solutions of problems and with which he outwits Flambeau? They are entertaining, handsomely framed in every kind of paradox, Chesterton's favorite and most resourceful rhetorical device, and never absolutely inapposite. But one cannot help thinking that it may be a good thing for the fat little priest's career as a detective that in time he came to have the assistance of Flambeau, who was able to add to Father Brown's theological wit his own thief's wisdom.

But whatever limitations there may be to Poe's tales and to the Sherlock Holmes and Father Brown stories, we can come back to them with some pleasure. We can even accept and support and add to the vast parascholarly apparatus with which the Baker Street Irregulars have surrounded Holmes, because there is so much style in his conception and such unashamed art in all his performances. His is a counterfeit personality, a perfect set of symbols, bringing together the hedonist, the learned man, and the mystagogue. He is larger than any of Conan Doyle's writings about him, as the speculations and meditations about him which fill the *Baker Street Journal* indicate. He stands for what the devotee expects from the really distinguished detective story: a large amount of pure pleasure, with no particular purpose or plan; a certain degree of instruction, preferably in obscure and useless fields of knowledge; and some increasing insight into the darker areas of deduction.

How often does any modern detective story yield that much? Rarely enough, and almost never in one of a series of volumes featuring the same detective. Distinction in the detective story, commercial though the genre may be and tailored though it must be to fit a large and quite precise popular demand, does not come by formula. Thus it is not surprising that there are very few writers who have turned out many detective novels of high quality, and not many more who have produced consistently fine examples of the short detective story. Often, writers in this field will bring their skills to an early peak and never again match it. Thus Dashiell Hammett turned out three novels in two years, 1929 and 1930, and by the third, *The Maltese Falcon,* had achieved the perfection of his staccato style and the most fully fleshed plot and atmosphere he was ever to attain. He had very few books left in him, and after the success of *The Thin Man,* surely his most feeble work, was content to work as a film writer, turning out near parodies of himself. Similarly *The Big Sleep* and *Farewell, My Lovely,* the first two Marlowe novels, published in 1939 and 1940, are much the best of the seven Raymond Chandler devoted to his detective, the definitive example of the private eye. In the follow-ups, in spite of some attractive variations on the basic theme, one of the most supple styles in American detective-story writing and perhaps its best cadenced prose, the aridities of a dying imagination are evident amid the empty outlines of formula.

The writers who are safest from the deadly attacks of formula are those who not only set themselves a new puzzle each time but a new detective to solve it. Even in this classification there are not many who have produced a quantity of works of distinction, but there are a few Americans who have done well enough more than once to rate special mention. The set of writers that uses the pseudonyms Q. Patrick and Patrick Quentin, in which one writer, Richard W. Webb, is a constant performer, has a number of fresh and quite original works to its credit, notably *The Grindle Nightmare* (1935) and *Puzzle for Fools* (1936). Cornell Woolrich, one of the most securely professional of crime-story writers, demonstrates the mathematical satisfaction, not to speak of the corollary pleasures in carefully induced fear, in two excellently plotted works, *The Bride Wore Black* (1940), issued under his own name, and *Phantom Lady* (1942), under the name of William Irish. If a domesticated Anzac may be made part of a list of Americans, Paul McGuire's name should be entered here, for his two masterpieces, *A Funeral in Eden* (1938) and *Enter Three Witches* (1940). Both are literate far beyond the call of detective duty. Neither, however, falls into the trap of self-conscious psychologizing or uncontrolled intellectualism, in spite of the author's unmistakable interest in religious issues and even some degree of theological authority. He gives just enough passing witness to his interest, like a dutiful Christian, and then passes on to the more pressing details of the puzzle. How felicitously he introduces his interest can be gathered from a passage in *A Funeral in Eden,* where the sultan of the unfortunate isle, which is the center of the book's events, is expatiating on his Scottish great-uncle, founder of the tropical dynasty. His entertaining forebear is a red-haired tugboat captain on the Clyde who took an even dimmer view of mankind than the founders of predestinarianism.

"As his view of his fellow-men grew darker and darker, he drew more and more comfort, as others have done before him, from the extreme discomfort of his doctrine. He believed that he had a new revelation. Calvin had been wrong, Knox had been wrong, all the most grim prognostications of the ultimate population of hell had been wrong. They had all been too optimistic, if optimistic is the word. Too conservative. To Buchanan it was revealed that but one man in each generation should be saved. He proved it out of Genesis. The case of Lot. Fortunately, in Buchanan's generation, the choice had fallen on Buchanan."

Still, we are told, Great-Uncle Buchanan was kind enough, in his own way, a reflection that leads his grandnephew to a fine piece of invective:

"It grieved him to go on living and working and eating and occasionally drinking with a race of the damned. There was also the example of Lot. Sodom and Gomorrah should be shaken off, before they fell about one's ears, though I should like to have seen Sodom and Gomorrah fall about my great-uncle's ears. He was a hard man when he was roused." [2]

Others of the race of the distinguished have used material of such substance to fill out their plots, their characters, or simply the background of both, and, happily, have been similarly discreet in their use of it. Anthony Boucher, in his early detective novels, sometimes had rather too obvious a type as his investigator, an Irish-American named Fergus O'Breen, accompanied by the usual complacent collaborator from the police force, but the use he made of the tarot deck in *The Case of the Seven of Calvary* (1937) and of the Los Angeles little theater movement and the Hollywood movie colony in *The Case of the Solid Key* (1941) is just about right. The world of the secondhand bookstore enters with the same sort of delight into *Fast Company* (1938), written by a professional bookman, Harry Kurnitz, under the name of Marco Page.

Discriminating attention to detail is the special achievement of American writers of crime fiction in the fifteen years before World War II, with the development of a writing style to match. One recognizes, looking back over their work, a growing awareness of the possibilities of their medium as a serious art, a popular one, but no less full of technical requirements and resources for being so. The "had I but known" sort of gaucherie, irrevocably associated with Mary Roberts Rinehart, and the sprinkling of stories, short or long, with large numbers of false clues were fast disappearing. There were beginning to be numbers of Americans one could compare with the best of the British, after Doyle and Chesterton, R. Austin Freeman, Dorothy Sayers, Margery Allingham, E. C. Bentley, and Anthony Berkeley. And a kind of attractive bluntness had entered into the writing of crime stories in this country, largely as a result of the success of the *Black Mask* writers. The style was as self-consciously virile and as artificial as Hemingway's. But at its best, when not too ostentatiously hard-boiled, it covered events with an exhilarating dispatch and gave to those happenings that same cheerful vitality which made some of the writing in the tabloids and the pulps so entertaining to read.

In the years after the war, detail has continued to fascinate American detective-story writers, but a new set of elements has entered, the inevitable product of our time. Their books have become more and more concerned with psychology. It cannot be missed at any point in the postwar narratives of the well-educated men and women who now write our mysteries. One possible explanation for any crime or any criminal is aberration, temporary or permanent. At worst, psychology hangs over the reader like a clumsy disguise or a deliberately misleading clue in one of the inept performances of the early decades of this century. There is no villainy then; just schizophrenia. As a plea of temporary insanity may do when accepted by a judge, it throws the case out of court. The book is no longer in serious contention as a work of entertainment. It is the wrong kind of case history—The Case of the Kleptomaniac, the Case of the Unsublimated Death Wish, The Case of the Infantile Regression.

At best, psychology adds a highly desirable depth to the detective story, reminding us by hints and suggestions of the complexity of our inner lives rather than by confident assertions. Such psychologizing is not content with the simple formulas to which Freud's speculations have been reduced in popular folklore. It is not, as a matter of fact, content with any single source for its psychological overtones. When, for example, Jack Webb uses William Blake's "The Sick Rose" as epigraph for *The Deadly Sex* (1959), the resonances are as rich as our associations permit us to make them, in Blake, in Freud, in the modern crime story, in the theology of original sin:

> O rose, thou art sick:
> The invisible worm
> That flies in the night,
> In the howling storm,
>
> Has found out thy bed
> Of crimson joy,
> And his dark secret love
> Does thy life destroy.

This is not to say that in reading such a work as Margaret Millar's *A Stranger in My Grave* (1960), perhaps the best of a series of fine mystery stories in which psychology has always played a part, that we must examine Daisy Harker's dream that she had died years earlier with the care of an analyst looking for useful clues to effect a therapy. Ours is not the role of a therapist, nor is Margaret Millar writing for a journal of psychiatry. It is enough, really, that what we know of psychology and psychiatric medicine is not offended by such volumes.

The urge to exactness is greater still in the many series devoted to policemen that have flourished since the war. The ordinary man knows enough of police methods, if only from newspaper accounts, so that he will no longer accept romantic versions of the working patrolman or detective. He expects from detective-story writers more rather than less detail of laboratory techniques and ballistics, of fingerprint analysis and lie-detection machinery, and he is getting it in abundance. It is true that it is often well mixed with a Baseball Joe kind of hero worship, such as that the late Ben Benson shows in his tales of Captain Wade Paris and Trooper Ralph Lindsey of the Massachusetts State Police (written in the decade from 1949 to 1959). But the police procedures had been so well researched by

Benson that his books must be placed several cuts above the juvenile category to which they would otherwise have to be relegated. The same is true of Evan Hunter's stories of the 87th Precinct Squad (written under the name of Ed McBain since the middle fifties)— Steve Carella, Meyer Meyer, Cotton Hawes, etc., and of Lawrence Treat's longer-lived series featuring separately or together a policeman, Mitch Taylor, and a laboratory technician, Jub Freeman, *V as in Victim* (1945), *Q as in Quicksand* (1947), etc. The police work in the novels of Jack Webb (who is not, incidentally, the radio and television actor of the same name, who has similar detective-story associations) is just a little farther in the background, pushed there by the attention given to the relationship between the professional detective involved, a sergeant on the Los Angeles force, Sammy Golden, and the inspired amateur, a parish priest, Father Shanley.[3]

Webb's work hovers on the edge of the hard-boiled novel, with just too much concern for the commercial possibilities of his uniting of Irish and Jewish personalities to keep it tough. Fortunately, there is also enough intelligence shown in the handling of other characters to keep the whole thing from turning sloppily sentimental. And the work of detection is at least professional, with psychological overtones always audible, even if just barely.

The great temptation for men like Webb is the one to which S. S. Van Dine succumbed so thoroughly, to display their erudition, mixed with another temptation, to show skill in one of the acknowledged techniques of the modern detective story. Raymond Chandler dealt with the two temptations with admirable directness after reading John Ross Macdonald's first novel featuring Lew Archer, *The Moving Target,* in 1949. Equally admirable is the fact that he says nothing about Macdonald's debt to his own Marlowe stories, on which the first and all the other Archer books have obviously been modeled. "I could use it as the springboard for a sermon on How Not to Be a Sophisticated Writer," he wrote James Sandoe, the reviewer of detective stories for the *New York Herald Tribune:*

What strikes me about the book (and I guess I should not be writing about it if I didn't feel that the author had something) is first an effect that is rather repellent. There is nothing to hitch to; here is a man who wants the public for the mystery story in its primitive violence and also wants it to be clear that he, individually, is a highly literate and sophisticated character. A car is 'acned with rust,' not spotted. Scribblings on toilet walls are 'graffiti'; one refers to 'podex osculation' (medical latin, too, ain't we hell?). 'The seconds piled up precariously like a tower of poker chips,' etc. The simile that does not come off because it doesn't understand what the purpose of the simile is.

. . . This is of course a very simple example of the stylistic misuse of language, and I think that certain writers are under a compulsion to write in recherché phrases as a compensation for lack of some kind of natural animal emotion. They feel nothing, they are literary eunuchs, and therefore they fall back on an oblique terminology to prove their distinction. . . .[4]

Macdonald has improved over the years in his handling of the Archer-Marlowe gambit and the slight variations on it that he performed with a county probation agent replacing the private eye in *Meet Me at the Morgue* (1953) and a young lawyer in *The Ferguson Affair* (1960). But Chandler's criticism is still apposite, as it is in the case of all writers of this sort of book who take themselves too seriously. "Why is it," Chandler wrote his agent in 1949, just a few days before the letter on Macdonald, "that Americans—of all people the quickest to reverse their moods—do not see the strong element of burlesque in my kind of writing. . . ." And then, as if to put the statement in its proper perspective, he offered a handsomely compendious definition of his craft:

The mystery writer's material is melodrama, which is an exaggeration of violence and fear beyond what one normally experiences in life. (I say normally: no writer ever approximated the life of the Nazi concentration camps.) The means he uses are realistic in the sense that such things happen to people like these and in places like these; but this realism is superficial; the potential of emotion is overcharged, the compression of time and event is a violation of probability, and although such things happen, they do not happen so fast and in such a tight frame of logic to so closely knit a group of people.

Chandler's achievement, as mystery writer and mystery critic, is that he sees merit in these exaggerations and compressions. That is why the best of his stories, like all the best examples of the species, are so satisfying. They are, in the best sense of the word, orderly.

SCIENCE FICTION AND FANTASY

THE VOICE of science fiction and fantasy is by convention prophetic. The time is always the future, if only a few years or a few months in the future. For the instrumentality of prophecy allows the writer of science fiction or the fantasist not only to make predictions about the world to come but to say all sorts of things about the world that is here through the most transparent of allegories.

Let there be no mistake about it. These writers have lots to say, both about the achievements of our present society, very frequently ugly, and about the achievements *in potentia* of the society to come, very frequently uglier. They have dreamed unpleasant dreams about the cruelties of conformism under scientific management that make wars between worlds and invasions of several phyla of BEMs—bug-eyed monsters—seem kind by comparison. They have some information and more conviction of a sociological, anthropological, and psychological kind and all the necessary imagination to translate a small tincture of fact and a large dose of belief into a tale of terror.

Sometimes it is terror mixed with humor. Sometimes no terror is intended at all. But the prevailing vision is of disorder or of an order so preternaturally thorough, so complete in its accounting for every human thought and action, that the effect is of the greatest disarrangement of all, the one by which the human species is transmuted into something quite different. In the conformist nightmare, it is merely humanoid or android, to use two of the favorite terms of science fiction—like the human, but not the real thing. It is not a reassuring vision, though some, delighted by the high place accorded reason in it, find themselves entranced. These great supporters of the genre make the firmest of distinctions between the sanguine vistas of science fiction, in which reason runs away with everything, and the doomful meditations of fantasy, in which everything runs away with reason.

It is certainly understandable that the devotee of science fiction insists on making such a distinction. His is likely to be a categorical mind, feeding on a kind of fiction in which category is all, as humans and humanoids, variously dominating and dominated, make their way across interstellar spaces and through galactic wars, into the future, the far-distant future, calculated in multiples of millennia. But for all his taste for categories, and perhaps even a talent for making or perceiving them, he goes too far if he makes this distinction too firm. Science fiction and fantasy cannot be separated from each other on the basis of positive and negative attitudes toward the future or the present. They have very much in common with each other and something too that links them to the stories of the supernatural that so often share the pages of their magazines with them. For all these different kinds of story present the essence of the tale: a narrative moving relentlessly to a conclusion. A tale, in this sense, is to be distinguished from the kind of brief descriptive effort that for so long went by the name of sketch or vignette, and from a study of character, and from the modern short story. It is beyond everything else what, according to the roundest definitions of grammar, a sentence is supposed to be—a complete thought. The thought is generally magnified a hundred times or more, but it usually is just one thought, a single one, no matter how many subordinate clauses it picks up in the telling. And sometimes the magnification is very slight indeed; some of the very best science-fiction stories are just a few paragraphs, a couple of pages. They tell their tale, make their point, and quit. Anything more would be extraneous, and perhaps just as important, would severely diminish the moral tone of these little fables, something, one gathers, their authors would lament.

There is no getting round the exemplary nature of science fiction. Almost every piece speaks to some special concern. The speaking is not done in whispers, either. There is nothing subtle about the moralization. To call it Aesopian would be to simplify by reducing several devices to just one, but it would not be too simple a category of moral tale with which to associate the genre.

There is a hortatory note to most science-fiction writing. At its most naïve it takes on the colors—hardly new in the world and far from dead—of meliorism mixed with imperialism. It is hard to know whether the do-good colonizers of science fiction are trying to colonize Mars, Venus, the moon, or the intellect. Whatever it is in precise detail that they are trying to do, it all adds up to Space Man's Burden. An excellent idea of the delights and demands of Space Man's Burden can be gathered from A. E. Van Vogt's Introduction to a collection of his stories, *Destination: Universe!* (1952).

Van Vogt begins with a vigorous expression of faith in the literary potentialities of science fiction: there is no "great literature" yet, but the future for the form is excellent because of the relatively small number of restrictions under which it is written. Then he congratulates science-fiction readers on their intelligence. According to surveys, more than half of them are professionals, doctors, lawyers, scientists; according to Van Vogt's "educated guess," one out of every five Americans with an IQ of more than 120 reads science fiction. Now, then, just how good is this entertainment of the intelligent with the high literary potentialities? Van Vogt does not flinch from the task.

It is my personal conviction that science fiction is good for people. I mean good in the sense of healthy and worthwhile. Science fiction stimulates the imagination. . . . What we know about the importance of positive suggestion points to the possibility that science fiction is having a far greater effect than might be suspected.

It is a field of writing where, month after month, every printed word implies to hundreds of thousands of people: "There is change. Look, today's fantastic story is tomorrow's fact." [1]

Nobody can fault him on the last statement. The circulation of the leading science-fiction and fantasy magazines is, in aggregate, somewhere around three hundred thousand, and unquestionably the magazines, like the extraordinarily large number of anthologies, are read by doctors, lawyers, beggarmen, thieves, scientists, engineers, and Indian chiefs. It may even be that all of them, at one time or another, exclaim over the shift from fantasy to fact which is one of Van Vogt's—and other science-fiction writers'—proudest boasts. It has been exaggerated, but these writers do have a predilection for hard scientific prophecy along with their wilder wanderings in the realms of the implausible and the improbable. They did anticipate the atom bomb. See, for example, Anson MacDonald's 1941 story "Solution Unsatisfactory," which was four years ahead of its time, anyway; or, for a wilder speculation and a more startling reach into the future, Frank Stockton's *The Great War Syndicate* of 1889, which suggests in some of its big bangs the explosive force, direction, and conformation of the nuclear weapon. Both are collected in one of the most satisfactory of the anthologies, Groff Conklin's *The Best of Science*

Fiction, which is organized on systematic principles and—a rarity in this field—is not just a culling of the pages of one magazine.[2]

Van Vogt is disinclined to keep a box score of science-fiction writers' "hits and misses," at least in precise numbers. What matters is the attitude they inculcate:

I don't think the misses or near-misses are important. The hits outnumber them by a great deal. But what really matters is the attitude that is being fostered. Science fiction has helped, and will—I am sure—continue to help form the forward-looking attitude. It has fostered and will—again, I feel sure of this—continue to foster the great notion that the universe is an area of endless potentiality. Science fiction, as I personally try to write it, glorifies man and his future.

Surely this is, in a more than merely metaphorical sense, coming out on the side of the angels. But it is not only outer space that Van Vogt looks to science fiction to liberate; it is also the enslaved on the humdrum home planet. All over the earth, slavery reigns. Man is in great trouble.

All the powers of misused positivism are arrayed against him. But he will free himself if scientific knowledge can ever penetrate into his prison.

It may seem arrogant for me to claim that science fiction is the medium best able to infiltrate the individual's instinctive defenses against the knowledge that can save him. But I do claim it. . . . He can be rescued because the sugar-coated pill is still the most effective method of breaking down the resistances of the inflexible personality.

From one point of view, that last sentence suggests a conditioning process as sinister as anything science fiction is fighting in that noble combat to which Van Vogt has elected it. But one can be fairly sure that Van Vogt would not have noticed that. Science-fiction writers tend to be naïve, in attitude, in style, in plot construction, in characterization—to the extent that any such skill, or even an interest in developing the skill, ever enters their work. They are out to entertain, to enlighten, and to form forward-looking attitudes, and in at least the first happy aim, many of them are highly successful. It can be argued, however, that in spite or because of a certain negative enlightenment about the society of the future, they do anything but form a forward-looking attitude. In fact, after a sufficient quantity of their worlds to come, one devoutly hopes that, in the quite literal meaning of the word as Sir Thomas More coined it, these utopias are definitely nowhere, that they do not and will not ever exist.

The world of The People that Zenna Henderson has been writing stories about since the early fifties is a typical one, in which a large-scale benevolence directs the rebuilding of deformed humans with synthetic replacements for almost all damaged parts. But it is also, in its easygoing flights across the spheres, one that seems to be pervaded with nostalgia for the dimensions and dignities of earth. The benevolence seems to be more in the interests of antisepsis than charity. Love is, as almost always in these stories, the missing element. There is a great deal of violence, either direct or about to burst forth, hovering over everything. In this, they follow the oldest patterns of stories in this tradition, reaching back to Jules Verne and H. G. Wells. There is a parallel amount of space exploration, a similarly venerable pattern for these tales, full of changes of temperature, of pressure, of vegetation, of all the forms of creation. And since the stories encompass most of the devices of the simple narrative, the gestures and postures of love appear in many of them, but not love itself. These writers are so engrossed in worlds variously mechanical and electronic, in which everything, including life itself, is at one time or another synthesized, that they have lost the ability to deal with love or with people in love—or perhaps they never had it. In any case, for what it may be worth, they bear solemn, if perhaps unwitting, witness to the fact that love cannot be synthesized.

Love apparently cannot be synthesized on scientific principles but a good story can. That is the abiding fact of science fiction. In spite of every solecism of language and construction, its stories entertain. Often they continue to hold interest right through fatuities of plot and awkwardnesses of expression that one would have to go back to the chronicles of Tom Swift and his flying machine and the Merriwells, Frank and Dick, to match. The dialogue is at about the level of the gangster melodrama of the early thirties, clipped, ungrammatical, with the rich tone of the exchanges to be heard any day in the backward classes of American junior high schools. Racial stereotypes continue depressingly too into the twenty-first century, as shown for example in this touch of life on a submarine in C. M. Kornbluth's *The Syndic:*

"No Frog has staying power. Give a Limey his beef once a day and he'll outsweat a Frog."

"Yeah, but you can't whip a Limey. They just go bad when you whip a Limey."

"They just get sullen for a while. But let me tell you, friend, don't ever whip a Spig. You whip a Spig, he'll wait twenty years if he has to but he'll *get* you, right between the ribs."

"If a Spig wants to be boiled, I should worry." [3]

The failure of logic here is hard to understand. These writers have recognized almost every possible category of change—of earth and sea formation, of galaxy and nebula, of the universe itself—but they do not seem to be able to imagine any alteration of speech over the centuries. What is worse, they have settled for a remarkably toneless lingua franca, closer to the grunt and growl than to any significant kind of communication.

When we are treated to what passes for the interior life of the characters of science fiction, the writing does not often improve; it just becomes more sluggish. Even when the subject of rumination or meditation is science itself, the technique remains wooden. With few exceptions, these writers, so much indebted to modern cosmology and atomic physics and at least the larger and bolder concepts of recent psychology, seem utterly unaware of any of the accommodations to the different layers of human consciousness made by novelists since the time of Dostoevski. When we are presented with the central character of Clifford D. Simak's *Ring Around the Sun* (1953), running some ideas about man's senses over in his mind, we get something like one engineer's memorandum to another—a retarded one to a regressive one:

Five senses, Vickers thought—the sense of smell, of sight, of hearing, of taste and touch. Those were the five that Man had known since time immemorial, but did it mean that it was all he had? Were there other senses waiting in his mind for development, as the opposable thumb had been developed, as the erect posture had been developed, as logical thinking had been developed throughout the years of man's existence? Man had developed slowly. He had evolved from a tree-dwelling, fear-shivering thing into a club-carrying animal, into a fire-making animal. He had made first of all, the simplest of tools, then more complex tools and finally the tools were so complex that they were machines.

All of this had been done as the result of developing intelligence and was it not possible that the development of intelligence, the development of the human senses was not finished yet? And if this were true, why not a sixth sense, or a seventh, or an eighth, or any number of additional senses, which in their development, would come under the general heading of the natural evolution of the human race? [4]

Vickers, incidentally, is by profession a novelist! And still one reads on in this book, to end in a kind of eternal countryside—"It was Manhattan as it must have appeared before the white man came, finally to build upon it the man-made half-wonder, half-monstrosity. It was a primeval Manhattan, a world unspoiled." There, in Simak's Acadia, a moderately complex plot is quickly ended by a sharing out of one person among three, a benign split personality, which permits Vickers, or at least the one-third of him that still goes by that name, to hold on to his girl—who may not be altogether herself either.

The writing of science fiction has improved—hard as it may seem to believe—since the early days of *Weird Tales,* which was founded in 1923, and *Amazing Stories,* the vital organ of this literature, which was founded by the great man for forward looking, Hugo Gernsback, in 1926. Gernsback goes farther back than that, however; he had himself begun to write science fiction before the First World War for another magazine he edited, one with a typically euphonious name, *Modern Electrics.* He looked forward for a long time and gradually gathered around him others with the same vision. They could not write very well, but they could see for a remarkably great distance, far, far into the future. And, perhaps inspired by the honorable progenitors of their craft, they could turn out a simple but engrossing plot, still the special mark of distinction of science fiction.

Depending upon how one classifies this material, its early masters include, in addition to Jules Verne and H. G. Wells, Edgar Allan Poe, Mary Shelley, and even Nathaniel Hawthorne (*Rappacini's Daughter*), Henry James (*The Turn of the Screw*), and Robert Louis Stevenson (*The Strange Case of Dr. Jekyll and Mr. Hyde*). Among the significant contemporaries of the Gernsback writers, if one accepts this kind of classification, would be Algernon Blackwood, Arthur Machen, M. P. Shiel, Walter de la Mare, Lord Dunsany, James Branch Cabell, H. P. Lovecraft—all the writers of fantasy whose plots and characterization involve more than a merely whimsical suspension of the laws of nature. Perhaps a more distinguished practitioner, and one closer to the procedures of science fiction than any of these, is Lodovico Ariosto, whose *Orlando Furioso* presents a voyage to the moon by that early space traveler, Astolfo, in 1532.

No one of the dimension of Hawthorne or James—not to speak of Ariosto—has turned up in American science fiction or its corollary fields. But there are some writers, especially among those who have come to maturity after World War II, who certainly bear serious comparison with any of the writers of the supernatural, such as Blackwood or Machen, and perhaps with Poe and Stevenson as well. Ray Bradbury, the best known of them, is only one of a half-dozen or more who have been unusually inventive, even in an area where the use of the imagination is not rare in science fiction and fantasy, the construction of plots. These men have done more, however; they have gone well beyond the simple expression of contumely for our conformist civilization or of ingenuous hope for others to come; they have developed modes of satire and psychological analysis in which they are content to express discomfort about our present society, rather than scorn, and, occasionally, some pleasant possibilities about its successors, rather than a foolish optimism.

Bradbury's most considerable work is *Fahrenheit 451* (1958), a large-scale version of the horror that he has made his own: a future in which the special enemy of totalitarian society will be works of fantasy and the imagination. With a thoroughness which even the Nazis did not attain, the firemen of this society burn down houses containing the dangerous volumes, their fires stoked to reach 451 degrees Fahrenheit, the temperature at which books, we are told, are combustible. In "The Exiles," Bradbury makes the same point in a few pages: A rocket lands on Mars from Earth. The captain steps forth with his crew, takes a quick look around, and asserts his faith in "science and progress" by a burning of books, monstrosities he has carted from a historical museum on Earth for just this purpose—*The Willows, The Outsider, Behold, The Dreamer, Dr. Jekyll and Mr. Hyde, The Land of Oz, The Land That Time Forgot, A Midsummer Night's Dream,* etc. The cognoscenti will recognize volumes from the precious shelves of fantasy. On Mars, a distinguished collection of writers rallies; Poe tries to get Dickens to join him and Machen, Coppard, Bierce, Blackwood, but he is as adamant as Scrooge before the visitation from Marley's ghost. "The worlds we created are falling into ruin," Poe reports. "Even gods must fight." "I admit," says

Dickens of the enemy, "they are stupid and rude, but that is all. Good day!" But at the end of the story there is hope: a green city near a lake, the Emerald City of Oz, splits in two. Fantasy has its resources, as it does in another of Bradbury's stories with this concern, "Usher II." In it, an Investigator of Moral Climates, whose special nastiness is the destruction of the Great Books, i.e., of fantasy, is walled up in the catacombs as the last act in a vast ritual of revenge in which members of the Society for the Prevention of Fantasy are murdered by methods drawn from Poe's tales.

Bradbury is at his best when he mixes horror and satire in almost equal parts, with a few sadistic touches to sharpen the point of his story. A fine example is "The Small Assassin," in which a four-month-old baby accounts for the deaths of both his parents before the doctor who brought him into the world begins to make toward him, scalpel in hand. Another is "The Watchful Poker Chip of H. Matisse," in which the title apparatus, designed by the painter as a false eye, is just one of several used to attract a crowd of visitors by a man who, after twenty years of loneliness, has become gregarious to the point of frenzy, and will do anything to keep people coming—pluck out an eye, kick away the tip of a finger, give up a foot. A similar blend infuses the Prologue and Epilogue of *The Illustrated Man* (1960), a collection of short stories framed by the tale of the title character, a horrendously tattooed man whose pictures come to life—they become the book's stories.

Robert Sheckley laughs more openly in his stories than Bradbury does; his humor is often more broad. But he seems just as determined to expose emptiness in society wherever it can be met. He develops a lovely scheme, in "A Ticket to Tranai," to preserve women's youth: wives live only one year to their husbands' twelve, by having their animation suspended for all but a short period each week. In "The Special Exhibit," a small man takes his wife, a woman of Brunhilde proportions, to see "a new experiment in descriptive anthropology" —headhunters working at their craft. "Educational," says the wife, winking back at a beckoning "native." The Special Exhibit, we are told, is "noted for its swiftness."

Sheckley's stories all stay close to the recognizable world. And even when they fall over into extravagances like those of more ordinary performers, such as in the visit to a second-rate planet that sets the scene for "The Sweeper of Loray," there are splendid touches that almost inevitably redeem the story. In "The Sweeper," the somewhat involuted narrative is justified by the irony with which it frames the title of the book written by the anthropologist who is its major character: *Underlying Causes of the Implicit Inferiority of Non-Terran Peoples.*

This genre is capable of polished ironies and a fine, dry, philosophical wit. Nothing, in fact, of the novelist's or short-story writer's art need be excluded from it, in spite of the rareness of art of any kind in science fiction. Howard Schoenfeld has shown how entertainingly, how wittily, the contrasting procedures of induction and deduction can be worked into a short story—"Build Up Logically"—and a short short story—"Built Down Logically." In a wry examination of atomic Armageddon, he shows the world saved from destruction by a twelve-year-old realist after whom the story is named, "Fillmore Y. Brightforks." By the application of an entirely suitable *Machtpolitik,* Fillmore brings peace and plenty to the world:

> Planes that had dropped bombs on enemy cities now landed in backward areas of the world to discharge cargoes of refrigerators and sewing machines.
> Consumer goods were created in abundance. Housing was erected on an unheard of scale. With poverty and the slums wiped out, crime all but disappeared. Capital punishment was abolished except in the cases of the inventors of the juke box and the portable radio who were tortured to death in Madison Square Garden while millions cheered.[5]

The story is—quite deliberately, of course—unconvincing.

Some of the same sort of laughter lights up the work of Frederik Pohl, either alone or in collaboration with the late C. M. Kornbluth. His story "The Midas Plague" is a finely edged presentation of the amusing horrors of oversupply and under demand in a booming society. In *The Space Merchants* (1958), he and his collaborator carry on with essentially the same theme, blown up to the proportions of a utopia as the advertising world might arrange it—"giant-size" is obviously the appropriate term. Apparently Pohl, like Van Vogt and others in this field, has a sense of mission, but he wraps it well in caricature and comedy that make his case—the title of one of his collections of stories is the 1957 *The Case Against Tomorrow*—only more convincing. His sense of proportion also makes him an uncommonly good anthologist, as is perhaps best demonstrated by the eight volumes of the paperback series, "Star Science Fiction Stories."

Other writers are not so consistent, perhaps, as these, but several are good enough to be worth examining at some length. Isaac Asimov, who teaches at the Boston University Medical School, is more trustworthy than most in his scientific detail, and often more than that, altogether absorbing. He is also capable of a wry tale with touches of Sholem Aleichim, certainly a fantastic figure to find wrinkling the corners of a page of science fiction. See, for example, his entertaining fantasy "Unto the Fourth Generation."

The details in Richard Matheson's science fiction are hardly of comparable scientific interest, but he tells his stories with a fine comic ardor. Fair samples are "SRL Ad," the tale of the outsized Venusian Venus, Loolie, who advertises in the personal columns of the *Saturday Review* for an "earthman of like fixtures," and "F——," the story of a bedraggled society where all eating and drinking is by injection, where food is a dirty word and everything associated with it is considered obscene. Matheson has also managed a somewhat too neat but not unmoving trip back through time to the Crucifixion on the part of an unbelieving professor.

Science fiction and fantasy do not often produce novels of quality. Like the ghost story, this sort of tale needs to be expeditious, as in the fine collection of mathematical stories, puzzles, and related entertainments gathered together by Clifton Fadiman under the title of *Fantasia Mathematica* (1958). When the narrative languishes, disorder is heaped upon disorder, and diversion vanishes. There are just a few honorable exceptions, books that manage to survive their *longueurs*— Bradbury's *Fahrenheit 451,* Pohl and Kornbluth's *The Space Merchants,* and James Blish's *A Case of Conscience* (1960). In this last a Jesuit biologist goes in his scientific capacity to a distant planet, where he finds his priestly vocation threatened by evidence that the planet is the creation of the devil. For at least half its length, this is a far more absorbing intellectual exercise than anything in the fantasies of C. S. Lewis and Charles Williams, good as they are. If it finally loses some conviction because it is not *durchkomponiert*—constructed on a direct line all the way through—as its kind of baroque fantasy requires, that is not enough of a failure to count seriously against it. It is most of the way a superb piece of storytelling. And isn't that— no matter what other pretensions it makes—the particular function of science fiction?

THE DANCE

A CASUAL LOOK at the beginnings of the American dance might lead one to laugh. Loie Fuller, in her Serpentine and Flame Dance, evolved just before the turn of the century, was more a magician with undulating silks and dazzling lights than a dancer. Isadora Duncan, a near contemporary of Loie Fuller, was more a personality with an eloquent torso than a dancer. She drew her inspiration from her ganglia, from bare feet, and the flow of a Greek toga. She had strong convictions which she was only too happy to impart to newspapermen who were only too eager to listen. She not only believed in love without benefit of wedlock, she practiced it openly and bore her two children without the usual trip to the justice of the peace. Hoping for a child of exemplary body and mind, she proposed a coupling for that purpose to Bernard Shaw, who turned her down with an irrefutable argument—the child might grow up with his body and her mind! Then, just to be difficult, she did get married, in 1922, to the distinguished Soviet poet Sergei Yessenin. And then her life sputtered to an angry close. She was quickly separated from her husband, who two years later committed suicide. Her children died by drowning. She drank a good deal and began to grow fat. Finally, while driving at Nice, her taste for flowing garments killed her: her long scarf got caught up in the wheel of the moving car and she was strangled to death.

Loie Fuller was also a personality. She was a scientist of sorts, designed her own lighting, and once, playing with explosive chemicals to try to produce phosphorescent costumes, she ripped half of her hair off. She was the great good friend of Queen Marie of Rumania. She founded a famous troupe of dancing girls named after her. She was a fascinating center of attention for Europeans long before the American dance had established itself as a significant branch of the art. And like Isadora Duncan she was always available to newspapermen, always equipped with a finely turned and provocative phrase for almost every aspect of human activity.

As much as anything else, it was the spaciousness of Isadora Duncan's and Loie Fuller's approaches to life that made them such good copy, such comical figures, and such excellent founders of a large tradition in the dance. Their views embraced the whole world. And if their seeing was sometimes cockeyed, it was also remarkably farsighted. They both recognized not only the beauty of bodily movement, but its aptness as an expression of interior states of being. Loie Fuller got caught up in lights. Isadora Duncan fastened her attention —for as long as she could fasten her attention—on inner activities. No word was so consecrated in her vocabulary as "inner." Though her translations of Beethoven symphonies added no great revelation to anyone's understanding of the music, and her choice of works like the "Marseillaise" and Tchaikovsky's "Marche Slav" for paeans to human freedom was something less than inspired, she did begin the movement away from mere pantomime in the dance. In her own dancing, in the work of her sister Elizabeth and of her adopted daughters Anna and Irma and others, inner emotion found outer motion. Though one had to look hard to see more than the ruffling of loosely hung cloth on women's bodies, with enough effort one could find something of enduring value for the dance there. This was no mere comic spectacle.

Similarly, in spite of a surface resemblance to the Orientalism of Theda Bara, to Little Egypt's hootchy-kootch and Rudolph Valentino's Turkish-towel and bare-chest histrionics, Ruth St. Denis and Ted Shawn were serious dancers, who did more to move American dance toward the rich abstractions and speculative drama of recent decades than anybody else. Both have always been highly theatrical, by choice and by accident. David Belasco changed the New Jersey farm girl's name from Ruth Dennis to Ruth St. Denis when she was acting and dancing for him. A cigarette poster in Buffalo, advertising Egyptian Deities with a picture of the goddess Isis seated on a throne, inspired that long series of dances with an Oriental setting with which, since the early years of this century, Ruth St. Denis has been associated—*The Incense, The Cobras, Radha, The Green Nautch, O-Mika, Egypta*. Some of the story lines and some of the movements were clichés, even then, before the First World War. But her careful framing of every gesture and her making of every inflection of her body part of a totality of movement, every bit of it consciously conceived, was not at all hackneyed. Europeans, at least, recognized the power of her dancing. After she joined forces with Ted Shawn in 1914, in marriage as well as in dancing, Americans began to see the possibilities in this conception of the dance. The work of the Denishawn Dancers and the Denishawn schools was remarkably quickly accomplished. All over the country, after the First World War, audiences responded to the vitality of this kind of dancing. Young dancers took up as a cause a conception of their art which recognized the possibility of using sacred writings, Eastern and Western, the work of poets such as William Blake and Emily Dickinson, myths of all kinds—anything that led mind, body, and spirit to some coherent movement together—as the basis of the dance. When Ruth St. Denis moved to Hollywood in 1947, it was to create a Church of the Divine Dance, there to combine dance movement and the words of theologians and philosophers in interpretations of the Christian tradition, having in her late years abandoned the Orientalism of her youth. Ted Shawn, who began his career as a student for the ministry at the University of Denver, has long mixed interpretations of Christian hymns and figures like St. Francis with whirling dervishes, the bound Prometheus, and a kind of universal figure of faith, *The Divine Idiot,* in his large repertory.

Shawn's special contribution to the American dance was to give a secure place in it to large-boned, heavily built male dancers like himself. He was much too big for the classical ballerino, and he had been forced to concentrate on rebuilding his muscles and keeping them limber after an overdose of a diphtheria serum left him paralyzed. He had brought himself alive again with ballet exercises. Then he brought the American male dancer alive with choreographic exercises for every part of the body, demonstrated in his own performances with Denishawn and then, after his separation from Ruth St. Denis in 1932, in his work with his own company, the Ted Shawn Men Dancers. The verbalization was clumsy but the performances were not.

Out of Denishawn came not only American dance, but American dancers. Martha Graham, Doris Humphrey, and Charles Weidman were all products of the Denishawn system. Martha Graham spent seven years with Ruth St. Denis and Ted Shawn before moving on to two years as a featured dancer in the Greenwich Village Follies. Then she began her teaching career at the Eastman School of Music in Rochester. Her style was not an overnight development, but she did not rest long with the fragile themes and Debussyan accompaniments which at first occupied her attention as a dancer on her own. Like all the dancers in her general tradition, whether they come directly or indirectly from Denishawn, Isadora Duncan, or the German Mary Wigman, she was dedicated to making manifest in physical terms her own ideas, her own feelings, her own convictions. By the early thirties, she had isolated some of the most lasting properties of her style— the great-skirted dress, as often as not a nondescript woolen; the wide-arched movements of arms and legs, culminating in a 180-degree sweep of the left leg; the severe hairdo and stern face of repression.

Repression has often been Martha Graham's theme: the withheld love of Emily Dickinson in *Letter to the World,* the joyous fantasy life of *Punch and the Judy,* the grim fantasy life of *Every Soul Is a Circus.* There has also been a strong sense of the conflicting impulses of American life, Puritan and voluptuous, withdrawing and outgoing, all visible in single and group movement in works like *Frontier, American Document,* and that most considerable of her dance dramas, *Appalachian Spring.* The dance is social history for her and almost all her works part of a continuing documentation of American life. In them, tenderness wells up out of a great reservoir of unhappiness and aberration much of the time, but not always. And even when the tenderness comes, as it does come in *Appalachian Spring,* or in her philosophical meditation on the nature of man, *Dark Meadow,* it seems like a passing smile on a ravaged face, the briefest of illuminations, however long it may actually last as movement or gesture or music.

So compelling is the state of sorrow or anguish or agony—it seems to vary only in intensity—in Martha Graham's work, many of us recalling a performance of hers are likely to retain in our minds only a stationary image of it, an emblem of grief, to summon it to life for us. This is not entirely the result of sheer concentration on a single state of being, since there is in her work a variety of moods, a taste for satire, and even on occasion a simple joy. The static image is more significant as an indication of a gift for the abstract, which transcends every other inclination of hers for narrative drama (sometimes complete with narrator) and dramatic movement. That is why, perhaps, the still photographs of her dancing taken over the years by Barbara Morgan are so arresting. At any given moment, her bony face, her bold and dissonant movement, and her total absorption in conveying a tortured emotion, are themselves as absorbing to contemplate as one of the not unrelated compositions of the abstract expressionists.

Motion was more essential to the work of Doris Humphrey than anything else, downward and upward motion, following a principle of fall and recovery. Her entire technique, she said, was the result of the investigation of the "process of falling away from and returning to equilibrium." This, she insisted, "is the very core of all movement. . . . Youth is 'down' as little as possible, gravity holds him lightly to earth. Old age gradually takes over and the spring vanishes from the step until the final yielding, death." [1] None of this should be interpreted in theological terms, for Doris Humphrey's thinking was very different from Ruth St. Denis's, very self-consciously different after her tour of the Orient with Denishawn and her painful discovery of the difference between Denishawn Orientalism and the real East. But there was in her work a philosophical depth, growing out of her rejection of the ethnic dance, Oriental, American, Slavic, or anything else, for her culture was urban and suburban (she came from Oak Park, the suburb of Chicago where Frank Lloyd Wright did his fine early work). And so she worked endlessly at dance form, at integrating gesture into other bodily movement, at drawing the essential content of music, or of a setting, or of a poem into the dance. How successful she became as a choreographer can be seen in her trilogy, *Theater Piece, With My Red Fires,* and *New Dance* (when that trilogy is performed—not often, assuredly, since the disbanding of the Humphrey-Weidman dance company at the time of the Second World War). In the centerpiece of that remarkable work the systole-diastole motion of the trilogy coalesces in a systematic investigation of two lines by William Blake, through three characters conceived as types, as in the expressionist theater, a *Young Woman, Young Man,* and a *Matriarch.* The lines are from the second chapter of *Jerusalem,* the last line of section 33 and the first of 34:

> For the Divine appearance is Brotherhood but I am love
> "Elevate into the Region of Brotherhood with my red fires."

Dark lines from a dark work, these, but quite suitable for Humphrey's kind of philosophical dance, half-speculative and half-assertive. Furthermore, her principal assertion was brotherhood, and

she found its most compelling allegory—analogy—metaphor—
whatever one wants to call it—in the unity of body, mind, and soul
which was the center of Blake's faith. Thus form and content are one,
at least by intention, in Doris Humphrey's choreography, as can be
seen in the trilogy, again in her most passionate work, *Inquest,* and in
many of the works she did for her longtime student and associate,
Jose Limón, when he formed his own company after the war. The
unity may not always be apparent, but something like a modality of
compassion is almost inescapable in the work of Doris Humphrey, a
feeling for human beings that pulses through her dance designs, not
unlike, one suspects, the ingratiating quality that attaches all who
knew her, as teacher and as friend, so warmly to her memory.

Warmth of a very simple kind, a sense of humor, and a fine
rhythmic drive were the liberating factors in Charles Weidman's work
when he finally found himself as a dancer, some years after leaving
Denishawn. Doris Humphrey was an enormous help to him and he in
turn gave her some first-rate dancing and not a few handsomely
turned designs. Nothing in modern dance quite matches his mood of
fun and games as it permeates *Flickers,* a dance about silent films, of
course; *And Daddy Was a Fireman,* about early settlers in his native
town, Lincoln, Nebraska; *This Passion,* all about the Snyder-Grey
murder case; and his conversion of James Thurber's *Fables for Our
Time* into dance. He is also a first-rate choreographer for musicals, as
those who remember *As Thousands Cheer* and *I'd Rather Be Right*
can attest.

Jose Limón, to some of those who saw him in his early years with
the Humphrey-Weidman company, represented little more than a
pulsating sexuality, warm and cold, delicate and coarse, as his assignments required. But his seriousness as a dancer and a choreographer
is now unmistakably established, first through the brilliant foundation
given his repertory by Doris Humphrey, and then by his own additions to it. Perhaps the most intriguing of the Humphrey items is her
translation of Federico García Lorca's magnificent poem memorializ-
ing a bullfighter, *Lament for Ignacio Sanchez Mejías,* into a *pas de
trois.* The three roles are those of Ignacio, Destiny, and Woman, and,
as always with the mature Humphrey, the particular person is only an
opportunity for generalizations about the race of man. Here it is a
familiar one: Woman's body, in an agony like that of parturition,
frees man (Ignacio) for his destiny, a highly masculine one. In the

most celebrated of Limón's own works, *The Moor's Pavane,* he uses the music of Purcell, as elsewhere he has drawn on other baroque composers, to frame intense emotion, in this case drawn from the passions of Othello, Iago and Desdemona, Limón has also become an effective choreographer of religious themes and of narratives drawn from his own Mexican Indian background, designed both for his own company and for the Mexican National Ballet. It is not difficult to see why he has become a box-office success, a rare thing in modern dance.

In the Limón company are a number of highly skillful dancers, among them the choreographers Lucas Hoving and Pauline Koner. Like Martha Graham, from whose company came a whole generation of dancers and choreographers, Limón has become a central resource of the modern dance. The dance needs such resources now. The days of controversy are over. Dance recitals are no longer great events to followers of the art. It is not unusual to see a hall so sparsely filled at a dance recital that it looks more like a gathering of relatives and a few interested friends than an audience. That, in fact, may very well be what it is—relatives, friends, pupils come to pay their respects, but not, in spite of appearances, their last ones.

The funereal pall that hangs over dance recitals is not a fair indication either of the quality or the quantity of modern dance today. Hanya Holm, Mary Wigman's protégé, is still teaching, and the steady flow of invention that she showed in such of her American works as *Trend, Tragic Exodus,* and *Metropolitan Daily,* is now a part of the musical theater. In *Kiss Me Kate, The Golden Apple,* and *My Fair Lady,* she demonstrated a lightness of touch that one might not have expected of Wigman's closest collaborator. But there was also a precision and clarity of movement which can be traced to her radical dance origins. Helen Tamiris has been more active still on Broadway, creating dances for *Annie Get Your Gun, Miss Liberty, Inside U.S.A., Up in Central Park, By the Beautiful Sea, Fanny, Plain and Fancy*—an unending series of deftly made patterns reflecting her broad background in ballet (with the Metropolitan Opera and with Fokine), as a Broadway dancer, and as a serious choreographer who has never lost her sensitive feeling for jazz.

No modern dance choreographer has ever had a richer sense of the possibilities of jazz for her art than Anna Sokolow. Her collaborations with Teo Macero reach with increasing imagination into the satirical resources of the saxophone, the trumpet, the trombone, the tuba, and the rhythm section as patterns for dance movement. The method is superbly demonstrated in *Le Grand Spectacle,* a cycle of pieces illustrating the humor and the pathos of second-rate dancers employed in second-rate places, without forcing either end of the emotional scale beyond its proper limits, as too often serious choreographers do when they become involved with the more obvious manifestations of sorrow or joy. She showed the same restraint in the dramatic movement she built into the Kurt Weill version of *Street Scene,* especially in her designs for crowds. Anna Sokolow has a rare gift. She can be as bawdy, as poignant, as satirical, or as lugubrious as her material requires, but with more than taste, with tact, she understates at just the point at which most choreographers would let themselves—and their dancers—go. The results are such adventures in psychological isolation as *Rooms,* entirely her own, and *Metamorphosis,* her adaptation of Franz Kafka's eviscerating allegory of a young man, in retreat from his family, who turns into a beetlelike insect. Hers is more than choreography in works of this kind; it is dramatic invention made all the more affecting by a detailed logistics of movement.

No one can fault the imagination of the choreographers of the modern dance as it has touched movement. They have gone everywhere in search of it—to prizefights (Sophie Maslow's *The Champion*), to African life (Pearl Primus), to the Caribbean (Katherine Dunham), to Greek myth (Myra Kinch's *Along Appointed Sands,* the story of Hero and Leander), to sheer abstraction (Sybil Shearer and Merce Cunningham). They have not only turned film and television assignments into fresh explorations of the possibilities of ensemble movement, but have—a few, anyway—made the traditionally thankless role of ballerina or choreographer at the opera into a fresh opportunity for eloquent motion. Janet Collins, in the first category, made her brief moments at the Metropolitan into suggestive comments, small epitomes of the points, such as they are, of the warhorses of the repertory, Italian, French, German. Ruth Page, Chicago's mainstay in ballet, has also added touches of interpretive dance to her choreography for Verdi, Rossini, Lehar—whatever has come her way or that she has made come her way.

In all such works, by definition, something of pantomime remains. A story must be told or a character delineated. The true eloquence of movement is not in this sort of dance. It is not filling its central role as an expression of interiority, as Isadora Duncan, Ruth St. Denis, Martha Graham, and Doris Humphrey understood it, each in her own way. And so one turns with particular interest to the work of Sybil Shearer and Merce Cunningham, hoping that their stubborn addiction for the abstract will prevail, that they will not be discouraged by its patent lack of commercial appeal, and that they will simply go where their talents should logically lead them, to a dance that is entirely outside pantomime and narrative, to the higher levels of contemplation, contemplation somehow made over into movement.

The extent to which American ballet has become permeated with the spirit and the forms of modern dance may be gathered from the fact that Anna Sokolow and Merce Cunningham have both taught classes at the School of American Ballet, the official teaching institution of the New York City Ballet, and that for that company's tenth anniversary season (1959), Martha Graham shared the choreography of a series of *Episodes,* set to the music of Anton von Webern, with George Balanchine. But then there is almost nothing of quality in the dance, old or new, which Balanchine has not somehow made a part of the performances of the New York City Ballet. Balanchine is the ranking doyen of American ballet, and as choreographer, teacher, philosopher, and director of its finest performing organization has had more to do with the development of a native tradition in ballet than anyone else, including his impresario, Lincoln Kirstein.

Balanchine was a mature choreographer, dancer, and musician when he began his career in the United States in 1934, with a full-scale background of training at the Imperial Russian Ballet School, at the Maryinsky Theater, at the St. Petersburg Conservatory, and under Serge Diaghileff. Perhaps as much because of this fact as any other, ballet in America has not been self-consciously nativist, in spite of some moments in the early days of Ballet Caravan when works like *Billy the Kid* and *Filling Station* set the tone for the repertory. American ballet has become in its choreography, in its dancing styles, and in the very structure of its companies as various as ballet can be and still retain some of the identifying elements of this kind of storytelling pantomimic dance.[2]

There are repertoires within repertoires in American ballet, reaching back through the years when classical technique and the ballets which best displayed it were *de rigueur* in American companies. It was to develop something much more open to native talent that the School of the American Ballet was founded, and with it first the American Ballet and then the Ballet Caravan. But Balanchine's personality obtained in the various dissolutions and re-formations that followed until the New York City company was established in 1948. And so, in spite of ballets by Jerome Robbins, Todd Bolender, and Lew Christensen, a few contributions by the Swedish choreographer Brigit Cullberg and the Anglo-American Antony Tudor, and a single collaboration by Martha Graham, the repertory of the company, like its governing spirit, remains Balanchine's, and the ranking composer, in spite of the use of many others from the classical, the romantic, and the modern traditions, remains Balanchine's favorite collaborator, Igor Stravinsky. Balanchine has himself touched on American themes, with *Western Symphony,* for example, set to music by Hershy Kay, and *Variants,* scored by Gunther Schuller and making use of the Modern Jazz Quartet. But Balanchine's West is far too statuesque for any close associations with the cowboy tales that the title may evoke, and his jazz piece works out a geometry of groups as ingeniously as anything he has done with music by Bach or Webern or Stravinsky, with barely a nod in the direction of the bodily motions usually associated with jazz, hip or pelvic or any other kind.

Balanchine is no more restricted by conventional associations of movement or mood than he is by plot. He rarely uses any kind of story line, though he has not been averse to restaging—and rethinking—such plot-filled ballets as *Swan Lake* and *Firebird.* But even in these and the children's-corner suite he has made out of *The Nutcracker,* his métier remains form, assiduously pursued through the groups of dancers and the individuals he has himself trained so thoroughly to become his spokesmen, his extraordinarily supple representatives on the stage—Maria Tallchief, Melissa Hayden, Tanaquil Le Clercq, Diana Adams, Patricia Wilde, or the less startling but by no means untalented men, Francisco Moncion, Nicholas Magallanes, Todd Bolender, Herbert Bliss, Jacques d'Amboise, Arthur Mitchell, Edward Villella, and so on and on through a distinguished company. Form in Balanchine's works is so engaging to the speculative—and meditative—mind that it can be caught up in ballet after ballet, season after season, without any great consciousness of either the repetitiousness or monotony of motions and gestures that the antipathetic critics of the New York City company are fond of pointing out. From the profound investigation of visual and aural form that marked the beginning of the company, *Orpheus,* to *Agon* and *Episodes,* Balanchine's has been a restless, stirring art, poking inquisitive fingers and feet into places where ballet otherwise simply would not or could not go. For works like *Orpheus,* some sense of the underlying myth was always a clear motivation for the choreographer, for the composer (Stravinsky), and inevitably, then, for the audience. For *Agon* and *Episodes,* only a wandering athleticism and a sense of the inner motions of twelve-tone music seemed to be guiding lines. But those with an acquaintaince with ballet history in general, and Balanchine's contributions to it in particular, would not be likely to feel so helpless in the presence of such determined movement. Determined? Yes, determined in every sense of the word— determined by the music itself, as Balanchine's work always has been, whether by Bizet, as in the handsome formalities of the *Symphony in C,* or Tchaikovsky, as in the adaptation for a virtuoso corps de ballet of the *Serenade for Strings,* or Bach, as in the translation of Bach's double violin concerto in *Concerto Barocco,* or Hindemith, Stravinsky, or Webern. And determined by a constant reflection on the history of ideas which is instinct in the history of ballet, from Petipa and the Russian ballet at home in Russia to the effect of American tunes and tempos upon Balanchine, upon Stravinsky, upon the dancers who have grown up with the designs of both. Whatever may be the difficulties of the New York City Ballet when Balanchine's career is finished, as in time it must be, they will not be too great a price to pay for his contribution. With him, ballet found a new grandeur, and not merely that domestication or naturalization that ardent nativists always demand. Ballet is not only at home in America now, it has a technical vitality it has never had anywhere else in the world and a philosophical depth and a company altogether capable of expressing both.

One should not fault the American Ballet Theatre for smaller ambitions and thus smaller accomplishments than the Balanchine company or condemn the Ballet Russe de Monte Carlo or the half-dozen or more small companies that play the community-concert circuits for still more confined aims and purposes and achievements. The Ballet Theatre has moved far beyond the elaborate pantomime of Fokine's *Bluebeard,* with which it was at first associated, when it was founded in 1939. It became for a while a center of psychoanalytical choreography with the ballets of Antony Tudor—*Dark Elegies, Jardin aux Lilas, Pillar of Fire,* and *Undertow*—and then a finely conducted vehicle for the work of Agnes De Mille, notably her adaptation of the Lizzie Borden murder case, *Fall River Legend,* and of Jerome Robbins, with most distinction in the engaging *Fancy Free* and *Interplay* and the more brooding *Facsimile.* It has kept alive such significant accomplishments of American ballet as *Billy the Kid* and Agnes De Mille's *Rodeo* and Valerie Bettis's *A Streetcar Named Desire.* It also has room in its commodious repertory for the standard works—*Giselle, Les Sylphides, Swan Lake*—as well as some of the most typical work of David Lichine, Adolph Bolm, and Frederick Ashton. A liberal education in ballet can be gleaned from several seasons of the Ballet Theatre. If one fills it out with the ancient sweetmeats of the Ballet Russe—*Gaîté Parisienne, Le Beau Danube,* and *Scheherazade*—one can begin to speak with some authority, if also, it may be, with some weariness, of this art.

Unfortunately, in spite of the performances of superb dancers over the years—Nora Kaye, Alexandra Danilova, Igor Youskevitch, John Kriza—the Ballet Theatre companies, like the groups that are formed by dancers like Alicia Markova and Anton Dolin, Mia Slavenska and Frederic Franklin, and Marina Svetlova, can make only a fitful appeal to the mind that finds its deepest satisfaction in Balanchine's choreography. Even the best of their perfomances have by now been equaled or surpassed by the groups gathered together for Broadway musicals to do similar patterns, designed by the same choreographers, Jerome Robbins, Agnes De Mille, Eugene Loring, Michael Kidd, and all the others. The investigations of the dark side of human psychology by Antony Tudor, once startling and provocative, have by now become commonplace, not only on Broadway, but in film and television musicals. What is more, the smug and self-satisfied imitations of Tudor that turn up all over these days, have made even the originals hard to take. For this sort of Freudian choreography was always a little fragile, and certainly never strong enough to survive hundreds of clumsy duplications by hacks.

Most television choreography is designed in fairly simple terms for audiences certainly long adjudged to be fairly simple by the self-appointed wise men who each year fix the intelligence of audiences at some low point somewhere near their own so that they can then comfortably arrange their tastes for them. Television dancing is, however, technically adept when managed by choreographers of the skill of John Butler, Tony Charmoli, and James Starbuck, as it is much of the time, and danced by dancers of the craftsmanship of Melissa Hayden and Nicholas Magallanes, as it is some of the time. There was a real wit about Charmoli's Hit Parade designs; he made over the trivia of television-era pop tunes into entertaining parodies, never too wearing on the consciences of those who liked the songs, but with unmistakable ironies for those who enjoyed looking for them. John Butler did choreography for Menotti's *Amahl and the Night Visitors* that made most viewers very happy; it did not violate the cheerful religiosity of the television opera, but neither did it sink into the bathos of movement that the music might have been thought to invite.

For all the good cheer of the *Amahl* dances and the Hit Parade exercises, however, television choreography comes very close to the general line of middlebrow nonsense, full of outward show and inner emptiness. It is almost always sleekly produced and danced superbly well by some of the most accomplished dancers in the profession. The result is a gloss that hides the essential feebleness of the works involved, say *Amahl,* or the great hollow displays which accompany singers like Mary Martin and Dinah Shore, Bing Crosby and Perry Como, or comedians such as Bob Hope and Victor Borge and Danny Kaye, and make them also seem hollow much of the time. By contrast, Balanchine's *Noah and the Flood,* written to music by Stravinsky as a television celebration of the composer's eightieth birthday, is a work of meditative brilliance, for all its brevity and obliqueness. It remains impressive in the memory in spite of a strange peristaltic production that presented first an excerpt from the ballet as a teaser, then a commercial, then a highly literary introduction to the work, then the ballet, then a commercial, and then a review of Stravinsky's life and works. In his choreography, Balanchine made very few concessions to the submarginal audience that is generally supposed to congregate around television sets. As the musician he is, he allowed Stravinsky's serial composition to dictate the formal structure of his work and upon it grafted some intriguing variations on the imagery usually associated with the Fall, Lucifer's as well as Adam's, and on the story of Noah. Masks and a fanciful set, designed by Reuben Ter-Artunian, may have lost something in the reduction to the dimensions of the TV screen, but they indicated, even within the patent limitations of the medium, how well the kind of invention that produces ballet of quality on the stage may fit into television.

Nothing of the same quality has ever quite been attempted in film choreography, in spite of the persuasive examples of Agnes De Mille's ballets for *Brigadoon, Oklahoma!, Carousel, Paint Your Wagon,* and *One Touch of Venus,* Hanya Holm's *Kiss Me Kate* and *My Fair Lady,* and Balanchine's various Rodgers and Hart assignments. Ballet has been integrated into films, however, perhaps most successfully in *Seven Brides for Seven Brothers,* in which all but two of the principals were professional dancers and Michael Kidd's designs were drawn into the plot and made part of the characterizations, such as they were. For the general public, there is little question that Jerome Robbins' *West Side Story* is the triumphant arrival of ballet on the movie screen. In it, all the peculiar elegances with which the rumbling gangs were endowed onstage are magnified a hundredfold by the most inflationary of modern film processes, Todd-AO. Nonetheless the ballet in it remains almost a caricature of the art, constantly attacking the credibility of the film's characters by its embarrassing perversion of their motions, of their gestures, even of their sitting and standing attitudes. Its mixing of an intense naturalism, in the story and the acting and the direction, with ballet of the most romantic kind is even more flagrantly wrong in the film than it was on the stage, for the conflict is much more awkward on the screen, where the naturalism is so convincing, where reality seems twice as real as life, and there is no constant awareness of the proscenium arch and the foreshortened stage to remind us that the medium is necessarily and even happily artificial and that in it life is only imitated, not relived.

Gene Kelly made better use of the film as a medium for the dance in *An American in Paris,* following what was by no means a new idea—a clean break with story, if not with characters, to present his dances. The dances themselves were almost fresh adaptations of tap-dance conventions, with touches of a rhythmic vitality that Kelly does not often get into his work, and with a constant enrichment from a profusion of color that spilled into and onto everything.

Fred Astaire has never been seriously hampered by the restrictions of plot or character or such mild touches of realism as his writers or directors or fellow actors may have tried to inject into his films. He has always remained himself, down to his belts, made of four-in-hand ties, and suede shoes, a performer of incomparable insouciance and individuality, not only with every facility as a dancer, but with almost as much ease as a singer. And to insure himself every opportunity to use all his skills, he has had scores made to order for him, some of the best writing ever done to order by Cole Porter, Jerome Kern, the Gershwins, and Irving Berlin. He has had only one partner who seemed, at least for a while, to match his nonchalance in the moves on screen from dance to plot and back again—Ginger Rogers. But he has never failed to make his skillful mixture of tap dancing, ballroom and ballet movements into a festive occasion, a moment in which to celebrate the simple but altogether joyous fact that man can move and move with a beat.

Nothing done by other American dancers in films has come close to Astaire's standard of performance, not the high-hipped, high-heeled stepping of Eleanor Powell and Ann Miller at one end, nor the elongated points of Cyd Charisse at the other. The only passages in films to approach the ebullience and technical mastery of Astaire were those brief moments entrusted to Negro teams in the musicals of the thirties and forties. In them, for a few frames, one could see something of the startling balance of absolute control of movement with rhythmic abandon of teams like Buck and Bubbles, the Nicholas Brothers, the Giants of Rhythm, the Step Brothers, and the Berry Brothers, or of single dancers like Baby Lawrence and Bill Bailey. But for the full weight of this sort of dancing, uninhibited by movie plot, the poor judgment of directors and producers, and the envy of Hollywood stars, one had to go to theaters like the Apollo in Harlem, the stage-presentation houses in the big cities, such as the New York Paramount and the Balaban and Katz Chicago Theater, and certain special nightclubs. There one could discover an art of extraordinary dimensions, far richer than its surface elements indicated. There were always, of course, military formations, the more exact and the more elaborate as the teams grew in size. There were shining dinner jackets and tails, black and white and every color, and rhinestone-studded derbies and top hats that were bright enough to read by. There were prodigious acrobatic feats, like the long sequences of splits by the Nicholases and the combination of air shows and drumming exercises with canes put on by the Berrys. But beyond all of this there was a tradition of swivelings from the hip and struttings from the thigh and flutterings of the hand and shakings of the head that reached back at least a century into plantation life and minstrel shows and social occasions in the life of slaves still far from clearly understood or documented by historians of American culture. These were dancers like the jazz musicians with whom they most enjoyed working: beautifully prepared by rehearsal exercises for every possible rhythmic opportunity, and not only rhythmic, but melodic and harmonic. For their ears, like their feet, were geared to improvisation, and improvisation of a fullness that had never been dreamed of on the plantation or the minstrel stage.[3]

These dancers are almost all gone now, dead or retired, and with them an art has almost died, too. John Bubbles, the surviving partner of his team, is still around to demonstrate a soft-shoe routine with felicity of step and sweetness of body motion. John Berry, of the disbanded Berry Brothers, has an awesome repertory of dances and fragments of dances, covering almost every aspect of jazz dancing, from its early antecedents, through the broad showmanly routines of Bill Robinson, to the complex improvisations of Baby Lawrence, as abstract and compelling in their dry hip way as Balanchine's permanently fixed designs. Here and there around the country other virtuosi of jazz dancing can be found, but not many of them are regularly employed in what was once a flourishing segment of the American dance. Nobody has thought to find a place for them in television. The kind of movie musical that used to employ them is no longer made, and there is no place for them in the grand operatic works that now make up the bulk of the American musical theater. If there is a future for this kind of dancing, whether through the few veterans that are still around or through younger dancers reviving and developing their art, it will have to come through a conscious effort on somebody's part to prepare that future for them as for all the rest of the American dance. It will come, if it does, because in recital halls and on college campuses and community-concert auditoriums around the United States, audiences have been worked on by American dancers, by those who dance to jazz, by ballet dancers, and by the inheritors of the tradition of Duncan, Denishawn, and their highly gifted pupils, recognizing that though the dance in America is essentially a private art, it has the closest of connections with every kind of human movement and thus with every kind of human being.

THE THEATER

THE DEVELOPMENT of the American theater from 1900 to the 1960's has been from players to playwrights and then all the way back again, as the producers, who had never been altogether shy about their participation in the art, have once again taken over and made the theater into a branch of investment banking. The result is an expensive dullness, unrelieved by anything except a few imports, a cabaret act or two, and yearly reports from the swamps of psychopathia sexualis by Tennessee Williams and Edward Albee. One can be driven into a defensive stupor by the Broadway season of the sixties, but it is not worse, really, than the 1900's, when plays like *Captain Jinks of the Horse Marines,* by Clyde Fitch, represented the best of the native dramatists, and Shakespeare, Shaw, and Ibsen kept the theater alive—if "alive" is the right word to describe the romantic postures of Richard Mansfield, Julia Marlowe, E. H. Sothern, and Robert B. Mantell, the country's leading Shakespeareans. Then as now there were superb imports—Shaw with Mrs. Patrick Campbell and Ellen Terry, Eleanora Duse in a season of D'Annunzio, Henry Irving mixing Shakespeare and Sardou. There were several gifted actresses who worked to keep the theater open to playwrights of genius, notably Mrs. Fiske and Nazimova, for both of whom there was for a long time only one modern writer, Ibsen. But the most consistent successes—and perhaps the most consistent performers— were teams like Weber and Fields, McIntyre and Heath, and Lew Dockstader's Minstrels. The public found its chief enlightenment in the plays of James M. Barrie, preferably with Maude Adams, and its warmth in *The Music Master* with David Warfield and *Rip Van Winkle* with Joseph Jefferson. Those who wanted more substance had to search out the little semiprofessional groups beginning to bring the modern theater onto the American stage.

The most vigorous and best-advised of the off-Broadway groups was the Washington Square Players, founded in 1915, who after some years at the accurately named Bandbox Theatre on 57th Street, emerged as the Theatre Guild, and the Provincetown Players, which in 1916 gave Eugene O'Neill his first production, at the Wharf Theatre in Provincetown, Massachusetts. The first group performed Maeterlinck, Chekhov, and a variety of American playwrights, of second-rate but not worse talent, chiefly in one-act plays, before it became the Theatre Guild and moved to Broadway. It began its auspicious career at the Garrick Theatre, with Jacinto Benavente's masterpiece, *The Bonds of Interest,* a dismal flop, and St. John Ervine's much less demanding *John Ferguson,* a success. Then came an incomparable set of seasons, which should not be forgotten in the light of the dolors which later attacked the Guild or its lackluster productions in radio and television. For the Theatre Guild in the twenties was responsible for the first performances anywhere of Shaw's *St. Joan* and *Back to Methuselah* and for keeping a large Shaw repertory going, for the introduction of Americans to German expressionism in Georg Kaiser's *From Morn to Midnight* and Ernst Toller's *Masses and Men,* for presenting such significant American experimental plays as Elmer Rice's *The Adding Machine* and John Howard Lawson's *Processional,* and for almost the entire career after his one-act plays of Eugene O'Neill, the Provincetown's special playwright.

The American theater came into being with Eugene O'Neill. For all his debts to Strindberg and Kaiser, he had something very much his own, which was to pass intact into the drama in this country, with all its crudities of technique retained alongside its finesses of insight. O'Neill has never been an impressive playwright to read, unless one has a remarkably attentive eye for the details of stage direction and a sufficient fullness of imagination to hear the clumsy dialogue come alive as it does on the stage and to see the action move out from behind the heavy rhetoric and into the actors' bodies. O'Neill is essentially a writer for the stage, whose coarsest mannerisms on paper often are his most convincing mannerisms in the theater, as for example the dialects he assigns his sailors in his one-act plays about the sea. The accents he labored to give phonetic conviction on the printed page—Russian, Swedish, Irish, Scottish, cockney, American —mean very little until one has heard a good actor turn the futility and frustration of his Ivan or Olson or Driscoll or Cocky or any of the others into an affecting portrait of the despair and degradation of the great nations of the sea reduced to the dimensions of a tramp steamer. Like Moussorgsky, or Verdi at the end of his career, O'Neill was so fully persuaded himself of the intrinsic dignity of the people of his—and the world's—melodramas, that he almost persuades us that the fuss is not out of proportion to the worth of his characters. And so we accept melodrama, only slightly hidden under the apparatus of expressionism which O'Neill gradually learned to use; and we are not so embarrassed by an impoverished language, and a symbolism not much richer, that we cannot go along for an hour or two with the terms of his sadistic dramas.

From the beginning O'Neill's characters long for everything, for life, for love, for fulfillments of various kinds, only sooner or later to reveal a consuming longing for death. O'Neill's audiences are punished along with his heroes and heroines, as they are drawn with them into plots that must end in disaster. With all the subtlety of an opera libretto, the story of *Beyond the Horizon,* O'Neill's first full-length play (1920), forces its central character out of his dreams of the sea into an eviscerating life on the farm. His love for his brother's girl traps him; the farm is a failure; his baby dies. Finally, tuberculosis saves him—it cripples and kills him, leaving him a dream to see at the end, beyond the horizon, to be worked out by his brother and his widow. The trapped dictator of *The Emperor Jones* (1920), a former Pullman porter who has become the wealthy tyrant of a small West Indian island, has not even death to rescue him: he has fired the silver bullet he had reserved for the ultimate emergency in his fear of being caught by his pursuing subjects, half of whom exist only in his terror-filled imagination. The end of *Anna Christie* (1920) is hopeful; the daughter of a barge captain is not so much morally regenerated as vindicated by the last events of the play. Though she has led the life of a whore, she has not lost her hold upon herself. She triumphs when her father accepts the finality of her love for a sailor and the marriage that must follow. But both her father and the sailor have been so shaken by her revelation of her life as a prostitute that they have signed up for another voyage at sea. A tumultuous scene, filled with drink and strong rhetoric, convinces the men that Anna is theirs, as daughter and lover, but its conclusion must wait; everything is still beyond the horizon, a little closer now, but still not close enough.

Even the small touch of hope at the end of *Anna Christie* was too much. O'Neill never tried it again quite that way. His one altogether sunny comedy, *Ah, Wilderness!* (1933), presents hope in uncompromising terms, but despair has never come closer in that little fable than an adolescent boy's mix-up with a chorus girl on a one-day drunken toot. Nothing of greater consequence than an evening's entertainment has ever been involved, except, perhaps, O'Neill's own dreams of a family life no more complicated than this one.

What sets the people of *Ah, Wilderness!* far apart from all the others in O'Neill's plays is that they belong to each other. Theirs is a family that mishap draws together. Nobody in it is more than a one-day outsider. Nobody in it is cut off from civilization like Yank, the stoker, who is the title character in *The Hairy Ape* (1922), or the impossibly mixed mates, Negro and white, of *All God's Chillun Got Wings* (1924). There is no place for Yank, not in the polished world of the daughter of the owner of his ship, not on "Fifth Avenue in the Fifties on a fine Sunday morning," not in an IWW union, not even at the zoo with a gorilla that he himself has freed. His great hulking presence, all body and no mind, frightens everybody, and even turns the gorilla into an enemy. Yank has extended his hand—"Shake," he offers; "de secret grip of our order." The gorilla is not amused; he crushes him with "a murderous hug" and throws his body into his cage. There Yank dies, with a last groan, more of tragic acceptance than protest, O'Neill's Pagliacci:

Say—dey oughter match him—wit Zybszko. He got me, aw right. I'm trou. Even him didn't tink I belonged. (*Then, with sudden passionate despair.*) Christ, where do I get off at? Where do I fit in? (*Checking himself as suddenly.*) Aw, what de hell! No squawkin', see! No quittin', get me! Croak wit your boots on! (*He grabs hold of the bars of the cage and hauls himself painfully to his feet—looks around bewilderedly—forces a mocking laugh.*) In de cage, huh? (*In the strident tones of a circus barker.*) Ladies and gents, step forward and take a slant at de one and only—(*His voice weakening*)—one and original—Hairy Ape from the wilds of——(*He slips in a heap on the floor and dies. The monkeys set up a chattering, whimpering wail. And, perhaps, the Hairy Ape at last belongs.*)

CURTAIN [1]

The attempts to belong of Jim, the colored man, and Ella, the white woman, of *All God's Chillun Got Wings,* are equally unavailing. They have been able to get married only when Ella has been rejected by a roughneck white man and she has lost her child by him. They can stay together only when Ella has rejected herself and an adult life, driven back by her hatred and fear of race differences into dreams of the only time in which she had ever been happy, her childhood, which she had shared with Jim. Like the diseased lungs which consume the hero of *Beyond the Horizon,* like the gorilla's hug that "perhaps" permits the Hairy Ape to belong, the peace that Ella finds is in death—the death of the mind. Insanity fair: nothing but insanity is temperate in such a world.

There is no peace in the normal, the so-called sane way of life, in O'Neill. Peace comes with death or its imitation, utter isolation from people. Isolation may be the result of insanity. It may come from the total destruction of one's own family, as it so often does in the plays of O'Neill, leaving an old man in demented but happy possession (in *Desire under the Elms,* 1924), a wife in sane but unhappy possession (*The Great God Brown,* 1926), a homicidal emperor in demented but unhappy control (*Lazarus Laughed,* 1927), a mother in moderately happy closeness to her son, who has only some disturbed inner feelings to tell him who his real father is (*Strange Interlude,* 1928), a sister and daughter remaining as the miserable survivor of one of the least savory of all the retellings of the myth of the House of Atreus as it appears in Aeschylus's *Oresteia* (*Mourning Becomes Electra,* 1931). The man in possession is the object of O'Neill's most explosive wrath. Everything that gathers around Ephraim Cabot in *Desire under the Elms* is made ugly by his snarling presence: a man who hates anything that stands between him and total possession, hates his sons, hates his wives, hates all who will live on after he dies. Though not the actual instrument of the murder, he is responsible for the killing of his young wife's child by his own youngest son. Of all the incubi of possession in O'Neill, he is the most oppressive, the one who is closest to being possessed himself, as his lines at the end of the play make abundantly clear: "God's hard, not easy! . . . I kin hear His voice warnin' me agen t'be hard and stay on my farm. . . . I kin feel I be in the palm o' His hand, His fingers guidin' me. It's a-goin' t'be lonesomer now than ever it war afore—an' I'm gittin' old, Lord —ripe on the bough. . . . Waal—what d'ye want? God's lonesome, hain't He? God's hard an' lonesome!" [2] And so he looks almost happily at his wife and his son as they are taken off by the sheriff; and then he goes about his chores, undisturbed.

Superb designing by Robert Edmond Jones placed a two-story farmhouse on the stage for *Desire under the Elms,* the walls of which could be removed to reveal whatever rooms were necessary. The setting was a fair indication of the distance O'Neill had traveled from the conventions of naturalism, in spite of the marks of *East Lynne* in the dialogue. He had cautioned against naturalistic treatment of any of the scenes of *The Hairy Ape* in the opening scene directions. In *The Great God Brown,* he used masks whenever he wanted to show his characters' numbing fear of revealing themselves, a better device, for all its obviousness, than the elaborate asides with which he presented the streams of consciousness in *Strange Interlude,* if that is the right term to describe the mawkish confessions of those silly people out of soap opera, who are around almost as long as the sad singers of Procter and Gamble's lyrics—for nine acts, God help us.

The Nietzschean drama of William, the Great God Brown, and Dion Anthony, is less than engrossing in itself. The war between the states—a Dionysian "creative pagan acceptance of life" and "the masochistic, life-denying spirit of Christianity as represented by St. Anthony"—is hardly civil. And the ultimate message, "Always spring comes again bearing life," conveyed by a whore with the grand symbolic name of Cybel, old Earth Mother herself, is, one would think, less than deeply moving, even to those, brought up on Dostoevski, O'Neill, and Tennessee Williams, to whom all whores have hearts of gold. But the technique of masks, drawn from Jung, is a striking one, that keeps the play fresh, for all its reduction of complex personality differences to a few grossly simplified conflicts.

The great ambitions of O'Neill in the trilogy *Mourning Becomes Electra* are frustrated by a language that does not begin to achieve the grandeur of the Aeschylean tragedy and is even weak as an attempt to convey the speech of a New England town just after the Civil War. The driving forces of fate, as a result, often seem little more than awkwardly managed coincidences; Frank Sullivan's parody of the play, "Life Is Just a Bowl of Eugene O'Neills," with its family of Badduns (for Madduns) and its puns on the names of famous psychologists ("I'm afreud . . . I'm so afreud. . . . Life gets Adler and Adler. . . ."), still seems witheringly apposite. Similar failures of language and a much weaker structure of plot and characterization crippled *Dynamo* (1929) and *Days without End* (1934), parts of what looked like becoming a series of plays, three or even four, about the contrasting appeals of large-scale determinisms for modern man's faith—the machine, religion, and whatever else O'Neill might have had in mind.

The size of O'Neill's gropings after language, symbols, plot, and characters appropriate to his grand themes can be gathered from his last four plays, the one that was produced with no great success on Broadway in his own time, *The Iceman Cometh* (1946), the one that he saw fail out of town, *A Moon for the Misbegotten* (1947), and the two that were produced after his death with good and with great success respectively, *A Touch of the Poet* (1957) and *Long Day's Journey into Night* (1956). None of them is a less than absorbing play. The *Iceman,* as Jose Quintero's revival at the Circle in the Square showed, is a brilliant blast at life, with a character in Hickey, the salesman who deals in despair, as James Barton showed in the original production, of the proportions of the central figures in the last plays of Ibsen and Strindberg—huge, like his own great speech in the last act, twenty-five minutes long. The special interest that *A Touch of the Poet* holds is that it is the only remaining play in finished shape of the eleven that O'Neill had planned and begun to write to fill out a cycle to be called *A Tale of Possessors Self-dispossessed.* Its terms are the old ones for O'Neill, of possession and its prototypes and antitypes, reduced to a day's doings at a run-down tavern near Boston in 1828. The play's humors are disturbing, its mixture of dramatic textures hard to follow with consistent interest or understanding. But the marks of a brilliant playwright are on the play, especially strongly in the central character of Con Melody. By comparison *A Moon for the Misbegotten* is a far from consistent performance, one that suffered, too, from being produced the year after *Long Day's Journey,* O'Neill's most considerable work and perhaps the finest play in the American theater.

Not much will stand up to *Long Day's Journey,* for this drama reaches, with a conviction no other play by O'Neill can match, into the destructive forces of family life. The family is his own—his actor-father, James O'Neill, and the rest of his family, mother and brother, translated into the tragic Tyrones. Tragedy is theirs, without any fall greater than Mary Tyrone's into drug addiction and the elder brother's into drunkenness. We are not made to weep over the tuberculosis that afflicts Edmund (as it did Eugene). Our tears, if they come, are elicited by the miserliness of the father, the pompousness of the father, the possessiveness of the father, who is finally, as all men in possession in this reading of life must be, self-dispossessed. Or they spring to life to compassionate the bitterly isolated mother, out of touch with everything except her childhood with the nuns, as a result of her having been addicted to morphine by the incompetent doctor hired by her economizing husband. In the most pejorative sense of the phrase, James Tyrone is a mean man. But he never becomes a merely melodramatic figure of meanness. We may not accept his long and elaborate self exculpations, but we do not find it difficult to understand that some of the time, at least, Tyrone himself finds them acceptable.

The techniques used in this play are almost a roll call of O'Neill's dramatic history. The setting is worked out in naturalistic detail, down to the last book in the bookcase, every author in which is named by O'Neill. But the play rolls around in a rich Connecticut fog as well, reaching long symbolic fingers across the action. The masks are all verbal, but for once the dialogue is up to it, long as the day's four-act journey is. This is one O'Neill play that reads very well. The stage directions are fascinating in themselves, and the violent struggle of the Tyrone family is so satisfactorily set in the Connecticut seaside house described in such detail by O'Neill that even the plethora of extra-long speeches does not weigh too heavily on the reader and onstage is only wearying when directed by a slow-paced technician who wants, probably contrary to O'Neill's own intention, to make every word count. The result, however one comes to the play, on paper or in the theater, is an overwhelming sense of the power of the drama. For a lifetime's meditating on the various forms the art can take seems to have gone into this play, and to have found, for once in the American theater, a genuinely meditative texture. That is what keeps *Long Day's Journey into Night* from ever becoming the exercise in grim dishonesty, in unbearable self-delusion and family hatred, which its surface events might lead one to expect it to be.

The texture of the American drama has not often been meditative. Skillful, extravagant, handsomely produced, brightly played, with entertaining people playing engaging characters—these things it has been again and again, although never again with such frequency as in the twenties, when almost every theatrical mode except the finely meditative had its exemplary representatives on Broadway. Expressionism was rather quickly domesticated, from *The Emperor Jones* to

Elmer Rice's *The Adding Machine* (1923), from the *Beggar on Horseback* of George S. Kaufman and Marc Connelly (1924) to John Howard Lawson's *Processional* (1925). Rice put an adding machine on the stage, a hundred times as big as life, to dramatize the metamorphosis of a harassed office worker, Mr. Zero, into a cipher, and a nothing at that. Kaufman and Connelly gave a thin romantic drama substance with a dream anticipation of the horrors of assembly-line songwriting which shatters the composer-hero and brings everything to a happy ending. Lawson's melodramatic allegory never had very much conviction as a narrative or as a presentation of character; American life simply stands condemned in it, as in everything the author ever wrote. But there are some effective employments of jazz in it and a good use, too, of vaudeville scenery, burlesque rowdiness, and of almost everything raucous in the popular theater.

With its new consciousness of the technical resources of the modern stage, the American theater came alive. Its scene designers reached a maturity almost all at once in the twenties which gave even second- and third-rate plays at least the appearance of theatrical quality. Robert Edmond Jones surrounded his productions with atmosphere, mood, using a misty machinery of suggestion in his sets that brought Gordon Craig's ideas into the American playhouse. Lee Simonson was a serious, scrupulously responsible designer. Norman Bel Geddes, the most generously gifted of all, ranged in his sets from the abstract designs in light and platform of his full-length *Hamlet* to the extraordinary realism of his *Dead End* production, for which he constructed, on stage, a full-size city street at the waterfront—complete with water. Like the theater which he served, he could touch all the stops—night-club carnival for a musical (*Flying Colors*), medieval cathedral for a morality (*The Miracle*), metaphysical space for a meditation on the wandering history of the Jews (*The Eternal Road*).

A majority of the ranking American playwrights achieved their maturity or their first box-office successes, or both, in the twenties. There were about 250 plays in every season, in that extraordinary decade, and plenty of room in that vast number for plays about the war (Maxwell Anderson and Laurence Stallings' *What Price Glory?* 1924), for plays about the deceptions of middle-class married life (Anderson's *Saturday's Children,* 1927), and for sleek comedies of American life, chiefly upper-class, such as Philip Barry's *You and I* (1923) and *Paris Bound* (1927) and *Holiday* (1928) and S. N.

Behrman's *The Second Man* (1927) and Robert E. Sherwood's *The Road to Rome,* which, in spite of its ostensible concern with Hannibal and the wife of the Roman dictator Fabius, was a comedy of American manners, and a splendid debut for the somewhat dyspeptic film critic and editor of *Life*—then, as older readers will remember, a comic weekly sans photos.

The best thing about all of these plays, as about almost everything else that Barry and Behrman and Sherwood were to do, was a constant flow of amusing situations, well set out with dialogue to match. Even *What Price Glory?* survives by virtue of its feud between Sergeant Quirt and Captain Flagg of the Marines, scored for invective and practical joke, an almost unbeatable combination for popular art, as a sequence of wildly successful films employing the same characters (played by Victor McLaglen and Edmund Lowe) proved shortly after the advent of talkies. On the basis of that comedy and some bright exchanges in *Both Your Houses* (1933), Anderson's noisy exposé of corruption and venality in high public places, and *High Tor* (1937), his often incisive allegorical attack on modern American businessmen, effected by means of some seventeenth-century Dutch ghosts who pop out of Anderson's favorite Hudson River country, one can only regret the playwright's determination to give tone to American drama with blank verse. There was some excuse for the acres of iambics assigned the title characters of *Elizabeth the Queen* (1930) and *Mary of Scotland* (1933) and their aides and enemies; at least all were contemporaries of the great masters of blank verse, Shakespeare, Jonson, Webster, etc. But listening to the little people who live under the Brooklyn Bridge—a Jewish family, gangsters, and so on—speak the same sort of verse in *Winterset* (1935) can be an excruciating experience. Why such an eagerness for tone—and that particular sixteenth-century tone—one wonders? And where, oh where, has Anderson's sense of humor gone?

Sidney Howard was also a generally humorous writer, but not without his own quite effective ironies. His only really funny play, *The Late Christopher Bean* (1932), is an adaptation from the French, with some entertaining anticipations of the central situation in Joyce Carey's Gulley Jimson novels: A servant in a small Massachusetts town has had the sense to recognize the true stature of a down-and-out artist, and when, after his death, his paintings turn out to be valuable, she makes the profit from them that she thoroughly deserves. As in all of Howard's very well made plays, the scenes move along at a fine clip and there is a suitable if not quite profound irony in the revelation of crooks as less shrewd than the most honest of servants.

Howard's *They Knew What They Wanted* (1924) several times pauses on the verge of a meditative examination of the conflicting claims of religion and science, with some entertaining possibilities for a contrapuntal line to be set against the play's main point, endorsing young love between lusty specimens of the sexes, as against the mating of people generations apart in age. In the cheerful irony of the play, carefully revealed in the title, all is made to come right: the older man gets his child and the young couple have their affair. The Earth Mother is rather better served in this play than in *The Great God Brown,* even if the theatrical strategies involved are a good deal less startling.

Howard was a fine craftsman. Even the dated indictment of Oedipal attachments in *The Silver Cord* (1926) and the documentary drama paying tribute to the scientists of the Walter Reed Commission who discovered the cause of yellow fever, *Yellow Jack* (1934), continue to hold interest because of the precisely plotted rise and fall of the action in each of them. A similar precision made Howard's adaptation of Sinclair Lewis's *Dodsworth* (1934) and of Humphrey Cobb's antiwar novel, *Paths of Glory* (1935), compelling, if less than deeply moving, theater. His last play, *The Ghost of Yankee Doodle* (1937), is not a polished work of the same kind; Howard's indignant protest against the drums-of-war propaganda constantly stands in the way of the precisions of which he was an early master. Unfortunately, too, such fury as the play contains fizzles out, finally, in an impassioned plea for neutrality, not the most attractive position to take at the time of Anschluss and Munich.

Most of the playwrights of the twenties had become too slick in their craftsmanship by the middle of that decade to be able to make speculative philosophical drama convincing. Lacking the depth of Bernard Shaw, their plays skidded around embarrassingly in a welter of wisecracks and nothing much better. Philip Barry tried several times to get away from the urbane comedy he did so well and into allegories thick with meaningful ambiguities. But even in *White Wings* (1926), the best of them, because the closest to Barry's usual comic mode, he makes much too much fuss over his issue: the passing of the horse and its replacement by the automobile. In *Hotel Universe* (1930), Barry jumps back and forth between the problems of common garden-variety guilt-ridden people and a fairly rarefied upper-class Catholic guilt, and shows too little wisdom about either set of difficulties. He settles, finally, for an embarrassing God-the-Father-substitute in the form of a benevolent old physicist who seems to suffer himself from a David Belasco complex, as he goes around explaining the sources of everybody's problems and then pops off himself for the next world, slipping noiselessly out of this life. In *Here Come the Clowns* (1938), the most ambitious of his allegorical plays, Barry translates the search for values in American life into what one of the vaudeville people who make up the cast calls "A still hunt for the Almighty!" The chief hunter is a stagehand, who just before his death announces the success of his quest in spite of all the evil in the world. Why is there so much unhappiness around us? Because men are "bad by their own choice":

. . . The proud will of Man is my answer! The free will of Man, turned the wrong way. By the grace of God, free to think and choose for himself, was he?—Free to make his own world, eh? The fine job he's made of it!—With pride at the top and despair at the bottom and all manner of misery in the between—turning lies into truth and truth into lies until nobody knows the one from the other—

But there is a better answer, implicit in "the other":

But know we will, know we *will!*—For it's a fine instrument, the free will of man is, and can as easy be turned to Good as to Bad.—Ah, it's the grand thing, is man's will! Whatever it's sunk to, it can rise again. It can rise over anything, anything.[3]

And even death, says the prophet stagehand, can overcome death, "it can live and die and resurrect itself!"

The difficulty about allegories of this kind is that they proclaim themselves so openly. Their signs and symbols are too clamorous, crying for substitution like letters in a cryptogram. We do not feel the need for the allegory to begin with; nothing in particular is gained by the extensive vaudeville apparatus, except the uncomfortable feeling that Barry's intention is a lot more profound than his effect. He is really much more impressive in his long series of investigations of the pretensions and the accomplishments, the honesties and the dishonesties of marriage. On the surface, *Paris Bound* and *Tomorrow and Tomorrow* (1931), *The Animal Kingdom* (1932) and *The Philadelphia Story* (1939) are nothing much more than bits of beautifully blown froth. But they do not dissolve as quickly as froth should. As a group, these comedies make a striking plea for monogamy, wherever it is true and thus lasting, even if, as in *The Animal Kingdom,* it is with a mistress rather than a wife, and just as resolutely and entertainingly, even if it is with one's wife rather than a mistress, as in *The Philadelphia Story*. One has something to carry out of the theater of such plays. With the allegories, it has all been said. That absolute finality, leaving so little to think about, must account for their failure, though nobody seems to have pointed it out.

As with Barry's comedies, so with S. N. Behrman's, Robert Sherwood's, and George Kelly's: Their brightly polished surfaces often conceal material of substance beneath. Behrman posed the dilemma of this sort of playwright in *No Time for Comedy* (1939): When a civilization is at one of its great crossroads, as certainly this one was in 1939, should not everybody, even one who is strictly a skillful producer of light comedy, deal with the issues of the day? By the deft means of a play within a play within a play, Behrman resolves his dilemma. *Chacun à son genre* is his answer. His playwright, with the impossibly chic name of Gaylord Easterbrook, turns his own situation into an amusing comedy—namely, *No Time for Comedy*. The issues in Behrman's other plays are not all disposed of so tidily. His characters do tend to choose opportunism and personal ease, when there is any problem of a choice, but there are exceptions, like the election of what passes—not quite convincingly—for working-class poverty in *End of Summer* (1936). The special merit of Behrman's comedy is that en route to a conclusion no more profound than that of *The Second Man*—"You have the two great requirements for the wife of a poor but intelligent man: money and tolerance"—the conversation is entertaining, the people engaging, and the opportunities for light acting endless. Ina Claire in *Biography* (1932) and *End of Summer* and Laurence Olivier and Katharine Cornell in *No Time for Comedy* are fair samples of the kind of performance his scripts elicit. His skill as a theatrical journeyman is also revealed in his adaptations, of Jean Giraudoux's *Amphitryon 38* (1937), of Franz Werfel's *Jacobowsky and the Colonel* (1944), and of Marcel Pagnol's *Fanny*

(1954) as a musical, the last a particularly impressive reworking, reducing a trilogy to a single play and stifling every urge to grand opera which the prevailing winds of the musical theater could very well have prescribed.

Robert E. Sherwood became one of Franklin D. Roosevelt's most trustworthy voices before he died, a fine craftsman of political speeches who managed to make issues tremble without allowing them quite to become fearful. In his comedies, *The Petrified Forest* (1935) and *Idiot's Delight* (1936), he accomplished the same trick, making in the one his indictment of a spineless American civilization and in the other of an irrational European civilization doomed to war, all done with amusing characters and serious ideas adroitly mixed. Each comes to a quick boil, in a small, speedily dispatched melodrama within the larger structure of the play, a fine piece of dramaturgical invention. If one wants, one can plot social significance into *Reunion in Vienna* (1931), too, about the displacement of the Hapsburgs in Austria—the old order passeth, etc. But most of all it was an elegant frame for the rococo motions of Alfred Lunt and Lynn Fontanne, just as *There Shall Be No Night* (1940), in spite of the playwright's unmistakably genuine indignation over the Russian invasion of Finland, turned out to be little more than a vehicle for the same actors. In *Abe Lincoln in Illinois* (1938), many found much more than an unparalleled opportunity for Raymond Massey's acting, with Lincoln somehow made surrogate for everything good and lasting and true in American life. But some of us were not moved by what seemed, in spite of a shining production, little more than a high-school pageant, slicked up for Broadway.

Writers of comic gifts, like Sherwood and Behrman, Barry and George Kelly, are not without their depths. But when they have practiced their comic trade so long, it becomes difficult for them to turn their profundities into plays of great conviction. George Kelly was primarily a social satirist, who worked in large, broad, and obvious strokes and was not less effective for doing so. Though he manages a convincing portrait of a woman of unconscionable addiction to security and a perfectly managed home in *Craig's Wife* (1925), he does not give the character sufficient depth; he leaves us too uncertain about the hidden psychological motivations of such a woman. His true métier was caricature, whether loud and funny, as in his classical cartoon of a braggart and a Babbitt, *The Show-Off* (1924), or the more contained sketches of women, variously adequate and inadequate, wise and foolish, such as *Daisy Mayme* (1926), *The Deep Mrs. Sykes* (1945), and *The Fatal Weakness* (1946).

George S. Kaufman mixed satire and caricature with tenderness of heart to produce a long series of highly successful sentimental comedies, none of them of any great consequence, but all excellent examples of theatrical craftmanship. Before the expressionistic experiment of *Beggar on Horseback,* he wrote three other plays with Marc Connelly: *Dulcy* (1921), which brought Lynn Fontanne stardom, as a woman of endless fatuities; *To the Ladies* (1922), one of Helen Hayes's most impressive early performances, as a woman of large psychological resources, though of a simple kind; and *Merton of the Movies* (1922), a dramatization of Harry Leon Wilson's entertaining novel, and still interesting as a kind of unintentional period piece, about Hollywood and about tastes in popular art in the early twenties, suggesting, as it does, a certain bemused self-criticism in the American air, as Merton Gill, our hero, achieves Hollywood success because he is such a brilliant farceur in his unconscious burlesques of Western stars and other film heroes.

Kaufman went on, after Connelly, to other lucrative partnerships. With Edna Ferber, he accentuated the sentimental, in a study of the Drews and the Barrymores, *The Royal Family* (1927), in an attack on high society, *Dinner at Eight* (1932), which could offend no one, and in *Stage Door* (1936), a potpourri of sketches of ambitious young girls who live at a theatrical boardinghouse, the Footlights Club. With Morrie Ryskind and the Gershwins, he did *Strike Up the Band* (1930), *Of Thee I Sing* (1931), and *Let 'Em Eat Cake* (1933), an incomparable series of political satires set to music, in which the writers avoid, happily, any kind of operatic posturing and still take full advantage of most of the devices so well developed at this point in the history of American musical comedy for the purposes of lampoon, satire, and farce. Some of the same attitude, often expressed with a fine acerbity, can be found in his first collaboration with Moss Hart, *Once in a Lifetime* (1930), in which Hollywood is ridiculed, and in *I'd Rather Be Right* (1937), in which the object of satire is the New Deal. But in this last, there is more good fun than ridicule, as there is in *The Man Who Came to Dinner* (1939), ostensibly a savage study of Alexander Woollcott, but not so savage that Woollcott himself could not play the title role on tour. With

Hart, too, Kaufman rolled off a technically impeccable study of an eccentric family, *You Can't Take It with You* (1936), and the most determined series of flashbacks in the American theater, *Merrily We Roll Along* (1934), in which a successful playwright's unfortunate concessions to a tasteless public are contrasted with his early uncompromising attitudes, as the play moves in reverse order from the present to the past.

Kaufman was at the center of the American theater in his era, a craftsman without compeer. He worked well with all his collaborators, those with whom he did many plays, such as Connelly and Hart and Ferber, or those with whom he worked only once, such as Ring Lardner, his partner in a gentle takeoff on life in the song factories of Tin Pan Alley, *June Moon* (1929), and Howard Teichmann, with whom he did a Wall Street farce of unmatchable momentum, *The Solid Gold Cadillac* (1954). Pace was something Kaufman could contribute to any play, as writer, doctor, or director. And those who worked with him usually became equally adept in the split-second timing which is always a special attraction of popular art in America. Thus, the elegantly ordered direction of *My Fair Lady* by Moss Hart. And thus, too, the restraint of *The Green Pastures* (1930), Connelly's masterpiece, which was, because of its delicacy and grace of theatrical state, a considerable improvement on its source, Roark Bradford's *Ol' Man Adam and His Chillun*. Connelly did not make his version of Genesis and Exodus any less anthropomorphic than Bradford's: it remains a Negro preacher's vision, word-simple and deed-proud. But it comes to the ear sweetly, with none of the clumsiness of dialect on the printed page, and with that secure sense of theater with which Connelly's generation and the next were so generously endowed.

The dramatists of the thirties were no less skillful in their timing, no less attentive to climaxes and denouements and to carefully contrived expositions that did not announce themselves, than their distinguished predecessors. Their plays were equally very well made. But they were products of the Depression and their themes were hardly comic: the struggle for recognition of the unions, poverty in all its guises and all its settings, homosexuality male and female, Nazism, tyranny in the South, tyranny all over—the tyranny of the economic system, the tyranny of the family, the tyranny of the American dream. Clifford Odets had the most immediate impact of these writers in his short-term role as playwright-in-ordinary to the Group Theatre, in which he had been an actor for several years. *Waiting for Lefty* (1935), a one-act play crude in content but rich in expressionistic form, broke the way for Odets. His use of the audience as the body of the meeting of taxicab drivers considering a strike was startlingly direct, with actors planted all through the house and the stage bare, as it would be at the meeting hall. But for all the vitality of its devices, the play never rises beyond the simplest exploitation of political slogans. Its people have about as much depth as those who inhabit the paintings and cartoons of William Gropper, the *New Masses* and *Daily Worker* artist. In *Awake and Sing!* (1935), which Odets wrote before his one-act play, he exerted himself to bring a Bronx family alive, type by type, person by person. The life of the Jewish family is as destructive as any family in O'Neill, but the play exudes the warmth of the grandfather whose compound of Biblical wisdom and Marxist dialectic gives the work whatever depth it possesses.

Odets was always able to manage at least one figure of stature in his plays, usually the pillar of strength upon whom others depended, or, more seriously, upon which the audience had to depend for bursts of wisdom and enlightenment. In *Paradise Lost* (1935), the role is assigned a radical thinker of much smaller dimension than the grandfather in *Awake and Sing!;* in *Rocket to the Moon* (1938), it was a part-time function of the girl whose agonizing choice between a married dentist and another man, too old for her, makes up the plot; in *The Country Girl* (1950), it was the job of the stalwart wife of the alcoholic actor whose life she had to reconstruct with the aid of a young friend and admirer. Neither in these plays nor in the almost hopelessly disjointed *Night Music* (1940) and *Clash by Night* (1941) did Odets show the formal ease which keeps the people of *Awake and Sing!* alive, even the worst of the whiners. But for all the imperfections of such a play as *Rocket to the Moon,* it is preferable to the glib allegorizing of *Golden Boy* (1937), in which the creative gifts of a poor young violinist are made to knuckle under to his more marketable skills as a prizefighter. Even the broad humor of *The Flowering Peach* (1954), in which Odets retells the story of Noah in a kind of Jewish *Green Pastures,* is preferable to the simplifications of this sort of proletarian play, which are in some ways more offensive than the crude barricades drama with which the Theater Union followed Eva Le Gallienne's Civic Repertory group at the old house on 14th Street. The class struggle is certainly effective theater, but when it is trundled forth in such perfectly oiled dramas, it becomes hard to take; it loses conviction and gains quite unintentional ironies which make villains out of heroes and turn the bad guys into nothing worse than psychological misfits.

It may be that Sidney Kingsley's *Men in White* (1933) and *Dead End* (1935) were never more than peripheral to the proletarian theater, in spite of the production of the first by the Group Theatre and the sharp current of criticism of The System that runs through the second. Kingsley is rather a manufacturer of modern Sardoodledum than a man with a cause. He anticipated Dr. Kildare and Ben Casey at St. George's Hospital in *Men in White,* if he didn't actually give birth to them. Out of *Dead End* came a whole spawn of class B films featuring the noisy, nasty, nimble characters he had created for that play, the Dead End Kids. The offspring of *Detective Story* (1949) were nothing more unpleasant than a series of mystery novels and television serials set in precinct houses.

The fatal weakness of the writers of the left is their attraction to the well-made play, with its simplifications all the way through and its much too neat tidying up at the end. Lillian Hellman has always suffered from such reductions of value, in spite of an ever more secure technique and deepening interest in her characters. The terms of *The Children's Hour* (1934) are unremittingly dramatic, if not melodramatic: Lesbianism, real or imagined; a self-dramatizing young girl who is also a pathological liar and an effective blackmailer of her contemporaries; an indulgent grandmother, and a weak fiancé. There are, happily, a few ironies in the play, not the least of them the self-contained one in the title, and for all the careful joining of contrivance to connivance to make the drama end in suicide, followed by apologies all around, *The Children's Hour* is not without a certain dignity. The same sense of the intrinsic worthiness of subject and central character keeps *Watch on the Rhine* (1941), an intensely felt anti-Nazi play, from fading into the long list of works done for a noble cause that no longer need doing.

One can hardly say the same thing about the hateful Hubbards of *The Little Foxes* (1939) and *Another Part of the Forest* (1946), or even about the righteous indignation which the two plays exude. The villainy is too obvious and uncontrolled, either by anything resembling decent instincts on the part of the villains or by such depths of psychological analysis as a playwright of more subtle modulations might have felt bound to offer. Simplifications of another kind make the patronizing treament of an American diplomat in *The Searching Wind* (1944) sometimes difficult to bear, but the complexities of the play's construction—framing an orderly view of the past between opening and closing scenes in the present—are fascinating to behold, perhaps more on paper than in the theater. The people themselves become interesting by the time of *The Autumn Garden* (1951) and *Toys in the Attic* (1960); they have motivation; they reach for our sympathy. If we continue to offer them in return more pity from above than compassion at the same level at which they live, it is probably because the retarded child whose adult problems confront us in *Toys in the Attic* seems such an excellent surrogate for all of Miss Hellman's characters in almost any of her situations. She seems to have committed herself to a negative judgment about the world in which the summary conclusion of *Candide,* in her excellent adaptation of Voltaire for musical purposes, remains no more than a faint hope, for all its modest terms: "We will not think noble because we are not noble. We will not live in beautiful harmony because there is no such thing in this world, nor should there be. We promise only to do our best and live out our lives. Dear God, that's all we can promise in truth." [4]

"We will not think noble because we are not noble."—Is there a better description of what happened to the American theater after *A Streetcar Named Desire* (1947) and *Death of a Salesman* (1949)? Arthur Miller had given notice of a small talent for highly contrived class-struggle melodrama, without any character of more than two dimensions, in *All My Sons* (1947). Tennessee Williams had shown a considerable stagecraft in his adaptation, with Donald Windham, of a D. H. Lawrence short story, *You Touched Me* (1947), and a gift for atmospheres in his translation of that old standby among dramatic themes, self-delusion, into the figurines of *The Glass Menagerie* (1945). Neither had indicated the commanding stature that both have since assumed in an admittedly weak theater. Miller did it with the expressionistic staging of *Death of a Salesman,* which, down to the flute motif associated with a missing character who represents a missed life, has all the range and depth his protagonist, Willy Loman, does not. So persuasive is the play's solid theatricality that most audiences go away convinced they really understand why Loman commits suicide, why he must end his life and leave his dimensionless family with the substantial proceeds of his insurance policy. But their understanding, like their tears (if the drama has elicited tears), is probably, as one of the London reviewers of the play suggested, for themselves. Miller's kind of misery insists upon company—or total rejection, a response sentimental audiences addicted to the vicarious are not likely to make.

There is a larger reach, if a smaller box office, in *A View from the Bridge* (1955). The full range of the modern melodrama is in it—homosexuality, the system, the inhumanity of democratic government to democratic man. In its one-act version, at least, it has some of the "breathtaking simplicity" that Miller heard in the tale when it was first told to him, and one understands his conviction that "its absolutely unswerving path, its exposed skeleton, so to speak, was its wisdom and even its charm and must not be tampered with." [5] But he did tamper with it. He made it into a two-act play, approaching full-length, and asked his new audiences to examine motivations, purposes, actions, characterizations at greater length, a length ultimately insupportable for this sort of story unless there stands behind it someone of O'Neill's dogged persistence in supplying dialogue by the page, by the scene, by the act, until enough has been revealed to absorb one, if only as a monumental document of human frailty.

The plays that followed the short and long *View*—*After the Fall* (1963) and *Incident at Vichy* (1964)—were embarrassments to some of Miller's admirers, major and minor embarrassments. *The Fall* was Marilyn Monroe's—so quickly dispatched by her own hand, so quickly dispatched by Miller's hand, in uncompassionate combat which many felt was as poor theater as it was poor taste. That was a major discomfort. *Incident,* a medium-length excursion into Nazi villainy in 1942 France, was minor in every way—in the smallness of the insights, in the dimness of the characterizations, in the obviousness of the plot. It held some attraction, however, for those to whom any examination of Nazis, no matter how clumsy, is morbidly fascinating, just as the well-made melodrama of Miller's *The Crucible* (1952) was fascinating to those who leaped at every opportunity to draw parallels between McCarthyism and such earlier tyranny of the same kind as the Salem witch trial dramatized there.

Some of the fascination people find in Tennessee Williams is in the sheer accretion of detail about his humanoids, about as wretched a collection to come along in the theater since *The Duchess of Malfi.* Certainly they are well documented, disease by disease, malformation by malformation, in all their glistening horror, in *The Glass Menagerie, A Streetcar Named Desire, Summer and Smoke* (1948), *The Rose Tattoo* (1950), *Camino Real* (1953), *Cat on a Hot Tin Roof* (1955), *Orpheus Descending* (1957), *Suddenly Last Summer* (1957), *Sweet Bird of Youth* (1959), and *Night of the Iguana* (1962). One can do nothing but admire the fullness of the documentation as Williams moves his animals from the smaller cages of his one-act plays to the larger confinements, hardly restricted at all, of his full-length dramas. It is zoo-keeping of a remarkable kind, in which all the habits of the inmates of the menagerie are duly recorded—bathroom procedures, lovemaking proclivities, and such small skills as a few of them may have for using the upper regions of their bodies. Williams' characters do not have any talent for the vertical, that is for sure, unless in the area of perverted sexuality there may be some small variation possible that way. But one doubts it. They would long ago have explored the possibilities of verticality and found them, like all the other positions in life, wanting. The only thing certain about the lusts of these pitiful practitioners is that they exist to be unsatisfied, for no satisfaction, as the word is normally used in this context, can bring anything but a tortured reminder of the gross incompleteness of their lives, in this as in all other respects.

What, then, apart from the shabby impulse of the voyeur, holds audiences so rapt in the plays of Williams? What is it about old light-bulb-smashing Stanley Kowalski of *Streetcar* that is so attractive? What is there about those two mountains of vulgarity, Big Daddy and Big Mama Pollitt, of *Cat,* that makes them so "exciting" to viewers and readers of the play, especially that master of the Anglo-Saxon expletive, Big Daddy? What is there about the cannibal kids of *Suddenly Last Summer* or the mother who acts as procurer for her own son that exercises such pervasive charm on motion-picture as well as theater audiences? Is it the plea for understanding, implicit in all the plays, explicit in the last lines of Chance Wayne in *Sweet Bird of Youth?* The brief speech is delivered on the apron of the stage, to the audience: "I don't ask for your pity, but just for your understanding —not even that! No—just for your recognition of me in you, and the enemy, time, in us all!" [6]

Surely one of the major appeals of Williams is to the mourner in us all, lamenting the ebbing vitality in us all. Big Daddy is dying of cancer; he will do as a figure of human attrition in the great allegory of death in life that Williams has been constructing, play by play, year by year. Blanche Dubois (in *Streetcar*) is dying of nymphomania, no longer so easy to practice now that she is without fortune or youth; she will do as another of the figures of depletion in the multiplay parable. And so will they all, the real ones and those of fantasy, from *Camino Real*. Whatever their problems, whoever they are, a faded movie queen left over from a previous era (in *Sweet Bird*) or a faded character left over from a previous literature (Marguerite Gautier in *Camino*), they are all seized in Williams' arms and whirled roughly, to use the words of Hart Crane in the epigraph of *Sweet Bird of Youth,* in a

> Relentless caper for all those who step
> The legend of their youth into the noon.[7]

The most open of the allegorical tales is *Camino Real,* because it is the most unashamed about its allegorization. Jammed together in this tour de force are figures of life and literature and half-legend. All draw Williams' warmest sympathy, except the ignoble *conférencier* of the affair, the hotelkeeper Gutman, who is anything but a good man. Out of Proust comes Baron Charlus; out of Dumas, Marguerite Gautier, to mix with Don Quixote, Casanova, Lord Byron, and Kilroy, the noble creation of the American soldiers of the Second World War, here turned into an ex-prizefighter with a weak heart. All fight to stay alive, to ward off being taken away by the Street Cleaners, death's uniformed emissaries in the tropical seaport that does duty for all the continents of life in *Camino Real*. Collapse is the inevitable denouement of the exemplum. After sixteen blocks of hard running—the play is divided into blocks, scenes of life on the *Camino Real,* the Royal Road—all that the leading characters have left in them is Don Quixote's hoarse cry, which serves as the curtain line for the play. But Williams' audience has, for once, a cityful of meditation, a plenitude of matter for lengthy concern, even prayer, like the splendid orison the play's ingenue offers up for con men and hustlers and "all two-time losers who're likely to lose once more" in the last scene. No violence has been done to anyone's sensibilities with that ostentatious effect in which Williams so often delights, unless it has been in the scene of attempted fornication (Block Twelve), which does not come off because of the essential innocence of the people involved, Kilroy and the ingenue, who remains innocent, like the perpetual virgin of Boccaccio's tale, in spite of her mother's constant sale of her favors.

Much of the effect of Williams depends on the director. The director of Williams has usually been Elia Kazan, a heavy-handed man with a scene, who bludgeons an audience rather than tickles it. A man of considerable craft, Kazan has given Williams' plays their identifying spirit—a roisterousness that is more noisome than bawdy. When Jose Quintero revived Camino Real at a Second Avenue loft playhouse, some seven years after Kazan's original Broadway production, a great change in style was made. Colors emerged that one could not see in the first performance; tints and shades, delicacies of characterization, delights of plot. Many will feel that the changes in the third act of Cat on a Hot Tin Roof that Kazan ordained were very much in the interests of the play. (One can easily decide for oneself, since the printed version of the play contains both Williams' original last act and the rewritten one, following the director's suggestions.) But few, surely, will want always to have a playwright of Williams' skill held to one key, to one dynamic, to one note.

Williams himself explains his concern, his ambition, perhaps one might call it his directing purpose, in his plays in a note added to the stage directions just before the pivotal exchange between Big Daddy and his son Brick at the end of Act III of Cat, in which Brick reveals his inclination to homosexuality:

The bird that I hope to catch in the net of this play is not the solution of one man's psychological problem. I'm trying to catch the true quality of experience in a group of people, that cloudy, flickering, evanescent— fiercely charged!—interplay of live human beings in the thundercloud of a common crisis. Some mystery should be left in the revelation of character in a play, just as a great deal of mystery is always left in the revelation of character in life, even in one's own character to himself. This does not absolve the playwright of his duty to observe and probe as clearly and deeply as he *legitimately* can: but it should steer him away from "pat" conclusions, facile definitions which make a play just a play, not a snare for the truth of human experience.[8]

Williams has seemed to be making pat conclusions because of his obsession with the association of death and sexuality. It is an ancient and honorable association, long observed by the poets, but with Williams it becomes a bore, and worse, an obstrusive nuisance. He does not leave enough mystery in his relentless conversion of everything devitalizing and corrupting into phallic terms, terms of tumescence and detumescence. There is something much too facile, too, in his constant arraignment of women as enemies of men, as their undoers, responsible for bringing them down, because they are disposed by nature to be antiphallic. One misses in these simplifications the deep probing of a playwright responsible to his gifts in the way that the quotation from *Cat* suggests Williams feels, at least some of the time. A few visceral observations cannot provide the hoped-for "snare for the truth of human experience"; wisdom lies deeper than that.

Dissatisfaction with the work of Tennessee Williams has been mounting. Some of the same people who had been most vociferous in their praise of Williams in past years have now become fearful of the effects of his plays, quite apart from their accuracy or inaccuracy as a record of human corruption. The fear is rather too late. If the effects, whatever they may be, have been felt, it was a long time ago. By now, no one is likely to be shocked by mutilation, perversion, or any of the other happy hobbies of the Williams humanoids. They are altogether too familiar with the processes, courtesy of the films. Now they may, instead, find both the time and the discrimination to search out the compassion in the Williams plays: for the spinster in *Night of the Iguana,* dying in the service of her ancient grandfather; for Maggie (the Cat on the Tin Roof), made frantic by her husband's taunting, disordered, nonfunctioning sexuality; for the widow in *The Rose Tattoo,* happily only temporarily doomed to sleep with the dead; to the bruised mother in *The Glass Menagerie,* very close in her fatuous life to becoming the Christian martyr she prattles on about. These recipients of Williams' passing sympathies are the dividends of grace in the work of a man of superabundant theatrical energy, who will, one hopes, live a richer life to find a richer life in his plays. For like O'Neill before him, everything turns into viable theater in his hands. O'Neill was only once or twice capable of dialogue that reflected his wide range of people accurately and thus, in a special sense, euphoniously. Williams has the ear O'Neill never had, but not his heart nor his soul, and thus not his range of characters or stories.

If not in Williams, then in whom else can one find the necessary range and depth in the recent American theater. In William Saroyan?

In Thornton Wilder or William Inge? In Edward Albee, in Jack Richardson, or Murray Schisgal? There is not exactly a wide choice.

What a lot of hope was once held for William Saroyan! After the sweet lines of *My Heart's in the Highlands* (1939), surely one of the most eloquent one-act plays in the American theater, he was expected to give poetry back to the stage, without any great fuss over techniques, just in the gladsome cadences of his prose. After the exhilarating vaudeville of *The Time of Your Life* (1939), his contribution was thought to be character—or characters—in both senses of the word, people of dimension, people of fiber, people of enduring friendship, however small their assigned roles. In *Love's Old Sweet Song* (1940), there was still wit of a soft and eccentric kind, such as that involved in reading aloud the names of all the editors of *Time* magazine, in a hillbilly accent, and some fine parody of John Steinbeck's use of the plight of the Okies to make a best seller. But afterward he seemed to lose his touch with the antic and the bedizened, and his enthusiasm for life and those who lived it most aimlessly either became embarrassingly confidential and coy or simply seemed out of place in the grown-up world of the war and afterward. In *The Cave Dwellers* (1957), however, something of the original quality came back. On the musty stage of a deserted theater on the Lower East Side of New York, a fine collection of dissolutes gathers, a kind of positive inversion of the miserable ones of Gorky's *The Lower Depths*. There the old man known as the King offers Saroyan's helpful hint for the helpless. It is *Candide* in a bright light: the message still is to cultivate one's own garden, but now to look at the flowers above as well as the weeds below:

Well, if anyone here should be angry, it should be *me*. Angry only that we know nothing, and that we can't learn. But I am not even angry about that . . . and there is no need for you to be, either. This is how it is. If we were in a palace, instead of in this cave, this would be how it is. If we had everything, and *more* than everything, this would be how it is. If we loved God and God loved us, this would be how it is. And I am not angry. I cannot be angry. This is the world, this is us, this is all there is, and we do not understand.[9]

Thus fortified, the cave dwellers can face the destruction of their cave, that is the theater, on "the last day of the World," for World turns out to be the name of the theater. The allegorical implications are obvious enough, in a world on the brink of the Bomb, but they are not forced, and not without some small comfort. Whatever there may be for Saroyan, there is still hope, if not for the World, at least in the world.

Saroyan is one of a small company of cheerful fellows in the American theater, just this side—the side of credibility—of reckless optimism. For a while the ranking member was Paul Osborn, with his handsome adaptation of Lawrence Watkins' novel *On Borrowed Time* (1938), in which self-sacrifice proves strong enough to vanquish death, delightfully personified as Mr. Brink, and with *Morning's at Seven* (1939), the least self-conscious and folksy of folk comedies, and one of the most attractive pictures of small-town life in the modern theater. Lynn Riggs belongs because of *Green Grow the Lilacs* (1931), more famous now as the source of *Oklahoma!* but a better play when unadorned by Broadway folk music, and *The Russet Mantle* (1936), an uncommonly warm and attractive endorsement of the inspirations and aspirations and essential decency of young people. There also should be added to the list, at least for individual plays, James Thurber and Elliott Nugent for the happy indignation at bigotry and bromides of *The Male Animal* (1940), Thomas Heggen and Joshua Logan for the good cheer, only occasionally edged with indignation, of *Mister Roberts* (1948), and Frances Goodrich and Albert Hackett for their adaptation of *The Diary of Anne Frank* (1955), not only touching and encouraging to a sad postwar world, but remarkably entertaining as well.

Thornton Wilder remains one of the most entertaining dramatists of the American theater, if an infrequent contributor to it. His plays, one-act or full-length, have the additional felicity of being eminently playable, by amateurs, semipros, or the theatrical mighty who have toured the world doing their best for American culture with his *The Skin of Our Teeth* (1942) as their touring vehicle. It tours well: it is a cyclical drama. But all of Wilder—little things like *The Long Christmas Dinner* (1931) or slightly bigger ones, like *The Matchmaker* (1955), or the biggest, *Our Town* (1938) and *Skin*—tours well or rests well. There is about all his work a calm and calming gentility, not unlike the medieval virtue of *gentilezza*. Death is welcomed, graciously and gracefully, on *Our Town*'s bare stage, with a stage manager, out of the Chinese theater or Pirandello or both, acting as master of eternal ceremonies. Life is ushered in, with some

noise and much gusto, but not raucously, in *The Skin of Our Teeth,*
with the human race reduced to a family of Antrobuses—an obvious
play on the word *anthropos,* Greek for man—and mankind's not
very deep-seated sexual urges converted into a maid of all work, Lily
(for Lilith; really our old friend the Earth Mother). Vaudeville sets
the tone for the tales from Genesis, the *Golden Bough,* and *Finnegans
Wake,* and as with all the best of that fine species, the jokes stand up
in repeat performances. Not quite as much can be said for the funny
business of *The Matchmaker,* which was once *The Merchant of
Yonkers* (1938), and before that a farce by the nineteenth-century
Austrian Nestroy. The essential matchmaking situation is funny; the
central role is funny; but where *Our Town* moves softly and easily
into its final somnolent moments and *The Skin of Our Teeth* bursts
happily into the creative future, *The Matchmaker* simply shuts up
shop. Which may be all to the good: the day's business is completed.[10]

William Inge seems to have moved the angry household gods of
Tennessee Williams to the Midwest and there to have found the
beast at bay in the damnedest people, that is to say, the least damna-
ble, the most ordinary. What keeps them from being as well the least
interesting is Inge's good ear and well-worked scissors. Nobody talks
too long. There is leg motion to go with jaw motion in the boardinghouse of *Come Back, Little Sheba* (1950), in the summer's-day
revels of *Picnic* (1953), in the winter's-night revelations of *Bus Stop*
(1955), in the large battles of the small people of *The Dark at the
Top of the Stairs* (1957). Just enough of everything to make a lusty
naturalism shake, rattle, and roar through three acts—with lust acting
as the energizing fuel. Sex is always rearing its head in Inge's plays,
its happy hearty head. It always comes onstage to a blare of
trumpets—not necessarily audible. For Inge hangs a great deal upon
the polarity of repression and expression: his is a simple sexual determinism. It is all oh, so familiar, but not often so prettily polished. It
is, if the footlight Freudians can bear to hear it, the same thing that
kept the high-comedy writers—Barry and Behrman and all the rest,
English and French and American—going during the twenties and
thirties, just moved down a class or two. It is middle class now,
because the sixties is the time of the middle—middle-middles and
lower-middles—the time they have had coming to them after so long
spent with the toffs and the prols. The middles aren't quite as fast as

the uppers, and they haven't the gusto of the best of the depressed and the submerged, but they aren't as stuffy as the two extremes either, and that's a mercy.

There are some rather self-consciously bitter ironies at the expense of America's much put-upon middle class in Arthur Kopit's *Oh Dad, Poor Dad, Mamma's Hung You in the Closet and I'm Feelin' So Sad* (1960) and some much less self-conscious and much more tender mockery of middle-class wooing, winning, and losing in Murray Schisgal's *Luv* (1964). Both are quick-witted playwrights. Neither calls for any great cerebration or meditation on the part of his audience. Both slip and slide in and out of vaudeville techniques and vignetting of a more naturalistic kind. Schisgal in particular seems to have found a shrewd adaptation for himself of theater-of-the-absurd techniques, comic, inventive, and no great strain on the audience.

Edward Albee is also a chronicler and a taunter of middle-class foolishness and misery, but no straightforward naturalist, he. Neither is he simply another member in good standing of the theater of the absurd, as for a moment he seemed to be in his first appearance as a playwright, *The Zoo Story* (1958), which shared a bill with Samuel Beckett's *Krapp's Last Tape.* In *The Zoo Story* he twitted and up-braided and finally blew up conformist conventions, with a macabre humor, but without taking his unhappiness too seriously, in spite of the violence of the play's ending. It was a kind of one-act *Hairy Ape* for man-sized puppets, in which a vegetable existence—the con-formist's—finally turned into an animal's, when his taunting com-panion on a park bench forced him into the murder of his life. Whose life? The conformist kills the taunter, but since the taunter leads him to it, it could equally well be said that the taunter takes his own life and by turning the conformist into a killer takes his as well. The story is a zoo story; it is a story of animals. So is *The Death of Bessie Smith* (1959), which is a not altogether adroit melodrama of the world of the South in which Bessie Smith's death was made inevita-ble. The bitchy Nurse of the play is a kind of earlier incarnation of the central role in Albee's first major work, *Who's Afraid of Virginia Woolf?* (1962). For her and the Negro Orderly who is her foil and every white person's as he tries to make his peace with the white world, the play is worth examining. For its record of its ostensible subject, it has the requisite kindness and ironic grief, even if it lacks the dramatic directness of *Zoo Story* and the conciseness of *The*

Sandbox (1959), a very small exercise in the spinning down of a middle-class Grandma's life that sounds like an addendum to Ionesco's *The Chairs.*

In *The American Dream* (1960), Albee shoots comic bullets at middle-class aims and aspirations, but he never quite hits. Others have been there before, many others, and his allegorical variations on the ancient theme are not arresting enough. We know the playwright is revolted by the coyness and the pretense, the cute language, the empty language, the vapid lives caught up in the American Dream, of a family which is not really human at all. But being revolted is not enough. Still, in Albee at this point in his career, as in the plays of Jack Gelber and Jack Richardson, the repudiation of the conventional mechanics of Broadway writing and Broadway production is larger than a mere revolt or the discovery of another way of expressing dissatisfaction with the Establishment. Far more than angry young men, they are observers of anger looking for the best theatrical ways of recording the wraths involved—the wrath of the undergraduate, the wrath of the hipster, the wrath of the artist. In *The Connection* (1960)—but not in *The Apple* (1961)—Gelber has wrapped up his strident voice convincingly in marihuana and heroin. He fiddles too much with devices, but he listens well, or at least once seems to have heard and to have found ways to make others hear. Richardson's hearing goes fairly far inside people in *Gallows Humor* (1961). In that fast-moving play, an exchange of identities that at first seems only a theatrical device hardens, upon reflection, into a shrewd comment on the imprisonment of personalities that regularity of all kinds, especially the sexual, may impose upon persons. Albee worked his way through all the devices and back into something like a conventional structure to produce the consuming anger of *Virginia Woolf.* That terrible argument *à quatre* is the chamber music of the dying family whose airs Albee had been scoring play by play until then. Having learned all the themes and fumbled with them through a variety of forms, he was able to write a work of tightly chambered horror. Though it may owe a great deal to Strindberg's *Dance of Death,* it is a play that also has its own eviscerating angers.

What is the anger of the middle-aged furies of a New England college in this play, husband and wife, academic and academic's daughter? What is the anger of the younger couple, the biologist and his wife, the furies-in-waiting? They are all impotent and sterile, by nature and by plan, nature leading to plan, plan leading to nature, until the only children they can have are of the imagination and the only pleasure they can have is by a kind of demonic dream brought to life on the insults and taunts and threats they distill out of their sad empty unlikable almost unlivable lives. The play's success is in its restraints. It does not achieve the terror of Strindberg's duel of fallen angels, but the battle is, happily, not so prolonged. For all the ugliness the four characters hurl at each other, they are large enough to hold us through three acts of such lobs and blasts and off-scourings. Once or twice Albee cannot quite contain himself; there are a couple of theatrical jokes, references to O'Neill and to Tennessee Williams, as if to set Albee off somewhere at a tangent to those men. But the tone is rarely off. The exchanges are as precise as in a tennis match in hell. Hell? Listen to Martha, the play's central character, who once, for a moment, in the third act of the play's three, explains herself, and thus explains hell, as she explains—to the young biology instructor who has proved impotent in his big scene, offstage, with her in the kitchen,—who it is who has made her happy. It is, she makes clear, nobody but that special object of all her execration, her husband George, who is also her only true lover:

> . . . whom I will not forgive for having come to rest; for having seen me and having said: yes, this will do; who has made the hideous, the hurting, the insulting mistake of loving me and must be punished for it. George and Martha: sad, sad, sad.
> . . . who tolerates, which is intolerable; who is kind, which is cruel; who understands, which is beyond comprehension. . . .[11]

This is an anger worth hearing, as the anger of *Long Day's Journey into Night* was worth hearing. Whatever Albee's precise level of accomplishment, it is the ancient anger, the murderous wrath of Hamlet, the terrible befuddlement of Lear, the demanding arrogance of Oedipus and Job. That is the anger of artists, not of undergraduates or of hipsters, asking questions that are not filed on examination papers, suggesting answers that drugs cannot cope with. For these questions and answers, Hamlet left his university, Lear gave up his kingdom, Oedipus struck out his eyes, and Job shook his fist at God. In the American theater until now, only O'Neill has dared to take on such themes—if I may be allowed to skip Archibald MacLeish's little tent-show Job, *J.B.* (1958). And if O'Neill only once reached exactly where he aimed, and Albee has come close at least this once, well, once is enough in such company. Once or twice.[12] They may be enough in the American theater to remind others of what the theater is capable of doing.

THE MOVIES

HOLLYWOOD wrapped itself around the work of F. Scott Fitzgerald like a chrysalis. It shaped some of his sentences for him and more of his characters. It constructed many scenes for him. It gave direction to his last years, even when they seemed to be most disorganized; it laced the seventeen Pat Hobby stories, written to a hack-writer's deadline, into something like a connected work, even when they seemed to be most aimless. It finally drove him to pull his thoughts together, jotted down in notebooks or gathered in dreams, to produce his most thoughtful novel, fragmentary and incomplete as it is, *The Last Tycoon.*

The view from West Egg to East Egg in the opening pages of *The Great Gatsby* is a camera-eye view, a panoramic shot from one side of the bay to the other:

My house was at the very tip of the egg, only fifty yards from the Sound, and squeezed between two huge places that rented for twelve or fifteen thousand a season. The one on my right was a colossal affair by any standard—it was a factual imitation of some Hotel de Ville in Normandy, with a tower on one side, spanking new under a thin beard of raw ivy, and a marble swimming pool, and more than forty acres of lawn and garden. It was Gatsby's mansion. Or, rather, as I didn't know Mr. Gatsby, it was a mansion, inhabited by a gentleman of that name. My own house was an eyesore, but it was a small eyesore, and it had been overlooked, so I had a view of the water, a partial view of my neighbor's lawn, and the consoling proximity of millionaires—all for eighty dollars a month.

Across the courtesy bay the white palaces of fashionable East Egg glittered along the water. . . .[1]

The story gets under way when we dissolve from the pan shot to a close-up of the narrator in his car, on the way from West to East Egg: ". . . the history of the summer really begins on the evening I drove over there to have dinner with the Tom Buchanans."

The writing in *The Great Gatsby* is movie writing, the focus that of a cameraman-director. Almost every scene is doubly directed, to the people in it and to the objects that surround or accompany them, objects only dimly symbolic, but easily photographed and recorded for sound. When Nick Carraway arrives at the Buchanans', he is shown over the place by Tom—and a camera:

> Turning me around by one arm, he moved a broad flat hand along the front vista, including in its sweep a sunken Italian garden, a half acre of deep, pungent roses, and a snub-nosed motor-boat that bumped the tide offshore.

The camera moves indoors a little creakily:

> We walked through a high hallway into a bright rosy-colored space, fragilely bound into the house by French windows at either end. The windows were ajar and gleaming white against the fresh grass outside that seemed to grow a little way into the house. A breeze blew through the room, blew curtains in at one end and out the other like pale flags, twisting them up toward the frosted wedding-cake of the ceiling, and then rippled over the wine-colored rug, making a shadow on it as wind does on the sea.

The set is familiar; the dressing is obvious. We can hear the grips move around, and the camera dolly is audible in the hall. But there are few creaks out of doors. Fitzgerald is a master of the long shot. The billboard across "the valley of ashes" that rises halfway between West Egg and New York is justly famous:

> . . . above the gray land and the spasms of bleak dust which drift endlessly over it, you perceive, after a moment, the eyes of Doctor T. J. Eckleburg. The eyes of Doctor T. J. Eckleburg are blue and gigantic— their retinas are one yard high. They look out of no face, but, instead, from a pair of enormous yellow spectacles which pass over a non-existent nose. Evidently some wild wag of an oculist set them there to fatten his practice in the borough of Queens, and then sank down himself into eternal blindness, or forgot them and moved away. But his eyes, dimmed a little by many paintless days under sun and rain, brood on over the solemn dumping ground.

Fitzgerald recognizes the value of the shot and returns to it often, usually in connection with Tom, whose mistress lives "along the road under Doctor Eckleburg's persistent stare." The stare follows us through the book to its dismal ending and makes perhaps too obvious the sense of guilt that hovers over all of Fitzgerald's characters:

That locality was always vaguely disquieting, even in the broad glare of afternoon, and now I turned my head as though I had been warned of something behind. Over the ashheaps the giant eyes of Doctor T. J. Eckleburg kept their vigil. . . .

The last shot is a lap dissolve. As Carraway comes to take his leave of the Eggs, the sounds are muffled, the millionaires have moved on: "Most of the big shore places were closed now and there were hardly any lights except the shadowy, moving glow of a ferry-boat across the Sound." The director cautions the cameraman: there will be a blending of views:

And as I sat there brooding on the old, unknown world, I thought of Gatsby's wonder when he first picked out the green light at the end of Daisy's dock. He had come a long way to this blue lawn, and his dream must have seemed so close that he could hardly fail to grasp it. He did not know that it was already behind him, somewhere back in that vast obscurity beyond the city, where the dark fields of the republic rolled on under the night.

Fitzgerald cannot stop there, as a modern motion-picture director would. He must translate the pathos into words and write a title for the last scene: "So we beat on, boats against the current, borne back ceaselessly into the past." D. W. Griffith would not have objected to the pithy sentimentality of that.

In a sometimes embarrassed, sometimes open and unashamed way, Fitzgerald believed in Hollywood, took it seriously, trusted it. He used its people and its pleasures and its miseries as subjects and objects for his moralities. He relied heavily on its devices. He defended it against "the money men . . . the rulers," who unless they had a guest with them sat and "ate in broken silence" in their private dining rooms, "sometimes asking questions about each other's wives and children, sometimes discharging a single absorption from the forefront of their consciousness." He defended Hollywood in his incomplete last book, *The Last Tycoon,* through the figure of Monroe Stahr, who "had first sat with most of these men when he was a boy wonder of twenty-two." Stahr, modeled clearly on the delicate bones

of Irving Thalberg, believes that producers really do have the responsibility to the public that their public rhetoric so solemnly proclaims.
It would even be "a good thing for the production schedule to slip in
a picture that would lose money."

Fitzgerald saw Hollywood with difficulty, saw it darkly and only
in fits of illumination. That, he said in the opening paragraphs of the
Stahr story, was the nature of its mystery. The voice is that of Cecilia
Brady, his narrator:

You can take Hollwood for granted like I did, or you can dismiss it
with the contempt we reserve for what we don't understand. It can be
understood too, but only dimly and in flashes. Not half a dozen men
have ever been able to keep the whole equation of pictures in their heads.
And perhaps the closest a woman can come to the set-up is to try and
understand one of those men.[2]

Stahr is the most important of "those men," but all have high
standing in Fitzgerald's narrative, for they are the producers of the
baroque fantasies that somehow compel Stahr's and Fitzgerald's admiration. For them, Stahr acts as gadfly and social anthropologist,
depending upon the distance from them he is able to maintain. In
either case he stings. When he sits down in the commissary with one
wing of the moneymen, he is quick to analyze, quick to bite:

Stahr went to the table where he was expected and sat down with
the Cafe Society group—from Wall Street, Grand Street, Loudon County,
Virginia, and Odessa, Russia. They were all talking with enthusiasm about
a horse that had run very fast, and Mr. Marcus was the most enthusiastic
of all. Stahr guessed that the Jews had taken over the worship of horses
as a symbol—for years it had been the Cossacks mounted and the Jews
on foot. Now the Jews had horses, and it gave them a sense of extraordinary well-being and power.

He is also respectful, reverent almost, about film and about the film-
making process. "Making" is the word: Stahr is a maker. Into a few
scenes Fitzgerald was able to cram the poetry he saw in Stahr. In two
of them, the producer explains movie-making to a novelist who is
horrified to find himself writing for the loathsome medium. Stahr
teaches him a few simple lessons. There must be no excess motion or
verbiage: ". . . nobody has moved violently or talked cheap dialogue

or had any facial expression at all. There was only one bad line, and a writer like you could improve it." Motion pictures catch the viewer's interest by moving, and as they move by distracting, distracting from one's own pains or from one's awareness of the pains of others. The distraction, Stahr instructs, need not be a murder; it could be a spider crawling on a windowpane.

The novelist objects to mass production. But that, Stahr explains, is the dispensable thing:

"There's always some lousy condition. We're making a life of Rubens— suppose I asked you to do portraits of rich dopes like Bill Brady and me and Gary Cooper and Marcus when you wanted to paint Jesus Christ! Wouldn't you feel you had a condition? Our condition is that we have to take people's own favorite folklore and dress it up and give it back to them. Anything beyond that is sugar. So won't you give us some sugar Mr. Boxley?"

How far does the sugar go? About as far as a sweet can go, to the point where it becomes nearly unendurable. All of Stahr's intercessions in the fantasy factory are directed to keep the cloying from clawing. When the sugar seems about to eat up the exposed audience, he intervenes on the side of the laws of nature and good taste: "There's no use printing stuff like that. She doesn't believe what she's saying—neither does Cary. 'I love you' in a close up—they'll cluck you out of the house! And the girl's overdressed."

The well-instructed novelist finally sees Stahr "like Lincoln": he is "a leader carrying on a long war on many fronts; almost singlehanded he had moved pictures sharply forward through a decade, to a point where the content of the 'A productions' was wider and richer than that of the stage. Stahr was an artist only, as Mr. Lincoln was a general, perforce and as a layman." He has, even in Fitzgerald's incomplete and uncorrected manuscript, reached a high promontory over the Pacific where the narrator sees him, finally, in a kind of divine role: "You could say that this was where an accidental wind blew him, but I don't think so. I would rather think that in a 'long shot' he saw a new way of measuring our jerky hopes and graceful rogueries and awkward sorrows, and that he came here from choice to be with us to the end."

Of how many film men would one dare use such fanciful language? The accredited heroes in this country are D. W. Griffith, Mack

Sennett, Erich von Stroheim, Robert Flaherty, and a small group of directors whose careers extended well into the era of the sound track, Josef von Sternberg, Ernst Lubitsch, King Vidor, Lewis Milestone, John Ford. Of the actors—perhaps "personalities" would be a better word—a handful of comedians and one lady hold such cachet as the medium affords those on the exposed side of the Hollywood camera: Charlie Chaplin, Buster Keaton, W. C. Fields, the Marx Brothers, and Greta Garbo. Directors and actors, all of these; not one was or is a producer of the Stahr-Thalberg kind, though certainly Griffith and Sennett had much to do with budgets and bankers and all have known what it was to worry about why they were staying away in Minneapolis or booing in Brooklyn. It is not likely that in any serious analysis of the art of the film, the producer will receive more than glancing attention, and then usually as an obstacle in the way of the artist-director or artist-actor or artist-cameraman or cutter. In the patterns of culture which the film sociologist draws, the producer's image is a curious mixture of despot and imbecile, whose hands can only maul the American dream like a monster out of a class-B movie, a Blob, a Creature from Another World, or one of the numerous progeny of Frankenstein.

What, then, are we to think? That such art as has made its way into the American film is the result of open combat in which the artist has triumphed over the producer or of the sly manipulation of the latter by the former? Anyone who has ever spent more time on a Hollywood lot than an official studio tour knows that the manipulation of Louis B. Mayer, Samuel Goldwyn, Harry Warner, or Darryl F. Zanuck was never a likely achievement, no matter how cunning the director or how crafty the actor. Open combat, one knows, has been waged against producers and won—but the victory thus arrived at has rarely been other than financial, increasing the income or the comfort or the prestige of the artist but hardly the artistry of the product. Von Stroheim and Flaherty lost their battles with Hollywood producers and the film art lost with them. Chaplin won his early struggle for independence by the simple maneuver of asserting it, becoming producer-director-actor without any administrative machinery or administrators to oppose him—and the art of the film won with him. But the others whose achievements are unmistakable had to rely on chance, the occult art which remains the central study of all good and true Hollywooders, even in the television era.

In the game of film chance, even the machinery of projection came slowly and tantalizingly out of hiding, as if loath to admit its existence or even the possibility of it. The illusion of a moving picture was conceived many times in many countries by many men before Thomas Edison and William Dickson conveyed a sequence of pictures on sprockets over a cylinder, and the brothers Lumière made the illusion stick with their projector.

It was not much of an illusion in the early days; it was the science of motion presented with very little art. But the audience's vision persisted. A succession of still photographs projected at a sufficient speed convinced the viewer that the movement was continuous. But who moved and what were the movements? The girls who worked for the French film-makers in *Lunch Hour at the Lumière Factory;* a railroad train arriving at a station; a baby girl eating cereal while one of the Lumières plays piquet with a friend and drinks beer; French bourgeois and petit bourgeois of 1895. A couple of prizefighters; a strong man at a circus; a couple of dancers; a half-dozen frozen-faced actors in the *Cripple Creek Bar-room;* a hedge-moustached man and a bulbous woman in the *May Irwin–John C. Rice Kiss;* the ax chopping off the head in *The Execution of Mary Queen of Scots* and the head tumbling in the dust; American actors and actresses and sideshow performers in 1893 and 1896 and 1898.

The end in view in American film-making in the first years was the peep show or the vaudeville bill, such as the program at Koster & Bial's Music Hall on April 23, 1896, in which Edison's reels made their first public appearance or at Hammerstein's Olympia Music Hall where the American Biograph films were first shown. Stills clipped from these films have a certain quaintness, a little of the charm of a daguerreotype or of an early Impressionistic painting. In motion, however, the films lend themselves much too easily to the sort of heavy-handed humor with which they are treated when every five or ten years they are revived by a more sophisticated industry for a two-reel glance backward at our artless grandparents or turn up on television programs to be smirked at and lampooned. The wit and fantasy of Georges Méliès is not to be found in these frames. Nobody in the American films of the nineties planted an umbrella on the moon and turned it into a mushroom; nobody here created sets with such Surrealist precision, as in the massive collection of machinery gathered on the drop for *Voyage à Travers l'Impossible,* or assembled such a permanent vaudeville as the toys painted or pinned to the symmetrical set in Méliès's studio; nobody here had the taste or the talent to combine the figures from a waxworks with the landscape of a steel engraving.

Americans did understand the literal power of the camera. They filmed American troops in Cuba in 1898 and English soldiers in South Africa during the Boer War. They shot brief and busy little travelogues as far away as Alaska. And one American, Edwin S. Porter, followed his actors out of doors in *The Great Train Robbery* in 1903 and pulled away all at once from the squareness and hollowness of the studio and the stiff pretentiousness of the studio actor. These are cowboys; this is a robbery. The atmosphere is at least bloody by suggestion as the engineer is hustled out of his cab. The power of the camera is at least suggested in the parallel cutting, the quick contrasts of telegrapher and mail car and dance hall, and the concluding close-up of the pistol being fired right at the audience. It is not difficult to understand the compulsion exerted by such a film on nickelodeon crowds or the erection on its foundation of an industry.

The furriers, the cloak-and-suiters, and the traveling salesmen who created the industry out of shops and showrooms and run-down burlesque houses were not prepared to produce art of any kind. Their passion was for the box office and the share of common stock. But both needed mass support and masses of Americans would not keep coming to brief moments of religious instruction or of death and destruction or of patriotic fervor or even of humor of the French kind as domesticated by Porter in the 1906 *Dream of a Rarebit Fiend*. For an expanding audience, an expanding film was needed. In 1908, the French provided the Film d'Art. A producing company of that name offered the *Assassination of the Duc de Guise,* a historical reconstruction shaky in every detail, including the sets and the actors. But the impression made by a long narrative and what seemed to be an authentic background was of embossed enchantment. Audiences responded and so did writers, actors, composers—everybody to whom the pomp and power of the medium recommended themselves. The well-made play of the mid-nineteenth century came back in all its tufted emptiness. The spacious gestures of a costume drama that concealed little flesh and no blood were broadcast around the world. In France, Edmond Rostand and Camille Saint-Saëns worked for the industry; in Italy, Gabriele D'Annunzio contributed a story for which

Carthage itself had to be rebuilt. Réjane brought the tearjerker in tights to the screen in *Madame Sans-Gene* and Sarah Bernhardt carried the burdens of *Queen Elizabeth* (seen from across the Channel) and *Tosca* onto celluloid. If what moves can be called stillborn, then as much can be said of the history (Pompeii's last days, Nero's Rome, Robespierre's Paris) and the classics (*The Divine Comedy, Othello, Hamlet*) translated into films in the years just before the First World War.

To match the furious scenery chewing of Europe, American movie men offered "Broncho Billy" Anderson and Tom Mix, Mary Pickford and the serial film. The Western adventures of the first pair and the saccharinity and suspense of the second two were of no great significance in themselves. But as antecedents of masters and mastery to come, they deserve honorable mention. Broncho Billy took pains to provide authentic settings in Colorado for his films; Tom Mix rode a horse with style and brought Good to a clear-cut climactic victory over Evil without descending from his horse or picking up a guitar; Little Mary communicated a state of being best identified as innocence, hopelessly sweet by later standards, but ingratiating to 1910 audiences and allied to a recognizable personality; the serials made the chase and the cliff-hanger into techniques of some complexity if little subtlety. There were almost enough ingredients now to make a full-length film of quality in the United States. Whatever was missing David Wark Griffith supplied.

Griffith and his cameraman, Billy Bitzer, provided the film with its enduring rhetoric, a rhetoric of motion and emotion. To do so, they made the camera move, to follow actors at all the distances, plausible and implausible, from which people take up their conflicts and concurrences, their single or double or multiple actions, their moments of dramatic participation or static withdrawal. The close-up gave depth rather than point to Griffith films, bringing the audience closer and closer to the person within the actor rather than the personality outside, brushing aside all the apparatus of war to reveal a mother's love for her son as a woman's arm reaches out from a doorway to catch a returning Confederate soldier and bring him inside, or to show a soldier's love in his long, lingering look at Lillian Gish visiting a hospital ward.

There is no single viewpoint in Griffith films. The actor and the event meet all across the lot. Now one, now the other is highlighted. The treasured intimacy that bares an emotion dominates even the Civil War in *The Birth of a Nation* (1915), and overshadows the combined grandeur and misery of ancient Babylon, Calvary, sixteenth-century France, and twentieth-century America in *Intolerance* (1916). The absence of any one center of vision, even when the theme is as precisely denominated and exploited as it is in *Intolerance,* gives Griffith at least the surface of objectivity. It is an objectivity haunted by the human person constantly destroying the gross fabric of human existence, tearing down religions, cities, and civilizations in his search for the precise experience, usually small and poorly managed, in which he can either declare himself or be found out. This is, if anything is, the unifying power of Griffith's films, the purpose for which the camera was made mobile, the several focal distances observed, and the cutting, the fade-ins and fade-outs, and dissolves practiced: that somehow, somewhere the person might be revealed.

The revelation is significant enough to make of no great importance the blunders of taste and solecisms of interpretation which permitted Griffith to make dark faces darker with shoe polish and burnt cork in *The Birth of a Nation* or to choose to film Thomas Dixon's epic of the Ku Klux Klan, *The Clansman,* in the first place. The revelation is enough even when, at the key moment, it is reduced to a smirk or a strut or a pair of bulging eyes. The actors Griffith chose—Henry B. Walthall, Wallace Reid, Robert Harron, Lillian Gish, Mae Marsh, Constance Talmadge—were not always able to compete with the long shots of soldiers stretching back into a perspective that would have made a Renaissance painter gasp with astonishment or with any of the shots of a Babylonian palace that seemed to realize Scriptural proportions. But they were not overwhelmed by their surroundings or turned into the mere machinery of spectacle. Lillian Gish, always the most flexible of Griffith's company, survived even the shattering of the ice in *Way Down East* (1920) and a hundred and forty rehearsals in a Vermont river. She triumphed over the novelty-store Chinoiserie of *Broken Blossoms* (1919) in which Richard Barthelmess was so effective that even a close-up of his glue pot Oriental eyes did not distract his audiences. Mae Marsh in the courtroom scene in *Intolerance* showed a concern over her husband's fate on her face and in her tightly clenched hands that continues to have the power to touch the viewer in still photographs; the close-up was never used more movingly.

Revelation in Griffith may have been—as it has been suggested —more the result of accident than of planning. But he edited his films with a kind of intuition that seems only to have disappeared when the vehicles became not his but those of the producers to whom he owed vassalage in the last dozen years of his career. He never lost entirely, however, his genius for crosscutting, for turning over all or most or just a handful of the frames in rapid succession, in order to bewilder or to cozen or to elate his audience or bring it to tears. His figures on the screen commanded audiences. By the shock tactics of his editing—however little he may himself have understood what he was doing or why—he changed heartbeats and induced or stopped the secretion of glands. By the very disorder of his films, by their lack of any one point of view or any single conviction, he persuades his audiences of their essential accuracy and honesty—persuades them as he probably persuaded himself, by intuition and projection, by the assumption of identities quickly undertaken and almost as quickly thrown aside. Others, unfortunately, thought even less than Griffith about what they were doing, and, lacking most of his talent, reduced his rhetoric to one simple metaphor, that of the vicarious experience. This they learned from him, but by controlling and directing it with more and more skill and less and less understanding, they turned a valuable device into a frightening weapon. The assaults on the emotions of audiences by American directors and producers after Griffith are extraordinarily like the political use made of the same techniques by Soviet film-makers. The Russians were more conscious of their indebtedness to Griffith and more aware of the value of the film as an arm of government than their Hollywood counterparts, but no more skillful in pursuing and capturing an audience's emotions.

Griffith's most gifted contemporary among directors was Thomas H. Ince, who is best remembered by American audiences for the film he made with William S. Hart and by European critics and film historians for a rawness and a hard simplicity that some of them have thought worthy of comparison with Rodin and Aeschylus and the makers of Eastern myth. One thing Ince achieved in a dozen years of strenuous production was a directness and an honesty that are still unmistakable in the few films of his that can still be seen. Both the cowboys and the Indians in the Hart films are convincing; they are as dirty, as badly dressed, as unshaven and as uncombed as the real figures of the West of a century ago. The saloons they inhabit could never double as Broadway nightclubs. Everything about these films has a realistic quality, everything that is, except Hart's self-sacrificing exits. One may accept, then, such a description of these films as that of the French film historians, Maurice Bardèche and Robert Brasillach: "Thomas Ince and William S. Hart have the honor of having given the cinema its first lyrics of the open air, those crude Iliads so well suited to the taste of young people with their intense love of life." But nothing seems quite to justify Jean Cocteau, who says of a fight in *Carmen of the Klondike* that it evokes the struggle of Jacob and the angel and that "M. Ince may be proud of himself, for a spectacle such as this seems in recollection to equal the world's greatest literature." One can only hope that enough prints of the work of Ince will turn up in future to permit a thorough review of the French claims for them. Until then, he may be better known as the first of the masters of conveyer-belt production and of autocratic authority at the head of the studio, though he may pique curiosity more because of his death in obscure circumstances in 1924, at the age of forty-four, than because to Frenchmen viewing his films in the years just after World War I he seemed to have an Attic power.

Fortunately, there is no dearth of films with which to judge the comedy of the period. And where the original films are missing, there are descriptions by the hundred and photographs by the thousand. Something like an accurate impression of the art of custard-pie throwing and receiving can still be achieved. Some idea of the underlying principles which governed the construction of the Mack Sennett two-reel comedy and the Charlie Chaplin is still to be had. The impression is of high skill. The idea is of low comedy.

Mack Sennett, like Griffith, started at Biograph. Like so many others, he learned a great deal from Griffith, worked under him as an actor, and worked alongside him (and later Ince as well) as a director. The awe he felt for Griffith helps thread together the chapters on his early film-making in his autobiography, *King of Comedy*.[3] The respect he felt for the camera—learned from Griffith—helped to make brilliant comedy even out of a Shriners' parade, hastily photographed just a half hour after Sennett, Ford Sterling, Fred Mace, and Mabel Normand had landed in Los Angeles in January 1912 to establish Keystone pictures. The original Keystone Cops, Sennett says, were the members of the Los Angeles Police Department who, in the magnificent manner of all of the director's representatives of law and disorder, chased Sterling and Miss Normand, who were happily improvising an elaborate drama of outraged womanhood and its outrager on the sidelines of the parade.

Sennett is willing to admit that he and his odd-sized, odd-shaped, oddly behaving human beings and their animal associates created "a new kind of art." But, he insists, it was without any pretentiousness or even premeditation. Improvisation was the special art of the Sennett clowns. It was not a profound art as they practiced it. It entailed sudden and totally unexpected charges of electricity and inundations of water that burst over the newly electrified actor. It involved lots of slapping with a stick, usually a bed slat. It sent round little men with tiny corkscrews of hair on the top of their heads up the sides of buildings and large square ones with great wads of hair on the sides of their faces sprawling in the dust. It was an art of the custard pie, a difficult art in itself, requiring not only a good throwing arm but a face wholly open in its innocence and—at least as far as the world was concerned—able to take the dripping pastry on the chin or anywhere else it happened to fall. Del Lord, one of Sennett's best directors, was also his best pie-thrower. Roscoe "Fatty" Arbuckle was a master: he could throw with either hand and sometimes with both left and right at the same time, though he did not always hit his targets as planned. Almost everybody was "splurched"—to use Sennett's word for the art—at one time or another, but few received the pies as well as George "Fat" Lobeck or Ben Turpin, and no one ever responded with such an eloquent slow burn as Edgar Kennedy.

There is no need to analyze Sennett in the terms he finds so uncongenial. His art did not come from the classic ballet or from *commedia dell'arte*. Its source was as ancient as the day after the Fall: the desire to puncture pomp and belabor circumstance. The stuffier the figure, the more comic the pratfall—that was the Sennett creed. And his figures—cops and robbers both, bankers and plumbers and railroad engineers, beautifully made maidens and terribly made matrons—were stuffy enough and their falls right on the prat as often as not. The humor was the same universal kind that lights up the *Canterbury Tales,* the *Decameron,* and *Gargantua and Pantagruel:* Man provides not only a tragic but a comic spectacle as he tries to wrest some dignity from his fallen state. The harder he tries, the funnier he becomes and the more satisfying. And what he satisfies is something more profound and significant than the risibilities of his watchers. The democracy of the banana peel is invoked every time a banker joins a plumber and a dowager slips down beside a bathing beauty, whether the clothing is medieval or modern, the scene a fourteenth-century bathtub or a twentieth-century hotel lobby. As long as not too much damage is done to flesh or bone, and the narrator or the camera avoids any description of any blood that may be lost in the democratic process, all who read or look will be delighted. They will also be delivered of anxieties at least as important as the pity and fear of which spectators at a tragedy are purged. Justice has been done. An even scale of humanity has been reasserted: Not only under the skin, but right on top of it, we are all remarkably alike.

It makes sense that in Renaissance Italy and England and France and in twentieth-century America this series of insights should have served comic genius so well. In the several revolutions of the last six hundred years, it has always been essential to level estates and bring upper classes at least halfway down toward the middle and lower. It was not simply a matter of *épater le bourgeois,* but of whacking the stuffing out of anybody who could be considered one notch higher than anybody else in the going Establishment. Sennett, an Irish-Canadian (born Michael Sinnott), and irreverent as only a Catholic growing up in a Catholic country (in this case, Quebec) can be, was a specialist in tearing down. As his career gathered energy, he multiplied his ranks. He grew from a director, one-third of the Triangle Company that featured Griffith and Ince at the two other corners, to Hollywood's major producer of two-reel comedies. He contributed something—backing, a place to work, and vehicles in which to work; timing, a personality, an identity, to race across the few perfectly measured minutes on screen—to most of the great comics of the silent era and to quite a few of the sound years. Roscoe Arbuckle was an acrobatic fat man with a stoic disregard for misfortune—at least on the screen—who paired brilliantly with round-faced, innocent-looking Mabel Normand. Buster Keaton developed his stone-faced impassivity on the Sennett lot. Harry Langdon first turned a powder-faced shyness toward the camera there. W. C. Fields recorded some of his vaudeville routines for Sennett's two-reel productions and Harold Lloyd passed through a few. All sorts of women decorated his films: Mabel Normand, Phyllis Haver, Marie Prevost, Gloria Swanson, Marie Dressler, Louise Fazenda, Carole Lombard. Bing Crosby made his film debut for Sennett and so did Charlie Chaplin.

All that Mack Sennett's minions—the versatile Ford Sterling and Hank Mann; the tiny Ben Turpin, Chester Conklin, and Billy Bevan; the huge Mack Swain and Kalla Pasha—could do, Chaplin could do at least as well and often better. He had had every kind of theatrical experience, on the streets and in the music halls, in a vaudeville which was more like a flea circus, and in melodrama with a Grand Guignol flavor. He was entirely up to the improvisatory spirit of the actors he joined at Keystone at the end of 1913. From their wardrobe—as Chester Conklin tells the story—he selected the big pants (Arbuckle's), snug jacket (Charlie Avery's), gigantic shoes (Sterling's), derby (Arbuckle's father-in-law's), crepe moustache (Swain's), and bamboo cane which gave his tramp his unmistakable outer identity. From them he gathered the house of props which he used more sparingly, more pointedly than they ever did. From them, he must have taken some of the irreverence toward the Establishment and the Established—whatever or whoever—of which the films he directed for himself were full. But in his work for himself, the irreverence becamse something closer to isolation, as the farceur turned into a master of pathos.

Charlie tripped over everything as he shuffled around his sets. He made chairs and dog leashes, doors and clothing into impediments of the size of railroad trains, the slipperiness of banana peels, and the elusiveness of fireflies. But he was, like the directors who came after Griffith, more in control with each move from one studio to another, until he became his own producer and writer, composer and designer, a whole moving-picture company in himself. With each step up, the degree of pain, of sentimentality, of concealment, and then of revelation increased. He was a buffoon at Keystone, a foil for Mabel or Fatty, a scared little man trapped again and again by frightening big men. At Essanay and Mutual in 1915 and 1916, he was an agile pantomimist, a vaudeville comedian who mugged at the props (*The Floorwalker*), made gags with the props (*The Pawnshop*), or transcended props altogether (*Carmen*). The heightened revelation begins with films like *The Immigrant,* in which Charlie, draped over a ship's rail, obviously very sick, turns out to be a successful fisherman and pulls in a very large fish. *Shoulder Arms* (1918) was his masterpiece at First National. This was the secret life of all the men in or out of the army who dreamed of great military undertakings as, behind a desk or on a farm, any place far removed from the war, they read about Sergeant York: A dogsbody private becomes a virtuoso of the trenches, striking a match on a bullet whirring by, using another bullet to open a bottle, sleeping happily under a flooded dugout by breathing through the small end of a phonograph loudspeaker, as the fugitive from a chain gang sucked air through a reed under water, and ending by capturing Kaiser Bill and the German Crown Prince. Thereafter, Chaplin's films became contrasts of dream and reality, moralities in which a Golden Age far removed from the shabbiness of this world stirs uneasily under the derby. In *Sunnyside* (1919), the dream links Charlie arm in arm with some Rubenslike nymphs— Rubens as the decorators of Loew's theaters understood and adapted him to their purposes. In *The Kid* (1921), the nymphs have become angels in a dream sequence which is as out of place and unconvincing as is the contrived ending in which the Kid leads the tramp from the flophouse to the mansion in which the child's mother, who had earlier abandoned him to fate (i.e., the tramp), now lives. At the end of *The Pilgrim* (1923), the dream becomes a nightmare, when a sheriff's benevolence to Charlie, an escaped convict, is challenged by terrifying figures who leap up at the tramp from both sides of the Mexican-American border and send him away, walking on both sides of the border line, a man of no country, no class, no friends, no hope, no future. There is a brief trip to the tramp's Arcadia in *The Gold Rush* (1925), to watch two rolls speared on the end of a pair of forks dance together as Charlie waits for the girl for whom he has prepared a banquet in a prospector's cabin. In the same film there is an even more successful fantasy, when, close to starvation, he gobbles up his shoes and shoelaces as his cabin rolls to the brink of a precipice.

The succeeding Chaplin films are variously successful allegories. In *The Circus* (1927), Charlie ranks a little lower than the animals; he is pursued by monkeys, he is potential food for a lion, a toy for a donkey, and, as always, incapable of getting the girl. In *City Lights* (1931), goodness must be its own reward: the tramp does not reveal himself to the flower girl as the benefactor responsible for her rescue from blindness. In *Modern Times* (1936) and *The Great Dictator* (1940), the clumsiness of some of his techniques makes his solemn sermons sometimes seem merely preachy and obvious: the Machine Age and totalitarian dictators required the economy of incident of *Shoulder Arms* or the concentrated horror of the end of *The Pilgrim;* Keystone comedy was too small to handle Hitler. *Monsieur Verdoux*

(1947) was more successful, an inverted attack on American society through the device of a kind of defense of a French bluebeard, a cynical film that was at least all film. The last of the series to be shown here, *Limelight* (1952), was almost all sentiment, combining the worst features of *City Lights* and *The Kid* with a few vaudeville turns exquisitely executed by Buster Keaton and a plot of a dreariness that was matched only by the theme song Chaplin himself contributed. The generally inept mounting of the whole long work fitted only too well the melodramatic late-Chaplin plot: once again an elderly gentleman rescues a poor waif and gains her admiration but not her love. But this time, Chaplin took full advantage of the sound track and the audience to confide pearls of wisdom in reel-long strands to the properly appreciative young girl (Claire Bloom). One was sadly aware, watching the gray film plod along, that the little man with the private woes had become too public a figure ever to be little again. As in his personal life he was taking on the United States Government, the West, modern civilization, in headline-to-headline combat, so in his film adventures he seemed to want to fight the same forces reel by reel. But Chaplin's windmills were too much for him. He was far more successful a Sancho Panza than a Don Quixote.

It was impossible, long before Charlie Chaplin turned from lyric to epic statement, to halt the megalomaniac march of Hollywood. Southern California, it had been discovered, was wide open. Its spaciousness licensed brief Sennett chases to the bluffs of Santa Monica and long caravans through the desert that terminated in nearby San Bernardino. After Cecil B. De Mille's *The Squaw Man* (1914), Hollywood was the center of the new grandiloquence, spitting up whole frontiers (*The Covered Wagon,* 1923; director, James Cruze), reconstructing railroads (*The Iron Horse,* 1924; John Ford), finally, in the forties and fifties, taking liens on Monument Valley and Yellowstone National Park to assure audiences of a satisfactory vicarious experience. But bombast was far more often the achievement than grandeur. The heroic, as Hollywood measured it, was simply larger than life-size and any resemblance to persons living or dead was entirely coincidental. Nonetheless, within the limitations imposed by the ex-furriers and made-over traveling salesmen, a craft was fabricated that often entertained and frequently instructed.

The entertainment came from all the obvious sources. Harold Lloyd peered earnestly through eyeglass frames that contained no lenses, knocked knees nervously together when he saw a girl, dangled from the hands of a clock high over a street, proved a happily inept sailor, doctor, college freshman. Buster Keaton manfully faced everything, standing on his flat feet, with his flat hat pancaked on his head: a sinking ship, the waters gurgling slowly over him (*The Navigator,* 1924); a horse's rear, as he stood high in the saddle surrounded by miles of yawning desert (*Go West,* 1925); the transition from bellboy to spy in the Civil War (*The General,* 1926). Douglas Fairbanks leaped from one moving vehicle to another, jumped from all manner of high places with a reckless abandon that made the most athletic fantasies seem realizable to those who watched him. In fortythree films from 1915 to 1931, he burst the bounds of a juvenile Babbittry, satisfying viewers whether in mufti, in the dress of Zorro (1920), D'Artagnan (1921), Robin Hood (1922), or of the Thief of Bagdad (1924), because he so obviously leaped his own leaps and jumped his own jumps—or at least could when he wanted to. His personal life, linked for so long with Mary Pickford's, gave him a special place in the fan magazines, the glowing one handsomely compounded of suntan oil, klieg lights, and the sepia tones of the rotogravure printing process. It was a happy contrast to the green tint that best served the shining hair, shining eyes, shining teeth, and shining costumes of Rudolph Valentino—all of which seemed to be pasted on him. It was clear, however, that the muscles were his own: the costumes were shed just often enough to assure that. And it was equally clear that even if Valentino could not act, he could dance, he could pop his eyes, he could retract them, he could languish in a doorway, he could make a muscle, he could leer. It seems incredible now that he should have been cast opposite Alla Nazimova in *Camille* (1921), but it needs no special pleading to account for his roles in *The Four Horsemen of the Apocalypse* (1921), *The Sheik* (1921), *Blood and Sand* (1922), *Monsieur Beaucaire* (1924), and *The Son of the Sheik* (1926).

Manners of a more subtle kind than Valentino's made the comedy of Ernst Lubitsch's films move. Move they did and leer they did, too; but where eyes and buttons popped in Valentino movies, doors opened and closed in Lubitsch's, a bed was caressed by the camera, an eye was raised by an actor, almost imperceptibly. Lubitsch made Pola Negri into a weapon of satire in *Forbidden Paradise* (1924) and blew up the sexual engagements begun by Chaplin the director, in the film in which he did not appear, *A Woman of Paris* (1923), into full-scale battles in which every implement on the set signified something sexual.

Instruction in the film of the twenties came through such touches. Taboo was made into totem in the American movie. De Mille lingered over the sins of the fathers and the fathers' fathers in *The Ten Commandments* (1923), making abundantly clear and not altogether unattractive what was proscribed in the Decalogue. The pattern was not hard to follow, and with European blueprints and models available in quantity—not to speak of European actors, directors, cameramen, and writers—Hollywood went merrily into the circles of hell, camera and debenture trailing close behind. Some of the classic cinematic deflation of human dignity that accompanied the inflation of German currency was brought over in the first American films of that monument of a man, Emil Jannings, *The Way of All Flesh* (1927) and *The Last Command* (1928). The first was directed by Victor Fleming, the second by Josef von Sternberg. For his weary-faced, hulking-bodied portrayals of two men, one wealthy in the wages of sin (*Flesh*), the other reduced in rank from Russian general to movie extra (*Commando*), Jannings won the first award of the Academy of Motion Picture Arts and Sciences. For his fine support of actors, of little or much merit, with photography in every key, but especially the low ones, Von Sternberg was given the opportunity to look down many streets with his camera, to find despair at the end of most of them. In *The Salvation Hunters* (1925), he found it in a pimp's exploitation of a river-barge family; in *Underworld* (1927) and *The Dragnet* (1928), he found it in the faces of criminals and the look of the alleys and avenues they inhabited; in *The Docks of New York* (1928), he found it in the sea setting, and again in faces, particularly the many heavy folds of George Bancroft's massive face. Von Sternberg returned to his study of Jannings' facial geography in *The Blue Angel* (1930), made in Germany, and coupled it with explorations of Marlene Dietrich's legs which made Dietrich and his treatment of her into a formidable Hollywood device, much imitated but never quite equaled, not even by Dietrich and Von Sternberg. Two of their best attempts were box-office failures. *The Scarlet Empress* (1934) was a study of Catherine the Great's sexual exploits, translated into every sort of symbol, including a brisk gallop by Dietrich on horseback down a cascade of marble palace stairs. The performance of John Lodge as the most admired of her lovers in this film assured his comfortable escape from acting into politics. In *The Devil Is a Woman* (1935), Von Sternberg matched the obsession with sexual symbol of the French writer Pierre Louÿs, from whose novel *The Woman and the Puppet* the film was adapted by John Dos Passos, translating rain into a positive fertility rite. But the Spanish government, notably sensitive at the time to any suggestion of unrest in its country, took offense at the part of a revolutionary played by Cesar Romero, made strong representations to Paramount, and the film was withdrawn.

Lots of offense was taken by many groups as Hollywood snapped its garters, undraped its shoulders, pointed its pistols, and threw its hand grenades or "pineapples," as gangsters called them. Censorship was inevitable after the investigation of immorality and crime became so thorough that there was no room left at the ends of the sagas of sinners for indignation or preachment. Will Hays, as head of the Motion Picture Producers and Distributors of America, waved a good man's finger at the badmen in Hollywood after 1922. After 1927, when the Production Code was promulgated by the industry, measurements could be taken within a millimeter to determine the precise amount of aphrodisiac sweater or thigh or the rate of the flow of blood a film ought to contain to stay "moral." The result of this sort of thinking was anything but a heightening of moral tone. It simply assured endings in which badmen met their just deserts and good men, were rewarded with the assurance of their own virtue. Skirts were lifted and bed-curtains parted with carefully calculated gestures. Crime paid everywhere and every time except in the last flickering moments of a film when a scarfaced villain, a Little Caesar, a public enemy, simply could not be allowed to get away. The only men who could be allowed quick and early exits were the temperamental or the eccentric, the woolly-headed intellectuals, the speculative social philosophers of the film, like Erich Von Stroheim or F. W. Murnau, or the documentary rhapsodists, like Robert Flaherty.

Both Von Stroheim and Murnau had something like a feeling for the public pulse. But Von Stroheim appeared to his Metro-Goldwyn-Mayer superiors to have lost the feeling when he compounded forty-two reels of *Greed* in 1923 in an effort to capture every detail of financial and sexual cupidity in Frank Norris's *McTeague*. Murnau retained the feeling at some loss to his own product when he came to this country after doing *Faust, Tartuffe,* and *The Last Laugh* in Germany. His *Sunrise* (1927) mixed beautiful shots with calendar art after a bold beginning, but whatever its limitations, the film was a fine parable of the perils of city life to country folk. Unfortunately his chief contribution to *Tabu* (1931), which he did with Flaherty, was the artificiality of story and prop which Flaherty had always eschewed.

The planning in Flaherty's films was not his, but nature's. For *Louisiana Story* (1948), for example, "We couldn't write scenes of what the alligator was going to do; we had to take what we could get." His first successful film, *Nanook of the North* (1922), grew out of the failure of the filmed notes he took on a mining expedition to hold together. The successor, made in a little port in the northeastern section of Hudson Bay, was a definitive example of cohesiveness and continuity, probably because the people and their surroundings carried everything before them: "My urge to make 'Nanook' came from the way I felt about these people, my admiration for them; I wanted to tell others about them. This was my whole reason for making the film. In so many travelogues, you see, the film-maker looks down on and never up to his subject." But *Nanook* was the product of a decade of exploration and film-making. The film that followed, *Moana* (1926), required two years of living in Samoa before it could even be begun. The same reliance on the people themselves and their natural world made *Man of Aran* (1934) a tone poem of the primitive Irish of the northern islands, of the feeling and the value of the Synge plays that have the same setting. Flaherty had achieved "a musical rather than a prose form . . . music and not words is used to motivate the story." Why? "Music and film have movement, whereas words tend to slow movement up. And movement, we still feel, is the essence of good film as a good form of art." [4]

Movement was not exactly the essence of the sound films that followed the Vitaphone shorts (Will Hays, Anna Case, Giovanni Martinelli, Efrem Zimbalist, Mischa Elman) and the score for John Barrymore's *Don Juan* (1926), and Al Jolson's singing of "Mammy" and the "Kol Nidre" in *The Jazz Singer* (1927). "All sound" or "All talking"—as long as they justified the banners that streamed outside the thousands of theaters that hastened to convert to sound, the films that fell off the Hollywood assembly line were acceptable. The only motion that signified anything in the first sound films was that of the actors' lips. A crude entertainment was provided by the novelty of actors, second- and third-rate even by moving-picture standards, suddenly become audible; by the fresh impact of ordinary street noises swelling and diminishing almost as they did in ordinary streets; by the dramatic power of a pistol shot or a scream. An offstage whisper, magnified with remarkable accuracy by the excellent equipment Western Electric produced for the purpose, had an enormous suggestiveness. More important, the economy of gesture and grimace which the spoken word permitted very soon raised the level of the run-of-the-mill film almost as much as the amplifiers did the average voice.

Extravagant gestures did not disappear with sound. Elaborate contortions of the face were still the major dramatic resources of hundreds of actors and actresses. Indeed it was well into the sound era when one famous actress proved that the nostril could serve as surrogate for a whole apparatus of grimace and another established the potency of the twitching shoulder as substitute for every known gesture. Those who restrained their nostrils, shoulders, and other parts as Greta Garbo did or made use of their bodies and voices with conscious rococo exaggeration as John Barrymore did were not victims but masters of the new art.

Garbo's ability to project onto the screen a large range of emotion and even what looked like a small reserve of contemplation was not new with the talkies. Neither was it a silent-film technique as the most stubborn defenders of the old movies insisted until the Swedish star showed herself the screen's most distinguished actress in *Anna Christie,* accent and all. She made her talking debut with something less than a great line: "A viskey for me, kid—an' don' be stingy!" She made it memorable, as she did *Camille* (1937) and *Ninotchka* (1939), and films of no great intrinsic quality such as *Susan Lennox* (1931), *Inspiration* (1931), *Romance* (1932), *Queen Christina* (1933), *The Painted Veil* (1934) and the piece of dross that made her believe her retirement from films was inevitable, *Two-Faced Woman* (1942). She was not less persuasive as a vocal Anna Karenina (1935) than she had been relying entirely on the power of the camera in the silent version with John Gilbert (*Love*), in 1927. As a matter of fact, although she was never less than impressive, her silent films made in the United States were all of the intellectual weight and spiritual depth of the Valentino movies. She was a foreigner, after all—"Discovered by Metro-Goldwyn-Mayer in stark

Sweden," the film company boasted—and foreigners were best cast in passion plays, such as Blasco-Ibáñez's *Torrent* (1926), which became, at MGM, a "Rushing flood of mighty emotion" and permitted Garbo to set "the heart of America aflame." And since Ibáñez was as suitable for Garbo as he had been for Valentino, her second film, *The Temptress* (1926), was also drawn from his works, with Antonio Moreno expected to be as "dashing—gallant—torrid" as Ricardo Cortez had been in the first. John Gilbert radiated more heat in *Flesh and the Devil* (1927) and *Love,* but neither he nor Garbo was very warm in *A Woman of Affairs* (1929), a clumsy film based on Michael Arlen's *The Green Hat.* The other Garbo silents were sad affairs, too: a feeble set of variations, on the life of Sarah Bernhardt, *The Divine Woman* (1928); *The Mysterious Lady* (1928), which at least described Garbo; *Wild Orchids* and *The Single Standard* (1929), in both of which Nils Asther made some Valentino moues and stared straight ahead with the requisite solemnity of a great screen lover; and *The Kiss* (1929), which, though directed by Jacques Feyder, had no wit, acid or otherwise, no warmth, no complexity beyond what Garbo's extraordinary face seemed to suggest. Garbo spoke in *Anna Christie,* laughed in *Ninotchka,* even danced in *Mata Hari* (1931), but only occasionally was she allowed to sit or stand still, as in the beautiful close-up that ends Queen Christina, or the early scene of *Conquest* (1937), in which she stares almost incredulously at Charles Boyer, who is rigged out as Napoleon. Few facts condemn Hollywood more persuasively than the witlessness of her producers in finding fitting vehicles for her quiet, meditative personality, for that brooding mysteriousness that she alone among the Hollywood ladies seemed to lift above the level of the counterpane.

   John Barrymore's cinema career was a very long one, stretching from 1914, when he made his debut in *An American Citizen,* to the year of his death, 1942. He made his share of stinkers, especially in the early years (*The Man from Mexico, Are You a Mason? The Incorrigible Dukane, Here Comes the Bride,* etc.) and the late (*The Great Profile,* 1940; *Playmates,* 1941). But he also managed in *Sherlock Holmes* (1920), *Dr. Jekyll and Mr. Hyde* (1920), and *The Sea Beast* (1925), Warner Brothers' version of *Moby Dick,* to create character. And in costume, with and without words, he made a convincing *Don Juan* (1926), a superb Mercutio (*Romeo and Juliet,* 1935), a witty Louis XV (*Marie Antoinette,* 1938). He compli-

mented audiences by assuming that they would see through his burlesque of stereotypes. There was always in his playing, even at its most
enfeebled, an implicit grand manner. In his performances, the tradition of John Drew and Henry Irving was kept alive and joined to a
satirical gift not unrelated to that of W. C. Fields. His special
achievement was to move with a cinematic grace, with that bold
athletic energy that Fairbanks had, that the saddle-sore Western stars
pretended to have, that the strange suddenly silenced figures from the
stage who were framed in the *film d'art* never had.

Acting was not the particular grace of many films, before or after
sound. Direction and camera work often made personalities into performers. But in spite of the frenzy that the personalities aroused in
audiences because they seemed not only the most beautiful people
ever created but the most thoroughly in control of their destinies, it
was the directors who were actually in control. Something of the
credit directors deserve has been meted them in histories of the film
and the few works that attempt a serious critical evaluation of the
medium, but with the exception of a handful of men celebrated by the
fan magazines or the studio publicity staff or both, they have not been
appreciated by the mass of people to whom their films are directed
nor has their role in the making of a film been understood. When the
Screen Directors Guild won the concession from the producers of the
last credit on the screen before the beginning of a film—a solitary
appearance, without so much as a copyright notice or a union bug
crawling on the same frames—they created for themselves a certain
splendor, often enhanced by a heightening of the theme music to
herald the opening scene. They did not win the necessary notice to
gather a substantial audience for such director's films as King Vidor's
Hallelujah! (1929), John Ford's *The Long Voyage Home* (1940),
or Orson Welles's *The Magnificent Ambersons* (1942).

There had been every sort of acclaim for Vidor's *The Big Parade*
(1925), a war movie with a small irony and a big cast, and some sort
of respect for *The Crowd* (1928), a sympathetic tale of little people;
but nobody had noticed in Vidor the sensitivity which showed itself
all through the all-Negro film. The sensitivity was there, in shouts and
silences and in handsomely integrated pauses in the concluding chase
through the swamp. Everything—talk, singing, camera close-ups,
medium shots and long—had continuity. Vidor achieved in *Hallelujah!* the *portamento* of a conductor, tying every little detail into

place. The long line was also John Ford's contribution in the films he did from the scripts of Dudley Nichols, *The Lost Patrol* (1934), *The Informer* (1935), *The Plough and the Stars* (1936), *Stagecoach* (1939), and *The Long Voyage Home*. Ford's limitation was a tendency to simplify, to make a simple plot simpler with uncomplicated characterization, often with no clear motivation at all. O'Casey's Black and Tan mosaic (*Plough*) became a black and white halftone. But the tale of Gypo the informer had the simplicity of a legend told many times. Since the Ford film it has been told many times, in radio and television, in short story and novel, but rarely with acknowledgment of the source, probably as much the result of the film's place in a writer's subconscious as the desire to plagiarize. The same sort of leanness, entirely apposite to the material, gave structure to the one-act plays of the sea of Eugene O'Neill that Nichols and Ford strung together under the name of the best known of them (*Voyage*). There is no overpowering complexity of characterization in the O'Neill plays, but much more a fading of men into their background, which, Ford was smart enough to see and to show, was as much the ships they lived and worked in as the waters in which they sailed.

The sea has not been as well used by filmwriters and directors as one would have expected it to be. But the houses of America have been photographed and dramatized even less expertly. Orson Welles, always aware of the least obvious piece of stage furniture, carried his cameras up the stairs and around the rooms of a turn-of-the-century mansion in *The Magnificent Ambersons*. He inspected every façade in the Midwestern town Booth Tarkington had first described—not half so thoroughly as Welles's cameras—and made the wood and the stones protagonists in the drama. The crude psychologizing of *Citizen Kane* (1941)—Welles's inverted tribute to William Randolph Hearst —was replaced in the Tarkington tale by a softer, sounder, more subtle analysis, one fitting in a world of shadows. Whether by chance or by understanding, Welles found the perfect set of symbols for his frustrated lovers of two generations in great houses with small windows which let in only pinpoints of light and surrounded every object with a gallery of suggestive shadows. Even in the truncated version of Welles's film that RKO released, cut to sell at the box office, there is a harsh brilliance that the jerky transitions and incomplete characterizations cannot compromise seriously.[5]

Other directors have managed to make inanimate backgrounds

into dramatic actors in their films. Vidor did it with a Welsh mining town in *The Citadel* in 1938, though, understandably, the English director Carol Reed did it better a year later with *The Stars Look Down*. William Wyler, inheriting Norman Bel Geddes' stage-set reconstruction of a New York cul-de-sac, made bricks and water into strong actors in *Dead End* (1937), as later he did a Southern mansion in *The Little Foxes* (1941), a middle-class Midwest homestead in *The Best Years of Our Lives* (1946), and a Washington Square brownstone in *The Heiress* (1949). John Huston evoked character by planting his actors right in the Mexican soil in *The Treasure of the Sierra Madre* (1948). Elia Kazan used Hoboken mud and splintered, splayed wood for the same purpose in *On the Waterfront* (1954).

What the serious film critic easily forgets is that for this sort of art one does not need social significance of the pointed kind Lillian Hellman offered William Wyler in the Hubbard family drama (*Foxes*) and in her screen collaboration with Sidney Kingsley (*Dead End*), or of the less obvious sort that the German who wrote under the name of B. Traven provided Huston (*Sierra Madre*). The drama of low-key lighting can be played out in films of no discernible significance whatsoever, such as Jacques Tourneur's *The Cat People* (1942), or Robert Florey's *Experiment Perilous* (1944), or *The Naked City* (1948), which showed some of the depth of Jules Dassin's directorial imagination more than a decade before *He Who Must Die* (1959) and *Never on Sunday* (1961). Crime films excited hundreds, perhaps thousands, of nervous camera pirouettes of a more than merely diverting variety; there were brilliant variations on the themes of betrayal, of loyalty, of cowardice, of braggadocio, of fear, of fury, of latent sentimentality, of gleeful sadism, by such competent professionals as William Wellman (*The Public Enemy,* 1931), Lewis Milestone (*The Racket,* 1928), Billy Wilder (*Double Indemnity,* 1944), Rowland Brown (*Quick Millions,* 1931), and Edward Dmytryk (*Farewell, My Lovely,* 1946). Of the tendentious films of the thirties only the antilynch tracts have the same sort of power: Mervyn Leroy in *They Won't Forget* (1936) translated the snapping of a hanged man's neck into a mailbag being spiked by a mechanical arm reaching from a train. Fritz Lang in *Fury* (1936) showed a lynch mob coagulating like the blood it was determined to let.

By comparison the well-meant polemics and preachments of Frank Capra (*Mr. Deeds Goes to Town,* 1936; *Meet John Doe,*

1941; *It's a Wonderful Life,* 1946) seem embarrassingly self-conscious, flatulent almost with self-righteousness. One does not quarrel with the meliorism of the exposés—if that is not too strong a word—of anti-Semitism released in 1947, *Gentleman's Agreement* and *Crossfire,* or the revelations of ugly anti-Negro feeling released two years later—*Home of the Brave, Intruder in the Dust,* and *Lost Boundaries.* One merely wonders why these bursts of indignation must always come so late, so limply, and in waves, as Hollywood suddenly arouses its conscience to coincide with an increase of sympathy with minorities on the part of the mass audience or the growth of minorities as part of the box-office mass. Cycles of musicals, of slapstick comedies, of horror films or of Westerns are more in character and come with far better grace from the American movie lots. Besides, they do them much more convincingly and with far more art. Perhaps distance has finally lent enchantment to the military formulations of the dance director Busby Berkeley. Perhaps one can now admire the geometric forms he conceived for the camera, concentric wheels of dancers that could only be seen from the flies or wings of a stage or some impossible point on a scaffold. When the wheels spun or the troops marched, the backstage plots of such films as *Whoopee* (1930) or *Forty-Second Street* (1933), *Gold Diggers of Broadway* (1929), *Gold Diggers of 1933* or *Footlight Parade* (1934) came to a quick halt, which was certainly no great misfortune. The first musicals had established the felicitous habit at the major studios of utilizing everybody under contract who could sing, dance, do a comedy routine, even a scene from Shakespeare (as, for example, John Gilbert and Norma Shearer did in *The Hollywood Revue*)—or who could not sing or dance or do any kind of skit but could be marched through his paces to look as if he could. Bing Crosby started his movie career in earnest in such a *meringue glacée, The Big Broadcast* (1932), which also introduced Burns and Allen to films and featured the Mills Brothers, Cab Calloway, Kate Smith, and the Boswell Sisters. Fred Astaire had to graduate from one such collation at MGM (*Dancing Lady,* 1933) and still another, not quite so sumptuous, at RKO (*Flying Down to Rio,* 1933) before it was realized that his talents were better displayed in more intimacy, with one partner—preferably Ginger Rogers—and a chorus of twenty rather than a hundred and twenty. Before his career had reached its apogee, he was once more involved with the baroque musical in which MGM had specialized ever since the Broadway melody reached Culver City. But even in the gargantuan productions, his taste for the virtuoso solo performance obtained, and one could watch him (and the cameraman) dance along the ceiling and walls of a stateroom on a ship, in and around an island in the Seine—wherever his nimble feet and nimbler fancy took him and the large crew his producers were happy to supply him.

Astaire's singing had the tonelessness and tentativeness of an amateur on any given note, but he found the nuances of Gershwin lyrics and Porter, Kern, and Berlin tunes with a sureness that many professionals envied and at least one (Mel Tormé) was willing to acknowledge. He did not exactly talk his songs, but he did converse in them. Audiences recognized their own bathtub and canoe styles in his singing. His technique was that of a *diseur,* the American equivalent of the art of Maurice Chevalier, whose collaborations with Ernst Lubitsch (*The Love Parade,* 1929; *The Smiling Lieutenant,* 1931; *The Merry Widow,* 1934) had a satirical element that Astaire's films did not possess, but whose work was never as marvelously relaxed as Astaire's.

Satire was not a significant part of many Hollywood films. The esthetic distance it required was not often achieved by anybody on the Coast. Producers had bankers to please; directors had producers to please. Actors were subject to directors and cameramen; writers, designers, and composers were subject to both. On the rare occasion when the edge of a film cut, it was usually with the sharpness of a cleaver. Ben Hecht's *Nothing Sacred* (director, William Wellman, 1937) made a point about the exploitation by press agents and newspapers of a handsome Vermont girl (Carole Lombard), apparently dying of radium poisoning contracted in a watch factory. And then it made it again and again and again, just about as often as it underscored the laconic bad manners of Vermonters. The temptation that beset every Hollywood satirist was to turn the daring knife of criticism into the safe bed slat of farce. Preston Sturges, a journeyman playwright (*Strictly Dishonorable*) turned comedy director, yielded every time, but with such deft employment of the wizened faces and marvelously misshapen bodies of the W. C. Fields Stock Co. that one easily forgave him his excesses and credited it all to a nature too good to be ironic for long.

Sturges did manage a continuing theme through most of his films of the early forties, the combined greed and inefficiency of politicians, which he lambasted and laughed at in his first film, *The Great McGinty* (1940). But wit and sympathy defeated severity. Sturges could not conceal his admiration for the roistering rapaciousness of politicians or their smoothly greased machinery of inefficiency. The result was such a scene as that in *The Great McGinty* when all the Honest Johns are told by a lugubrious male telephonist to get out of town, an investigation is coming; or the lumbering plot of *Hail the Conquering Hero* (1944), in which the union of war and politics is blessed by a plot that turns a hapless medical discharge (Eddie Bracken) into an honest marine. The most thoroughly blessed union in Hollywood annals was that of Eddie Bracken and Betty Hutton in *The Miracle of Morgan's Creek* (1944), a film funny because sexual potency is made to reside in what seems an unlikely habitation (Eddie Bracken again), and the much debated virility of the American male is turned into the comic subject that at least some of the time it surely is.

Sturges did not often allow sentimentality to mix with his satire, but, in the Hollywood tradition, when farce entered so did romance. When the structure of ridicule and irony was weakened by workmen slipping on banana peels, it was easy for what American youngsters for years have rightly called "mush" to slip in. And so it did, as expected, in the films that immediately followed *McGinty, Christmas in July* and *The Lady Eve* (both 1941), but not in the fourth of the series, *Sullivan's Travels* (1941). This was Sturges' one acid film, an attack on Hollywood routine and customs, more sorrowful than angry, though not without bitterness. A pause in a bedraggled Negro church in the South, filled with the most submerged members of American society, invited the audience's meditation: the minister asked for prayers "for those less fortunate than we."

W. C. Fields did not make any important changes in his own patterns of behavior, personal or theatrical, when he moved permanently from the vaudeville stage to the Hollywood screen in 1932 with his canes and hats, billiard cues, bent golf clubs, and cigars. He was an "original," in both the eighteenth- and the twentieth-century sense of the word, endlessly suspicious of people, endlessly trusting in his distrust. He had the naïveté of greatness, making the well-aimed words and kicks he directed at the sacred totems of American society, babies and dogs, into a harmless sort of indoor sport in which genuine doglovers and the firmest admirers of babies could join happily. But underlying the friendly fun was an almost Swiftian contempt for human weakness, as demonstrated in the cuffing daughters and wives gave and husbands took, in the domination of families by little animals, canine and human, and the overwhelming control of the animal and human subject by the inanimate superhuman object. The dictatorship of airplanes and automobiles, billiard cues and golf clubs, hats and canes, milk and water increasingly occupied his attention in Hollywood. Compared to humans these objects were really of no account but they exerted a tyranny from which refuge had to be found, preferably in the anodyne of whiskey. Fields' own skills as actor and writer—under such names as Mahatma Kane Jeeves and Otis Cribblecolic—were always joined to others, character actors, stage-door characters, and just plain characters. Tammany Young's soft gray face, with the wide-open (though not wide-awake) eyes, was the perfect foil in color and texture for Fields' hard physiognomy, with the round red nose and the tight suspicious stare. Franklin Pangborn's long-jowled righteousness added an emotional dimension to Fields' exploits, alternately justifying and condemning his low opinion of human kind. Central Casting never did as well for anybody else as it did for Fields, except perhaps Sturges. Both men realized the fullness of resource of Hollywood veterans, especially those men and women who had long-lived show-business backgrounds. Maude Eburne and Alison Skipworth had the necessary background—which showed in every movement of their ample busts and bustles and the constantly moving topography of their faces. Mae West was splendidly built to stand up to Fields, and so she almost did in *My Little Chickadee* (1941). In all the films after *Million Dollar Legs* (1932)—in which Fields played, of all implausible roles for him, the president of a Graustark liberally endowed with superhuman track-and-field athletes—actors and actresses of various skills almost stood up to him. The lightweight acquired a brief substance in fencing with him; the really substantial were given an opportunity to show their stature—whether they were of the size of Baby Leroy (who almost outlasted Fields in a fair fight) or Freddie Bartholomew (to whose young David Copperfield he played Micawber) or puppets (among whom he disported himself as Humpty-Dumpty in *Alice in Wonderland*) or the well-corseted ladies mentioned above. But best of all, he did almost all by himself, as in the magnificent trilogy with which he concluded his career, *You Can't Cheat an Honest Man* (1939), *The Bank Dick* (1940), and *Never Give a Sucker an Even Break* (1941). The three films were loosely tied together by a running satire on films—on their advertising, their chases, their versions of love and family life. In the first of the three, he played Larson E. Whipsnade, father of a girl with ambitions to marry into society, as represented by the Bel-Goodies. In the second, he was Egbert Sousé, a no-account who proves himself of some account by his capture of bank robbers, but, the audience and Fields know, entirely inadvertently. In the last, he ran everything together inadvertently, to produce a bundle of comic fragments so loosely tied together that any excerpt from it is satisfying in itself and no one scene needs any other to be understood. It is a *mélange vitale* of scornful glosses and comments on life in America that constantly hovers on the brink of the Boccaccian or the Rabelaisian gulf and but for the production code would fall in.

Scorn for human failings leaks out of the corners of Groucho Marx's mouth every time he opens it. Sometimes his replies to contestants on his former television quiz program became offensive; they were often genuinely funny. He was once an improviser with an endless flow of insults, witty, generally apposite, and occasionally wise. In pictures, the contempt was heaped on his brothers—the aimless affable Zeppo, who left the act in midcareer; the one-finger pianist Chico, with the stage Italian accent, who always dressed like a barrel-organist's monkey; the sentimental harpist and inventive Harpo, who always wore a fright wig and a costume that looked like a parody of the velvet suits of *la vie bohème*. Chico and Harpo were stand-ins for the outside world, slow to understand anything but amiable enough. The three Marxes burglarize a darkened house. "Flash," Groucho hisses at Harpo, reasonably enough. Harpo produces a whiskey flask and a broad grin. "Flash," Groucho repeats with irritation. Harpo reaches into his pocket for a fish and the grin becomes idiotic. "Flash!" Groucho is exasperated. Finally, the flashlight appears. The embroilments of an insane world were endlessly parodied by the Marx Brothers, best of all, perhaps, in their fifth film, *Duck Soup* (1933), which intermittently took an antiwar line and with a little more organization could have been a pointed satire. In it, the predilection of Hermann Goering for sumptuous uniforms was anticipated by Groucho, who in one sequence changed military costume by the second. Some of the dialogue manufactured for or by the

Marxes had an Elizabethan briskness usually intended to expose the foolishness of conversational conventions. *Question:* "What is your pleasure, Sir?" *Answer:* "Women. What's yours?" *Question:* "How do you keep your youth?" *Answer:* "I don't. He keeps me."

In their first films, adapted from vaudeville or musical-comedy patterns with few concessions to the camera, there was only a modicum of plot to clutter up proceedings. But after those undignified stews—*The Coconuts* (1929), *Animal Crackers* (1930), *Monkey Business* (1931), *Horsefeathers* (1932) and *Duck Soup*—came super-productions at MGM. The Marxes' version of *Il Trovatore* in *A Night at the Opera* (1935) was funny enough, with Groucho as a witch and Harpo bringing the song "Take Me Out to the Ball Game" alive in the orchestra, in a game with the musicians and their instruments and everybody and everything onstage. The number of talking characters, mute extras, chorus girls, and Marxes crammed into a tiny stateroom in the same film set a record that collegians in later years vainly tried to surpass in telephone booths. But there was also a plot, taken seriously enough to include sober tenor arias. And again in *A Day at the Races* (1936), plot intervened too frequently and too heavily, as it did in *Room Service* (1938), much too mechanical a stage farce for the Marxes. The opportunity to rag Westerns in *Go West* (1940) was accepted only halfheartedly, but the film did offer an addition to protocol for swooners; a fainting Groucho, flat on his back, lifts his head, opens one eye, and croaks, "Force some brandy between my lips!" Finally, in *The Big Store* (1941), the second or third of the Marxes' "farewell appearances," a department store at night becomes a hippodrome for Harpo, who roller-skates across the counters with the helpless joy of an uninhibited clown. The sting was taken out of the Marxes in their later films, but not the wild humor, always directed, however lazily, at sham, hypocrisy, and repressive convention.

The ethical content of Walt Disney's animated cartoon films seems inoffensive. Children have been pleased for more than three decades by the balance of sweetness and violence to which Disney's empty-eyed animals are predestined. Adults might have been expected to question the abuse to which apparently only the most ingenuous species in Disney's cosmos, as represented by Donald Duck and Pluto the dog, have been regularly subjected. No medieval torture chamber ever held instruments more ingeniously devised to eviscerate, strangulate, inflate the body or deflate it than the pens and brushes of Disney's drawing boards. By comparison to the sadistic exercises of the cartoons, the "true life adventures" photographed by Disney cameramen make it seem as if some animal Gandhi has sold satyagraha to the jungle and forest. Violence was almost justified by the faces, movements, and voices of Snow White, Cinderella, Sleeping Beauty, the cast of *Fantasia* (1940), and most of Alice's Wonderland friends and enemies in Disney's version of the Lewis Carroll book (1951). That Disney could do better with line and color, and could even give texture to some of his characters and plots, he demonstrated in the long films that followed *Fantasia*. Dumbo, the little elephant with the ears so large he could use them as wings and fly, managed to scrape off much of the treacle with which Disney figures are covered at birth. Kenneth Grahame's Reluctant Dragon and Toad of Toad Hall (from *The Wind in the Willows*) reached a mass audience without any significant change of character, and moments in the South American musical anthologies, *Saludos Amigos* and *The Three Caballeros,* and the North, *Make Mine Music,* suggested that the wit that had given motive power to *Steamboat Willie* (1928) and *Three Little Pigs* (1933) was not entirely dead even if animated cartoonists at other studios seemed to be.

Wit has reared its pointed head from time to time in Hollywood, but producers and administrators have been suspicious of pointed heads, and rightly so. They are freaks. And so are witty films. They bite the wrong people, if they are any good at all. If they are really witty, they have only a critical success, and not even necessarily that: Film critics have, like film directors and film actors, tended to have a rudimentary social conscience and a well-developed sentimental nature; but their sense of humor seems to start at bawdy innuendo and to stop at anything more indirect. Hollywood lets who will be clever —somewhere else—and itself does lovely things rather than dream them, making Life, Death, and that vast Forever one grand sweet song.

The sweetest of Hollywood songs are Western. Into the blithe airs that always accompany the journey west, some of the handsomest strains of contemporary music have stolen—a little Richard Strauss, a soupçon of Debussy or Ravel, a snatch of early Stravinsky. Into the camera has gone the most rugged territory and the most handsome on Hollywood's side of the Great Divide, fitting terrain for the hirsute heroes of the horse epic. The Western film—at least the class A, Technicolor, Cinemascope genus—contains almost all that makes Hollywood a significant part of world culture. Its protagonists are the Cuchulains, Achilles' and Hectors of the American imagination. They are men of myth, but unlike the Irish hero and the Greek and the Trojan, they inhabit a world we know, no merely legendary Atlantis or Olympus. The prodigious feats they perform can be seen. If the tightly-corseted cinema star has to be lowered into the saddle from a derrick, if a stand-in has to do the slugging, if a camera trick has to account for the bull's-eyes, it is nonetheless true that somebody has done these things sometime or other, or that somebody could, or that Gregory Peck or Gary Cooper or Henry Fonda would if called on by the harassed townsfolk of Tombstone or Dodge City.

The words of the gunfighter, the fast-drawing marshal or sheriff are few, homely, and wise, the words of a man apart. He is not himself a frightened banker or Wells Fargo official, but rather a one-man deposit insurance corporation and armored car company. Without him, the pittances of widows and orphans and pretty young schoolmarms would never be safe, in or out of a bank. Without him, the mails, especially when they contain the gold shipment that is about to save a whole town from destitution, would never go through. He is beloved of trollop and vestal virgin, gambler and solid citizen. He himself seldom goes to church except to be married or buried, but neither sacrament nor sermon would avail overmuch, since he is a demiurge, although whether for good or evil is not always clear. He tries to do good; that much is apparent. But men—or boys—work mischief and provoke out of the holster the gun he has sworn to keep quiet. He is the peace officer only constant harrying will bring to war. He will do everything up to and including marrying a Quaker and keeping by her discipline until the boy he sent up comes a-callin' at high noon and there's nothin' to do but fight it out on the dusty street between the saloon and the bank, those two poles of Western-town culture, with every signboard, pickle barrel, and wagon concealing an eager but suitably frightened or awed spectator. All of us crowded behind buckboard and barrel know that no unshaven outlaw is a match for even an aging hero—as the late Gary Cooper proved again and again. As when we watch Sophocles or Euripides, we know the ending, but our suspense is just as great as if we did not. Besides, this might be the terrible moment when some daring independent producer will switch from the upbeat to the downbeat ending and Gregory Peck will get his right in front of our eyes instead of in that distant ambush to which he and all the others are constantly journeying over the extravagantly colored horizon in the waning light of the sun. The image is the popular one most Americans hold of their own country in time of international conflict, a peace officer drawn only very reluctantly out of retirement and as tardily as decency and the arsenals of other countries will permit.

In keeping with the greater realism with which Americans now face themselves and their failings, Western films look more searchingly now at the faces and figures and personal histories of their stars. The marshal is older—partly force of circumstance: Gregory Peck and Henry Fonda are older, much older, and nobody seems to have quite the right stoop in the shoulder or lank in the hip to replace them; partly the courage to see a character through to the end the way Skeezix was allowed to grow up in the comic strips. The marshal is closer to retirement, his past farther behind him. As he grows older, he grows more honest, too. He is willing to look himself in yesterday's eye and admit that mebbe he shouldn't've killed everybody he did and that he did his share of cheating at cards, too. As for his relations with women, they can only be hinted at. He is weary of the world with good cause but still willing to instruct it, if it will come softly and listen attentively. He dresses better than he used to and likes to surround himself with beauty, not only in the flesh, but sometimes also in furniture, or paintings. There is no suggestion yet of literacy, but at the rate he is going, that ambush for which he is headed may be some Southwestern literary conference.

The beauty of Western films has been enhanced by their new honesty. They look as earnestly today into front and backyards, up and down streets, in and out of stables and saloons as they do at the marshal. The whore at the end of the bar looks as if her fame should be ill. The houses are not often painted; the chief coloring agent is the weather. And even some of the interiors show signs of age and use. The steps and slats on the boardwalk that lead to the swinging doors are bowed and bushed, broken and tired, like the men who walk them. The sun is hot enough to bring out a sweat and a flush and a stain beneath the armpits and between the shoulder blades. It's not only the villains now who do not shave. Sometimes the camera compositions seem too clean, too correctly balanced, but the houses across the mesa do look that way; it is not simply George Stevens' taste (*Shane*, 1953) or John Ford's (*My Darling Clementine*, 1946). If there is the neatness of an Edward Hopper painting about the streets (*Warlock*, 1959), it may be because the streets have such a neatness, faded in the sun as they are, braised by the sand and bruised by the bullets. If there is a great deal of Frederic Remington and Charles Russell in these cowboys and Indians, it may be because the West that offers itself to be filmed does in fact have a great deal of Remington and Russell about it. What makes it all more convincing than ever before is the honesty of the cameras: if they find peeling paint and broken fences, ragged stubble on a man's face and dirty clothing on his back (*Yellow Sky*, 1955; *The Gunfighter*, 1957), then perhaps the rest that they report may be true as well. Or perhaps it may not: in *Cowboy* (1958) and *The Sheepman* (1957) the Western tradition is taken only half seriously. An agreeable irony insinuates itself through both films, now in the dialogue, now in the plot, occasionally in the acting (Jack Lemmon in *Cowboy*, Glenn Ford and Shirley MacLaine in *The Sheepman*), often in the settings and in the direction.

We must be grateful for this last of movie genres to hold its own. The contemptuous comedians have departed. The large-scale personalities have almost all died or retired or turned to making fun of themselves in nightclubs. In place of Garbo, we had for a while Marilyn Monroe, who progressed to the point where in films like *How to Marry a Millionaire* (1955) or *Some Like It Hot* (1959) she could at least recall Clara Bow or Sue Carol or Jean Harlow. There are still vast agglutinations of stars and extras, paper models and wooden reproductions to make miniature Romes and life-size Babylons, but they resemble *Grand Hotel, Dinner at Eight,* and *Gone with the Wind* far more than *Intolerance* or *The Birth of a Nation*. There are moments of convincing spectacle, as in the battle scenes in the Italian-American *War and Peace* (1958) or *The Pride and the Passion* (1957). There are ridiculous reconstructions of places and people such as *The Brothers Karamazov* (1958). There are visits to real streets and neighborhoods such as *Marty* (1955). But the essence of Hollywood still comes in a burst of color and bullets amid Ferris wheel and sky jump, as in *Some Came Running* (1958), where Vincente Minnelli used a tent show on the streets and open lots of a small town to dramatize an insane murder at the end, or in the same director's use of Paris as seen directly by the camera or as filtered through Impressionist and Post-Impressionist painters' canvases in *An American in Paris* (1951) and *Gigi* (1958). Painting has made its way in Hollywood: there was the explicit biography of Gauguin (*Moon and Sixpence,* 1942), of Toulouse-Lautrec (*Moulin Rouge,* 1953), and of Van Gogh (*Lust for Life,* 1955), which Minnelli directed. Hollywood actors, directors, and producers own large holdings in paintings from 1860 Paris to 1960 San Francisco. It is one of the acknowledged signs of arrival in Hollywood to hang a Monet, a Gauguin, a Klee, or even a Tobey or Graves over the mantel to give shelter and stature to the Oscar. Minnelli's taste for the art extends to the production drawings in line, which he commissioned David Stone Martin to do in order to set the haunted mood for his tale of a sanatorium of psychoneurotics *The Cobweb* (1959), to deliberate evocations of Toulouse-Lautrec and Henri Rousseau in the *American in Paris* ballet and the prism of *fin-de-siècle* French painting through which he and Cecil Beaton saw the figures of Colette's *Gigi*.

Painting has probably had a stronger influence upon the experimental film in America than any other art, including the movie. Georgia O'Keeffe, Emlen Etting, Jackson Pollock, and two artists in mobiles, the founder of the form, Alexander Calder, and James Davis, have made films or had films made about their work. From the first clumsy translations of tones and textures onto the screen by means of the color organ, through the supple manipulations of paint right on film by Len Lye, the painter's eye has directed the work of the most adventurous American film makers. John Hubley's *The Adventures of an Asterisk* (1957) restores humor to the short animated cartoon while it defends abstract art by inference and implication. Hubley used jazz—Benny Carter and Lionel Hampton—for his music, as so many of the experimental film-makers of the last fifteen years have. Hollywood has made use of the music, too—Duke Ellington's score for *Anatomy of a Murder* (1959) is perhaps the best recent example —but usually with a heavy production and the sort of fanfare that classical trumpeters play more convincingly than jazzmen. Perhaps the most significant of the several reminders of the eloquence of the film that experimental directors, cameramen, musicians, and painters have made is of the economy of line and brevity of statement of which the moving picture is capable. "Film," Robert Flaherty said, "is the great pencil of the modern world . . . Man started with pictures, and in the Twentieth Century he has discovered that pictures —motion pictures—provide a more graphic and cosmopolitan method of communication than the printed word. Film has given mankind its first universal language." [6] Some of the time, at least, it is good to have that language spoken quietly and in short sentences.

The quiet speech and the short one are not for mass audiences. Experimental films, whether abstract and recondite or concrete and clear, are played at the so-called "art" theaters when they are shown at all, setting their haunch beside the paunch of a Brigitte Bardot. Hollywood has given up one- and two-reel films, except for newsreels or an occasional Disney short. Those studios that are not given over entirely to making television films concentrate on longer and longer and wider and wider movies, movies so long that one needs a barbiturate to stay awake through them and so wide that only the walleyed can see them. Not even the vicarious experience is protected by this sort of spectacle. Film audiences like to have their fantasy lives invaded but not stupefied, and so many have made a dignified retreat from the cinema womb to the living room, preferring to take their technological art in small doses and electing the two-hour reruns on television, with all the time-outs for deodorants, hair sprays, brassieres, and tobacco, in preference to the all-night session in ancient Rome, ancient Egypt, and ancient Israel.

And how dismal the all-night epics of recent years have been, how long, how repetitious, how tedious in their elephantine display of misspent millions! One can always stay awake during the three or four hours one of these terrors takes by trying to estimate where all the money went. Did it go to rebuild ancient Rome or the Peking of the Boxer Rebellion? Did it go on people—thousands of Italians and as many Spaniards? Or did it go on makeup, transforming Italians into Egyptians and Spaniards into Israelites and Arabs into Arabs? Or did it go into the hold of the *Bounty* in the form of yards and yards of calico to cover all the bare breasts in Tahiti? When this wondering ceases to entertain, one can speculate on the extraordinary lapse of judgment that permitted Lewis Milestone to take on that large, clumsy, and utterly unmoving remake of *Mutiny on the Bounty* (1962), in which the only satisfactory moment really was the death by frying of Marlon Brando, whose foppish eighteenth-century Englishman looked and sounded more like a twentieth-century Japanese dancer. And equally, one can meditate on the marvels of vicariousness that will make Charlton Heston believable to anyone as Moses and Ben Hur and El Cid, that will sit still for Jeffrey Hunter as Jesus, and can find Richard Burton and Elizabeth Taylor acceptable as Antony and Cleopatra. By comparison, the fact that Peter O'Toole, a very tall man, plays Lawrence of Arabia, a very short man, is of no significance, and that the producers of the movie version of *Bye, Bye, Birdie* (1962) had to cast a Swedish actress, Ann-Margret, in the part of an American teen-ager, is unimportant —at least she looks the part, even if she doesn't quite pronounce every word with the right bubble-gum inflection. None of this, one may conclude, is any more upsetting than the relentless casting of veterans of the Yiddish theater and the Moscow Art as Spaniards, Frenchmen, Italians, Nazi Germans, everything except Jews and Russians. One must be sad, however, to see the practice exported. Carlo Ponti's production of Sartre's *The Condemned of Altona* (1963) sports a German family, the head of which speaks in Fredric March's flat American accent, with one son, Robert Wagner, out of the same cloth, another, Maximilian Schell, in his own loud German accent, and Sophia Loren playing Wagner's German wife with a splendid Italian accent—'Amburg, she pronounces the city where all the disagreeable events of the film take place.

Some attempt to counteract this foolishness has been made in American films. Such films as Martin Ritt's *Hud* (1963) can be made in Hollywood, using well-trained performers like Melvyn Douglas, Paul Newman, and Patricia Neal in parts that appeal to professionals, making sense out of its Texas settings, making, in sum, a mature commentary, almost a biting one, on the inevitable decay of the cowboy and his way of life in the mechanical world of modern agriculture. Marlon Brando's use of color and composition in *One-Eyed Jacks* (1960) showed a directorial skill rather larger than his mannered acting had ever suggested he might possess; it also, like *Hud,* came a little closer to the reality of Western life than has been usual in this sort of film, especially impressive in a story of the past. What makes it of lasting significance, perhaps, is its reliance on film techniques to accomplish its end rather than a superimposed sociology of narrative or dialogue. A little bit of wit was allowed to slip into the dialogue of *Wives and Lovers* (1963), and the actors involved—Van Johnson, Janet Leigh, Shelley Winters, Martha Hyer

—seemed to understand their lines. A great deal of wit was forced into two thin plots by Blake Edwards' direction and Peter Sellers' acting and as a result *The Pink Panther* (1963) and *A Shot in the Dark* (1964) seemed in the dim days of the American film positively lustrous narratives of a brilliantly inept detective. Joanne Woodward continues her steady course across the South of Tennessee Williams and William Faulkner and the Middle West of William Inge, making their kind of undercover girl understandable, lovable—in a manner of speaking—if not quite admirable. All the best efforts of Elizabeth Taylor, Carroll Baker, Geraldine Page, the best Technicolor sets in the West, lots of local color, and oh, such candor, have not been enough to turn Williams, Inge, O'Hara, or any of the other bad providers into good movie material. For all its sophomoric gray-grim naturalism, Sidney Meyers' *The Savage Eye* (1959) made more sense of Los Angeles in its tour of B girl sinks and revival meetings and third-rate hotels than Hollywood has ever done with its next-door neighbors. John Cassavetes' *Shadows* (1961) was amateurish, but it swung, swung life out of New York streets onto film, and Shirley Clarke got some convincing atmosphere, if not much else, into her film version of Jack Gelber's *The Connection* (1961). And the best of these films made with small budgets and large concerns for the film, *David and Lisa* (1962), and *Nothing But a Man* (1964), were at once the most economical in their techniques and the most convincing, full, as only works that communicate by sign and indirection can be, of emotions that came from beneath the surfaces of the scenes and the actors in them.

What films like *David and Lisa* and *Nothing But a Man* suggested was, if not a New Wave of the quantity and quality of the French films of the late fifties and early sixties, at least one that relied like them on brevity and obliqueness. The French had discovered the always engaging, often brilliant devices of the skilled directors of Hollywood's B films of the thirties and forties. These men, with small budgets and the briefest shooting schedules, had had to use their imagination instead of thousands of feet of excess film and hours of leisure in the cutting room to shape and form their movies. It was enough in their films to show a door, indicate a house, point to some stairs; it was not necessary to shove an actor through, into, or up; audiences were hip enough to make the connection. The French have gone a step further in films like *Breathless* and *Cleo from Five to*

Seven. They have reached into the truncated metaphor of symbolist poetry, the dangling symbol of Valéry, the wild wandering episodes of an Eluard, to make their not always clear narratives. Alain Resnais has drawn from the heaps of facts of the so-called antinovels of writers like Robbe-Grillet and Nathalie Sarraute part of his technique and added to it his own enormous resourcefulness as a maker of shots and frames to create what looks like an entirely new sort of film in *Hiroshima, Mon Amour* and *Last Year at Marienbad.*

Resnais's technique is fresh, but not quite new. It rests upon long meditation, a shifting of time sequences, and the kind of slanting indirection that all capable silent-film directors could rely upon to give their work depth, even sometimes a depth they had not intended. François Truffaut showed in *Jules and Jim* how much could be done with ancient film devices, compounded by a setting in the time of silent films. In *To Live Her Life,* Jean-Luc Godard made a dozen titles, brief, elliptical, into the structuring device of a film that did not altogether succeed in paralleling the misery and defeat of an unnatural prostitute with the misery and defeat of Joan of Arc, but that did show the kind of respect for film techniques and traditions upon which the Nouvelle Vague and all good filming today must depend. It is that sense of the reality of film history and all the useful wit and intelligence that have gone into it that makes Ingmar Bergman's films so compelling, even at their frostiest, and makes some of us sit long hours through Michelangelo Antonioni's by-now-all-too-familiar examinations of moral failure in modern society. But however frigid Bergman's *Virgin Spring* and *Winter Light* and *The Silence,* however somnolent Antonioni's sociology of *The Adventure* and *The Night* and *The Eclipse,* the perceptions are in the cinema, of the cinema, by the cinema. As in the magnificent *Apu* trilogy of Satyajit Ray or the eviscerating films of Akira Kurasawa (*Rashomon, Ikuru, I Live in Fear*) or the terse thrillers of the Polish directors Roman Polanski and Andrzej Wajda (*Knife in the Water, Kanal*), the film offers its own speech, its own silences, its own textures and tonalities. Most of these come, ultimately, from Hollywood. They go back to films famous or almost unknown. They reach back and forth across directors and actors and cameramen, from the silents to the talkies, from spectacle to low-budget economy. They are artists with a profound respect for their own art, a great art.

Some sense of the possibilities of their own art occasionally turns up in the work of Hollywood producers. Stanley Kramer's *It's a Mad, Mad, Mad, Mad World* (1963) has a few moments with the sweet lunacy of a Laurel and Hardy comedy and even some felicitous pantomime, but in the end it succumbs to the ancient afflictions of length and lavishness. Stanley Kubrick's *Dr. Strangelove or: How I Learned to Stop Worrying and Love the Bomb* (1964) makes its acid point with a mock eroticism that springs from a careful culling of silent film techniques. When it came time in Hollywood to appraise the achievement, *Dr. Strangelove* was, inevitably, an also-ran; the Academy awards went to the noisy kitschy confections, *My Fair Lady* and *Mary Poppins*.

Hollywood's long-practiced evasion of reality has made the community either incompetent or unwilling to see what has happened. It has never recognized the size of the audience for a film art of brevity, understatement, and adventurousness, and does not even now when hundreds of cinema societies have been formed in the United States to revive the masterpieces of the past, American as well as European, and to support the experiments of the present, domestic as well as foreign. It found even the Monroe Stahrs of the twenties and thirties difficult to live with and blessed the only brevity it understood, a short life, for ridding it of a troublesome kind of man, Stahr-Thalberg, who insisted on linking quality to quantity. Perversely, Hollywood always pays its greatest respects to the uncompromising individualist while it does everything possible to compromise his individuality. It buys up and encourages with long-term contracts talents that by its standards can only be called eccentric, and then bottles up the men or their work or both. It sets up a production code childishly silly in its reduction of morality to measurement and then sabotages the code even more childishly with films that boast of their prurience in advertisements that, regardless of the true nature of the films being advertised, in themselves invite the aphrodisiac itch. The Hollywood producer may not be the imbecile or despot his detractors make him out to be, the Blob or Frankenstein monster, but he comes very close to being a creature from another world. For above everything else he has failed to assess the size, the nature, or the significance of his own achievement.

RADIO

NO MASS MEDIUM in the United States resisted becoming an art so long or so successfully as radio. First there were technical problems to solve, to broadcast sound as far and as clearly as possible. When these were disposed of, approximately two years after broadcasting began in 1920, the second set of obstacles appeared, advertisers' resistance to buying time. By far the more interesting of the two kinds of problem to radiomen, this one was attacked with a vocabulary, a logic, a dialectic, a rhetoric, a zest that almost made owning, promoting, and sustaining a radio station into an art. When in another two years, stations were linked from New York to California and networks began to spin their webs, selling became the principal concern of broadcasters. Programs had a recognizable content, but the recognition that counted was in the provinces of the two divisions of the philosophy of radio: esthetics, or sponsor identification, and ethics, or sponsor loyalty.

To begin with, the identification of sponsors was rarely left to chance. Products and programs were linked together as firmly as the stations of the network. Soft drinks were sold by an orchestra called the Cliquot Club Eskimos, in imitation of the parka-clad figure that served as the trademark of the sponsoring soda-water firm. The music played was not gathered from under the well-rubbed noses of Eskimos: it was of that tepid variety better known in salons than in igloos. Groceries were vended by "The A&P Gypsies," none of them with any ancestry in Romany but all of them dutifully clothed in silk shirts with billowy sleeves to look, at least in publicity photographs, a little like the kind of gypsies that played in tearooms. And so the tags went. Tires: the Silvertown Orchestra. Milk: Whiting's Milk Milkmen. Radio tubes: the Radiotrons. Toothpaste: the Ipana Troubadours.

Sponsors made every effort to keep America clean from toes to teeth, to keep it from coughing while smoking cigarettes or spitting while chewing cigars, to keep its women happy while cooking and its men amiable when eating, to keep all Americans of any age safe against the perils of constipation, diarrhea, or headaches of any kind.

Regularity as a goal was natural in every way to broadcasters. Nothing was more important, it became clear within a couple of years after network transmission began, than that millions tune in tomorrow and tomorrow and tomorrow. And thus began the baleful tales of love invited, love unrequited, too much love and too little love, girl internes and boy doctors, one man's family, Jake and Molly Goldberg's family, Amos and Andy's families, Myrt and Marge's families, and all the others who turned out to be the best salesmen soap ever had.

Sponsor identification began in the evening with gypsies and Eskimos and troubadours of every kind. Sponsor loyalty developed in the daytime. Women listened avidly and were quickly caught up in the turmoil and torment with which the heroines of the daytime serials were so liberally afflicted. Every harassment was spun out at tantalizing length. No decision could be made; it had to be confronted. No choice, no matter now simple, could be elected without a degree of agonizing. To mount or not to mount stairs was an issue. When the stairs were finally undertaken, each flight brought a commercial. Women stayed close to their speakers, while the stairs were being mounted. Before Our Gal Sunday or Helen Trent reached the top, a vast number of boxes of soap flakes or detergent had been sold. And when they reached the top, there was always the trip downstairs and at least as many opportunities to hawk products as there had been in the journey up.

Sociologists have made much of the fantasies encouraged and the symbol systems inculcated by daytime serials. They have demonstrated with a fair show of evidence that in these programs dreams became reality for the average woman listener, her way of life was defended, her values approved. The family as the basic unit of society had no more zealous champion than the daytime serial. Adultery had no more deadly enemy. The moral superiority of the woman who pursued her maternal and wifely roles earnestly was a constant theme in these programs and with it what seemed to be an empirical truth: the "other woman" always loses. If by some chance, to vary the monotony, an "other man" entered the story, he merely confirmed the fact that a woman of thirty-five can be beautiful, that a mother of three can be admired by a man other than her husband and loved by somebody other than her doting—always doting—kids.

What sociologists and psychologists did not investigate or demon-

strate with any conviction were the supplementary fantasies that inevitably accompanied the sense of security bred by soap operas. This
they could not do satisfactorily, or at least not with any large and
useful sampling, because these were the dreams locked well below the
surface, the hostilities that emerged clothed in an endlessly variable
wardrobe of indirection. This was the topsy-turvy fantasy life, the
inverted dream that the daytime serial gave substance. This was the
dream of becoming the other woman or attracting the other man.
This was the pleasure stimulated by the secret life of revolt against a
comfortable maternity and a secure marriage. There must be long
pauses between the triumphs of the true believer in any tale that takes
a lifetime to narrate, and as in any normally abnormal lifetime of the
kind in which the mass media specialize, the pauses were filled with
deftly dramatized erring-do. No woman with a standard supply of
blood could help but be stirred to dreams of infidelity by such tales,
in which those destined to be unhappy took so long to arrive at their
miserable end, and so obviously enjoyed themselves on the voyage.

Radio developed a whole battery of sounds to dramatize pain and
misery. Art entered here if anywhere in broadcasting. No daytime
serial heroine could suffer without sibilants, long-drawn hisses of
agony. Sighing became the music of soap opera, the natural complement to the snatches of electric organ with which each day's episode
began and ended and which clicked off the climaxes on the stairs.
Everything but the death rattle was recalled by actresses intent on
communicating the effects of the diseases of love, including, unfortunately, sounds more suggestive of the turbulence of an upset
stomach than of a suffering heart. Actors whispered asthmatically to
indicate passion, licit or not. Nobody actually howled, except in moments of terrible distress, such as when a woman was informed that
her husband had been seen at a nightclub with his secretary. And
then the sound she made was more like a whinny than a howl.

Sound effects on radio programs, daytime or nighttime, dramatic,
melodramatic, or comic, were unusually good in every respect but
one. Cats in heat, dogs in a fight, snakes crawling out between rocks,
bears making the noises of hibernation (say a ten-decibel snore),
mosquitoes in wedge formation, gnats in retreat—any animal noise
could be simulated by means mechanical, electronic, or human. A
building going up, a building coming down, every kind of outdoor
traffic hum or indoor machinery buzz—any sound made anywhere by

anything inanimate could be duplicated. But human sounds escaped actors, directors, producers, and the remarkable human beings who imitated animals or buildings or machinery for a living—all except, to be as accurate as possible, certain human sounds, a baby's cry or an old woman's cackle or the snaps and thuds that were meant to suggest the breaking of bones or the sudden flow of blood.

The radio voice joined what Max Picard calls "the cinema-face"; like the physiognomy molded by the camera, it was "merely . . . mobile . . . hasty . . . provisional, unstable . . . taken out of the live and set into the mechanical." [1] The effect was monstrous, as of a group of disembodied voices clattering around the acoustical chambers of the broadcasting companies. But listeners came to accept it, and even more, to admire it. An imagery of the ear developed that was almost all exaggeration. This was the way emotion was conveyed, emotion that was powerful enough all at once to build the image of an eternal love, to create an enduring taste for a breakfast cereal or a deodorant, and to hold the audience glued to a particular spot on the dial at a particular time in the day or the week.

Obviously the relation between an actor's looks and his sound did not have to be very close. The illusion of romance could be achieved by a fat man who was bald and pockmarked, as long as his voice had the necessary quiver. It was amusing to see how many men played leads in radio dramas who were not conventional romantic types— though not necessarily fat or bald or pockmarked. Allan Joslyn, for example, spent half a career languishing in the day and simpering in the night over the whispering Bernhardts of radio, and then went on to another career as a comedian of very different sounds and manners in the Broadway theater and in Hollywood. But he had in the first of his acting roles an air of conviction, somewhere between the sound of a tire decompressing and a man being asphyxiated, that peculiar sound that came in the arrangement of voices in radio to be equated with romance.

The pattern was a familiar one in America, or for that matter in any of the leading democratic cultures of the West. When a new form of public entertainment was in the process of development, the first methods and manners established were always exaggerated, with an inclination to pomposity and bombast. Even stranger than the tonal range of romance and family drama in early radio was that assigned the announcer. Unctuousness was all. In the roundest, most pear-shaped tones ever directed at the human ear, commercials were caressed and the news was oozed. And announcers, some of them very able men indeed, were confirmed in their oily ways, first of all by public approval, and then by the awarding of a gold medal each year by the American Academy of Arts and Letters to the announcer with the voice the Academy liked best, which turned out to be, like most things academies like best, hollow and pretentious.

Globular sounds in the lower register, such as David Ross's, were much favored. His was the task of sifting through the coin of "Poet's Gold"; culture was his domain. One never knew quite how seriously to take Norman Brokenshire. When he announced through clenched teeth, "Brokenshire speaking . . . ," the accents were Shakespearean, no matter what the content to follow, and at the same time engaging, in the way that W. C. Fields' orotund oratory was. Others balanced words like burning food on the tips of their tongues, hesitating either to pronounce them roundly and clearly or to swallow them and get them out of the way. The congestion around the microphone, a cumbersome object in those early days, was considerable, but never so heavy as on the occasions when the British Broadcasting Corporation version of Oxford English welled up in the diaphragm. That form of speech is best described by a number of men quoted by H. L. Mencken in *The American Language: Supplement II*. One man called it "emasculated insipidity"; another, "impeccable bleating." Still another spoke of "the thin, high-pitched bleat that a certain type of person associates with culture and a great many others with effeminacy." Almost all those quoted by Mencken—all of them British—express a preference for "the virility of American" or suggest, as a Scotsman of some authority does, that this "silliest and dwabliest of all the English dialects," that "obliterates distinctions, tends to reduce all unstressed vowels to the same natural grunt, and then—as if by some obscure process of psychical compensation—diphthongizes and breaks up vowels that in other Standards are cleanly and simply articulated," really must "be taken out into the open air, and buffeted by trans-Atlantic winds." [2]

The winds were all from the other direction in the first decade of radio. Commerical radio spurned the example that the BBC gave of radio licensed by the government, sponsored by the government, run by the government. But it was impressed by the bleats of BBC announcers and BBC actors. Upper-case Culture and England were often confused with each other in those days, and the broadcasting companies listened in enchantment to the accents of Oxford and Cambridge, consulted with imported phoneticians and gave serious thought to establishing the bleats and grunts of the British universities on Madison Avenue (CBS) and Fifth (NBC). Some of the public and several publications were moved to protest. Others were charmed, as intended. Fortunately, before the whole thing got out of hand, CBS hired Frank H. Vizetelly, well known as an expert in speech and diction, who conducted a column in the *Literary Digest* and a radio program on the meaning and pronunciation of words with the same title, "The Lexicographer's Easy Chair." His advice, when he started to teach CBS announcers in 1931, was to talk to be understood. He and his successor, W. Cabell Greet, introduced standards of reality into the broadcasting studios, balancing the need for clarity and spontaneity with a respect for the correct pronunciation of foreign names. Within a few years, NBC took unto itself a speech clinician, James F. Bender, and most of the wind departed from that network, too. A great change had been effected. One of radio's most important contributions to American culture had begun to be made: to teach Americans to be at ease, if not downright pleased, with the way they talked naturally; to establish communication as the goal of speech and not a mincing air or any other vocal atmosphere that disguised or effaced the true person, and to develop at the same time an understanding of the speech patterns that expressed other countries, other cultures, other kinds of personalities, allowing foreign words that could not be decently domesticated to be given their native pronunciation.

Pomposity did not depart the networks with the hiring of the experts. Of all the identifications a news commentator could have, this one conferred the richest rewards. Listeners often confused a seeming stateliness with an oracular wisdom, and as a result appointed men whose voices had the requisite majesty as their prophets. Many took advantage of the role to make pronouncements that rivaled the yearly predictions of the coming destruction of the world that came out of Zion, Illinois. A few, more modest in their prophecies, were content to "reveal," to "expose," or to "predict" a scandal or two in high places and in low, or to restore by their own editing the balance of the news that had been upset by the networks' own agencies or the wire services. Manner was always more important than matter, however. The accents of the Morse code that gave dash to H. V. Kaltenborn's analysis of the news were undoubtedly far more significant to his listeners than anything he actually said: few ever could identify the brand of Republican politics with which he could or should have been associated. What Floyd Gibbons reported each night was less important than the speed with which he ran through the news, racing past the items like the cars past the stands at Indianapolis. He also wore the first patch over an eye to intrigue the American public. The resonance of Edwin C. Hill's voice was the most human of the elements that made up his "Human Side of the News"; the personal reminiscences of Lowell Thomas, associating him with famous names and obscure places all around the world, gave his news programs appeal, but without a percussive beat to his narration, the tales would not have been enough to hold listeners. Boake Carter's irascible and irresponsible attacks on government, labor, the military, and the English were acceptable to listeners in the years from 1932 to 1942 because he had an English accent.

There were many opportunities in the early years for commentators to convert listeners to a point of view. Not many tried. None succeeded until the beginning of the second decade of radio, when the Depression made home entertainment mandatory for most families. Radio offered itself happily as the major resource for the purpose. Most of its technical problems had been solved. Stations could be linked by the throw of a switch. Men like Father Charles E. Coughlin and Huey Long could start a movement to bring to America a Fascist brand of social justice or to make it possible for Americans to share the wealth. Long was stopped in 1935 by a bullet in Baton Rouge, Louisiana; Father Coughlin was silenced in 1940 by his bishop. Both had long demonstrated how magnetic a radio voice could be. The Middle Western twang of the priest and the Southern drawl of the Senator were irresistible to millions. At least sixteen million followed Father Coughlin's attacks on the Jewish financiers who dominated nations and prevented them from turning to silver, the currency that might have saved the West. At least nineteen million joined Long's Share-the-Wealth clubs, each one in anticipation of receiving no less than $100 a week and becoming a king, as Huey promised to make every man. All were cozened by voices, sounds with fingers attached, calling them to their promised lands.

What Coughlin and Long offered in politics, Dr. John Romulus

Brinkley held out in medicine. From a 1,000-watt station in Milford, Kansas, in 1923, he promised to rejuvenate almost anybody of almost any age or condition with a goat-gland operation and to cure all manner of ailments with a series of numbered prescriptions. After he was allowed to increase his station's power to 5,000 watts in 1927, he was able to organize more than a thousand druggists into the Brinkley Pharmaceutical Association to dispense his nostrums. His station, KFKB, mixed hillbilly singers, educational programs prepared at State College in Manhattan, Kansas, and the medical advice of the Goat-Gland Doctor. When the American Medical Association persuaded Kansas authorities to revoke his license to practice medicine, Brinkley moved to Mexico and built a 100,000-watt transmitter for a new station, XER. His business boomed until 1940, when the Mexican government finally approved the Treaty of Havana, three years after the United States, Canada, and Cuba had signed it. The pact brought order into radio in the Americas, reassigned frequencies to give stations clear channels, and stopped the pirates on the Mexican side of the border whose booming voices had shouted down all competition on the American side. Brinkley declared himself bankrupt. His American imitators had been muffled by action taken earlier by the Federal Radio Commission. The only shamans left in broadcasting were the revivalist preachers and the sports announcers.

Religion was generally left to responsible voices in radio. From the beginning, individual stations and networks opened their microphones to ministers, priests, and rabbis who came well recommended by the size of their congregations or the circulation of their books or the frequency with which their sermons were reported in the press. Not many were accomplished speakers. Sunday mornings on the air were early consecrated to well-intentioned, good-mannered, poorly-produced programs. Children's gambols alternated with clerics' solemnities. For all the sweetness, not much light was shed. For when a man had theological authority, much too often he did not have oratorical skill. There were exceptions, ministers and priests who either had a compelling manner or matter or, more rarely, both. Ralph Sockman, Harry Emerson Fosdick, Daniel Poling, and Fulton Sheen proved themselves capable of holding audiences year after year. Bishop (then Monsignor) Sheen helped make the Catholic Hour on Sunday afternoons on NBC into a program more consistently and more carefully listened to than any other his Church ever attempted in radio or television. But neither Monsignor Sheen's very successful series of broadcasts analyzing Communism nor any of the addresses of famous Protestant clergymen ever stirred as much response as the assorted revivalists whose bellowings generally were to be heard (and still are) on small stations on Sunday nights. Because of the weak wattages of the stations on which they were heard, not many achieved national fame. But their incomes, or those of their churches, swelled after their broadcasts as none of the other men's did. Some idea of the excitement these medicine men generated can be gathered from the passage which concludes James Joyce's parody history of English prose styles in *Ulysses*. Joyce wrote this passage before the time of radio and with only newspaper accounts and a few visiting American evangelists upon which to base his parody. But his ear was accurate. Alexander J. Dowie, his tent-show evangelist, is a fair example of the species.

Come on, you winefizzling ginsizzling booseguzzling existences! Come on, you doggone, bullnecked, beetlebrowed, hogjowled, peanutbrained, weaseleyed fourflushers, false alarms and excess baggage! Come on, you triple extract of infamy! Alexander J. Christ Dowie, that's yanked to glory most half this planet from 'Frisco Beach to Vladivostok. The Deity aint no nickel dime bumshow. I put it to you that he's on the square and a corking fine business proposition. He's the grandest thing yet and don't you forget it. Shout salvation in king Jesus. You'll need to rise precious early, you sinner there, if you want to diddle the Almighty God. Pflaaaap! Not half. He's got a coughmixture with a punch in it for you, my friend, in his backpocket. Just you try it on.[3]

Not all the revivalists were equally loud or offensive. Not all were Sunday shouters. Elder Solomon Lightfoot Michaux, an African Baptist minister, led a congregation of singers, clappers, and stompers in Saturday noon broadcasts from his temple in Washington, D.C. He and his coreligionists brought to network listeners some of the art of gospel singing, rhythmic, robust, inevitably cheerful, and never synthetic.

Synthetic cheer was the profession of the sports announcer. No matter how feeble the baseball game, how uninspired the tennis match, or how mechanical the prizefight, some sort of excitement had to be generated. "Enthusiasm, you see, for the pageant or game immediately at hand," Graham McNamee explained, "is my stock in trade.

And my spontaneity can't be forced—because my listeners would be the first to recognize it. I just happen to be lucky in that by temperament I'm naturally enthusiastic and excitable." Nonetheless, McNamee could not leave spontaneity in the hands of Babe Ruth or Chris Cagle, Helen Wills or Jack Dempsey. If no home run were hit, no long runs made around left tackle, no lobs or uppercuts worth commenting upon, the drama would have to be provided by the announcer. McNamee, trained as a singer and hired as one at WEAF in 1922, was used to preparatory scales before a concert; he did setting-up exercises that were the equivalent before going on the air, revving his motor up to the necessary tension. Ted Husing, who performed the same chores at CBS as McNamee did at NBC, was generally more impassive; but when the moment came that could be called "electrifying" or "breath-taking" or "tremendous" or "terrific," he did not hesitate—he ran with the adjective. Both men covered all the major sports and a few of the minor, all the championship games and final matches to which their networks could buy the rights—McNamee for more than fifteen years after 1924, Husing for as long a period after 1927. Both reported a large number of what radio calls "special events," ticker-tape parades for Lindbergh and Byrd, the landing of the Graf Zeppelin, the funeral of Floyd Bennett, the inauguration of President Hoover. Much of the excitement in the late twenties was over airplanes: special-events announcers talked from planes over New York to famous fliers, such as Captain Frank M. Hawks, flying over New York or more distant places, and covered every significant occurrence in aviation history at which a microphone could be present. Elections produced a useful agitation, too: radio had become a part of American entertainment with the KDKA broadcast of the Harding election returns; they quickly became as much a ceremony as a service. Ted Husing broadcasted the results of the Hoover-Smith contest in 1928 all by himself, from eight in the evening until six in the morning, with enough music between the reports of balloting to permit him to keep his voice. That was before CBS brought in an army of machines and pundits to sum up elections and give them significance. That was when men rather than machines were electrified, most of them sports announcers.

Pundits, or at least those who could make the motions of the learned, soon replaced sports announcers as broadcast commentators on political contests. The grammar and syntax improved noticeably at the all-night sessions on first Tuesdays in November. News commentary generally sobered up in the second and third decades of radio broadcasting, until an academic severity had almost entirely replaced "Enthusiasm . . . for the pageant or game immediately at hand." Only in sign-ons and sign-offs did excitement fill the air as commentators lingered over the solemn words that told America who was about to pontificate or who had just shared his wisdom with them: "Baukhage speaking . . ." *"This* is Edward R. Murrow . . ." The new gravity had emerged bit by bit.

Sportswriters were among the first to complain about the old excitement. As a class they were increasingly bitter in the thirties over the millions who turned to McNamee and Husing, Clem McCarthy and Bryan Field, Sam Taub and Steve Ellis for the official word on baseball, racing, and fighting. They had good evidence of the misdeeds of the sports announcers, who in their "natural" enthusiasm and excitement often indicated that the losing fighter was winning or that unmistakable fouls and easy outs were being knocked for home runs. Listeners began to complain after a while, too. The combined protest brought the roar that accompanied sporting events down to a respectable holler and even led to the hiring of a few experts, semi-pundits anyway.

Another force that led to change was that exerted by Alexander Woollcott, who brought to an anecdotal radio program from 1929 to 1940 a voice that reasoned in whispers and rambled in murmurs. He made the mildest announcement sound like a great secret confidence. Culture curled around his microphone like a cat. Woollcott talked about the Algonquin circle, about writers, about actors, about the famous people who visited him on his island. He didn't drop names, he picked them up; for clearly they were all about him on the studio floor, in piles. Millions were titillated.

Millions were also delighted—not necessarily the same millions —by Rudy Vallee, whose ultimate effect on broadcasting was much the same as Woollcott's. He too performed at a lower volume level than had been usual in radio, for he had long "determined," he explains in his autobiography, that if he should ever have his own band, his "music would be what is commonly called *commercial,* that is, music that would readily sell itself, that would easily reach the heart, that anyone and everyone would like and understand." Vallee understood that "hot" music did not reach the heart; "at its best," it is "rhythmic and quite loud with little melody in evidence." Even "a wild peppy tune" could be "played ever so softly, because *pep* is not *volume,* and loud raucous notes have never delighted the ear of anyone."

Rudy Vallee also did his best to raise the cultural level of radio. When he was at Yale, he had been, he tells us, a great admirer of Professor William Lyon Phelps. Rudy's father, who, "in his own small way, is somewhat like Phelps," was another inspiration to him: "he speaks French and English fluently with no betrayal of accent in either. During the War he delivered some beautiful four-minute speeches in both languages to the inhabitants of our little mill town in Maine." From the two men, Vallee learned the value of the anecdote, the "little" anecdote: "I felt that in my radio announcements, little anecdotes and entertaining facts about each tune would be of human interest." [4] Whether it was the anecdotes and "entertaining facts" that stimulated the "human interest," or the commercial style—the "wild peppy" tunes "played ever so softly"—or Vallee's own toneless nasality, no one will ever know. But the combination was effective beyond any other in 1929, when the Vagabond Lover and his Connecticut Yankees began to dominate American popular music.

The way radio used Rudy Vallee's band in 1928 and 1929 was typical of broadcasting practice in the formative years. There were "remotes," broadcasts on WABC and WOR from wherever Vallee was playing, a nightclub such as the Heigh-Ho, or a theater such as Keith's 81st Street. There was a sponsored program, the Sunday afternoon "Herbert Jewelry Program" on WMCA, a small New York station, "the only one," Vallee says "that dared to broadcast dance music on Sunday afternoons." There were the unscheduled shows, when somebody failed to show up at the studio and a sudden call would come to Vallee at the club or theater, telling him to be ready to go on in a few minutes. The pattern was not unpleasing. It assured the band of four or five programs a week, and sometimes nightly representation on the air. It built for Vallee an audience that had been saturated with his sound and naturally came to equate it with popular music.

For almost forty years now, the reigning popular music has been defined and popularized by radio. To begin with, it was the ignoble pottage called "salon music," although the only "salons" in which it has been played in the last century have been the public rooms of ships and of the lodging places by the sea that cater chiefly to the aged and decrepit. This pabulum for the unparticular was the staple food of radio for a decade; on it the Eskimos, Gypsies, Milkmen, Minstrels, Sparkers, and Troubadours subsisted. Gradually, the diet changed. The singers crooned, gurgled, stuttered, and wobbled their way in; after Rudy Vallee came Bing Crosby, Russ Columbo, Ozzie Nelson.

Crosby and Columbo started out in radio at about the same time in 1931. They were on the air opposite each other at exactly the same time, 11 P.M., Eastern Time, Columbo on NBC, Crosby on CBS. Both to some extent relied on devices, but both also had voices of quality, as popular singers go; both phrased with intelligence, sang in tune, added little improvisations with a small jazz flavor to their performances. They were certainly the best of the singers who dominated radio in the early thirties—the crooners, Vallee, Will Osborne, Ozzie Nelson; the Irish tenor, Morton Downey; the large personality, Kate Smith, who had had honorable beginnings in the Gershwins' *Girl Crazy* before taking to the microphone.

There were bands in radio besides Vallee's and Osborne's and Nelson's. Guy Lombardo offended only jazz musicians, and that left 99.99 percent of the rest of the country to enjoy his musicians, who had great appeal for those who were moderately alert—they played the notes of popular-song melodies quite distinctly—and also great appeal for those who were not alert—they offered them a soporific. Even more syrupy music, usually in waltz time, was played by the Wayne King Orchestra.

Those who liked their music loud had a choice of brass bands or the next thing to them, orchestras in which the strings and woodwinds played an inaudible obbligato to trumpets, trombones, French horns, tubas, and drums. B. A. Rolfe led that sort of organized clatter for years, following the prescription of his sponsor, George Washington Hill (American Tobacco), perfectly: "nothing but choruses of nothing but hits and all in fast tempo." It was a brass band led by Arthur Pryor that Bing Crosby replaced when he moved from 11 at night to 7:15 "across the board," every week night. For years, Saturday-evening band concerts were sponsored by Carborundum, and then Cities Service took over with a Friday-night band series. Unfortunately none of these bands played anything but routine rise-and-cheer numbers, music that must have made it possible for old soldiers to fade away just a little more slowly but that did little to advance the art in radio.

Occasionally, a band of musicians would be hired to play jazz or well arranged dance music. Don Redman's distinguished band accompanied the Mills Brothers for Chipso in late 1931. Jimmy Dorsey turned up at the end of 1935 as Bing Crosby's support when the singer turned *compère* of the "Kraft Music Hall." Hal Kemp's band, a little too nervous in its staccato accents by today's standards, but an orchestra of spirit and musicianship, was a familiar radio sound in the mid-thirties. So were many of the small tenor bands, the so-called "society" orchestras that mixed three tenors, doubling fiddles, a thumping beat ("the businessman's bounce"), and show tunes, more or less agreeably: Eddie Duchin, Al Kavelin, Henry King, Charles Baum. There was something like good dance music between Ben Bernie's metrical chomps on his cigar and his effusive, affectionate sign-ons ("Greetings and salutations, all youse guys and youse gals") and sign-offs ("A bit of an au revoir, a fond farewell"). Paul Whiteman led large orchestras in radio programs of different degrees of pretension, playing "symphonic jazz," a music that was far more symphonic than jazzlike, except when one of the talented soloists in the band—Bix Beiderbecke or Eddie Lang or Joe Venuti or Tommy or Jimmy Dorsey, early on; Jack or Charlie Teagarden later on—would unaccountably get loose for a few measures.

Jazz did not make much of an impression on radio until the swing years—1935 to 1939—when Benny Goodman, who had made a substantial contribution to the National Biscuit dance-band program on Saturday nights in 1934, was a fairly regular broadcaster. There were unexpected programs around the country, such as the fifteen-minute recital that the pianist Art Tatum did daily in Toledo in the early thirties. There were "remotes": program directors who did not know any better gave time to the sprightly little bands at the Savoy Ballroom in Harlem on a late-afternoon or early-morning schedule, and so Chick Webb and Willie Bryant and Teddy Hill were heard in the early and middle thirties; Don Redman broadcast from Yoeng's Chinese-American Restaurant in New York at noon or a little after in the same years; all sorts of bands, in which jazzmen were featured or were managing to stay alive during the Depression years, were allowed a whack at the mike in broadcasts from clubs and ballrooms and theaters from the late twenties until swing and Benny Goodman emerged together. Then radio took open notice of American music and acknowledged that everything that it had been calling jazz was not necessarily so. At CBS, the "Saturday Night Swing Session" was, to use the words of the script, "called to order," and at NBC the "Chamber Music Society of Lower Basin Street" mixed gentle satire in the announcing of Gene Hamilton and heavy Dixieland jazz in the music of Henry "Hot-Lips" Levine, and weekends in the late thirties took on a little lilt.

There was more to come before radio regretted its hasty adoption of the tempos and tastes of jitterbugs. John Kirby's band had a Sunday afternoon show on CBS that presented fair jazz, coy continuity, and a rich voice to read it, Juano Hernandez's. Chick Webb came back to radio in 1937, with Ella Fitzgerald and the Ink Spots, in a sustaining program on NBC called "The Good Time Society," in which the script was only patronizing some of the time. A few years later, several jazz musicians were hired at the networks, to play regularly in the studio orchestras or to take part in sponsored programs that permitted eight bars of mild improvisation from time to time. Raymond Scott's band at CBS in 1943 was the most impressive of the newly seasoned orchestras: there were no less than seven jazzmen in his augmented quintet. Teddy Wilson and Specs Powell were in the Chesterfield orchestra, back of Perry Como. Finally, in the last years of World War II, it became a matter of policy to hire good musicians to play in the dance orchestras at the networks, even if they were primarily jazzmen and might be expected to cut loose from the hackneyed scores every time a few bars were marked "tacit" —left open—in their parts.

The conscious employment of the talents of studio musicians is restricted, as it always has been in radio, to the conventional arrangements that are used to support singers and the "bridges" or "cues" that tie scenes together in a drama or introduce them. A director or producer or writer may make use of the wit that is in musical instruments, the parodies of human sounds or animals, the clucking comments on a situation comedy, the rhythmic or melodic glosses of a murder mystery. But even when instruments are used this way in radio, the purposes are only too obvious, the wit is only too broad; reality, instead of being heightened by the music, is trumped.

Subtlety is not the way of radio in music. When it turns to classical music, it does so with many bows to itself for its courage and good taste in doing so. The pompous airs with which symphony orchestras and the opera are surrounded have long made it difficult for many to listen to them on the air. One understands the urge to verbal fustian every time "the great gold curtains are parted" at the Metropolitan. But discussions that presuppose a technical knowledge of music and music history, and that are offered in sepulchral tones, do not advance anything except the listener's hand along the dial.

There was a time in radio when classical music was presented with much less fuss. Paradoxically, it was in the late twenties and early thirties, when the average radio announcer sounded like an unemployed Shakespearean actor of the 1890's. Even the networks had lots of sustaining time to fill. The disc jockey was not yet a fixture in radio and the networks still disdained the use of records. String quartets were presented regularly by the networks. There was a quartet in residence at WOR, the Perole, even as in later years at WQXR, which is far more solemn about its obligations to "music lovers" and the American Federation of Musicians. These chamber music programs were offered quietly; the music was introduced quickly. Occasionally an announcer would break loose his Grove's Dictionary of Music and Musicians and confide a few weighty insights about the late Beethoven quartets or the middle Mozart. But generally, the decorum on these broadcasts was impeccable: it seemed to be assumed that those who tuned into a string quartet wanted to hear music. Besides, if they wanted their musical tone raised they could always turn to Walter Damrosch on Friday mornings on NBC or the "American School of the Air" on the right afternoon on CBS or to Deems Taylor or Olin Downes between innings at the Philharmonic on Sundays.

There was usually more pleasure, if less edification, in the appearances of Feodor Chaliapin, Lauritz Melchior, Lotte Lehmann, Leopold Stokowski, and Kirsten Flagstad on the "Kraft Music Hall" with Paul Whiteman or Bing Crosby and on the Rudy Vallee "Variety Hour." Vallee was less and less a crooner and more and more an emulator of William Lyon Phelps in the thirties. For eight years on Thursday nights he brought the standard brands of culture to the masses for Standard Brands—opera singers, concert pianists, comedians, snippets of drama from Broadway plays—all introduced with "little anecdotes and entertaining facts." As Vallee became skillful in his new role, the anecdotes diminished, the facts increased in entertainment and relevancy; there was then about his performances a becoming modesty, a chasteness that almost justified the constant hankering back to New England in his autobiographical confidences to newspapermen.

Radio came close to art in these variety programs. It had practiced the technique and polished the format for a long time. The first sponsored show of any significance on the networks was a variety program, "The Eveready Hour." Vaudeville, which had been forced to decamp from movie houses, had supplied radio since its beginning with entertainers. The variety program was one in which the brief attention span of American audiences, brought up on vaudeville, short short stories in the slick magazines and narratives not much longer in the pulps, and films that guaranteed at least a dozen climaxes an hour, could be catered to explicitly. It was tailored to performers and to audiences both. And it all made sense to the technicians as well, engineers, directors, producers, writers, *conférenciers*. The perfectly cut, glistening three-minute or five-minute spot became a medium in which all involved showed themselves small masters, like the specialists who did similar jobs in producing phonograph records of the same duration.

Those on whom all this loving attention was lavished, the "guest artists," responded in kind, whether in fact they were "artists" or not. Baseball players and classical musicians, burlesque comics and classical actors, jazzmen and opera singers mixed well. With their uniforms or greasepaint off, their pomposity or nervousness disappeared as well. Wheeled quickly on mike and off, they offered touches of their persons and their art: a moment of poignancy, a breath of whimsy, a suggestion of virtuoso skill. Sometimes the dialogue assigned the visiting firelady was embarrassing or the Wagnerian *Heldentenor* was made to unbend rather more than his corsets permitted and the squeaks became audible. But most of the masters of ceremonies were craftsmen and could talk their way out of any emergency—Bing Crosby with notable fluency. The tone of these programs was one of relaxation, though planned to the last fraction of a second. Though much indebted to other arts, the variety show was radio's own genre and, during the brief Golden Age of broadcasting, the mid-thirties, it was rehearsed constantly and performed constantly, remarkably often with distinction.

Large-budget shows like "The Chase & Sanborn Hour" presented

Maurice Chevalier, W. C. Fields, and Edgar Bergen and Charlie Mc-
Carthy and managed much of the time something like the atmosphere
of a small revue. The format was fixed by programs like this one: a
comedian, a band (preferably with a leader who could handle
lines), a singer or singers, and an announcer with at least the outlines
of a personality, even if it were only girth, that would provoke laughter. To their efforts those of a guest were added each week. That was
the pattern of the Jack Benny and the Bob Hope shows. It was so
successful a formula that even when the featured performer was of a
different species, a comedian, a bandleader, and guest stars had to be
added to fill out the prescribed number and kinds of people and to
maintain what the producers or sponsors or advertising agency fondly
believed was an equilibrium. Thus, when Fred Astaire was sponsored
by Packard in 1937, there was no time for him to give his singing and
talking personality a clear airing, because there had to be so much
time for Charles Butterworth, a skillful comedian, but one slow to
make his stuttering points, for Johnny Green's Orchestra, with its
long arrangements in the film-studio manner, and for guests. When
Artie Shaw, at the height of his career as a bandleader-clarinetist-
eccentric, was sponsored, he was reduced almost to a background
noise, with no time for the kind of amusing, informative, or belligerent
conversation which could have made him into a fresh and entertaining radio personality, Instead, Robert Benchley was hired to keep
numbers and kind complete, guests were added and neither Shaw nor
Benchley nor the guests had enough time to do anything much worth
doing.

Inevitably megalomania set in. Before radio ran its course as the
dominant mass medium in America, it lost the respect it once had
had for talented performers who could project their personalities
through sound alone. It engulfed its personalities, surrounded them
with so much of the apparatus of showmanship that the shows
themselves never got going. Tallulah Bankhead and Meredith Willson
made an excellent program in themselves, conversing, filling time
between band numbers. But they were only the stage waits in the
brontosaurean vaudeville called "The Big Show," which used to
lumber across the NBC network on Sunday nights in 1947. Fred
Allen needed little more than a small band of some small musical
quality to spell him and his wife, Portland Hoffa, but he was almost
always surrounded by a large hack orchestra, and guests, and gim-

micks, including an amateur "hour" of his own, a regular part of his weekly olio, to take advantage of the insane popularity of Major Bowes's competition for homemade performers.

Allen did well enough. Each additional device was an additional opportunity for parody. While he was too kind a man to tell his amateurs—or the audience—what he really thought of them, his satirical nuances were never entirely lost. In his long career in radio, he developed a high talent for ridicule which could get by sponsors and agencies. His caricatures of the stereotypes of broadcasting were soft at the edges but hard at the core, satirical portraits of excessively genial masters of ceremonies, of excessively Chinese detectives, of excessively coincidental radio dramas. He and Tallulah Bankhead did an acid impersonation of the husband-and-wife teams whose cloying breakfast-table conversation was for so long an indigestible early-morning radio diet. He adapted *The Mikado* to fit the person of the emperor of music in America: the refrain "Tit-willow, tit-willow, tit-willow" became "Pet-rillo, Pet-rillo, Pet-rillo." On occasion, he could himself make good use of stereotypes, as he did in the dialect comedy of the inhabitants of Allen's Alley, Mrs. Nussbaum (Minerva Pious), Titus Moody (Parker Fennelly), Senator Claghorn (Kenny Delmar), and Ajax Cassidy (Peter Donald). When he appeared himself it was always as himself, in a voice that was an intriguing compound of the sound of the heavy in *East Lynne* and of Charley's Aunt. He was consistent, generally funny, rarely tasteless. His only serious lapse was to indulge himself or his advisers or his press agents by participating in a running battle with Jack Benny, which had all the offensive manufactured elements of that mock feud which so often cluttered the show-business lives of Bing Crosby and Bob Hope.

All such bric-a-brac in radio was designed for one purpose, to create an identity. Repetition is the lifeblood of the medium. Steady plugging could make popular a song, a daytime serial, a nighttime comedian, a breakfast cereal, a laxative—and not just popular, but epidemic. The only limitation was in complexity. The item plugged had to be fairly simple, of the order of "Mairzy Doats" or "The Music Goes 'Round and 'Round" or the character assumed and developed by Jack Benny. Because parsimony is not unknown in a materialist civilization and because humbug is not unfamiliar in any society, Benny's constant haggling over money and clamorous pretensions to culture, to position, and to prestige delighted Americans. They saw them-

selves in him, but exaggerated, they assured themselves; or they saw
friends, relatives, neighbors, to the life, caught by the microphone in
midharangue. What was to a few a tiresome joke was to most a
brilliant comic character, supported by others almost as satisfying—
the Negro servant who really was his master's superior in wit and
wisdom; the woman, half-wife, half-mistress, who knew more than
master or servant and was honest and generous by instinct; the pug-
nacious bandleader and mildly belligerent tenor, who, like their
employer, could be easily gulled; the announcer, also bellicose on
occasion, who could be quieted even more quickly. There was a little
sham in all of them; all were always being exposed. It was like a
child's version of Molière in which the comedy is explained as it goes
along.

Comedy in radio relied on familarity and simplicity. The cast had
to be the same every week and the characterizations could not
change fundamentally, or become complex. There had to be a costume in sound, the verbal equivalent of funny hats and outsize panta-
loons. Thus Jack Pearl's Baron Munchausen character could always
be relied upon to assert the logic of his lie with a rhetorical question,
"vas you dere, Sharlie?" Thus Joe Penner would invariably inject into
a conversation a lisping inquiry: "Wanna buy a duck?" and Ed Wynn
would puncutate his gags with a high piercing giggle. As a result of
this reliance on a phrase, a sound, or a rudimentary character, situation comedy never got beyond one situation and most comedy never
rose to the level of a situation. Only the satirists or farceurs could be
counted upon for something better. From Colonel Stoopnagel and
Budd, who were both, something like wit could be expected. In a time
when advertising contests required that all participants submit some
part of the box in which the sponsoring product was packaged,
Stoopnagel asked his listeners to tear off the top of their grocer's head
and to send it in to him. The sponsor was a mythical one, needless to
say. Stoopnagel and Budd were not eagerly sought by sponsors. Bob
and Ray in the fifties brought this kind of humor back to radio with
their daytime serial, almost too accurate to be funny, their portrait of
Arthur Godfrey, their tireless parodies of interviewers and inter-
viewees, of special-events broadcasts in which the event is anything
but special, of great moments in science (at which radio is privileged
to be present) that sputter feebly to an anticlimax.

One of the special merits of the art of Bob and Ray is its

economy. If more than two speakers are called for, then they change their voices as often as necessary, becoming old men, young men, and women of all ages. As female impersonators they are absurdly unconvincing, to themselves or anyone else, which only adds to the charm of the performance. Stoopnagel and Budd had the same versatility and about the same degree of conviction. Listeners were more awed by the range of Negro voices that two white men, Freeman Gosden and Charles Correll, could adopt when they played Amos and Andy, the Kingfish, Madame Queen, and the other members of a cast the size of which was never limited by the sex, race, or number of the actual performers. A similar bravura display was put on by the two men who played Lum and Abner and everybody else in Pine Ridge, Arkansas.

The art of radio is economy of sound. It is of all the technological arts the one in which only the essentials count. Ornament is merely frivolous in radio; it not only wastes time and money and energy, it interferes with communication. Voices may be effaced by music cues or backgrounds that come up too soon or too loud. An abundance of voices may make it impossible to sort out the important speakers and to remember what they have said or what they stand for. Voices too much alike in timbre make for confusing listening. Voices in which there are no sharp contrasts in tone are hard to follow, and tend to become monotonous: The even scale of the average trained woman's voice is not only unattractive in the disembodied form which radio imposes, it creates intolerable ambiguities of meaning and emphasis.

Even in American radio, where drama has not been pursued with much interest and economy means only retrenchment, the single voice has often been used imaginatively. The central figure in every significant radio performance except that of music is the announcer. It is the announcer, or alternatively the MC, who gives to a quiz show such quality as it may have and its lasting identification. No matter what the intrinsic merit of the question-and-answer pattern of the show, it achieves its effect through the voice that asks, the voice that knows, the voice that dramatizes. The memory and wit of John Kieran, Franklin P. Adams, and Oscar Levant were the essentials without which "Information Please" would have had no endurance on the air; but it was Clifton Fadiman, the MC, who gave the program its lasting aural personality and who emerged from the program with a radio career. Producers have long recognized this fact in their choice of quizmasters—comedians such as the late Phil Baker and Walter O'Keefe and Joe E. Brown and hypertensive announcers such as Bert Parks. The drama or the amusement or the charm, however the listener might describe it, is in the single voice. That is the essential to which all radio sooner or later is stripped.

Discussions of literature or politics or almost anything at all by a panel of experts more often than not fail to recognize the compelling power of a clear, bold single voice, and the repelling effect of a poorly defined jumble of voices, no matter how distinguished the men or women who possess them. When the "Town Hall Meeting of the Air" was fortunate enough to be able to present contrasting attitudes in contrasting voices, it achieved a drama that needed little comment from the chairman. When, as frequently occurred on the Town Hall program and "Invitation to Learning" and others of the same kind, clear distinctions in idea were presented by voices with no distinctions in tone, the audience was the victim of the unmistakable limitations of the medium. Pious talk and good will could not overcome those limitations; they were technical; they were matters of production and required (but did not get) the same forethought that went into the choice of narrators or principal actors for a detective drama or a mystery story.

The voices that for many years identified "The Incredible Dr. Fu Manchu" and "The Shadow" were shrewdly chosen. The catarrhal melodrama of the Oriental villain was comic as each week he turned to his implacable enemy and crowed in triumph, "Ah-hah, Dr. Nayland Smith!" It was also magnetic in its way, like the perfectly polished tempera exaggerations of an early Surrealist painting. The ostentatiously ghoulish laughter of the Shadow did not frighten many, except the most susceptible youngsters and the most willing elders. But it did define the tone of mystery which the program courted: all trumpery and a yard wide.

Gangsters found persuasive voices in radio, especially when they were given monologues in which to outline their personalities, their situations, their dramas. Little advantage was taken of this narrative technique by writers who had more significant subjects than the rackets and presumably the necessary techniques with which to dramatize them. When radio writers turned to serious drama, in this country, they turned to the poetry of Carl Sandburg for form and to the plays of the Group Theatre and the Theatre Union for content. A self-conscious rhetoric made intrinsically poetic situations and characters merely prosy.

Archibald MacLeish turned to radio drama with the natural enthusiasm of a poet for a medium that is all words and sound: "the imagination works better through the ear than through the eye." But in his radio plays, he did not give the ear enough. In *The Fall of the City* (1937), he made consistent use of the single voice, starting with an announcer and following with a sequence of monologues: a woman returned from the dead, a messenger, a soapbox speaker, another messenger, priests, a general, a conqueror bringing dictatorship to the City. What the play lacked was drama. The terrors of Fascism were not half as frightening as those of Fu Manchu. Falling somewhere between the understatement of a news broadcast and the overstatement of cops-and-robbers melodrama, it lacked both the cold chill the first can generate and the hot fear the second can sometimes spread. In *Air Raid,* a year later, he created more conflict and thus a more convincing drama. But the speeches were long-winded; the horror of war rained on civilization from the skies was so attenuated by words used uneconomically that it became as unaffecting to many listeners as the headlines about the Spanish Civil War or the Japanese invasion of Manchuria—just streams of syllables without the ability to hurt or even to make one wonder.

The same year, 1938, Orson Welles demonstrated what could be done with the theme of an air raid. Using H. G. Wells's novel *War of the Worlds* as the substance of his drama, Welles turned science fiction into broadcast fact. He used the commonplace techniques of ordinary radio to dramatize the story of an invasion from Mars. A weather report opened the drama; it was followed by dance music ostensibly from a hotel in New York ("the Meridian Room" of "the Park Plaza"), interrupted by a news bulletin: "At twenty minutes before eight, Central Time, Professor Farrell of the Mount Jennings Observatory, Chicago, reports observing several explosions of incandescent gas, occurring at regular intervals on the planet Mars." The dance music was returned to; it was interrupted again and again. Bulletins announced the landing of the Martians in New Jersey, and then all over the country, equipped with an array of munitions out of H. G. Wells and Buck Rogers—death rays, flamethrowers, and so forth. The results were convulsive. In some communities, evacuations began. In others, defensive steps against gas warfare were taken. Many listeners had been so narcotized by the drama and were so used to ignoring commercial announcements and station breaks that they simply did not hear the four clear statements made during the program that it was a dramatization and that the names were fictitious.

The commonplace forms of radio are most persuasive. Welles understood that and persuaded thousands that their country was being invaded by Martians. Writers for German radio before the coming of Hitler had the same grasp of the structure of broadcast drama. Bertolt Brecht's *Lindbergh Ballad* (1927) is written in the leanest terms of radio. It begins:

> My name is Charles Lindbergh
> I am 25 years old
> My grandfather was Swedish
> I am an American
> I chose my own machine
> It goes 131 miles an hour
> It's name is *The Spirit of St. Louis* . . .[5]

The voice of the announcer is heard again and again in the radio dramas of the Weimar Republic. Inanimate objects are given voices. The split personality is dramatized by assigning each of the persons a voice. Inner conflicts are given outer action by the same device: every point of view has a corresponding radio sound. In a more gentle way, the BBC Third Programme has demonstrated the vitality of the commonplace in rambling reminiscences such as Stevie Smith's *Syler's Green: A Return Journey* (1947). The mode could not be simpler; it needs only the voice of an actress experienced in radio, one capable of shadings and tintings, to give it conviction. The speaker has been remembering the "dear suburb of my infancy," and some "gentle woods" nearby. This is the way it ends:

Only those who have the luxury of a beautiful kindly bustling suburb that is theirs for the taking and of that "customary domestic kindness" that De Quincey talks of, can indulge themselves in these antagonistic forest-thoughts. And of course we may observe that only these ever do. And was there ever such a suburb as Syler's Green for the promotion of briskness, shrewdness, neighbourliness, the civic sense and *No Nonsense?* There was not. And so with this sniff of regional pride and smug selfrighteousness I will say goodbye to the happy place of my childhood. And where is, where is it? [6]

Radio drama still prospers on the BBC Third—and on the Light and Home services as well. Its effectiveness springs from the simplicity, the spareness, the directness of its technique. The poets who write for British radio—and they are almost all the British poets of distinction—do not write down to radio; they write up to its needs and their own resources. The result is no loss of poetic strength but a gain in dramatic power. The writing remains allusive, and for many elusive. Poetic drama as practiced by C. Day Lewis, Lawrence Durrell, and Dylan Thomas is not a mass medium, but it is a living one and a most effective kind of public speech for the poets, even if the public is by design a small one. Philosophers and theologians join dramatists in this sort of speech on the Third in Britain and on corresponding services of Italian, German, and French radio. They debate with each other; they form three sides of a triangular exchange on the morality of atomic warfare or capital punishment. They come along in formal addresses, cut to the demands of radio speech. They participate in impromptu broadcasts in which they are called upon to improvise comments, develop ideas as they go or at least give them the spontaneity of utterance that they might have in the common room or the pub. Often a philosopher—or anthropologist or chemist or poet—is tedious on this sort of outing, hopelessly dull or helplessly obscure. But just as often, when he and his producer respect each other and their audience, he is lively and engaging. He may not be informative—he should feel under no compunction to be so; he should be, in a very broad sense, entertaining.

A few years ago, these would have been meaningless injunctions for American radio. It would have been unthinkable that Bertrand Russell and the Jesuit F. C. Copleston should be heard discussing together the existence of God, as they did on the Third, or that Gilbert Ryle or his American opposite number should be heard marking the death of Ludwig Wittgenstein with "a set of impressions, interpretations, partly, of mere echoes of echoes," in an attempt to answer the question, "what is the difference that he has made to philosophy?" But now with the proliferation of FM stations in the land, philosophy too has begun to be audible in the air, on transistor radios of all sorts, including, at last, one which brings FM into the automobile. Music is the special achievement of FM. The fantastic reach of recordings makes it possible for a station with a staff of one, a combination of announcer, engineer, and janitor, swept into a corner of a derelict university building, to go from Albéniz to Webern in the course of a year, touching almost every genre and composer and performer of quality. Discussion programs are still not as free as they are in England and on the Continent, but FM panels are not cautioned, either openly or by unspoken tradition, as AM ones were for so long and television groups still seem to be, to remember the enormous limitations of that hypothetical audience, half-cretin, half-imbecile, which radio for so many years imagined it was addressing. The more self-conscious among FM speakers sometimes err in the direction of a hazy pomposity through which only a determined listener can penetrate. And the supply of dull ones continues unabated, especially those poor university lecturers, not usually afflicted with this sort of sluggishness, who yield to the importuning of the undergraduate managers of campus FM channels and turn up to go through one or more stuttering reductions of their course lectures or to pronounce judgment on a "significant" new book or "important" new play. They cannot altogether be blamed if the best they can do for these chattering outlets is to raise the level from total tedium to intermittent ennui.

FM, for all its virtues, has too often fallen prey to the contagious disease of the educational missionary to the American millions, in-structivitis. Instead of assuming a small but sensitive audience, as by this time it might always safely assume, some several FM stations, even as their louder, brasher, ruder TV brothers and the AM networks, have entrusted themselves with the mission to the millions. There are few programs more enervating than those which seek to educate in this fashion, or I suppose in any fashion. Patronizing in tone, shackled by a lack of information as great as it is deep, produced only in the sense that they go on at a scheduled time and, *grâce à Dieu,* depart as advertised, they add little to the wisdom of radio and nothing to its charms. All they contribute is weight, sheer dull weight. Even a disc jockey might be preferable.

The assault on American eardrums that began in the mid-thirties in California and New York gathered such force in twenty years that when television seemed about to blow radio out of the sky, the networks, independent stations, big ones, little ones—everybody in broadcasting—turned to disc jockeys. They promised—and they delivered—audiences; children, it is true, not retarded adults, but teen-agers and much younger ones, hordes of those who had just reached puberty or were about to. They promised—and delivered— sponsors; peculiar people advertising peculiar products, but what else would one sell to youngsters who wear clothing three sizes too small for them in order to make their pubescence unmistakably clear to those who might doubt it? They did not promise music—except, if they were conservative, the top fifty hit songs; if they were more daring, the top hundred; if they were altogether without caution, the top two or three hundred. Most were without caution, and so since about 1950 radio has been mostly popular music, and since 1955 rock 'n' roll. Hillbilly sexual litanies have alternated with speculations about which version of twang 'n' bang would be successful next, Elvis Presley's, Pat Boone's, Conway Twitty's, the Everley Brothers', Fabian's, or the Beatles'. In order to get a little balance into the day's programming—and a few listeners outside the jeans and leather-jacket trade there has been time out for news and weather every hour or half-hour, with special bulletins every time an event has occurred of the significance of a Martian invasion or a revolution behind the Iron Curtain or the death of a rock 'n' roll singer in an airplane accident or the induction of a major twang 'n' banger into the army.

In four decades, AM radio has come full circle. It is back where it started. In its first years, it devoted four out of five of its hours to what used to be called "syncopation." In 1928, Charles Merz described the situation:

The radio ought not to be criticized if it fails to take over the functions of laboratories, books, and art museums. They are out of its line. It has a function of its own.

This function is tympanic. Into a nation that lives at top speed most of the day and comes home much too wide-awake to settle down, the radio brings a stimulus for tired nerves and something to distract us from the dull business of staying put at home. We tune in, and let it play while we wash the dishes, read the evening's news, or entertain a neighbor on the porch. We tune in—on a mighty rhythm to which millions of people are marking time, the pulse-beat of a nation. All over the country the trombones blare and the banjos whang and the clarinets pipe the rhythm. All over the country the same new tunes that will be generations old before the week is out are hammered home at the same vast audience from a hundred different places. . . . If it is true that from twenty to thirty million Americans are listening in on the radio every evening, then for a large part of that evening they are listening in on the greatest single sweep of synchronized and syncopated rhythm that human ingenuity has yet conceived.[7]

Today, there are over ninety million radio sets in the United States and more listening is done during the day and after midnight than in the early hours of the evening, which are consecrated to television. But the sound is the same as it was in 1928, with voices substituted for trombones and with electric guitars substituted for the banjos, but no less "blare" and "whang." Tunes are still "generations old before the week is out." And laboratories, books, and art museums are in no more danger of having their functions usurped by radio in the sixties than they were in the twenties. On FM stations and educational outlets there are hours of what is called "good music"; there are talks and interviews and panel discussions; there are a few university courses. On the larger AM stations around the country, there are some good, if sometimes too informal and protracted, interview shows and several service programs that intersperse news and traffic information and weather announcements with background material that amplifies the news and ties together all the announcements. On NBC, there are laborious efforts on weekends to distinguish network broadcasting from the record-saturated independent broadcasters: a few brief interviews, very brief; a number of comedy spots, just as brief; the inevitable news briefs, and the equally inevitable records, given a certain seasoning by the addition of remotes from clubs at which the microphone catches the singers and bands that make the records—briefly. This is what the variety show has come to in radio in the post-television era.

Has AM radio finally succeeded in wiping out all pretensions to art among its performers and producers? Tune in tomorrow . . .

TELEVISION

BY 1950, after three years of enormous success in selling sets to viewers and programs to sponsors, television was established as the most popular of the mass media. By 1960, it was a tired old medium, looking back with wistful eyes at its entrancing youth, and speaking reverently of the years of the "Philco Playhouse" (1948–55) and the "Goodyear Playhouse" (1951–57) and the first few seasons of "Studio One" (1948–57) and the "Kraft Television Theatre" (1947–58) as its Golden Age. It had aged at a fearsome rate. It had developed all the ills of radio and had contributed to the physicians of culture several new ones for diagnosis. Its prevailing mood was cynical, bitter, discouraged. What vitality was left in television in the sixties seemed to come from other arts, other media: from films, from the theater, from vaudeville, from people unscarred by the disease-charged atmosphere of an industry that could not quite relinquish its claims to being an art.

Nobody would deny that television is an industry. The figures are clear enough. The three networks show annual profits of ten to twenty-five million dollars each. More than a fifth of the 530 television stations in the United States gross a million dollars or more a year each. The number of viewers must be close to saturation point since well over fifty million sets are in operation in the United States and one must figure three or four viewers to each set. And in spite of all the hopeful predictions of a diminishing audience, of vast numbers of viewers surfeited with Westerns and mysteries and situation comedies and prepared to forego all TV rather than take another trip down a dust-filled street to meet a blazing pistol at the end of a quivering psychotic's fingers or jump over another crate in another warehouse to avoid being confronted by a popeyed little man with a shivering tommy gun or simply go to sleep rather than be startled with any more canned laughter—in spite of the predictions, the ratings keep going up and the advertisers continue to line up for the privilege of sponsoring street fighters and hopheads and doctors and nurses and situation comics.

Many people will deny, then, and with cause, that television is an

426

art. Its major concern is billings. Its vast structure—producers and directors, camera crews and electricians, carpenters and wardrobe mistresses, graphic artists and propmen, set and costume designers, casting directors and publicity men and composers and musicians and dancers, editors and readers and all the others—is dedicated to one great purpose: to swell the profits. In passing, it is true, pretensions to quality are asserted and even occasionally served. And when, rarely, there is a coincidence of financial function and artistic achievement, congratulations are exchanged all around and words go forth from the upper echelons to the lower ones and out to the world that NBC or CBS or ABC has once again made its contribution to culture. It is all part of the American way of life, David Sarnoff tells us, not failing to touch a single base:

> The American system of broadcasting is part and parcel of the American way of life, the essence of which is freedom tempered by a sense of responsibility. Broadcasting, like the rest of our industry, is financed by private capital that is put to work to earn a profit. If we are to maintain and enlarge our capacity to serve the public, the various elements of our broadcasting structure must be kept in sound financial condition. It is a case where self-interest and public interest coincide.[1]

Television's hostile critics have no trouble discovering television's self-interest. It is the coincident public interest that they cannot quite find.

Has television served the public interest? On occasion. It has developed a considerable skill in the production of documentary programs, which are notable for a surface precision, if not any great depth of analysis. The cameras of the networks do explore dirty political corners. They have touched the trembling bodies of drug addicts, have rumbled along the back roads walked by migrant farmers, have perched on desks in classrooms, and stared far inside the perforations made by a surgeon's scalpel. They have traced the development of cancer in a distinguished victim, Dr. Tom Dooley, and the efforts made to arrest the disease. They have looked back on war and forward to war with films of distinction. A fair number of famous people—a fair number of distinguished people—have been shown in full face close-ups, if not in full mind and soul. Every once in a while a live issue has been caught alive in debate before the cameras and the best defended people in the world—senators, gangsters, film stars—have been caught defenseless by merciless lenses. If these are public services, television has served. But the news programs in which it takes such pride are far from adequate service to the public. They are too infrequent. They are too static—a stolid commentator alternating with very brief film clips. They are too thin—usually a series of headlines, with only the briefest elaboration of the headline facts. They are too stale—after a four-hour interval only the weather seems to change; the film clips too often remain the same; the quotes are unchanged; even the jokes may be the same. It may be true, as the president of the Columbia Broadcasting System, Frank Stanton, insists, "that no news or public affairs program at CBS, however expensive to the sponsor, has ever been subject to his control, influence, or approval. There is a total and absolute independence in this respect." But the independence ends there. With rare exceptions, news programs at CBS—and NBC and ABC and most independent stations —have a grim sameness about them, a flatness even in the midst of great events, a lack of attention to detail, and a remarkable resourcelessness as to picture coverage.

One notable exception over the years to the monotony and lack of inspiration of news programs has been a half-hour program on CBS on Saturdays in the early afternoon. It has shown what can be done with film pulled out of the network's morgue, with a mixture of old and new clips, and with an attention not only to the headlines but to what for once might aptly be called stories of "human interest," since most news programs on television are so clearly lacking in it. A similar invention has been displayed in the continuing stories which sometimes extend over most of a week on the CBS morning news half hour. Racing to the scene of fires or plane disasters or the corridors of legislative houses with a portable microphone and a script which amounts to little more than "Say something" or "How did it strike you?" is no substitute for this sort of imagination. One is impressed by the mileage covered, by the stubbornness and eagerness of the man with the out-thrust arm. But one could be more than impressed, one could be edified by the program that shows the kind of attention to detail and special television requirements that the Saturday-afternoon program does, as it moves in substantial lengths of film and commentary from topic to topic, from front-page to back-page stories, from heavy to light tones. But even this exemplary show is to some extent at the mercy of its commentator. Lacking the light touch, the sure touch, of its longtime newscaster, Robert Trout, it too has lost some of its luster.

Television does not often earn high marks for imagination. Its producers and directors early recognized the resemblance of the small screen housed in a wooden or metal box to the large one framed by a proscenium arch on a stage. Unfortunately, they have not fully conceded the difference in size between a screen that can curve into the wings of a full-size theater and one that can be set up on a small table between stationary candlesticks or the mobile ears of an indoor antenna. The images projected across the television screen are still cluttered much of the time by heavy sets and large numbers of people. Westerns, Easterns, Hawaiians, situation comedies, dog stories and all the rest are still filmed as if they were going to be inflated to the massive dimensions of the movie screen. Intimacy, the great gift of the medium to cameramen, and directors, and writers, is only rarely exploited by cameramen, directors, and writers. When the close-up is emphasized and no figures are reduced to the size of insects in meaningless crowd scenes, it is just as often a small budget that is responsible as it is a discriminating judgment on the part of producer, director, or writer. In spite of all the evidence that television does not achieve its own identity and the status of an art except in close-up and middle shot, it continues to rely on long shots to put large numbers of people on the screen at once, and to ape the elements of quite different media—film, theater, and radio. There remains among television executives and performers and sponsors only one clear conviction, one clear bond: ratings.

The terrible need to get high ratings is, as everybody must know by now, a crippling limitation for television, far more serious in television than it ever was in radio, where it also worked its inflexible deterministic way for so long. Costs in radio were low compared to those in television. It was possible sometimes to experiment in radio for one-quarter of a year, sometimes for two or three, with a sustaining program (as broadcasting jargon describes a show that is in fact not at all sustaining, being without sponsors, without much of a rating, and with no assurance of returning). The sustaining program in television usually languishes in the pilot stage, a certain number of reels of film intended (by network or advertising agency or package producer) to demonstrate beyond argument to projection-room audi-

ences made up of sponsors or sponsors' representatives a high rating
potential. Unless it does so demonstrate, the pilot film is doomed to
end up as a summer replacement, with only the faintest hope of
adoption as a regular-season show, or to die in the cans. Experiment
in television is confined to a few odd moments in programs which the
networks grudgingly cede to the requirements of the FCC Blue Book,
or which have some participating sponsorship by a govenment educational agency. Here, for just a few moments, television leaps into the
half-light of art. "Camera Three" on CBS on Sunday mornings, for
example, may look at the jazz dance or the influence of jazz on poetry
or bring characters out of Dostoevski into a kind of examination that is
more interview than dramatization and more satisfying and more faithful to Dostoevski than a dramatic adaptation would be. Various programs by which the networks confess their religious obligations, or at
least their obligations to other people's religions, lean heavily on the
angular thrusts and convulsive sprawls of dancers trained in the
Wigman and Graham manners to communicate the subtleties of the
life of the spirit and the contrasting blatancies of the life of the flesh.
But this is the exception, the risk that is by careful calculation so low
it can hardly be called a risk—low budget and poor viewing time
when sponsors are hard to come by. And thus are fulfilled the new
obligations networks have to provide programs in the public interest.[2]

Television likes to offer other examples of its virtue: "Omnibus,"
"Wisdom," "Victory at Sea," "Wide Wide World," "Person to Person," "Sunrise Semester," a whole series of regular public-affairs programs such as "Twentieth Century," and "Meet the Press," and its
heavy coverage of the national political conventions, of the Olympics,
of parades and sports events and royal weddings and Senatorial investigations and grand and glorious spectaculars which bring the
world's most famous and highly paid entertainers into everybody's
living room. One element links all these projects: a fatal pretentiousness which at one time or another has vitiated the best efforts of the
most earnest participants in these series. "Omnibus" has been the
chief offender. It was always conscious of its high cultural duties and
oh, so anxious to remind the viewer that he was undergoing culture.
"Omnibus" had its relaxed moments—recollections of burlesque with
some amusing lines by S. J. Perelman and entertaining performances
by the veterans of the old burleycue wheel who were still around in

1956, Bert Lahr, Bozo Snyder, and others; Peter Ustinov as Dr. Johnson; an effective dramatization of the effects of capital punishment. But in spite of a great show of relaxation by Alistair Cooke, the program's *conférencier,* "Omnibus" was a show stiff with the significance of its self-appointed task to bring art to the masses. It provided a full curriculum—a few of the classics of the drama; a once-over heavily of the dance by Gene Kelly and, a little less heavily, by Agnes De Mille; a little jurisprudence with Joseph Welch, who proved the power of his television personality if not necessarily the weight of his legal philosophy in the Army-McCarthy hearings; a little night's music—Bach, jazz, opera, musical comedy—with Leonard Bernstein; a little history—say the Renaissance—neatly tied together in spacious generalizations and entertaining pictures, all in one hour and a half. "Wisdom" did rather better with its collection of distinguished elders—Pablo Picasso, Bertrand Russell, Arnold Toynbee, Robert Frost, Carl Sandburg, Frank Lloyd Wright, Herbert Hoover, Igor Stravinsky, Wanda Landowska, Edith Hamilton, Sean O'Casey, Pablo Casals. It filmed them in their native habitat, studio or library or country home, by the Devon seashore, the Vermont hills, the New York towers. The interviewers were generally knowing. But their reverent hush in the presence of greatness sometimes reached the point of lugubriousness, as if they were calling at the bier of an ancient just about to settle himself comfortably for eternity.

Less self-consciousness attends the funeral games of politics, those sessions in which reporters pick over a tired Senator, an ebullient Cabinet member, a one-week headline wonder. Members of the panels of such programs as "Meet the Press" and "Face the Nation" must act the parts of prosecuting attorneys, learned commentators, masters of ceremonies, and comedians all at once. They must keep one eye carefully cocked on the Congressman or Cabinet member or one-week wonder, and another at least as shrewdly directed at the camera. Occasionally a miracle of coordination occurs: a serious exchange of views is effected, an intelligent question gets not only a sharp but an honest answer, and the camera, far from being forgotten, is all caught up in the exciting art of photographing vigorous minds at work.

The camera is the key. Surrogate for the audience, it moves sluggishly or with alertness, cuts beneath surfaces or settles for conventional frames that simply meet each subject flatly, head on. When the camera pries relentlessly, looking for a hand, a piece of clothing, a tapping foot, anything that may reveal a little more of the person being filmed, then it establishes the strength of television, the special warmth of television, the unique skills of television. The prying need not be an invasion of privacy; it is enough if it catches a small suggestion of personality that the still photograph or the microphone or the verbal description cannot by itself communicate. The man in motion, audible, seen close up and somehow found at ease—that is the revelation television promises, and occasionally delivers. It is what some interviewers are able to produce. Dave Garroway did it often enough in his morning show, "Today," and again in "Wide Wide World." Edward R. Murrow did it with some of his subjects in "Person to Person." Howard K. Smith was capable of it with the least likely of people, a cigar-smoking Southern legislator, for example, and as a result he sometimes brought the man out from behind the political clichés. Whatever else may have been his limitations as a nightly performer, Jack Paar was often able to pull a moderately bumbling show-business personality up to his desk and by a not quite contrived mixture of fatuities and near insults produce a suddenly masterful wit where the only mastery before had been of banalities. Mike Wallace, with only the slightest change of stance, could move from a toneless boy singer to Tennessee Williams and elicit something of value from the conversation, not merely gossip, occasionally offering a real clue to the person. The insistence of such interviewers on their own marks of personality is, under the circumstances, forgivable. We can put up with Garroway's oversize spectacles, Murrow's slit-eyed flattened stare behind smoke rings, Wallace's imitation of Murrow, Smith's schoolboy folding of the hands, Paar's constant reiteration of his own importance by a kind of Uriah Heeping of the coals of humility on his head. These are trademarks. They identify a product. They produce a rating. They also add a useful atmosphere to a program, just enough theater to remind viewers that none of this should be taken altogether seriously: it is still a game intended to amuse; it remains show business. By comparison the marathon "Open End" sessions of David Susskind, who sometimes takes himself and his large and not always quite apposite vocabulary much too seriously, are just plain dull, and the eager efforts of Johnny Carson and Steve Allen and their imitators and competitors to get into almost everybody's act, seem gauche.

Television is, of course, a form of show business. When it was playing everything by ear, in the golden days of its childhood, it turned by instinct to vaudevillians, gave Milton Berle and Ed Wynn the run of the camera and let them and others bring into the studio the broadest stooges, the crudest shills, all the little fellows who in older days, before the talking film, used to fill up space between the opening trapeze turn and the big act at the end. Competing with Uncle Miltie, Bishop Sheen won his audience with devices not so far removed from vaudeville, with an angel acting as his invisible stooge and a reading from Shakespeare, when necessary, to bring his act to a throbbing finish. One tires after a while of the obvious patterns of such performers, especially when they keep turning up week after week. But one does not as a consequence reject comedy or comedians or give up show business as a debased form of art. One turns to other comedians—however infrequent they may be—or to variety shows that promise to relieve the monotony with a constant change of acts. But the change is not constant. Every time a new comedian is discovered on one of the variety shows, he turns up quickly on all the others, and inevitably repeats his routines until he runs out of them or achieves conversational status on the late-night programs. In that last eminence, he can break up his routines into fragments and splice them together with dialogue, variously hip or naïve, sensible or inane, apposite to something or packed with nonsequiturs.

Comedy has not made a singificant contribution to television, nor has television been wise in its use of comedians. A very few venerable clowns, schooled in vaudeville and radio, have managed to survive as once-a-week performers, as much because their ancient images have long pleased their audiences as because of any genuine week-to-week freshness. Jack Benny's characterization suffered no change in the transition from radio to television; his Zasu Pitts-like gestures and his tightness of lip were so obviously right for the role of the epicene miser his writers have worked on for so long that few listeners felt any let-down. Red Skelton had an enormous repertory of vaudeville routines to buoy him up and a contagious good humor that triumphed over poor lines, missed lines, and feeble supporting dancers and singers. Jackie Gleason managed well both as a situation comic and as a vaudevillian and came closer than any of the regular performers in the medium to making the gestures and grimaces, the postures and prattfalls and elaborate costuming of vaudeville fit the small screen.

But these men are rare exceptions to the television rule. For it is with comedy as it is with drama in this medium: only a situation series with stock characters can last week after week and season after season. To that rule, Lucille Ball, Danny Thomas, Dick Van Dyke, Phil Silvers, Joey Bishop, Andy Griffith and countless others have sacrificed themselves—if "sacrificed" is the word. They have lost most of their individuality as comedians, but they have gained enormous profits, and there is no immediate end in sight. Even if the weekly show palls sufficiently to make millions turn their dials elsewhere, there remain the endless re-runs in the morning and the afternoon, in which old weekly shows become daily programs and new generations can become conditioned to canned laughter and the kind of corn that deserves no better response.

There have been some moments in television comedy that rose above the level of shrewd investment-banking, almost all of them single appearances. Victor Borge and Danny Kaye were exactly the same in their first TV programs as they were on the revue stage; Kaye made the mistake of turning to a weekly series, and as is almost invariably true, his performances lost their freshness and he came to depend upon the same guests who turn up on all the other variety shows. There was something like adult satire in the sketches of Nichols and May, Shelley Berman, and the first few programs of the American version of the BBC varsity show, "That Was the Week that Was." Jonathan Winters brought his appealing Babe Ruth-like face, his larynxful of sound effects, and a sometimes mordant wit to an early high boil in television in a fifteen-minute weekly program. Television gave a fair share of its time to Negro comedians and let them bring to program after program the full weight and the full wit of their disillusionment with white America. But even the considerable grace of Dick Gregory's and Nipsy Russell's and Godfrey Cambridge's humor about racial tensions began to pall after too much exposure; Russell was lucky to have his skill as a dancer to sustain him after the jokes began to lose some of their appeal. The jokes may change, but the styles of delivery and the faces and the figures remain the same, and even the most generously gifted of comedians must, on constant exposure, begin to seem hackneyed, as Sid Caesar and Imogene Coca discovered after filling several television seasons with wit and charm of a very high order. No single writer, even one with the gifts of a Molière or a Congreve, can supply the same comedian with material good enough to hold audiences for years and years, nor can a whole team of writers, as Bob Hope finally seemed by the mid-sixties to have discovered. Nor, as television has now long proved, can extravagant production numbers or a constant round of guests, no matter how famous or high-price, relieve the tedium.

Such an assault on the senses is bound to jade. It does not matter whether the quality is first- or second-rate. It is entirely too much for undiscriminating masses whose only serious critical judgment is the one exercised when a choice must be made among comedians or variety shows or situation comedies competing for their attention at the same time. Finally, overwhelmed by the sheer quantity of the stuff, the whole television audience turns, as one, to a new kind of program, the Western, or the private detective saga, or the crime show with a setting in the 1920's, or the doctor-and-hospital saga. And, once again, the audience is saturated—"Gunsmoke," "Wyatt Earp," "Maverick," "Wagon Train," "Bonanza," "Rawhide," "Have Gun, Will Travel," to name just those Westerns that have occasionally shown professional skill; "Dragnet," "The Untouchables," "Peter Gunn," "Perry Mason," "77 Sunset Strip," to name just those crime and detective stories that have revealed a Hollywood glitter, if nothing much else; "Dr. Kildare," "Ben Casey," "The Nurses," "Breaking Point," and "Eleventh Hour," to name a group of highly professional, highly exaggerated, and often highly irritating shows. This is saturation of a more deadly kind than comedians and singers and sentimental family tales. This is a drenching in violence and misery and psychopathy which nothing in radio could possibly match and only nightly visits to the motion pictures could come close to equaling. Here it is all exhibited to the eye, in copious detail, night after night, hour after hour. The child or the adult who lives suspended between Prohibition-era gang fights, contests between top guns in the old West, medicine at its bloodiest, and psychiatry at its most melodramatic cannot return quickly or easily to school or business or family life. Ordinary events must pall by comparison. The rather simpleminded devotee of the ritual of the gun or of the couch can either slip into a world of fantasy, shutting out the apathy of ordinary existence with loud and colorful dreams, or make over the tedium of his life into a shattering drama with the aid of real firearms and real fights and, if necessary, real killings.

Nobody will ever know with certainty what the precise relation is between television violence and the growth of juvenile deliquency. A parallel can be shown. As the number of hours devoted to violence and misery has increased so has the number of juvenile crimes and of arrests of youngsters. Mere coincidence? A response on the part both of television and of young people to the spirit of the times? Does it really matter? Isn't it enough that television standards, never very high, have slipped to the point where any film of the early thirties shown at any time between 11:00 P.M. and 6:00 A.M., offers a bright moment, simply as a historical record, and that the freshest, most entertaining faces and voices belong to cartoon characters?

The heavy reliance on the serial drama is a fair indication of television's retreat from its own reality. Like the little boy wrapped up in dreams of gunplay, television cannot or will not face the facts of its own life (except, of course, the financial ones). The industry recognizes, with a certain nostalgia, that it achieved at least a small distinction in the fifties with the dramas of Paddy Chayefsky, Reginald Rose, Rod Serling, Robert Alan Aurthur, William Gibson, Gore Vidal, and James Costigan. It prides itself, when it works out its chronology of distinguished moments, on Toscanini's ten telecasts, on its coverage of presidential inaugurations and the coronation of a queen and pivotal sessions of the United Nations. NBC cites its introduction of "Kukla, Fran and Ollie" as one of a handful of events in 1949 of signal importance in its history. CBS lists among its special accomplishments all the programs that political and economic crises bred—the Hungarian revolution, the Suez conflict, a whole sequence of Algerian outbreaks, civil defense, sputnik, muttnik and all the ascents of missiles and men from Cape Kennedy. In 1958, Frank Stanton, speaking to a conference of CBS television affiliates on "The Dangers of Opportunity Denied," summed up television's "primary responsibility":

It is nothing short of providential that television has had a decade of constant growth to bring us to a position where we have a real chance of meeting that responsibility. It will be nothing short of tragic if, through our own fault we muff it or through the faults of others, we are kept from meeting it. In the simplest way that I can put it to you, that responsibility is to use television as fully and as effectively as we know how to help take up the slack that is characteristic of democracies between the time of a need for action and the time of action itself. In the age of ICBM, only by taking up that slack can a democracy match a dictatorship without imitating it.[3]

The urgency is compelling: "we do not have the luxury of time." What must television do? The CBS president is clear about that:

Our first and vital job is to speed up and improve the dissemination of the information that is the primary step in the decision-making process; for if there is a failure at that step, the whole democratic scheme will have failed. And these new demands for speed, for reaching all the people simultaneously, for immediacy, are put squarely up to us in television.

And how have the networks met the demands? Well, in 1958 Frank Stanton boasted that CBS News had "more than 600 correspondents, located in 263 cities around the world. . . . the Washington Bureau alone has a staff of 63. . . ."

The rhetoric and the figures are impressive; the performance is not. For all its wealth of correspondents and fullness of staff, CBS offers news programs that are not notably richer or more searching than the programs compiled from the wire services and a thin collection of publicity photos by the small independent radio stations. More important, apart from crisis coverage, the networks offer so little news, and news covered so superficially, that one is better off waiting for a weekly newsmagazine or the compendia published in the Sunday editions of the larger newspapers. Even the tabloids offer more facts.

The other boasts have about equal merit. "Kukla, Fran and Ollie" started in Chicago in 1947, went to the NBC network in 1949, lasted there until June, 1954, moved to ABC for three years, and departed from television at the end of August, 1957, to return only for five-minute spots in 1961. Toscanini did half a dozen programs before the cameras in the 1948–season and four more two seasons later. There are few regular telecasts of symphony orchestras, and except for an occasional culture session with Leonard Bernstein and his band (the New York Philharmonic), none on the networks. Concert artists turn up only on the "Bell Telephone Hour" and a few specials, and when they do they are usually restricted to the mushy flow of that terrible music that is identified with Muzak—the worst of opera, the least of operettas, music to gum milk toast by—or to bravura exhibitions of the kind that violinists and pianists relegate to the end of a recital.[4]

To get regular news of the United Nations, one has to wait for an early-morning program on Sundays or turn to educational television stations. For educational television, one has to turn to the nonprofit outlets, in Boston, in Minneapolis, Pittsburgh, Chicago, New York, and a few university campuses around the country. What sort of educational television is it that offers academic discussions at 6:30 A.M., as CBS did with its "Sunrise Semesters," or offers a series of weekly programs crudely planned, flatly directed, and poorly filmed, and which do not show up in the same time spot for very long, such as NBC once provided on Saturday afternoons? One can argue the merits of teaching by television. One can question the whole concept of educational television. But it is beyond argument that commercial television stations, whether linked together in a network or individually, have shown themselves either indifferent to educational responsibilities or incapable of discharging them.

It is not really the proper function of television to educate. Its executives do not have the equipment to run a university themselves, nor, one would gather from their performance thus far, do they have either the respect for those who are qualified to do so or the humility to allow others to run it for them. Education might well be left in the hands of educators, who have enough trouble running their own institutions without trying to take over any part of television. Television would make a far more useful and lasting contribution if it were to take up again the art of the camera, to return to the procedures it once established as its own and to attempt new and bolder uses of film and sound.

No dramas for the ages were uncovered in television's Golden Age, but several techniques of considerable reach and depth were polished in the years of the playhouses. Paddy Chayefsky demonstrated a fine ear for Bronx dialogue, a kind of late echo of Clifford Odets, in *Marty* and *Middle of the Night*. Rod Serling wrote the familiar exposure of big business in *Patterns,* but wrote it tightly, to fit comfortably within the clumsy conventions of an hour of fragments —so many commercials, so many scenes (pretentiously called "acts"), so many station breaks, with opening and closing "billboards" and a fair variety of spots so brief that they almost could be called subliminal. William Gibson selected episodes brilliantly for his dramatization (on "Playhouse 90") of the early years of Annie Sullivan's tutelage of Helen Keller, selected so well and written so economically that when his script was blown up to the proportions of a full-length drama for Broadway (*The Miracle Worker*), it seemed extravagant, melodramatic, and lengthened beyond the needs of the material. Television drama was—and is—at its best when it reduces ornament to a minimum, strives for understatement and irony, and depends at least as much on the camera as on the word. Hence the taut power of Reginald Rose's *Twelve Angry Men,* which translated well into motion-picture idiom, but required in the move some softening at the edges, some unnecessary underscoring of character and belief. Rose showed again that he had control of the medium in his quiet two-part study of a celebrated example of injustice in the courts, *The Sacco-Vanzetti Story.* Anger came slowly through a scrupulous examination of the documents, through precise reenactments of sessions at the 1921 trial, and through the simplest kind of dramatic irony which awarded all the hysteria to those who condemned the shoemaker and the fish peddler, those who were in fact hysterical, and saved the soft articulation of a passion for justice and truth for the two accused, who were in fact soft and articulate and passionate. A similar understanding of the inner resources of the small screen gave eloquence to Robert Alan Aurthur's *Requiem for a Heavyweight* and *A Man Ten Feet Tall.* "The Defenders," Reginald Rose's frame for a series of courtroom dramas built around a sensitive and compassionate pair of lawyers, father and son, continued week after week to present the case for righteous indignation and merciful justice, and to do so with occasional bursts of eloquence and even a show of characterization now and then. But because each week's play had to be tailored to fit a serial-drama pattern, there was little room for the imagination, the structure was all too predictable, convention too often replaced invention.

This sort of modest achievement will always be possible in television, no matter what any year's trend or fashion may be. There will not often be room for drama apart from that associated with fixed characters, but we may from time to time get a series like the Armstrong Circle Theater, which occasionally used to cram into an hour something like a full-length portrait of a man of great stature, such as the Burma surgeon, Dr. Gordon Seagrave, or the Nobel Peace Prize winner, Father Dominique Pire. Such a magnetic figure as the late Dr. Thomas Dooley will always find support and sponsorship for a program such as the one he did shortly before he died, on his experiences as a cancer patient. We can always be sure of lavishly produced intensifications of crisis—Cuba, Mississippi, Viet Nam— sudden eruptions in television the same day or night as the crisis or

just a day or so later. Inaugurations, coronations, World Series baseball and bowl-game football, Olympics, political conventions, state
funerals, even assassinations. Television missed the killing of President Kennedy, but it was right there when Ruby shot Oswald. It was
also present for every tasteful and significant and touching moment of
the rest of that searing weekend. It *was,* in fact, the whole weekend;
in television's detailed and disciplined and thoughtful coverage of the
events following the assassination, America found something like
assuagement for its grief and shock. This sort of thing we have in
television, and very well done, too. This, at least, we have, and this
apparently we shall always have.

We are apparently also bound to have the classics, television
style. That means Maurice Evans' version of Shakespeare, productions of *Hamlet* and *Macbeth* and *Richard II* that were thin enough
on the stage but that reduced to the small dimensions of the television
screen are almost entirely devoid of insights. It means slightly more
acceptable Shaw: Evans has some communicable feeling for the
causes Shaw supported and the comedy with which he decorated
them in the early years of this century. It means Broadway drama of
the second and third order of merit: *The Petrified Forest, The Good
Fairy, There Shall Be No Night, The Corn Is Green, The Barretts of
Wimpole Street, Ah, Wilderness, Dial M for Murder, State of the
Union.* It means an occasionally well-conceived, effectively cast performance, such as *The Green Pastures* or the *Time Remembered* of
1960 or the *Hedda Gabler* of 1963. But more frequently the "classics" mean those extraordinary abridgments of nineteenth-century
novels in which David Susskind's Talent Associates specialized.
Dumas, Dickens, and the Brontës, ancient poaching ground for
second-rate movies, are now wide open for third-rate television programs. The acting is generally inadequate, sometimes execrable; nobody seems much at home in the costumes, and unfortunately for the
actors, every nervous wriggle—the slightest twitch of irritation, the
most minute manifestation of discomfort—is revealed in the merciless close-quarters examination of the television camera, whether the
instrument is in the hands of an artist or of a clod. The final effect is
rather like a grade-school pageant, with some of the wrinkles in the
costumes pressed out but with none of the great smiles of joy with
which youngsters greet their every action as George Washington or
Abraham Lincoln or Betsy Ross.

Resorting to modern novels is no particular advantage to producers of this kind, especially when the novels are such pastiches of
style and language and characterization as *For Whom the Bell
Tolls,* with dialogue that is embarrassing to read and absolutely impossible to say, and the cast that is meant to portray Spaniards speaks with
accents and moves with gestures learned at the Actors Studio, which
is on Manhattan's West Side, a location one never fails to grasp in
any of the performances of its alumni. Laurence Olivier as Somerset
Maugham's conception of Paul Gauguin in *The Moon and Sixpence*
developed as convincing a case of leprosy as ever a makeup artist
conceived and every once in a while seemed to reach beyond the
superficial understanding of the painter with which the novelist had
burdened him. The collapse of *The Bridge of San Luis Rey* was not
entirely the one engineered by Thornton Wilder; it fell to pieces in the
hands of Judith Anderson, Viveca Lindfors, and Rita Gam as the
leading women, actresses whose styles could not and would not mix.

If novels do not work, and most television adaptations of plays are
inept, then certainly miniature versions of Hollywood films are not
likely to be satisfactory. Not persuaded by the logic of the case, the
"Twentieth Century–Fox Hour" and the "Lux Video Theater"
offered empirical proof of the foolishness of this procedure in several
seasons in the mid-fifties. It was one more set of demonstrations that
television, like any other popular art, would feed itself endlessly on
other arts, popular and private, and inevitably give itself indigestion
that way. It was also, along with the badly managed novels and plays,
a further demonstration of the cheapening effect of this kind of distillation for mass audiences. Certainly the process never achieves
essences. The relentless cutting away of what from the point of view
of an adapter or producer of an hour-long program must seem like
extraneous material only results in the barest outlines. The narrative
is clearly visible—in silhouette. But there is no development of character, no meditation on person, place, or event. There is only a kind
of synopsis which forever after millions of viewers will accept as the
substance of the work.

There is nothing sacrosanct about *Wuthering Heights* or *Jane
Eyre* or *The Count of Monte Cristo* or *A Tale of Two Cities.*
Holocausts will not be visited upon those who dare to tamper with
Hemingway or Wilder or even Shakespeare. But whatever vitality
may still remain in the novels or the plays after bad movies and

magazine and comic-book digests has been sapped to the point of exhaustion by television adaptations. Much the most widely watched of all, they not only stamp the original works with an indelible meretriciousness, they lead audiences to expect a similar flashiness, all on the surface and quickly presented, in other "classics." The exasperation of masses of readers with all discursive writing, with any reflection and speculation that may interrupt the forward motion of a narrative, is confirmed. Even the briefest digression in a television drama is not likely in future to be tolerated, unless it adds to the flash or the sentimentality or the obvious humor of the piece. Far more than cuts to satisfy censors, expurgations to meet the lowest level of public taste, or the time limits of a program, or to leave room for commerials, are offenses against the integrity of a work of art.

As long as American television is dominated by commercial sponsors and their bawds and body servants, expurgation is bound to be the main business of the medium. Minority tastes will continue to be suppressed. Quality will remain a euphemism to describe the unpalatable stuff that must from time to time be aired—as far from prime time as the twenty-four-hour day will permit. And such sense of responsibility as may remain with government administrations or educational foundations will be discharged in the awarding of channels—preferably the least accessible channels, on ultrahigh frequency waves—to educational stations. These stations sometimes do their job with distinction—whatever their job may be. They teach courses, not as well as they can be taught in the classroom, and perhaps not as economically, but they do reach thousands of people at a time. They not only offer folk singers, they tell their viewers something about the songs. They present discussions no duller than the Sunday discussions on the networks. They present the drama, if that is not too large a name for the amateur performances that move off the campus onto the camera. And because they are so unmistakably amateurish, even at their best, they generally increase the taste of their viewers for the sleek facility of the networks.

European television works entirely differently. It makes large concessions to mass tastes, but it seems to recognize them as concessions. Quality is not resented but served in British and French, German, Italian, Swiss, Swedish, Polish, Czech, Belgian, and Russian television. The Western countries buy a lot of trash from the United States, and even produce their own trash. But they also, like some of the Iron Curtain countries, encourage producers to put on variety programs and musicals in which style is given a specifically photographic dimension and the size of the screen is accepted as a positive element. All sorts of camera effects and studio sets are used, rarely very expensive, but with a pleasing mixture of Mondrian lines, Surrealist maskings and distortions, and every sort of graphic manipulation of the textures and tones of abstract art.

In the drama, too, European television continues to be adventurous, to be experimental and open, week after week, to quantities of new writers. And this it does within the limits of one or two channels, which are on the air for only a few hours a day, generally from about five in the afternoon until eleven or twelve at night, with a longer day on Sundays and an occasional Saturday-night program that crosses the dateline. The most consistent of the European networks, BBC, has risen from the creaky security which had won it the well-earned name of "Auntie," to thrust aside almost all censorship, to allow writers every reasonable freedom in the situations and the people and the language they present. The result has been a great loosening of the drama, a real grasp of camera and microphone techniques and of the small television image.

Discussion programs of various kinds turn up on the Eruopean channels. Many are as tedious as their American equivalents. Those that are alive usually are so because a man of intellectual vitality has been given time and freedom to use that time as he wishes.

One of the best things about British television is its irregularity. It suffers very few programs for a whole year, even its most popular. Programs turn up for one or two series a year, and that is all. A one-shot is not necessarily a "special" or a "spectacular"; it may simply be a telecast of the Warsaw Philharmonic from a cultural center on the edges of London, or a half-hour performance of a chamber work by a Soviet string quartet, without anything but a quick title for introduction and another for ending, and no talk of any kind, not even an announcement for those whose sight has atrophied after years of having the words read aloud for them by booming announcers—and this last on the commercial channel!

Commerce is understood differently in British television. The Independent Television Authority has not been licensed to besiege its viewers with hard sell, soft sell, or any other kind of persuasion, hidden or open. It must win sponsors and its sponsors obviously must win sales, but the only opportunity the dozen producers for ITA and their sponsors have to get at audiences is in short sequences of spot announcements, rarely more than a minute long, and never run more often than at fifteen-minute intervals, and in dramatic or musical programs or vigorous discussions, in which communication would be interrupted or taste affronted by spots before the viewers' eyes, they are postponed until the natural break. One way of gathering just how unnatural American TV breaks are is to see any American program (except, perhaps, a Presidental press conference) on BBC. The precipices come and go at a terrifying rate, but the program moves on, simply skipping over the commercials and allowing one to laugh away the foolishness of the contrived suspense every eight or ten or twelve minutes.

Apart from the British, the best television I have seen in Europe is the Polish. It does not have the gusto of Italian quiz games or the flair for educational programs which the Italians also have, a skill that has actually brought literacy to hundreds of illiterates in the south of Italy. It offered no singing as good as I heard over German television and no variety as good as I saw in Sweden and in France and Belgium. But the use of film techniques on Polish TV is at times as good as in the movies of Roman Polanski and Andrzej Wajda; the film has been studied by television producers in Warsaw with as much care as it has by the critics who have turned directors in the French cinema; the best book on the subject is Polish, a small, well-illustrated encyclopedia by Lech Pijanowski called *Films in Television,* published in 1962. Propaganda has little to do with the choice of dramas or of music or of art of Polish TV; nationalism is far more noticeable. Chopin remains a favorite subject for any kind of program; while I was in Warsaw, a play built round an episode in the composer's life with George Sand was the principal item on the week's schedule, a splendidly acted play, so well performed, in fact, that the difficulties of the language for one whose approach must be through the back door—that is, through Russian—were easily overcome. And in Denmark, I saw a Polish TV film which used every silent-film technique to make broad propaganda overtures to the general subject of democracy across races and classes and did so with such skill in pantomime and music that the clichés and banalities of the Marxist esthetic seemed insignificant and inoffensive.

Russian television, like so much in Russian art, is heavy. Its political programs lumber across the screen on slogans that move as clumsily as the wooden swan in *Lohengrin*. Its news announcers, male and female, have an urbanity not unlike BBC's extraordinarily voluble Richard Dimbleby, and, like him, they are not fazed by a film that slips in backward or the wrong news clip or a guest who stumbles over his lines or forgets altogether what he is in the studio to do. But unlike Dimbleby, they have no fresh comments of their own to add to their dull copy, and the films, whether they go in straight or upside down, are hopelessly dull. It is in other areas that Russian TV comes alive. Its most popular program, "Blue Light," should be its most popular program. It is a weekly show, of an hour to an hour and a half or more. The format is a night club, with guests gathered at tables on the club floor. From the tables, in the course of the program, come singers to sing, dancers to dance, and tumblers to tumble, but also actors to speak great lines from Pushkin or Gogol or Lermontov, scientists to talk about their work, poets to read their poems.

The Russians invariably turn to singing and dancing when they have a special event to celebrate. When an international women's congress was convened to coincide with the space flights of Bykovsky and Tereshkova, the first female cosmonaut, the Palace of Congresses in the Kremlin, one of Moscow's few really modern buildings, was thrown open to dancers from all over the Soviet Union—Ukrainians, Georgians, ballet dancers from the small and the great companies, and singers of all sorts. And inevitably it was televised—hours and hours and hours of it. It was too long. It sagged in dozens of places. But it also leaped with the folk dancers, pirouetted with the ballerinas, and settled down deep into the voices of the basso profundos. The dancers were not photographed from under the crotch or over the topknot as they are so often in the West by frustrated cameramen led by ambitious directors. That would be as dubious a procedure in Russian television as concentrating on Khrushchev's warts or shiny red nose. The dance was preserved in all its aspects. One could forget that one was looking at a TV presentation of a Georgian sword dance or adagio from *Swan Lake*. And almost equally well, we were shown the singers, whose pulchritude was quite forgotten by the cameramen in favor of their voices—but then that may have been because they had no pulchritude.

Children's programs in Russia are also presented with very little fuss of any kind. A tale is told, a cartoon run, a technique of model-ing explained. There are not many such programs; Russian television is not on the air any longer than other European TV. But as in all the Iron Curtain countries and in Germany, children's programs are taken very seriously. Budgets may be small, but the care is great. That is why when English networks assemble their programs for children—usually two a day—they use so many Czech, Polish, Hungarian, Russian, and German films, along with an engaging series from Australia about a group of boys called "The Terrible Ten," a couple of French adventure serials, some simple vaudeville acts, a very few of their own productions, and a few imports from America.

No contrast with American television is more striking or more unfavorable to our performance than that in this area. Our children are sated with cartoons. Hour after hour, day after day, they are barraged with the sadistic maneuvers of Felix the Cat and his pro-fessorial nemesis; with Bugs Bunny, no mean tyrant himself; with Heckle and Jibe and all the other slapbangboom horrors which make one regret the technique of animating drawings was ever discovered. The same cartoons turn up again and again. How could they help it when the consumption is at such a fearful rate? And the alternative shows do not rise far above the insanity fare of the cartoons: a few low budget Westerns, no more inventive than their nighttime proto-types, just more inept; a couple of circus shows that could conceiva-bly bring wit and variety to the medium if they were not required to fill time every Saturday morning in the year; and just occasionally, as a kind of lapse into forgetfulness, an animal film or two to remind us of what American television once promised to bring its children. It is possible that Shari Lewis, a ventriloquist of skill, would be more welcome, nasal New York accent and all, if she had not been a daily visitation for so long and then a weekly one for almost as long again. Mr. Wizard's science program would not have become a bore if it had not been so familiar. Captain Kangaroo, mistaken by some as a boon to children, did once provide fresh, if not exemplary, fodder for kids. But the fodder is well chewed by now. For more times than agitated parents can count, the same books have been digested, the same songs sung, and the same inane waltz conducted around the same silly set by the same limp characters—Mr. Greenjeans, Dancing Bear, and the porcine Captain. To add subornation to the other crimes, the heavily sponsored program now makes the same appeal that the other shows do to the children to demand this or that brand of shredded steel or puffed iron or tin crispies or sweetened ester of cherrylemongrape.

Television is a child's art. It is at its best when it displays the wonder of a child at the smallness of an inchworm or the largeness of a giraffe, at the miracle of a parrot's speech or a goose's, at the grandeur of a lion or at the madness of a panda. One of the most distinguished of its interview programs in its early years was "Zoo Parade," in which Marlin Perkins exchanged ideas with animals at the Lincoln Park Zoo in Chicago. When television cameras gawk at a parade or stare open-lensed at a skier or a skater or a diver or a swimmer, it is a joy to have television around. When American crooners sing in the streets of a European city, trying to stir up interest in their own faltering voices by the quality of their backgrounds, one forgives the dodge and delights in the streets, the rivers, the buildings, the people, as the cameras move restlessly up and down London, Paris, Lisbon, Salzburg, Copenhagen. It is only when the performers suddenly become aware of adult responsibilities, political responsibilities, sociological responsibilities, philosophical responsibilities, as Jack Paar did in Berlin, that one loses patience and respect as well.

Television has the intellectual development of a child, but it insists too much of the time on acting like the adult it may one day be, but has not yet become. Thus its everlasting pretensions to educate, to bring art and culture and political wisdom to the Kallikaks and the Jukes, who, if they are as dumb as television seems to think they are, probably will never get art and culture and political wisdom anyway. Thus its constant crisis psychology, turning every political and economic event into an occasion for shattered nerves, so that when a true crisis occurs, viewers are incapable of distinguishing between it and a false alarm.

Perhaps one day in an effort to face itself as it really is, not as its pretentious fantasies make it think it should be, television will go out into the woods and up into the sky and down into the ocean and across the streets and avenues to see the world as it really is, as uniquely among the popular arts its equipment permits it to do. Perhaps it will sometime return to the aerialists and tumblers, the cyclists and prestidigitators. Perhaps it will look long and happily at the inflated cheeks of the tuba player in the symphony orchestra, at the pursed lips of the flute player, at the furrowed brow of the triangle player or tympanist waiting for his cue—look and listen, not explain. Maybe after all these years of flirting with color—since 1946, to be precise—the television industry will produce color sets at reasonable prices and bring into our homes paintings, birds, flowers, all the things and beings that have color and should be seen in color—just bring them, not explain them. It may even be that television will be willing to admit that it finds itself enchanted with the simple wit and wonderful wild faces of old vaudevillians and will do everything possible to keep them alive on the screen and to encourage others to follow in their improbable footsteps. In the meantime, we will have to be content with the handsome photography and funny faces of the better commercials, such as the antic physiognomy of that strangely intense man who a few years ago shifted to a mentholated cigarette, and we will celebrate as emancipated and imaginative those who a few years ago began giving prizes to such commercials at foreign film festivals.

CRITICISM AND CENSORSHIP

WE ARE a people obsessed with judgment, judgment of ourselves and of others. In this we are not unlike our contemporaries. The French and the English have hardly contained their impulse to examine and criticize. The Germans and the Italians, though always of course with an eye for the deeper philosophical issues involved, have been earnest weighers and balancers, too. But no people has so strenuously employed its energies in the profession of criticism as the Americans. There is not a genre of criticism that has not had its representatives in the States; not a school, not a movement without American roots or cuttings or graftings. The Marxist, the Mythical, the Archetypal; the historians of Literary Theory, the makers of Literary Theory, the writers of Literary History; the Rhetoricians, the Logicians, the old critics who are still called the New Critics; the defenders of Allegory, the offenders against it, and those who are offended by it—all are well spoken for, plentifully spoken for; the magazines and the review supplements and the learned journals are full of them. But more important, for all the waste motion and the mere display of academic heat and energy, there can be found among the critics men of sufficient wit and skill to keep one intensely interested and indeed some of the time to persuade one, however foolishly, that the work or artist being criticized is somehow less important than the critic. For a great deal of the time in the United States, the critical occasion is more important than the occasion which produces a work of art.

The reason for all this concentration on critical writing is not difficult to find if one examines the growth and development of the forms of criticism. What starts as a genteel exercise, somewhere between reviewing and an autobiographical memoir, ends as a species of sociological, psychological, or linguistic analysis. Criticism has become the nonspecialist's brand of philosophy. From it he has been able to gather a political position, a taste for psychoanalysis, a quick introduction to positivistic philosophical disciplines masquerading as textual criticism. He has found, if he has wanted it, a religion, and not necessarily a religion of art, for in several of the more articulate defenders of the critical faith he has bumped up against a more traditional apologetics as well. And at their best, literary criticism and some very specialized writing about the visual arts and music have offered the selective, the private reader a generous introduction to the meditative mind at its discursive best.

There is no better example of criticism as meditation than the celebrated essay of Henry James on *The Art of Criticism,* written in 1884 as an answer to the popularist position adopted by Walter Besant in a lecture on the same subject. For James, in spite of his amiable chiding of himself in *The Sacred Fount* for quite "fatally" lacking a sense of tone, had in fact just that sense beyond all other things, and it is his tone that, directly or indirectly, American practice has followed. It has been a tone faintly or firmly polemical, alive with personal experience and definitions that grow out of that experience, and inevitably instructive. The deities of criticism are all tutelary. Viz and to wit from James:

[Mr. Besant] seems to me to mistake in attempting to say so definitely beforehand what sort of an affair a good novel will be.

A novel is in its broadest definition a personal, a direct impression of life: that, to begin with, constitutes its value, which is greater or less according to the intensity of the impression.

Humanity is immense, and reality has a myriad forms; the most one can affirm is that some of the flowers of fiction have the odour of it, and others have not; as for telling you in advance how your nosegay should be composed, that is another affair.

There are bad novels and good novels, as there are bad pictures and good pictures; but that is the only distinction in which I see any meaning, and I can as little imagine speaking of a novel of character as I can imagine speaking of a picture of character.

Catching the very note and trick, the strange irregular rhythm of life, that is the attempt whose strenuous force keeps Fiction upon her feet.

Nothing, of course, will ever take the place of the good old fashion of "liking" a work of art or not liking it: the most improved criticism will not abolish that primitive, that ultimate test.

There is one point at which the moral sense and the artistic sense lie very near together; that is in the light of the very obvious truth that the deepest quality of a work of art will always be the quality of the mind of the producer. . . . No good novel will ever proceed from a superficial mind; that seems to me an axiom which, for the artist in fiction, will cover all needful moral ground: if the youthful aspirant take it to heart it will illuminate for him many of the mysteries of purpose.

The last quotation comes very close to the strengths and the weaknesses of critics and critical movements in the last four decades, the years in which criticism in America has left far behind its genteel tradition and become an art of considerable strength and grace. "Criticism, at bottom, is indistinguishable from skepticism," H. L. Mencken was writing more than forty years ago. "A critic who believes in anything absolutely is bound to that something quite as helplessly as a Christian is bound to the Freudian garbage in the Book of Revelation. To that extent, at all events, he is unfree and unintelligent, and hence a bad critic." [1] Leaving aside Mencken's theology and psychology, the substance of his point remains. A critic tied to a creed or a method in his criticism is helpless much of the time. He or his beliefs will be upset by any strong enough mutation from the procedures on which his beliefs have been structured. He will be more a reformer than a critic, working on the "false assumption," as Mencken calls it, "that immutable truths exist in the arts, and that the artist will be improved by being made aware of them." It is a notion Mencken finds absurd, "as much so, indeed, as its brother delusion that the critic, to be competent, must be a practitioner of the specific art he ventures to deal with, i.e., that a doctor, to cure a belly-ache, must have a belly-ache."

The creedal methods and movements in criticism have demonstrated again and again how true these anticreedal statements of Mencken are. Those bent on reform have either collapsed or had to be reformed themselves. It is not movements or schools or methods that have lasted in American criticism, but men. The Marxists have gone from the scene as a serious body of critics and scholars, but those talented men who trained with them, however briefly, have remained—Meyer Schapiro, Lionel Trilling, Edmund Wilson. Nothing much remains today of the concentrated assault on Philistinism of Mencken and George Jean Nathan and their less talented associates of *The Smart Set* and the *American Mercury,* which too often became a kind of caricature of *l'art pour l'art* in which astringency became an end in itself, and the pleasure of the game of *épater le bourgeois* (the "booboisie," Mencken called the class) soon obscured its purpose.

But Mencken left some notable examples of slanging and Nathan helped open the theater to serious inspection as an art in a full shelf of volumes from among which a dozen or more critical essays continue to hold interest. Mythists—Archetypalists—New Critics—they must all go the same way if a code of true belief or a method of methods instructs their every critical writing. Even the supporters of patently more enduring and more endurable positions, say the Freudians or the Eliotic Christians, must sooner or later find themselves dated, *passés* or *déclassés,* curios more important to Ph.D. candidates specializing in their brief moment in literary history than to living breathing human beings. But though the movement goes, more than just a man or two remains.

The perceptions of the Marxists about the nature of society are vital to our understanding of our own world, at least as vital in this larger context as they were when applied to Matthew Arnold and his world or to the development of Marxist ideas from the founding fathers to the Russian Revolution or to the shaping forces of Cubist painting. We may no longer go careering through literature or art looking for those saints of the Marxist pantheon who were prescient enough to intuit or actually predict and describe the class struggle. We are still concerned to understand that struggle and to make sense of it in any time, any era, past or present, whatever value we set upon it, whatever side we take, whether or not we take sides. And so with the greatest concentration on the *Text an sich* of the New Criticism. Only the most ingenuous of practitioners will really seriously question the value of historical and biographical information, as the New Critics once did; today, that sort of New Critical orthodoxy is only for the worshipful graduate student who cannot abide the thought that any statement of Ransom or Tate, Brooks or Warren or Wimsatt, made at any point in their careers, should be considered as less than oracular. Others will be content to discover the marvels of a masterpiece that concentration on the work itself may reveal, leaving aside only for the moment its epoch, its place in an artist's life or among his other works, and its moral value, if any. And there may be still another group of very private readers who will accept some critical performances of Ransom, Brooks, & Co., and their critical cousins, Kenneth Burke, R. P. Blackmur, Francis Fergusson, and Yvor Winters, as very private writings, splendid pirouettes, imaginative studies that may say almost nothing of any value about the works under review but still make enchanting reading.

We look in our criticism not for a final judgment but for a first-rate mind making judgments or fishing *aperçus* from the critical sea. It may be a poem that occasions it; it may, once or twice, actually be a perception about the poem or, rarest of all, about the poet. Whatever its distance from the occasion of the critical essay, if it is really a perception that the critic has served up to us, that is enough, it will do; it is our substitute for philosophy, and we must feed on it as if our thinking lives depend upon it, for they do.

And so, it may be, James's dictum holds for criticism as for the novel: "The deepest quality of a work of art will always be the quality of the mind of the producer." We can say with him, making the few necessary change of words, "No good criticism will ever proceed from a superficial mind; that seems to me an axiom which, for the artist in criticism, will cover all needful moral ground: if the youthful aspirant take it to heart it will illuminate for him many of the mysteries of purpose." It will certainly obviate, as it should, the apparent foolishness which permits so good a critic as F. R. Leavis to make a tiny little druid's circle of great novels and novelists, leaving out one first-rate performer after another to follow the quaint quarrelsome dictates of *The Great Tradition* as he sees it. What he has to say about George Eliot and Jane Austen is good enough, wise enough, clearly enough the work of a mind in no wise superficial, as in his writing on D. H. Lawrence and Gerard Manley Hopkins, where the men and their works and their times are all illuminated. Such an approach to quality in criticism will make it possible to put up with R. P. Blackmur's determined autobiographical anecdotes, with the temperature in Cambridge (Massachusetts) when he went looking for *The Wings of the Dove* in the public library and then sat himself down to read it—all this and a great deal more about boyhood and many other books by James as an introduction to *The Spoils of Poynton* which is almost useless as an introduction to that novel but which has its own charm and its own enduring values, not, as it purports to be, as a brief conspectus of James's tour of human sensibility, but as a view of Blackmur's way of touring round human sensibility.

The perils of this sort of tour are obvious. It depends so much on the tour leader. If he has the necessary stature, if he has the right sort of quality of mind, we are likely to remember it as a grand tour and to come away with a new vocabulary or an old book clenched firmly to our bosoms; if we are not in fact keenly illuminated, at least we are convinced for the moment that we are. We have moved into a kind of spiritual exercise, one of the higher sort, the equivalent of acquired contemplation. If we go along with Lionel Trilling's analysis of "Art and Neurosis," for example, we find an illuminating gloss of the *Urtext,* that is, Freud himself, with applications to all branches of intellectual activity, and a remarkable peroration on the phrase "We are all ill" which has the richness of a set of well-sung antiphons, whatever it may or may not contribute to our understanding of "the nature and source of art even in our grim, late human present." [2] There is something of the nature of an incantation about the concluding paragraphs of this essay from which it may be difficult to extract ideas. But the structure of the piece is built around an important distinction between Freud's early reduction of the artist to "a neurotic who escapes from reality by means of 'substitute gratifications' " and his late understanding of art and artists as collaborators with psychology in revealing the nature and scope of the unconscious. Style is always the means with Trilling, a musical style, with quotations and footnotes used as appoggiatura decorations and even in the shortest essays apparent in a formal introduction and again in a conclusion that acts like the briefest of recapitulatory codas. But no matter how much he or we may be bemused by the style, it is style in the service of ideas, in defense of the liberal imagination and its exemplary servitors, of whom Freud is the leading example, the one most concerned to alleviate human suffering.

In general, the early adherents of the sociological method stand firmly in their critical tours on the side of criticism as a humanistic discipline. The best of them are much too subtle, and much too scarred by their struggle to establish the class struggle as the central truth of human existence, ever again to be snared by the simplifications of Stalinist politics and its corresponding esthetic or any of the palliatives which have succeeded it in the camp of Socialist realism. The concern for suffering remains, however, and the recognition of the place of the artist in diagnosing the conditions of human misery, even if he is not always, or even often, equipped to prescribe for them. Criticism with this understanding is never a means of winning converts to a cause; it is a means only of penetrating to some deeper awareness of where and who and what we are. It is a philosophical activity, whatever the faith or practice or equipment of the critic, "an attempt," as Edmund Wilson has written of all kinds of intellectual effort, "to give a meaning to our experience—that is, to make life more practicable; for by understanding things we make it easier to survive and get around among them." [3]

One of the reasons for Edmund Wilson's enormous appeal as a critic-philosopher is the range of activity he has undertaken in order to understand things. In his elegant spiral onward and upward from Marxism, he has learned all manner of languages, Russian, Hebrew, political science, psychology. He has developed a sensitivity to people and to places as containers of people that makes him a model humanist of the newest of the new humanisms. His attempts to translate that sensitivity into story, play, and novel have not ever quite achieved conviction as story, play, or novel, except insofar as they present more of Wilson and less of the nymphs of Hecate County (see the *Memoirs* thereof) or their Greenwich Village prototypes (in *I Thought of Daisy*). For the fact is that Wilson is the most interesting subject in Wilson. The caricature of one of those lengthy monologues of his which used to appear as book reviews in *The New Yorker* that *Punch* ran as part of its brilliant parody of its American counterpart is not very far from the tone of Wilson's criticism:

I had a short acquaintance with the British writer, Mr. William Shakespeare, but only one extended conversation with him when he stayed overnight to ask my opinion about *King Lear,* the next play he planned starting. . . .

That week had already been a hard one for me, teaching Scott Fitzgerald and Ernest Hemingway how to write and explaining to them about T. S. Eliot and Henry James. . . .[4]

Wilson's running autobiography with letters and conversation can be almost as solemn and humorless as that, especially when the subject veers close to the dear days at Old Nassau with Scott and Dean Gauss, when Bunny Wilson put modern American literature on its somewhat unsteady feet. But though his accomplishment may be somewhat smaller than that, he has served valiantly as spokesman for the sensitive reader in America, for the man who is much more than a dilettante though something less than a scholar. He has helped not only to point the way to those works and artists that patently give meaning to our experience, but by his own skill as a writer of imaginative criticism has himself added to the list of such works.

A critic of this kind becomes what Delmore Schwartz writing about T. S. Eliot has called a "culture hero," that is, "one who brings new arts and skills to mankind." [5] Certainly Eliot as a poet and critic has done something of that sort. Following Ezra Pound's example, he has preached the good book (but not always the Good Book, even in the years after conversion; he has always been open to quality in writing, of almost any kind; he has not been a prig.) He has fought to extend the consciousness of his readers as far back into tradition as their learning and his would permit. And, perhaps because better dressed than Pound, in his prose as in his clothes, clean-shaven, with a banker's manners, he has succeeded, as Pound did not, in reaching all sorts of readers, especially critics. Others might have accomplished as much, but it was Eliot, not others, who made modern literature safe for Dante and the French writers of the nineteenth century, for the Elizabethan playwrights and the Anglican Divines of the seventeenth century. It was he who set poets and critics thinking about the "objective correlative" of an emotion or an experience that a symbol, a metaphor, or any figurative weapon in the poet's armory might be. In spite of later desertion of the cause, it was he really who established the techniques of textual criticism, upon which the New Criticism rose and foundered. His habit of seizing upon perceptions as they seized him, in the middle of things, became the habit of almost all American and British critics, as it had been Pound's before Eliot and Baudelaire's before either of them. His practice, once he had become convinced of the truth and centrality of Christian traditions, did much to establish the possibility once again of working openly from a position of conviction, with a creed, in literature generally, in criticism in particular. He became a spokesman for Europe, for the West, not to repudiate the East or any part of its traditions, but to asseverate the immense dignity of man that Christian thought in the West had at least conceived, if not established.

"I do not expect that all men of letters, in every country of Europe, will concur with my *views*," he wrote; "but I venture to hope that some of them will agree, that there is a range of public problems in which we all have, irrespective of nationality, language or political bias, a common interest, and about which we might hope to have a common mind; and I hope that some will agree that I have stated some of these problems." [6] Even those who disagree most strongly with the spirtual and intellectual and moral disciplines Eliot has advocated as a convinced Christian would not often today disagree about his statement of the central problems. And is there, really, anything more useful that a philosophical mind can contribute than this, the posing of the right questions? Schwartz says of the kind of prodding of consciousness that Eliot has done, that "nowhere better than in Eliot can we see the difference between being merely literary and making the knowledge of literature an element in vision, that is to say, an essential part of the process of seeing anything and everything." The terms are not very different from those of Edmund Wilson's definition of the purpose of intellectual activity, nor are they excessive as a description of the aim, if not necesarily the achievement, of most serious criticism in our time. The special concern of Eliot, however, was to make vision prescriptive. To the extent that he has made the prescribed vision attractive and reminded his readers of its ancient place in human society, he has worked differently from almost all others in criticism, even from those who have been most anxious to emulate his example. His is not an apostolicity that settles in the bone with an acceptance of the articles in the Apostles' Creed. It does share some of the same mystery, however, for it is in the order of grace, whatever the source of that grace may be.

In spite of his great concern to speak as a European for Europe, or perhaps because of it, Eliot's vision remained a personal one. Whether such a view is up or down, it is a contemplative view that springs from one's powers over oneself or one's attempt to secure that power. The critics, philosophers, and literary historians whose prime concern is the American imagination look at things very differently. However covert their language, however restrained their figures, somewhere bubbling beneath their rhetoric there lurks a consciousness of manifest destiny. They know the land, they love the land. Even when they are most scathing in their narratives of the helter-skelter culture the land has produced, the love is there, often urging them on to contempt, or at least a show of it, that special kind of opprobrium that a disappointed child reserves for its failing parents. They are involved as persons, but it is not a personal vision that they pursue or that pursues them; it is the pursuit of a national ideal, of a utopia, one, like all utopias, that never was nor will be, but that entrances a certain kind of visionary, a Walt Whitman, a Hart Crane, a Lewis Mumford, a Van Wyck Brooks. Such men do not know their country like a book. They know their books like a country. They move through literature, architecture, politics, people as if through forests and gardens, mountains and plains, lakes and rivers and brooks. They are variously proprietary, critical, descriptive, prescriptive. But the main concern always is what the land has produced, what the land can produce.

In almost every way, Van Wyck Brooks found himself out of sorts with Eliot's thinking, Eliot's early thinking, Eliot's late thinking, Eliot's thinking at any time. In the last volume of *Makers and Finders,* his History of the Writer in America, 1800–1915, Brooks translated his argument into the terms of Renaissance humanism and the "new confidence in life that enabled Hugo Grotius to establish the science of international law on a fundamental faith in human goodness, the faith that Eliot called a 'myth'. . . ." [7] This faith, predicated upon the natural brotherhood of man and a central conviction "that peace, not war, was the normal condition of mankind," Brooks saw as the foundation of this country and its most lasting traditions—at least until the time of the First World War. Eliot's sinfulness lay in his distance from this faith and his power to draw others away from it; he was one of those writers, as Brooks put it in *The Opinions of Oliver Allston* (1941), "who were at odds with their homeland." But more important, he had made that alienation into a literary fashion, and worse still, after his conversion, "connecting his religious views with his literary criticism, he spread a philosophy of literature through the academic world, especially in America, the basis of which was a virtual denial of whatever gave literature in America its historic importance." [8] That philosophy purposed the reestablishment of orthodoxy in the land and the literature, which, as Brooks saw it, could be fatal to the "heretical" (the quotes are his) American tradition and temperament and the literature which reflected both.

Brooks's conduct of his fight with Eliot and Elioticism, especially in the words and person of his alter ego, Oliver Allston, did much to discredit him with the literary quarterlies and their academic editors, contributors, and readers. They granted him a continuing place in American letters for his acerb pamphleteering in *America's Coming-of-Age* in 1915 and *Letters and Leadership* in 1918, in which like a

Thomas Paine of the literary left he tried to rouse a sleeping literature and to draw a poetry from the land. They gave him good marks for his psychoanalytical approach to the lives of Mark Twain and Henry James, an approach which he himself in time repudiated. But Brooks's new humanism they found as objectionable in its way as Irving Babbitt's and Paul Elmer More's was to Eliot. In fact, of course, Brooks's rise from skepticism and an aversion to Puritan tradition to a warm respect for almost the whole body of nine-teenth-century literature was no great rise at all. He was always the most Americanist of Americans, the least European of critics, except in the sense that a firm confidence in the ability of men to mold their own destiny and to mold it well could be found in such European sources as Rousseau and Locke. And so he collected and supported the minutemen of American literature: even if their contributions were no larger than a minute, they had spread the news, beat the bonfires, kept the faith. And the faith was good and was worth keep-ing. It had come upon hard times in the terrible years after the First World War, the years of Eliotic philosophy and of Ezra the Prophet. But it always had had its great-hearted and noble ad-herents, Jeffersonians, Jacksonians, partisans of the "Left" (once more, the quotation marks are Brooks's), from the time of the con-version of Irving, Cooper, and Bryant to the wisdom of Thomas Jefferson to the time of Hemingway's support of the Loyalists in Spain. Who stood behind the faith? Scott Fitzgerald in *The Crack-Up,* William Faulkner at Stockholm; Mencken in his *Treatise on Right and Wrong;* Thomas Wolfe and André Gide in their plentiful support of utopian dreams. Even the Prophet Ezra could be quoted on the side of the American faith, and all who raked muck or worked to improve the world were in the American grain: Ibsen, Shaw, Wells, for example. Could the faith be defined? There was Gide: "Without the idea of a possible progress, life would no longer have any value for me." There was Jefferson, talking about "the unquestionable re-publicanism of the American mind." To which Brooks contributed his solemn amen:

In a day that was too late for parochial sovereignties, too late for race-conceit, this defined the claims of America on the imagination—the im-agination that would have to return, if America lost its belief, to the humanistic tradition of which it was an offshoot. This had always been the American wager, and might one not say of it what Pascal had said, referring to another wager,—involving no less than this an act of faith,— that nothing could be lost and much was to be gained if, considering which held the greater value, one placed one's bet on the faith rather than the doubt.[9]

The difference between Brooks and some of the lesser men who moved as he did to fervent support of the *Festung* America is that he never hesitated to denominate his fervor as a faith. Nor did he fear for his integrity as he felt the nettles of skepticism slipping from him and a genial glow replacing the guarded look. And all this with thousands watching. That ease in the face of a staring audience marks the public critic, who no less than the public poet must constantly stand exposed in all his opinions, if not in his separations and divorces and trips to the analyst's couch. At least as much as a political commentator like Walter Lippmann, he espouses a public philosophy. Far more than any man whose texts are the commonplaces of Presidents and Congressmen, he works on the great issues, the lasting ones, and in the precise terms which assure their endurance, as works of literature. The social contract, as Brooks deals with it in his large-scale history and small-scale memoirs and memoranda, is thus reviewed and redefined and still found acceptable, worth reaffirming, worth keeping.

Without making Van Wyck Brooks and T. S. Eliot into wooden figures in an allegory of critics, it can be said, I think, that they represent the two extremes of American criticism and of the philosophy which informs them. Brooks's public philosophy is one to which the thinking of friends and associates such as Paul Rosenfeld and Lewis Mumford can be approximated, with some connection at one end of his career with Randolph Bourne and Matthew Josephson and all the others who identified and attacked modern industrial society as the special enemy of the artist, and at the other end with the special brand of America-first thinking supported by Archibald MacLeish in *The Irresponsibles*. Eliot's private vision is one which recommends itself with large variations in language and liturgy, to the New Critics and all adherents of straight textual analysis, to rhetoricians and to dialecticians, and even, with certain reservations, to hunters after myth and seekers after archetype. Even so resolute an independent as Yvor Winters obviously has close ties with Eliot, in his distaste for romanticism and his insistence upon objective procedures as a way of preparing and justifying critical judgments. To the extent, too, that Eliot both as editor and publisher showed himself to be sympathetic to the specialized modes and insights of philosophy, psychology, and scientific method, he may be said to have had much to do with the development of those intense interdisciplinary approaches to literature and the arts which at one time or another have touched every field of learning of our time. It does not matter precisely how much he has or has not influenced a writer like Kenneth Burke or Susanne Langer, Lionel Trilling or Northrup Frye. The fact is that the warmth of the reception accorded their application to the arts of the insights of rhetoric or linguistic philosophy, psychoanalysis or cyclical historical theory is in some degree a result of Eliot's preparing of the way—or, as Brooks in the mood of Oliver Allston might put it, of his poisoning the wells.

The two critical philosophies are not in every way antipathetic or antithetical to each other. The learning and the dedication of the men involved make such a polarity impossible. But the fundamental differences are clear enough and should not be underestimated. The proponents of a public philosophy in the arts tend to be censorious, however little they may want to invoke the machinery of censorship in support of their positions. The scholar-critics, while far from a bland indifference to other men's points of view, tend to fight out their differences in comparatively recondite language, in the pages of journals somewhat remote from the interests or competency of the large reading public.

There are entertaining ironies in this conflict of ideas and attitudes. Brooks, with something approaching scorn for the religious orthodoxy of Eliot and a central concern that is really entirely based on tradition, falls back on the language of faith and the most apologetic argument of a defender of the faith, Pascal, to make his appeal. Eliot, for all his orthodoxy, relies largely on the argument from literary tradition to make his appeal. We seem to be instructed here by each man according to the lights and convictions of the other. This is not as paradoxical as it may for a moment appear to be. Eliot, for all his devotion to the Apostles' Creed and the particular Christian sect to which he belongs, is not a full-time apostle, nor even much of the time a working proselytizer. His vision, as his poetry and plays have made abundantly clear, is so insistently personal and private that all sorts of people far removed from the particular terms of that vision can accept his critical modes, his concern for the text, his own respect for other men's modes. And equally, for all his dedication to the full library of American literature, in almost all its contrasting styles and personalities and points of view, Brooks is in the best sense of the word an apostle; more and more as he followed the direction indicated by Walt Whitman's lines, "Poems and materials of poems shall come from their lives, they shall be makers and finders," so more and more did he come to be a full-time defender of the American faith. To that faith he gave his time, his energies, his emotions, his eloquence, for in it belonged, he believed, the future not only of this country, but of all countries.

We can be well instructed, I think, by the different kinds of zeal involved in these critical philosophies. There are large measures of selflessness displayed by the critics as they develop their methods and modes. However much the most autobiographical of them confides of his personal life as he introduces a book or a writer or a moment of literary history, he is clearly motivated by something or someone outside himself. Here if anywhere in our arts men pause to contemplate ideas. When they introduce themselves into their speculations, it is generally in a meditative sort of way, as stand-in for the reader or as exemplar of an idea or an experience. They are genuinely concerned to give meaning to their lives and to ours, to redeem human experience by adding to our understanding of it. And this concern, both selfish and selfless, gives even some of their inept performances the stature of philosophical discourse, the stature to which their best writings have all succeeded in our time.

The several audiences, public and private, respond eagerly to the critical performance. Simply as a performance, it often eclipses in interest for its audience the work of art that has engendered it. Whatever its deficiencies of scholarship or exaggerations of a critical position, it underscores some of the procedures of meditation and contemplation, and more important than the procedures, it suggests the kind of wisdom that emerges from prolonged reflection upon an idea or a vehicle of ideas. The contemplative posture is an enormously winning one, always has been, always will be. In a time and in a place where it is little known and rarely adopted, the critic-philosopher is bound to be an appealing figure, for he is bound to follow at least the superficial structures of discursive meditation.

When inspired or preternaturally gifted, he can rise far above these to those exercises of the spirit that lead from exaltation on his part to a corresponding exaltation on ours. Then indeed we have reached that "point" of which James speaks "at which the moral sense and the artistic sense lie very near together . . . in the light of the very obvious truth that the deepest quality of a work of art will always be the quality of the mind of the producer."

The mere reviewer can almost never achieve the level of the contemplative. Exaltation is not for the dailies, nor is it often for the weeklies. But rare as it is in the performance of the so-called critic who passes books or plays or music or painting under review in newspapers or magazines, it is rarer still in the life of the censor. A kind of darting elation may be his as he strikes another blow for church or country, but hardly any sort of useful or edifying or enduring perception about the work he is in the course of rating or slating. His standards must be simple or rating would be out of the question altogether. Except in the case of the grossest possible work, evaluation cannot be reduced to a number or a letter or one of three or four categories, and even then it is hard to know which is the more gross, the performance under review or the performance of the censoring reviewer who is content to reduce all the elements involved in, say, a film—the acting, the direction, the writing, the photography, the music, the cutting, the setting, etc., etc.—to one crude judgment, usually in the realm of morals. This is one point at which the moral sense and the artistic sense lie very far apart.

One recognizes in the public arts the need to exercise some standards of moral judgment. The inundation of television or film programs by the ordure that now turns up at stag parties and the other abattoirs that specialize in collecting audiences for sewage is not of course to be supported. Nor does one want children picking up the kind of sleazy magazine which barbershop critics find so titillating. A strong case can be and has been made against films and comic books and radio and television programs of violence and horror. But are these the sole or even the chief offenders? Isn't there something worse than the lewd and the violent to which the critical performance, with its very different concerns, calls our attention with force? I am speaking about the attack on values, all values, upon value itself, which is the staple diet of our mass media. What sense of value can a child who feeds on television commercials develop? What kind of value system can emerge from the popular song of the rock 'n' roll era? Is there any violence or lasciviousness worse than the constant appeal to envy, greed, and pride which the writers and producers of television programs and their set and costume designers have taken over bodily from the worst films of the worst periods in Hollywood history? These films, of course, rarely were or are rated less than morally acceptable by the agencies of moral betterment; they do not fall into any of the categories which a simpleminded censorship finds repugnant to its sensibility. Pride, envy, and greed do not rank with lust and anger in the twentieth-century version of the deadly sins. And lust and gluttony, if they are sufficiently disguised by the masters of subliminal advertising, cannot be detected. It takes a remarkable alertness, apparently, to penetrate the hidden horrors of cigarette commercials which use every ancient sexual symbol at its most degraded to persuade Americans to stay with or pick up the habit.

No one has yet discovered an altogether reasonable way of conducting a moral examination of a work of art, perhaps because such an examination offends against the very nature of a work of art. Intention in art is never as precise as this sort of examination must suppose. Moral values develop in mysterious ways, even in works designed with the most clear and open moral purpose. For Christian writers, the central value is charity, and charity is not inculcated by any merely human agency. All values are subtle ones for the Hindu moralist, or the Taoist, or any modern philosopher, for that matter, who recognizes the atomic elusiveness of values in a world of chance. What is involved in any serious attempt to preserve rather than erase moral value, in the public arts as in the private, is the same sort of reflective probing of ideas and attitudes in the context of a work of art as one finds in the essays of Eliot, Brooks, Wilson, Trilling, and the rest. Probing, not judgment in a court of law. Graham Hough's critical examination of the effect of *Lady Chatterley's Lover* upon the literature that followed it is immeasurably superior to a court trial of the book, even with the most articulate and intelligent and trustworthy witnesses. Hough is able to show the real moral depth of Lawrence's accomplishment, making the sexual act as logical and significant a part of literature as of life.[10] This sort of demonstration neither belongs in court nor can it be effectively staged there, for obvious reasons. It requires the detachment and meditative calm that are uniquely possible in the writing and reading of a carefully reasoned, slow, and deliberate philosophical essay. It requires, too, the recognition that we are in the area of what the theologian would call *pudor,* decency, which has to be redefined at least once a generation, among what the sociologist would call shifting standards of taste. A judicial weighing of *pudor* or taste necessarily takes place out of court.

Can one hope in time to find censoriousness a matter of tone—as among serious critics—rather than a matter of public action—as in committees of censors? And if such a change should take place, as recent state and Federal court decisions seem to presage, are we inevitably doomed to a reign of terror and indecency in the public arts? The answer is, I think, that terror and indecency will always hover over the public arts as long as critical judgment is suspended, whether to give way to the depressive simplifications of the censor or to the manic simplifications of enthusiastic children, who often are the only ones to take these arts with any great seriousness. What is clearly called for is an informed seriousness, at least a modicum of the gift of contemplation, and, to return to James, the conviction that "Humanity is immense, and reality has a myriad forms; the most one can affirm is that some of the flowers . . . have the odour of it, and others have not; as for telling you in advance how your nosegay should be composed, that is another affair." That is another affair, an affair best forgotten while we spend our time as critics sniffing out the flowers that have the odour of reality, in all the forms of reality. That could in time bring the critical performance in the popular arts to something like the plane of the critical performance in the private arts in America, to the point at which it is as important as the works of art which make it possible.

CONCLUSION

THE ONE THING that is certain about American culture is that it is not only one thing. It moves across arts and attitudes with the recklessness and intensity of a summer storm. It seeks novelty like a bored child on a long Sunday afternoon. The only article of faith to which it has sworn constancy is change.

Many reasons can be found for this total commitment to change. Some can be located in American society. Some must be sought in the world outside. It is clear that we live in a time in which change and chance hurtle across all societies with terrifying speed, and not only with speed, which could perhaps be calculated, but with an imprecision of aim, like the antiaircraft fire of the Italians in the last world war, which cannot be calculated or predicted. In the United States every effort is made to trace the imprecise lines of change and to hold it down to mathematical description, especially in the great organizations of mass culture, where change is held to be fairly gentle, not too difficult at all to domesticate. All one has to do is to obtain and keep up-to-date a good set of statistical averages and change will work for you, not against. And so, with every market survey, every best-seller list, each television and radio rating, each list of the top two-hundred pop songs, the commitment to change increases, and with the commitment to change the search for novelty. Thus, what starts as a confident series of maneuvers to control change ends with change firmly in control.

The decline in standards that has followed the spiral path of change across the entertainment arts is well enough known and has been often enough commented upon. Television programs and motion pictures are not significant to their producers for any intrinsic values but rather for how well they follow a trend, for how quickly they establish and maintain a rating. Box office is the basis of value judgment. The cruel corollary to this *Weltanschauung* in the popular arts is an almost equal and opposite one in the private arts. There, too, trends establish values. In television, there are Western cycles, gangster seasons, a trend to internes and hospital-corridor histrionics. In painting, there is abstract expressionism, pop art, op art. In the

466

history of ideas, there is an existentialist period and then one for the religions of the East, expecially Zen Buddhism. Quick translations are made from the obscure books of the philosophers of *Existenz*. Zen is not only percolated in the coffeehouses, it is explained in terms any man can understand by popularizers—any man, that is, except a Zen Buddhist, but then he is not able to understand through words, as *he* has made clear enough, perhaps the only point he has made clear. Abstract expressionism, or action painting, or the work of the New York School—take your pick—is explained in a piece among many others in *The Saturday Evening Post* dealing with the cobbles and bobbles of contemporary thought in a fine lucid style, is spread before the eye in *Life,* and followed exhibit for exhibit, wall-sized canvas by wall-sized canvas, drip-artist by drip-artist in the pages of *Time,* which covers all the action.

The popularizations are much better than they used to be. The explications are fuller. They come from men of much greater authority than the adult educationists who used to write the books that made philosophy, psychology, and scientific method clear for the millions who read Star Dollar and Blue Ribbon Books in the happy years before the Second World War when it was thought that almost anything could be explained to anybody by somebody, and if not by somebody then by several bodies quickly gathered together under the editorship of Samuel Schmalhausen. Now the attitude is a little closer to reality, perhaps. It is recognized that the confusion felt by small numbers of people about existentialism or Zen or abstract painting can be shared by large numbers of people until by constant repetition of certain jargon words and phrases and frequent reprinting of the same sort of picture it will all become, if not clear, at least familiar. And with *The New Yorker* and *Look* and the *Post* and all the others ready to lend the destructive wit of their cartoonists to the effort, how very quickly it does become familiar and just the least bit contemptible. The contempt never becomes strong enough, however, for anyone to raise any significant protest about the silliness of trying to explain everything to everybody or even just attempting to share and spread the confusion. Lots of little and large programs follow the popularizations across the country on television and radio, with more and more programs coming all the time, now that these mass media have been won for education. Now it is possible to read about it, see about it, and hear about it the same week, even the same day, if one happens to come home to the right issue of the *Saturday Review* or *Time,* the right program on FM or the local educational outlet. And these failing, there is always Sunday on the TV networks when discussion is king for a day.

It stands to reason that some responsible effort to introduce large numbers of people to the thought of their times, to the art of their times, must be made by those articulate enough to do so in terms masses of people can understand. The democratization of education has made such a movement up and down necessary. The question is how far the movement must go, or rather, how far the explanations can go, without the whole thing turning into a farce and incidentally killing a great deal of art at the source. The private artist remains what he has always been, a man equipped by taste or temperament or the peculiar kind of skill or intuition with which he is gifted to communicate only to one man at a time, however many he may eventually reach. He is not a box-office performer. He is not meant to make sense to masses of people, nor does he—initially, at least— mean to make such sense. Something unfortunate happens to his art or thought when its gritty subtleties and complexities are reduced to an easily digestible mush. Something equally unfortunate happens to the audience for whom the flaccid preparation has been made. It begins to think that there was nothing frightfully complex or subtle about the art or the ideas in the first place; it was just a question of getting someone clearheaded and entertaining enough to straighten out the muddle. Of course anybody can understand anything, or at least nobody understands anything any better than anybody else. We are all in the same muddle together in this great democratic society, the thinking goes. And soon enough, we all are—elucidator, elucidated, and elucidatee; artist, reviewer, and audience.

None of this would be very serious, except for the corruption of vast chunks of the population, who now think they really do *know* what they like and who as a result lose all humility before works of art and artists, and for the greater debasement of a smaller part of the population, the private artists, who now begin to work for an audience to whom they have little or nothing to say. The transformation of a private into a popular artist is not always conscious. It is very hard when one has made one's mark with a particular kind of painting or novel or poem or play not to return to the same kind of work again and again. This is standard practice in the popular arts, where most actors are cast according to type, where a comedian finds a basic routine and comes back to it every time around even if he is on a once-a-week broadcasting schedule, where a detective-story writer finds a character—district attorney or Scotland Yard superintendent or eccentric old lady or corpulent polymath—to whom he can return as often as twice a year in books and once a week on the air. In spite of the indelible marks of the human person that make their way into the work of all artists, no matter how obscure, this is not the deliberate practice of private artists who remain private. Their identities are not paraded like brand names or trademarks, to make purchase easier or the purchaser more secure. But when a private art or private artist turns popular, this is almost always the first sign: an identity is quickly established; the same tricks of style are repeated again and again; none without this mark is genuine.

The degree of consciousness on the part of the artist who transforms himself from a private into a popular artist is hard to ascertain, even for the artist himself. The degree of chicanery is even harder to run down. It is lost forever in the brambles and thickets and marshy ground of artistic intention, where critics and historians of the arts and artists have for years—for centuries, in fact—wandered hopelessly. But the artist who makes the switch is obviously conscious of some significant change, sooner or later, when he becomes aware of the beguilement of his identity mark or deliberately fixes upon one, or discovers, as so many artists do, a loss of artistic power along with a gain of prestige and commercial success. That is the point at which many artists seem to decide that, whether or not they have cheated anybody else, they have cheated themselves. That is the point at which self-mockery and cynicism enter their works, disguised as ironies, perhaps, but only thinly disguised. And how often in the years of the great movement from private to popular art, from just after the First World War to the present, that sort of mockery and cynicism has set the tone of the arts, especially the mass arts! Inevitably that cynical tone, that mocking air made its way into the screenplays that relatively serious and well-equipped writers did for Hollywood. And of course it also permeated the stories and novels that the same sort of writers wrote as they moved from the little magazines to the big, from obscurity to success, from obscurity to transparency. The examples can be multiplied with the arts. In almost every case, the move from private performer to public has been accompanied by a growing taste for mockery and an increasing talent for derision, which on close analysis seem more and more to be directed by the artist at the artist.

Of course the artist is a useful and even a necessary critic of society. However often we hear that truism stated, we all accept it, and much more warmly still, we accept the criticism of society itself when it is made with the high skill of a Kafka or a Swift, a Dante or a Fielding or a Dostoevski. We accept, too, the mockery that is often one of the best devices of a social critic, but when that mockery turns into self-ridicule we may be less grateful, especially when it becomes, as it seems to have become in the years since the Second World War, endemic in the arts. The warm laugh of a Joyce at himself and others like him in the early stages of a writing career, in his *Portrait of the Artist as a Young Man,* is one thing. The curdling smiles of all those who cannot deal with love, marriage, faith of any kind, intense feeling of any kind, without a note of scorn and suspicion is something else again. Theirs are the antiheroes that rankle, not the figures of Camus's Stranger or Gide's Immoralist or Mann's Tonio Kröger, who is torn between the appeals of the blond and blue-eyed Nordic bourgeois and art, not the ambiguous accretions of bloodless documentary fact that populate the novels of Nathalie Sarraute and Alain Robbe-Grillet.

Most often the private artist who becomes a public performer turns naturalist. Naturalism is, as it has been for some six decades or more, the going method in the halfway art of the halfway artist. It allows the playwright, the novelist, the screenwriter or director or photographer, the painter, the sculptor, and even the composer to feel himself a superior moralist in the midst of his naïve auditors and viewers. He brings them the world as it really is. No fantasies. No evasions. Stark reality. And so we get the bathroom and the strait-jacket on the stage in *A Streetcar Named Desire,* a limb-by-limb, genital-by-genital homosexual encounter in *Another Country,* all the rump-scratchers of Method acting, the random switches and twitches of radio dials in a work by John Cage, and Coca-Cola bottles, soup cans, and a multiplicity of movie faces in the combines and smears of pop art. And in hundreds and hundreds of novels and short stories that present the rites of puberty—all those groaning, surging, grip-ping, tearing volumes that reach from Thomas Wolfe to Philip Roth —we must live again the awkwardness and anguish of adolescence, always in terms of the dog beneath the skin, but never of the heart or soul.

Nothing in the world of popular art is quite so feeble or so pathetic as the public artist who convinces himself and tries to convince you of his mission to the masses. His every naturalistic work brings not only art but truth to the millions. They will be saved for themselves or from themselves—the precise accent depends upon whether the mission is more markedly psychological or sociological— by his fearless presentation of the world as it really is. And so we get narratives of futility and despair in television, squeezed into crime series, social-worker series, medical series, any series, and those gloomy documentary reports which alternate with the fatuously sunny ones in which a report "in depth" turns out to be a rehearsal of Washington saloon conversation. And we get the "courageous" films which "dare to face the truth"—for which read, "dare to break the motion-picture code"—by concentrating, like the novels from which they are taken, on illegitimacy, abortion, and the early development of young girls, which we all know is very early indeed. With every respect for the achievement of D. H. Lawrence in bringing the sex act out of the bushes and back into the books, and the accomplishment of James Joyce in opening up the dammed streams of consciousness of the man on the street and the woman on the john, how much respect can we have for the kind of naturalism that continues to show us what surely most people must know by now, that there are two sexes and that they tend to make for each other in ways that, considering the number of people and the number of works about them, are remarkably alike.

A sense of mission does go a long way toward mitigating the self-mockery from which the ex- or would-be private artist so often suffers. It can even appease the doubts of a working intellectual hired to go through many weeks on a quiz program as a kind of public performer, with the answers to questions supplied to him. His success, we were told at the time of the television-quiz-show scandals, was a way for at least one of them, or so he convinced himself, to achieve a high rank and position for his profession and then to use that position to do work of quality in television. The same excuse has been used to defend the cruelly shrunken versions of novels and plays of distinction which first the movies and now television indulge in as a mark of respect for art.

The excuses should not be necessary, nor should any other way be required to appease the doubts or to assuage the sense of ridicule or of false pretensions with which popular artists are from time to time quite properly afflicted. It is time for a definition of separate purposes and precincts for the two kinds of art in America and with that definition time for an end to the ridiculous missionary effort which succeeds only in converting the missionaries and in providing bad art with an elaborate apologetic which it really does not need. Of course I am not proposing a definition of any precise location of place or intention on the part of any artist, private or popular, but rather a clear license for both kinds of art.

One might think that popular art has all the freedom it could possibly want. One could be forgiven for thinking so. But it is not so. For all art in the United States has constantly to prove itself, to prove itself at the box office, to prove itself in the market survey, to prove itself in the phone check or the specially wired television sets, to prove itself over the counter and in the jukebox. Folk songs are *in* because folk songs, or rather the synthetic products of television and records, have been plugged mercilessly and have found favor as a respite from rock 'n' roll which is—the kids have happily discovered —not too different from that earlier form of musical hypertension. But jazz is *out,* as it has been since the early fifties. And the witty music, the warm songs and the entertaining instrumentals from the back country in the South and the Southwest and the Southeast are out, too, except for an occasional Library of Congress or specialized Folkways record that can be heard on FM or on the more enterprising disc jockey shows on AM radio.

Vaudeville, which seemed to be coming back in the first feverish days of television, when time had to be filled somehow, is not exactly a large part of mass art in America, in spite of a tumbling turn for a few minutes at the beginning of an Ed Sullivan show or a quick trip across the trapeze ropes at the end or an occasional itinerant juggler who confronts the bored cameramen about 3:00 A.M. on an all-night show in aid of some famous show-business personality's favorite charity. The dance is insignificant in popular art except for moments of national mania, when a new style such as the Twist genuinely catches on or another such as the Madison is pushed hard by its commercial sponsors and almost catches on. But in spite of all the time given to dancing in films and television and Broadway (and off-

Broadway) musicals, it is a distorted kind of dance we are given in the mass media, at once pretentious and feeble, filled with the desultory frills of the pseudo-ballet and almost untouched by the vital art that used to be practiced in the ballrooms and the back alleys, the beat-up nightclubs and offbeat presentation houses and still can be found at the outer edges of big cities in what remains of ballroom and back-alley and presentation-house atmospheres.

That sort of popular art should still be very much a part of our popular culture, no matter how popular it actually is as popularity is measured in the surveys and the lists and the ratings. Minority tastes should be catered to; minority tastes should be developed; minority tastes should in every way be encouraged in popular art as in private. What it amounts to, is that every taste should be encouraged the only way a taste can be encouraged, by exposure. But here the most powerful form of censorship the world has ever known intervenes, the censorship of majority tastes, a censorship rigorously developed and maintained by the majority's representatives, the producers and sponsors and bankers and agency men who run the mass media, managers of majority tastes, who impose those tastes upon everybody, majority and minorities, whether or not the majority wants them imposed.

The excuse is used again and again that majority tastes are indeed carefully consulted, through surveys, checks, etc., etc. But two fundamental assumptions that underlie those taste-hunting expeditions on the part of management are rarely defended because rarely questioned. One is the assumption that this crude reduction of the principles of democratic procedure to one mass, one taste is quite right and proper. And the other is the related conviction that the managers of the mass media who got there first are both morally and esthetically entitled to their extraordinarily powerful positions. And so, to take the most glaring cases first, the several dynasties of radio and television can perpetuate themselves as long and as tyrannously as they please, just as long as they can follow the impassioned rhetoric of a Federal Communications Commissioner suddenly inflamed with the desire to see mass media raised to some level of quality with an equally impassioned rhetoric in which they protest their devouring need to do exactly what the FCC torch carrier wants done. But, of course, it never gets beyond rhetoric and a handful of programs ostensibly in the public interest because they are so doggedly dull and interest so few people as they make their solemn pronouncements about the water supply or the movement of migratory workers or the condition of education in the states. And then these too gradually disappear, along with the rhetoric and the FCC firebrand, and we are right back with the quiz shows and the serial comedies and the doctors and the nurses and the psychotic cowboys.

It is only a dynastic system as unrepresentative as ours of any tastes that would so blandly, so securely go on imposing the tastes it discovers at the end of a market survey or a telephone check, that would take media designed for millions of listeners and viewers and spin them round the results of a sampling of a few thousand people. Both procedures are repellent and reckless. Both toss away casually, heedlessly, what for once deserves that much-abused, much-mocked phrase of the politicians, a sacred trust.

There have been dozens of inquiries, public and private, into the conduct of mass media in the United States, but no serious attempt to reassess the enfranchising of a private enterprise with the freedom of the air on the part of those with some power to do something about it. In no other country in the world has so much profit of a financial kind been made with so little profit of a cultural kind as in American radio and television. And yet it continues to be assumed by almost everybody—or to be assumed that it is assumed by almost everybody—that this is the way things must be. We must have ABC and CBS and NBC forever. They are part of the American landscape. And who but a dangerous radical would propose any serious alteration of our great system of free enterprise?

What requires examination now is the extent to which these media are conducted as systems of free enterprise, which means not an inquiry into stock plans and holding compaines, but into the freedom of the air—the openness of broadcasting schedules to all kinds of taste, to minority popular art and even to that least representative of tastes, minority private art. For there is a substantial potentiality for private art in radio and television, as the European performance has long demonstrated in radio, as FM has begun to show in this country, and as any number of European countries have made clear in their television offerings. The thought would make a network executive shudder, but it is reasonable to expect some time, even prime time, to be given over to the tastes and skills of writers, actors, directors, musicians, singers, lecturers, conversationalists, painters, sculptors, architects—anybody and everybody who could make intelligent use of the time—even if the audiences for their tastes and skills are tiny, less than one million, less even than a hundred thousand. It is reasonable to expect this time to be shared and developed in this way even though it does not balance on the books, the rating books or the budget books. The time given to the networks is given to them by all of us, those of us with majority tastes (whatever they may be) or minority tastes, those of us who find our joy and our understanding and our growth in private art or popular or both. The same sort of moral obligation to open their enterprises to all tastes devolves on the managers of mass media as it does to open their employment to all races.

The one mass–one taste foolishness never quite worked in the film industry, in spite of every effort to achieve a generally palatable, thoroughly inoffensive, and mediocre mass medium. There were always a few directors, a few writers, a few cameramen, even an actor or two, who could make a private presence felt, if only through the exigencies of B-film budgeting, which made obliqueness a necessity and indirection a virtue. Now the era of private tastes is really upon the film industry, as Hollywood becomes a monument to a civilization almost as dead as Ozymandias's and the means of filmmaking become open to anybody with an income larger than that required to feed and clothe and shelter him or his family. The result of such a proliferation of the means may be a spate of naturalist documents, in which the savage eyes of young filmmakers search out the dirtiest, the sleaziest, the most unappetizing haunts of their cities and towns and come up with the triumphant discovery of sexuality. A whole group of such perfervid peepers has formed itself already, with an aesthetic which boldly comes up to the taste and times of Emile Zola. But it will not all go that way, as films like *David and Lisa* show, and the simple fact that Greenwich Village and the hills of San Francisco are crawling with film units suggests that a freshness and freedom are available to this art that have hardly existed in America since the days of Griffith and the Keystone Cops. Whatever the ultimate result, the art of the film is being reexamined and rediscovered and that is enough for a new beginning in America.

The enormous success of abstract painting has made it possible for almost anyone who can make what looks like a professional scrawl across a piece of canvas to get gallery space—at least once.

The result has been a great deal of trash hanging, not only in galleries, but in florists' shops, restaurants, bars, almost anywhere that there is a spare wall. And with the trash, so the complaint goes, a great many charlatans have found easy pickings, for we all know how difficult it is to discriminate among the abstracts and how simple to fool the great masses of people who can barely tell the difference between an abstraction inside a frame and aimless graffiti scratched into the plaster of a urinal wall. But suppose there has been and is and will be trash on the gallery and restaurant walls and many other places as well; hasn't there always been? Is a poorly executed abstraction any more offensive than boats at eventide (or dawn or high noon) or sunset over the Grand Canyon (or sunrise) or daisies (or black-eyed Susans or goldenrod) swaying in the wind, tra-la? And suppose masses of people are fooled by imitation De Kooning or gyp-drip artists? Is that worse than being fooled by imitation Picasso or Renoir? Or pseudo-Hopper or O'Keeffe? And isn't there a great deal to be said for hanging a real live painting in the home rather than just another reproduction of Van Gogh? It is quite true, I think, as I have said elsewhere in these pages, that too much private art and too many private artists have moved in an ungainly and even dishonest fashion from their proper precincts, the private, where they can be themselves and paint what they feel, to a domain that is not really theirs, the popular, where no matter how hard they try they cannot be themselves and often cannot even know what they feel, much less paint it. But the fact that in this mass migration to the masses a prodigious amount of wall space has opened up to the abstract artist, and his cousins and his sisters and his aunts, is something to cheer about. Perhaps the time will soon come when anyone who paints will be able to find hanging room somewhere—for his paintings, not for himself—and not simply on the fences and the sides of buildings in the great open-air exhibits, entertaining as they are, but indoors, where each work can be examined with care, slowly, meditatively, and the most private of communications can seek out its audience of one or the most public communication can find its crowd. How good it is that we have come to that point in our response to the visual arts where such a possiblity can even be contemplated!

And how sad it is that nothing remotely resembling such a possibility exists for the American composer. The composer must find a sinecure for himself at a university or a conservatory or a record company or turn hack writer of broadcasting or film cues, if he is to remain a working musician. Not only is it impossible for him to earn a living at his composing, he is wildly successful if he manages to hear all his compositions at least once before he dies. He, too, is tempted to turn popular artist, with less likelihood of success than the abstract painter, but always in hope of a short run as a composer of tone poems of the lone prairie or patriotic cantatas or folksy choral pieces that college glee clubs can do. But why shouldn't he too be supported, and in everything he does, by at least a handful of performances, to the point where he—and we—can say something with some assurance about his talent or lack of talent? The American Federation of Musicians used some of the money it made after it won its fight for a union royalty on every record sold in the United States to present concerts where concerts had not been heard till then. The same source of funds could be used to present music that would not otherwise be heard in concert. Perhaps foundation support could be won for such a project. Certainly the radio and television networks should be involved. It is urgent, not in order to have an American music, but simply to allow Americans to be musicians, any kind of musician. For this goes for jazz as much as for composers in what is solemnly, if not quite accurately, called the classical tradition. Unless jazzmen can follow a modish style or create a new mode with a distinct box-office following, they also must languish unheard. And they, too, at this point, are divided into private and popular precincts and have the right, it seems to me, to follow their skills and inclinations where they lead, even if they lead far from public success.

Perhaps the most crucial of all the areas for the private artist is the drama. For in this art, even the public artist is severely limited by staggering costs which have transformed a sometime art into an always business. Off-Broadway production has now reached the point at which its budgets compare with prewar Broadway expenditures, and its prices have reached about the same level, about twice the cost of going to the theater in England, France, or Germany. And so, though it is off-Broadway that the great achievement of the earlier twentieth century can still be appreciated—Ibsen, Strindberg, Chekhov, Shaw, Pirandello, Giraudoux, Yeats, O'Casey, O'Neill— and the more striking new American playwrights discovered—Albee, Schisgal, Richardson—it is not in the boxes and lofts and basements and made-over movie houses of New York that a great new theater is being made or will be born. It is too expensive to give just anyone a hearing, much less a setting and a cast and a competent director. And even out of New York, costs are high enough and audiences fickle enough and critics unfriendly enough so that producing new plays has become a business venture and a rather dubious one at that. On the college campuses, the shows that bring in the audiences and satisfy the trustees and the alumni are first of all the musicals and second of all the farces and box-office hits of fairly recent seasons, and while a fair number of drama departments keep a fairly good repertory alive, the university is not an eager sponsor of young playwriting talent. Equity does not have the resources of the musicians' union, though it has made an attempt to bring the drama to the outlying districts of the New York metropolitan area with its Library Theater, which gives employment to young aspirants in the theater while it develops something like a new audience for the theater, but nothing like a clamorous demand for plays in the Bronx or Queens.

Must playwrights depend upon clamorous demand? Are we so tied to our tradition of self-subsistent arts that the theater, like rock 'n' roll and "Gunsmoke," must pay for itself or be delivered entirely into the hands of the traveling salesman and the stay-at-home salesman, who will give their undying support to Rodgers and Hammerstein and their lineal descendants? Somehow the principle has been established that grand opera need not pay for itself. With the aid of a great oil-company sponsor for its great radio broadcasts and contributions from the great unseen audience, the great gold curtain of the Metropolitan will continue to rise as the great costs continue to rise and nobody will complain as the great money is spent for Mascagni and Verdi and Puccini, a little Mozart and a lot of Wagner, and such new works as Alban Berg's *Wozzeck*, written in 1925, and such daring American operas as Samuel Barber's *Vanessa* and Gian-Carlo Menotti's *The Last Savage*. Perhaps the new Lincoln Center repertory company, whoever directs it, will achieve a similar preferred status for the theater, but even if it should become much more adventurous than its first seasons suggest it intends to be, the theater in America must find less grandiose undertakings if it is to develop new playwrights and directors and actors and even new audiences. It must exist in neighborhoods. It must be set up at the center of life in small and large towns and more loosely organized country regions, as was recently proposed when a group of entrepreneurs made plans for a series of theaters in shopping centers around the country. They did not suggest a particularly bold set of plays. Their vision did not extend beyond the well-chewed hash of the summer theaters. But they were right about their locations. And perhaps with an outer covering of pabulum, it would be possible to present something more solid at the center. Certainly it would make sense to join a season of the dance to material from the experimental theater, as is done regularly in Paris in the brilliant summer festival of the Théâtre des Nations, and then to add to that some small-cast operas and other music.

Three sets of opportunities converge upon the sponsors of art centers that really reach across the arts. One is an opportunity to free the artist to be himself, whatever kind of artist he is, popular or private, in whatever art he practices, music or theater or the dance, painting, sculpture, photography, architecture, or almost anything else that needs exhibition or performance to reach people. Another is an opportunity to expose the sorely tried adult population of the United States to much more of their own culture than they are likely now ever to see or hear within the constricted confines of radio, television, the movies, and the jukeboxes, which are their usual channels of culture. Still another, and surely the most important, is the opportunity to offer some breadth and depth of experience in the arts to the untried children of this country. Without such a confrontation, American children are doomed as American children never have been before to a mechanized culture, in which the highest grace they can hope for is a temporary respite from the insanity of rock 'n' roll or the inanity of pseudo-folk song in the form of a Frank Sinatra or Ella Fitzgerald recording, or an equally brief interlude from cowboys and Indians and situation comedies when, by some fluke of scheduling, all the television channels in their area have programmed music or talk or drama of quality.

It is probably too much to expect Americans to support the right of artists to be themselves, especially if that means producing an art that has no commercial appeal whatsoever and cannot pay for itself. It is equally unlikely that many of us who have reached the age of consent in the arts will take very seriously the privileges and responsibilities that go with it; it is much easier to continue in a state of mute acceptance of everything that is thrown at one, muttering occasionally at the cost of a new television set or movie prices, reserving one's passions for occasional involvement in the melodrama of justice of "The Defenders" or the nostalgia that is evoked by a late late show revival of a film of the thirties. But just possibly we may be aroused by the implications of our passivity for our children. The fact that they may not only be deprived of the bulk of the rich cross-grained culture of their country in their time, but may turn into cultural robots, grotesque parodies of persons, as a result of constant exposure to machine art—that may alert parents. But alert them to what? To take what measures? What alternatives do they actually have?

In spite of the pious assurances of the managers of mass media, letters and phone calls to radio and television stations and to film companies really do not accomplish very much. They may help to bring a Gary Cooper out of the obscure background of a war film and into stardom or confirm the aphrodisiac effect of a Marilyn Monroe; they may help to determine the precise accent of a trend—just how sadistic gangsters may be allowed to be or precisely how pathological the cowboys. But they will certainly not bring about any large-scale changes in the entertainment arts, for all the sensitivity of networks to ratings: it is a statistic that decides a program's fate, something cold and clear and mathematical, not the imprecision of a complicated expression of opinion that may go on for two or three paragraphs or even more. And if letters and phone calls cannot achieve much in the entertainment arts, how much less, one would normally reason, can they do in the private arts or in the expression of minority tastes in the popular arts. But here, I think, one might be reasoning wrongly. The open show of support for FM radio of high quality has brought that medium out of obscurity and into prominence at least as much as the dollar-and-cents contributions of listeners to keep the Pacifica Foundation stations alive in Los Angeles and New York. The eagerness of women's clubs to listen to lecturers on the new arts and the new artists in America has been a barometer of some significance to the entrepreneurs of these arts, one which they have not been slow to follow in their investments of time and energy and money. And, of course, much has been accomplished by the enthusiastic response of crowds at the various museums of modern art around the country, at jazz festivals and symphony concerts, and at film series on university campuses. It seems reasonable, then, to expect that something could be done through letter and petition and phone call and every other means of expressing a firm opinion in support of the more obscure arts and artists in America. The questions that remain are what form that support can take and into what mists of obscurity it will extend.

It seems to me that when one examines the range and depth of the arts in America in our time, as I have tried to do in this book, one sees soon enough that the accomplishment is such as almost to demand support, support of every kind for every kind of art. If they are not supported, they will continue to develop. There is not much doubt about that. The compulsion to compose or to paint or to write or do anything else in the arts continues with or without financial ease and critical acclaim. But the development may be less and less reflective and more and more cynical and bitter, as more and more we are subjected to the mocking tonalities of a popular art that is constructed out of the compromises of private artists. We face the constant possibility of an art that is little more than mere novelty, for all the brilliance of its techniques, except for the performances of those men of many endowments or multiple opportunities who have been able to live well enough as lawyers or insurance men or obstetricians to be able to support themselves as poets or musicians without making any concessions to popular taste, or the work of the brothers and sisters of the monasteries of the Atomic Age, the universities. Perhaps the universities on the one hand and the business-supported artists on the other will be able to provide us with enough private art of quality to offset the worst depredations of popular art. But even that cheerful thought we should not be too quick to accept, for in it we accept too easily a narrowing of our resources and the reduction of our private artists' experiences to worlds that, as the authors of all the college and big business novels of recent years are only too quick to assure us, are irremediably cramped and cramping.

No solution presents itself as altogether satisfying as long as, uniquely in the modern world, American government monies remain unavailable for arts and artists, and the foundations, for all their generosity in these areas, continue to work, as they must, with selective vision based on restricted budgets. It will be enough, perhaps, if for the present Americans are led to give more serious thought to the large achievement of American culture and its even larger potentialities, to see how small or how great their share in it has been and how much more substantial that share can be. To give such thought to art is not an American habit. We would rather allow chance to work its changes and to make our value judgments afterward, if we make judgments at all. In this, as in so many other things, we are an unrecollected people. We do not like to conduct discursive colloquies with ourselves about ourselves. We prefer our dramas and all the rest of our arts to deal with the seeking body rather than the seeking soul. And yet sooner or later we must discover that the body's appeasement is very sudden and quite incomplete if there is not with it some assuagement of the spirit. There is no better evidence of that than the work of the best of our artists in all the arts. For ours is not simply a waist-high culture. It is a culture of many kinds, of many levels, addicted to change, it is true, but change by definition can be in any direction or in every direction. If we point in every direction at once, we obviously cannot arrive at any single goal, but we may arrive at many goals and among them a large number of high quality. That is the hopeful point of this book.

NOTES

INTRODUCTION

1. In his essay "What Is American About America?", in *The Beer Can by the Highway* (New York: Doubleday, 1961, John Kouwenhoven concludes that "America is process." It is neither a precise ideal nor any other kind of orderly structure: "neither is it chaos except as that is chaotic whose components no single mind can comprehend or control." This is a view that seems to look to the future as much as to the past in its recognition of the fundamental importance of change in American culture. It is a point, I think, that must be made about any Western culture of size. The rhapsodic words of Nietzsche, with which Rudolf Rocker concludes his *Nationalism and Culture* (New York: Covici, Friede, 1937), are apposite here: "Not where you come from will from now on redound to your honor, but whither you are going! Your will and your foot, which tries always to outrun you—that shall be your new honor." This is an attitude much in favor in our time, though not often held with such fervor. I have tried to indicate some of the limitations of a process-centered attitude of mind in my *Seeds of Hope in the Modern World* (New York: Kenedy, 1962).

2. The Russians are not without some feeling for the vernacular in art, but it is almost always the most pretentious version that achieves—or is permitted to achieve—wide circulation, such as the souped-up arrangements of their popular songs, the grotesque rococo decoration of their subway stations, the involuted narratives of their ballet librettos. It is not only the techniques of jazz that are foreign to Soviet Russian tastes, but the spontaneity of the music and its fine, noisy vulgarity.

3. This is a point that still needs to be made again and again. Obscurity is not the special ambition or achievement of poets (or any other group of artists) in the twentieth century. The allegorical structures of medieval and Renaissance poetry have more obvious symmetries than the symbolism of late-nineteenth- and twentieth-century poets, but the veils are at least as hard to strip away from the earlier as from the later verse, and not only because of the distance in time and the remoteness of the idiom of medieval or Renaissance poetry. No poet of quality ever wrote for instant comprehension, not even Dante when he was seeking to make the eloquence of the vernacular tongue self-evident.

MUSIC

1. American singers and instrumentalists no longer suffer from this form of inverted snobbism. They have been accepted in Europe; they have won international competitions; they are now accepted at home. American composers have not been so fortunate. They have had foundation support. Each year there are many festivals at which their music can be heard. But the "names" in contemporary music continue to be foreign or, at best, naturalized. One can understand the ruefulness of American composers when year after year their experiments go nearly unheeded, while attempts no more felicitous than theirs, and often a good deal clumsier, are taken up with such sympathy by conductors and recitalists and audiences.

2. Many performances of modern works (as well as of ancient ones) are required, but so are many performers. Unless one believes that there is one single "right" performance of a work, which can be defined, demonstrated, and imitated, one will be restless until one has heard a variety of interpretations. Only an electronic work, written for "synthesizer," can be done once and for all time, and even it is susceptible to limitations of recording or playback equipment and may have to be changed with a changing technology of sound reproduction. But that aside, how uncertain our grasp of most American music is! Compare what we know of even the most frequently performed American works with our knowledge of and feeling for works contemporary with the American, works by Debussy, Ravel, Richard Strauss, Prokofiev, Vaughan Williams, Britten, and so on.

3. See Robert Browning, *Paracelsus,* V. The speaker is Paracelsus.

4. Psalm 67 is the very definition of a psalm. Though it invokes God's blessing, its seven verses are almost all praise, and its central line—"O let the nations be glad and sing for joy . . ."—is made to Ives's musical order.

5. See Aaron Copland, *Copland on Music* (New York: Doubleday, 1960), p. 138.

6. See, for example, Copland's *Piano Fantasy* (1957), which he himself identifies as "absolute music. It makes no use whatever of folk or popular music materials. The composer's purpose was to attempt a composition that would suggest the quality of fantasy, that is 'events' that would carry the listener (if possible) from the first note to the last, while at the same time exemplifying clear if somewhat unconventional structural principles." By 1957, Copland's return to the precincts of private art required such a disclaimer and explication. It also deserved some celebration.

7. Schuman has never been guilty of the kind of ostentatious pledge of allegiance with which left-wing composers were making concert halls and movie theaters and radio studios noisy in the late thirties and early forties, a time when Carl Sandburg's *The People, Yes* was regarded as a religious document by those for whom communism was "twentieth-century Americanism" and to whom the sounds of the prairie seemed most appropriate for a confession of faith, even if it was a faith born in Brooklyn and nurtured in Hollywood.

8. The English translation of Menotti's Italian libretto for *The Last Savage* (1963) makes his attack on tastes and tempers in the modern world into so much mush, which nothing in the conventional score relieves. For what it reveals of Menotti's hostility to almost everything of consequence in the contemporary American arts, the opera has a certain documentary importance. A much more engaging document is Samuel Barber's *Piano Concerto* (1963), which sounds much of the time like a recapitulation of the central modes of concerto writing in this century, with particular reverence for Prokofiev's *Third Piano Concerto*. Like the best known works in this genre, it is a fine vehicle for a bravura pianist.

9. One can whistle Henderson's two- and four-bar figurations; nothing in Cage is quite so easily picked up. But his fragments often do "swing": they catch the attention and focus it, forcing a response which may be as much to his theater as to his music, but which is not any less valid as a result. His piece for silent pianist and silent piano is good drama and amusing theater; it also makes a useful point about the sounds of coughing, the turning of buttocks in the seats, and the shuffling of programs, which are also part of the sound of music in the twentieth century.

POPULAR MUSIC

1. Negro life as reflected by white librettists and composers in *Porgy and Bess* and *Carmen Jones* is without depth or dimension, even when one makes all the necessary allowances for the simplifications inherent in opera narrative and dialogue. The events are violent, the characters crudely motivated, and the diction in which they set forth the unmitigated anguish of their lives is a caricature of the language spoken by Negroes in the South. A fitting irony in all of this is that the Gershwin songs and Oscar Hammerstein's adaptations of Bizet are most often sung by trained singers, white or Negro; their educated accents inevitably make *dese-dem-dose*-ing and the *gwine*-ing seem not only inapposite, but ridiculous.

2. Weill's lack of pretentiousness was not always good box office. But it did offer a pattern of performance for those who want to be serious without being ostentatious about it. If a composer in this genre could somehow combine the Broadway melancholy of Weill's late years with

the Berlin acerbity of his early years, what a splendid musical style he would have for a tale of futility and frustration!

3. The special failure of this inflated popular music was that it did not take any significant advantage of electronic techniques. Apart from the echo chamber and the opportunities that tape provided for splicing together bits and pieces of different "takes" of the same number, nothing reflects any awareness on the part of composer, arranger, or performer of the enormous technological resources now accessible to musicians. In this branch of popular music, as in most channels of private music, the working musician still has an eighteenth-century conception of his craft.

4. Johnny Burke is best known for his songs written in collaboration with others, to most of which he contributed the lyrics. He was capable of skillfully made tunes as well as lyrics, and not only in collaboration, as his performance as composer and lyricist for the musical *Donnybrook* (1962) demonstrates.

5. The success of the title song of *Hello, Dolly!* (1964), which more or less mimics a gay nineties' tune, in keeping with its setting of Thornton Wilder's *The Matchmaker,* has prompted some to suggest that good new pop tunes will in future be written only as imitations of good old pop tunes. Haven't they always? No particular daring is expected of a composer in this genre. But it should also be remembered that the song in question became a hit in large part because of Louis Armstrong's swinging recording of it. Jazz procedures have still not been much studied or employed by the writers of musicals. There is still a large new territory open to them. But it does require some small invention and a modicum of daring to enter it.

JAZZ

1. The affinity of jazz for things sexual is real enough, but that it is any more significant or solid a tie than that between, say, poetry and sexuality is debatable. The ecstasies that jazz reports and records are generally small-scale; the passions of jazz are usually short-lived. What makes the sexual glosses and comments of jazz so entertaining is their mixture of biting acid and tolerant irony. Sentimentality is usually the butt of a jazzman's joke, and sentimentality has no more certain environment than the congress of the sexes. The major contribution that the association of jazz and the bordello provided was familiarity. While the jazzman of post-New Orleans music is no longer dependent upon the same housekeepers for employment, he still plays in a world close enough to that of the bordello. In this area of human enterprise, he still speaks with authority.

2. "If only he had lived. . . ." Early death is so fundamental a part

of jazz history that an examination of the work of the distinguished early dead is almost enough in itself to convey the quality of the music at every stage. Bix Beiderbecke, Frank Teschemacher, Jimmy Harrison, Bessie Smith, Eddie Lang, Chu Berry, Chick Webb, Bunny Berrigan, Charlie Christian, Jimmy Blanton, Mildred Bailey, Sonny Berman, Dick Twardzik, Serge Chaloff, Charlie Parker, Fats Navarro, Clifford Brown, Eric Dolphy —the list is astonishingly long, appallingly long. Longevity in jazz is too often a function of mediocrity or obscurity. And success much too frequently requires a life that neither head nor heart nor stomach can long sustain.

3. It can be argued, I think, that no other pianist in jazz made such a contribution to the art as Earl Hines did. Certainly no other has proved so long-lived as a soloist of distinction, capable of adapting himself to the changes in time, in texture, and in playing procedure from Louis Armstrong's *Wunderkind* years in Chicago, through bop and the years of cool, to the confusion of the sixties, and still very much his own person. Among performers on other instruments, only Coleman Hawkins has shown a comparable flexibility and control over so long a period.

4. The quality of Bessie Smith's work survives about as well on records as that of John McCormack or Enrico Caruso. It is flawed by inadequate recording techniques; its robustness is only suggested; its deeper timbers are not presented with the fullness of resonance that they had in person. Nonetheless, the beat is there; the commanding way of shaping a phrase and the great reserves of power waiting in the lungs are more than suggested. If one is not moved by Bessie Smith on records, it is not because her substance was never collected between the grooves.

5. Many bands in the swing years and just after came close to the high distinction of Henderson and Ellington—for a season or two, sometimes for as long as a decade, long enough to leave behind some excellent records. Such bands were those of Chick Webb and Jimmie Lunceford, of Don Redman and Benny Carter and the various organizations with which they had their playing-arranging-leading associations. Such bands were Charlie Barnet's and Tommy Dorsey's, the former's when he was most slavishly imitative of Duke Ellington, the latter's when he was most determined to capture some of the quality of the Lunceford powerhouse. But none of these bands was so consistent as Henderson's various personnels or so imaginative as Ellington's.

6. A standard lament in jazz circles since the late forties has been over the decline and fall of the big band. An equal cause for joy has been the sudden appearance of any new organization that indicated that another big-band era might be at hand. Thus almost every edition of Stan Kenton's band has been greated with eager applause. Thus Maynard Ferguson's attempts to build a band of distinction around his loud, far-ranging

trumpet have been received with hopeful enthusiasm. Unfortunately, the American economy has not responded with equal enthusiasm. Until there is a deflation great enough so that it does not seem so fearfully expensive to go dancing where a "name" band is playing or until the Department of Commerce decides to underwrite big-band tours of the United States as the State Department has paid for band tours of Asia and Africa, there will be no large number of big bands again, the laments and the sudden bursts of eager and hopeful applause will continue, and jazz will not have the hold it had on the American imagination in the thirties and the forties.

7. Like all the popular arts, jazz bogs down in clichés with a deadly periodicity. Every few years, a school having made its mark on hundreds of musicians, a particular way of playing can be heard, almost phrase for phrase and note for note, all across the land. Each new school is a revolt against the old one, which has become revolting in a very different way as it prepares to die. No revolt of this sort was ever so violent, so upsetting to so many, or, for a while at least, so triumphant as bop.

8. Not only trumpeters imitated Dizzy Gillespie; not only instrumentalists imitated Charlie Parker. Singers also picked up the new ways, especially two gifted, musicianly singers, Billy Eckstine and Sarah Vaughan, who remained closely identified with bop throughout its formative years. Eckstine developed his rich sound and shrewd phrasing with Earl Hines and then with a band of his own from 1944 to 1947, a band which at one time or another included among its musicians Charlie Parker, Dizzy Gillespie, Miles Davis, Fats Navarro, and Sarah Vaughan. Sarah Vaughan was quite entitled to a listing among musicians in her years with Eckstine and just after. She worked out her cadences, like Eckstine, with a musician's understanding of structure, selecting her notes for improvisation with a sureness of touch that one would have expected in a pianist like Bud Powell. Her tones were large, warm, dependable. In solo or duet with Eckstine, she could be listened to as a jazz musician. The failure of both these singers to maintain the same level of performance is in part the result of trying to fix themselves in a commercially attractive style, in part the loss of the brilliant musical support that the best of the bop musicians, playing at their best, gave them.

9. Jazz dies in a jazzman when commercial success becomes his major goal. He depends upon spontaneity, and spontaneity generally fights the badges of identity without which commercial success is not possible. There are exceptions to this grim economic law, but they do not come quickly to mind. The worst of its effects is that once the major concession has been made to it, a performer is helpless to recover his freedom to experiment as widely or as daringly as Lennie Tristano has, for example, in his development of a kind of polyrhythmic improvisation that permits him to play two lines with each hand—four lines altogether and at once—as

well as in two different times and with an elaborate system of borrowings and anticipations that gives his piano solos a tension and a breadth unequaled in jazz.

PAINTING

1. Everybody still talks about Duchamp's descending *Nude*. Many, much too young to remember the Armory Show, still think of it as the special blazon of modern painting, and they use it to whip the art with philistine fervor, to confess their confusion in the face of everything that has followed it, or to indicate the deviation from naturalistic representation that has given painting its identifying character, good or bad, in this century.

2. See José Ortega y Gasset, "The Dehumanization of Art," in *The Dehumanization of Art and Other Writings on Art and Culture* (New York: Doubleday, 1956). This essay, originally published in 1948, is an unusually coherent statement of the reasons why painting inevitably stopped offering its viewers the lure of the vicarious and withdrew more and more into the processes of abstraction.

3. See *America and Alfred Stieglitz, A Collective Portrait* (New York: Doubleday, 1934), pp. 245, 234–235.

4. See Ben Shahn, *The Shape of Content* (Cambridge, Mass.: Harvard, 1957), pp. 38–39.

5. No geometrician was ever more incisive than Ad Reinhardt, whether with paints or words. He has done explications of modern painting for newspaper readers, for critics, for painters. He has mocked his tormenters and tormented his mockers with a raillery in prose and cartoon that has always been entertaining, has often been perfectly aimed, and has never failed to say something of some value about the nature of modern painting and the modern painter. His most incisive performances are on canvas, however, a small history of the possibilities of formal design in the painting of our time, with touches of nearly every kind of hook, square, line, and plane in the geometrical designer's vocabulary. He has even made black on black into something more than an eccentric's comment on the eccentricities of abstract expression. Like John Cage's silences, Ad Reinhardt's blacks call attention to unexplored realms of possibility in art, things that need to be looked at, thought about, and used.

6. Statement by Barnett Newman for the exhibition *The New American Painting* (1958). See the catalog of the exhibition, published under the same title (New York, 1959).

7. Hopkins' speculations on the *thisness* of an object derive from his reading of Duns Scotus. What he has to say in his *Notebooks* about

490   N O T E S

*thisness—haecceitas—*is quite useful as a commentary on the abstract painter's approach to an object, though he makes his comments as a poet and priest professionally involved with philosophy and theology, not as a painter.

8. See *The New American Painting,* p. 36.

9. There is a color reproduction of *Burst* in *The New American Painting,* but no very significant impression of the painting can be gathered from it: its great size, 96 by 40 inches, has been reduced to 9 by 3¾ inches. A similar caution must be made about most reproductions of painting, in black and white or in color, but especially about the huge canvases of the New York School, which lose much of their vitality and become little more than amusing graphic art when diminished to less than one-tenth their original size.

10. Alfonso Ossorio, quoted in *The New American Painting,* p. 64.

11. Willem de Kooning, quoted in *ibid.,* p. 52.

12. The preoccupations of pop and op artists with the surfaces of things suggest that it will be quite a while before manipulating and maneuvering lose their appeal or develop well beyond the superficial machinery to which pop art has dragged the procedures of abstract expressionism.

13. See Larry Rivers, "A Discussion of the Work of Larry Rivers," *Art News,* March, 1961.

14. The development of figure painting along lines close to abstract expressionism is most evident, perhaps, in the New York galleries, but it can also be seen in the work of artists who do not show often or regularly in New York or the cities that depend upon it for their tastes. An excellent example is the work of Byron Burford, a painter in residence at the State University of Iowa, in Iowa City. All his figure paintings of the late fifties and sixties show the firm sense of design characteristic of the new figure painting, but they are also a remarkable record of his own fascination with the uprooted men who made up the armies of the First World War, with jazz musicians (he himself has been one), with people whose flattened lives fill a flattened space with particular aptness and eloquence.

SCULPTURE

1. The discussions in Caffin's book reflect the quality of the sculptors and sculpture Caffin admires very well. The tone is one of reverent awe before the might of the past that can be made to live again by the mighty artists of the present. For a considerable contrast in tone and attitude, see Herbert Read, *The Art of Sculpture: The A. W. Mellon Lectures in the Fine Arts, 1954* (New York: Pantheon, 1956). "For good or ill we

now demand from the artist an expression of *truth*," Read says just before the end of his book, "and in judging the success of the artist in this task our criterion is the subjective criterion of vitality rather than the objective criterion of harmony. We say of a work of art that it *moves* us, that it appeals to us, that it fascinates us, that it excites us—all expressions that indicate a psychological and not an intellectual reaction." Truth, as Read suggests in his last paragraph, may be "just as ambiguous" an aim as beauty, but it does mark another significant stage in the "evolving sense of reality" to which art gives constant testimony.

2. See Elizabeth C. Baker, "The Late Lachaise, Uncensored At Last," *Art News*, March, 1964. One hopes that the reader will not make judgments on the basis of photographs of Lachaise's sculpture. They do not give an accurate sense of proportion. Their textures are those of photography, not of sculpture. The sexuality in the pictures of the sculpture is literary, illustrative, not bulging with life, as the actual sculpture is.

3. The sculpture of Lipschitz is admirably adapted to gardens and large open spaces. It demands long and meditative viewing. Perhaps as municipal commissions and private donors find themselves more at ease with the procedures of modern art, they will think of the appropriateness of such sculpture in the large open spaces of our great cities.

4. The strength of sculpture like Zorach's and that of his contemporary, the Spanish-American José De Creeft, is in its bull-like masses. De Creeft's feeling for stone textures is communicated in contrasts of finished and unfinished surfaces. John Flannagan's attempts, in his short life, were less ambitious, but perhaps more graceful in their acceptance of the direction afforded by the stone itself.

5. See E. C. Goossen, R. Goldwater, and I. Sandler, *Three American Sculptors: Ferber, Hare, Lassaw* (New York: Braziller, 1959). For discussions of these and other American sculptors of the present, see Carola Giedion-Welcker, *Contemporary Sculpture: An Evolution in Volume and Space* (New York: Wittenborn, 1960), and Michel Seuphor, *The Sculpture of This Century* (New York: Braziller, 1960). The Giedion-Welcker volume has a useful selective bibliography by Bernard Karpel.

6. For some of the background of this attitude toward the object, see Robert Motherwell (ed.), *The Dada Painters and Poets* (New York: Wittenborn, 1951), and Robert Lebel, *Marcel Duchamp* (New York: Grove, 1959). Duchamp's wry comment, *"Il n'y a pas de solution parce qu'il n'y a pas de problème,"* is an excellent guide to recent sculpture in America.

7. Great distinction has accrued to the New York State Theater at Lincoln Center because of its use of sculpture. In addition to the Bontecou monument, there are excellent pieces by Nadelman and Lipton.

Philip Johnson's great entrance hall, so much like the halls at the Deutsche Oper in West Berlin in its large theatrical flying spaces, makes a splendid setting for Nadelman's odd, open-bodied women.

PHOTOGRAPHY

1. See *America and Alfred Stieglitz, A Collective Portrait* (New York: Doubleday, 1934), pp. 116, 285.

2. Stills have been ingeniously used, from time to time, in television commercials and, less adroitly, in TV news programs and documentaries. The possibilities for the employment of the still photograph in television, at different speeds, in different lights, in whole shot or in fragment, are being examined with far more care by European studios than by American, perhaps because of economic necessity.

3. See Jerry Mason (ed.), *ASMP Picture Annual* (New York: Simon and Schuster, 1957), pp. 20–21.

4. *Ibid.*, p. 130.

5. Moholy-Nagy had shrewd perceptions about the relationship between photography, painting, sculpture, and type design that were often clear in his own work as an artist, a theorist, and a teacher. Photographic composition has been used effectively in American typography, but the sort of thing Man Ray was doing has only been suggested in some of the designs of men like Paul Rand and the late Alvin Lustig. For further indications of related conceptions of design in which photography has a role of significance, see Ladislaus Moholy-Nagy, *The New Vision* (New York: Norton, 1938); Gyorgy Kepes, *Language of Vision* (Chicago: Theobald, 1945); Paul Rand, *Thoughts on Design* (New York: Wittenborn, 1951).

6. See Jerry Mason (ed.), *The Family of Man* (New York: Museum of Modern Art, 1955). There is an extraordinary difference between the full-size original edition of the book and the version in pocketbook size. Both have their separate and individual eloquences, but what is intrinsically and essentially photographic in the larger format tends to become literary, an elaborate accompaniment to the brief texts, in the small pocketbook.

7. See Chapters 10, 13, and 15, in Edward Steichen, *A Life in Photography* (New York: Doubleday, 1963), for a fuller discussion of the photographer's "creative act."

8. Some indication of where abstract photography may go can be gathered from the collection of photographs by three Americans, Nathan Lyons, Syl Labrot, and Walter Chappell, *Under the Sun: The Abstract Art of Camera Vision* (New York: Braziller, 1960). Several of the photographs, both in color and in black and white, seem to justify Chap-

pell's comment, "The art of creative work in any medium is, for me personally, to unify my discovery of Nature with the growing discovery of my inner being. . . ."

ARCHITECTURE

1. See Louis Sullivan, *The Autobiography of an Idea* (Gloucester, Mass.: Peter Smith, 1956), pp. 257–258.

2. The acoustical failure or near-failure of so many recent auditoriums is more than vexing; it indicates a scandalous disregard for liveness of sound on the part of architects who would be appalled if their architectural designs revealed such a loss of vitality. The fact is that steel, concrete, and glass have not yet revealed the warmth of response and the openness to resonances in music that are inherent in wood, and no treatment thus far devised has been able to compensate for the loss of sound in the modern concert hall or theater. The construction of a theory justifying dead sound, that is, sound that stops the moment it is uttered or played, is an almost offensive reminder of how unpleasant listening to music or speech can be in a dead acoustical chamber.

3. Root, speaking at a symposium in 1887, said, "Our architecture will probably remain practical. This means not only that structures of purely decorative character will be few in number, but that each important detail of a building must have some immediate, easily recognized and practical use." The "Chicago window," with its large horizontal span, was easily recognizable and had an obviously practical use. It brought light into Chicago buildings—and those in other cities—and onto them as well, in the breadth it afforded the designer. See Harriet R. Monroe, *John Welborn Root: A Study of His Life and Work* (Boston: Houghton, Mifflin, 1896), and John Burchard and Albert Bush-Brown, *The Architecture of America: A Social and Cultural History* (Boston: Atlantic Monthly, 1961), p. 207.

4. See F. Gutheim (ed.), *Frank Lloyd Wright on Architecture* (New York: Duell, 1941), and Frank Lloyd Wright, *Autobiography* (New York: Longmans, 1932).

5. Richard Neutra, quoted in John Peter, *Makers of Modern Architecture* (New York: George Braziller, 1958), pp. 38–39. See also Richard Neutra, *Life and Human Habitat* (Stuttgart: Alexander Koch, 1956), pp. 22–23.

6. See John Peter, *Makers of Modern Architecture*, p. 39. Neutra's separation of his architecture, in these words, from the theory and practice of those architects who are most closely associated with painting and sculpture seems to ally him with an architecture that is either self-consciously functional or commercial or both. Need these approaches be

mutually exclusive? Later practice, more flexible than Neutra's and more open to the architect's personal vision, suggests that such an opposition or dichotomy is false. After all, beauty, even if it comes through "some over-simplified, static, geometrical, or mystic 'modulor,'" is also functional.

7. Recent alterations and additions have not made the Metropolitan Tower and associated structures any more attractive or any less anthological, nor have they taken any better advantage of the insurance company's handsome site at the east end of Madison Square Park.

8. Whatever the sexual force the Empire State Building manifests, it is a misfortune for American architecture that its sheer size should have made it the central symbol of skyscraper design in the country's largest city. Whatever the limitations of Minoru Yamasaki's designs for the twin towers of the World Trade Center, his huge boxes, topped and bottomed by interlaced arches, will be far more attractive in the role of architectural heraldry, to which their height—the world's highest—destines them.

9. See Christopher Tunnard, *The City of Man* (New York: Scribner, 1953), especially Part I, "In Search of a City," and Part II, "Tradition and Experiment."

10. The eighteenth-century translation of Alberti's *De Re Aedificatoria Libri Decem, The Architecture of Leone Battista Alberti,* translated from the Italian by James Leoni, has been reprinted with some corrections and additions (London: Transatlantic, 1955).

11. Urban sprawl is an ugly blight on American cities, but city planning that is based on the premise that everything in a district must be razed before intelligent designing can begin rates the mementos of the past, as well as its architectural performances, too low. It not only threatens to wipe out Middle Monstrous and Late Hideous, but offers us the ugly possibility of cities without a past, except in dusty archives. Even a crank antiquarianism is preferable to this sort of unfeeling surgery.

12. The New York World's Fair of 1964 was less successful architecturally than Lincoln Center, but it had its moments, such as Saarinen's eggshell housing for the IBM show, a fine union of typographical and architectural design; and Edward Durell Stone's series of peaked-hat roofings for the small Christian Science building, a piquant merging of styles to provide a delicate eye-catching display outside and a frame for a sequence of exhibits inside. There were other acceptable designs, but the general effect was of 1925 *moderne*. As is so often true in popularizations in other arts, so is it in architecture: to find public acceptance, a style must be loud, familiar, and highly decorated. If the World's Fair styles had been a little louder, they would have been quite acceptable as good carnival: instead, they were too frequently merely nervous throw-

backs to a bad period in our architecture and interior design, when almost everything was imported—and imported by people who knew little about what they were bringing over to this country or why they were bringing it.

13. Yamasaki's appeal is obviously broad. His arches have some of the same appeal that rows of classical columns do: they proclaim the power of a simple repeated motif, of proportion, of measurement that the eye can quickly take in. They do not disturb the viewer used to the touches of Renaissance and Gothic architecture in American design from the late nineteenth century to the Second World War. Yamasaki is a *popular* architect in every sense of the word.

14. See *Louis I. Kahn; Architect Alfred Newton Richards Medical Research Building,* Museum of Modern Art Bulletin, Vol. 28, No. 1, New York: 1961, p. 3. See also the two statements by Kahn in Vincent Scully, Jr., *Louis I. Kahn* (New York: Braziller, 1962), pp. 113–121.

POETRY

1. See "Solipsism," in *The Poems of George Santayana* (New York: Scribner, 1923).

2. See "On Some Shells Found Inland" and "Live Blindly," in *The Poems of Trumbull Stickney* (Boston: Houghton, Mifflin, 1905).

3. See "Bryan, Bryan, Bryan, Bryan," in Vachel Lindsay, *Collected Poems* (New York: Macmillan, 1923).

4. See "The Man Against the Sky," and "New England," in Edwin Arlington Robinson, *Collected Poems* (New York: Macmillan, 1937).

5. See "Once by the Pacific," "Acquainted with the Night," "Desert Places," and "Directive," in *The Complete Poems of Robert Frost* (New York: Holt, 1949), and "A Cabin in the Clearing," in Robert Frost, *In the Clearing* (New York: Holt, 1962).

6. See Wallace Stevens, *The Relations Between Poetry and Painting* (New York: The Museum of Modern Art, 1951).

7. See "The Sense of the Sleight-of-Hand Man," in *The Collected Poems of Wallace Stevens* (New York: Knopf, 1954).

8. See "The Idea of Order at Key West," *ibid.*

9. See "The Widow's Lament in Springtime" and "Rain," in *The Collected Poems of William Carlos Williams, 1906–1938* (New York: New Directions, 1938).

10. See "Poetry," "In Distrust of Merits," and "Armour's Undermining Modesty," in Marianne Moore, *Collected Poems* (New York: Macmillan, 1951).

11. See Canto LXXXI in Ezra Pound, *The Cantos* (New York: New Directions, 1948).

12. See *Homage to Sextus Propertius* and "E. P. Ode pour l'élection de son sépulchre," in Ezra Pound, *Personae* (New York: New Directions, 1926).

13. See *Ash-Wednesday*, in *The Complete Poems and Plays of T. S. Eliot* (New York: Harcourt, Brace, 1960).

14. See Pound, *Homage to Sextus Propertius, op. cit.*

15. See "Survey of Literature," in John Crowe Ransom, *Poems and Essays* (New York: Vintage, 1955).

16. See "Apology for Bad Dreams," Part II, in *The Selected Poetry of Robinson Jeffers* (New York: Random, 1938).

17. Bishop's novel remains a deeply moving presentation of the effect of sexual relations between the races—and not simply as an historical record of attitudes. It is a poet's transcription of an act of darkness, in which persons transcend politics, even if they do not transform it.

18. See "Overture to Today," Part II, in Conrad Aiken, *A Letter from Li Po and other Poems* (London: Oxford, 1955).

19. See "The Harbor Dawn" and "The River," in *The Collected Poems of Hart Crane* (New York: Liveright, 1933).

20. See "Pity This Busy Monster, Manunkind," "What If a Much of a Which of a Wind," and "My Father Moved Through Dooms of Love," in E. E. Cummings, *Poems 1923–1954* (New York: Harcourt, Brace, 1954).

21. See "The Abyss" and "The Far Field," in Theodore Roethke, *The Far Field* (New York: Doubleday, 1964), and "The Cow," "The Sloth," and "Open House," in Theodore Roethke, *Words for the Wind* (New York: Doubleday, 1958).

22. See "Elegy Written on a Frontporch," in Karl Shapiro, *Poems 1940–1953* (New York: Random, 1953).

23. See "The Quaker Graveyard in Nantucket," in Robert Lowell, *Lord Weary's Castle* (New York: Harcourt, Brace, 1946), and "Aeneid," in Lowell, *The Mills of the Kavanaughs* (New York: Harcourt, Brace, 1951).

24. See "Heart's Needle," in W. D. Snodgrass, *Heart's Needle* (New York: Knopf, 1959).

25. See "Art," in Denise Levertov, *With Eyes in the Back of Our Heads* (New York: New Directions, 1959).

26. See "Someone Talking to Himself," in Richard Wilbur, *Advice to a Prophet and Other Poems* (New York: Harcourt, Brace, 1961).

THE SHORT STORY

1. See Edgar Allan Poe, "Twice-Told Tales by Nathaniel Hawthorne: A Review," written in 1842. He makes the same point about the initial

effect of a story in his essay "The Philosophy of Composition," written four years later. The essay, though chiefly concerned with the writing of poems, starts with some preliminary considerations about the construction of a story.

2. The quotation starts at the third sentence of the opening paragraph of "The Beast in the Jungle." The date of the story is 1903.

3. See "The Teacher" and "Departure," in Sherwood Anderson, *Winesburg, Ohio.* Both stories are reprinted in *The Portable Sherwood Anderson,* ed. Horace Gregory (New York: Viking, 1949), pp. 96, 114–115.

4. See Ernest Hemingway, "The Capital of the World," in *The Hemingway Reader,* ed. Charles Poore (New York: Scribner, 1953), pp. 572–573.

5. See "Old Man," in *The Faulkner Reader* (New York: Modern Library, 1959), p. 378.

6. See "That Evening Sun," in *The Portable Faulkner,* ed. Malcolm Cowley (New York: Viking, 1946), p. 464.

7. See *The Ballad of the Sad Café: The Novels and Stories of Carson McCullers* (Boston: Houghton Mifflin, 1951), pp. 24–25.

8. See "Beatrice Trueblood's Story," in Jean Stafford, John Cheever, etc., *Stories* (New York: Farrar, Straus, 1956), p. 86.

9. See John Cheever, *The Enormous Radio and Other Stories* (New York: Funk, Wagnalls, 1953), p. 181.

10. Roth's *Letting Go* (New York: Random, 1962) takes us a long way farther into the processes—thought processes, gland processes, all sorts of processes—of adolescents trying to escape from adolescence and getting more and more mired in it with every clumsy attempt. Mostly, they seem to be suffering from a bad case of campus cramps, which short stories dramatize rather better than very long novels.

11. Baldwin has preferred in recent years to concentrate on the novel and essays. But in his polemics, perhaps his best written pieces, he is still telling the same tale of suffering and delight and possible triumph, and the note of conviction is the same—a small light in the darkness still raises hope.

THE NOVEL

1. See Henry James, *The Wings of the Dove* (New York: Scribner, 1902), pp. x–xi.

2. See the Introduction to Paul Valéry, *Monsieur Teste,* trans. Jackson Matthews (New York: Knopf, 1947), p. x.

3. See Henry James, *The Golden Bowl* (New York: Scribner, 1905), p. 63.

4. See Edith Wharton, *The Reef* (New York: Scribner, 1912), pp. 12–13, 21.

5. See Edith Wharton, *The Fruit of the Tree* (New York: Scribner, 1907), pp. 4–5, 615.

6. *The Golden Bowl*, p. 273.

7. *Ibid.*, p. 290.

8. *The Wings of the Dove*, p. xi.

9. See "Letters and Leadership," in Van Wyck Brooks, *America's Coming-of-Age* (New York: Doubleday, 1958), p. 154.

10. *The Wings of the Dove*, pp. xxiv–v.

11. See Letter to Henry Adams, in *The Portable Henry James*, ed. M. D. Zabel (New York: Viking, 1951), pp. 675–676.

12. See William James, "The Dilemma of Determinism," in *The Will to Believe and Other Essays in Popular Philosophy* (New York: Longmans, 1907), pp. 172–173.

13. See World edition of Theodore Dreiser, *The Financier* (Cleveland: World Pub., n.d.), pp. 254–255. For a similar response to the *things* of a city, the furniture of rooms and of streets, see Chapter 31 of *Sister Carrie*, "Broadway Flaunts Its Joys," especially the opening and closing pages.

14. See Compass edition of Saul Bellow, *The Adventures of Augie March* (New York: Viking, 1960), pp. 3, 438, 99–100.

15. See the splendid discussion of Ellison and his book in Marcus Klein's *After Alienation: American Novels in Mid-Century* (Cleveland: World Pub., 1963), Chapter III. "He embraces the *blackness* of blackness," Klein says of Ellison's man, "and thereby becomes an underground man—like Dostoevski's hero, an incarnation of that which is just beneath the surface of things that is treacherous, irresponsible and mad. He embraces that fate to which he was 'before of old ordained,' and thereby inherits that 'power of blackness' which Melville said 'derives its force from its appeals to that Calvinistic sense of Innate Depravity and Original Sin, from whose visitations, in some shape or other, no deeply thinking mind is always and wholly free.'" (pp. 143–144) Ellison's special achievement may have been to see the "power of blackness" in nearly metaphysical terms, to have taken it, as Dostoevski took the power of powerlessness, into the philosophical latitudes, to have taken it where it surely needs to go, beyond social struggle and political and economic combat, to have raised it to the *n*th power.

16. See Compass edition of William Styron, *Lie Down in Darkness* (New York: Viking 1957), p. 386.

17. The little horror tale that hovers somewhere between the serious novel and the mystery story does not often rise above the light air necessary for successful hovering. These tales usually rise as the result of a

determined effort on the part of their writers to make their horrifying events signify something about the nature of human evil. They do not often achieve great heights. Their central characters remain too horrifying, figures more of fantasy than of reality, with an insufficient complexity of motivation or action to give them psychological depth. But they can produce a considerable degree of terror, and notably in the case of Patricia Highsmith, a more than matching revulsion at the depraved humans who are responsible for the terror. Less self-consciously literary than works like *Set this House on Fire* (New York: Random, 1960), unmistakably popular art, they can also be unmistakably artful.

18. The recurring lament over the novel, either given up for dead by its mourners or tiptoed past out of respect for the past accomplishments of the poor dying old thing, seems to me to be justified in some small part by the hundred and one clumsinesses of the cult of verisimilitude. The new naturalism is no more attractive than the old, first of all because it is bound, under a sense of duty on the part of the naturalistic writer, not to be attractive, and secondly because the highest meditation to which it aspires is one on the evils of our sick society—economic evils, mostly, with psychological side effects. But even if this is not the case, as it is not in the later novels of Swados or in the novels of R. V. Cassill, the accretion of naturalistic detail is not made to serve a large enough purpose. The books too often fall into mere detail, even when it is shrewdly observed detail—details of the warfare that love breeds as much as hate among three brothers, as observed by Swados; details of the pointless appetites of a Wolfe-like American writer and of the pointed hunger of an American housewife who demands sexual violation, as observed by Cassill.

19. See Jean Stafford, *The Mountain Lion* (New York: Random, 1947), pp. 31–32.

20. See Mary McCarthy, *The Company She Keeps* (New York: Harcourt, 1942), p. ii.

21. See Ellen Glasgow, *The Romantic Comedians* (New York: Doubleday, 1926), pp. 1, 345–346.

22. See Ellen Glasgow, *They Stooped to Folly* (New York: Doubleday, 1929), p. 350, and *The Sheltered Life* (New York: Doubleday, 1932), pp. 383, 395.

23. See Willa Cather, *Death Comes for the Archbishop* (New York: Knopf, 1927), pp. 166–7, 95.

24. See Willa Cather, *The Professor's House* (New York: Knopf, 1925), p. 265.

25. See Willa Cather, *Lucy Gayheart* (New York: Knopf, 1935), pp. 199, 221.

26. See Elizabeth Madox Roberts, *The Time of Man* (New York: Viking, 1926), pp. 82–83, 379, 380, 382.

27. See Elizabeth Madox Roberts, *A Buried Treasure* (New York: Viking, 1931), pp. 26, 255.

28. See Signet edition of Elizabeth Madox Roberts, *The Great Meadow* (New York: N.A.L., 1961), pp. 71–72, 119.

29. See Elizabeth Sprigge, *Gertrude Stein: Her Life and Works* (New York: Harper, 1957), p. 126. See also Anderson's sketch of Miss Stein, in substantially the same words, written in 1919 for *The New Republic* and reprinted in *The Portable Sherwood Anderson* (New York: Viking, 1939), pp. 551–552.

30. See *The Portable Sherwood Anderson* (New York: Viking, 1939), pp. 401–402.

31. See Permabooks edition of Ernest Hemingway, *To Have and Have Not* (New York: 1953), pp. 191, 192, 140–141.

32. See F. Scott Fitzgerald, *The Crack-Up* (New York: New Directions, 1945), p. 69.

33. On and on we go, through the ganglia, through the gonads, through the hopped-up veins and hardening arteries of our troubadours of visceral enchantment, Henry Miller, J. P. Donleavy, Jack Kerouac, William Burroughs. How much it is the same, page after page, book after book, writer after writer—"outblownness, cut-off-ness snipped, blownout-ness, putoutness, turned-off-ness, nothing-happens-ness, gone-ness, gone-out-ness, the snapped link. . . .", as Kerouac puts it in *The Dharma Bums* (New York: Viking, 1958). "What is that feeling," Kerouac asks in his most disciplined (or perhaps best edited) book, *On the Road* (New York: Viking, 1957), "when you're driving away from people and they recede on the plain till you see their specks dispersing?—it's the too-huge world vaulting us, and it's good-by. But we lean forward to the next crazy venture beneath the skies." Kerouac's leanings are leaner and leaner with each book, but in his mapping of the American road, he produced something with at least the shape of a novel, with one memorable character, Dean Moriarty, who "drove on with his mouth hanging in awe, ten miles an hour, desirous to see every possible human being on the road." Even Dean is flat, like the people in the new figure painting, but he has some dimension; he is more than the sum total of his secretions or his bludgeonings with drugs. Kerouac's wanderings in the higher metaphysics of Zen have nothing much to recommend them except as witness to the intensity with which a writer and his characters will pursue experience, any experience, as long as it promises a continuity of explosions. Burroughs' lucubrations on behalf of the drugged and the inverted, *The Naked Lunch* (New York: Grove, 1959) and *The Ticket That Exploded* (Paris: Olympia Press, 1962), are interesting as samples of the new ped-

antry of dirty words and dirtier experiences. Like a composer who writes everything triple *forte,* he offers no contrasts of tone or feeling or dynamics. There are no people, no events, but only a verbal combat, in which neither drug-taking, nor homosexuality, nor the good fight against repression and repressors triumphs. What might have been an entertaining fable of the foolishness of most people's sexual attitudes turns out not to be *The Ticket* at all, but just another dose of verbal dysentery. Donleavy is the best of the crowd, though he is as repetitious as the worst of them. At least his boys, *The Ginger Man* (New York: Random, 1961) and *A Singular Man* (Boston: Little, Brown, 1963), the one in his endless tiltings and tittuppings in the fleshyards, the other in his massive construction and frenzied leading of an imaginary life, have gusto. Both have some of the sound and a little of the wit of Ireland. In both, Donleavy shows so much compassion for his central characters, Sebastian Dangerfield, the Ginger Man, and George Smith, the furious fantasist, that something like love bursts through. That is almost enough to make the repetitiousness acceptable.

34. See *The Faulkner Reader* (New York: Random, 1954), p. 4.

35. See William Faulkner, *A Fable* (New York: Random, 1954), p. 354.

36. See *The Faulkner Reader* (New York: Random, 1954), pp. viii-ix.

37. Knowing when to stop is a rare gift. Joseph Heller's *Catch-22* (1961) and Thomas Pynchon's *V* (1963) are robust novels, inventive novels, witty in their adaptations of eighteenth-century elaborateness and involution to a twentieth-century world. But they are not inventive enough to hold one's interest all the way through unless one has a positive addiction for necrophile jokes *(22)* and schoolboy surrealism *(V)*. Cutting would have made both books far more cutting.

THE MYSTERY STORY

1. What makes the public eyes of Georges Simenon (Maigret) and John Creasey (Roger West and George Gideon) so satisfying over so many books is that, with a minimum of sentimentalizing about family, friendships, and the like, the writers concentrate on the viewing from the vantage point of the Sûreté and Scotland Yard. We see the body, the pursuit, the criminal. The passions are not neglected, as they cannot be in tales of detection, but they are presented in a simple sort of arithmetic of feeling in the case of Creasey's detectives, or a somewhat more complex algebra of *sentiment* in the case of Maigret. Descartes would have approved.

2. See Paul McGuire, *A Funeral in Eden* (New York: Morrow, 1938), pp. 40–41.

3. The really well equipped priest-detective remains to be invented. Neither Father Brown nor any of his American successors has enough theology or psychology to do his calling as a priest any real justice in his avocational pursuit of criminals. A thorough Thomist would be a cool detective. A well-rounded Augustinian would be a master of the inspired digression and thus a match even for the most imaginative schizophrenic—at least in a mystery story.

4. See *Raymond Chandler Speaking*, ed. Dorothy Gardiner and K. S. Walker (Boston: Houghton, Mifflin, 1962), pp. 53–54.

SCIENCE FICTION AND FANTASY

1. See A. E. Van Vogt, *Destination: Universe!* (New York: Pelligrini and Cudahy, 1952), pp. x, xi, xii. There was more joy and less self-consciousness in the stories that turned up in the first science-fiction magazines, Harold Hersey's *Thrill Book,* published just after the first world war, and Hugo Gernsback's *Amazing Stories,* which followed soon after. There was more wit in fantasies like that of the Dada writer Jacques Rigaut, "A Brilliant Theme," published in Paris in 1921. Time's spiral, as conceived by Rigaut, permits a sentimental young man, one Skullthorn, to retrace the steps of his affairs, to discover the reason for the loss of his mistress, to make love not one time after another, but one time before another, until, as a result, his mistress dies at the age of seven. Skullthorn's girl makes Lolita seem positively decrepit. The story exists in an excellent English translation by Simon Watson Taylor.

2. There is nothing more uneven than the average science-fiction anthology, but one must be thankful to publishers for producing them in such number, for in these collections some stories of real merit are preserved. One wishes the same sort of procedure had been followed for sea stories and other adventure tales, which in the years between the world wars were turned out with frequency and often with distinction to fill the pages of the pulps.

3. See C. M. Kornbluth, *The Syndic* (New York: Doubleday, 1953), p. 90.

4. See Clifford D. Simak, *Ring Around the Sun* (New York: Simon and Schuster, 1953), pp. 105–106, 230.

5. See Howard Schoenfeld, "Fillmore Y. Brightforks," in *Fantastic Universe,* May, 1957, p. 128. "Build Up Logically" appears in *More Penguin Science Fiction,* ed. Brian Aldiss (Harmondsworth, Middlesex, 1963), p. 103; "Build Down Logically," in *Fifty Short Science Fiction*

Tales, ed. Isaac Asimov and Groff Conklin (New York: Collier, 1963), p. 227.

THE DANCE

1. See Doris Humphrey, *The Art of Making Dances* (New York: Holt, 1959), p. 106.
2. One wishes the variety of style and content of American ballet could be better and more widely known. A sort of tributary theater of the dance does exist. There are regional companies in this country and a fair number of dancers lead troupes on tours of the major cities and the colleges and universities, major and minor. But until other cities support a dance company with something like the largesse shown Balanchine's New York City Ballet, the large resources of this kind of dance in America will be known only to a hard core of enthusiasts. And if not cities, why not states? For the occasion of a State Fair or a political convention or even a Shriners' conclave, *Billy the Kid* and *Filling Station* would be fine fare. And then, between such very public occasions, a state dance company could attend to its more serious business of exposing its potential audience, bit by bit, to the delights of imaginative ballet.
3. The revival in the early sixties of a rhythmic social dance that allows some scope for improvisation suggests that Americans are still eager for jazz dancing of quality. Most of those who do or have done the Twist, the Frug, the Watusi, the Mashed Potato, and other gyrations of the same sort, follow the simple lead of sexual exhibition—first you lift your foot and then you drop your head, then you twist your hip, or whatever. But some actually add their own variations, a few, in the less well-known places, with great invention that recalls the dear dead days of the Lindy Hop and Trucking and make one sanguine—perhaps recklessly—about the future of the jazz dance.

THE THEATER

1. See *The Hairy Ape,* in Eugene O'Neill, *Nine Plays* (New York: Modern Library, 1932), pp. 87–88.
2. See *Desire Under the Elms,* in *Nine Plays,* pp. 204–205.
3. See Philip Barry, *Here Come the Clowns* (New York, 1939), pp. 186–187.
4. See Lillian Hellman, *Candide* (New York: Random, 1957), pp. 141–142.
5. See "On Social Plays," in Arthur Miller, *A View from the Bridge* (New York: Viking, 1955), p. 17.

6. See Tennessee Williams, *Sweet Bird of Youth* (New York: New Directions, 1959), p. 114.

7. See "Legend," in Hart Crane, *Collected Poems* (New York: Liveright, 1933), p. 62.

8. See Tennessee Williams, *Cat on a Hot Tin Roof* (New York: New Directions, 1955), pp. 98–99.

9. See William Saroyan, *The Cave Dwellers* (New York: Putnam, 1957), p. 105.

10. What I am trying to suggest here is that business may be adroitly worked into a symbolic apparatus in *The Matchmaker,* an apparatus of form strictly tied to content. Wilder is appropriately close-mouthed about his techniques and his meanings. He is also, however, a very close reader of the drama, as his shrewd plumbing of his resources indicates. It would not be forcing symbolic structures upon him, I think, to make this suggestion of a business, in *The Matchmaker,* which is at once stage business and merchant's business. The play certainly improves with the kind of critical attention that reveals such a possibility.

11. See Edward Albee, *Who's Afraid of Virginia Woolf?* (New York: Atheneum, 1962), pp. 190–191.

12. If Albee continues on the downward spiral of *Tiny Alice* (1965), he may never again achieve such telling intensity. The spleen vented at religion and the religious in *Alice* seems merely diseased. The play is noisy, ineloquent, tortured in form, and pretentious. Saddest of all, apart from some well-placed invective in the opening scene, it seems to come only from spleen, not at all from accurate observation or well-instructed reading. This is Hamlet before he ever got to high school; this is Oedipus in kindergarten, but not half so interesting as those men would be even in the cradle.

THE MOVIES

1. See F. Scott Fitzgerald, *The Great Gatsby* (New York: Scribner, 1925), pp. 6, 8, 19, 94, 137.

2. See F. Scott Fitzgerald, *The Last Tycoon* (New York: Scribner, 1941), pp. 3, 74, 105.

3. See Mack Sennett, *King of Comedy* (New York: Doubleday, 1954), pp. 89–90.

4. See Robert Flaherty, "Film: Language of the Eye" (*Theatre Arts,* May, 1951), pp. 30–36.

5. But do not judge either *Citizen Kane* or *The Magnificent Ambersons* in the cruel diminution of the television screen. Both, but especially the second, require a full-size screen for Welles' intricate drama of light and shadow, which throws everything into relief, like sculpture in mo-

tion, and offers enough interest of its own to offset the rather simple-minded psychoanalyzing of William Randolph Hearst in *Citizen Kane* or the slightness of the Tarkington tale.

6. One cannot say that the experimental film has made much progress over its decades of fitful life. It does achieve economy and a becoming obliqueness often enough, even in the hands of student directors and cameramen. But it draws its significant lines with a large instrument and thus must draw them large, to fit the inflated image the screen demands. The result is rarely anything like a private meditation, a private symbol system, or private art of any kind. Abstract forms, surrealist inventions, color-organ impressions, drawings cut into the film itself—all appear at least a little precious in the experimental film; few seem to have any great staying power. The film stubbornly remains "the great pencil of the modern world," as Flaherty said, and it imposes not only its size on everything it touches, but also a kind of clarity and directness of utterance, even when clarity and directness are not wanted.

RADIO

1. See Max Picard, *The Human Face* (London: Cassell, 1931), p. 129.

2. See H. L. Mencken, *The American Language: Supplement II* (New York: Knopf, 1948), p. 40, and *The American Language,* 4th ed. (New York: Knopf, 1943), p. 328.

3. See James Joyce, *Ulysses* (New York: Random, 1934), pp. 420–421. This is the culmination point of Joyce's ingenious tracing of the development of English prose by parody in the "Oxen of the Sun" episode of *Ulysses.* From Anglo-Saxon to American Tent-Show—thus have the gods ordained.

4. See Rudy Vallee, *Vagabond Dreams Come True* (New York: Dutton, 1930), pp. 93, 60.

5. See Rudolf Arnheim, *Radio* (London: Faber, 1936), pp. 179, 182–183.

6. See Stevie Smith, "Syler's Green: A Return Journey," in *From the Third Programme,* ed. John Morris (London: Nonesuch Press, 1956), p. 93.

7. See Charles Merz, *The Great American Band Wagon* (New York: Day, 1928), pp. 49–50.

TELEVISION

1. Sarnoff Senior's words, glossily packaged in a special issue of *Wisdom,* are echoed by Sarnoff Junior, Robert, that is, Chairman of the

Board of NBC, talking to the National Association of Broadcasters on March 16, 1959. He is out, he tells his listeners, to "help others achieve a more valid understanding of our function and contributions." There has been "a fundamental misconception of the role of broadcasting." One major cause of the misconception is "honest confusion," which can, perhaps, be eliminated by making "explicit the fact that broadcasting in a free society is and must be a service designed primarily for the majority. . . . We must recognize that it is minority distaste for programs chosen by the majority that has triggered the slogan of mediocrity—and we must label this slogan for what it truly is, a failure to respect freedom of taste, an effort of the few to impose their tastes on the many." Robert Sarnoff, who was "privileged to study" under Alfred North Whitehead, as he explained in a commencement address in 1959 at Franklin and Marshall College, surely recognizes the illogic of his argument, as well as its considerable distance from the facts. Clearly it is the many who have imposed their tastes on the few—if the networks are accurate in their samplings of the tastes of the many. And clearly, mediocrity in television needs no underscoring from the "few"; it must be self-evident by now even to those who are its most slavish addicts.

2. The failure of the Federal Communications Commission to define, to defend, and to demand a substantial percentage of prime viewing time for programs of high quality, demonstrably in the public interest, is the result of another failure, this one on the part of the large minority in America of educated and intelligent men and women who constantly express their discontent with television, as earlier they did with radio, to everybody except those that matter. Private conversations are full of the fatuity and the tedium of TV. But those only too eager to pour their scorn on the medium privately do not express themselves publicly. They do not write the FCC, their Congressmen and Senators, the President. As long as the federal government hides behind the rhetoric of "our American way of life," when radio and television come up for discussion, without any protest, even at the scandalous misrepresentation of what free enterprise means, so long will television remain a second- or third-rate popular art, in which quality is largely a matter of coincidence and bad taste is the deliberate object of the producer.

3. Frank Stanton, President of CBS, in a speech at the Fourth General Conference of CBS Television Affiliates, in Washington, on January 13, 1958.

4. The lack of interest of television in music is as astonishing as it is total. Neither jazz nor so-called classical music nor popular music is ever taken up at length or in depth in television. With the largest number of symphony orchestras of quality of any country in the world, with a vast number of chamber organizations, of recitalists, of singers; with a near

monopoly of jazz musicians, and with mountains and fields full of genuine folk who sing (as distinguished from night-club singers trying to sing like folks), America is without any clue to its musical attainments. Television could let Americans know something about their music, not as an educational service, but simply as a logical and proper use of its resources. Of course, the resources would have to be studied. It would not be easy to do jazz or symphonic or chamber music, *Lieder* or folk songs on television. It would require thought, care, concern. The ratings would not be very high for such programs, but millions could in time be brought to think a little more about their music, to care a lot more about it, even to enjoy and admire it. And that might justify some of the fancy talk about "the American way of life" and "our capacity to serve the public" on the part of the broadcasters.

CRITICISM AND CENSORSHIP

1. See "Footnote on Criticism," in H. L. Mencken, *Prejudices: Third Series* (New York: Knopf, 1922), p. 97.

2. See "Art and Neurosis," in Lionel Trilling, *The Liberal Imagination* (New York: Viking, 1950), pp. 176–180.

3. See "The Historical Interpretation of Literature," in Edmund Wilson, *The Triple Thinkers* (New York: Oxford University Press, 1948), p. 269.

4. See *Punch,* April 7, 1954, insert, p. vii.

5. See Delmore Schwartz, "T. S. Eliot as the International Hero," in *Literature in America,* ed. Philip Rahv (New York: Meridian, 1957), p. 334.

6. See T. S. Eliot, "The Man of Letters and the Future of Europe," in *Sewanee Review,* Summer, 1945, p. 342.

7. See Van Wyck Brooks, *The Confident Years* (New York: Dutton, 1952), p. 584.

8. *Ibid.,* p. 603.

9. *Ibid.,* p. 611.

10. See Graham Hough, *The Dark Sun* (New York: Macmillan, 1957), pp. 148–166.

INDEX

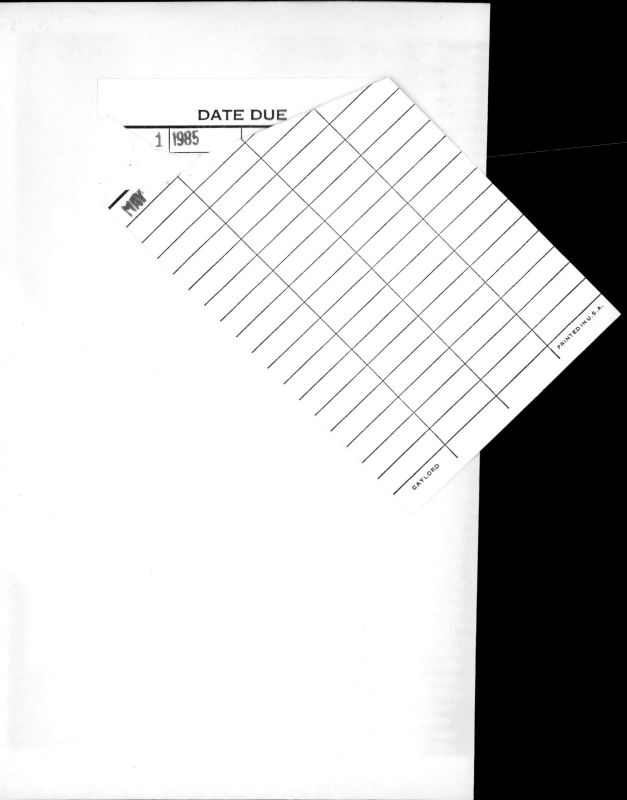